Cover: Photomontage, Jan van Toorn; *Page 1*:
Adorno's Hut, 1987, Ian Hamilton Finlay (photo,
Antonia Reeve, courtesy Galerie Jule Kewenig,
Frechen)

First published in Great Britain in 1994 by
ACADEMY EDITIONS
An imprint of the Academy Group Ltd

ACADEMY GROUP LTD
Editorial Offices
42 Leinster Gardens London W2 3AN
ERNST & SOHN
Hohenzollerndamm 170, 1000 Berlin 31
Members of the VCH Publishing Group

ISBN 1 85490 285 7 (HB)

Distributed to the trade in the United States of America by
ST MARTIN'S PRESS
175 Fifth Avenue, New York, NY 10010

Printed and bound in Singapore

Why have practical men not acquired credit?
For the reason that architecture is born of
discourse. Why not the Men of Letters?
For the reason that architecture is born of
construction. To be an architect, one must seek
discourse and construction together.

Vitruvius

The problem of this world is that the problems of this world are no longer reflected in the lives of those who are in a position to do anything about them.

Gregor Gysi

*Multiplicity is never in the terms, whatever their number, nor in the set, or totality, of them. Multiplicity is precisely in the **AND**, which does not have the same nature as the elements or the sets. (...) The **AND** is neither the one nor the other, it is always between the two, it is the boundary, there is always a boundary, a vanishing trace or flow, only we don't see it, because it is scarcely visible.*
And yet it is along this vanishing trace that things happen, becomings are made, revolutions are sketched out.

Gilles Deleuze

The Invisible i

Editors Ole Bouman and Roemer van Toorn

h Architecture

Essays   Interviews

Pictorials

Questions, comments, interviews and criticisms by Ole Bouman and Roemer van Toorn (additional research: Dave Wendt)

Preface

From 1987 to 1988 seventeen speakers in the Faculty of Architecture of the University of Technology, Delft, explored the social conditions of architecture in depth. It was the first time the title 'The Invisible in Architecture' was used.

We thank Giancarlo de Carlo, Henri Raymond, Ernest Mandel, Geoffrey Broadbent, Amos Rapoport, Jean Leering, Michael Müller, Franziska Bollerey, Cees Hamelink, Charles Jencks, Rod Hackney, Santiago Calatrava, Peter Eisenman, Rem Koolhaas, Wolf Prix, Rob Krier and Kenneth Frampton for their contributions.

Their ideas were various and their points of view often decidedly contradictory. One could not say that there was any real exchange of ideas during the organised series of lectures. We felt that for an exchange of this sort to happen it needed to be given the right setting. To this end we pursued our project by preparing and compiling this manuscript which you now have before you in printed form.

No one person, or even two people, are capable of organising a conference or writing a book unaided. Many people have helped us during our long journey towards realising our goal. To all of them our heartfelt thanks are due. We think in particular of Dave Wendt, whose intellectual insight and editorial support have been invaluable. In no small part, the present book is also his work; he wishes to thank Suzanne Olde Monnikhof for her ongoing support. We also thank the writers who sent us their essays, the architects who answered our critical questionnaires and generously made their material available to us, the people we interviewed who welcomed us warmly giving us hours of their time, and the many artists, photographers and others who have put their work disinterestedly at our disposal.

Our gratitude also goes out to the student association, Stylos, in Delft, which offered us accommodation and facilities for the duration of the series of lectures. The same goes for the Ministry of Welfare, Heath and Cultural Affairs, the Ministry of Planning, Housing and Environment, the Faculty of Architecture of Delft University of Architecture, Prins Bernhard Fonds, the Royal Institute of Dutch Architects and many architectural offices, who, despite their faith in our project being repeatedly put to the test, have continued to believe in its successful outcome.

'To steal from one is plagiarism; to steal from many is research.' We would like to thank everyone for 'lending' us the intellectual properties that we needed to write and compile this book.

No words can express our deepest affection for Liesbeth Janson and Mirjam Westen for their love and critical comments during our lengthy saga.

Finally we would like to thank all those who have been of such immense assistance during this process and without whose support we would have been powerless to do anything: Herman Albers, Christine Baart, Frank Bakker, Mirjam Beerman, Manon Beerman, Hans Bos, Karst Bouman, Machteld Bouman, Titus Bouman, Arnold van den Broek, Hans van Dijk, Tjeerd Dijkstra, Rients Dijkstra, Joop Doorman, Oliver Draxler, Kees van Drongelen, Kenneth Frampton, Donald Gardner, Michael Gibbs, Marcel van Heck, Arjen Hoogedoorn, Anne Hoogewoning, Hans Ibelings, Victor Joseph, Guus Kemme, Margot Knijn, Arjen Knoester, Michel Korsse, Liesbeth Levi, Birgitte de Maar, Ron Miltenburg, Gerrie van Noort, Ingrid Oosterheerd, Pearl Perlmutter, Wilma Peterse, Stephan Piccolo, Johan Pijnappel, Angela Pohl, Hans Rijnja, Erna Rijsdijk, Axel Roest, Sjon van Rossem, Wienke Scheltens, Ineke Schwartz, Joes Segal, Petra Slegh, Frans Spruijt, Ed Taverne, Jan van Toorn, Tessel van Toorn, Yvonne Twisk, Frank van Unen, Steffen de Vries, Anouk de Wit and Arthur Wortmann.

Ole Bouman, Roemer van Toorn, Amsterdam, September 1993

Ministerie van
Welzijn,
Volksgezondheid en
Cultuur

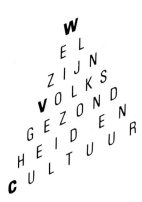

Minister van Welzijn, Volksgezondheid en Cultuur

Architecture is a social and cultural process. It not only fulfils a functional need for shelter and territorial boundaries, it also gives expression to the prevailing values and standards in a particular society. Architecture not only renders a service, it is also a narrative form.

It is a task of government to ensure that justice can be done to both these aspects of architecture. On the one hand the government is bound by the need within society to construct adequate accomodation for people. In this regard it has taken a material obligation upon itself within the social contract. On the other hand, in its capacity as custodian of the arts the government is concerned to preserve the cultural dimension of architecture. To the extent that building implies a measure of thought about society, the government can create conditions that will give full rein to such reflectiveness.

Over the years the Netherlands Ministry of Welfare, Health and Cultural Affairs and the Ministry of Housing, Planning and the Environment have taken a serious view of their responsabilities in this matter. On the basis of the policy document on architecture entitled *Ruimte voor Architectuur*, or Space for Architecture, conditions have been created in many areas that aim to provide scope for a thoughtful attitude to building as well as earmarking resources for the construction process itself. One example of this is the Netherlands Architecture Institute, whose rich collection forms the heart of its presentations and discussions of Dutch architectural culture. Another is the Berlage Institute, which offers an international postgraduate course in architecture, urban design and landscaping. And finally there is the Architecture Promotion Fund, which provides active and financial support for initiatives from the field.

The institutions referred to are the most important of a broad range of policy measures and policy instruments, the objective of which is to improve the climate for architecture and to encourage and properly equip the main parties involved in the construction process -in particular architects, clients and public authorities- to strive for the best possible quality, both in an architectonic sense and with regard to urban planning.

In this connection, the initiative taken by The Invisible in Architecture, which has brought together science, technology and the artistic side of architecture, is an important one.
I anticipate that the conference and this substantial publication will make a valuable contribution to the debate on architecture, and hope that this book finds the wide readership it deserves.

Hedy d'Ancona
Minister of Welfare, Health and Cultural Affairs

The Invisible in Architecture

Ole Bouman, Roemer van Toorn

With regard to the invisible, there is a theological and philosophical tradition as old as the distinction between truth and untruth. A cloak of invisibility has always been the favourite guise of the truth. The truth was something you had to strive for. The invisible was the infinite, the absolute, the unreachable, and it was seen as being one with God, with the Platonic Forms of the True, the Beautiful and the Good, with the ghost in the machine or with the *Weltgeist*. Faith in the invisible truth has been so steadfast that five hundred years of Humanism, two hundred and fifty years of Enlightenment, a hundred years of Modernist creative destruction and twenty-five years of Post-Modern radical doubt have proved insufficient to unmask it decisively. The invisible truth has invariably seduced the rational biped.

Our intention in celebrating the Invisible in Architecture is not to uphold this tradition of an 'underlying', invisible truth. We cherish no iconoclastic longing for a pure, bare essence, uncontaminated by the deceit of representation. It is not our aim to reinstate a spiritual transparency. This book is the result of our wish to react to a culture whose products appear more and more to be nothing but representations. Seeing is believing, as the proverb would have it – but now literally so: seeing is the only believing. The truth still seduces, but invisibility is no longer its favourite stratagem. We have abandoned the metaphysical perception of the universe that made us long for the reality behind appearances. When the contract on this essentialism expired, all we had left was the image, the sign. From that moment onwards, the truth lay in the image itself and must hence also be sought there. Truth now no longer seduces through image, but *as* image. And that is quite a different matter. Once the arbitrary relation between image and meaning, between signifier and signified, was discovered, the way was open for total manipulation and fictionalisation of the image. In these times, the signifier has supplanted the signified, the representation has usurped the original, the semblance has displaced the essence, and verisimilitude has ousted truth. Deprived of its former metaphysical certainties, the eye, that actively searching, documenting organ, has taken on an immeasurable importance. The visual now seems to determine the entire agenda of existence. Our life owes its rhythm to a bombardment of images. This optical cadence is not all there is, however. Inevitable though it is that the visual opens the way to the truth, the time is now ripe to refute its pretention to *be* the truth. And if there is one medium, one art form, that can prove useful for the purposes of this refutation, then it is surely architecture. The simultaneous double role of architecture, as both participant and critical bystander in the process of advancing simulation, is thus our guiding theme. What is visible? The sign is visible, not the content to which the sign refers; the object is visible, not the action taking place in and around that object; the elegant, unique signature is visible, not the humdrumness of collective manners; the solution is visible, not the problem; our Brave New First World is visible, not the peripheral Third World to our south and in the ghettos of the affluent West; and the Self is visible, not the Other in that self's selfness. In this book, however, we shall not continue to attempt to probe the truth behind the visible in such a cut-and-dried, dialectic way. That would do meagre justice to the complexity of that truth. Oppositional thinking must make way for complementary thinking. Instead of bewailing the gulf between visibility and invisibility, we would prefer to emphasise the connection of the two by an intervening transitional zone. That is the region where we may fruitfully seek the invisible *in* the visible, and where we can escape the documentary pretentions of images by exploring the agendas concealed in them.

This book also aims to offer a cross-section of contemporary pluralistic architecture – not so much a Who's Who, as a Who's What and Why, of present-day architecture. For that purpose, we must cut right across contemporary culture. Most architects offer immense resistance – with renewed force in recent years – to the view that their work is ideologically loaded, that it has political consequences and that their formal choices and spatial concepts institutionalise relationships of power. This book's explicit aim is to probe and to discuss these particular dimensions of the craft, and thereby to stimulate debate on the social motives that give added legitimacy to, and receive added legitimacy from, architecture. Perhaps the architect's goal should be not to make political architecture, but rather to make an architecture with politics. In other words, should an architect's thinking about social constraints and possibilities not manifest itself in her or his work? Therefore one thing we would like to emphasise in this book is the

considerable potential of architecture as a medium of dialogue on current social conditions – and, of course, on potential alternatives.

Gradually, the entire architectural discourse has come to centre around design. Design discourages critical thought and action – and by probing the politics of design, the present book aims to rehabilitate precisely those attitudes. Architectural and urban design will be considered not only as affairs of autonomous, poetical inspiration (which can of course be a source of much pleasure) but as *loci* where individual artistic creativity intertwines with cultural, social and economic processes. We hope this book will stimulate a form of criticism that has a bearing on (architectural) practice; and vice versa.

Criticism must never be an indulgence, a let-out for an otherwise autonomous *métier* that unblinkingly and unthinkingly throws off one masterpiece after another. Criticism of that kind lives on a reservation, out of touch with the rest of culture. We hope to make it clear that there exists a kind of criticism that really does enmesh with society, a criticism that forms part of a practical strategy. Criticism should not be primarily about other criticism, but about the object that was its original *raison d'être*. That is the only way to break out of the vicious circle of academic scholasticism. Real criticism is marked by intellectual generalism, and does not confine itself to its own specialist idiom.

Architectural criticism often takes a passive stance, reflecting on the work but refraining from any explicit standpoint. It operates introvertedly, from the viewpoint of the architect or of the architecture, while the critic herself or himself hides behind marginal notes on the architectural object. When architecture is intrinsically empty of any stimulating philosophical, ideological or poetic vision, then criticism, too, usually lacks the power to escape this emptiness. Criticism degenerates into project documentation, becomes entangled in quasi-profundities or starts describing its own impotence and alienation. Such criticism is little more than a travel guide for the omnivorous cultural tourist. But, even when the object of criticism is not ostensibly 'about' anything, that criticism should surely not ape its object's superficiality. Perhaps this calls for effort, independence and nerve – or at least some other angle than the usual architectural jargon. Criticism must create a picture of reality through its own cogency. It must maintain an independence towards the object of its attentions and not merely take sides. When architecture tends towards endless mystification, towards a rhetoric of functionality, beauty, force, utopia, communication, cultural fragmentation or (by contrast) tranquillity and order, a rhetoric that casts a smoke-screen over the real social forces within which it operates, then criticism must act as the conscience of that rhetoric and make the doubtings visible. Only such criticism can elevate architecture to a mainspring of intellectual and moral understanding, and at the same time promote an architecture that demonstrates this understanding in practice, in the kind of use the building sanctions. Such criticism can bring architecture into contact with a public sphere that is more than just a market or the sum of private interests. The present book must be seen as an attempt at such criticism. It argues for cultural analysis as the backbone of architectural discussion, and for architecture itself as a cornerstone of the ongoing cultural debate. It advocates the creation of conditions for a new scholarly and critical mentality.

None of the architectural intelligences discussed in this book is to be interpreted as the exclusive product of an ideological, economic or geographical context. After all, intelligence and talent travel beyond the frontiers of their origins. However, the result of their expression is never located in a historical or cultural vacuum. Nowadays there is a widespread interest in the creative achievements and ingenious practical solutions of architecture. We would like to widen this interest to cover the world in which architecture is practised, and how that practice is defined by institutional and social factors. It is this world and these factors that generate the meanings crucial to the functioning of the architecture and thus vital to its proper understanding. The influences and pressures must be recognised, even when they are denied. We must escape the rigid dichotomy between 'us' and 'them', between architecture and the world at large. Our conviction that these spheres are really interdependent will accompany us throughout this book.

A fair treatment of today's kaleidoscopic architectural culture will inevitably be a tangle of intersections and overlaps. We intend to bring countless 'inherent' aspects of the craft, such as buildings, models, drawings and the accompanying architectural jargon, into relation with matters usually regarded as being external to it, namely politics, culture and economics. On the one hand, this intention reflects our wish to approach architecture architecturally, i.e. in accordance with the specific laws of the discipline and with respect for the profession's attainments. On the other hand, we wish to probe the programme behind the architectural discipline – a programme which may be latent, implicit or explicit. In other words, we are prepared to raise questions about how architects could or should go about their business.

We must move from a situation in which reality tolerates criticism in a non-committal way towards a situation in which criticism is a match for reality. Thus the question is not how architectural criticism can serve architecture, but how architecture can be a medium of critical activity. This book is an attempt to sketch the world as it looks today on the basis of its architecture. To achieve that, architectural criticism must be taken to the elliptical point at which this genre completely undermines itself, and makes way for a different, conceptual mode of criticism that is not primarily occupied with media, genres and disciplines but with issues that concern us all – issues in whose service media, genres and disciplines can be deployed. Amid 'this century's most important art form' (Berlage), amid the star-struck profession, amid the pluralism of today, and amid an ocean of ostensibly autonomous and isolated built objects, the gaze is inevitably held by the 'luminous' architecture – the kind of architecture that can be seen to stand out in the spotlight of media attention. This book hopes to reveal the cultural shadow of that architecture, the invisible in architecture.

At first sight, this book may look like a labyrinth, a myriad of *faits divers*. In fact, our subject matter has a specific if somewhat complex conceptual structure, and this will take a little explanation. Firstly, we have identified eight 'vectors', current dimensions of interest and debate in both architecture and culture at large. Secondly, we have divided the contemporary pluralistic spectrum into three 'strategies', three prevailing ideologically motivated approaches to contemporary architecture. Together, these variables form a matrix of 24 'positions', and this is the backbone on which the subject matter of this book is structured. On partly subjective grounds, we have associated each of the positions in the matrix with a specific architect or bureau; and for each of these architects or bureaux, the book includes an essay, a project description, visual documentation and a selection of quotations from the architect(s) concerned.

Our eight 'vectors' are as follows: **durée, context, border, topos, programme, space, identity and representation.** Durée is the long term. Context is the situation in which the long-term factors become concrete. Boundary is the transition between context and object. Topos is the place contained by the boundary. Programme is the *raison d'être* of the place. Space is the container of the programme. Identity is the cultural value of the space. Representation is the form in which this value re-enters the discourse and so reproduces the durée.

The vectors are concepts which have the potential of bridging the gap between practice and theory. Besides being terms that crop up in the ongoing intellectual debate, they also form part of the architect's theoretical frame of reference. Hence not only are these vectors aspects of a concrete reality, but they provide points of entry to a less concrete (but equally real) invisibility. The vectors are not just instruments for seeing architecture through the eyes of an architect. They are, rather, tools with which we can break out of the constraints of a specific and perhaps biased architectural vision; like all tools, their value must ultimately become apparent in use, by yielding results.

One could argue that these eight vectors form the core of the reaction against Modern Architecture that has taken place during the last twenty-five years. The internationalism, utopianism and universalism of the Moderns has made way for a situational ethics. This historical transformation has extended to all aspects of society. But architecture, as situation-creator *par excellence*, is directly caught up in this change and has in fact made a considerable contribution to it. It is not insignificant that Post-Modernism has developed into a movement above all in architecture. Issues of duration, context, boundary, place, identity and representation figure repeatedly in philosophy as well as in architecture. We could even argue that programme and space are 'Post-Modern' notions, in the literal sense of the word. After all, for the Moderns, with their love of flexible structures, the programme was often nothing more than a retrospective addition to the architecture. In their emphasis on architecture as a 'platform' or a 'facility', they left the programme for others to think about. And this brings us to the Modern space. New technical resources made it possible for the Modern architect to achieve the ideal of an isotropic space. Modern space was no more than a precondition for existence. And although the adulation of space in countless writings might lead us to expect otherwise, the whole discourse was aimed at a breakthrough measurable in *time*. That was the utopian progress and the vertical uplift. Our recent concern for the Other, for our fellow being, is actually a manifestation of the renewed currency of the space theme. When mankind proved incapable of actualising utopia, his puzzled gaze turned to the environment of that failed

Ole Bouman Roemer van Toorn

15

enterprise. It turned out to offer plenty of material for investigation.

A final reason for choosing these eight vectors is that they enable us to side-step the problem of cultural incommensurability. When anthropologists and philosophers realised that every time and every cultural entity has its own interpretation of reality, making it difficult to penetrate elsewhere with our own cultural frame of reference, they also discovered that there were some subjects – actually dimensions of existence – about which everyone, regardless of culture, had either a conscious or an unconscious opinion. Thus no sooner did universal theories become impossible, than they discovered universal themes. By concentrating precisely on universal themes of this kind, it becomes possible for us to penetrate everywhere. True, this is theoretical imperialism. But the eight vectors are also illuminating categories, which enable us to peer into architecture and society. Moreover, they indicate exactly the extent to which the whole conceptual framework of architecture is currently under fire. They are also compelling: no wonder they have become the subject of furious debate.

This book falls into eight main divisions, corresponding to the vectors we have defined; each division contains an introduction in which we explore the nature of the vector in greater detail. The three 'strategies' we mentioned, which intersect with each of the vectors, also deserve a more detailed examination; and we have chosen to discuss them in this main introduction, below.

During the last thirty years, the purpose of architecture has been redefined. Architecture has abandoned many of its utopian pretentions and has found itself faced with the challenge to survive in a building process that is increasingly carved up into specialisms. The architect's self-respect could only endure with the role of artist replacing that of saviour. It is this artistic reorientation that runs like a thread through the past few decades of architectural history. Structurally speaking, this re-orientation can be broken down into the three dominant strategies we have already mentioned. Firstly **archaism,** the retreat into the 'dumb' architectural object. This strategy places its emphasis on the durable *thing*. Archaistic architecture is *touchy-feely*. Secondly, **façadism,** a belief in style. Style proves capable of reconciling antagonisms at the level of form. This strategy places its emphasis on the representative *image*. Façadist architecture is *looky-glossy*. Finally, **fascinism** supplies experiential suggestions, whose content is a condensed expression of an issue but not a challenge to it. This strategy places the emphasis on a certain *atmosphere*. Fascinist architecture is *brainy-flashy*.

The architecture discussed in this book is an *architecture autre*. It is, without exception, of high practical, aesthetic and intellectual quality. It is, also without exception, more than just the solution to a pragmatic problem: it also addresses social issues. It bears witness to the courage needed to take risks, to enthusiasm and endurance. But architecture, even architecture that is not satisfied with an unquestioning acceptance of the client/investor's wishes, is to a substantial degree socially affirmative. This is quite simply because it serves a practical end and because it is so expensive. It unavoidably nestles into a cultural politics of consensus and status quo. By distinguishing the three strategies, we hope to show how architectural projects can bear witness to a critical capacity as well as to affirmative action. There are some questions we shall pose in each case: how does the work relate to what it institutionalises, how far does it respect the public domain, and what is the role of the work's author?

Ole Bouman Roemer van Toorn

Archaism The first strategy is Archaism. Archaism hopes to barricade itself against the destructive force of racing Modernisation. It refuses to accept the consequences of endless acceleration and tries to find a way of resisting it. Archaism seeks an escape from historical dialectics in the 'primitives' of existence. It studies the enduring attributes of the topos with the aim of thereby giving mankind his identity. Archaism resists Modernism by appealing to a timeless prehistory in which man supposedly still lived in innocent symbiosis with his cosmos. Although this strategy is unavoidably a representation of the symbiosis instead of the symbiosis itself, so that the cerebral aloofness of modern man continues to apply with undiminished force, it does in fact offer a 'way back'. The real object, the authentic thing, the phenomenology of space and material, the innocence of ritual: these are things we share with all peoples in all times. And that is where Archaism aims to lead back to.

Archaism places itself outside the Modern dialectics between form and content. All that matters is substance. It has an aversion to design. It insists on an architecture of reality, an architecture you can feel – feel with your eyes. We can also describe this strategy in psychoanalytic and biological terms. Archaism represents the unconscious, the *id*. Architecture that accords with this analysis does not work at a cerebral, cognitive, logocentric, rational or purposive level, but seeks its existence in the organic, phenomenological, symbiotic and holistic. These are areas that are difficult to treat discursively (although that does not apply to theories about this architecture!). You could perhaps compare archaism with the eighteenth-century romantic longing for the condition of the noble savage in his primitive hut. But it goes much further: in the interests of achieving a primal state, it would have us give up the consciousness that has made us into the aloof and calculating creatures we are. For some archaists, it even implies a figurative return to the maternal lap, to the womb. In some ways this architecture bears an unmistakably erotic tint, in that it strives to produce an almost orgasmic release through (the eye's) caressing of the object of adoration.

While the archaistic *id* can be understood in Freudian psychology as the libido, its neurological counterpart is the mid-brain, the reptilian substratum of the human spirit. Archaism appeals to the seat of the passions, the limbic system. Archaism is the architecture of *homo faber*. As such, it concentrates on the solid stuff, the touchstone, the centre of cosmology. Its method is a return to the *thing*, the *referent*, the *ground* on which all else is based. The main philosophical problem that besets archaism is that the return to roots and to mythical consciousness involves forgetting all that has taken place between 'then' and now. The past is romanticised. Interpersonal relations are offered up in favour of supracultural categories which can only be experienced individually, in lonely silence. Meanwhile, the (tectonic) world gets by perfectly well without the individual.

To identify archaism, take note of the following paradigmatic soundbites: *traditions, authenticity, essence, phenomenology, niche, Geworfenhei, immediacy, nearness, thingness, presentness, tactility, Heidegger, unconscious, eternity, place, texture, material, ground, métier, canton, autarchy, landscape, path, tectonics, haptic realm, silence, loneliness, modesty, harmony, participation, use, human scale, ontology...*

18

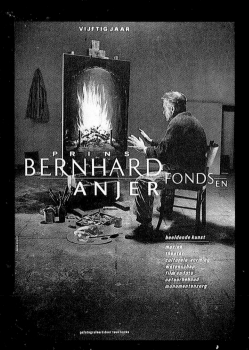

Teun Hocks

Façadism The second strategy, Façadism, operates largely within the dialectics of form and content. It is most tellingly exemplified by the 'decorated shed'. This strategy defines our environment principally in stylistic terms. Functions are represented by a stylised narrative couched in terms of ornament and figuration. The narrative, be it metaphorical, critical or speculative, is thereby separated from the substance and expelled to the surface. The façadist approach concentrates in general on the Semperian *Bekleidung* and is thus not necessarily restricted to the outer surface of the volume. Surfaces are treated in an overtly communicative way; the architectonic signs are like pictographs.

In psychoanalytic terms, façadists operate at the level of the *ego*. They wish to engage every user in a dialogue by means of multiple coding of form and meaning. They aim to attract everyone into the communication process at his own level. The façadist architect believes he controls the semantic scenario of his building, just as the ego has control over cognition. This architecture is thus in a certain sense humanistic. It places its trust in meaning – and in the happy ending. The façadist strategy is based on correspondence thinking, i.e. on the faith that the meanings 'behind' the signs are based on universally valid agreements. Man still forms the centre, even if he is just an anonymous consumer.

Façadism appeals to the cortex. It is the architecture of *homo sapiens* and *homo significans*. It is cognitive and assumes a reasonable communication of meaning. As such, it concentrates on meaningful *images*. Its method is the use of many separate *signs*. The work guards consciousness against doubt.

Façadism is not interested in the critical evaluation of its signs. The context offers all kinds of meanings, whether mythical or rational, and these territories are regarded as interchangeable. The presence of at least *some* meaning is the ultimate criterion. In the first instance, façadism seems to rely on a strongly developed consciousness of everything to do with meaning and communication. But when we examine this consciousness more closely, it seems to relate largely to the operation of the meaning process and not to the cultural causes and effects of that operation.

Facadism allies itself with the world as it is. It lives in harmony with the liberal tradition. History knows only gradual variations, not breaks or sudden changes of direction. Facadism seems to believe in democracy as the mitigating circumstance of capitalism, which offers everyone an equal chance as long as he or she takes the initiative. Its practitioners believe in open, free and meaningful communication in which the consensus functions by majority. The New World exists thanks to the people.

To identify façadism, take note of the following paradigmatic soundbites: ***representation, iconography, common sense, democracy, life-style, marketing, communication, Rorty, language, semiotics, sign, Jakobson, surface, varnish, eclecticism, visuality, city, monumentality, volume, classicism, dressing, figuration, decor, ornament, authorship, ratings, pragmatism...***

19

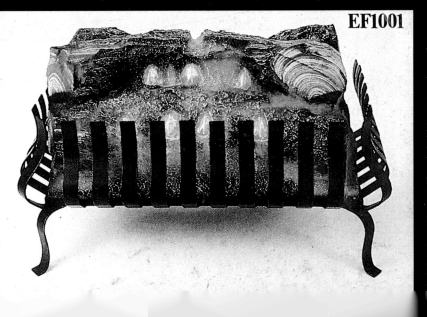

EF1001

Fascinism The third strategy we call fascinism.

Fascinism denies the dialectics between form and content. For this strategy, the surface is the deepest thing there is. The author, as genius and as producer, no longer exists. Intentionality makes way for modality. Representation *is* reality, in an endless semiosis. We can never stop this process, only succumb to it in fascination. How does the global village work? Despite its inhabitants, with autonomous chains of meaning-assignation and social processes. Fascinism treats us to a bombardment of images torn largely from a variety of historical and functional contexts, obscene fragments. And although fascinistic architecture harbours a vein of criticism, an intrinsically valid aesthetic revolt against the uniforming terror of teleology and system thinking, its nihilism makes it a ready vehicle for a 'charismatic' politics.

The architecture of fascinism is a construction in name only. It is dematerialised on all sides into a communication medium in which it is possible to 'write' meanings of every kind. Hence this tendency is 'post-historical', post-humanistic and post-structuralist, outside dialectic history, beyond Utopia and intertextual. What remains is a universe of signs that may be viewed positively as the source of an immense freedom, or negatively as a terror of simulacra in a pluriversum of so many different micro-meanings that every distinction is erased. However you look at it, it is a waste of time seeking anything 'behind' anything else – and certainly seeking truth behind a form.

The fascinists represent the dominion of the superego. It is not insignificant that they agitate keenly against the paralysing effect of too much knowledge, and long for a new innocence. Fascinists know too much.

Taking into account a whole complex of social, cultural and technological factors, they aim at an architecture that is up to date. Everything must be represented in this architecture (as a person or as an architect, you must spare no effort to follow the news). In negative terms, the superego is your own Big Brother. The media keep watch on everything, and even mould reality to suit the image. There is no escape from this condition, and architecture that does no justice to it is, intellectually speaking, utterly irrelevant. In positive terms, this architecture of the superego is a hypersensitive expression of what is actually going on in our culture. All in all, viewed positively or negatively, the superego stays on top: you, the architect, cannot know how things are, no, the here and now of current reality is always one step ahead. Anyone who wishes to disobey is suffering from hope for the past or yearning for the future (or vice versa). Hence fascinism is free of nostalgia, but by no means free of other impositions. Mandatory submission to the 'course of things', to a historical/futurological *Zeitgeist*, is a present-day variant of the seductions of totalitarianism. Hence this strategy is vulnerable to the same criticism as has been applied to cultural relativism: it offers no moral criterion to help us chart a course into the future. At the same time, the fascinist refuses to recognise the ethical choice implicit in this observation. Nothing is true, and not even that – everything is relative except that. Fascinism appeals to the extensions of the cortex, to the eye of television, to the binary brain of the computer, to artificial intelligence. Fascinist architecture is a feverishly progressive architecture, aimed at an impassioned *mood*, an architecture for *homo cyberneticus.*

To identify fascinism, take note of the following paradigmatic soundbites: ***post-humanism, metropolis, periphery, interface, fragment, rhizome, difference, Derrida, intertextuality, Barthes, speed, mobility, dromology, Virilio, atopia, simulation, nomadism, excess, hyper-reality, cyberspace, grotesque, dislocation, folding, event, tracing and mapping, elevated, skin, fire, obscurity...***

Jan Dibbets transformed the TV set in an electronic fireplace. For this time pure fire was transmitted. No introduction, no commentary. 24 min. TV as FIREPLACE, 1969

The heuristic matrix of eight vectors and three prevalent strategies gives us twenty-four intersections on which we can dispose a similar number of architectural oeuvres. Of course, this does not imply that the twenty-four architects have nothing to say about other intersections than that on which we have placed them. On the contrary, the speculative power of these designers would probably surpass every classification applied for the sake of argument. Partly for this reason, we asked our chosen architects to make a statement about all eight vectors, in order to clarify their positions (in some cases we have culled these statements from the published literature). Thus you will find a spread containing twenty-four statements, one from each architect, preceding each vector introduction.

In our interpretations of the individual oeuvres, we sometimes stick our neck out rather far. Therefore, to give a hearing to both sides of the argument we have included a documentation of at least one much-acclaimed or much-discussed project by each architect. We have also compiled a number of each architect's most important past statements, sometimes together with statements by apologists, exegetists, colleagues and rivals. This structure offers unexpected alliances, counterpoints, pure presentations, fictive dialogues and imaginary press conferences – all intended to clarify someone's standpoint and to make this heard in the current debate on the issues concerned.

In addition to the twenty-four monographs, this book includes thirteen scholarly or critical articles and eleven interviews with various architects. Our intention in including these articles is, on the one hand, to chart out the intellectual context of the architectural debate, and on the other hand, to create an arsenal of arguments that can prove useful in this debate. As an extra stimulus to this debate, we have provided additional comments, questions and answers in the margins of the articles.

The eleven interviews reproduced in this book gave us an opportunity to ask directly about motivations and mentalities. But they also reveal a variety of styles of talking about architecture. These styles demonstrate the relationship between discourse and form. In publications on architecture, the reader is all too often confronted with speechless objects, reduced moreover to two dimensions as photographic reproductions. To avoid this situation, we considered it worth creating verbal contexts, in which the architectural forms are given a voice, so to speak, through the voice of their makers. Conversely, we have striven to use the pictures not merely as illustrations to decorate the text, but as critical notes in themselves.

To sum up, this book aspires to being a documented interaction of practice and theory, of main and marginal text, of documentation and manipulation, of styles of speech and of thinking, of image and text, of description and criticism, of scholarly and practical disciplines, of quotations and dialogues. We hope that our readers will be able to use this material not only as a means of simultaneously refining and adding edge to the cultural debate, but also in developing new design strategies.

We can well imagine that after reading this book, you may believe that every architect who tries to do something more than build an illustration to an investor's brochure is a present-day Sisyphus. However much the architect does to create a new world, or to express an idea in form, someone is always going to try and pick holes. The reader will understandably raise his hands and ask, 'What is it you actually want, then?' With this in mind, we have chosen to present an outline of our standpoint with respect to the current state of affairs at the end of this book. This exposition takes the form of an epilogue in which we argue the case for an open architecture.

The Invisible in Architecture could be conceived as durée. The durée consists of historical lines and patterns that often unconsciously influence our individual thoughts and actions, and make the functioning of society durable and familiar. Durée is the mute certainty on which our existence is founded. It is the time dimension that joins objects to the forces which produce them. Durée is the substrata of every social, political and cultural behaviour, and stands for the persistence of the past in the present. Hence we might question whether the past really does lie *behind* us. An understanding of ourselves is impossible without a sense of durée.

The antithesis of the long-lasting, i.e. the event, now seems to dominate our lives. We forget durée; we take no interest in the hidden, permanent forces. We are so familiar with the self-reproducing order of durée that we fail to notice it. Conserving forces legitimise our daily practices in a complex and subtle manner. In the process, anthropological motives and ideological preferences hide behind a flexible, seemingly autonomous world of images. History seems to have stopped. Duration, the dimension that unites the *faits divers*, is de-activated. We undergo a bombardment of fragments which, seemingly isolated and value-free, add up to a staccato culture. The only permanence in that culture seems to be the eternal Now, a continual, all-moralising actuality. Countless questions concerning the self-evident character of our way of life – what, why, for whom, for what end, by what means, to what future? – succumb to the single inescapable message: *this!*...

We live in a time when forgetting the long-term has turned into a virtual ideology. Meanwhile, however, our lives remain richly regulated; we hang on to all kinds of cultural and societal codes and conventions, to our genetic passport, our climate, our social stratum and a clutch of other historical and biological factors, to our Superego and our Unconscious. Thus there are reasons enough to resist the ideology of forgetting. The durée vector places us in a position to investigate the relations between objects,

Durée

conceptual frameworks, institutions and interests, from a variety of angles. It unravels myths and rituals. And, the instant we observe durée, we realise how dubious the advantages of its objectivising grip on our existence. We had therefore better take account of it in our thoughts and actions, if we wish to become moral agents instead of remaining servants of power. And there is only one way to go about it: keep asking questions.

Since Hegel and Marx, history is no longer understood as a supernatural programme. History, in as far as it has succumbed neither to the temptation of interpreting its subject matter fatalistically as blind chance nor to a positivistic fascination for the fact, has developed into a search for the hidden agenda. The discipline stumbled on concealed factors that determined the course of events, such as dialectics and class conflicts. Where historians have managed to depart from this antagonistic view of their craft, they have sought the explanation of events in relatively timeless factors such as anthropology, climatology and demography. Alongside the rich tradition of a history of self-developing individuals, there has thus grown a new tradition of research into super-individual, anonymous processes and structures. One might almost say that, as a worldly substitute for the reassurance of the divine, historians have developed an eye for the long term, the epistemè, the paradigm, the collective world view, the system – categories that rise well above the individual action and its object.

The philosopher Henri Bergson was concerned with permanence, continuity and the irreversibility of history. He wrote of the *survivance du passé*. Fernand Braudel, a historian from the French *Annales* school, turned his attention to the long, slow time-scale of climate and landscape which gives whole cultures their character. Martin Heidegger devoted a life of research to the phenomenological relationship between man and his world, a relation stripped of its utilitarian features. And Michel Foucault recognised a civilising and disciplining offensive, extending over centuries and associated with the permanent reproduction of

power: a techno-scientific discourse governed by an autonomous logic which dominates society and totally determines human life.

These are all interpretations of durée that are so broad they could not possibly offend anyone. These versions emerge first in the rehabilitation process of the enduring. However, there are also other versions of durée that concern us both directly and morally. For instance:

1 Since the rise of mercantilism and, later, capitalism, we have lived increasingly in terms of quantity, goal-oriented rationality and economic value, the three techno-scientific faces of a society of commodities. In short, there has been a gradual displacement from the question of why we do things to the question of how we do things. This process, which may be alienation to one person while it is secularisation or even emancipation to another, has reached a pinnacle under late capitalism: the triumph of simulation. At first sight this triumph seems to bring in its train a total immaterialisation, a world of the radically new. But perhaps it is really just an endless reconfirmation of the same economic and social reality, expressed in a continually changing guise.

2 There exists a form of intelligence, not necessarily conscious, a practical mastery of current regularities and conventions, which is crucial to the perpetuation of social practices. This intelligence finds its application in the status game that is played according to characteristic rules in each social field. Neither participation nor success is possible without tacit recognition of the stakes of the game. Education and specialisation can elevate the status of the individual within a social field (for example architecture) to a position that Pierre Bourdieu has called 'naturalised distinction', a form of generally recognised superiority that depends on conforming with the inherent demands of the game. The acquisition of status is thus inseparably linked to perpetuation of the rules.

3 Even in their relativistic guise, our Western cultural mores still impose themselves as a universal criterion. Their malleability makes them all the more effective as a standard in relation to which everything is measured, adapted or subjected. High in Western esteem is the right of individual self-determination: everyone must be allowed to go about his life as he pleases, with a freedom that extends as far as the point where that of another begins. But, with the arrival of the global village, it has become clear that a universal morality can have the practical result of Eurocentricity. 'We' and 'they' are more real than ever before, with consequent xenophobia. We discover that a long-term, symbiotic bond exists between the idea of the autonomous individual and imperialism.

Broadly speaking, there are two tenable positions in respect of durée: that of *the ideology of forgetting* and that of *belief in the moment*. The ideology of forgetting gives durée a free hand. It accepts the restricted freedom that is allotted to the individual to intervene in time. After all, what use is it to you to penetrate the reality of durée if, at the same time, you are transfixed by the realisation that there is nothing you can do about it? This ideology takes its lead from whatever durée confronts us with. It describes and illustrates, but never ventures into explanations. Belief in the moment tries to escape the schizophrenia of the forgetting of memory. It tries to find a critical force through the trivial properties of the moment. It hopes, by this, to unmask durée and so to oppose alienation. What both positions have in common is that they can arrive at (no more than) an individual product within the domain of the specialism.

More than any other art, architecture is obliged to respect durée. It is as a rule meant to be enduring, solid and well-founded. It is never simply the substantiation of an autonomous idea of its maker, and thus an 'event', but also aims to satisfy the wishes of the user and investor. Since these wishes are typically based on durable codes and conventions, and since the investment must show a profit, architecture has little choice but to be durable. Perhaps architecture can itself be called the *keeper* of the past because it will always have a material form and be intended for more than a single moment. Even in the most unscrupulous take-the-money-and-run architecture, taking the money requires a short wait.

Architecture takes its place amid an existing configuration of climate, history, local context and socio-economic production relationships. It offers shelter by means of its tectonics, which are based on the 'eternal' principles of the joint in harmony with gravity. Moreover, it maintains traditions of form and responds to existing archetypes and/or other kinds of functional typologies and recognised spatial organisations of programmes. At the same time, it has to be flexible with regard to eventualities, for which it must provide a platform or a background; it must not aim to be an event in its own right at the cost of all else. Architecture is thus the condensation of an idea, of dominant values; it perpetuates them and carries them along into the future. Architecture is in that sense not only the bearer of durée but generates it too. It is the ideal medium for representing the past in the present. It is the *trait d'union* between past, present and future.

Three strategies and three architects In the reaction against Modernism, durée too has been rediscovered. Many architects have retracted from the wish to eliminate the enduring, and use their profession as an instrument to stage a revival of the long-term. Others perpetuate durable patterns in a less unequivocal way. We distinguish:

Archaism
The first strategy is super-historical, and honours only the eternal and transcendental. Time is reduced to a practically timeless essence. Morality and amorality are not directly relevant; only metaphysics and ontology count here. How could this goal be embodied except in matter? Hard, slow and naked matter is the medium in which the transience and shallowness of metropolitan life is problematised. The house is solid, robust and reliable. It is shelter and root.
Tadao Ando radicalises durée to the point of a spiritual experience of eternity that practically excludes historicity. Literally turning its back on the world of continual happenings, his introverted architecture principally aims to induce an ultimate serenity, an exclusion of all the tormenting problems that still cry out for solution. His architecture aspires to a reptilian level that eludes the grip of the vicissitudes of language. Ando's central purpose is to foster the spiritual exchange between mankind and the thing that manifests itself in loneliness. With its outspoken materiality, this architecture is almost a definition of the durable.

Façadism
The second strategy appeals to history, from which it hopes to learn and with which it aims to educate. The primary means towards these ends is an unambiguously canonised iconographic vocabulary that is meant to guarantee the enduring reproduction of 'eternal', classical, humanistic values. The archetypes of classicism must banish doubt and reinstate a clear morality. **Leon Krier** believes that the tide of the today can thus be turned: 'The *Zeitgeist* is there despite us; the more clever we think we are at dealing with it, the more stupid we will one day appear'. The facade is deployed to institutionalise a world of order and quiet. The self-aware, honest individual will not succumb to the chaos of the metropolis, but will find himself in a peaceful pedestrian world. Pictorial, monumental series of architectural objects and axes generate the necessary quotum of civilisation.

Fascinism
The third strategy would have nothing to do with a durable order. It shatters this order in an explosive game of form in which all is apparently permitted – a maximally individual interpretation of the Now condensed into the material of an ecstatic object. This attitude thus considers itself amoral and answerable only to the principle of simultaneity. The world is as it is, and the only adequate answer is fragmentation. This reality is fragmentary and momentary, and the appropriate architecture is always breathlessly frenetic. It seems that **Frank Gehry** wishes to turn everything on its head: the elite culture, the accepted values and norms. Everything must be possible *now*. But, at the same time, a durée is in fact perpetuated. Alongside the eternal ritual of daily life, the theme embodied here is also the ever-returning element of play. The carnivalesque aspect of Gehry's work, its hilarity, always looks like a denial of the past but is in fact a subtle reproduction of it.

The lack of beauty is the current architectural actuality. Materialistic functions are consistently emphasised instead of the function of the beauty of the building and its environment, which is equally important to man. Material functions are only valid temporarily, since they change constantly. Beauty is much longer-lasting and far sooner has a timeless function. **Ton Alberts & Max van Huut**

To question the interrelationship between architecture and nature is to capture architecture within the framework of time. By employing geometry as a methodology, I seek to synthesise past and present, East and West. *Tadao Ando*

This century is the century of the ephemeral. All is fragile, everything disappears. The image reigns, the image dies out, fashions pass, buildings comply with changing requirements. The Durée lies hidden within the gaze. The gaze will only rest on those objects which it recognises. One ought to build for this gaze. **Ricardo Bofill**

Duration is primarily achieved through grounding, to be bound to the earth. Buildings are bound to the earth. Not so much by gravity but by use and by our understanding of them. Today universal depresencing produces not strong but weak bonds. The task for architecture today is enormous, the sedimentation of new perceptual modes into the realm of the physical will result in new topologies + new forms, new scales. The responsible architect must today rethink both object + field. Simulation today is reality. It is the task of everyone to give it depth. **Julia Bolles & Peter Wilson**

Believe that the professional activity of an engineer lies mainly in the development of analytical models which describe nature in a realistic way. Working with isostatic structures almost inevitably leads one to sketching nature. When, for example a dog stands on his four legs it constitutes an isostatic body. The load is divided by the number of legs, there are no other forces present other than those supplied by the muscles. **Santiago Calatrava**

The very permanence of architecture can only be understood with the actions that take place in it as part of its structure. Then and only then can architecture entertain an intimate contact with the moment of perception – of being in it, of finding that it means something. **Nigel Coates & Doug Branson**

The duration of architecture has little to do with its physical life. Architecture changes under the attentive scrutiny of our gaze, and opens itself to new interpretations. It is the duration of continuous change. **Pietro Derossi**

Leonardo Da Vinci and Schlemmer constructed two fundamentally different models for the relationship between man and this world. As we slip further away from the model of Leonardo and past that of Schlemmer, into a time of revered artifice and spatial implosion, the relation of man to this world has become a subject of renewed interest. What could a new model of this relationship be? Could there be one? **Elisabeth Diller & Ricardo Scofidio**

Architecture is a bridge over time, spanning between those cultures of the past and the future. Buildings created today are sited in places which have evolved over the history of past cultures. Each of our projects attempts to be a special response to its own place, influenced by and sensitive to the past also shaped by an anticipation of the future. **Norman Foster**

Bouncing off the interior walls and ceiling (of the Joan Miró Library), the shimmering light becomes the permanent source of brightness, constant throughout the building. **Beth Galí**

You always have to work against your past. *Frank Gehry*

People criticise me for looking back to the past – for using hitorical references. I would love to be able to use only archetypal references, because I think that's the basis of the myth and ritual of architecture. But I get primarily that language from Rome – that kind of continuous language. I see architecture as a cultural continuity. **Michael Graves**

Architecture ought to be such that it allows us to hear the mysterious music of the universe and the rich, yet by no means transparent, world of emotions that have been disregarded by modern rationalism. **Itsuko Hasegawa**

There no longer are any traditions in the consistent and comprehensive sense of the word... Our architecture is not part of any actual tradition, but relates to earlier architectures through observation, critical perception, imitation or rejection. It is as if an earlier, mediating generation had been eliminated by an environmental catastrophe. This is the point of rupture where our contemporary culture begins... Such a culture only carries on earlier patterns of behaviour and buildings as apparitions of the original, comprehensive forms... **Jacques Herzog & Pierre de Meuron**

Architectural thought is the working through of phenomena initiated by idea. By 'making' we realise idea is only a seed for extension In phenomena. Sensations of experience become a kind of reasoning distinct to the making of architecture. Whether reflecting on the unity of concept and sensation or the intertwining of idea and phenomena, the hope is to unite intellect and feeling, precision with soul. **Steven Holl**

Man has always striven for – and built for – survival: survival during life but, equally important, survival after life. In human activity there is duality and my architecture reflects this in a dialectic between the natural and the artificial, the anthropomorphous (and amorphous) and the geometric. **Hans Hollein**

In traditional cultures, fundamental aesthetic and ethical principles are considered to be of universal value and this is where the controversy lies; namely in the question of a universal value transcending time and space, climates and civilisation. In traditional cultures, industrial rationale and methods are subordinate to larger themes, to larger concerns. In Modernist cultures, by contrast, invention, innovation and discovery are ends in themselves. **Leon Krier**

Respect for time and duration is not just nostalgia. It means making allowance for things as they are and refraining from imposing tyrannical utopias. On the other hand, it is absolutely clear that we can not extrapolate an existing context into the future (that is romanticism!). Our contemporary context is mobile, multi-racial, ever more diverse (what a wealth!). Thus the present situation calls for architects who are capable of working very personally but also with great complexity. **Lucien Kroll**

When attempting to transmit history through material objects, first history must be deconstructed into symbols and signs, and these fragments, endowed with a new meaning, must be incorporated into the work as bits of memory. Another method of achieving symbiosis between past and present is to incorporate the atmosphere or mood of the past – Japanese Buddhist thought or traditional Japanese aesthetics, or philosophy, or patterns of living, or arrangements of space – into Modern Architecture. In this case, the past that we are trying to incorporate is invisible, a spiritual legacy, and our intellectual task is to discover a way to make this spirit come alive in Modern Architecture in a sophisticated form. **Kisho Kurokawa**

We have no vision of the future. It is all happening so quickly. A vision of the future is outdated as soon as it is expressed. We can only keep thinking and keep saying it can all be much more beautiful. For us, hard work is a way of life. We just keep working. **Lucien Lafour & Rikkert Wijk**

The architect must have some idea of immortality to do his work. After all, history doesn't exist. **Daniel Libeskind**

There is a widespread yet largely unarticulated belief that buildings are going to disappear, and I share this sensation as well. Architecture is now prepared for being an ephemeral art. That is one of the reasons why architecture today so frequently appeals to the superficial image of its predecessors; today's society does not believe in the lasting condition of its own creations. The initial impact of the building is what counts, not its long life. My point of view, however, is that this durability – this condition of being built to last – is very powerful. One must still fight for that. **Rafael Moneo**

The once fashionable 'epistemological break' notwithstanding, ruptures always occur within an old fabric which is constantly dismantled and dislocated in such a way that its ruptures lead to new concepts or structure. In architecture such disjunction implies that at no moment can any part become a synthesis or self-sufficient totality. **Bernard Tschumi**

Architects should consider the need of several generations of users. This suggests political questions: Who shall decide for the future? and others regarding materials and the nature of spaces that will permit changes in both the philosophies and needs of future users. Long durée brings up consideration of the functions of space and the relations between spaces. Over the long run, should a building fit its present functions specifically, like a glove, or should it, like a mitten, satisfy a variety of functions, although the fit is loose for all? In our experience, adaptability does not necessarily require that space be bland. To appeal to multiple cultures over many years, a building might better be complex and multi-layered than bland and simple. Complex architecture may satisfy the avant-garde as well. Avant-garde architects have a right to enjoy their work. In civic, institutional, and other long-lived buildings we hope they can do so along with present and future users. Users today, who change their postures and opinions every decade, could be seen as the evanescent factor against which the building stands solid though not confrontational, supportive but not necessarily pliant. **Robert Venturi & Denise Scott Brown**

Virgin Islands in the Urban Chaos

The serene, austere, ascetic, thick-walled, geometrical buildings of Tadao Ando won the first Carlsberg prize for architecture in 1992 – the largest culture prize in the world, the 'Nobel prize' of architecture. Confronted by concrete hardness, starkness and colourlessness, the brewery jury could hardly fail to pause for a closer look. A pause for contemplation in the ceaseless flux of the metropolis. A pause for reflection on the eternal, amid the volatile images of here and now.

Tadao Ando tries to evoke a fundamental spiritual experience in the users of his buildings. 'The immaterial and formless elements, like the wind, the sun, the sky and the landscape, are transected and appropriated by the walls, which are the powers of the world inside. (...) Organic and continually changing nature must be captured by geometric forms that give it a spiritual dimension.'★ 'I hope my spaces will put down sturdy roots in a real earth of human life, and that they will embrace human existence in its utmost diversity.'★ His architecture manifests itself as a stubborn attempt to cool off the overheated machinery of the city. Thus it provides everyone, from the apologist of progress to the apocalyptician, with explosive material for discussion. One could almost see Tadao Ando as an envoy of the Virgin Islands, visiting the high-tech cyberindustrial world to attest to the charms of his homeland.

★ Ando, Tadao, quoted in Bertrand, Pascal, 'Ruimtelijke Strategie', *Archis* 11 (1991), p. 21.
★ Ando, Tadao, quoted in Bertrand, Pascal, op. cit. p. 22.

As a self-taught noble savage, he reaches an unequalled mastery in the architecture of serenity. His buildings are sanctuaries in which one can silently rediscover the inner truths of existence, immaculate islands of calm in the tortured agglomeration of screaming haste. Through his fusion of organic nature, monastic asceticism, pantheistic imagery and existentialist pondering, Tadao Ando enriches architecture with work that can be interpreted as a *testimonium paupertatis*, in several senses. Ando's buildings lay a finger on the spiritual poverty of the chaotic metropolitan pulse. But the buildings are themselves parsimonious, naked and ascetic in appearance. And nature, which plays such a prominent role in this architecture, attracts concern nowadays on account of its straitened circumstances. The best way to combat poverty, according to Ando, is with poverty.

Laconic Architecture

The essential thing about poverty is that you have to experience it *physically*. And Ando's architecture offers ample opportunity for that physical experience. The space, *ma* in Japanese, is physically and spiritually interpreted in this work, and obtains its character though a subtle game of continually changing incident light and geometrical proportions. It is not just the emptiness between the walls, but also that between successive events. Hence the space always forms a bridge between the Actual and the Possible. In the Row House (Osaka, 1976) this is made completely clear by the alternation of inside-outside-inside in a single house. When you wish to go from one part to the other, you have to go through the open air, with its associated experiential verities.

Children's Museum, Himeji, 1990

Besides being a bridge, a space is also a place. Ando creates a hermetic microcosm, circumscribed by massive walls. Often you can only access it via a long passageway which prepares you, as it were, for the atmosphere you are about to encounter. This *rite of passage* is meant as purification, and is accompanied by a little physical discomfort: you have to stay outside for a bit longer than you would like.

Ando's use of materials is also fundamental. His concrete, made using the latest technological methods, is generally strong and pure. Sometimes it is like silk, rough and soft at the same time. In the city, the bunker-like walls function as ramparts against the metropolitan chaos. Inside the building, the elementary predominates. The walls cast you back on yourself. In country locations, Ando assimilates features of the natural landscape (or what is left of it) into the building by making interior and exterior intersect, and by creating a long *promenade architecturale*. The elements of light, wind, water, sky and earth are written into the experiential scenario. The total impression made by Ando's work, which has shown considerable consistency throughout his career, is one of a supremely laconic architecture where silence and meditation go hand in hand. He offers a physical framework in which this can take place – a matrix for people, their movements and their gaze.

Tadao Ando hopes to offer us something more than an artificial solace. He aims to rediscover the essential elements of the 'human sojourn' that have been left behind in the pell-mell economic growth. These elements are, in his view, as follows: the primary relation with nature and with materials; the minor discoveries people make in their daily living environment; the pleasure that can be introduced into a simple lifestyle by a creative intervention. He reduces space, material and light to a naked essence, a union that coincides with emptiness. This emptiness must not be dismissed as nihilistic, according to Ando, but should be understood as the core of existence to which everything in life is related. This can only be reached through a spiritual experience.

28

These works, with their intangible qualities and poetic images generated in actual experience, eventually transcend the level of visual or verbal communication and reach the deeper subconscious regions of perception whereby we are compelled to approach them through an internal or intuitive understanding while being immersed in them. At this deepest level they do not stand for anything; they are only themselves hermetically closed within ourselves. This is a primordial ontological condition, a point where architecture steps out of space and time, and the 'terror of history' is suspended. Here the past as much as the future is real and permanently exists. At its best, the new Japanese architecture is the result of poetic inspiration and sentiment rather than a merely problem-solving or scientific analysis; its unique qualities defy quantitative measurement and evaluation.
Botond Bognar

Whereas Western thought is hinged on individual consciousness, the Japanese have traditionally held a pantheistic view of nature and entrusted consciousness to God, who is seen to dwell in all things of the universe. Accordingly, within an architecture's form a spiritual and invisible something is felt to lie concealed.
Tadao Ando

Like a fortress built in the desert, a wall is not only a protective barrier but a spiritual bridgehead, clearly asserting its presence in the changing flow of the city and rejecting any preconceived notion of community.
Tadao Ando

Literary Museum, Himeji, 1990

Row House, Osaka, 1976.

Reticence and Charisma

There are many ways towards an understanding of the spirituality that Tadao Ando wishes to serve in his work. Thus we could concentrate exclusively on the typically Japanese references. For example, the paradoxically prominent visual sobriety of Ando's architecture can easily be seen in the light of Zen philosophy. The outsider might expect this sobriety to arouse an experience of 'nothingness', but its real intention is a sense of totality. Zen aims to bring man into a state where he feels united with reality. Zen art thus never aspires to represent, but to present nature as it *is*. The artistic medium must remain as invisible as possible in order to maximise the pure experience. Or, as Ando himself formulates these ideas in relation to his bare walls, 'they become abstract (...) and approach the ultimate limit of space. Their actuality is lost, and only the space they enclose gives a sense of really existing'. ★

Another Japanese reference: isn't Ando's architecture a petrified *haiku*, the art of omission, poetry in concrete, the expression of an *unmediated* relation with the universe? From a slightly greater distance, the work also seems to be inspired by Shintoism. That is not altogether surprising since there is no clear boundary between Zen and Shintoism. Shinto is a religion that exalts Nature. Because the concepts of good and bad are not really recognised in Shinto, all things in Nature are given the status of *the sublime*. Not only are natural objects deified in this way, but also objects that represent nature. Shinto does not involve anthropomorphism, however – it does not ascribe a human identity to the things it worships. There is no metaphor intended. The holy Mount Fuji always remains the mountain Fuji. Shinto architecture, in line with this thinking, does not attempt to adorn nature but to become one with it. Rather than imposing itself on its surroundings, it conducts itself in sublime harmony with them. This traditional reticence can also be recognised in Ando's architecture. Therefore it is

★ Ando, Tadao , 'From Self-enclosed Modern Architecture Toward Universality', *The Japan Architect*, May 1982, p. 9.

all the more remarkable that his work is now the focus of so much attention. Ando claims no more than a wish to restore the 'sense of light, wind and rain that is being lost in Japanese cities'. But amid the hectic modernity and rampant chaos of the urban environment, this introversion has acquired the charisma of heroic resistance. Hence the Carlsberg prize.

Mineralisation of the Soul

Ando recognises his inevitable role as critic. He stresses his wish to support cultural resistance to the juggernaut of modernity. 'I believe that, however anachronistic it may sound, it is important to ask the fundamental question "What is architecture?". The creation of architecture must be a criticism of problems of today. It must resist existing conditions. It is only when one faces up to today's problems that one can really begin to deal with architecture.' ★

Ando's architecture aims, in fact, to enhance the experience of the phenomena of time, place and space; and it pursues this goal by excluding everything that could distract from those phenomena. By taking this approach, he engenders an existential (i.e., in these times, critical) experience whose import is clearly and comprehensively embraced in the Heideggerian *Fundamentalontologie* paradigm, which was introduced into philosophy as a way of taking the criticism of Western civilisation to its extreme. This brings us to a way of comprehending Ando's work that is more familiar to Western thinking. In *The Concept of Time* (1924), a finger exercise for his principle work, *Being and Time* (1927), Heidegger proposes that the true nature of *Dasein*, namely the *Sein* part of it, is *Temporality*, which Heidegger interpreted principally as being our capacity to form an image of our own future 'being in the past', i.e. of our own mortality. This image is characterised by a large measure of certainty and a total unsettledness. Heidegger refers

★ Ando, Tadao, quoted in Bretagnolle, Alain, 'The Timeless Message of Nature', *El Croquis* 44, (1990), p. 193.

29

to '*die Unbestimmtheit der Gewißheit des Vorbei*', and resists the rationalist '*bestimmung*' of the '*unbestimmte Zeit*'. His principal aim is to rescue the authentic moment of certain transience and unsettledness in a universe that is ever further strictured. Heidegger's essay ends with the words: 'Then *Dasein* would be: being questionable'. Only the authentic experience can evince the vulnerability and openness that the present-day city dweller has so lamentably sacrificed.

We can also view Ando's architecture as being an appeal to this kind of stable and the durable experience, as invoking a profounder, almost unchanging existential layer beneath the giddying onrush of historic events that seems to dominate our notion of time. 'My approach to the person who will use these spaces', he says, 'amounts to acting as an intermediary in a deep dialogue between him and architecture, because my spaces transcend theory and appeal to the deepest levels. In other words, my spaces

Sloterdijk, 'healing the wound of time with eternal stone, by mineralisation of the soul'. That is where the unique existential experience enters the public domain, and it is this that gives Ando's architecture its social significance.

Reptilism

Admirers claim Ando's work has indisputable social significance. All the same, this architecture is intrinsically rooted in a strategy of rising above social concerns. Society is a temporal matter, whereas man is only capable of rediscovering himself in the universe when forced into introspection, detached from daily concerns. Ando's work is aimed at that individual anchoring in the domain of the presocial. The work remains noncommittal about what has to be achieved beyond that, after reintroduction of a social context. It does not lay itself open to a further explanation because it lacks a nar-

Forest of Tombs, Kumamoto, 1992

Japan Pavilion, Sevilla Expo, 1992

relate to the fundamental aspects of humanity'.★ Amid the suffocating strictures of Japanese conformism, and at the same time confined by the straightjacket of Western conventionality, Ando thus highlights a fundamental uncertainty of being that in principle leaves room for

★ Ando, Tadao, quoted in Bretagnolle, Alain, op. cit. p. 193.

a different way of doing things. His architecture seems to propose a change of course towards (in the words of Peter Sloterdijk) a world of the still present, away from the world that is still to open. It involves a relaxation of the cramp of modernity, a transition from a resolute vision to an acquiescent vision, allowing oneself to be overtaken by the unreachably nearby instead of chasing after the unreachably far away. His buildings stand for authenticity and durability. They seem to be capable of, refering to Peter

rative quality that can be discussed. It offers no stimulus to take a specific subjective standpoint, and hence no invitation to a dialogue. Representation is rigorously excluded so as to arouse, in its total serenity, something that can best be described as a deep-freeze ontology. The work does not attempt to activate this quiescent, perpetual, deathly conception of existence simply by presenting us with a sign. That would split the world unnecessarily along linguistic lines and thereby plunge us deeper into the ubiquitous entropy of meaning. The architecture of Ando aims to arouse the senses only at a non-linguistic, almost *reptilian* level. It is humourless, cold-blooded, acortical. The message imparts itself and we have no need of a cerebral language centre.

You may well wonder what this strategy has to offer in the public domain. Even though

I think the task for architects is to provide environments that in some way confront the sensibility in which we live.

Peter Eisenman

To gaze at the river made of time and water. And recall that time itself is another river.

Jorge Luis Borges

The concrete covering vanishes under the action of the light and the space then oscillates between the visible and the invisible, the opaque and the transparent, it leads from shadows to light, i.e., in a spiritual sense from the sensible to the intelligible, from imperfection to perfection. This negation of constructed space aimed at replacing it with the simple idea of space modifies the perception of duration and operates a fixation on time in space, i.e., a spatialisation of time.

Alain Bretagnolle

In you, my spirit, I measure time; you I measure, as I measure time. Do not cross my path with the question: How is that? Do not mislead me into looking away from you through a false question. Do not obstruct your own path with the confusion of what may concern you yourself. In you, I say repeatedly, I measure time; the transitory things encountered bring you into a disposition which remains, while those things disappear. The disposition I measure in present existence, not the things that pass by in order that this disposition first arise. My very finding myself disposed, I repeat, is what I measure when I measure time.

St. Augustine

Kidosaki House, single family house,
Tokyo, 1986

Zen Garden

Koshino House, single family house,
Ashiya, 1984

Ando's architecture succeeds in staging – and sometimes actually invoking – a spiritual experience, its minimalism threatens to succumb to deaf-mutism. Architecture must naturally generalise in order to answer to the needs of society at large. It can only express itself in broad terms and can never be as subtle as writing or speech. But perhaps the deliberate degradation of its expressive capacities to a level of bare tectonic substantialism constitutes all too small a contribution to a critical counter-culture. Ando's architecture continually runs the danger of losing contact with the object of criticism, the madness of modernity. Unfortunately, architecture that says no more than enough is liable to say too little.

The main requirement that the nature of the message here places on the architecture, viewed as a medium, is simply that it must be a thing in the world, subject to experience. The signified and the signifier may merge here into a (literally) material basis; but the basis is so primitive that nobody could conceivably object to it or be inspired by it to even the faintest stirrings of a political programme. Admittedly, the architecture's geometry, its terseness and the brutalist use of materials, generate a sense of absolute conviction, but at the same time you are thrown into total confusion over the question of 'What next?' It is concerned with *being* and not with *doing*, with non-historic time as a modality of being but not with time as a historic material you can do something with. Ando's durable contents are minimal in the programmatic sense. Perhaps that is why they are so perfectly at home in the atavistic medium that architecture, in its tactile guise, has always been.

Henny van der Steen-Schakenraad, *With money you can be everywhere*, 1989.

Time-out

Just as we breathe without thinking, Ando seems to wish us to undergo his architecture without mental reflection. In the full spirit of the Shinto and Zen traditions, immersion in the architecture must be total and not distracted by contemplation of the experience itself. By the same token, we are not expected to muse on matters such as wealth or poverty. We are only truly poor when we no longer realise that we are so. At that point, a remarkable Zen paradox comes into operation, one which is clearly visible in Ando's portfolio of clients. For if we no longer realise that we are grindingly poor, it is equally possible for us to be oblivious to the fact that we are nauseatingly rich. The monastic asceticism of Ando's work is paradoxical in relation to the wealth of its occupants. In Zen, experiencing the fullness life may be preferred above self-awareness, and sometimes there can be a good reason for it. So should we fail to forget our wealth and continue to feel pangs of guilt, Ando's architecture may offer a useful remedy: a means for daily penance, as we are forced to endure the cold and rain on our way from one space to another. These ideas will surely not be foreign to Ando, considering the background of some of his clients, including the Church. It is noticeable how, as Japan's economy prospers, Ando's entry rituals increase in length.

Marx's observation that 'all that is solid melts into air', Baudrillard's 'death struggle of reality' – Ando can only be commended for distancing himself from such scenarios. He aims to offer mankind an authentic experience, a benchmark in a world where things are all too fuzzy. This attempt to pin humanity down to a fundamental experience, with the intention of offering a shield against the dehumanising logic of its own culture, has developed into something of a tradition for a certain critical tendency that operates from the periphery of the modern world. There are countless intellectual heavyweights in that fringe who have sought and still seek a way out of that predicament described by Max Weber as a 'disenchantment of the world' – a predicament where practically anything can be achieved by rational operation while not even a fragmentary moral basis apparently remains to help answer questions such as Tolstoy's 'What shall we do and how shall we live?' Culture's efforts to make life easier have become a burden too heavy to be borne.

But perhaps Ando's paradigm shift, confined as it is to an impressive series of architectural accomplishments, does not have enough to offer the world at large. It would be far from fanciful to suggest that the serenity of Ando's architecture is ultimately not so much creative as recreative: that it offers a brief and refreshing time-out from the headlong pursuit of higher corporate profits, no more than a sanctuary for the status quo. Here, in fact, Ando's architecture touches on questions that are outside the competence of the architect. What, with the wisdom of the Virgin Islands, can he teach us about the space we should reserve for peace and quiet, about the cultural options that will cultivate that tranquillity and give it meaning? Is there really any prospect of the re-enchantment not just of architecture, but of the world?

Although the impact of Modernism has declined at the cultural level, its essential functions still remain valid in contemporary society. We have yet to see the end of it. Based on this assumption, I apply Modernist vocabulary and technology to my architecture, overlaid with distinct contextual elements such as regional identity and lifestyles of the users.

Tadao Ando

Regionalists advocate minimalists like Ando, Botta, Siza, etcetera. But minimalism can't articulate regionalism. That's the paradox. To be truly regionalist you have to use enough codes of the region so that the people in the region understand the language you are using. Siza, Ando, they do the reverse. They use international architecture, concrete architecture, abstract architecture, which is decontextualising, deregionalising and which no one in the region can understand. That's why it's anti-regionalism.

Charles Jencks

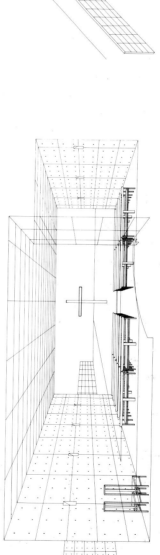

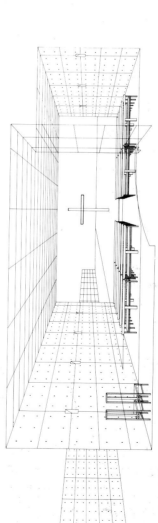

The building is situated on a plain in the central mountains north-west of Yubari Range in Hokkaido. The site is surrounded with wild trees, and covered with green foliage in the spring and the summer and with silvery snow in the winter. An artificial lake was built by channelling the water from a nearby stream. In this project, I tried to contemplate in what way the water, as an element of Nature, relates to architecture and human beings. The whole layout comprises two squares having sides of ten metres and fifteen metres respectively which are overlapped and face the artificial lake. Elevated walls extend to surround them in the shape of the letter L. When one approaches from behind the building along the long wall, one only hears the stream but does not see the water. With expectation swelling, one goes through an opening in the wall and turns around by 180 degrees to confront the water. One is directed to an approach encircled by glass walls on all four sides as one climbs up a gentle slope listening to the sound of the stream. One finds oneself within the box of light. The top is open, and four crosses are standing facing each other under the vaults of heaven. Here one communicates with Nature as one listens to the sound of water, wind and chirping birds. I wished to build an architecture which would appeal not only to the eyes of viewers but to all the five senses of man. One is not oriented in any particular direction when going around the four crosses, and therefore the effect one feels when starting towards the church is intense. One appreciates the surrounding Nature while descending the spiral stairway. Climbing down a dark arc-like passage, one suddenly finds a church, and the sight abruptly opens out toward the lake to reveal another cross. The church houses nine inscribing spheres of five metres in diameter, and is defined with a glass door in front and a lobby in the rear. The lake starts under one's feet and joins a stream ninety metres ahead. The water surface extends in the great Nature in front of the chapel as if it were a mirror surface in the abstract. The scenery which is cut by the frame of the door changes with time and is reflected on the water. In the changes one feels Nature and the sacred at the same time. *Tadao Ando*

Location Tomamu, Hokkaido, Japan **Assistant** K. Okano **Client** Hotel Alpha Tomamu **Design** 1985-88 **Completion** 1988

► Tadao Ando Architect & Associates *Church On The Water*

Skeet McAuley, Portage Glacier, Alaska, 1990

O Tempora, O Mores!

Brace yourself: what do Cicero and Cato, Albert Speer and Paul Ludwig Troost, William Morris and John Ruskin, Quinlan Terry and Rod Hackney, Adam Smith and Thomas Jefferson, Thomas Hobbes and Edmund Burke, Burberry's and Laura Ashley, Camillo Sitte and Hendrik Petrus Berlage (with apologies to any we may have missed), all have to do with Luxemburger/Briton Leon Krier? It is personal – they all crop up somewhere in the chain of associations we have with the work of Krier the architect and anti-revolutionary visionary. In some cases you might think they really do have a direct influence on Krier's words and thinking, and that he would not exist at all without their historic work. But then you realise that this view of Krier isn't fair, and that the associations continue where Krier himself leaves off. His project touches on themes to which the Western world has become ultra-sensitive and whose diabolical colouring makes them strictly taboo. The question is thus whether Krier can be blamed for the fact that we tremble for the implications of his approach, while he himself restricts his role as prophet of doom to the area of architectural discourse and is primarily concerned with the design. He opts for art where a less creative spirit might have chosen a risky political course. Therefore Krier can not be dismissed with the usual liberal right-mindedness that is the common reflex reaction to conservatism. On the contrary, it is Krier's artistic skill that forces us to listen to his proposals, makes his work unignorable and tricks us into letting ourselves be seduced by what places him head and shoulders above the modern politician: quality. That is to say, his penetrating eye, his critical spirit, his biting words, his graphic skill, his organisational strength and his talent for mobilising his sympathisers into a Party with a Cause.

One of those sympathisers is the crown prince of what was once the world's mightiest royal house. Now both the nation and the Windsor dynasty are showing signs of decay. But Krier no doubt eagerly agrees with the uncompromising words that HRH Prince Charles addressed to the architectural profession, whom he accused of succumbing to the arbitrary aesthetics of the profit motive. And although it now appears that the sharper edges of the debate that occupied UK architects in the late eighties have been dulled, and that the fieriest of opponents have sunk back in exhaustion, Britain remains the theatre of the endless, titanic struggle between the nostalgics and the rest – the punks of progress, the Modernist marauders.

British die-hards traditionally refuse to reconcile themselves to the purportedly inevitable. For example, conservatives of all colours blench at the idea of a united Europe and even the supposedly pre-European government keeps its foot close to the brakes. Similarly, there are countless British architects who will simply refuse to have anything to do with the modernisation of town and country. This recalcitrance even goes so far as to produce an inversion of the usual conception of what is inevitable. It may now be 1993, but the Modernists still feel they have to justify their adherence to Modernism. The traditionalists have history on their side and are all too pleased to shift the burden of proof on to the other side. It is the reciprocal sense of superiority, for the *Anciens* on grounds of the rule book, for the *Modernes* on grounds of empiricism, that

gives the discussion such an emotional charge for those involved, while it leaves outsiders wondering what it is all about.

The World According to Leon Krier

It is not difficult to sum up Leon Krier's views on the decline of our civilisation, for they are more strident than original. As we know, trenchant messages on the urgency of change tend to be worded in the familiar terminology of doom and gloom. The apocalypse is just not very subtle, so it is not up to Krier to bustle about inventing a new language. The old language is good enough, and for the following reasons.

If our world is going to blazes, we have only ourselves to blame. If a significant part of that world is made by the architects amongst us, then a significant share of that blame goes to them. If we are not happy with that state of affairs (and who is?) then it is high time we sought redress against the architects. In this, Krier takes the lead himself and he is not averse to including the structure of the capitalist system in his crusade targets

House at Seaside, Florida, 1988

(or at least wherever this system promotes profit over beauty). Krier constantly denounces the cupidity that has so horribly disfigured the modern city in general and London in particular. Private interests overshadow public ones. 'The catastrophic state of great parts of our environment is a direct expression of how far urban politics are now dominated by factional interests to the disadvantage of the common good.' ★ Krier distinguishes here between capital and the public interest. After nearly three centuries of industrialisation and the architectural contribution to it, architecture has at last understood that its own decline is a consequence of being all too ready to equate the public interest to the private one. This equation, originating in Benthamist utilitarianism which also proffers the idea that 'every supply creates its own demand', can no longer be upheld in a

★ Krier, Leon, 'God Save the Prince', *AMA* 38 (1988), p. 14.

Urban legislation is clearly incapable of building decent cities and communities and instead is responsible for large scale urban ecological destruction.
Leon Krier

Modern barbarism can only be defeated by bringing urban civilization into the suburb, i.e. by building true urban centres in the suburban desert. Not expanding the cities but expanding the public realm by redeveloping the suburbs is, I believe, the main goal of civilisation.
Leon Krier

Urbanism will emerge from the revolution, not the revolution from urbanism.
Henri Lefebvre

The motivations of Krier's schemes for the reconstruction of cities such as Berlin and Washington DC are urbanistic and utopian (in the sense that they are unlikely to be realised). They are also traditional and idealistic in the straightforward manner that Post-Modernism is not. The way of life implied is paternalistic and monistic, but the plans would entail not the totalitarianism that his critics aver when they compare him with Albert Speer but an integrated culture led by a determined and sensitive elite.
Charles Jencks

Leon Krier and Duany & Plater Zyberk, Masterplan for Seaside, Florida, 1988

world that is visibly suffering both morally and ecologically from too much passing the buck (both in space and in time). The end of the nineteenth century was marked by a complete reorientation towards the *laissez faire* politics of high capitalism, together with the founding measures of the later welfare state. Now a similar shift is noticeable in the reaction against Thatcherism and Reaganomics. While Milton Friedman sounds the retreat, Leon Krier is one of the voices in the wilderness that people are suddenly listening to again. His words often turn to the time-honoured English stereotype of the man in the street, the possessor of a common sense directed towards the common good. It is redolent of the harmonious society as 'state of nature' of Shelley; but we encounter it even as long ago as the fourteenth century, in Wyclif.

Capitalism With a Human Face

If anyone supports Leon Krier's cause in word and writing, then it seems to be his Modernist colleague and formal antithesis Richard Rogers. In 1992, Rogers wrote *A New London*, together with Mark Fisher. This book gives a convincing sketch of the city's decline, caused by an unacceptable growth of traffic, impoverishment of the urban environment and the widespread malaise of government. London is descending into chaos. 'Trafalgar Square was once the heart of an empire, Piccadilly Circus the centre of the universe. Today they are just two more jammed roundabouts in a shabby city playing a less and less culturally central role. (...) We must seek policies that will reduce urban traffic, energy consumption and pollutants and will produce a London with ecological balance and self-sustaining communities.'★

This quotation seems to represent Krier's views rather well, too. He is also good at eleventh-hour rhetoric. He, too, hammers away at the need for a rapid turnabout in town planning and in the current commercial way of thinking. '*Domine dirige nos* is the city's pious motto. It is hard to escape the impression that it should more correctly say *Pecunia nos dominat*.'★ But however much similarity there is in Krier's and Rogers' published views on urban decay, their proposed solutions differ radically. Rogers pleads the case of opportunity, of creating the preconditions for urban improvement. But Krier takes a definite stand for values, and wishes to revive nothing

★ Rogers, R., London: 'A call for action', in Fisher, M. and Rogers, R., *A New London*, London 1992, pp. xiv-xix.
★ Krier, Leon, 'God Save the Prince', *AMA* 38 (1988), p.19.

less than *civitas*, the sense of community and middle-class morality. The city is important to Rogers because it provides a public space, and hence a context for the kind of public life that is becoming strongly undermined in this age of telecommunications. 'The paradigm of public space is the city square or piazza: without it the city scarcely exists. City squares are special because their public function almost eclipses any other use they might have – people come to them principally to talk, demonstrate, celebrate, all essential public activities.'★ As far as Rogers' own work is concerned, this usually means an architecture that gives the maximum amount of (neutral) space to this buzz of conversing, demonstrating and celebrating. What there is to discuss or celebrate falls, in his view, outside his sphere of competence.

★ Rogers, R., 'London: A call for action', in Fisher, M. and Rogers, R., *A New London*, London 1992, p. xv.

It is laudable that Leon Krier sees his task as more than just creating preconditions, and wishes to offer a concrete, *civitas*-fostering alternative. According to Krier, the community is served by the maintenance of certain civilised values, and architecture must not hide behind its facilitating function but must have some kind of message that manifests those values. If architecture is to be representative, then let it represent what is good. Why should it have to represent the crisis of the eternal values by being no better than a platform for debate of these values? It should support these values wholeheartedly and be a monument as well as a platform. It should bear witness to the community spirit in all respects – urban, architectonic and in details – like the architecture of the ancient Greeks. And if it proves impossible to do this for the entire urban programme, save your energy for the main image-defining locations. The aim should be to show that, in the words of sympathiser Prince Charles, 'capitalism can have a human face'.

Rogers wonders whether there is likely to be anything human behind that face too, and hopes that those responsible for urban disorder, the low profiteers, will be called to task. But Krier is not satisfied with this materialistic approach; he ascribes a self-regenerating power to culture in general and architecture in particular. 'The Prince of Wales is right to object to the Paternoster Redevelopment Brief and doubly right for blaming the architects who out of ignorance or timidity have done nothing to object to a brief which is positively ignoble. Listening to them on the BBC they told us that it is neither developers nor politicians nor indeed architects who shape our cities, that instead irresistible market forces, pressures and processes are at work here and that to resist them would be as futile as objecting to rain and sun. The Prince's message is instead one of freedom; he affirms that *we* shape our cities, and that *we* are free to choose what cities we build and how we build and use them.'★ And if we are free and responsible for our actions, we shall have to accept a positive principle to guide us. That clearly applies to influential architects too. 'If you fill a position of authority and you are supposed to teach architecture, you'd better be certain of what you are teaching. Otherwise there is no place for you as a teacher. Otherwise, you have a faculty of doubts, not of architecture.'★ In other words, now that the cultural contract no longer applies even-handedly to everyone,

★ Krier, Leon, 'God Save the Prince', *AMA* 38 (1988), p. 19.

★ Peter Eisenman versus Leon Krier, 'My ideology is better than yours', *Architectural Design* 58 (1989), p. 17.

Gypsotheca, Turin

we need 'the rules'. Prince Charles has already partly written them out himself: don't rape the landscape; a building must express itself; man is the measure of all things; sing with the choir and not against it; resurrect the principle of enclosure; use local materials; give us the details; architects and artists should be betrothed at an early stage in any major public project; don't make rude signs in public places; let the people who will have to live with what you build help guide your hand.

Categorical Imperative

Since the rules in the rule book have no absolute authority, they need further justification. Krier has repeatedly taken the trouble to define a moral basis for his approach. Immanuel Kant has proved useful here. Introducing his Atlantis project (1987), Krier formulated a 'Kantian' categorical imperative for architects, and this makes his principles clear: •'Build in such a way that you and your loved ones can find pleasure at any time in using your buildings, looking at them, living, working, holidaying and growing old in them.' •'Build in such a way that the concept of your design is valid as a principle of both architecture and urbanism.'

Before we consider the question of possible grounds for that validity, it would be a good idea to let the implications of this imperative sink in. Leon Krier's work is not a solution to a problem that has been raised, but an exemplar, or at least a suggested solution for the whole gamut of problems facing the city of today. Bearing in mind his reversal of the burden of proof, we must now listen while Krier unblushingly asks us 'Why not rather build like this?' The 'this' is a square-headed positing, against all Post-Modernist odds, of a visionary Utopia, a world organised and built through the wilful implementation of a set of chosen moral and stylistic values which the architect/demiurge conceives of as enduring certainties.

If we look closely at the blueprints for Washington DC, Atlantis (Canary Islands) and Poundbury (Dorset, England), we invariably see a blend of classic republicanism, eighteenth century pastoralism and contemporary neo-historicism. If virtue is in such peril, it seems, the answer is an explicit display of the historical vocabulary of virtue. Thus we see in outline the highlights of forty centuries of architectural history; we find names redolent of greatness; we see urban axes stretching beyond the eye's reach; and, in

bird's eye view, we survey islands of spotless civic probity. Surely nothing could disturb this virtuous rectitude. If we must create sanctuaries of intransigence, then they must of course exclude all the contradictions of everyday life. Krier's cities fall into the purest *città ideale* tradition, which has accompanied Western architecture ever since the Renaissance. How can we classify his projects – as a plea, a vision, a Utopia, an alternative, a salvation? To Krier, they are totally feasible plans, no more and no less.

The plans are architecturally spectacular in the sense that their cultural programmes are taken to such extremes. In the case of private dwellings, a traditional (vernacular) typology and materials are adopted. For the public buildings the idiom of (monumental) Classicism, presumably the best thing for expressing universal values, is found suitable. In the project for Seaside, Florida, we see how Krier's historic preference results in mixed functions and a compact, almost medieval street plan which restricts motorised traffic. Everything seems to be aimed at demobilising Modernism. The dichotomy of modesty and monumentality is analogous to the eighteenth century bourgeois concept of private and public life, in which the family-man at home becomes a citizen of the Republic when out of doors.

Spatium Virtutis

Although there is more than one intention behind Leon Krier's approach, we can understand his work as a plea for the resurrection of Classicism, as an expression of civil uprightness, as a *spatium virtutis*. In Krier's urban planning work, this space is thus named Atrium, Propylaea, Acropolis or Agora. His rhetoric is also strongly reminiscent of Marcus Tullius Cicero, the Roman statesman who used his legendary eloquence to defend the classical moral ideal which in his times (as always) was being increasingly perverted by self-interest, cynicism and stupidity. To Cicero and all his subsequent incarnations, every newfangled idea is treasonable and should be opposed with might and main. But there is invariably a hidden agenda behind the sermon. Someone who *systematically* denounces the state of affairs as shocking, corrupt and doomed is aiming to enlarge his own role. That is why Cicero branded his opponent Catilina as the most evil monster of all time. The *o tempora o mores* can also be heard dying on Krier's

Charles Robert Cockerell, The professor's dream, 1848

38

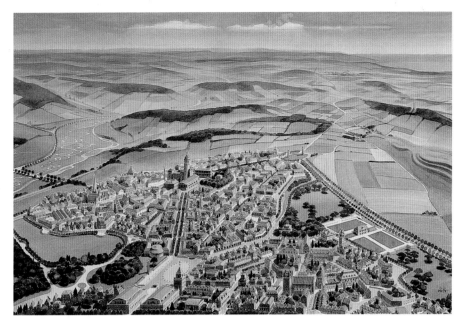

Masterplan for Poundbury, Dorchester, 1989

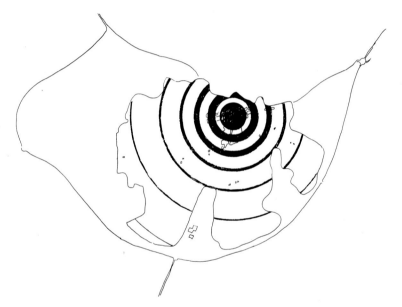

Present, monocentric Dorchester

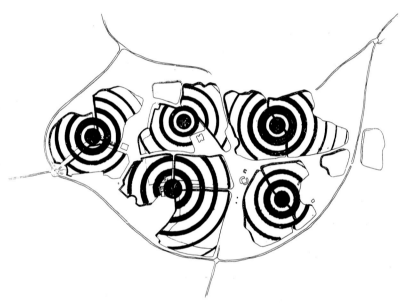

Future, poly-centric Dorchester

Street leading to market square

The unknown Alvar Aalto

lips. A *homo novus* among the English aristocracy, his manner is more British than the British. He stresses the earnestness of the situation. Just as Cicero, he preaches a major ethical reawakening with a return to *honor* and *virtus*, i.e. simplicity, diligence and above all incorruptibility. In the eyes of such a conservative there is no need to reform all of society at once: that would only release unpredictable forces. What is needed is to cut away the rotten parts – which happen to bear names like Eisenman, Rogers etcetera. The goal is to restore what there has never actually been: an orderly, stable and harmonious world headed by enlightened philosopher-kings – or at least enlightened aristocrats. In other words, a *Pax Krieriana*. And the tragic aspect is that everything points to such a peace no longer being needed.

Classicism: Style as Historical Compensation

Krier's Classicism is naturally the most obvious way of representing his Classical ideals. His Atlantis is the Aristotelian *polis* of mature, happy citizens. We ought to take the possibility seriously: if there really still is a durable, self-contained ideal to which a like-minded group could conceivably rally, then surely this classical ideal is the one that might expect to attract the most adherents. On the other hand, it is Krier's unequiv-ocal premise of an ethical politics that makes it impossible to accept his attitude as being a purely aesthetic programme. All Krier's references to harmonious cities, a good relation between human scale and monumentality and so on, can not be taken as suggestions for design principles without any thought of their moral connotations. Clearly this kind of morality has had time enough to prove itself during the course of history. But it has singularly failed to do so...

What is more, are there really any mature citizens out there, in a time such as this in which personal identity has to be fought so hard for, or has even been dismissed as completely obsolete? It is points like these that move us to find Krier's vision wanting, however much sympathy his incorruptibility deserves. Cicero ultimately overplayed his hand and was murdered. The values that Krier so emphatically supports have not been completely without effect on civilization, so he is unlikely to share the same fate. But the tragedy is that, in the long run, the exaggeration needed to delineate the problem of our times prevents the future sketch from achieving much in the way of realism.

Since the mid nineteenth century, Classicism has mainly been the style of the socially frustrated. The old aristocracy and a disgruntled middle-class were the social group-ings that were so keen to compensate their loss of historical meaning, their displace-ment from the social centre, with an appeal to the eternal classical values. It was also the style, in an almost purely formal sense, of the parvenus, for whom it was the prima-ry, recognisable means of expressing their newly acquired status. Therefore we should think extra carefully about the cultural meaning of Krier's *rappel à l'ordre*. His admira-tion for the work of Albert Speer, one of the last great Classicists to receive state assignments, explains a great deal. Part of the fascist iconography was shaped by the compensatory urge of a social class on its way down, the lower middle-class. Not only Speer, but Paul Ludwig Troost and Leni Riefenstahl supplied the ephemeral images of the supposedly solid world that was to last a thousand years. These images were very strong, but they owed their strength largely to the manipulation of propaganda media such as film and photography. Fascism was thus marked, in the words of Hal Foster, by 'both an extraordinary investment in the real and ★ Foster, Hal, *Recodings*, Seattle 1985, p. 80. an extraordinary manipulation of its loss'. ★ Krier is faced with the same contradiction in his work. On the one hand, he hopes his oeuvre will reinstate the Classical system of values of the Republic. On the other, this doughty aspiration indicates just how obso-lete that value system is. On top of that, this programme's own historical antiquity guar-antees that it will fail. It can go no further than pure image, pure façade. Hence it inevitably also retains an air of propaganda. Krier's urban planning ideas all imply recreating exactly the unsullied universe of the medieval class society – and that milieu no longer exists.

After Virtue

We must admit that few architects speak the truth as Leon Krier does. What a pity that his truth always has to be such a universal truth. He admits to no nuances. Particulars are foreign to him. Krier regards as relevant that which is timeless – and this in an age that has made relevance such a time-dependent attribute. His arguments are not quali-tatively incorrect, but they are demonstrably ineffective. His architecture, which serves as the necessary illustration to his arguments, thus fails in its advocacy of cultural renewal. He draws a categorical distinction between truth and falsehood, and then he poses a categorical imperative as his idea of that truth. Thus one can only be for or against him. But that distinction is inadequate for these times. We now live in the age of *After Virtue*, to use Alasdair MacIntyre's words, in which the clarity of classical lan-guage is seriously muddied by an ossified terminology of values. This situation is not, alas, just a trivial oversight that can be stuccoed away behind a historicist façade, but a reality we have to face up to. Defiant gestures are not enough; we shall have to dirty our hands. The atmosphere Krier conjures up in his architectural drawings, with their antiquated motorcars in the street and biplanes in the air, leads one to suspect that he would have preferred to stop the clock some time before the Futurists. But the Futurists are a fact, and at this very moment their heritage is shaking the author's attic with its limitless decibels.

In traditional cultures, fundamental aesthet-ic and ethical principles are considered to be of universal value and this is where the con-troversy lies; namely in the question of a uni-versal value transcending time and space, climates and civilisation. In traditional cul-tures, industrial rationale and methods are subordinate to larger themes, to larger con-cerns. In Modernist cultures, by contrast, invention, innovation and discovery are ends in themselves.

Leon Krier

Leon Krier is perhaps the most extreme contextualist at work today: basically, his paradigm is the urban fabric of nineteenth century Paris - the street, the square, the quarter. Such contextualism derives from a reactive reading of Modernism: its ruptures were posed against historicism, not history, in order to transform the past in the present, not to foreclose it. But the disruptions of the modern age are real enough, and the rheto-rical urgency of contextualism owes much to the 'catastrophe' of Modern architecture. To put it simply, this Post-Modern Style of History may in fact signal the disintegration of style and the collapse of history.

Hal Foster

I think it is terribly dangerous to submit one-self to the inexorable forces of history.

Leon Krier

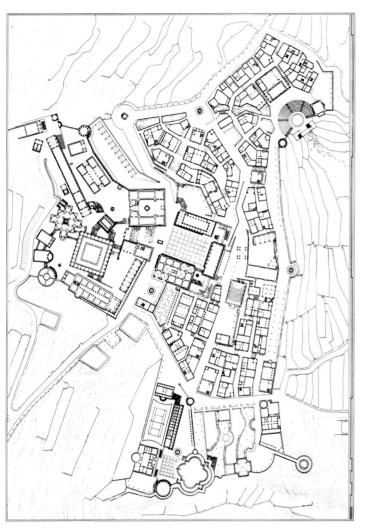

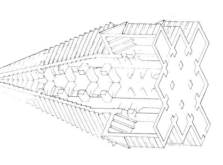

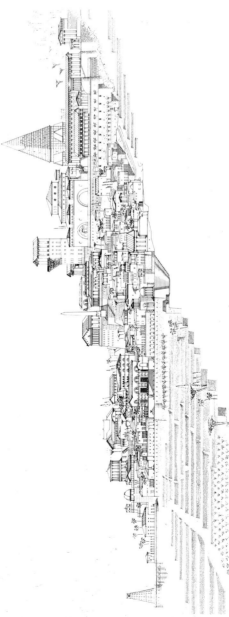

The site for Atlantis is a terraced southeasterly slope. In plan, as well as in silhouette, the city describes a roughly pyramidal figure whose base is the 350 metres long Corniche Promenade, 595 metres above sea level, and apex the church at 635 metres. In the centre of this triangle, lying at the foot of the Acropolis, is the Agora which is bounded on one side by the small mountain road between Arona and San Miguel. In Atlantis, the programme is split up into more than a hundred buildings both large and small, each of which can be simplified to its typologically irreducible core: church, baths, art museum, library, theatre, restaurant, workshop, house etc. These building types represent the hierarchic components of the city. With the exception of the Great Tower, all the buildings are only one or two storeys tall, although their heights vary considerably according to their use and significance. Whilst there are very few internal passages and staircases, there are some 31 external streets, alleyways and stairways, and nineteen squares. The streets are lined with plain-fronted houses, garden walls and pergolas, whereas on the squares communal buildings of a monumental character are located which both qualify and dominate the lines of sight within the city. The houses are on the narrowest alleys, but they all have a garden terrace with a view of the countryside. The great number and extent of alleys, streets and paths (4.5

kilometres over the five hectare site) permits the richest variety on the minimum space. The 42-metre high Great Tower and the four-towered Atrium Carrée form the *propylaeata* of the upper city, framing the stairs which lead from the Agora up the church. In the seventeen metres climb, the width of the stairs tapers in a forced perspective from 25 metres to two metres. The Agora sits like a bastion on an overhang 681 metres above sea level. The 24-columned *stoa* (open market hall) stands between the square and the open countryside. 45 houses and eleven studios, each with a garden terrace, comprise the real fabric of the city to the left and right of the main axis. The houses are of five basic types: linear, L-shaped, L plus tower, tower, polygon. The form and fabric of the city were largely determined by the topographic configuration of the site. The *cavea* of the theatre, the terraces of the city and the hanging gardens and the large *podia* of the Agora and the Acropolis all accentuate the natural topography. Respect for these features, combined with a complete freedom of grid, makes the form of the city naturally fluid. The methods used here are the same as those proven in the creation of great cities of the past.

Leon Krier

Location Tenerife, Spain **Assistants** R. Day, J. Maciag **Client** H. J. Müller **Design** 1987 **Completion** unbuilt project

Leon Krier *Urban Design Atlantis*

▶

Arrival from Arona, gate to agora

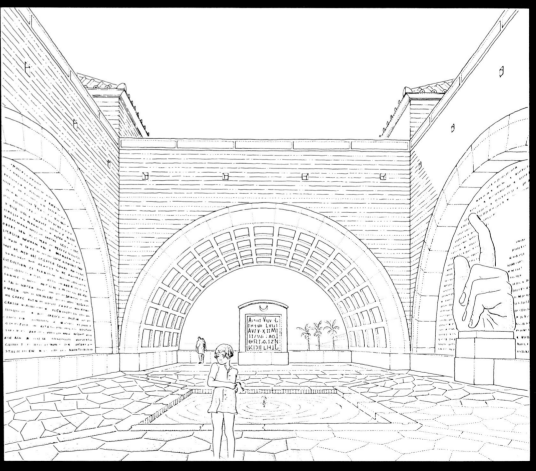

Atrium of Applied Arts Museum

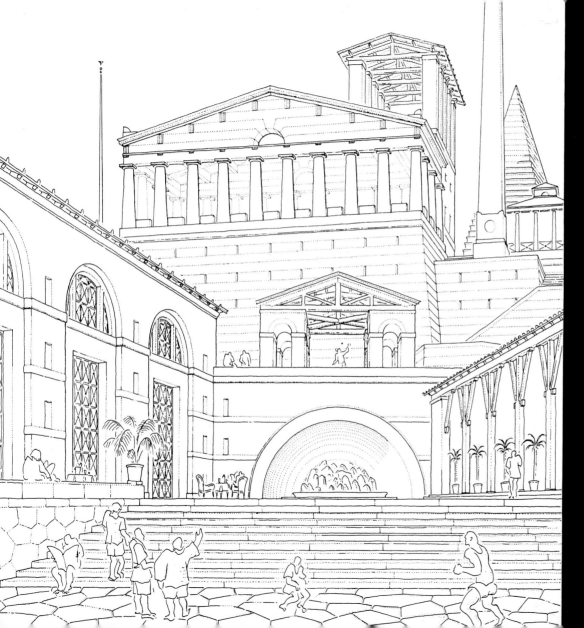

On the Work of Frank Gehry
Born to Be Wild

Los Angeles Vice might be a good name for Frank Gehry's brand of architecture. His work flouts so many conventions that at first sight it looks like sheer materialised malefaction. Using all the discipline's autonomous resources, Gehry tries to shake established architecture out of its slumber and offer it an invigorating cold shower, ultimately to its own good. First catharsis, and then... everything is allowed.

Frank Gehry was once likened to his fellow Californian Clint Eastwood as the notorious *Dirty Harry*, the cop who spurns all the stultifying legal niceties and meets crime head on with his Magnum 44.★ The powers that be at first want to strip him of his badge, but in the end

★ Davis, Mike, *City of Quartz, Excavating the Future in Los Angeles,* London 1990, p. 236.

they are visibly pleased with the lone combatant who takes the law into his own hands. At last, the city can breathe easy...

Perhaps the analogy looks a bit far fetched: Eastwood's neo-reactionary Harry seldom yields as much as a grudging smile, whereas Frank Gehry's playful avant-garde is closer to a Dionysian guffaw. But there is also an overriding similarity. In both cases, the nomadic wilfulness and provocative methods are widely enjoyed. And in both cases, too, this is really because whether intentionally or not, their wayward behaviour perpetuates a conventional morality.

The American Way

The media and the market have welcomed Gehry's work with open arms. His presence in the *Deconstructivist Architecture* exhibition at New York's Museum of Modern Art (1988), his invitation from Skidmore, Owings and Merrill to design offices and from Disney to design a concert hall, his commission for the American Centre in Paris, and his selection with Peter Eisenman as the official American representative at the 1991

Gehry House, Santa Monica, 1978

How to twist the rules of the game.

KnollStudio

Venice Biennial, all go to prove that Frank Gehry the architectural delinquent has made it to Parnassus.

So Gehry is not a real troublemaker, after all. Manoeuvring around the framework of personal expression with the legitimacy of artistic freedom to back him up, he bears no rancour against a world that is supposedly fragmented and without ideological *leitmotiv*. Gehry says yes to life. 'I think pluralism is wonderful. That is the American way. Individual expression. It hasn't hurt us in painting and sculpture. It hasn't hurt us in literature. And it won't hurt us in architecture (...) My perception has always been to deal with the world the way it is and to deal with it optimistically. I don't try to change it because I know I can't.'★

Gehry makes use of his autonomy primarily to help halt the decline of 'human' architecture. This places him in the much-followed tradition of Romanticism, which is forever attempting to unmask the darker side of the rationalist civilisation-offensive. But there is a further meaning to be read into his work, one that is specifically linked to recent social developments and is more their product than a form of resistance against them. Gehry's fragmentary architecture is a reflection of late capitalism, in that it releases the objects from their contextual obligations in a way that is reminiscent of the world-wide proliferation of identical Cultural Centres, McDonalds and Novotels.

★ Frank Gehry, quoted in Cohn, David, 'I Sing the Light Electric', *El Croquis* 45 (1990), p. 124.

My perception has always been to deal with the world the way it is and to deal with it optimistically. I don't try to change it because I know I can't.

Frank O Gehry

I was very annoyed with Post-Modernism. In the early beginnings I felt that we were just starting to find a way to deal with the present so why did we have to go backwards? I got very angry and I said: 'Well, if we're gonna go backwards, we can go to fish which are 500 million years before man'. And I drew many pictures in my sketchbook of fish and pretty soon I started to become interested in the fish itself. Inevitably you start becoming interested in what you are drawing.

Frank O Gehry

Perspective illusion and perspective contradiction are used throughout Gehry's house, and many of his other projects, to prevent the formation of an intellectual picture that might destroy the continual immediacy of perceptual shock. (...) Such illusions and contradictions force one to continually question the nature of what one sees, to alter the definition of reality, in the end, from the *memory* of a thing to the *perception* of that thing (...).

Gavin Macrae-Gibson

I had a funny notion that you could make architecture that you could bump into before you realised it was architecture.

Frank O Gehry

Vitra Design Museum, Basel, 1989

A Different Kind of Objecthood

Frank Gehry's work is noted for its experimental quality and for its intuitive, seemingly temporary *mise-en-scène* of form and space. The result is what appears to be an arbitrary clutch of spaces that evade every syntactic convention. 'I wanted the building not to look like buildings.★ I wanted to give them a different kind of objecthood.' In his own house in Santa Monica (1978), based on an existing dwelling in a characteristic local style, this effect is created partly by the use of found materials. Through their raw incongruity, these elements set in train a process by which the existing structure is questioned and qualified. More recent work, such as the Vitra Museum (Weil am Rhein, 1989) and the Schnabel House (Brentwood, 1989), demonstrates a much more abstract approach which concentrates on the manipulation of discrete volumes. These buildings no longer look as though they are in a permanent state of simultaneous construction and disintegration, but take the form of discrete, gleaming objects, geometrical volumes and archetypal forms, clustered in what appears to be a state of confrontation.

Something that has formed a consistent thread through his work so far is the distinction between interior and exterior. The exterior is industrial and hard. From the outside, we see an explosion of forms, volumes and materials that scores a direct hit. Its Expressionist tectonics can scarcely represent a programme or a function. Attack is the best defence against over-pedantic interpretations. Only a voyeuristic gaze is tolerated. The order-seeking eye is forcefully denied, and this strongly stimulates the viewer's inquisitive search for secondary visual and spatial cues.

The interior, on the other hand, is more yielding. It is often reminiscent of the homey world of the do-it-yourself enthusiast. You are taken up in a centreless *hyperspace*, with a multiplicity of shifting horizons, perspective lines with countless intersections

★ Filler, Martin, Eccentric Space: Frank Gehry. In *Art in America,* June 1980, p.114.

and disappearing points. This space is continuous, offering a non-hierarchical succession of explicit banalities. There is no focus, no totalitarian composition. The emptiness and the absence of normative messages give this architecture the character of a soft envelopment that is not so much to be grasped by mental decoding as by sensory experience.

Adhocism as Opportunism

Gehry's preference for the everyday, the temporary and provisional does not stand in isolation, but relates to a more comprehensive view of culture. An important source of inspiration is the typical American vernacular, an apparently all-out democratic architecture that spurns every trace of Classicism and leans towards an ad hoc attitude of healthy opportunism. In the North American idiom of do-it-yourself, unfinished materials such as metal, plywood, glass, corrugated aluminium are knocked together to form a structure of adjoining wrapped, cubed or framed volumes. It is a pseudo-poverty technique that evinces a collective creativity. Thus, to Gehry, it is not the pop culture of Scott Brown's and Venturi's Las Vegas that characterises America, but the 'architecture without architects' – the formal vocabulary of the common man who relies on his own resourcefulness. As Sinatra sang, 'I did it my way'. 'Venturi', observes Gehry, 'is into storytelling. (...). I'm really interested in this hands-on thing, and not in telling stories.' The result is a highly plastic kind of architecture. The realities of everyday experience are placed first, with the result that the traditional space is annulled, surcharged, volatilised, sublimated and transformed until the spectator can no longer be sure where he is. Gehry's work often looks ad hoc and it stimulates ad hoc usage – with the proviso that it is the architect who orchestrates the ad-hocism for the user. Of course, by the use stage, it is not the intention that there should be new ad hoc inter-

45

The decontextualisation of objects of everyday use, their estrangement through alterations in scale, and the rejection of closed languages in favour of mechanisms that generate meaning through semantic distortion: these are some of the operative methods shared by Oldenburg, Cage or Gehry with the Surrealists. The intention of this line of thought, originating in the same seed as Modernism, is finally directed at the *elimination of culture*, understanding by culture all

Meanwhile, the single family dwelling may also be less characteristic of the projects of the Post-Modern: the grandeur of the palace or the villa is clearly increasingly inappropriate to an age which began with the 'death of the subject' in the first place. Nor is the nuclear family any specifically Post-Modern interest or concern. Here too, then, if we win, we may actually have lost; and the more original Gehry's buildings turns out to be, the less generalisable its features may be for

What I like doing best is breaking down the project into as many separate parts as possible. So instead of a house being one thing, it's ten things. It allows the client more involvement, because you can say, 'well, I've got ten images now, that are going to compose your house. Those images can relate to all kinds of symbolic things, ideas if you've liked, bits and pieces of your life that you would like to recall (...)'. I think in terms of involving the client.

What is different about my house from the Schröder and other Rietveld houses, is that his houses demanded a kind of order (...). My house, on the contrary, is very comfortable. You can drop your coat and jacket. It is like an old shoe. So I am not such a purist.

Frank O. Gehry

ventions, since that would mar the integrity of the artist and his work. In practically all Gehry's projects, the programme components have an identity of their own; together, they form a close-knit community, a 'village of forms'. The construction as such is unrecognisable. If we note the technical structure and the symbolism in Gehry's work, it becomes clear that he is particularly interested in the cultural connotations of the materials and volumes. We encounter, at this point, subtler strategies than simply an iconography of populist debunking. They involve no less than the reinstatement of the myth of the everyday, an inversion of the process of civilisation of recent centuries and a firm rejection of the philosophical underpinning of that process.

Mythology

'The characteristic distinctive trait of mythic thought, like a *bricolage* over the practical plane, is that it builds structures not directly based on other structures, but rather using the residues and debris of phenomena; in English, odds and ends', wrote Levi-Strauss. And what architecture does this suggest more strongly than that of Frank Gehry? Gehry's *bricolage* is an attempt to undermine the representative value of architecture. His buildings are mythic inventions, or perhaps anti-myths of middle-class domestic culture. By appropriating and abstracting the com-   ★   Quoted in Foster, Hal, *Recodings*, Seattle 1985, p.168.
mon-or-garden banality of the typical American fam-
ily house, he defines a strategy of resistance. Ironically, he does it in the language of his 'opponent'. 'Myth is speech stolen and restored, not put exactly in its place',★ as Roland Barthes said. He realised here that when a sign is transposed from the myth to the countermyth, it can function only as a signifier of criticism. From that point of view, Gehry's early designs are surely exemplary of a subtle form of semiotic resistance. The dilemma, however, is that the mass media have managed to neutralise this

46

Pieter Breughel the Elder, *Battle between Carnival and Lent*, 1559

340

Main Street Building, Venice, California, 1989

antimyth's provocative character with devastating effectiveness. This kind of resistance has become so popular that its critical potential has sunk to zero: the process of mythical appropriation ('stolen speech') decontextualises the original sign and reduces it to an isolated, neutralised gesture that simply crops up somewhere. Appropriation can have its brief critical validity, but it soon decays into a simple undermining of the collective repertoire for expression. The media have done to Gehry what Gehry did to the vernacular: they have appropriated his antimyth to the point of familiarity. This work ultimately plays into the hands of the original butt of criticism, middle-class banality. The new myth serves only as a surrogate for a lively, open debate and as a subtle alibi for the marketing of the image. Gehry may divide, but the client still rules.

Recognising the mythical character of our daily surroundings, Gehry hopes, will enable us to experience them in a creative, spontaneous and anti-authoritarian way. His aim is not a defensive architecture of resistance, but an assertive architecture that punctures the armour of convention in search of a direct, sensory relation towards objects and people. But the fragmentary character of this architecture has lost its ambivalence: the only difference is that of form. What remains is a style, the style of the other. The myth makes way for the fetish.

Laughter as Strategy

Gehry seems to cock a snook at the established order in general, and the conventional choice of materials and typologies in particular. This, however, does not alter the fact that his architectural parody, while laughing in the face of the establishment, is meant in earnest. But the question is, what is the critical impact of such a burst of laughter on social reality? To answer this question, it is not enough just to examine Gehry's own development. The social significance of laughter has itself undergone important

Walt Disney Concert Hall of the Los Angeles Philharmonic, 1995

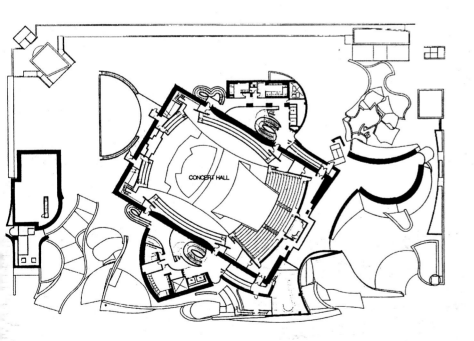

Walt Disney Concert Hall, Venice Biennale
presentation with preliminary studies, 1991

changes in the course of history. In medieval Europe, the serious world and the mirth-racked Land of Cockayne were seen as two complementary, coexistent realities. The feast of Carnival and fast of Lent belonged together, and neither was superior to the other. With the growth of a middle-class, however, the symbiotic balance between laughter and gravity had to make way for a dialectic in which laughter was increasingly marginalised. By the end of the seventeenth century, the Fool stood cap in hand before the Miser. The cultural domain of laughter had declined from parity to subordination and finally to a mere attribute of leisure, a spectator's privilege. Laughter no longer played a role in the ontogenesis of the world, nor was it a significant dimension of life. Seriousness was sacrosanct and laughter profane.

In the course of the nineteenth century, people rediscovered laughter (along with Carnival) but only as an anthropological phenomenon. It never reattained its liberating potency. Laughter, in social respects, had become a museum piece. Successive avant-garde movements, notable Dada, have attempted to resuscitate its subversive power, but the debasement of laughter to one of the minor phenomena of life has never been reversed.

This history of continual decline seems to repeat itself in Gehry's oeuvre. His early work, located amid the radical counter-culture of the sixties, ventured into as yet uncoded, unnormalised areas of architecture. But the territory, once conquered, had to be defended. The public, originally participants in the anarchistic process, became spectators entertained by a procession of droll forms – across the world, courtesy of the architectural press. It speaks for itself that laughter fades in the face of such massive technical reproduction. Finally all that remains is a faint grin and all Gehry provides is an aesthetic outlet valve for the powerful. Transgression? Forget it. In the , for instance, the anthropological functions – bed and three-piece suite (the sleeping and sitting areas) – remain unaffected as such, while they seem strange because of the anomalous space that surrounds them. We may be momentarily surprised at the imbalance within the context. But as long as this joke leaves the ideological identity of the function unimpaired, it is just a pretence at turning things on their head and actually underlines the status quo. It is laughter as repressive tolerance.

An excellent illustration of this process of degeneration from defiant laughter to the feeble resistance of the *bon mot* is to be found in the way Gehry handles the urban context when called upon to do so. In his California Aerospace Museum (1984) in Los Angeles, the transition to city space at the rear of the building is so abrupt that it is practically a clash between Carnival and Lent. And, as we know, Lent always comes out on top. The avant-gardist pose is absorbed by the unruffled social discipline.

From Undermining to Affirmation

Some of Gehry's works, in which the archetypal traditional house is interrogated in all kinds of ways, both as to function and to symbolism, generate experiences that reach further than what Fredric Jameson calls 'existential messiness' and 'psychic fragmentation'.★ Admittedly these projects go along with the idea of a decentralised subject, but they also

★ Jameson, Fredric. *The Cultural Logic of Late Capitalism.* London 1991, p.117.

actively challenge the powers of judgement of the user and spectator. They stimulate us to take a definite standpoint in relation to the dubious order. Here Gehry generates something more than a promenade for the aesthetic tourist. It is rather a kind of rambling around in which the deliberate oddness deliberately undermines the premises of the programme. In Gehry's recent work, unfortunately, the aesthetic scenario is becoming increasingly dominant. The programme is now left for what it is and the function is unquestioned. What remains are frivolous follies whose autonomous identity is only skin deep. They offer no trace of an undermining effect, let alone a provocation to redefine the actual function. On top of that, the projects on behalf of clients with well-filled purses display a use of materials that is far removed from the original impoverishment technique. Polished prestige takes the place of the former temporary shack. And it is becoming increasingly easy to perceive the interior as an orthogonal, functional box. (Perhaps we will be spared this disappointment in the impending Walt Disney Concert Hall, since in this case the design grows from the programme: the context, the concert hall, the music and the audience.)

In Gehry's quest for heterogeneous images, the homogenising forces of the transnational economy have escaped the attention of his anarchistic 'savage thought'. This has placed him in a position that has all the hallmarks of schizophrenia. After all, he originally professed to a critical strategy that was meant to unmask the totalitarian tendencies within culture. But the fragmented image to which Gehry now resorts has come to serve as an excuse for the underlying homogenising processes. The interests behind those processes no longer need the traditional, recognisable image. They can easily transmute the rebellion of form into merchandise while remaining comfortably invisible themselves. *Go ahead, punk*, says Frank 'Dirty Harry' Gehry, and he sends his built rebellion out into the world. *Go ahead, punk*, the world echoes back with a guffaw. He who laughs last...

According to Adolf Loos, the architect ought to concentrate on the mood a building invokes. This mood has to be refined and precisely adapted to the function. Gehry's work, too, conveys a mood – not that of the institution being built, but of the institution of 'contemporary architecture'. In contrast to Loos, the mood no longer relates to the specific character of the function, but only to external processes that clearly overshadow spatial and functional particularity. It presents affirmatively the ostensible visual heterogeneity of the Post-Modern age. In this connection, the work might have been expected to achieve something more than, to quote Jameson, 'posing its own internal content as problem or dilemma (...) even representing itself as a problem in the first place (...)'.★ Gehry's rebellion has created space. But that space is a territory of easily digested aesthetics. It's a bit like the tale of the hippie who became a stock market operator. Born to be wild – a box office success, particularly as a remake.

★ Jameson, Fredric. *The Cultural Logic of Late Capitalism.* London 1991, p.127.

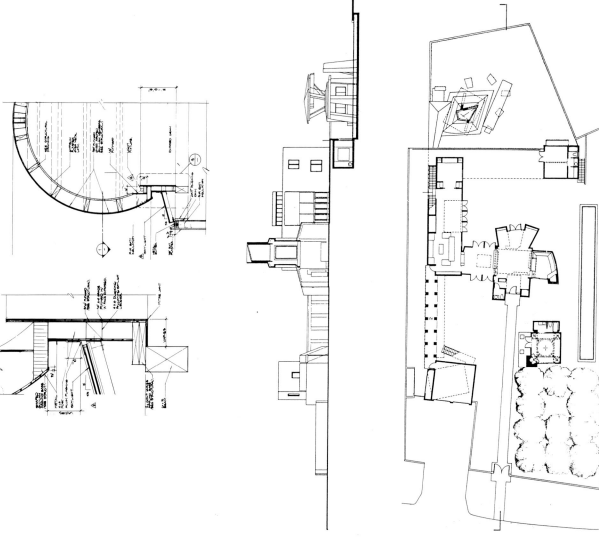

A number of years ago I was asked to design a tract house. I thought that one room buildings were so much more interesting because they eliminated all the baggage of function and all the things that one can hide behind. When you do one room there is nothing, just a roof and a space. Some of the best buildings in history are one-room buildings. I decided to make a house that would have separate pavilions. This is in California so you could go outside. It is a courtyard house and each piece would have a different character. I started to play with the site. To begin with I decided that what had to happen was that the grounds (only a 30.5 metre wide by 76.25 metre long) had to look open. So the living room became a pavilion in the middle. Because of a slight slope of the site at the back I cut the site and put a retaining wall and made a lower level with a garden for the master bedroom. The master bedroom and all of the dressing rooms and bathrooms together form a retaining wall that connects to

an additional terrace on the higher level. So there is a private garden at the back and one in the front, and then a private bedroom garden. In this way I sculpturally engaged the site. I wanted to make it look like a complete village. From each room you can look to other parts of your own house. In other words, you can create your own setting. The living room pavilion could be more open because it was set way back and there is a lot of privacy in the garden. When you walk into the bedroom, it almost feels like a boat sitting on a lake. It is very peaceful inside, and this Stonehenge, or whatever you will call it, creates a foreground, gives depth, creates a relationship with the landscape, creates privacy and gives the feeling that there is more happening, that there is more space. Inside the living room, it is very light and airy. The palm tree happened to be there by accident; it is not a John Baldessari painting. I claimed it. *Frank Gehry*

Location Brentwood, California, United States of America **Assistants** T. Buresh, K. Daly, C. Gregory Walsh and others **Client** M. Schnabel, R. Schnabel **Design** 1986 **Completion** 1989

Frank O. Gehry & Associates, Inc.

▶ **Schnabel Residence**

Your money talks

Barbara Kruger, 'Your money talks', 1984

Le Style, c'est l'Homme

A Conversation with Oswald Mathias Ungers

There exist at least two types of libraries: the labyrinth and the catalogue. In the first type knowledge is haphazardly piled up in dusty stacks and worm-eaten archives, seemingly without any system and inaccessible. The visitor browses, discovers a stimulating point of entry, reads a little, turns a page, looks further... Under the influence of chance, inquisitiveness and adventurousness, such a labyrinthine legacy generates knowledge. This type of library makes one think of the labyrinth of wisdom in Umberto Eco's *The Name of the Rose*, as described by Alinardo, one of the characters in the novel, 'the library is a great labyrinth, the sign of the labyrinth of the world. Once you enter it you never know if you will come out'. But this is not so far from a typical archive in Italy, where new documents are not infrequently dumped to the left of the shelf so that the old ones on the right fall off and become prey to damp and oblivion.

The other type is the systematic catalogue which has already reserved a place in advance for all new acquisitions. The catalogue is impeccable; everything can be found from a chair in front of a card index. Browsing is out of the question, the system obviously does not accommodate surprises. It is the library for people who know what they want, for the rationally ordering mind desiring logic in its quest for More and Better. Such a library, *gründlich und ordentlich,* is especially to be expected in Germany. Oswald Mathias Ungers, president of the Foundation for Architectural Studies that bears his name, is an architect who advocates the second version of the library. Indeed, he presides over a library organised according to these principles and where the first thing one encounters is its hospitable alphabetical arrangement. A second glance reveals his stock of books to be extraordinarily complete. You ask, the library answers. If you know precisely what your questions are, you can come a long way in this environment. Particularly if they are serious questions. But is there something that the library itself is asking?

Ungers' work can easily be characterised in terms of library typology. He is an architect who wants to have control over the situation, to hold in check the concrete facts of context, location and social circumstances, with the absolute, eternal values of the profession. In the course of his career Ungers has steadily worked at building up a monumental body of work, both built and on paper, that for an outsider has a well-nigh monolithic nature. Consistency and severity are his trademarks. The buildings, monuments for an endangered architecture, are solid, permanent, symmetrical and above all very much present as objects. His architecture is professional, conventional and without dissonance, the vocabulary is invariably learned. For the defenders of architecture's self-respect – Aldo Rossi, Giorgio Grassi and Rafael Moneo come to mind – a rationalist and conventional approach like Ungers will be most welcome. With Ungers' talent as a mediator between renewal and tradition, architecture should be safeguarded against its possible dissolution into the general semiotic pandemonium of today.

On the other hand, those who regard architecture as the reflection of culture in stone will not be so happy with the silent archetypes of eternity. Ungers himself is well aware of this dichotomy, as his comment during our discussion shows: 'If you look at my architecture very carefully, it has the idea of fragments and of discontinuity'. Even Ungers, it seems, wants to know about Post-Modernism; but is the interest mutual? Is there still place in the Post-Modern condition for a Platonic notion of architecture? Here speaks a man who focuses attention on the phenomenology of archetypes in the age of their technical reproducibility.

We are here in your new library, in the very serious atmosphere of the Oswald Mathias Ungers Stiftung für Architekturwissenschaft. *Forty centuries of civilization look down on us. What's your relationship with the written word?*

The architect in the Renaissance, like Alberti or Palladio, was *un homme de lettres*, a humanist, a very educated man, who was able to communicate through writing. There is a difference between communicating orally and ordering your thoughts and writing them down in correct grammar. This requires education, exercise and experience. To be an architect was not only to be a craftsman, but also to be a man who was cultivated and who longed for education; not only an education in technology, but also an education in the cultural development of mankind, of human thought. He had to be concerned with philosophy as well as several other disciplines. You find very few people today who have this concept of themselves and the will to become *un homme de lettres*. Usually the architect today is a *doer*.

You are talking about the Renaissance, but in the twenties and thirties many of the leading Modernists wrote well.

Oswald Mathias Ungers

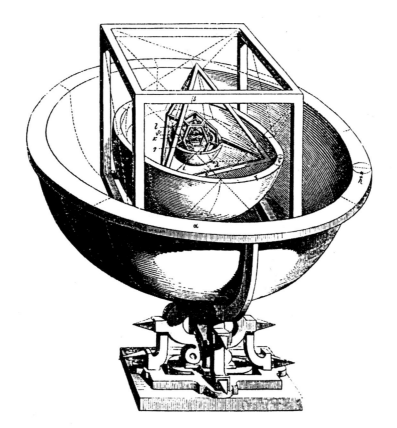

The platonic solids composing the universe, after
Johann Kepler

Absolutely. Many architects in the twenties were involved in publishing magazines. You won't find a magazine any more created by architects, like *G* was by Mies van der Rohe and El Lissitzky, or *Veshch/Objet/Gegenstand*, another rare magazine. They were concerned with expressing themselves intellectually. This is rare today. Maybe the process of building is so rapid and the task so huge that you scarcely have time to think. You just *do*. If you are not used to writing all the time, you lose the concentration and the ability to do so. It is difficult to sit down and write an essay when your constant concern is the building process itself and the techniques that go with it.

But as an architect you could say 'I'm speaking a visual language'.

The Germans have a saying for this: 'The artist should make art and not talk or write it.' But all the Renaissance designers, painters and architects, have a written *œuvre*. And look at Malevich, who developed an important theory. It's too limiting thinking that an architect or an artist should not be concerned with intellectual problems or with writing theories. Artists should take the time to reflect on what they are doing. It's not enough to look at whatever trend or *Zeitgeist*-movement might be 'in' or 'out' at the moment. It's necessary that, as an artist, you are concerned with writing something about your method or your theoretical concept.

Are you satisfied with the general reception given to your work, in the magazines, in architectural circles, and so forth?

It might sound a bit arrogant to say it doesn't interest me, but that is the truth. Of course I'm glad when I'm well received, but during my life I've had so many different experiences of not being well received. In Germany my work was criticised more than it was regarded highly or as of special interest. On the one hand I also enjoyed this controversy. If my work is regarded as radical to some extent, it provokes the controversy and therefore is part of it. I even try to strengthen the dispute, because my work benefits more from it than if I were praised as the most interesting and most fantastic architect around. On the other hand **I have reached a stage that I'm no longer interested in a present-day debate. What I am actually looking for is to achieve an archaic clarity and simplicity in my work.** But this is not acceptable to the public. They think it's without fantasy, too rigid, too static. They are all wrong, because it's highly dynamic and full of fantasies. It is very diversified, but in a subtle way, not in a way that is obvious to everybody. I'm indeed much concerned with the cube, the grid, the wall, things that are simple but of an archaic simplicity.

You mean the phenomenological value of these elements?

Title page of magazine G, no. 3 (1924)

Yes. These phenomenological elements create the idea of architecture. I'm not interested in dissolving architecture into some kind of transcendental world, or in some kind of transparency which behaves as if architecture as an archaic phenomenon no longer exists. When I'm talking about walls, stairs, doors, cubes, cylinders, volumes and things like that, I'm perfectly aware that this is exactly what the *Zeitgeist* at the moment is trying to neglect. Everybody wants to make the world transparent, very dynamic, walls not existing any more, interior and exterior no longer distinguished. The more architecture becomes literature or media-shows, the more I am moving in the other direction. I want to make clear that architecture consists of those basic elements. *I want to make the wall even stronger, because everybody wants to dissolve it.* I want the volume even more voluminous, to reduce it to the cube, which is *the* volume as such. I know perfectly well that this doesn't reach the front page. They might accept me because I'm known, old enough. They publish my work as well, but simply as a style. It doesn't mean anything to them. I have to live with the fact that I'm 'out'. And I enjoy it, it gives me much more freedom. When you are in, you always have to worry about staying in; it's a very tricky situation. But being free, my walls can become stronger, my volumes can become even more forceful. I don't have to compete with anybody any more, I'm left alone, and I love it. Being out is a beautiful experience, it's fabulous, it's marvellous, it gives me time.

But why, or for whom, are you actually building?

For me.

For yourself?

Yes.

You aren't building for the public?

No. Yes! We have to make some distinctions in this statement. Of course, indirectly, I might be doing it for the public. Beethoven wrote his music firstly for himself, because it was the only thing he could do, but the public enjoyed it. It's not a matter of choice. You cannot sit down and say 'I'm doing something for the public'.

But can you articulate your interest in the phenomenological part of architecture in terms of its social meaning?

It can *acquire* a social meaning. First of all you have to do the best you can. This perfectionism is frustrating. But you have to accept it as a basic desire, a basic push to create something perfect and beautiful.

Judgements are only made by yourself. However, your own possibilities are always too limited to match your expectations. This results in a very personal struggle. What counts is not whether the man next door accepts it or not, but the personal judgement: are you satisfied with your own potential? Is there still enough motivation to do the next thing, even if you continually experience some kind of defeat? If you want to express your idea as clearly as possible, you have to force it to its limits. If some of these ideas become real, visible, readable or touchable and they are enjoyed by the public, then that's fine, but it cannot be the motivation.

Should there be a dialogue between the public and the architect?

There can't be. The process of being creative – I'm a little bit hesitant to use this word but I have to do so – is a dialogue between you and your fantasy, your intellect, your ratio, your mind and your potential. That is the dialogue.

And the context?

Of course you can have conversations. But during the process of creating you cannot have the dialogue, because it's too fragile; it might disappear, or be disturbed before you were even able to formulate it. You rely only on yourself in this process. If you were to start with a dialogue immediately, you would never find it.

Is there a dialogue afterwards?

You know Seneca's saying 'I don't need them all. I don't even need a hundred, and not even ten. One would be enough.' If only one would understand what you are trying to do, it's enough. If nobody understands, I might as well talk to my beloved dog Jakob. It is not necessary for culture and art to communicate with everybody. There are a lot of other things that satisfy the general public, that make them wealthy, healthy, and happy. The public is not my concern and it will never be. If, later on, people enjoy looking at and living in my buildings, being stimulated to look at their own potential and fantasies, that would be enough. You can't do more.

Your work, done, as you say, in seclusion, has been published and discussed, and you are a well-known public figure. We now encounter you as a public figure and not as an artist; you create art when we are not here. Are you really interested in influencing this dialogue afterwards, or is that the business of journalists and critics, since you are polite enough to receive them?

I haven't discussed my work in public for almost ten years. I never take part in a discussion, go to a symposium, or to a presentation. It's not that I'm afraid, nor that I don't want to discuss it. But I cannot talk in public about my work, because every discussion or every presentation today unfortunately somehow ends up as a justification. If it comes to the point – and I'm afraid that it mostly does so – that I have to justify my work, since my work is my life, I have to admit that I cannot. The question 'Why did you do this?' is a very personal question. This kind of discussion doesn't lead you anywhere. The communication through a medium, writing, publishing, television, avoids the kind of direct confrontation with the public that asks you to justify your life. The last time I appeared in public, somebody came up after my presentation and asked me to sign a publication of mine. I gave it to him because I didn't want to disappoint him. He went back into the audience, waved his paper, and said 'Look at that important man! Who does he think he is. He signs his own things.' I was so deeply shocked that from that moment on my public appearances stopped. Nobody deserves that. I didn't want to continue that kind of game. I had a second shock some time ago. I *have* to go to presentations of course, when the city planning committee or the board of directors, or whoever, asks me to present the project. This is part of my professional life. To the community of Neuss, a small town north of Cologne, I had to present the project I did for the development of the town, including a few high-rise buildings. There was an audience of 250 outraged citizens; I really felt their hatred. They wanted to destroy me! It was absolutely horrifying, how they were yelling and screaming. I couldn't say a word. They didn't give me *any* chance!

So you can imagine a more positive situation in which you would really like to have a dialogue, but the present situation does not give you the opportunity?

Absolutely. We are living in a society where dialogue becomes more difficult every day. Some have the

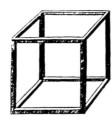

Leonardo da Vinci, platonic solid: cube (6 planes)

Wenzel August Hablik, Der Weg des Genius, 1981

audience on their side and others have not. If you are not going with the mainstream, whatever this mainstream might be, intellectually or on a profane level, you are in a difficult situation. Maybe it is because the media always show violence. If you go one step further they're going to stone you. Let me give you another example. We had the movement of Art for the People (*Die Kunst dem Volke*), which was terrible enough. When the public or, one step further, the 'mob', decides what is art and architecture and what is not, you are completely lost. We can forget about art entirely. The result is folk art and other art will be called corrupt art (*Entartete Kunst*). Who had to leave the country in the thirties? The so-called corrupted artists! Their books were burnt, their pictures were destroyed. The public prohibited architects building. They either had to leave the country or go into personal exile, to hide. Do you really believe the public could do you *any* good?

Do you believe in a democratic system?

Of course I believe in a democratic system, but in one that would secure the right of the individual. The democratic system doesn't mean the great majority. It means the protection of the extreme, of the individual. In such a democratic system I could believe, but I don't believe in the democratic system of the mob. I have never found public situations very friendly. Fortunately I found friends to whom I could talk and whose judgement concerned me. For example, I visited several meetings of Team 10, where some of the leading architects had to present their

Trade Fair Gate House, Frankfurt a/M, 1984

projects to a group of ten or twelve people. I have never seen them so nervous. They even lost their voices while presenting their work. They would have presented it to a thousand people without any problem, but not to ten friends. They knew that their judgement would be honest. It would not be killing, but it would be honest, strong, and such a judgement could hurt personally. I think this is more interesting than the question 'Is your work generally accepted or not?'

So you want to safeguard architecture as a discipline and you want to safeguard the individual within democracy. Let's simulate a controversy between you and your friend Rem Koolhaas, as a meeting between two extreme individuals who respect each other as intellectuals but who detest the mutual ideology.

We have worked together. I regard him highly as an intellectual, as a writer, and as an architect. But he tries to be a 'modern man'. He tries to transform the consumer-attitude into an artistic expression. He will never end this because he is always concerned with updating. There's no stability, no criterion to it. It's like collecting data all the time, you never come to a conclusion. They are already obsolete before you can do so. Koolhaas is creating obsolete architecture. He's surfing on the *Zeitgeist*. You can see it also in the work

Leonardo da Vinci, pyramid (4 planes)

of Jean Nouvel. Architecture becomes a medium, and the façade is only a screen. I feel like I'm in a different world because I'm struggling with the façade all the time to make some good architecture. But Nouvel tries to let the façade disappear, it doesn't exist any more, it could be anything, a billboard. There's no convention, while *I look for the conventions*. If I am talking about architecture as something more archaic and real, I'm trying to save the phenomenology of architecture. You can see his work in a dialectical relation to Koolhaas. If this kind of dialectical in-out falls back, there might be a possibility of fantasies, a new *ratio*.

From your point of view he's a dialectical opposite. But from his there isn't any opposite, so he cannot see your work as an opposite, because he hasn't such a solid position as you have. For him it is a flux of architecture, a non-identity, you cannot point at.

But he cannot escape. Malevich could not escape either. Every time art tried to escape art, one came up against art. There were many artists who tried to make art which would not fit in museums, which could not be categorised. Warhol's or Beuys' position is similar: they tried to make everything art. They tried to let the convention explode. In the end they couldn't escape it either. It seems that one is caught, like your mind is caught in the human body. It seems that Koolhaas' mind is caught as well. When Taut did his Alpine architecture, in the end everything became transcendental. He then found out that he had reached a stage where he absolutely could not continue. He turned back to something very profane: 'I want to make a

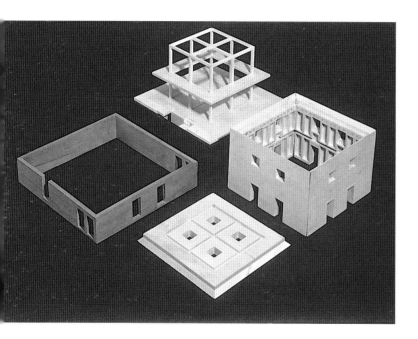

The architect's library, Cologne, 1990

house with a door and four windows and a roof'. Art cannot escape art. And Koolhaas cannot escape architecture. In the end it might be self-deception.

The other possibility is that he will drop architecture as his medium and turn to literature or film.

Yes. If he is really honest about what he is doing, he should turn into a 'Bladerunner', going on in the media, simulating anything. No convention any more. As soon as you talk about architecture you're back again at the wall, the roof, the door, the stairs.

In the meantime his architecture already functions as an expression of this mob society, which he would probably call the fragmented society, and not as a spatial background of a society of autonomous individuals.

I think it is a great illusion. His thoughts are so exclusive. *Bladerunner* is not a movie for the general public either. His architecture is not meant for the general public. Even if he thinks so.

And in what sense is your architecture of public value? Is it, in the end, in the way it meets functional needs?

The function is obvious, but it's not the real thing that concerns us. We are trying to go beyond that. I would enjoy it if my buildings were to change the attitude and character of the people who work or live in them. The bank building in Düsseldorf for example is very attractive. People identify themselves with the building. The special architecture gives them a certain self-consciousness. They even behave differently. The two directors of the building were mainly administrators. Now they have a new identity, they love to show the building, like museum directors. Now what more can I give to the people with my architecture than to turn them into self-conscious individuals, aware and proud.

This must give you an enormous satisfaction; the same criterion is used by Ricardo Bofill in his scheme at Saint Quentin en Yvelines near Versailles. You can give the people a very subliminal sense of self-confidence through a phenomenological approach, or you can give them a clearly defined set of ornaments which refers very directly to the palace and gardens of Versailles, giving them the feeling they live in a palace.

It's not what really matters to me. For myself, as an architect, I made no compromise to satisfy the public. I did *my* architecture, and in this case it was accepted. I didn't try to satisfy this kind of emotional concern. My architectural space and environment, without any compromise, turned out to be highly successful in terms of acceptance by the public.

So even if you want to safeguard architecture as a discipline, there isn't really a schism between your feelings as an architect and those of the people. They can coincide. But what if you are working on a larger scale? Can you work out your metaphors and symbolism on an urban scale?

Of course. I did the Tor house in Frankfurt, which was in the first place a synonym for the Frankfurt fair, being a gate, a metaphor for entrance and open to the outside. Later it became simply a sign for the city of Frankfurt itself, like the cathedral of Cologne or the Arc de Triomphe in Paris. There are certain pieces of architecture that represent entire cities or even regions. This is also a part of the power of architecture. The

Henri Labrouste, Bibliothèque Nationale, Paris, 1868

kind of metaphor suggested became at the same time a sign. The city exists through these high points or very articulated special environments. The rest is more or less filling in.

Does this description of the supra-public meaning of such a building reflect your former statement on the need to be left alone as an architect and not be involved in all these discussions?

Yes, you have to create the theme or the concept of a building yourself. If it is accepted, that is a lucky circumstance. Identifying with it, saying 'this is our building', is a marvellous kind of public relation. It can also be rejected and labelled in a very negative way. Then it is a stigma instead of a symbol. But that's the risk you have to take.

In your conception of architecture there are not many opportunities to correct yourself. Finished is finished.

Yes, as a Classical architect there is another great risk for me. Designing architecture is always a simulation. You are making models, videos, drawings, perspectives, always simulating on a smaller scale. The reality is only there at the moment when you think it's finished, often ten years after you actually made the design. And then it is irreversible. You have no way of checking your idea or your architectural conception

Leonardo da Vinci, octahedron (8 planes)

59

The architect's library, Cologne, 1990, columns and bust

beforehand. You avoid this risk if you are an architect for whom it can be anything. But when I walk in, I might see that I failed, or not. Therefore every time I go into a building for the first time when it's finished I go alone.

The architect for whom it could be anything is the one who delivers isotropic space, the maison domino, in which you can change the walls and the façade whenever you like.

There is a kind of human engineering involved which I don't like. This architecture doesn't want to commit itself, it gives you a kind of primary structure and the people do whatever they want to do. It is some kind of manipulation, correction, advice, giving people a stable as if they were guinea-pigs. This kind of guinea-pig-architecture is not my cup of tea.

There seems to be a problematic relationship between you as an 'extreme individual' and your architecture, in which people have to deal with a finished space...

Which hopefully is not going to be changed.

Exactly, because it has its own integrity, ...and on the other hand architects with a less strong personal identity who provide neutral space for people who can use it in their own way.

There are two kinds of architects. One only invents the connection and provides the components. The others, like me, define, and don't care about the connections and the components. There is a beautiful book by Adolf Behne, *Die Wiederkehr der Kunst*, in which he describes the garden sheds (*Gartenhutte*), the architecture of the people, as the most ingenious, inventive architecture that exists. For Behne we should all forget about the academic conventions of Classical architecture. We should look instead at the development of garden sheds in Berlin. There we would see the real creative force. I think this is naive. A space like the Pantheon would never have been created if we'd left it to this kind of unreflected, spontaneous, creative way of building. Bruno Taut went so far as to distribute his architectural programme in the streets. He wanted to have a school of non-academics, of these spontaneous unknown architects that built God knows what. He wrote a programme called *The Earth, a Good Home (Die Erde, eine gute Wohnung)* in which he describes a society – and this really frightens me – that is not ordered any more by conventions and common codes or the Law but by some curious wise men. Taut invented a whole legal and ethical system. As you know, there are historical parallels. They tried it, but it was a terrible disaster. It was tried in the twentieth century and it was disastrous. I rather prefer a man of reason and not a man of emotions and feelings.

But aren't you inspired looking at El Lissitzky's Prounenraum*, as a motivation to act?*

I'm not interested, nor in Kurt Schwitters' *Merzbau*. I was interested in it as a young man. I even wrote a pamphlet about Expressionism in architecture in which I discussed all these issues. I like the idea of abstraction very much, but the *Prounenraum* is romantic nonsense. And I don't like *Merzbau* either. Collecting found objects, putting them together. The *Merz* object grows like a city through the entire house. What do we see now? We see *Merzgebäude* everywhere. Cities growing, all over the place, because nobody risks coming up with a reason to create some kind of order.

Lissitzky and Schwitters offered free space as a stage for real life.

They think that's life, but the Common Code is more life! In another context. That we agree on certain conventions and that I have to control the emotions by *Reason*.

What you actually say is that Schwitters, Lissitzky and Taut all could have known better, even at that particular stage in history. But wasn't there some logic in the fight for freeing space after the battle of styles in the nineteenth century and its horror vacui.

Maybe, but that doesn't serve as an alibi for giving up straight reasoning. The point is one of emotions versus reason. Feeling becomes a cult in which people think everything that is regulated is rigid. I know that the chaos theory tries to rationalise a total freedom. At the same time, this coin has a reverse side: there is complete oppression. You know that complete freedom leads to complete chaos and chaos is more oppressive. Real freedom only exists within reason.

You can see the same distinction in the words Room (Raum) *and Space. Raum is a kind of controlled space, in a way, while space implies endlessness. Do you have a personal philosophy about why in one*

Leonardo da Vinci, dodecahedron (12 planes)

61

language a term is developed that is more specific than in another language?

Maybe the Germans are more concerned with order. I have always thought of space as a more pragmatic concept. Space is something completely open and *Raum* is something which is defined. I'm very much concerned with *Raum*. My criticism of Modern architecture is that there is no concern about *Raum* any more. Scharoun tried to dissolve the borders. He never wanted a *Raum*, no clear geometry, but a totally loose and open space. He didn't talk about the *Räume* but about the landscapes in his buildings. Mies used translucent material because he didn't want to define *Raum*, he wanted to have space. In the German Pavilion in Barcelona he only defines space but no *Raum*; therefore the slabs don't touch.

You are looking for Raum. *So, you have it conceptualised?*

It is programmatic, but it was programmatic for the late Baroque as well.

But we are aware of space as a concept. I don't think the Baroque architects were. They were aware of space, but the itinerary from the phenomenon to the concept is really one of our century, particularly since Germans like Chmarzov, Hildebrandt and Brinckmann conceptualised Raum. *They invented a whole vocabulary of* Raum, Raumbewußtsein, Raumgestaltung, Raumgefühl, *hundreds of words in which* Raum *figures. From that moment on architects were so aware of the concept of* Raum *that in their designs they tried to apply their concept of* Raum. *So, if you are looking for* Raum, *yours is a very distanced architecture.*

But in the category of *Raum* there might be a metaphysical aspect. Let me give you an example. Recently we have been designing a sphere and a cube as an interior space *(Innenraum)*, in a sequence. The sphere has always been a concern in architecture. The sphere as a *Raum* goes beyond the idea of the usual concept of space. A *Raum* as a sphere, defined as it is, has the idea of the unlimited, the idea of the universal space. In other words it's our intention to create this idea of endlessness through a defined space.

Your endlessness is quite different from the secular endlessness of the isotropic space. Yours is metaphysical, the other is physical.

The interesting thing is to see the cube as the opposite, as the most archaic limitation. It's like a cage. So there are two rules, the cage and the sphere. This goes into the question of the extreme possibilities of creating space. This is my kind of architectural vocabulary. I try to express those two extremes.

Your library is a cube, a cage in your terms. Defined and enclosed as it is, you can imagine the rectangularity and straight lines as suggestions of the conquest of the rest of the universe. Your cube is also a section of a three-dimensional grid.

The cube inside is a scaffold, surrounded by a wall. I try to investigate the dialectical relationship between the inside and the outside. This is a summary of my architectural thinking. The transformation of elements going through several stages is actually what I'm trying to do. You see it in the library, the column painted on the wall; you see the column in light, then the reflection of the column in a mirror. I made a sort of scenario where a world goes from illusion to reality and vice versa. It's the same with the heads of the revolutionaries on the balcony. Twelve revolutionaries, including Robespierre, were beheaded on 28 July 1794. I found them and thought they might be wonderful in a room that stores the basic knowledge of architecture. Usually you would have the philosophers or Gods in such a room. They do also fit architecturally and formally. But in this case there is a content to it, which has to do with the architectural idea of the Pantheon, with the architectural idea of the cube, with the light that's coming from the top. All the other elements have to do with the idea of transformation. There are indeed a lot of architectural conceptual things in it.

To return to the distinction between the sphere and cube: there is an outside to a cube, but do you think there is an outside to a sphere?

The cube is a cage, that's why there is an outside. But the sphere is endless. There is always speculation as to whether there is an outside to the sphere. I think you could conceive it as having no outside, as being endless. You could not conceive the cube as being endless.

The largest sphere is the heavenly dome, which has no outside by nature.

The sphere represents the universe. The sphere could not be labelled as a room any more. It's a universal space, while the cube, the cage, is an enclosed room. Let's check how it sounds. Universal space? That sounds okay, here 'space' is all right. Universal room? That doesn't sound good. A cubical space? That doesn't sound good either, but a cubical room would be okay.

After considering their spaces, we can also look at the shape of your two basic volumes. There is an opposition between the sacred quality of the sphere and the profane quality of the cube. The cube is a section cut out from the universe and made by human hands; the sphere is made by a Supreme Being. Perhaps the modern emphasis on the (white) box and its promise of freeing space is a secular impetus to give man his own destiny, a stage, neutral and anonymous, for his own life. The lack of any great dome in twentieth-century-Western architecture is another indication.

It's an illusion and I'll give you an example. If you have a free-parking lot, the one who comes first can make any choice. The one who comes last has no choice at all. The let-the-people-do-what-they-want concept that you describe has nothing to do with freedom. This kind of modern architecture is architecture for the one who comes first.

That is an important critique of modern architecture. But isn't there something more to say about it? There must be a connection between the ethical vacuum, after the 'Death of God', and the freeing of physical space. Since you are designing a sphere, what do you think that architecture, as the specialism of creating space, can do to answer this question of the ethical vacuum?

Of course there is a relation between architecture and philosophy. But I don't see philosophy or architecture developing in such an inescapable progressive way. It's true that there are certain priorities of thought, and it seems to be the main direction at present that would fit into a description such as you have given. But it is not exclusive, other spiritual concepts existing simultaneously as well. The development of human culture is no longer so exclusive that you can order it nicely into a series of categories. When a certain way of thinking becomes too exclusive, it provokes the contrary. Should it develop to the extent that all architectural space becomes formalistic, without content, it might be necessary then to bring back content. Anything produced by the human mind is mostly a matter of discovery. I do believe that messages exist all the time, everywhere, and if you have the right receiver, you can hear all of them. This might be a metaphor for the intellectual and artistic fields in architecture. There is too much technological fascination concerning the concept of unlimited space, leading to certain overstatements, or overreactions, which then become absolute.

The question is whether Max Weber's concept of the 'disenchantment of the world' (Entzauberung der Welt), which is the essence of all this, is universal and total, or if it's only one direction in the process of civilisation, with many counterparts.

I think there are many directions, which may be opposed or which may be subdued or enforced. For my personal orientation I need to rely on certain repetitive elements, which become a kind of archetype, let's say *topoi*. These *topoi* can be more or less visible, powerful or dominant. Actually my concern is to look for these *topoi*. It's not because the archaic is so desirable, but it's a search for what is general. This brings me to an architecture which could never be exclusive, because I always have to think of the antithesis. My criticism of Modern high-tech architecture is that it wants to be exclusive. I'm not exclusive, I'm ambivalent, that's the correct word. If you think in a dialectical way, your instruments and your vocabulary broaden enormously. When I'm able to reduce architecture to archetypal *topoi* and I'm able to integrate this in an ordinary environment, as here, in this kind of morphological unity, we'll have something possible for all stages, not only the extremes but also all the forms and structures in between as part of an intellectual concept. And, at the same time, able to realise it in material as well. This is then my kind of universe, an environment of universal context. My house might be a very good illustration because I've been building on to it for more than thirty years and it has become more and more dialectical. It's my own architectural history, started in 1958, which I not only express in words but also try to express in stones and concrete, forms and volumes and material, in actuality.

Is it correct to say that in your work every piece made at a given moment is a Gesamtkunstwerk, a synthesis? But, in the future, your family house together with your library won't be a Gesamtkunstwerk at all, but a kind of open structure consisting of thesis and antithesis.

Yes, only through a dialectical process, or through discontinuity, can you avoid one-dimensional exclusiveness. A village is one-dimensional because everything is in the same style and the same materials, but a complex environment has many aspects. I'm trying to express the fragmentation in this controversy, thinking of continuity at the same time as fragmentation. This suggests completely my philosophical conception, the morphological idea of pieces and transformation, the idea of pieces and discontinuity and fragments. This is what I'm trying very consciously in my architecture. I'm not trying to create an architecture which is

Leonardo da Vinci, icosahedron (20 planes)

63

64   The architect's house, Cologne, 1959

The architect's house, extension, Cologne, 1990

only this or that. If you look at it very carefully, the idea of fragments and of discontinuity is apparent. Returning to space and room, I would not see them as a dichotomy in the sense of either/or. I can see the concept of space as one legitimate stream in architecture, and I see room as another, and my concern would be to bring these two streams into some concept, either in the way of transformation or in the way of morphological development.

But you don't want to challenge the categories in themselves?

Let me show you something. You have a volume here, the enclosed cube, the library. In opposition to this absolutely enclosed space, I wanted to have a space without a roof, open to the sky. That is my garden. If I had not placed the columns in it, it would have been a court, but with the columns it could be that phenomenological room which has no roof, which is endless. This is dialectical design.

All right, but that is an additional system of elements. What I mean is do you challenge the elements in a fundamental sense? Would you ever make an inside as an outside and vice versa?

What I'm doing is not so obvious. Conceptually I'm trying to have those architectural phenomena, space and room, like a city in one place. The experience you get if you walk through is no accident. The order is conceived, there is orientation. I don't want to be labelled a conventional architect. Of course, like everybody, my handwriting has its limitations. **I'm trying to be as complex as possible within those limitations which you cannot escape.**

Hypo-Bank, Düsseldorf, 1991

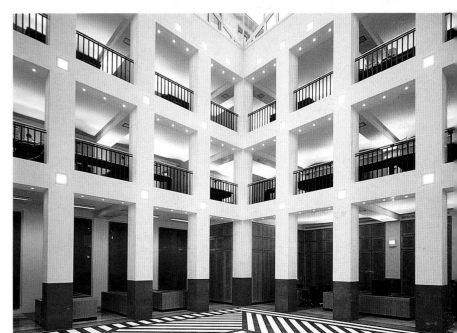

Is this way of building context-bound or programme-bound? Or can you use the same archetypes all over the world?

You have to be very careful that you don't turn them into clichés, which might happen if you don't control your work carefully enough or if your work is going too fast. Architecture as an art is a narrow path; if you take one step too far looking for a metaphor you'll have kitsch. If you take one step too far looking for an archetype you'll have a stereotype. It is a very narrow path and the more you try to define your thoughts the narrower your path will be.

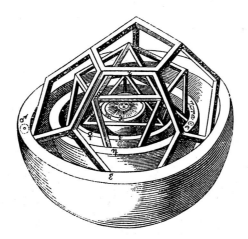

The platonic solids composing the universe, after Johann Kepler (detail)

On 'The Invisible in Architecture':
An Environment-Behaviour Studies
Perspective

Amos Rapoport

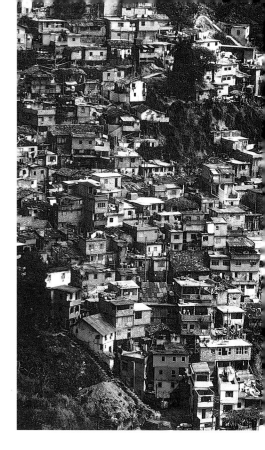

This essay will be structured around the implications of the title of this book. This I do by taking the title literally as my topic and attempting to interpret what it might mean or imply in terms of Environment-Behaviour Studies (EBS). Thus, one immediate change is that I will be discussing 'the invisible in environmental design' (a second change will emerge later). I have thus moved from considering buildings to considering built environments in the broadest sense, which I take to be what geographers call cultural landscapes. There are a number of reasons for this among which only two will be discussed.

First, from my perspective any purposeful modification of the surface of the earth is design. In fact it is almost unnecessary to say 'purposeful' because people rarely or never engage in the difficult task of creating built environments without a purpose.**?**

Thus all man-made environments are designed in the sense that they embody human decisions and choices: essentially a choice among alternatives (what I call the choice model of design). This is a much broader definition of design than is common, but it is an essential one. Designed environments include the planting or clearing of forests, diversion of rivers and fencing of fields in certain patterns. The placement of roads and dams, gas stations and settlements, are all design. Roadside stands and second hand car lots (and roadside strips which they inhabit) are as much designed environments as office blocks and cultural centres. The work of a tribesman burning off, laying out a camp or village, and building his

66 ***What has been studied is the work of a few designers, a minuscule portion of built environments. It is essential to study all environments, over the full span of their existence and in all cultures.***

dwelling is as much an act of design as the designers' act of dreaming up ideal cities or creating 'significant' buildings. In fact the apparently mundane activities just listed have a much larger impact on the earth and people than the invention of ideal cities and grand buildings. The way cities, regions and whole countries look depends, in the final analysis on the design activity of many individuals over a long period of time.

What all this activity has in common is that it represents a choice out of all the possible alternatives, that it tends to be lawful and systematic, and that it results in the cultural landscapes we inhabit.

In order to understand Environmental Behaviour Relations (EBR) one must be able to generalise *en route* to the development of an explanatory theory. For such generalisation to be even minimally valid, and in order to identify patterns which play an essential role in research, it is essential to study this totality of environments which comprises most of what has ever been built. Yet it has been ignored: effectively it has been invisible. What has been studied is the work of a few designers, a minuscule portion of built environments. It is essential to study all environments, over the full span of their existence (almost 2 million years) and in all cultures.

This brings me to the second reason why it seems so essential to shift from buildings to cultural landscapes. People do not live in single buildings. They move from buildings to other buildings, to streets, to public spaces, transport, open spaces, countrysides – to many other 'settings'. People live in 'systems of settings', a partial visible expression of which is the cultural landscape. Architect-designed buildings and complexes both now and in the past, only make sense in their context, the matrix of the largely 'undesigned' (vernacular) landscape. This has major implications not only for theory but also for the study of the history of the built environment, which I cannot discuss here.★ Yet all these matters and the complex issues which they raise have been to a large extent ignored by the mainstream architectural literature – it is part of the invisible in architecture.

★ Rapoport, Amos. *History and Precedent in Environmental Design*, New York, 1990.

? *Wouldn't it make sense if we distinguish between different kinds of purposefulness? For the biologist no behaviour is without a purpose, but from the perspective of civilisation there is a big difference between the purpose of a shelter, and the purpose of a folly, both versions of an architectonic structure. Can you work with such a distinction?*

! There are certainly different kinds of purposefulness, but I would approach it differently. If one considers, as one must, all that has been built, then the body of evidence becomes very large and varied. The variability of built environments seen cross-culturally and historically is most striking. Much of this variability is due to the latent aspects of activities (their meaning) and thus linked to culture. Therefore, the shelter of one culture may be the 'folly' of another. Moreover, from my perspective 'shelter' is not a good term since a major function of housing (or dwelling) (as of all environments) is to communicate meanings. And at that level, 'shelter' and 'folly' may communicate the same meanings.

Environment-Behaviour Studies

Some summary statement is essential to provide a common framework within which my remarks can be interpreted and understood.

I take EBS to be the scientific study of EBR which is, by its very nature, highly interdisciplinary. Its purpose is to understand how people and environments interact and eventually to develop explanatory theory on the basis of which design can validly be done. From this perspective, design is concerned primarily with deciding *what* should be done and *why*. *How* comes later and is less fundamental.**?**

This implies that design is primarily problem identification and discovery and then   roblem solving on the basis of research-based knowledge, the best available knowledge, at any given time. This means that any single solution, how any individual goes about dealing with the problem (e.g. a building) is less important than what one could call the equivalent of 'public science', the disciplinary base.

As a discipline EBS, like other sciences, aims to be self-correcting and cumulative, so that knowledge improves over time. This cumulativeness and improvement occurs not only through basic and applied research but also through the application of research (i.e. design) and its evolution.

Design seen this way becomes the generation of hypotheses of the form: if so and so is done, such and

? *Do you think that creativity, which is the quality-measure of the 'how' in our society of the spectacle, is less important? You are using a strict hierarchy of practice, but doesn't the process have its own dynamics which influence the 'what'?*

! I regard the (pathological) preoccupation with 'creativity' to be a major problem with architecture. Others, mainly scientists, are much more creative without ever worrying about it. Creativity plays a major role in discovering the 'what' (and 'why') – in fact, that is far more creative than setting one's own (often meaningless) problems. Moreover, even the 'how' is amenable to scientific research – one could do a much better job in achieving one's objectives, which is what 'how' is, if they were explicitly articulated and justified. The 'how' must clearly come after the 'what'; its importance and whether and to what extent it may affect objectives is an empirical question. My own view is that it is more a constraint (among many others) than a determinant.

Still from the 'Fountainhead' by King Vidor, 1949

Public education Hong Kong, 1991

such will happen. It must, therefore, be evaluated and such evaluation made part of the knowledge base. Evaluation is a two-stage process. One first asks whether the objectives (which must be made explicit) have been met (and also, how we know). If so, the second question (whether the objectives are valid) follows, and how we know *that*. But this once again, if pursued, is another topic-although a critically important one. Note, however, that from the perspective point of view of the present topic, this process is far more important than any single solution which is the tangible concern of most study.

I have long argued that EBS can be understood, or conceptualised, in terms of three major questions:
1) What characteristics of people, as members of a species and various groups, and as individuals, influence (or, in design, should influence) how built environments are organised and shaped?
2) What effects do which environments have on the behaviour, mood, well-being, satisfaction and so on, of which groups of people, under what conditions, and so on?
3) A corollary question: given a mutual interaction between people and environments there must be a mechanism linking them. Given the importance of mechanisms in understanding and explanation, what are these mechanisms?

Clearly much could be said about this. Also, each can be researched, greatly elaborated, articulated, developed and clarified. But our present concern is the environment and its design. Here again I have

? *What interdisciplinary knowledge does help to evaluate the objectives?*

! EBS provides (in principle) that knowledge. It identifies the bio-social, psychological and cultural attributions of humans (question 1), the effects of given environments (question 2) and the nature of this mechanism (question 3). By using the best current knowledge, setting objectives, considering design as hypotheses and then evaluating these (in lieu of what is called 'criticism'), design itself would contribute to that interdisciplinary knowledge – it would become applied research (and research application) to complement basic pure research.

Peter Eisenman and Philip Johnson having lunch

Le Corbusier, housing estate, 60 years after opening (1926)

argued that the design of the environment is the organisation of four variables: space, time, meaning and communication. These are largely invisible.★ One can also think of environments as being about the relationships between people and people, people and things, and things and things. Relationships are also invisible. This brings me to the first of my two major possible interpretations of 'invisible' within this framework.

The Invisible in Human Interaction with the Environment

I will mention just a few examples of invisibility starting with relationships. It has been argued, as I have done several times, that cultural landscapes (for example urban landscapes) have more to do with relationships among elements than with the nature of the elements. When elements are for example made of materials regarded as bad, the sometimes outstanding relationships are not seen. Examples might be spontaneous settlements in developing countries, markets composed of boxes and torn sacking and so on, which yet produce superb settings which work extremely well.**?**

★ It is often thought that space is visible but it is not; it is the hardware surroundings or enclosing space which is visible and even then the conceptual organization of the space is not visible. The fact that space can be effectively invisible is well shown by the case of the Maori Marae studied by Michael Austin among many other examples.

Other examples are provided by buildings which are seen as hovels because built of materials regarded as bad, having earth floors, no services, etcetera, when they are really environments of great quality which work superbly in terms of their congruence with lifestyle and culture generally, communicate clearly to users, climatically and in other ways. Many environments like these, and historically they are the overwhelming majority, which have much to teach us, have effectively been invisible. The evidence is that the architectural literature ignores them.

There are other reasons why certain environments are effectively invisible. Because of ethnocentrism one often fails to understand environments to the extent that one does not really see them. For example, one may look for a geometric order basic in one's own culture, in cases where the order is cosmological as is the case in most traditional preliterate or vernacular situations. Since one then finds no order, these environments are dismissed and effectively become invisible. Alternatively instead of a geometric order, the order is social. This again is the case in many traditional settlements. Again, the environments are rejected, ignored and become effectively invisible.

Australian Aborigines build relatively little – the visible built environment appears insignificant.

Yet they have a most complex culture and an extremely rich and complex cognitive environment. They live in an 'invisible landscape in the head' which is overlaid, as it were, over the natural visible landscape, overlapping, coinciding and being congruent with it at certain visible features. In this way the apparent barren and empty natural landscape is transformed cognitively, becoming endowed with extraordinary meaning, given great temporal depth and being humanised. None of this is visible to the outside (European) observer for whom there is nothing there.

? *In which sense?*

! They work extremely well in the most important sense of being supportive for the lifestyle and activities of people (including the latent aspects of these activities), by being culture-specific, by communicating their meanings effortlessly and extremely efficiently. They also often work extremely well even at the formal level – in their relation to site, light, and shade, spaces, massing, solid/void relationships, colour and so on. Even at that (mainstream architecture) level I would argue (as a subjective hypothesis, because this has not been researched empirically) that they often work far better than anything architects have done for a long time (see my 'Spontaneous Settlements as Vernacular Design', in C.V. Patton (ed.), *Spontaneous Shelter*, Philadelphia 1988, pp. 51-77).

? *From an anthropological point of view you may be right. But how do you consider the chaotic development of the late-capitalist periphery of the modern megalopolis? What is the organisational principle there. Here it seems that the hidden dimension is less human instead of more.*

! Your question perfectly illustrates my point above: you find the development of the periphery of the modern metropolis 'chaotic' because you dislike it, find it incomprehensible or unacceptable. Others do not – or it would not be built. People are abandoning those areas in which you like to live, shop, eat, etcetera for the periphery. Moreover, there is a clear order; this is shown by the fact that we use the periphery so effectively (often more so than older areas). There are, of course, many things wrong with it (possibly). The approach to that, however, is not to call it 'chaotic' but to understand it and the rationale behind it, and see whether one can do better. Attacking it is not going to change it, but if designers cannot suggests improvements they should not be in business.

? *You are emphasising the collective basis of design, the sharing of cognitive schemata as the basis for collective behaviour. But in the mainstream architecture of today unique individual creativity as a notion prevails. So while you mention what most literature overlooks, the authors could blame you for leaving out the need for uniqueness and distinction.*

! I see designing as a science-based profession, which at the moment doesn't have the base that it needs. To deal with problems, to understand it, even enhance it by suggesting other ways of doing things, one needs to have really basic fundamental knowledge which at the moment is totally lacking, and I believe personally that even art can be studied scientifically with very beneficial results. I'm not saying art is a science: you see that's why I'm constantly separating the disciplinary base from the individual designer working within it. If you read the literature on creativity what becomes very interesting is that creativity in science and in art is very similar and that descriptions of the ways artists and scientists work are extremely similar; the difference is that artists essentially put forward their individual intuitions, while in science these intuitions are first tested by the people themselves, and then by the people around them before they are admitted into the canon. And at that point, the question of where architecture fits becomes much more critical because I think it fits much more in the second than in the first.

This pattern is not unique to Aborigines. They can be created through naming, as they have been in many immigrant countries, for example the United States, how the landscape is actually transformed to express the images and schemata brought **★** The history of painting in Australia shows that the landscape was effectively invisible for quite a few decades. by immigrants who also express those through naming. It begins to be designed in my sense. In these cases, what is an incomprehensible landscape, and hence invisible**★**, is made visible by being transformed into familiar forms.

But there is a more important implication of the above discussion than that such landscapes are invisible. It follows that there are no such things as disorderly or chaotic cultural landscapes. The order can, however, be so incomprehensible or unacceptable that they are rejected and ignored to the extent that they become effectively invisible.**?** These various forms of 'invisibility' in people's interaction with built environments all relate to a single point. This is that all built environments are concrete expressions of *schemata* – a term I have already mentioned. I use this term in its 'cognitive anthropology' sense. In that sense a schema is some very abstract notion of how things should be. As such, schemata are a rather difficult and high-level concept, and there are a number of intermediate steps between schemata and their product. This material expression of schemata is usually imperfect (almost in the Platonic sense). Strong support for the existence of schemata is provided by cultural landscapes. These are never 'designed' in the sense of the common use of the term (and never by a single designer).**★?**

Of course, in most cases, all these invisible things: order, relationships, schemata, and so on, are made visible to some extent, they are translated into form. While the product is always at least potentially visible, it is the result of invisible processes which are however an essential part of the product. In the definition of vernacular design and spontaneous settlements (and this also applies to high-style, popular and other environments) process variables are at least as important as product characteristics.

★ An interesting comparison is with large-scale landscapes designed by professionals (e.g. those of the eighteenth and nineteenth century English country house estates). There the existence of a schema is quite clear. This concept is also very useful in interpreting many other studies of traditional architecture, e.g. Wittkower's study of Renaissance churches among others.

It has been my suggestion (and this is simplified for the purpose of this essay) that schemata are translated into built environments, which if they communicate (and currently they often do not) generate appropriate schemata in users' minds. This can be shown through a diagram I have used before:

69

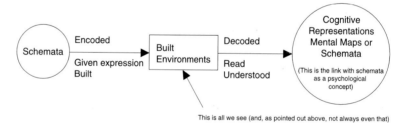

This is all we see (and, as pointed out above, not always even that)

Effectively environments are thought before they are built. Typically one wraps hardware, as it were, around schemata and cognitive domains and we have seen that Aborigines (amongst others) hardly build, although they establish 'place' or settings in many ways. They just do not wrap hardware around settings. This idea is not new. We find it even in a CIAM book of the fifties which, as an epigraph, gives a child's definition of a cannon as a hole with metal wrapped around it.**★** The difference is that we now have concepts such as schemata and methods for studying them. I have made the point that schemata are rather high-level, abstract concepts with a number of intermediate steps involving possibly lower-level concepts, such as images or cognitive domains, between them and built environments. One way of thinking about the creation of built environments is that hardware is being put around cognitive domains of various sorts. These can be domains such as private/public, male/female, front/back, sacred/profane, and so on; or such as living room, bedroom, office, men's house, and so forth, depending on the culture. These then enclose behaviour, and while some behaviour can be seen, some cannot. Behaviour is also typically missing in architectural literature and illustrations (whether criticism, history, or 'theory'); it is effectively invisible.

★ A similar point is made by Amos Chang in his application of Lao Tze's philosophy to the study of architecture (in his *The Existence of Intangible Content in Architectonic Form*).

Yet behaviour is the essence of the built environment, its *raison d'être*. Also, behaviour can occur without, or with minimal built environments, as in the case of the Aborigines or outdoor markets, for example, where the behaviour itself defines the place or setting. It is, however, important to note that environments do not just enclose behaviour. The way one usefully thinks of this in EBS is that built environments provide settings for behaviour. These can be supportive, or alternatively, inhibiting of various behaviours. In many cases, settings are not visible-and supportiveness never is. *Settings* also act as mnemonics, reminding people of how to act thus making co-action possible. This is a very important purpose of built environments and depends on visibility – it requires cues which are noticed and understood. These define the situation and guide behaviour. But these visible cues are only the tip of the iceberg; the invisible is most important. Moreover, in many of the more traditional ('exotic') situations used by anthropologists and by me, the cues can become extremely subtle, almost invisible and, in some cases, completely invisible. Being 'extreme' such cases show things more clearly.

Recall that the cues are the property of settings. What we see are buildings (offices, hospitals, shops, dwellings etcetera), streets, suburbs, neighbourhoods, cities and so on. But first, these all represent schemata, cognitive concepts etcetera which are variable, so that we do not actually see these, we construe or infer them.**? ?**

But secondly, and more important, one is really dealing with settings supporting behaviour; each of these environments (such as a building) consists of very many settings. Moreover, settings are often invisible, because the same space can become a different setting without the fixed-feature elements

changing. Often only the semi-fixed feature elements (furnishings' in the broadest sense) change the non-fixed feature elements (people and their behaviour). Architecture, however, is typically primarily concerned with fixed-feature elements. The 'invisible' in this case is what environments are all about – and they support and guide behaviour. Moreover, these settings are linked into systems through human-behaviour which is often invisible

The Role of the Invisible in Design

To deal with behaviour and the like in design (in the broad sense in which the word is used here) one needs high-level principles of concepts based on research, knowledge, generalisation and theory. This is so that a relatively manageable number of such concepts can be applied to the very many specific cases without each becoming unique. This means that concepts and theory are most important. But these are not objects, and hence not tangible or visible. This also applies to the human responses to the environment which are the *raison d'être* for design – clear schemata, satisfaction, pleasure, supportiveness, understanding, appropriate meanings, and so on. In terms of the previous diagram:

? *On the one hand you refer time and again to the reliability of theory as the basis of design, on the other hand your theory is very nominalistic. You define the environment as a mental construct. If you are right, how then can we really bother about the deplorability of architectonic culture? For you don't have an absolute standard to judge its moral deficiency.*

! My position is that designers are surrogates for users. In other words we are hired to do things that users either don't or can't do for themselves. Therefore it seems to me that the ethical obligation and the intellectual challenge is to try and understand what users would have done if they were doing it themselves. One of the big problems one then has is of course the problem of the unknown user. Many modern buildings are designed for known clients but unknown users. Again there is a problem of generalisation: what do people in general require? So the first thing, it seems to me, is that we need to understand how to design for people who are very different from ourselves. There is a distinction between the individual person, solving a problem, doing a design, and the public discipline, which sets the framework for it. I think we very often confound the two.

? *Architecture is not only built as an answer to material needs, but is also a matter of taste. How can we escape the preoccupations which are involved here? Even if an architect responds exactly to what people want, it is possible that what they want is bad.*

! I have actually emphasised above that design is not merely for material or instrumental needs (in criticising the use of 'shelter'). It is for the satisfaction of many latent functions, which include meaning. I have also emphasised that wants tend to be more important than needs. This is what you call 'taste'. But it is 'users' wants and tastes that are critical, not designers'. From that point of view a good design may be one the designer personally hates – his tastes are totally irrelevant. As for wants being 'bad' it is essential to be certain that they *are* bad – and *why*; this needs knowledge. I predict that most wants are not bad, only disliked by designers (like orders). If wants, however, are bad – and this needs to be demonstrated beyond reasonable doubt on the basis of evidence, data etcetera – one needs to understand what these wants express and to try and achieve them in different (and possible less 'bad') ways. Real creativity is to be found in this process of analysis and response. Finally, I agree that no professional ever gives anyone 'exactly what they want'. But professionals do not disregard wants, either.

In one sense one could say that built form relates two invisibles and the linkages between them are also invisible. Their understanding requires theory and this becomes the critical aspect of design understood as the translation of schemata, cognitive domains, images and the like into built form and the ability to achieve the proper human responses to such built environments. This is design conceived as a science-based profession based on explanatory theory (theory in a scientific sense). In this, the tangible, visible aspects are a relatively small part of the whole. Theory of that type consists of constructs and concepts related to each other in complex ways which are all invisible. The whole structure is linked to the concrete, empirical world which, ultimately, is tangible and hence perceptible. Theory and knowledge are both vast abstract domains and hence invisible, yet they must be the basis of design.

The left-hand side of the above diagram, which is where design occurs, can be of different kinds. In the traditional vernacular situations, in the case of buildings and in the case of cultural landscapes more generally, the users and designers were the same. The process occurs over long time-periods and is *selectionist*. What I mean by this is that it gradually achieves congruence with users' wants, needs, lifestyle, ideals, schemata, and so on in an almost 'evolutionary' way through many decisions and modifications over long time periods. In traditional architectural design, designers and users, while distinct, were close in sharing values, schemata etcetera; designers also were concerned with very few types of settings. Currently designers operate as surrogates for users, there are multiple groups of those and

Amos Rapoport

designers as a whole are very different indeed from users as a whole. Moreover, designers are expected to design types of settings which they never did in the past. As a result, they operate in a *instructionist* mode – they need to provide instructions for the organisation of system of settings over very short time periods.★ The only basis on which this can be done validly for people very different from designers, with highly varied cultures, schemata, values, lifestyles and so on, and who are often not known individually, is through knowledge based on research. The task is to know *what* to do and *why*.

But knowledge based on research also seems critical in the process of achieving the objectives once set – the how. Not only is this amenable to research but it crucially depends on it. One needs such knowledge in order to know how to achieve given objectives and whether people will like them, whether they will prove supportive. One needs knowledge of the repertoires of means available, how people perceive, how they recognise, how meaning is communicated and what meanings are communicated by which cues, to whom and under what conditions; what effects which environments have on which people and under what circumstances – and how important these effects are and so on.

Research is essential for all aspects of this facet of design. Research is essential in order to know whether one has achieved the objectives and if not, why not. Research from an EBS perspective even changes the

★ These terms, from molecular biology, were proposed by Lederberg (cited in Jacob, F, *The Possible and the Actual*, New York, 1982, p. 15-17. Although they refer to very different processes I first applied them through analogy in my 'Culture and built form – a reconsideration' in Saile, D.G. (ed.) *Architecture in Cultural Change*, Lawrence, 1986, p. 157-175.

way one thinks of perception: it makes one question the term 'visible' (the second of the changes to my title). From that point of view even visual perception is dynamic rather than static, and hence very different indeed to what is considered in mainstream design. Much more important however is the multisensory nature of perception. The physical, tangible built environment is more than its visible shape.

I would argue that a most neglected aspect of environmental perception, the perception of the built environment as artefact (in itself a small part of EBR) is its multisensory nature: it is much richer than merely vision. Environmental perception involves sound and the acoustic quality of environments, smells, textures, and tactile characteristics, thermal qualities, in general and of surfaces, air movement, kinetics; the only sense not directly involved seems to be taste. Also involved are light quality, views out, and so on, that are rarely considered in architectural criticism, history or theory.*? ?*

In effect one should speak not of visible but rather of sensible or perceptible. The preoccupation with vision to the exclusion of other sensory modalities in Western design and ignoring the combined effects of the various senses is a serious lacuna. Also while the emphasis on the visible implies an excessive pre-occupation with aesthetics. From an EBS viewpoint, this can be studied in the sense of experimental aesthetics, or by shifting to the use of concepts such as 'environmental quality'. These can be conceptualised as profiles consisting of many variables, only some of which may be perceptual qualities. Thus, the relative contribution of appearance and the like to preference and satisfaction becomes a researchable question and can be identified for various cases.

Also, while perception is almost by definition sensory and is most important to the way designers judge environments, it appears that most users react to environments quite differently – through their associational aspects. In other words, the physically perceptible elements and characteristics are cues which communicate meanings – and meaning is one of the most important mechanisms linking people and environments. It is users' meanings that influence preferences and evaluation through various levels of meaning related to identify, status, guides to behaviour in the settings etcetera. Therefore not only does the emphasis on the visible perpetuate the visual bias of designers at the expense of other sensory modalities, more important, it is misleading in the necessary understanding of users' interactions with built environments. While designers judge environments in the perceptual mode, users do so in the associational. I cannot develop the topic meaning here. I will only say that meaning is not additional to function.*?*

More important is that meaning is at the latent end of the function, behaviour and activities, away from the instrumental or manifest pole – and latent means hidden, non-obvious, and hence invisible. More specifically I divide activities into four levels, the variability of which goes up as one moves up from, (1) the activity itself (its manifest of instrumental aspects), (2) how it is carried out, (3) how associated with others into activity systems, and (4) the meaning of the activity (its latent aspects). The cultural specificity of environments is related to latent aspects of behaviour and leads to the extraordinary variety of environments. This variability is one of their most striking characteristics and raises most important questions about them. Because these latent aspects explain the variability of settings for the relative few things people do, they become most important in shaping environments.

Conclusion

My main argument in this brief and simplified essay is that the physical expression of design – built environments of cultural landscapes (let alone buildings) – forms only a small part of the whole domain, and not the most important one. This is even the case for users: their experience of the environments and their relationships with those goes far beyond the hardware. More important, however is the implication that most of what professionals need to know, understand and explain in order to be able to design validly and responsibly has little to do with artefacts which presently occupy them to the exclusion of anything else. It is what cannot be seen which is clearly by far the most important part of the design process in the sense that I use it – design for users as a science based, responsible profession based on a research-based discipline.

I have argued that research is needed for various reasons, and only mentioned a few of those. A major point is that *what* to do and *why* is far more important than how to do it – which is what typically preoccupies designers. The 'what' is the problem to be solved and the proposed solution; 'why' addresses the justification for the identification of the problem and rationale for the solution – and problem identification is possibly the critical issue. Problems cannot be set arbitrary as they typically are but need to

? *Why is this? Could you give an historic explanation of the present-day ignorance of architectural practitioners?*

! No, I cannot, since I have not studied this. I have however, suggested that it occurred when architecture, unlike other disciplines, rejected science. One result was that, unlike real disciplines, it only has practitioners. Other fields have begun to redress the balance. For example geography. Two geographers, Abler and Gould, have suggested that any real discipline must have four types of people:

Philosophers
Theoreticians
Researchers
Practitioners

They argued that in geography there were many researchers but the other three groups were lacking and that the field should begin to redress the balance; it has done so. In architecture there are practitioners but I believe the other three are lacking; they are badly needed. EBS now has researchers but theoreticians and philosophers are still missing.

? *But why is there a lack of theoreticians and philosophers in architecture? And aren't the idiosyncratic architects on the tip of the iceberg, the Deconstructivist or the Heidegger-inspired phenomenologists, the philosophers you are talking about?*

! No. This kind of philosophy is *not* what I am discussing. From my perspective the less said about Heidegger, phenomenology, deconstruction and the like – the better. I refer to the carefully worked out philosophical foundations of a given theoretical discipline, for example the philosophy of biology as an aspect of the philosophy of science. The latter is the only branch of philosophy (and needs to be combined with other fields) that I regard as relevant to the types of things I am discussing. Personal 'philosophies' or 'theories' have no connection at all with the public, communal, cumulative enterprise of theory building on the basis of empirical research and conceptual analysis. That, I would argue, is the only thing worthy of the name theory. The subjective positions that masquerade as 'theory' of 'philosophy' are just personal views based on no data or evidence or serious conceptual analysis.

? *So you will not agree with most architectural theory of the recent past, in which the need of symbolism on the façade has been emphasised? In fact, this statement of yours implies a strong dissatisfaction with any notion of meaning as an architectural element, whereas you will opt for meaning as a dimension of architecture?*

! Of course I take a very different approach to meaning than most, particularly in rejecting linguistic models and semiotic approaches in favour of non-verbal communication models. But that is another story. I have told that story in a book, and can only refer readers to it: Amos Rapoport, *The Meaning of the Built Environment,* Tucson 1990 (updated version). There are also several papers but the essence of my argument and approach is in the book mentioned.

Sao Paulo

Amos Rapoport

? *In mainstream architectural thought many aspects, dimensions and factors are effectively overlooked, as you say. What could be the interest behind this narrow vision? Another question is: what does the monomaniacal attention to the 'tip of the iceberg' actually produce? Does it have any positive side-effects, according to you?*

! I cannot answer the first part of your question – I do not know, and the reason is that I am really not interested so that I have not looked into it. It seems enough, for my purpose, to have identified the problem and the current situation. My answer to the second half of the question is rather brief: No!

? *Cinema?*

! You misunderstand my point: I am talking about the process of creating built environments. As the next line indicates one is dealing with conceptual structures and these cannot be filmed. As far as the products of design are concerned cinema or videotape may be somewhat better and holograms better yet. Acoustic quality could possibly be recorded and communicated. This still neglects the other senses – smell, kinesthetics, temperature and wind, tactile qualities etcetera. There may well be adequate technologies available now or in the future which are helpful in communicating the *ambiance* of settings which is multisensory. Even then, however, they would lack an important aspect of human interaction with the built environment – that it is active and hence dynamic, involving sequences of activities within systems of settings; that it is purposeful and goal-oriented and hence very different from the contemplation of images. But even the best of such technologies only deal with the perceptual product – which, I have been arguing, is a minute part of the field.

be identified on the basis of knowledge of the potential users and of EBR theory. It is only the final part of the solution, a very small part, although an important one, (because it is what one lives in) which is concerned with the hardware. It is only that part which is perceptible, i.e. capable of being grasped through the senses. And even that has to do with relationships and many other qualities which, I have argued, are only partially perceptible. Moreover, they are ignored in the material typically discussed by the mainstream literature. It follows that as analysts and researchers, and as designers, we cannot stop with the perceptible – and certainly not in the narrow sense currently used.

I have argued that *how* one goes about solving a specific problem, which is closest to traditional concerns of mainstream design, can be researched and can be approached scientifically, indeed it must be. Any term, for example 'privacy', has major conceptual complexity and is linked with other concepts in a theoretical structure. The physical elements provided to help achieve it (i.e. solve the problem) are only a small part of it. Thus the physical and the conceptual are rarely fully congruent or coincident – and do not need to be highly so. This is because most such concepts are highly variable, for example cross-culturally, and cannot be assumed, guessed or based on intuition. In the case of privacy, for example, the mechanisms may not involve martial means, as I and others have shown.

To understand that many concepts which design needs to address and satisfy require research and analysis not only of the concepts themselves but of the relationships between them and the physical equivalents or expressions. Design is much more than the arbitrary assembling of physical elements to satisfy designers' arbitrarily posed problems.**?**

I return to the three basic questions of Environment-Behaviour-Studies in terms of which the field, its domain and its theory can be understood and articulated: 1) human characteristics: perceptual, cognitive, cultural, lifestyle, etcetera, 2) effects of environment on people, choice, criticality, etcetera,

3) mechanisms linking people and environments, perception, cognition, meaning, instrumental, etcetera.

Each of them is very complex but comprehensible and researchable. They are not however, immediately (if at all) perceptible in the built environment one encounters.

The essence of the process of creating built environments and experiencing them is invisible. No photograph in a journal or book, and no slide can show these.**?** They require modes of representation and manipulation as complex as they are. One is dealing with conceptual structures, not material ones. The research needed to understand these processes at a sufficiently rigorous level to generate usable explanatory theory is also highly abstract and cannot be seen in the actual environment, although its role in creating acceptable settings is crucial. The built environment can only be understood as the final material manifestation or expression of a largely non-perceptible domain.

Classical Architecture is no Saviour

A Conversation with Quinlan Terry

It exists everywhere in the modern world: the conflict between progressive and conservative, between the shock of the new and the continuity of tradition. But nowhere, and certainly not within architecture, is this struggle fought so vehemently as in England, where, on the Modernist as well as on the traditional front, the form of architecture is taken as a manifesto of an attitude to life, one that is either vital or not. The traditionalists, in this case the Classicist's, gained unexpected and overwhelming support from Prince Charles The Prince of Wales's *Vision of Britain: A Personal View of Architecture* (1989), a vision of a pacified, corporate Britain deserving once again of the adjective 'great', touched a sensitive string. For in England, a land of extremes – its combination of modernist marching forward, economic decay, isolationism and unassailable traditions –, there are many who have lived through the *juggernaut* of modernisation. Nowhere has industrialisation taken place faster and more thoroughly than here, but nowhere else arose such a strong tradition of resistance as well. It was here that the *Luddites,* the destroyers of machines, the personification of the dialectic of the Enlightenment, originated. 'God made the country, man made the town', wrote the poet Cowper in the eighteenth century, thereby setting the tone for a fundamental dividing line through the culture which is also a division between two characters: of the man who respects the world as it is, and of the man who only endures the world if it is altered. The one aims at preserving the things of value that are already present, the other concentrates on the things of value that still have to be made real.

Quinlan Terry is clear-cut in his architecture and in his words; since the fetishisation of the new our civilisation has gone downhill. There is no place for noncommittal irony in his work, no time for frivolity. A rare exception in the contemporary pluralistic spectrum, Terry makes pronouncements of high moral calibre. What is especially noticeable is that the scorn of colleagues doesn't bother him at all; he just perseveres indefatigably with his investigation into the spiritual energy of a 'personal' Classicism. An ability to discriminate, quite unknown in modern terms, is naturally part of this morality. Anyone who waves the flag for God is obliged to damn diabolical modernity. And Terry does just that. What is very unusual is that he also remains faithful to his vision in the organisation of his practice. No absenteeism, no computer screens and rattling printers constantly spewing out the master's sketches which are then elaborated on by well-trained, highly educated architects. In the small office in rural Dedham there are only a few assistants who work according to the traditional principles of common sense, and under the maestro's continual direction.

If we examine the discussion of his work more closely, then it appears that one of the major reproaches levelled against Terry consists in the supposed static nature of Classicism which is seen as being insufficiently flexible for contemporary (commercial) programmes, and certainly not expressive enough of the fragmentary and nomadic qualities of contemporary culture. Besides an imperturbable belief in the futility of such *Zeitgeist* ideas, Terry counters with a flexible Classicism, as exemplified by the Richmond Riverside commercial complex, where it appears possible to combine the solidity of a traditional wall with the endlessly extendible space of the commercial office landscape. Classicism, whatever that may be, can dress up the anonymity of money apparently without any problems. Separating function and façade in such a way without any scruples, Quinlan Terry shows himself to be an architect bent on turning back the maelstrom of modernity with universal and timeless values. It is a matter of applying the eternal to the scale of the historical, however transitory that may appear to be. Terry seems to consider that only architecture is able to perform this noble work. But what would happen if he were to test his moral reductionism against the amorality of large-scale urban development and the periphery, where is it difficult to maintain the objective criterion of theological purity?

Cottage, Frog Meadow, Dedham, 1979

74

You are one of the most controversial architects in England. You have often clashed with colleagues on your opinions and buildings. Could you describe a concrete situation in which the reason for this confrontation becomes very clear?

Well, let's talk about competitions and the control over taste by the architectural establishment. A competition is only as good as the assessors. If the assessors are chosen by vested interests, you get Modernist architecture; so they make sure that Modernism continues and you will never break that influence. It's time to escape from that system. The architectural establishment is similar to the former communist establishment in Russia: it looks after itself. In the seventeenth and eighteenth centuries marvellous cities were built

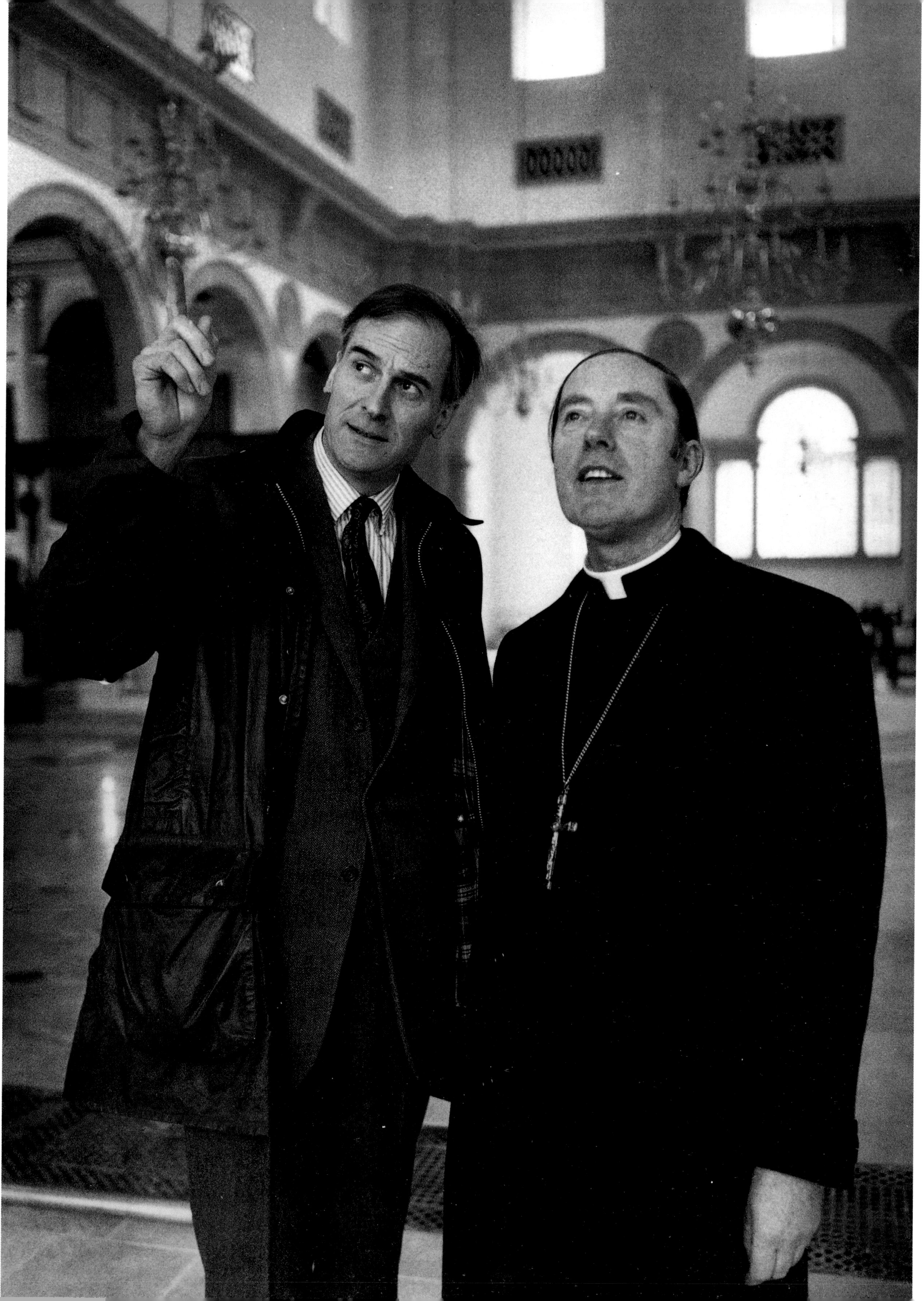

Quinlan Terry with bishop of Brentwood

Brentwood Cathedral, 1991

without having qualified architects. There was no planning authority. All there was was a good system of law and order; people worked their way up into an office, they didn't start by winning a competition. By the time they were forty-five they would be recognised and receive major commissions, if they had any talent. Nowadays the system is so doctrinaire that it's very hard for anyone with talent to survive. By the time students have been brainwashed for five years in an architectural school, by the time they have gone in for competitions and found out that all the assessors are institutional partymen, by the time they have gone in for various awards and found out that the gold medals are only given to the good boys, they will have given up the pursuit of excellence. Anyone who dares to criticise the system is persecuted. But their absolute control since the war is beginning to crack, in places. Critical books have been written and people have even said that they hate architects. That's at least something. When you are doing something which is classical and traditional and you say that what architecture has been doing for the last fifty years has been a complete waste of time, they will do everything to stop you.

When a poll was taken on favourite buildings, respondents reacted favourably to your Richmond scheme. Does this mean democracy, and will it result in democratic architecture?

I do believe that architecture reflects the society and the age. There's something about St Paul's in London which says 'England is a great country, the Protestants are as good as Roman Catholics, we stand for good values, honest living and beauty'. Of course you can envelope a building with an idea which wasn't intended. St Paul's was bombed but not destroyed in the Second World War, so everybody felt that was what they fought for. Nevertheless there is no doubt that architecture, like art, does reflect. Modern art in all its pluralism reflects a pluralist society that has no real principles, apart from a belief in progress. It seems it has something to do with the theory of evolution, which has taken away the old belief that we are created by God; that we come from some primeval slime and evolved by chance. So we have no purpose in the world, and we came to pass by accident. This differs totally from the view I take: an orderly world which was created in a certain way, mankind was put upon the earth with a certain task to do, and life will only come to an end when the Lord chooses to return. It is a very different conception of life, and somehow or other I hope my architecture expresses that. In that sense it is a political art and, if people support it, that must be a sign of the perseverance of a moral consciousness which enhances the quality of democracy.

If art reflects the state of affairs in society, do you believe then that if you could improve architecture you could improve society?

I think that is too simple. Some very good buildings were built during the era of decadence in the Roman Empire. You might say that in comparison with the age of Augustus the buildings were decadent in the Constantinian era. But the Arch of Constantine is a very great building; even Raphael copied it. I don't honestly think you can improve society by improving architecture. It is the other way round. If there is anything that really will improve society, it is in the end the spiritual reawakening of the Christian faith. Not emotional excitement of the charismatic sort, but a genuine revival on the scale of the Reformation in the sixteenth century. In Holland the whole country was changed by Calvinistic teaching. And though some would denigrate it, crime, adultery, homosexuality, all that sort of thing was reduced. The country was cleaned up; so was this country. When this belief really takes root again in a country, then all sorts of good things result. People will not work just for money, but they will work because they like to work. They work because they are working, *as unto Christ*. Of course they are working for money as well. But their honesty is watched by their conscience. If you have people, self-motivated to live clean and honest lives, you are bound to get a country which is powerful and strong. And then, little by little, architecture will improve, art will improve. I think most of these blessings will come from a new Reformation.

How can we escape from the repressive order you have described, other than to wait for a new Kingdom of God or hope that one day everything will be all right. Are there some hints we can already discover? Are there some signs from which you can derive hope?

I don't see many encouraging signs at the present time. Of course there are some very great men alive, men who are very inspired even today. And in spite of all the awful things, there are opportunities to practice one's architecture and to enjoy doing it, although every time I build a building it seems to lead to a pitched battle. It's a fight against planning officers, the architectural establishment, the media. Not against my client; my client just wants a beautiful library, cathedral or a house; they can see things like the ordinary man. But once I start to do a design, particularly if it is in a public place, all the party members scream their heads off and say this mustn't be allowed, it's shocking, it's backward-looking, it's derivative, it's turning its back on the present; it upsets all their expectations of how the world should be developed. They do what they can to stop it. What I do is, I suppose, an act of defiance against this age of permissiveness where anything can be built, except, for some illogical reason, what I design.

Richmond Riverside, second floor window

1986

Well it's quite natural that a small section of the pluralist spectrum which challenges this permissiveness should be expelled; banned from the scene. So it's a compliment that you're not accepted as just one element along a spectrum. Because at least it seems to imply that you are taken seriously.

It's not a matter of taking me seriously, I would like to think that I'm a threat. They fear that if this sort of architecture is actually allowed to happen at the end of the twentieth century, it'll catch on and if it catches on people will then realise that you don't have to be a Modernist to build. Vanbrugh, Hawksmoor, Gibbs, all the great architects of the past, went to work for another architect as an apprentice. The official course is unnecessary. Architecture isn't an academic subject. It's something that you're born with, which can be trained under the old apprenticeship system. So the only way to improve architecture is to get back to the sort of condition in society which we had before these nineteenth-century institutions came along. Now if traditional architecture were to catch on in a big way, the whole architectural establishment would collapse because the public – that is the developers and the clients – would begin to realise that **good architects do not have to be Modernist union members.**

But this is one of the main lines of modernisation, the institutionalisation of the profession. You are suggesting a traditional situation in which isolated master-apprentice workshops offer a few designs to a few other people and this in a quite recognisable unit. But what the professionals want, or rather reflect, is the nationalisation or even internationalisation of commerce. So that's another reason why you are not accepted: it is not only the meaning of your designs but also your suggestion of how to reorganise the craft in an anti-commercial way.

The professionals have replaced the craftsmen completely and so they never talk about beauty. Partymen architects never say 'What I want is to make this building easy on the eye'. They want it to look twentieth century, or powerful or brutal. We don't respect that eye which we all have in us, which appreciates beauty. We don't talk about beauty because nowadays we don't see that carving, plasterwork and stonework is the way to express something we actually enjoy looking at. We have now invented all sorts of other Gods which come before it: it must be economical, it must be built on time, it must have lettable area which sells, it must fit into the marketplace, financial equation. But these are not the only things in real architecture. The important thing is that you erect a sound structure which is easy on the eye and which makes you feel good. For example the village Dedham where I live. You walk down the street and you think 'What a peaceful world'. None of the buildings was built by an architect; they were just ordinary builders, but they did

Richmond Riverside, office space

Richmond Riverside Development, 1986

Richmond Riverside Development, 1986

have an eye for what worked. I work with people in my office who have never been to an architectural school. They can look at a roof and say 'That roof doesn't fit well on a building'. They have that sort of natural appreciation of common sense in art which country people have and which can be properly developed in a right society. But if you put these people in the middle of the city, into the architectural schools, and then brainwash them for five consecutive years, they will come out and say whatever you tell them to say.

You think the way everybody expresses and appreciates beauty is context-bound?

I wouldn't quite say it's entirely context-bound, because a lot of people who have been brought up in a concrete jungle hate it and want to get out into something which is more pleasant. My late partner Raymond Erith was born and brought up in a particularly ugly part of suburbia and when he came out to East Anglia he just could not believe it could be so beautiful. So he wasn't that context-bound to the world in which he was born. There is a certain independence of what's really important in all of us, but the problem is that we are not able to define this independence independently. However, we are not going to get very far by trying to establish fundamental principles about life out of architecture. A building – however beautiful – is not going to help you in your search for the Truth, which is the first thing that you ought to be interested in. Otherwise you are just talking about society. But what is society without the person who made society? You have to follow the argument right to its logical conclusion. Why am I here? Who has put me into this world? Why do I live such a short space of time? Why do I suffer so much and then die? Architecture may move our emotions but it will never help us to answer the important questions about life. In that search, architecture is an irrelevance.

So you will never believe in art or architecture as a legendary challenge to heaven, the genius and the hero as competitors to the gods? I don't only mean an anthropocentric architecture as such, but also the heroic architecture which denounces the old metaphysics of architecture, gravity, shelter, occupation, foundation, and the like.

Anyone who challenges God is bound to lose. The laws of gravity must be obeyed. Anyone who disobeys the laws of gravity falls down. He can appear to defy the laws of gravity, but he will never succeed.

Going through the history of architecture you perceive many examples of Promethean, if failed, challenges to the divine. Can't one even be inspired by these failures? It is not only success which inspires.

Yes, but inspire to do what?

To new Promethean acts.

In fact to insult God more?

Well, defy Him, at least. The insult is His projection.

Really! If that's the purpose of your life, it is a bit unequal, you, one little man, taking on the law of universe.

You don't think this legend, this myth of Prometheus, is of any value for Western thought?

Of course it has historical value, but it has no moral value. And it may be so that the whole drift of the Modern Movement is ultimately blasphemous. One of the greatest men I ever knew (a great preacher with a huge regular congregation of over 1,500 people) was very interested in architecture. I asked him 'what do you think about architecture?', and he said 'I don't know anything about it, all I can say is that it is blasphemous.' He saw something about it that is defying God and blaspheming and insulting. He felt it was an attack on an ordered discipline, on a loyal civilised society which recognises that God is in control of our destiny. That is in a way how I think the older ages were trying to live, although they failed in many ways. Then there comes this revolution, Marx and Darwin and Nietzsche, and all those nineteenth-century philosophers who really turned the whole thing on its head. Architecture following that revolution is Promethean. **The Modern Movement is Promethean in its concept, and in that sense it is blasphemous.**

Therefore you blame it. But it is not always that conscious. For example, the improvement of building techniques and the corresponding technology-push in modern times almost automatically led to flexibility and transparency. New systems of construction at the end of the nineteenth century suggested we could forget about the wall and use only columns. This was a revolution because the notion of the wall has always been a very strong mental concept, if we may believe the phenomenologists of Architecture. Now this concept has turned out to be obsolete.

I always like the walls to be thick, solid and load-bearing. If you have a load-bearing wall, you will get architecture without trying very hard because you have to put the windows in the right places and when you come to the top of the wall you will need a cornice to keep it dry. And if the cornice is to scale, it will need to project by so much. But you can't project a cornice if the wall is too thin; it will fall off. So either you have a lot of metal cramps holding it in place, which is a sham, or you build a wall thick and properly. If you have a solid wall, you have a perfect solution for elegant architecture. This is all you really need to know.

We never talk about spiritual things during work, it just isn't in the repertoire of the people in my office. They talk about brickworks, sash-windows, roofs, slates, getting the building done on time. But these deeper things, you can leave them to the King of kings.

Maybe this is the third reason why you are isolated and not accepted; these thick walls represent an Epimethean world-view, as if you are saying you shouldn't steal the fire from the Gods. Wait, don't make everything transparent! Of course Prometheus always considered his brother a bore and a stumbling block.

81

Yes, but don't you think we have opened Pandora's box? Once the box is opened, we have nuclear energy, nuclear bombs, drugs, the technology to keep people alive as vegetables. We invented all this and now we think it would have been better if we hadn't. Certainly, I think the world would be a great deal better off without half the things we have invented in the last fifty years.

Probably we are now touching on the insolvable incommensurability between les Anciens *and* les Modernes. *If you are an* Ancien, *the standards of the past are sacred and in a way you are paying daily tribute to the eternal values of Classicism. Is it these values which represent the* durée *in architecture for you?*

Respect for the long term in architecture simply involves constructing a building to last. One of the great advantages of Classical architecture is that it produces buildings that endure for hundreds of years.

The cathedral I have just built replaces a building that was built in 1973. The building only lasted seventeen or eighteen years. That cannot be of much use to the client. The man in the street wants a building to last so his great-grandson can live in it. Traditional architecture can do that, always has done it. But Modern architecture is like a car, the turnover time is too short. The materials in it are so unsuited to changes in weather, temperature and moisture that each year it's progressively nearer the end of its life. So a Modern building – quite apart from the philosophy behind it – will collapse in one generation, just because it's made of steel and concrete which, once the moisture gets to the steel reinforcement, will fail. Traditional architecture is built for hundreds of years, Modern architecture is built for decades. The developer gets a financial return for twenty years, after which it has payed for itself in rent. At Richmond the walls are thick, it has slate roofs, so there is little to go wrong. I admit that there are also concrete slabs with car parking underneath and as a modern construction I think that will be the first thing to go. But the actual buildings themselves are built on traditional architectural principles. That's what I am saying about *durée*.

It's quite remarkable that in the discussion about durée *as one of the secret layers of architecture, people often refer to it in terms of anonymity. Usually it is more about the mass of urban texture than individual Classical architecture. It's about the imperceivable slow mutations in the urban fabric. The Classical way of building is very persistent and durable but also very charismatic in a way. It gives a place a name, stands out from this anonymous urban fabric in its self-confident built rhetoric. So as a Classical architect you put 'time' in the* durée.

Thomas Gainsborough, Hon. Mrs. Graham, 1777

B. Spoerry, Port Cergy, Paris, 1991

The Classical architect doesn't put time in a building consciously. It happens accidentally. When I design I think of the Romans, of Palladio or of all sorts of eighteenth-century precedents, but I don't really intend to make an eighteenth-century building. In fifty years time you will pass that building and it will look like 1990. You don't think 1990 can be expressed in Classical terms but it can, because the age in which a Classical building is built will never be confused with another age.

Why then are you so very keen on telling the public that Richmond's from 1986?

Because I want to emphasise it's nothing to be ashamed of. At the moment it may look like eighteenth century to some people. But I'm sure in one generation it won't look like that. Lord Burlington was copying Palladio as carefully as possible when he built Mereworth Castle, which he thought was really a pastiche of the Villa Rotonda. But Mereworth Castle is absolutely the hallmark of the English eighteenth century. There is nothing of the Veneto about it, nor the cinquecento. Palladio himself, in his *Quattro libri,* says about a number of buildings that these should look like Roman houses. But they do not look like Roman houses at all, it's the Veneto and the cinquecento. The age and the place goes into the building – particularly Classical building – whether the architect does it consciously or not. What the architect wants is one thing. What it appears to be is obviously different. On one building in Richmond I added a little bit of Venetian Gothic to break the monotony of the Classical. But now it begins to look Victorian. I don't know what it is, it's just part of the age we live in; we can't help but put our own age, our own character, our own nationality into what we do. So it's a contemporary work which will have the qualities of the age, whether we like it or not.

Compared to your work the National Gallery extension of Venturi and Scott Brown is more obviously designed today, though it has many Classical details and motives.

You are talking about Post-Modernism, which has all sorts of hang-ups. It comes after, whereas I'm just doing what architects already did long before Modernism. Post-Modernists are terribly worried about misleading the public; they are always talking about the dangers of falsifying history. They have so many *-isms* running around in their brains that they can't just rely on themselves to build a simple extension to the National Gallery in a sensible way. I think it's just irritating. They are also too worried about the architectural critics who are here today and gone tomorrow. What will remain in 200 years time is the building.

And the Classicism in your architecture escapes from this erosion and matches the true standard? Where is the limit beyond which you don't agree with specific solutions any more?

Classical architecture, properly handled, is a living thing.

Each single building is slightly different, and when you use Classical principles you have to make many judgements. The Doric columns for example won't always fit exactly as they do in Palladio's book. So you may have to reduce the columns. Coming up to the frieze one will have to arrange triglyphs and metopes to fit between the columns. Another problem. Then you want an order above it which is perhaps Ionic, with modillions in the cornice; these have to correspond mathematically with the triglyphs below. Actually, you will start a three-dimensional game of chess trying to combine the lower with the upper order and you can't get that to fit without the triglyphs not meeting. So you reduce or widen the column. After you have been working on the thing for hours, perhaps weeks, you have little by little made a whole lot of intellectual judgements in terms of material, of texture, of proportion, of architectural detail, which is your contribution to the Classical tradition. It's your game of chess. You have to know the gambits, you have to move out your castles and bishop and knights. That's what architecture is. If you are good at playing the game, you will give a good performance; if you are an amateur, it will be obvious to everybody. It isn't a pastiche, it's a living tradition; that's where the limit lies. There are a million answers to the problem and yours will be different to mine, and therefore they will always be interesting to look at because not only will yours show a country and a century but it will also show whether you are foolish or clever. We can't help being derivative or being born into a world where we have things in our mind which we work out in our practice. But we shouldn't make this insight an alibi for pastiche without paying tribute to the tradition from which pastiches are derived. I think we have established one thing during this conversation: that Modernism and Classicism are opposites. This is important, because now in England everybody tells you that this debate has gone on far too long and it's about time it stopped; that it's not really a debate at all, it's a question of two sides of the same coin. That Norman Foster or even Robert Venturi does a thing one way and Quinlan Terry does it the other way, and they are just showing us the depth of Classical architecture. They say it's all the same thing. I don't know if Norman Foster thinks that, but I certainly don't. **The Modernists use the word Classical to make themselves more respectable!**

83

But don't they say that the Classical is in the measures and not in the orders?

Yes, they say that classicism is clean lines, grain, texture, careful thought, but they eschew ornament and mouldings and the orders. Having raised a fierce debate, they now say that it has gone on too long, and we should just stop this argument because it is not helpful; it is like a schism in the church, and we mustn't have the archbishops fight against each other. With tremendous effort a great blanket is put on top of all architectural debate. They say 'We like Quinlan Terry as long as he likes Foster', and when I say 'I'm sorry I don't see the point of it' they say '*shhh*, it has been for too long'. In fact the Modern establishment is going to win. The points that have been raised have been swept under the carpet. Healthy debate, that's all right, but don't actually say that the one is the opposite of the other. That's the point, they fear the consequence of opposite world-views.

Why are you so ambivalent? On the one hand you have emphasised the irrelevance for architecture of finding the meaning of life; on the other hand you are very fierce in defending the Classical as a super category with social implications.

Dufours Place, London, 1983

That's because it's a very complicated problem. I have been pondering the relationship between classical architecture and the Christian faith for a long time. The question is in what sense architecture is a way to truth. I've not quite worked it out yet. In the Old Testament God told the children of Israel that they must worship before a building. He designed the building, for Moses was given instructions about what this building should look like. Later, when David and Solomon took over the kingdom, they erected the temple in Jerusalem, an unbelievably beautiful building where His people should meet with God and bring their sacrifices. Worship then was architecturally bound. The whole history of Israel is connected with the destruction and rebuilding of their temples and all their zeal and all their fighting was centred around the temple. At that time architecture (and music and priesthood and all the trappings) was theological. When Christ came he said 'I shall destroy this temple in three days and rebuild it', referring to the Christian faith. He removed all that architecturally oriented worship which He required in previous ages. The temple was destroyed in 70 AD and was never rebuilt. From then on the apostles talked about the temple being the body of believers. So the Christians had to change their approach – from an architecturally oriented type of worship which was legitimate and proper until Christ came, to a way of thinking in metaphorical terms. The temple is just a metaphor for the New Testament, a church is not a building but a body of believers. A tremendous mental change is required; the building is no longer of any help to a man seeking God. The word church, *ecclesia*, means 'those called out', called out of the world, whereas we tend to think of a church as a building. In the Old Testament church, architecture is the handmaid of worship, but in the New Testament church the whole thing was revolutionised into a metaphor for the believers and the individual soul. Church history shows a return to that Old Testament idea that God is best served by bricks, by stone, by art and by music, and they have re-created the architecturally bound worship. The buildings got more and more lavish and they returned to this primeval feeling that you have to serve God in a particular place, with a particular art, in a particular building. In the Reformation Luther and Calvin had to say again that it isn't the building, it's actually a belief in certain doctrines and truths which are contained in the New Testament. Dedham church was built in Roman Catholic times, but the Reformation removed all the offending items, the stained glass, the altar, the idols. In the eighteenth century there would have been a simple Protestant church, with a simple service, whitewashed walls and a pulpit in the centre, thus returning to the Old Testament pattern. It would have been fine if it had stopped in the eighteenth century, but not a bit of it! In the Victorian Age all the sacramental things were put back. Now you have stained-glass windows again, a great big altar at the east end, the pulpit pushed away to the side, which is a return to the Middle Ages. In the mind of men there is a tension between a vague idea that God must be served through architecture and a conviction that God is served in the mind and the heart, through an understanding of the Bible. This tension we still have today and this is why I can't say that architecture is related to theology. The Bible gives the right answer. However, we still feel that buildings reflect truth; that's where our difficulty lies.

Perhaps this is the reason that you strongly emphasise the irrelevance of architecture for finding truth. Since your architecture is very material and durable, it would be Old Testamental if it was suggesting a way to God. Instead of bashing the spiritual meaning of architecture, the Moderns chose to upgrade the concept of space as an alternative to the godly substance expressed in material which was a standard in Classical times. Is the moulding of space a major concern for you?

In Richmond there are various squares within various buildings and one can feel that the proportion is more or less what you envisage.

In the same way that in a room you design a certain height, a certain length with a certain space running out of it. Yes, it is very important; the whole thing is enclosing space. It is the space that you enclose and the way you enclose it that is fundamental to what you are designing.

Okay, but now when I ask you you admit it is important. But do you often use the term space in your conversations? Is it a concept you are fond of?

No!

But you still use Modern space in projects like the Richmond scheme, where behind the façade you are just offering the isotropic space of any office-building, with open-plan floors, columns, modern lighting, air-conditioning, etcetera. Inside there is absolutely no Classical identity in your sense of the word. What's your opinion of such use of your buildings?

I'm in business to design office buildings. I have a particular client who believes, perhaps quite wrongly but economically he's right, that space can only be sold if it is open plan. That is what all the funds insist on; and all Modern buildings have this type of internal planning. If the client listened to me I would not have any air-conditioning at all, and because the windows are no more than six metres from the wall I would not think it necessary to have artificial light all day. A lot of things I could improve, but I have to follow instructions like everyone else.

So in Richmond you are forced to show your ideas on the façade and not at the level of the programme, even though you would like to do that.

We are always forced to compromise in some measure. But it is not just the façade, because in fact the span of all the buildings is no more than twelve metres, which Modern architects never do. So if electricity fails, you could live and work in these buildings without air-conditioning. You could open the windows. You would have enough light. All roofs are pitched. It's based on common sense. But it's true, it lacks consistency inside. The entrance halls are an indication of how the space could have been done. It's unfinished, an incomplete building. If a tenant were to ask me to design the partitions, we could do it with the greatest of ease. But the partitioning is always a subcontract, carried out by the tenant.

In your ideas we see a very exclusive dimension, one that doesn't fully correspond with your pragmatic approach as a professional. There is an intrinsic paradox in building a scheme like Richmond, which has inside it a programme which is in the end antagonistic to the message being told on the outside. It's a bit depressing that the message you want to advocate, extrapolated in your opinions about the thick wall, can also cover up the effect of money in making your own darlings transparent.

We have to realise that money as an end in itself is obviously destroying everything. But money as a servant is necessary for all of us. It's a matter of proportion. I had a client who asked for 100 square metres. And I said I wanted thick walls. Now the walls are at least about one and a half metres thick; most Modern walls are less than half that in thickness. If you make the wall thick, you can't provide so much extra space, which makes the building less profitable. However, good space can be let for a higher rate. This is what I can do within my competence. I'm not competent to change the brief.

However, it is strange to see you, an architect working under the banner of Cowper's famous assertion that 'God made the country and man made the town', working on an unspoiled form as a screen before the monetary forces of the city.

Maitland Robinson Library, Downing College, Cambridge, 1991

What you should realise is that I'm not a latter-day prophet. I'm not telling anybody that if they live the way I would like, the world will be saved, which some people tend to think. I believe that there is a length of time for the history of this world and as evil increases on the earth there will come a point when God will tolerate it no longer. The evidence as we look around us seems to suggest that something like that could happen. It could happen next year, it could happen in 100 years time. I live in the knowledge that these things will happen sometime, but at the same time we do an ordinary job. There are indications that there is a right way for man to live on earth and a wrong way. Since the nineteenth century, with progressive technology, the wrong way has been made available, whereas previously it just wasn't so easy. Now we have more ways of living in an unnatural environment. You might say that we live further from God. But Classical architecture is no saviour. It's common sense.

The Invisible in Architecture could be conceived as context. The context cannot be captured in a single truth; it is the rest of the world, that which is provisionally ignored but in fact has a bearing on the subject under discussion. There is always a context. It is unthinkable that we or our cultural artefacts could exist without it. In the absence of a sense of contextuality, there can be no sense of either reality or of viable possibility.

Our culture is permeated by the realisation that everything is relative, that everything acquires its meaning in relation to an environment. Objectivity does not exist, let alone absoluteness. He who fails to think in terms of context is politically incorrect and a shady customer. Since this is a reputation nobody relishes, our culture is engaged in a major undertaking to map out the context. All kinds of forgotten corners are being discovered, and formerly implicit agreements are being discussed openly. We have become conscious of the Other – and we have even become conscious of the fact that we become conscious of ourselves through the Other.

Before the days of Modernitas, this 'universal surround' had another name: God. He was the all-encompassing, the spiritual connective tissue in an infinity that was always presupposed although only partially visible. But now we have declared God dead and sanctified the context as His worldly successor. Belief in context takes the place of a waning belief in truth. In the circumstances, the search for what was previously overlooked easily becomes a goal in its own right, without the least emancipatory intent. The final result is a morally detached 'complexity' in which the context has become the text.

Although the context is actually infinite, we can only be aware of one or two aspects when we focus our attention on it. Thus we fool ourselves into thinking that we contextualise everything, but there are many aspects of the context we still prefer to dis-

Context

regard. The purveyors of today's culture restrict their attention to precisely those individual contexts that support their personal ambitions and their (contextualised) theoretical hobby-horses. The political contexts of social systems and their potential alternatives remain invisible. All attention is reserved for the symbolic context. Thus effectively a contextualisation takes place that remains restricted to the surface and does not extend to the social content under the surface. Awareness of context gives us an illusion of liberation, but it really leaves us trapped in all those contexts we would rather not know about. We often protect 'our' context by saying that we 'don't understand' other contexts and would therefore rather not express an opinion about them. Conversely, we reject the interference of those who do not share our own context.

With the 'context' vector as our tool, we should like to probe the limits of this selective awareness. We must avoid the pitfall of a deconstructive exercise that obfuscates the responsibility for our actions. Thus in our examination of architectural oeuvres, our attention to context must go deeper than merely a biography of the architect and an assessment of his position within the professional field. We must also consider non-professional contexts: these will shed a very different light on the 'autonomous' discourse.

One could say that Post-Modernism is a wide-scale rehabilitation of the context. The Modern project, although clearly of a secular character and thus different from the God-given metaphysical narratives, always presupposed a totalising, all-encompassing perspective. Things could be better in this world, and to achieve that betterment various matters had to be excluded. In this respect, Modernism was a destructive machine that ran on dissatisfaction and was accompanied by a perilous agenda of hypothetical utopias. Post-Modernism is a reaction against both the dissatisfactions and the enthusiastic projections by which they were stifled. This world is by no means the worst of all possible worlds. There is no reason to be either discontented or exaggeratedly optimistic. And you cannot allow yourself to exclude aspects, not even in the interests of a better world – after all, that invariably leads to catastrophes and deceptions. This is a nomadic attitude: it does not 'design' in time, but 'finds' in space. The cartography of the context that this nomadism so strongly stimulates has meanwhile brought us into contact with quite a few 'forgotten' dimensions of our existence.

And there is more. Inclusivism, the urge to recognise the forgotten, is the core of the contextualism in much of present-day philosophy and architecture. In succession, history, social background, ecology, race and gender have become the catchwords of the growing awareness of the Other – an awareness that plays a significant role in the difference thinking that has been so prominent in philosophy since Kierkegaard and Nietzsche. Initially stimulated by the idea of Enlightenment, this thinking has by now reached the very roots of that idea: the notion that things ought to be better than they are. Since even that notion is open to doubt, difference has become a drifting theoretical concept that lacks a project or goal but enters into everything. As a result, the context seems to have changed from being a subject of research into a new morality. But it is a morality of the culture reserve: contextualisation is becoming more and more a luxury problem for a privileged elite. Attention to context seems to have taken on the function of an indulgence, a remedy to lull the uneasy conscience. Admittedly, we are highly sensitive to context in our theories, our debates, our teaching and our art; but in daily life we get by without qualms under our capitalist consumerism, fret about our careers, never venture a thought about what could be different, and remain captive in patterns that sustain the misery of others. In our prosperous corners of the world, universal suffrage has given us freedom of speech and we make ample use of it in our contextual chit-chat. But in doing so we also sanction the impasse. We have become apolitical.

At first sight, the context in which we find ourselves is bafflingly complex. We have now explored countless contextual dimensions of our existence and live, as a result, in a heterotopia of opinions, roles and paradigms. A huge diversity of possibilities lies within our conceptual grasp and our freedom of choice seems vastly enlarged. But, remarkably enough, this does not give us the least existential angst or heightened urge to act. The media present us with the multiplicity of contexts in a comprehensible, entertaining and reassuring way. However, this domestication of heterotopia has become part of our context in its own right, and, moreover, precisely the part we do not talk about. The obsessive interest in personal micro-narratives has thrust the macro-historical and macro-economic context into the background. The context is our morality, but in this morality we ignore the context.

The relationship of architecture to context is inevitable. Architecture is an applied art. The building must inevitably relate to an institutional, material and spatial context. This has always been true, but in the last few decades the contextuality of architecture has enjoyed our special attention. Context is now a term that crops up with unerring regularity in discussions of architecture. The notion of context that figures here is generally narrowed down to the relationship of the built object to its material environment. Interest is focused on the relation of the project to the built environment. The architect chooses an aspect of the context that catches his attention and incorporates this into his project in some way or another, so that the building is 'in harmony' with its surroundings. In this approach, the context is usually regarded as a tradition of style or materials, or an urban or functional typology. References to social conditions, ecological problems or prevailing ideologies are much more unusual. And rare indeed is a critical intervention in the programme inherent in the context. Naturally, architecture always articulates a value judgement about the context. If this judgement is an unfavourable one, it can, in the best cases, stimulate a striving for an alternative. This alternative, too, is invariably 'contextual': it is located both in the context of the existing circumstances and in a context of current critical ideas.

Contextuality is inescapable. Nor is it easy to evade a specific context in the practice of architecture. The statements archi-

tecture makes about a context are often no more than marginal. They are recognisable in the three-dimensional structure but leave no mark on the programme it accommodates. Even in architecture that is intentionally critical towards the context, its functional content is often continuous with the programme implicit in the context.

Three strategies and three architects Practically all architects nowadays justify their work at least in part by an appeal to the context. In the arguments by which they back this appeal, there are clear differences of accent. We distinguish the following:

Archaism
Archaism seeks its context chiefly in enduring attributes such as topography, ground, location, region and nature. It is inclined to shield itself from excessive or excessively abstract context. Rather than latching onto the image of the instant, archaistic architecture seeks a relation with the tangible surroundings and with a concrete human being. This architecture summons to its aid a context conceived in tactile and tectonic terms, and deploys this to evoke an authentic embodied experience. For this purpose, a modest bearing is essential.

In his architecture, **Steven Holl** does not attempt to delimit the individual in any way. He wishes only to offer that individual some peace of mind. Materials and space operate in unison to produce a synthetic gesture. Holl concentrates increasingly on a psychological refinement of experience. His motive is to anchor his architecture in firm ground, both literally and figuratively.

Façadism
Façadism presupposes the notion that it is possible to refer directly to the (cultural) context by means of overt signs on the facade. After Modernism, which was context-free in this respect, it is now permissible to 'mean' things once more. Facadism uses the ABC of the visual language. It aims to achieve legibility, and is hence by definition contextual at a visual level. This architecture therefore relies extensively on a publicly recognisable formal vocabulary. In the architecture of **Robert Venturi and Denise Scott Brown**, the emphasis is on 'both/and' inclusivism. No semiotic idiom, no taste culture, is excluded *a priori*. Everything is aimed at 'serving' the public, whoever that may be. The public gets what it wants: legibility, identity and a little irony. In this, it is invariably the will of the majority that prevails. There is barely any questioning. The figuration is reassuring and seems to say: yes, this building is for you.

Fascinism
Fascinism does not interpret context as the spatial and visual surroundings, but as our current historical period. This is characterised by a profound decontextualisation, at least in the sense that everything merges into the flux of *Modernitas*. Under this strategy, it is a small step from contextuality to intertextuality: it is then no longer the value of the context that matters, but the context as a system of signs. Things, images, words, everything, can be read as text. This reading has moreover become a value-free activity. Where but in an urban periphery, a chaotic zone where absence of centre is palpable, can the fascinist attitude draw its inspiration? **Nigel Coates and Doug Branson** do not so much react to the context as become part of it. Since the whole culture is permeated with a metropolitan attitude to life, architecture can best aim to generate a metropolitan ambience. Thus Coates and Branson conceive a hyperactive, almost neurotic environment, in which a general atmosphere rather than objects predominates. There is hardly any room left for individual self-development in this context. It resembles Art Nouveau in which the biotope of nature has been replaced by that of the metropolis.

True organic architecture can only exist when it is in harmony with the totality, for through a limitation in one place, expansion elsewhere is possible. The point is to find one's organic place in the total social structure. **Ton Alberts & Max van Huut**

What is necessary is not to promote the myth that 'progress' is everything, nor to react to this myth by returning to the past or mischievously referring to the vernacular for expression. I value cultural treasures and would like to develop them in a creative way. My architecture basically follows the tradition of the Modernist compositional and formal methodologies; however, I emphasise the geographic and natural environmental context and climate, as well as historical and cultural heritage. My architecture evolves from the interaction of these elements. *Tadao Ando*

Context is physical, but it is also in the mind. The french mind for instance is made up of sweeping designs, ordered regularity, Classicism; and the projects we realised in France all integrate with this specific context. You have to dialogue with the context, yield to it, resist it, transform it, distort it, and create it. Pyramids are mountains. *Ricardo Bofill*

Context is where we find ourselves. In making architecture one brings contexts into being – they are presenced. **Julia Bolles & Peter Wilson**

It is my intention to produce buildings that are built for their environment and which seek a relationship with their surroundings. The aim is to reach once again an understanding between engineering and architecture in the sense of the creation of static, formal and plastic possibilities of the respective materials. Behind all this stands the search for a unity between the art of architecture and the art of engineering. **Santiago Calatrava**

The new city must use every conceivable technique to flip meaning and throw the control of events back to the people performing the
Nigel Coates & Doug Branson

The context is an intrigue of dialogues in different languages: that of physical forms, of history, economy, politics or love. **Pietro Derossi**

Today, conceptions of the body are radically changing. The Post-Modern is heterogeneous, indeterminate and ubiquitous. It is deterritorialised from cultries and information and in continuous flux between silicone, steel spandex and skin. We have come to understand the body as gendered and turally inscribed, a product of 'political technolog **Elisabeth Diller & Ricardo Scofidi**

Architecture is first and foremost about people and their needs, both priva as individuals and publicly as communities. In our work this theme of s context extends from the basics of shelter to the creation of symbolic spa the dynamic of movement and the poetry of natural li **Norman Foste**

The Joan Miró Library, situated in the Parc de l'Escorxador, lying in one of the clearings of the park's wooded areas, seeks the silence of the park while at the same time clearly belonging to the urban hierarchy of its surroundings. **Beth Galí**

My approach to architecture is different. I search out the work of artists, use art as a means of inspiration. I try to rid myself and the other membe the firm, of the burden of culture and look for new ways to approach the w I want to be open-ended. There are no rules, no right or wrong. I'm confus to what's ugly and what's pretty. *Frank Gehry*

One of my interests is to make the familiarity of my work such that society can get into it. I think there is lots to say once you have access to the work. *Michael Graves*

A building that is used by many people, whatever its scale, ought t designed not as an isolated work, but as a part of something larger. In o words it must have a quality of urbanity. My second major aim has been t to eliminate the gap between the community and architecture and to architecture a new social character. **Itsuko Hasegaw**

Context seduces people into believing they have a neighbour, they do have something to relate... **Jacques Herzog & Pierre de Meuron**

Building transcends physical and functional requirements by fusing with a place, by gathering the meaning of a situation. Architecture does not so much intrude on a landscape as it serves to explain it. Architecture and site should have an experiential connection, a metaphysical link, a poetic link.
Steven Holl

Everything is architecture.
Hans Hollein

I think it is terribly dangerous to submit oneself to the inexorable forces of history.
Leon Krier

Taking the context into account simply means feeling part of the geographical, human, cultural, economic world you have chosen to operate in, not shutting yourself up in abstract and destructive forms of logic. **Lucien Kroll**

Synchronicity is a way of describing the feeling of equal distance (or equal closeness) to all different cultures... The new syncretism must be based on the principle of equal distance between each culture of the world.
Kisho Kurokawa

When we design an office building that consists of large number of cells, we make those cells so transparent that the people who spend their time in them can feel they are working with other people, in a single building, in a single company. In our housing designs we try to avoid designing units that have no relationship to their surrounding, the world outside. **Lucien Lafour & Rikkert Wijk**

In a time when architectural traditions are in a process of dissolution, the 'language of architecture' suggests more probing questions in the mind of man than what is said in that language. Thus style takes precedence as a problem over the content or substance of architecture. The public is less interested in what is actually disseminated – what architecture makes blatantly visible – and more seduced by the preconceptions that have gone into its formation.
Daniel Libeskind

The almighty notion of freedom implied by a carte blanche acceptance of personalised creation is, in reality, delimited by the world that presses on it. The 'context' in architecture – the surrounding environment and the circumstances that it encompasses – should not merely serve as a platform for one's creations; rather, it should be thought of as and constitute the very soil in which the edifice will emerge and grow. This notion of context as fertile ground in which an edifice will germinate and by natural process foster its own individual character, as opposed to the common interpretation of context as the backdrop against or within which a building must melt, blend, or, in effect, disappear, seems to me the most true and productive understanding of the word. **Rafael Moneo**

One works within the discipline of architecture, as well as within an awareness of other fields – literature, philosophy, or even film theory.
Bernard Tschumi

To be relevant to their age architects should learn, from the cultural context, 'ways of doing things at a point in time'. Ways of doing buildings – how walls and roofs are built and doors are framed – can be discovered from the minor architecture of the day. Architects, we believe, should for the most part follow these conventions and, because in our time they derive from Modern architecture, we should, in general and in the major portions of our buildings, follow Modern conventions. In our opinion, contextual borrowings should never deceive; you should know what the real building consists of beneath the skin. For this reason our allusions are representations rather than copies of historic precedents. The deceit is only skin deep. As important, all buildings, even 'background' buildings, should add to their context, although the appropriateness of what they add should be subject to discussion.

This is the appropriate architectural role in the landscape and the city. Alternately, architecture that engages only in context is likely to be bland or banal. The architect who takes no care for context is a bore and the architect who cares only for context is a bore. **Robert Venturi & Denise Scott Brown**

On the Work of Steven Holl
Under, In, On and Over the Earth

Steven Holl's architecture is sober but immensely rich. Although his exteriors betray a unique hand, they never speculate in the shock of the new. The interiors often show an ingenious use of space à la Rietveld, albeit for the Affluent Society. In spite of Holl's sensitive use of colour, the impression that persists in the memory is one of black-and-white. That is to say, not the simple black-and-white of the monochrome snapshot but a true pre-war black-and-white, charged with historical meanings, intimating nostalgia and melancholy but also suggesting longing and purity. This black-and-white is a conscious choice, part of an aesthetic programme. The sobriety of the overall impression is deliberate. In fact, this kind of black-and-white is not really uncoloured: an earthy tint, an underlying alchemical hue that practically resists conscious perception, seeps through to the surface. And this coloration takes on a disproportionate significance precisely because of its false modesty, especially when the context is overwhelmed by a gleaming, sparkling extravaganza of colour, technically reproduced to its maximum extent. Holl's colours bring to mind the self-imposed restraint of the films of Jim Jarmusch: the world is dirty, the circumstances cruel, life is hard and the only true friend is a partner in adversity. In spite of his isolation and the wretched tricks of fate, the individual – in Holl's case the architecture – retains a towering dignity. It is the visual self-restraint that is responsible for a sense of elegance and grandeur.

The veiled opulence of Holl's architecture seems to be gaining wider and wider appreciation. There is no need to lay it on as thickly as before: the market for Post-Modernist glitter has passed its peak and architecture is gasping for a *Sinnpause*. At a time like this, Holl's kind of reticence may be the answer. It is not a real impoverishment (for the pampered eye is not willingly chastened), but a restrained form of luxury that strikes just the right note. Holl's architecture is delightfully designed and beautifully executed, and bears witness to a high degree of precision. At the same time, by appropriating tactilist techniques, he avoids becoming ensnared in the temptations of Total Design. Some questions are left unanswered. There are places in his buildings where we encounter a kind of vacuum, often due to a sudden jump in scale, a vacuum waiting to be filled by emotion or by a subjective experience. The experiences proffered by Holl's architecture compensate for a longing that is never mentioned but is felt by more and more people. If we regard his buildings as therapies, then Holl is not a surgeon but a psychoanalyst who proffers his patients the key to greater self-understanding. One question remains, however: does the cure also have a public significance, one that does justice to the programme of his buildings?

From Typology to Phenomenology

Steven Holl's speciality is character analysis. What is the nature of the elements from which architecture is composed, how can they be manipulated and into what entities can they be combined? He is an architect who seeks out experiment. Not only do his projects form a kind of laboratory, but his studies, publications and teaching work all bear witness to his passion for enquiry. A vital ingredient of his research is the phe-

View at elliptical passage, project for Porta Vittoria, Milan, 1986

nomenological value of architecture at various scales, from the interior to the city. But his phenomenology is anthropological rather than philosophical in nature. In other words, it is not so much the power of things *as things* that preoccupies Holl, but the general human experience of that power as it affects each of us separately. Holl's work exploits the power of things to communicate with people and with the functional programme at a somatic level. He takes a stand against the soulless mass production that has the building industry in its grip and argues for '... a kind of reasoning that joins concept and sensation. The objective is unified with the subjective. Outer perception (of the intellect) and inner perception (of the senses) are synthesised in an ordering of space, light and material'.★ At first sight this resembles an appeal for a more profound kind of architecture, but the stress Holl places on the *architectural* embodiment of the marriage between intellect and experience gives him a special position among the many who have summoned phenomenology to their side: their interest either fails to go beyond a theoretical appeal, or develops into a glorification of the experience of every detail as an end in itself. Holl is concerned not to dismiss the programmatic significance of the marriage, and this expresses itself in his capacity for both small and large scale thinking. His competition entry for the Palazzo del Cinema in Venice (1990) is an example

★ Steven Holl, 'Selected Projects', in *Quaderns* 181-182 (April 1989), no. 166.

Phenomenological intensity and a preoccupation with tactile experiences have both been salient characteristics of Holl's work over the past decade, and in this connection, one may claim that he is the only American architect of his generation to be directly influenced by the main lines in modern philosophy and music, that is to say, by the line leading from Husserl through to Heidegger and by the separate achievements of Bartók and Schönberg.

Kenneth Frampton

General theories of architecture are constrained by a central problem; that is to say if a particular theory is true, then all other theories are false. Pluralism on the other hand leads to an empirical architecture. A third direction, as potentially resilient as it is definite, is the adoption of a limited concept. Time, culture, programmatic circumstance, and site are specific factors from which an organising idea can be formed. A specific concept may be developed as a precise order, irrespective of the universal claims of any particular ideology. A theory of architecture

that leads to a system for thinking about and making buildings has, at its base, a series of fixed ideas constituting an ideology. The ideology is evident in each project that is consistent with the general theory. By contrast, an architecture based on a limited concept begins with dissimilarity and variation. It illuminates the singularity of a specific situation.

Steven Holl

Architecture is bound to situation. Unlike music, painting, sculpture, film, and literature, a construction (non-mobile) is intertwined with the experience of a place. The site of a building is more than a mere ingredient in its conception. It is its physical and metaphysical foundation.

The resolution of the functional aspects of site and building, the vistas, sun angles, circulation, and access, are the 'physics' that demand the 'metaphysics' of architecture. Through a link, an extended motive, a building is more than something merely fashioned for the site.

Steven Holl

92

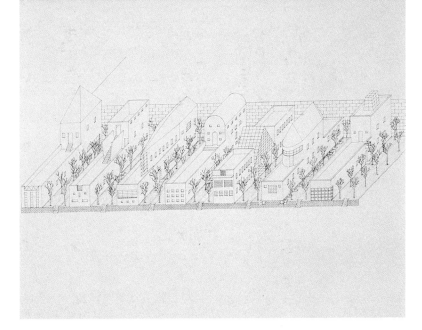

Autonomous Artisans' Housing, project, Staten Island, New York, 1984

that reveals the importance he attaches to the programme of his architecture. It is apparent in his remarkable treatment of the surface and in the great subtlety with which he manipulates incident light; in the way he stage-manages the architectural experience by means of an almost labyrinthine access to the space via the water, sloping ramps and promenades; and, finally, in his treatment of the auditorium.

Initially, his broad concern with form and programme was concentrated on typology, the American vernacular and existing building methodologies, as in the Hybrid Building, Seaside, Florida 1988. It becomes especially clear in his project for Autonomous Artisans' Housing, Staten Island, New York 1980-1984. Here Holl invented a specific type of form to reflect the specific activities of each hypothetical occupant – the paper maker, the wood worker, the glass etcher et cetera. The hitch was that the possible associations the public might have with the chosen typology would be largely prescribed, owing to the conventionality of the forms. Hence these associations would fail to elicit subjective experiences in the individual spectator. During the eighties, Holl therefore developed a more refined idiom in which the typology of forms was replaced by spatial scenarios and a more abstract image that was virtually no longer open to rational pros and cons. It appealed to the user at an almost unconscious level. The 'style' that Holl uses in his recent work, with its almost alchemical surface treatment, makes 'a permutable series of abstract correlations that can be brought to accommodate a very wide range of empirical programmes'.★ On the one hand, Holl has hereby ventured into a much freer area of design, in which he can cater for many different kinds of programme within the scope of his vocabulary, without bowing to the irresistible demands of specific formal conventions. On the other hand, the craftsmanlike quality of his work has made him practically invulnerable to conventional, external criticism. Now a critique will have to be found which does justice to the purely architectural perfectionism of his work, without thereby losing sight of the work's public meaning.

★ Frampton, Kenneth, 'On the Architecture of Steven Holl', in Holl, Steven, *Anchoring*, Princeton 1991, p.7.

The transition from typology to phenomenology is a transition from static observation of a subject with a name and a function, to dynamic interpretation of subjects without names but nonetheless with an irreducible existence. It is a change from iconography to anthropology. In later work, such as the Palazzo del Cinema, the building no longer offers a made-to-measure solution to the visual and programmatic problems, but leaves room for an interplay of associations. From this, we can make the crucial observation that Holl is not actually all that interested in coding the use, but in the irreducible, subjective moment of experience that is *possible*. The question of who will take advantage of that possibility falls outside the architect's competence. The spatiality of the recent work is no longer bound to the presumed identity of the occupant or user, but solely to the wishes and the spiritual and tactile needs of *specific* persons.

An abstraction has been made that offers more space for the concrete human experience. 'It is no longer possible to make a building for the mass of society', says Holl, 'without understanding who that anonymous mass is. Architecture must be done with a person in mind.' Holl is seeking a temporary assignment of meaning; not to the thing as phenomenon, nor to man as philosophical category, but to *a person* and his activities, which are reflected in the architectonic material. This architecture stands or falls by the instance.

Sweet Daydreams

A number of recurrent themes can be detected in Steven Holl's oeuvre. Firstly, he works from what he calls a *limited concept*. That means that no single aspect of his design method is universally applicable. Only meticulous analysis of the constraints imposed by the specific combination of location, time and programme can lead to a solution that 'joins concept and sensation'. Neither truth nor an established meaning prevails, but a *combination* of experience and meaning.

Secondly, he uses a technique he refers to as *anchoring*, in which the building is rooted into the existing context by simultaneously respecting and challenging it. Holl is concerned to elicit a certain idea of the location and to establish associations between his design and its urban environment. These are nebulous images and concepts that give him the leeway to develop a line of thought (and action) in give and take with the location. The intention is not to achieve a design that is at one with the existing environment, but an 'anchoring' that exploits the conflict inherent in the linking of a particular building to a particular location. This implies that anchoring always takes place from a certain distance, and we encounter this in a literal form in the conception of the aerial roots as 'legs' on which the project stands.★ The *Parallax Skyscrapers* project springs to mind here.

A third notable aspect of his work is his *alchemical approach* to form and material. Form is de-institutionalised and thrown open to discussion by means of a sort of elegant crudeness. Materials are not used for their own sake, nor do they betray a unequivocal reference to a conventional meaning. Their purpose always seems to be

★ Indebtedness to an article written by Arthur Wortmann, 'Het scheppend vermogen van de schaalversnelling. De architectuur van Steven Holl' (The creative potential of the acceleration of scale. The architecture of Steven Holl), *Archis*, 4 (1992), pp. 27-35.

93

The edge of the city is a philosophical region, where city and natural landscape overlap, existing without choice or expectation. This zone calls for visions and projections to delineate the boundary between the urban and the rural. Visions of a city's future can be plotted on this partially spoiled land, liberating the remaining natural landscape, protecting the habitat of hundreds of species of animals and plants that are threatened with extinction. What remains of the wilderness can be preserved - defoliated territory can be restored. In the middle zone between landscape and city, there is hope for a new synthesis of urban life and urban form.

Steven Holl

In the yet-to-be-built city, notions of passage must be addressed. Consider the city as it might appear in a series of cinematic images: zoom shots in front of a person walking, tracking shots along the side, the view changing as the head turns. At the same time, the city is a place to be felt. Notions of space, shifting ground plane, plan, section, and expansion are bound up in passage through the city. Consider movement through the city framed by vertical buildings. Each change of positions reframes a new spatial field. This parallax of overlapping fields changes with the angles of the sun and the glow of the sky. Premonitions of unknown means of communication and passage suggest a variety of new urban spaces.

Steven Holl

Materials interlocking with the perceiver's senses provide the detail that moves us beyond acute sight to tactility. From linearity, concavity, and transparency to hardness, elasticity, and dampness, the haptic realm opens. An architecture of matter and tactility aims for a 'poetics of revealing' (Martin Heidegger), which requires an inspiration of joinery. Detail, this poetics of revealing, interplays intimate scaled dissonance with large scale consonance. The vertical patience of a massive wall is interrupted by a solitary and miniature cage of clarity, at once giving scale and revealing material and matter.

Steven Holl

Texas Stretto House, Dallas, 1992

Museum of Modern Art Tower, New York, 1986

94

to bring about a chemical reaction with the mind of a further unspecified person who literally *comes into contact* with Steven Holl's architecture through some (ostensibly) random quirk of circumstances. This treatment of material turns even the most tranquil moment into an *event*; it is a process of sublimation or condensation that is meant to lead to a real experience. The architect must rigorously avoid revealing any of his intentions in advance since that would channel the reading along a fixed route.

This brings us to a fourth aspect of Holl's work: straying through a labyrinth. By taking us along a *promenade architecturale*, along stairways and ramps, Holl aims to bring us face to face with the Other. Advantage is taken of that unpremeditated encounter – no contrived meetings, please. Thus the aim is certainly not to create a tourist attraction, but the *amazement* of that sudden contact with the Other. Only amazement proves the authenticity of the encounter, a view that places Holl within the paradigm of existentialists such as Jean Paul Sartre and Martin Buber. The meeting is the criterion of a successfully designed space, in both the social and the architectural sense. This irreducible and authentic meeting is the only *raison d'être* of this architecture. In this respect, spoken language can even be an obstacle. In the attempt to create maximum *nearness*, Holl shows himself pupil of Heidegger. It is not a matter of the space as a neutral container, but of space as existentially experienced potential:

'The psychic core of a room is like a *reverie*. The room, an individual's place of periodic repose, either inspires or inhibits creative thought. Insight, fantasies, and imagination are fueled by the psychological space of the private interior. (...) At the direct encounter with interior space, architecture changes the way we live.' ★

But this change does not take place according to a rational communication pattern. The architecture is meant, rather, to invoke an atmosphere which is unaccented, hardly perceptible to consciousness, and which clears one's head of all over-evident messages, leaving it open to Experience in the broadest sense of the word.

★ Holl, Steven, 'Edge of a city', in *Pamphlet Architecture* 13, New York, 1991, p. 12.

With this thought in mind, and not forgetting Heidegger, we arrive at a fifth main theme in Holl's oeuvre, the idea of *Geworfenheit*. Man does not choose the conditions under which he lives, but the conditions choose him. Holl's work is never an objectivising platform for convincing arguments. On the contrary, it is the modality of those arguments that will itself assume the characteristics of Holl's space and material. The literal basis for this architecture is the earth, which can be subject to four main relations: 'Under the earth, in the earth, on the earth and over the earth'.★ Holl goes into more detail about these relations as follows: '... a series of primary syntactic proximical correlations such as rear, over, atop, under, within, against, between, through, across, beside and from'.★ The very essence of existentialism, thus – an orientation in life by means of the most fundamental thing mankind has at his disposal, namely space, particularised as prepositions in masonry! His tectonics are not traceable by the usual methods, for rational construction

★ Steven Holl, quoted in Frampton, Kenneth, 'On the Architecture of Steven Holl', in Holl, Steven, *Anchoring*, Princeton 1991, p. 7.
★ Kenneth Frampton, op. cit. p. 7.

does not play a major role. They involve, rather, a compositional ordering of volumes and lines that makes a conclusive statement not about the edges, but about the (psychological) space itself. The spirit finds its place and there is room for the daydream.

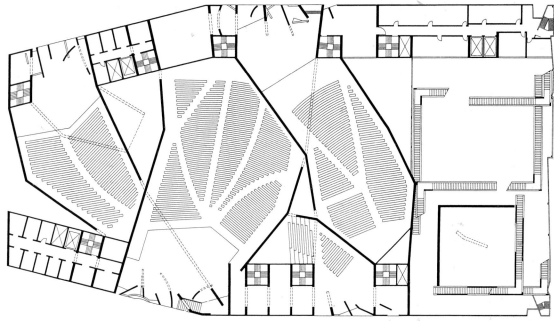

Palazzo del Cinema, competition entry, Venice, 1990

The important thing is thus the associative potential, and this ultimately plays a role in generating new context. The context – the social, the physical and eventually also the tectonic conditions – is a precondition for experience. Experience, in turn, is a precondition for continuity of the context.

Elbow-room versus Force Majeure

Holl's work is intriguing for the way it exemplifies both the strength and the impotence of architecture as an autonomous participant in the ongoing cultural debate. From the functional and programmatic point of view, his work is extremely difficult to characterise. On the one hand, Steven Holl writes about the 'the interior as harbour of the soul'. If the architectural interior space were to respond to a spiritual appeal, it might well change our lives. But Holl remains silent on the question of what that new lifestyle should be like. On the other hand, he clearly takes a great interest in the programme of the architecture at various scales. In this connection, he deliberately refrains from polished designs. By using an ontology of architectonic design elements (volumes, access, material, mathematical structures), he ensures that the image transmits its content to us through its tactile qualities, in spite of, and at the same time due to, its highly aesthetic qualities. The transcendental spirituality is thus dimmed and the earthy character of the programme is unmasked. He succeeds in softening the constraints of the programme by strictly architectural means and is hence not forced to seek that elbowroom outside architecture. Perhaps this is the only route open for strategic action if we wish to isolate architecture from its political dimensions. The merit of Holl is that he tries to read reality anew from things themselves, and he strives for an experience that leaves room for continual reinterpretations of things and in relation to things. An ambiguity, a non-metaphorical moment, arises and this can repeatedly inspire life and permanently refresh communication between things, culture and the public sphere. But when it comes down to it, it remains questionable whether the work is not too

phenomenological. In spite of its disarming openness and modesty, it becomes bogged down (deliberately, so it seems) in a purely architectural language. Hence it side-steps a confrontation in which the programme relates to a broader cultural context – a context that can not be translated into a purely architectural language, but could in principle be captured by tectonic means. Holl accepts the total context of the environment and the programme as it is given. He is vulnerable to the criticism that applies to all phenomenological strategies: the interplay of context and programme is reduced to the level of sensation. There is no explicit narrative which might otherwise restrain the power of the media to confiscate Holl's rough, indistinct and recalcitrant forms and to transform them into ornamentation. Only in an explicit relation to a definite programme, can form and material hold onto their cultural meanings and so evade the decline into representation.

Parallax Skyscrapers, Manhattan, Penn Yard, study project, New York

28 housing units are divided into 18 variants of five types: 'L' (L-shaped plan), 'I' (straight plan), 'D' (double level, 'DI', 'DL'.
Units interlock in plan and section, interconnecting the different court spaces

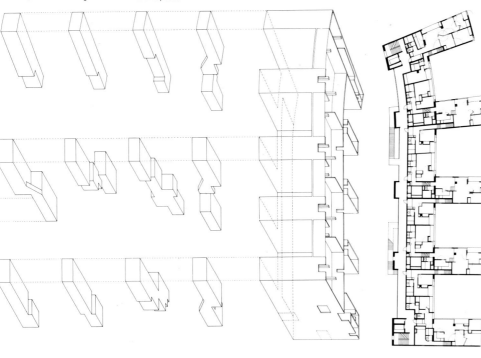

Four active north-facing voids interlock with four quiet south-facing voids to bring a sense of the sacred into direct contact with everyday domestic life. The south voids are meditative spaces held apart from day-to-day activity. To ensure emptiness, these voids are flooded with water; the sun makes flickering reflections across the ceilings of the north courts and apartment interiors. The north voids are set as play areas for children, seating for a ground floor café, etc., and face onto a common garden. Each pair is joined together by a large opening and a flight of steps. Light from the water court spills into the paved court; in return, the sounds of children playing and of conversation percolate into the meditative space. The opposition of phenomena corresponds to the sheared section of the voids. Interiors of the 28 apartments revolve around the concept of 'hinged space', a development of the multi-use concepts of traditional Fusuma taken into an entirely modern dimension. One type of hinging – diurnal – allows an expansion of the living area during the day, reclaimed for bedrooms at night. Another type – episodic – reflects the change in a family over time: rooms can be added or subtracted to accommodate grown children leaving the family or elderly parents moving in. An experiential sense of passage through space is

heightened in the three types of access, which allow apartments to have exterior front doors. On the lower passage, views across the water court and through the north voids activate the walk spatially from side to side. Along the north passage one has a sense of suspension with the park in the distance. The top passage has a sky view under direct sunlight. The apartments interlock in section like a complex Chinese box. Individuation from the standpoint of the individual inhabitant has an aim in making all 28 apartments different. Due to the voids and interlocking section, each apartment has many exposures: north, south, east, and west. The structure of exposed bearing concrete is stained in some places. A lightweight aluminium curtain wall allows a reading of the building section while walking from east to west along the street; an entirely different façade of solids is exposed walking from west to east. The building, with its street-aligned shops and intentionally simple façades, is seen as part of a city in its effort to form space rather than become an architecture of object. Space is its medium, from urban to private, hinged space. *Steven Holl*

▶

Location Eastern Fukuoka, Kyushu, Japan **Assistants** H. Ariizumi, P. Lynch, T. Jenkinson and others **Clients** Fukuoka Jisho – Ken-ichi Toh **Design** 1988-89 **Completion** 1989-90

Steven Holl Architects *Void Space/Hinged Space Housing*

Per Barclay, Untitled (steel, wood, motoroil), 1987

Twin Dolphin Resort Hotel,
Cabo San Lucas, Baja, Mexico

Two Cheers for Democracy is
One Too Few

In the course of their career, Robert Venturi and Denise Scott Brown have distanced themselves further from the kind of architectural criticism that deals not so much with the buildings themselves as with the philosophical implications of those buildings. For these architects, who have two of the most influential books on architecture of the latter half of the twentieth century to their credit, it has become clear that words always fall short of practice. In the course of their professional life they have found out that architecture is a *craft,* and that an architect's philosophy can better be one of action. This emphasis on the deed has kept them out of the centre of the theoretical arena in recent years. Nonetheless their appeal for an architecture that 'communicates', even if it dates from a quarter century ago, has become utterly relevant to today owing to the soaring growth of the communications industry. Communication – admittedly of a very specific kind – has meanwhile become a human right. Owing to this contemporary relevance Venturi and Scott Brown remain susceptible to criticism that goes deeper than the architectural object as such. The repercussions of the widespread tendency to equate architecture with language are affecting people all around the world. These repercussions are the subject of the present essay.

To apocalypticians, revolutionaries and other progressive types the status quo may well be unbearable, but there are people who frankly accept what it has to offer. Since *Complexity and Contradiction in Architecture* (1966), and especially since their inspiration by Pop in *Learning from Las Vegas* (1972), Robert Venturi and Denise Scott Brown have been the most important representatives of the latter group within architecture.

100   In *Complexity and Contradiction in Architecture*, Robert Venturi formulated a critique of post-war Functionalism, which he argued was characterised by a utopian attitude coupled to a contempt for historical structures. The homogeneous Cartesian grid, the purist formal principles of the International Style, and the rationalist principles of modern industry had, according to Venturi, brought us predictability and a monotony of form. In these circumstances Venturi was in favour of complexity and contradiction, as his title suggests, which he saw as representing a more humane approach than the rational humanism of the Moderns. In practice it amounted to a plea for a break with the moralising dominance of functionality. 'Architects can no longer afford to be intimidated by the puritanically moral language of orthodox Modern architecture. (...) I am for a messy vitality over obvious unity. I include the *non sequitur* and proclaim the duality. (...) Less is a bore.' A multiform and hybrid answer to the abstraction and uniformity of Modernism was anything but humdrum. 'I think life is so complex today you go essentially for richness of effect over purity of effect: any aspiration to clarity would be naive; viva ambiguity', wrote Venturi.

Venturi's plea for complexity met with broad sympathy within the architectural profession. It was not for nothing that Vincent Scully compared the influence of his book to Le

Guild House, home for senior citizens, Philadelphia, 1961

Gordon Wu Hall, dormitory of Butler College, Princeton, 1980

Corbusier's *Vers une Architecture* (1932). Venturi's ideas of the sixties were mainly about an aesthetic correction. This has made a lot of headway in architectural circles, since most architects have a better grasp of architecture's aesthetic dimension than of its social one. The architectural profession seemed perfectly happy with an aesthetics that goes along with the world the way it is.

Las Vegas as a Perfect Parody of Living for Tomorrow

Learning from Las Vegas radicalised the formal correction to Modernism by adding a social dimension. The effect of this book on the architectural world was therefore not so much liberating as controversial. Whereas form was Venturi's main concern in the sixties (in retrospect the author would have preferred the title *Complexity and Contradiction in Architectural Form*), he and Scott Brown used their research and photographs of the Las Vegas Strip to express a quite different, more fundamental critique of Modern architecture and its revolutionary and elitist pretensions. In *Learning from Las Vegas*, Venturi and Scott Brown (together with Steven Izenour) made mincemeat of the obstetric idiom of Modernism. The Strip, with its enormous billboards and neon signs, can be interpreted as the ultimate metamorphosis of the Enlightenment Utopia. Unburdened by the cultural pessimism of much contemporary philosophy, they saw the commercial vernacular of the American Main Street as the source of a bottom-up architecture that would be 'closer to the people' than the top-down strategy of the Modern Movement.

It was no longer necessary for architecture to be a forerunner of tomorrow's world, nor an impartial stage for the life of today's. Venturi and Scott Brown, richly under the influence of the relativising tendencies that had been at work in all aspects of culture since the sixties, wished to break with the habit of always taking a mortgage on the future. Instead, their point of departure was the world of the here and now – and what image could better express this world than the permanent makeshift of Las Vegas, which

Our design philosophy is based upon appropriateness of design to context, directness and economy of means, and careful tailoring of the architectural expression to the needs of the client, the program and the budget. Because each of our completed works responds to different natural, cultural, and architectural surroundings, each has its own distinctive identity. While our designs have been widely recognised as innovative and eloquent, it is also true that most of our buildings have been produced within modest budgets.
Our firm has served corporate, commercial, institutional, governmental and individual clients in executing a broad range of building types. These have included offices and retail showrooms, educational facilities, municipal buildings, museums, theatres, medical research laboratories, multiple and single housing units, libraries, and recreational facilities. In addition to the design of new structures, the firm has extensive experience in the rehabilitation and reuse of buildings of historic importance.

Robert Venturi & Denise Scott Brown

Today a family that chooses lower-middle class or low taste culture does not feel the need of an architect, an 'effete Eastern snob'.

Denise Scott Brown

Any architect who steps out of the elitist box today courts trouble from design review boards and architectural critics.

Denise Scott Brown

For whom shall the large civic building or the city-wide facility be programmed? In such projects, people must add their own symbolic meanings mentally rather than physically, and the architecture should be evocative rather than anonymous in order to enable them to do so. Here the something-for-everyone approach to values seems to be most suitable, although one balks at the task of defining the architectural equivalents of Archie, Edith, the Jeffersons, Gloria and Mike, in, say, the design of a city hall.

However, I suspect that cultural pluralism may be less of a problem in urban design than the social critics lead us to believe, and that further investigation into subcultural urban values in design will demonstrate that there are enough shared values to allow architects to find something for almost everyone in civic building and urban design.

Denise Scott Brown

Today the mass media have accelerated the flows and muddied the distinctions between cultures, but outrage still results if intercultural movements go in the wrong direction, if high culture turns toward low. Upper-middle culture saves its strongest salvos for those who debase its taste canons and retains its

lacked the least atom of metaphysical pretention and delivered the imagery which 'meant' the most in practice (both to the passer-by with a hunger for images and to the bank balance of the owner of Caesar's Palace).

The book *Learning from Las Vegas* is more than just a provocative gesture towards the architectural establishment. It is a monument of acceptance of the human condition, of liberation from the yoke of futuristic legitimisation. Las Vegas *is*, and that's all you can say about it. What Las Vegas ought to be, or what it will be in the future, are not of the least importance to its existence. From that point of view the city with the world's highest density of roulette tables per square mile is also the best extant metaphor for the acceptance of the now. Las Vegas earns its living literally from the myth of reckoning ahead. Where else could the authors find inspiration for an attack on this particular pretention of Modernism? Las Vegas is the ideal parody of the rationalist fixation on the future. In its sanctioned façadism, it is a first-rate source for cultural history.

If the now has become the criterion, then it is self-evident that Modernist experiential asceticism is no longer acceptable. The architecture that Venturi and Scott Brown stand for is no longer an alienating prelude to the future. The architecture of here and now is figurative, affirmative, literal and above all immediately gratifying. It is no longer concerned with a predetermined social deficiency that may potentially be overcome by architectural means, but with a *moment of recognition* that it can offer us. On the basis of the here and now, Venturi and Scott Brown have built up an oeuvre that can not be considered part of architectural Post-Modernism in a formal sense, but can in a moral sense. The world is the way it is, and nothing can remedy it – certainly not architecture. The world does not exist thanks to people but in spite of them.

Language as Context

A highly effective method for confirming the condition of the here and now and relieving oneself from the burden of looking after the future is to interpret architecture as language. This approach has its historical precedents and Venturi and Scott Brown have made a speciality of it. During Late Modernism the reduction of architecture to a package of standard solutions for a limited range of quantifiable problems resulted in the neglect of its social and historical context. From the late fifties onwards, a wider interest began to be taken in the historical transformations of the built environment, the demands of the topos, pre-existing social bonds, psychological needs and, above all, the communicative value of architecture. Alongside this, the autonomy of architecture was soon assailed by a host of sociological disciplines that specialised in such matters. Architecture risked being discussed to oblivion in an effort to redefine its cultural significance. The three-dimensional reality of architecture was being smothered by the textual discourse. But suddenly there dawned a potential way out of the predicament: define the essence of architecture as language. The discipline thus came to terms with language by turning the tables; that is to say, it started justifying itself more and more frequently in linguistic terms. If you can't beat them, join them.

From this new point of view language was both the context and the content. Architecture could escape the stranglehold of the social-scientific context by defining itself as part of that context, namely language. In the logic and terminology of the period, i.e. the late sixties and early seventies, if everything is language (Roland Barthes) and architecture is also language (Umberto Eco) then everything must be architecture (Hans Hollein). That is to say, by identifying itself with the one universally applicable contextual aspect, language, architecture could avoid being swallowed up by all those other aspects, especially the social and psychological ones (which after all could also be reduced to language). To this extent, the undertaking was successful and the mother of arts could breathe easy again: architecture was still alive. What is more, a whole new universe, that of language, opened up for it.

But an enormous problem soon emerged. By borrowing its new self-respect from the means originally used for conveying that self-respect, the linguistic sign (*signifié*), architecture sacrificed its third dimension. It was reduced to representation, and for that purpose its content, space, was no longer strictly necessary. The architectural design thus became a graphically manipulable object instead of a three-dimensional consequence of intellectual, aesthetic and technical considerations and choices (the *signifiants* of earlier times). In Venturi's words, 'We want architecture that deals with meaning more than with expression'. In short, the institution of architecture saved its skin by capitulating its historic strength as an unconscious metaphor for the rest of the world. Meaning is no longer a fact after the event but an *a priori* objective – and countless signs can be brought into play to guarantee that this objective will be achieved. Architecture thus rescued itself by semiotic disengagement, by uncoupling of the sign from the content. Practically this meant erecting 'decorated sheds' (see the American pavilion at the World Expo, Seville 1992) and figuratively it meant consciously working towards a multivalency of meaning (Venturi: 'If you are designing City Hall, you have to appeal to a broad community like a successful T.V. show.'★ For that purpose a gripping iconography is sufficient. This strategy of disengagement could be seen as blasé: two-dimensional architecture leaves no latitude for the subsequent formation of a patina. Its meaning has already been assigned in advance. The user is confronted with a pre-programmed interpretation. The construction has the character of a stage set. Time loses its status as a determinant of meaning.

★ 'Choosing Richness', interview with Robert Venturi and Denise Scott Brown, *Domus 747*, 1993, pp. 24-26.

Less is a Bore, Language is More… of What?

Credit to whom it is due, it was Venturi and Scott Brown who gave the distinction between language and content, which had already been felt as a problem in the heyday of the neo-styles, the nineteenth century, a radical rethinking in respect of architecture. Their passionate interest in the value of the visual sign as an autonomous carrier of meaning, which was clearly present in their study of Las Vegas and in their launching of the term 'decorated shed', throws explicit light on the sign's arbitrary character (with which we have had to struggle ever since Ferdinand de Saussure). Their intention was to restore communication between architecture and 'the people', and for this to happen a consensus on the symbolic order was a necessary precondition. But unexpectedly this consensus started crumbling at exactly the same time as the 'natural' bond

101

choicest epithets for those in high culture who go 'slumming' in lower-middle culture: they are called supine, arrogant, and patronising; they 'sold out', 'betrayed their responsibilities as architects'; and they 'wouldn't live there themselves'. Upper-middle critics take Gans to task for spelling culture without a capital C, and us to task for learning from Las Vegas. The outraged tone of their reviews and letters to the editor sounds startlingly similar to the tone lower-middle culture uses when it encounters pornography. In matters of aesthetics, it is easy to *épater the bourgeoisie*. (…)
If one recommends nonjudgementalism as a heuristic method for architecture, it does not follow that one must therefore be nonjudgemental about social or economic conditions as

well. It is a poor reflection on the intellectual level of architectural critical thought in America that we find it necessary to point out that one can learn from suburbia and yet be in favour of social justice and civil liberties.
Denise Scott Brown

For all architects a broadening of the terms of reference to include more than their own personal tastes can be a means of sharpening and refining their aesthetic sensibilities. Ranging beyond the confines of one's own taste culture and conditioning provides an aesthetic jolt. It opens the eye to new possibilities of beauty and revives the creative energies. At least, it can help architects to understand the context in which they build.
Denise Scott Brown

The architectural autocracy of total design applied to all objects from ashtrays to company headquarters may suit the need for prestige of a giant corporation, but for large-scale architecture and urban design, it is often unjust, usually unbeautiful (to pundits *and* people), and an inadequate expression of our society and time.
Denise Scott Brown

Although most architects are destined to remain the creatures of a limited number of taste cultures, they should take the wider view, if only to make themselves and the influential taste publics they serve more sympathetic to the needs of others. Designers who hope to plan with and for the American city need to take a wide-eyed nonjudgemental look at it first.
Denise Scott Brown

We Americans, like other former colonials, are xenophobes, yet in some areas of life, we clutch the apron strings of our mother cultures. We are proud of our indigenous styles, yet at times we still require European endorsement to validate them in our own eyes. The United States is artistically both precursor and follower, and the pendulum swings quite rapidly. But in architecture, discovery by latter-day European 'colonisers' – a Reyner Banham for Los Angeles, an American-born Charles Jencks for Post-Modernism – is still needed to dignify, for Americans, those artistic forms that originate in America.
Denise Scott Brown

City edges study, 1973

ing. The 'decorated shed' resembles a materialised semiotics and the design process becomes dominated by linguistic considerations. Thus heuristics descend into dogma and architectural complexity into linguistic abstraction; the remedy becomes a new debilitating factor and architecture declines into a packaging industry.

This unpleasant outcome of a discussion that was started on good grounds, must also be a reason why Venturi and Scott Brown are no longer keen to get involved in the public debate about their 'signs'. They have long noted that this debate remains incurably theoretical. They prefer to concentrate on the further professionalisation and refinement of their craft, i.e. designing. It appeared, after all, that there was a great deal of three-dimensional design work to be done behind the billboard façade. Even with Venturi and Scott Brown, ascending a museum stairway is not a graphic but a spatial sensation.

Democracy as Totem and Taboo

Once language becomes so objectivised that it changes from being a medium into a formal objective, it is no longer possible to attend to anything other than how the process of meaning operates as a mechanism. For example, the gold-anodised television aerial on the Guild House (Philadelphia, 1962), the polyvalent signs in the House in Northern Delaware (1978), the flat ornamentation above the entrance of the Gordon Wu Hall (Princeton, 1980), and the fading of the Classical ornamentation of the main

between words and things. If architecture, in particular the façade, is seen as a 'means of expression' then the question of what is to be expressed inevitably arises. And that is where the trouble starts; for architecture had barely been recognised as a medium of meaning when it began to lose hold of the intrinsic meaning for which the medium was traditionally meant. In other words, once we know how language is organised, we lose our simplicity of communication. Our expression becomes forced, out of respect for the Organisation.

Although it is no longer obvious *why* and *what* has to be meant, it is at least clear *that* there has to be meant, if only out of biological necessity. Everyone who has wished to enrich the architectural language for this reason has developed an idiolect of signs with which the façade can be dressed up, as though in a two-dimensional variant of *horror vacui*. Signs, conscious and abstract, are on offer at all levels of perception and intellectual development. Not one square millimetre in the field of view or in the analytical capacities is left unexploited; after all, such an empty patch might evoke reminiscences of Functionalism. Everything is filled up with ornament, symbol, colour – in short, with anything, for it is sure to mean something.

The miracle drug which people tried to use to revive the communicative powers of architecture was no longer a totally consistent historical style, as in the nineteenth century; now it was a consistent pluralism, an awareness of the systematic (and obligatory) many-faceted nature of reality, which led to the open use of a motley of Classical, modern, exotic, kitsch, serious and ironic elements. The critical distance needed to temper Modernistic Functionalism and to pillory an architecture that had become one-dimensional could only be obtained by identifying the meanings of architecture at a meta-level. Thus the introduction of semiotics has made an extremely important contribution to the enrichment of architectural culture and has enlarged its versatility and pluriformity.

But it only proves possible to step back from an analysis in the meta-language of semiotics, to real building in the object language, by decoupling the façade from the build-

Ski House, Vail, Colorado, 1977

102

United States Pavilion, Sevilla Expo '92, competition entry, 1989

Duane Hanson, Tourists II, 1988

Italian Village, tea and coffee service in porcelain, 1984

building into the façade of the new extension to the National Gallery (London, 1991) are more in the nature of references to the elements of which the users (local or otherwise) already avail themselves in their cultural communication, than of a self-conscious choice of a desired new usage. The meaning itself changes from a penetrating force, an unconscious metaphor, into a readable message for whoever cares (perchance) to take an interest in it. The meaning of a sign has become the sign's own responsibility. Those who were once creative artists – architects, authors, speakers et cetera – turn into arrangers and co-ordinators of semiosis, minders of the established language machine. At this point, criticism, the criterion for a flourishing democracy, becomes outmoded. There is no chance of bringing anything into 'crisis' or doubt because the grounds on which criticism takes place have also been transformed into impartial signs. Left or Right, Radical or Conservative, each avails itself of its own kit of signs and everyone is heartily welcome to do so. The only surviving metaphysics is the meta-language that we employ to speak of the processes of meaning and the structures of language.

The architectural symptom of this situation is the continual substitution of new signs in a linguistically idolatrous architecture. One can hardly be surprised at the architecture of 'ironic references', 'double coding' and 'polyvalencies' when public space has lost all connection with a democratic conception of what is public. Even in the designs for Franklin Court (Philadelphia, 1972) and Welcome Park (Philadelphia, 1982), which were meant as public or semi-public territory, the public interest cannot have been a factor of any significance in the project, considering the neutralised character of that

publicness. All the attention has gone into the signs and the form, and not into the function or a possible manipulation of the programme. Urban design, in the sense of a complicated pavement or of a subtle articulation of space, seems to be the highest achievable good.

But that is not all. An *a priori* pluralism expressed by multiple layers of signification is defended as being the most democratic thing around. Democracy is no longer the political result of confrontation between ideologically-driven individuals, but a feature of our personal mental worlds. The inner life of the 'politically correct' individual is a pluralistic theatre. Democracy is transformed from a political system into an unquestioned state of the psyche. The democrat no longer acts *in* the forum of events, he or she *is* a forum. The highest possible aspiration is to become chairman of this permanent internal debate.

From Totem to Lifestyle

Venturi and Scott Brown repeatedly present their design principles as democratic and humane. Their work has far more to do with what people really want, they suggest, than could ever be the case in Modernism or in several Post-Modernist strands. And they are not just referring to a uniform mass, but to a differentiated group with differing lifestyles. As Scott Brown has said, 'I have certain tastes, other people have other tastes. I share some with everyone. I, as a creator, have a right to my own appreciation of that building. But I would be wrong to ram that, and only that, down the throat of someone else. There should be room in one building for lots of types of enjoyment.' The problem with this is that those lifestyles are presented as genuine choices. But lifestyles are a matter of the projected needs of specific market segments, seen as consumers, whereas architecture should not be about market preferences but about experience of life today and in the future. If we reduce architecture to a consumer good chasing a market share, we fail to discern what the public wants – apart from instant gratification – in a social sense and what it may hope for in a political sense. The almost biological need for 'meaning' is not the same as the longing for a meaning. Architecture that devotes itself to the former, with its legitimacy derived from marketing concepts, and pushes the latter aside as a non-architectural problem has an exceedingly narrow base. This also immediately puts the claimed democratic character of Venturi and Scott Brown's thesis into perspective. Democracy is not just about what people wish to *have*, but about what people would like to *be*. The works of Venturi and Scott Brown do not appear to get as far as stimulating the posing of the latter question. With its stress on different significations for different market segments, each with its own characteristic need for meaning, this architecture contributes both to the cacophony that stands for the democratic process and to a massive consensus on the way our society should be organised. Everything is neutralised and the status quo is primary. If we persist in giving people what they want, then thinking about what people are capable of wanting, about ideologies that might transform the folly of the day into durable values, fades into the background. The 'democratic' architecture of spectacle clears the way for those totalitarian tendencies that its proponents think so far from their bed.

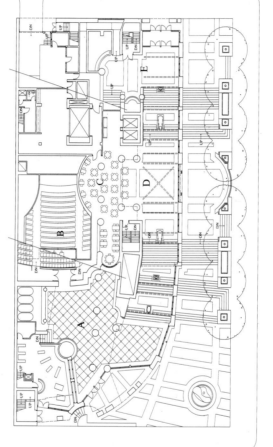

The Seattle Art Museum's new building in downtown Seattle is a 150,000 gross square feet building with main entrances on both First and Second Avenues. It is set back thirty feet from University Street to preserve the view corridor to the water. This setback allows the creation of a terraced stair. As the museum will eventually be surrounded by tall skyscrapers, we have employed large scale to emphasise its presence. The south façade is constructed of limestone that is scored with vertical fluting and incised with large letters across the top that announce the museum's name. The west end of this façade pulls back dramatically from the hillside terrace to create an entry plaza at First Avenue and to accommodate a large-scale sculpture. In contrast to the formality of the fluted limestone, the ground level is a lively juxtaposition of granites, marbles and intensely coloured terracotta. Large windows between groups of piers reflect the rhythmic progression of the terraced stair and enhance the continuity between inside and outside. This play of windows and piers is reinforced by alternating pediments and arches tied together in a continuous band of light pink granite. Inside the building, the entrances at First and Second Avenues are connected by a wide stone stair which exactly parallels the outdoor terraced stair.

The main lobby is located at the First Avenue entrance, and on this ground level are found information and orientation functions as well as an auditorium, classrooms and service areas. At the mid-level of the stair, a broad landing terrace opens both into a mezzanine restaurant and onto the terrace outdoors; the restaurant area can be extended onto the landing, and even outside, for banquets and receptions. At the second floor level is the lobby and admission desk for the Second Avenue entrance, and a large flexible gallery for travelling exhibitions. The third and fourth floors house the permanent galleries for the museum's substantial holdings of Asian, ethnic and modern art. The east-west circulation on these floors is defined by a progression of columns with a large window at either end of the building. The galleries to the south of this area are smaller rooms connected en suite which house objects of more intimate scale; the galleries to the north are larger and loft-like. Their long-span beam structure allows the flexibility to arrange the galleries in various ways. Each of these floors also contains a classroom which permits the orientation of students near the art being studied. The fifth floor houses the administrative offices as well as the library and the conservation laboratorium. *Venturi, Scott Brown and Associates, Inc.*

Location Seattle, Washington, United States of America **Assistant** J. Bastian **Client** Seattle Art Museum **Design** 1984 **Completion** 1991

Venturi, Scott Brown and Associates, Inc. *Seattle Art Museum*

▶

Jeff Wall, Eviction Struggle, installation photo/video, 1989

Neuromancing in Cyberia

No introduction needed. With Nigel Coates and Doug Branson we plunge straight into life – or, perhaps better, into hyperreality.

The Imaginary City

Perhaps it doesn't really exist, but most people recognise the idea: the city of light, the city of the electronic paradigm, a thermometer going off the scale, the laboratory of global degeneration, the entrails of society, the dream factory, a place of solitude and multitude (Baudelaire) where self-immersion in the masses produces only a feeling of isolation. The metropolis is creative nihilism, an amoral, indifferent vigour that is potentially an unceasing source of inspiration; it is the preserve of the blasé whose icy gaze is their only defence against the barrage of lacerating images. The city is a collage, a ruin, a system of signs in permanent danger of succumbing to semantic entropy, yet continually fed with new energy by the perpetual flood of youthful arrivals. It is intangible yet of the greatest possible significance for its inhabitants. A real metropolis has eternal youth. This idea originated in the old world but has only been achieved on a modest scale there. For the real city, writ exponentially, we must look to the east – to boom towns like Hong Kong, Singapore and above all Tokyo.

The city is a picture composed of countless allusions. Everyone has his individual experiences, and these are many and diverse. But in the end that multiplicity and diversity make the concept of the city identical to all. The townscape has become a mass medium and has shaped a common psychological framework for all its inhabitants. Rivalry between Mods and Rockers faded into the urban spectacle, which became the same for everyone. Social and economic differences become submerged in the common Difference, The Other. In this dimension the city is a *cyberpunk stage*. It walks a tightrope between vitality and apocalypse. The difference from the past is that these two extremes effortlessly coexist. *Les extrêmes se touchent dans la métropole.*

In the city you breathe freedom, as we have known since the Middle Ages. Since then, too, new Cassandras have regularly materialised to warn us that the same freedom can also corrupt. These two tendencies in appraisal for the city have been present in every vision ever to be applied to it. On the one hand, the city is a refuge, a public ambience, a fount of creativity and a breeding ground of poets and thinkers. On the other hand, the city is a pit of vice and a conspiracy of the ungodly. The outsider, the average inhabitant of Kensington, say, or of St. Cloud or Brooklyn Heights, can always understand this as a neutralising polarity. But for the woman behind the soup stall in Bangkok or for the salaryman in Tokyo, the distinction is not at all clear. They are in the middle of it.

Building for the Night

Nigel Coates and Doug Branson. What are they? Architects? Interior designers? Creators of atmosphere? Or are they merely set designers in the theatre of the idle class? To them, the city is a gushing spring of inspiration to which they are addicted.

But the dark side of the city fascinates them too, the refuse, the abandoned remains, the scum of the earth. The image of the city in their mind is a strange blend of high-tech constructions and ruins from bygone times, whose physical residues remain but whose moral significance is long exhausted. It is the result of beachcombing among the flotsam and jetsam of the past, but without the usual accompanying nostalgia. The players in this world sometimes seem like romantic heroes in dark times, but their existence is alleviated by countless video screens and laser flashes, by the incessant electromagnetic throb in the veins of the universe. Their city is a far cry from the *civitas* and the *urbs*, from the community and the fabric, from Augustine and Livy; their city is Cyberpolis, virtual, imaginary and without roots. Everyone has to become a performer – not to promulgate a message but to enter into a practically erotic relationship with the fragmented world, a game of flirting and ogling in that open air club people call a city. Coates and Branson, as will already be clear from the lyrical phraseology, are not primarily interested in the profession of architecture and the workmanship of an ancient craft. What matters to them is the state of our culture at this moment, with its strivings and its failures, its fatal course, extrapolated into the very near future.

Coates and Branson build for the night. It is the night that the new times have welcomed with open arms. Leave the daylight to fade the already yellowing conventions of yesterday.

From Revolution to CyberProp

Although it may be an injustice to the special character of their work, we would like to attempt here not only to undergo their architecture but to understand it too. Nigel Coates began his career as a student at the Architectural Association in London, under the leadership of Bernard Tschumi. In the experimental atmosphere of the AA, architecture was not so much regarded a specialised craft but as a territory for cultural research and (in the present case) cultural action. This is underlined by the fact that the theoretical foundations were provided by the work of Superstudio, the situationist Guy Debord and the French sociologist Henri Lefebvre. Lefebvre's dictum that 'Urbanism will emerge from the Revolution, not the Revolution from Urbanism' meant, in practice, taking a very unconventional approach to architecture: the important thing was not building, which served only the interests of the bourgeoisie, but a critique of this degenerate world embodied in an architectural dimension. In the studies that were carried out, the accent lay on the communication between architecture and the public and on making the *flaneur*, a city dweller free to make his own decisions, visible. Here we can trace the choreographic approach which was to remain characteristic of Coates' and Branson's architecture. It was not a matter of supplying architectural properties, but of creating an appropriate setting for urban behaviour.

We can see this in 1983, for example, when Coates founded NATO (Narrative Architecture Today). After boundless and fruitless neo-Marxist discussions on the economic infrastructure, the cultural superstructure and the role of the intellectual between

---

In the initial stages I try to visualise the building as a place after it is built. I think of the people in it and the way they will look at it – find the sources in that. I use the sketchbook as a catalyst. I love the irrationality of drawing-just to draw a line and see what happens. It's not quite automatic drawing, but it's starting with something you know, such as the outline of a site. You draw it and very often it develops into something else and it's

that development which you can't do simply by sitting down and analysing something and redrawing it using the usual logical processes of design. I much prefer a process which uses sequential operations to allow the unpredictable element to emerge. It's a conversation between the mind and the paper.

Nigel Coates

The very permanence of architecture can only be understood with the actions that take place in it as part of its structure. Then, and only then, can architecture entertain an intimate contact with the moment of perception - of being in it, of finding that it means something.

Nigel Coates

The simulacrum implies great dimensions, depths, and distances which the observer cannot dominate. It is because he cannot master them that he has an impression of resemblance. The simulacrum includes within itself the differential point of view, and the spectator is made part of the simulacrum, which is transformed and deformed according to his point of view. In short, folded within the simulacrum there is a process of going mad, a process of limitlessness.

Gilles Deleuze

Caffé Bongo, Tokyo, 1986

Frans Smets-Verhas, De Vijf Werelddelen, Antwerpen, 1901

these two, it became clear at least that there was no point in waiting for the revolution to happen. Practice enticed. Utopia, a motif always implicit in Lefebvre's work, evaporated and made way for the Big Chill. But at the same time a feverish spate of activity was directed towards fathoming and manipulating the city's immanent and autonomous powers, which patently cared not one whit for any kind of progressive vision. The disillusionment of lost ideals and the relief that times were going to be less predictable than any little red book might have foreseen combined to form a blend of despondency and zest. The essence of this transformation was a shift of focus – from what life ought to be, to what it is. The NATO periodical revealed plans for this new urbanity. The initial basis was the contemporary life style of a certain type of Londoner, the rootless urbanite. What Lefebvre had already pondered in theory, namely the potentially subversive effect of manipulating a banal mythology, was now to be explored forcefully in the form of architectural design. In design, irrational, ritual behaviour on the part of the individual was not a disruptive element but an inspiring one. Nothing merits preferential treatment – pop music, modern dance and fashion were just as interesting as Art and Architecture. High Modernism was infiltrated by the Low Modernism of mass culture. 'Low Modernism wants to work towards an ethic, but an ethic without blueprints. Its universalism is one which fosters cosmopolitanism, but cosmopolitanism without emancipation.'★

It is the hybrid character of metropolitan life, pre-eminently visible in the nightclub, that fascinates Coates and Branson. Here, in the flush of conviviality, conventions are flouted and the cultural ★ Lash, Scott, and Friedman, Jonathan, *Modernity & Identity,* Oxford 1992, p. 3.

spectacle is at its most vivid. Theatre is too restricted as a metaphor, since the distinction between the performer and the public remains intact. But in any self-respecting nightclub, the spatial barrier between the stage and the auditorium vanishes. The

spectacle of the self is given total freedom, the sensuous faculties of the body are on display. Everyone becomes a performer. The clubs that Coates and Branson have designed so far are thus not just so many completed projects; they are, as Rem Koolhaas puts it, retroactive manifestos of an achieved Utopia. The boundaries between body, clothing, movement and architectonic hardware are blurred.

Architecture was looking the other way when this Valhalla became a cultural fact, but now that things have come so far, architecture can still supply heaven on earth with satisfactory cyberprop. Propaganda for the post-agit age, in other words. The Revolution? That was years ago.

Rétro-garde or Post-orgiastic Triste?

The meaning of the city resides not in its buildings but in the fact that it is the place where the modernisation process proceeds, full of conflicting or supporting ambitions. That is why Coates' and Branson's work is concerned neither with Style nor with the making of architecture as such, but with the city as a continually changing decor, so rich and varied that it passes everyone's understanding. That quality that makes the city what it is, is located in the memory and fantasy of its inhabitants and is hence personalised to the individual psyche. In the words of Coates himself, the city is 'a lexicon of all that goes on in it, both physical and abstract'. Just as the nightclub is a condensate of the city's hybrid nature, so is the city a magnified nightclub.

Coates' and Branson's executed work has so far mainly taken the form of interior design, largely in Britain and Japan. Clients for their kind of choreography and architectural props are few and far between. Having seen their urban visions, we long to see their ideas realised on a greater scale, but so far that seems not to have fallen to their lot. To the architects themselves, this restriction of their radius of action does not

109

The new city must use every conceivable technique to flip meanings and throw the control of events back to the people performing them.
Nigel Coates

It was a cruel city, but it was a lively one, savage city, yet it had such tenderness, a bitter, harsh and violent catacomb of stone and steel and tunnelled rock, slashed savagely with light, and roaring fighting a constant ceaseless warfare of men and of machinery; and yet it was so sweetly and so delicately pulsed, as full of warmth, of passion and love as it was full of hate.
Thomas Wolfe

It's a city that's in tune with the shifting desires that inhabit it - where the material, communicative and social worlds combine to make one infinitely balanced 'cyber' urbanism. It's a city where architecture and the physical landscape put forward cultural and functional challenges strong enough to stimulate collective highs - a city where the private world of love finds its double in an erotic world of shared spaces. It's a place where buildings seem to be alive, to have feeling!
Nigel Coates

The process involved standing in for the users of buildings and learning to use one's body as a source for an enriched handling of the elements of architecture and the real life situations they contain.
Nigel Coates

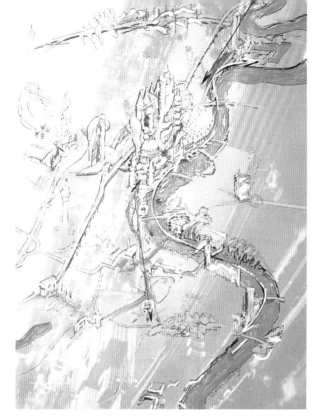

London 2066, journalistic manifesto for Vogue, British Edition, June 1991

The Shiba Driving Range, Tokyo

appear to be too great a problem. Interiors have just as much potential as complete buildings, in their design philosophy, because the important thing to them is the creation of a super-urbane atmosphere. Projects like bars, shops, restaurants and other semi-public spaces make it possible for them to confront the challenge of the metropolis. 'To some people, interior projects are second class to new buildings, but to me they're a real opportunity to bring the physical nature of the city as a whole together with the experience of people that live in it. Just about all the spaces we have done are derived from the "excellence" of the city experience, or what I call Ecstacity.'★

In their current portfolio of work, transience is already present in the nature of the commission. Firstly, this is because fashion has a big say and the laws of marketing dictate a regular facelift; secondly it is because the new interior 'overwrites' the old, in itself suggesting a
★ Hatton, Brian, 'Arcadia and Epicomedy', in *Ottagono* 94 (1989), p.132.

less than scrupulous attitude towards the design. There is no reason to suppose Coates' and Branson's work will be spared the next little shock of the consumable new. The architects have thus made a virtue out of necessity by linking the conditions under which their architecture is created with the ephemerality of the city on the one hand and the provisional status of their work on the other. That way everyone is satisfied. At first sight, the spaces are one enormous *bric-à-brac* of found objects, inventively deployed industrial materials and elements scattered as though at random. But although these items lack a logical ordering, they are extremely effective in mutual relation. The *bricolage* method runs counter to so-called good taste, but the totality is a perfect grotesque that represents the disorder of the metropolis just as tellingly as the

classical orders of the past did for feudal and, later, middle-class power.

In the new order of chaos, no single system of representation can be valid. Coates therefore reverts to a mythical kind of thinking that restores desire to its former prominence. What is concerned here is not the deferred satisfaction of needs that we know from the Modern project, but the hedonistic life style, uninhibited enjoyment of the here and now. This Surrealistic ploy (comparable to André Breton's 'reintroduction of desire in the very centre of our existence') is part of the strategy to demolish the barrier between *Lustprinzip* and *Realitätsprinzip*. There is not a message being promulgated with which we are expected to agree, but a narrative which we can allow to sweep us along. Decorative features from the repertoire of good taste have been replaced by an anti-decorum in which public performance is possible.★ The scientifically dissected life-view of the
★ Coates, Nigel, 'Ecstacity', Royal Australian Institute of Architects Conference, 1992.

Moderns, with its concomitant functionalism, is now replaced by the 'art of life' (Herbert Marcuse) for which the appropriate architecture is one of sensation. What we should now like to know is the following: is this a new avant-garde or a *rétro-garde* – or must we now beware of a post-orgiastic depression? We are waiting... for Godot. As always.

The Irony of the Arrivé

Coates' and Branson's Industrial Baroque offers a false architecture, an inverse world as seen in the mirrored toilets of a house party, with sudden glimpses into the depths of the soul. It is carnivalesque, a hilarious excrement-slinging match. Everyday banality is deployed in an ironic game (in the romantic sense of Friedrich von Schlegel: *'Ironie is*

To make clear the reality of our world behind the ideological and material curtain and to show how it could be changed, art should break the identification process of the audience with the theatre. Neither feeling nor empathy is needed, but rather distance and reflection. The effect of alienation should accomplish this break and lead people to recognise their true position. Daily life should be abstracted from the sphere of self-evidence.

Berthold Brecht

I believe banality could be salutary. Ushering into banality is one of the major strategies at our disposal. It seduces because feeling is directly and automatically hit. And this is exactly how subversion works, because everybody feels threatened by it.

Jeff Koons

It is reality itself today that is hyperrealist. Surrealism's secret already was that the most banal reality could become surreal, but only in certain privileged moments that are still nevertheless connected with art and the imaginary. Today it is quotidian reality in its entirety - political, social, historical and economic - that from now on incorporates the simulating dimension of hyperrealism. We live everywhere already in an 'aesthetic' hallucination of reality.

Jean Baudrillard

Ecstacity embraces my challenge of excellence.

Nigel Coates

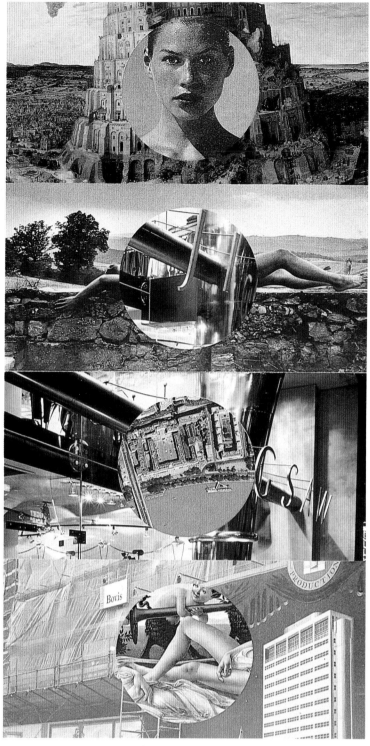

Pages from Ecstacity, London, 1992

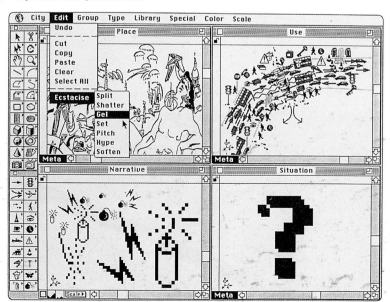

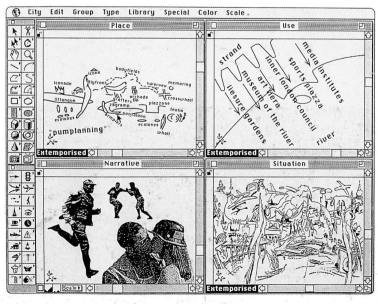

Café Bongo, Tokyo, 1986

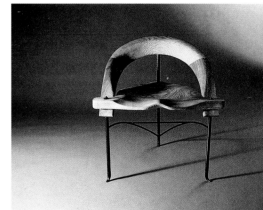
Chair for the l'Arca di Noè restaurant, Sapporo, 1988

klares Bewusstsein des unendlich vollen Chaos.' ['Irony is a clear awareness of the infinitely rich chaos.']) But besides the clearly recognisable affirmative irony, they also aim for an alienating effect that is meant to make the individual much more sharply aware of his public exposure and hence foster genuine communication. The problem with this is that in the avant-garde tradition alienation has lost much of its vitality as an artistic device. Perhaps the pre-war avant-gardes really did succeed in setting themselves up as opponents of reality, and from that standpoint were able to highlight the asymmetries between ideology and reality, and between intellectual and material productivity, while maintaining, in their isolation, their artistic integrity. But recent history teaches us the impossibility of this sort of critical distance. As Herbert Marcuse observed, the cultural centre becomes 'a natural part of the shopping centre, the city centre or the centre of government. The result is cultural uniformity, while the domination continues unabated.' The double stakes of irony and alienation have come to look highly dubious as a way of arriving at any standpoint that rises above the level of the *salon*. When this incongruity between the artistic and public realms remains unconscious, even the most intelligent architecture becomes no more than an ineffectual fascination. The world-despising bohemian in search of *bonheur* turns into a cocky arrivé. The beautiful literary notion that irony should guarantee our freedom seems here to find its Waterloo.

Non-design in the Non-context of Cyberpolis

The architecture of Coates and Branson is design in as far as that it supplies a certain pattern of cultural values, in name still anarchistic, with legitimising images. This architecture creates, moreover, an undeniable distance from other cultural domains and practices, and generates a clearly recognisable identity. But it is also non-design in that it evidently undermines that process and tries to stay ahead of an institutionalised version of itself.★ It aims to be the outcome and the living evidence of a culture, not a fossilised relic. And as long as they can continue pulling it off, against the background of anti-decorum, they can also keep up the ambition of non-design. It's not the form but the performance that matters. The role-determined action stands or falls by virtue of its context. The context – or rather, in the case of Coates and Branson, the immediate situation – is bounded by the triangle of use/narrative/urban location. Within that zone lies the cultural value of their architecture, their field of action. But this triangle is itself embedded in the hard-to-define field of Cyberpolis, the source of countless impulses. In the metropolis, the notion of space transforms into the notion of time. The city is a self-perpetuating instant, an enduring flash of light but a flash nonetheless. The context is therefore the moment of the present. *Architecture is Now!* At the moment of the present nothing can retain a permanent identity. Nothing still refers to itself but everything melts away in the crucible, the tapestry of culture, the intertext of all imaginable impulses. The city in which this all takes place is barely reminiscent of the economic entity of the machine age. Time and space have long fused under compression to become a slideway for the flexible accumulation of capital. Centre and periphery dissolve into the great sprawl.

★ See Agrest, Diana, 'Design versus Non-design', in *Architecture from Without,* Cambridge, Mass. 1991, pp. 30-65.

112

The context no longer bears a relation to architecture, morphology or even texture. Everything depends on the performance. The action, conceived by the Moderns as a consequence of architecture, has now become a precondition of architecture. Without (night)life, this architecture does not even exist.

Nigel Coates and Doug Branson have no wish to acquiesce to the circumscriptions of a feeble architecture, and they pronounce dauntlessly on the state – sorry, flux – of this world. It is to their credit that they also make inescapable, powerful visual statements about our late-capitalist society. Because their manifestos are retroactive, we are given to understand how *panta rei*, how unexceptionally exceptional this world is, how hyperbanal and super de luxe. Just observe, as you meander tipsily home after a long night at one of Coates' and Branson's establishments, how the panorama of slight disarray that unfolds before you is not all that different from what the architecture had to offer in the hours just gone by: a hotch-potch of consumer vernacular and good taste, a surfeit of *arte povera*, a blend of decadence and asceticism. And the whole affair is half obscured in spaces resembling subterranean labyrinths, not unlike the confusing maze of shadows through which you now head home to your bed. The main drawback, however, is that the world around your bed has become so flexible that critisism will have to make flexibility its second nature if it is to stand a chance of reacting appropriately. And once that second nature has been established, the object of criticism, which was originally so clearly in view, starts disappearing behind the continually approaching horizon. Having noted the existence of Utopia realised in the hyperworld, criticism loses its ethical and aesthetic grounds. In short, the horizon of experience extends beyond the horizon of expectation leaving no scope for criticism at all.

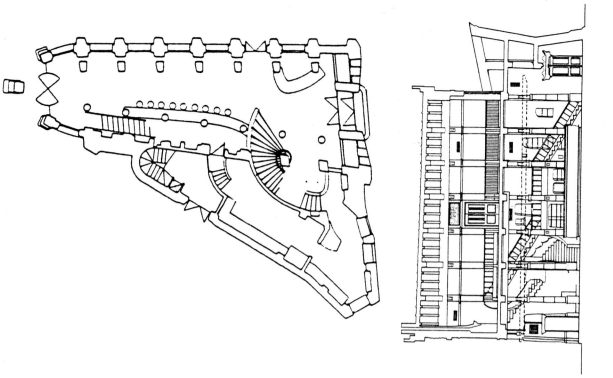

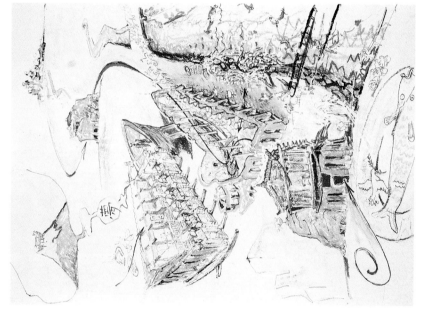

The Ark's hull is fashioned from a poured concrete base, treated to look like weathered sandstone. The interior is spatially complex: an elliptical spiral staircase, lit from above by a skylight, collides with a second, linear staircase. The mood is positively baroque, with the feeling of a Piranesi engraving. Interior and exterior are heavily loaded with cosmic iconography and symbolism. The imagery combines illusion and illusion, eroticism, archaeology and mysticism. The aim was to design a building that would transport the imagination as well as the body. It pretends to be a 'pavilion in a park', even though it is surrounded by ten-storey hotels. The Ark fuses an Etruscan temple with a boat-Berg in sprayed concrete around an inner spiral stair. The building's simple representational conceit is that of Noah's Ark run aground on a mountain. However arbitrary it might seem, the narrative idea was primarily a response to the limitations of a narrow triangular site. The client's original suggestion of a temple could never have worked. On one side, the prow emerges from a formless mass of rock housing kitchens and services; on the other, windows lean out over the picturesque river like the stern of a pirate galleon. The upper storey and roof are Etruscan in style inside, plaster finishes with the texture of sandstone are remarkably effective in suggesting a petrified wooden structure. Despite the heavy post and lintel construction,

the effect in the daytime is light and open. Entrances at the prow and stern increase the flow of customers, and solicit a desire to explore the building, turning the visitor from a passive onlooker into an active participant required to make choices. The theatricality of the ground-floor bar is emphasised by the use of non-structural columns to form a sequence of sectional slices resembling the wings of a stage. By directing attention to the windows while breaking up the plane of the wall, the columns help to engage the building with the river outside (upstairs the leaning windows and dipping external canopies perform a similar function).

A stairway like a ship's gangway, or a ramp of the original Ark, runs in a straight line from the prow door to the top-floor restaurant, where it collides unexpectedly with a second, more conventionally palatial spiral staircase serving the other entrance; they converge in a Piranesian double-height space. This, the building's single most impressive spatial moment, is the point at which its alternative channels of movement are consummated and resolved. Museum-like, the building is full of Etruscan-inspired objects and art works, from Coates's Noah chairs to wall paintings by Stewart Helm and Adam Lower. *Based on:* Brian Hatton in *Prospero's Software, Ecstacity Nigel Coates, The City in Motion,* London, 1992, *and:* Rick Poynor, *Nigel Coates, The City in Motion,* New York 1989.

pour l'Architecture, Brussels and Architectural Association, London, 1992, *and:* Rick Poynor, *Nigel Coates, The City in Motion,* New York 1989.

▶

Location Minami 8 Jo, Nishi 4 Chome, Chuo-ku, Sapporo, Japan **Assistants** D. Naessens, C. Egret, M. Tonkins **Client** Jasmac Co., Ltd. **Design** 1987 **Completion** 1988

Branson Coates Architecture *l'Arca di Noè Restaurant, Bar and Patisserie*

Henri Cartier-Bresson, A Fire at Hoboken, New Jersey

Architecture for King Client

A Conversation with Denise Scott Brown

Strangely enough, she did not share in the 1991 Pritzker Prize; it was awarded just to Robert Venturi. But anyone who is really familiar with the architectural work of their design office in Philadelphia knows that the name of Denise Scott Brown is not on the letterhead for nothing. The profession, and in particular the prize-giving bodies, aimed as they are at unique artistic achievements of 'brilliant' individuals, generally have little interest in the social dimensions of design, and so Scott Brown's speciality, the converting of historical and sociological research into concrete design strategies and developing the methodology of that research in the direction of practice, is destined to remain in the background. The same goes even more so for her work in urban planning and development. Scott Brown has published numerous studies about morphology and American city planning. She is interested in the mutual relationships between the various material and social ingredients of the design process. The professional world, concentrated as it is on matchless projects, finds it difficult to perceive these connections, however much Scott Brown, in her own words a 'philosopher of action', wants to apply her sociological knowledge practically in concrete cases.

Scott Brown's speciality is crucial to the way the studio approaches the design process, where what comes first is to pay attention to the effect that forms have for various segments of the public. It is also vital for the worldwide intellectual significance attributed to the bureau since their triumphal progress began with the publication of *Complexity and Contradiction in Architecture* (1966) and *Learning from Las Vegas* (1972). Denise Scott Brown sees her work as strictly belonging to the domain of the visible, but her involvement with the social research that has for many years been part of this, prompted us, as editors of *The Invisible in Architecture*, to set out for her office in Philadelphia, situated (how could it be otherwise?) on *Main Street*. Not surprisingly, the conversation was completely 'almost all right'.

On a number of fronts Denise Scott Brown's work reveals a strongly affirmative attitude and the acceptance of today's *faits accomplis*. The titles of several of her essays contain the phrase 'learning from'. She is always concerned with empirical research, fuelled by Popperian 'conjectures and refutations', into provisional hypotheses. In this respect she belongs to a rich Anglo-Saxon scientific tradition. Her empiricism is well expressed, for example, in her numerous studies and designs regarding the reorganisation of the urban landscape. Averse to planning abstractions, she works at the level of urban design, directly connected with concrete experience at street level. That explains too her ever-increasing interest in the symbolic dimension of designing that stands out so emphatically precisely at that level. Her field of activity is formed by the façades, the street furniture, the pavement, in short the empire of signs of daily life. This leads straightaway to her great social involvement, for without an active concern for the actual people who will make use of the executed design, and will be able to identify with the symbolic order, such research has no meaning.

Ultimately, however, her work betrays something even more fundamental, something that, for Europeans in general and poets and thinkers in particular, gives her work such an elusive character. ('No one loves the truth and the good, unless he abhors the multitude.') It is the typically American way of working she prides herself upon: 'One should not merely understand the way a society operates but should try to work with its forces, to the extent that one can without too far compromising goals. I think it's called 'American pragmatism'. It is also an effort to develop a green thumb for cities. (...) We try to talk about important things in an easy, straightforward way; speaking American, not translated French, German or Italian. We have an old fashioned belief in being understandable to others and even to ourselves, so, don't hold us suspect if you find you understand us.'

To want to be understandable, or to think that you automatically are so, and leaving it at that; it does make rather a difference. About the same difference as between rhetoric and an ordinary conversation. To want to practise rhetoric is in fact something that we are not always *willing* to understand. But who's going to fight against this now, since every culture has the right to avow its own identity? Now that the 'Other' in culture is attracting such a great deal of attention, we ought to summon respect for the 'American Dream' too of course, even if this has transpired only very partially and/or for the few. But there exists an intrinsic and problematic relationship between the globalisation of American culture and the threat to regional and cultural identity. Should we see the American way of life as a way like any other, or has its universal success perhaps placed it on a level where it should be evaluated with something other than anthropologically-based relativism? In any event, the vision of 'all you need is a dollar and a dream' (used as well to promote the New York lottery) seems insufficient for a critical attitude with an eye to the future. Perhaps 'the action of philosophy' can offer solace?

Denise Scott Brown

117

You have always been very aware of the necessity for someone who wants to become an architect to stop
talking and start building. How do you estimate the current stature of theory?

There have always been oscillations in architecture between theory and practice. Although we can deal
with architecture as architecture by the rules internal to its making, we have also to relate architecture to
life. But what aspects of life and how? There is a tendency in the United States now to see theory of architecture as a discipline in itself, unrelated to practice. This is evident mainly in the schools, where there has
been a proliferation of theory of architecture courses and where the ratio of academic faculty to practitioner
faculty has increased. You could cynically say that's because there is no work for architects; when we
didn't have work, we wrote theoretically, but we theorised about design and practice. If we are philosophers, we are philosophers of action. The new theoreticians in the schools seem to feel they don't need a
strong link to the making of architecture; they are involved at the moment, I believe, with the theory of psychoanalysis. Architects tend to read a book and then to organise their thoughts and work around that book.
Kenneth Frampton read *The Human Condition* by Hannah Arendt, other people read the semiologists, and
now they are reading Lacan and Derrida. (Or is that already over?) We did not read the semiologists; at

least not at first. We looked at Las Vegas and said 'It's very exciting to us, why?' Then we began to theorise. When going from the concrete to the conceptual we found semiology to be relevant, but we didn't read Jakobson until we had learned from Las Vegas. We don't know if we hate it or love it but we feel a certain shiver when we see it. What is the reason for this shiver? That question comes afterwards. I think practical philosophers and architectural activists should work in this way.

Do you mean an empiricist, inductive way of looking at things and trying to make use of them in practice?

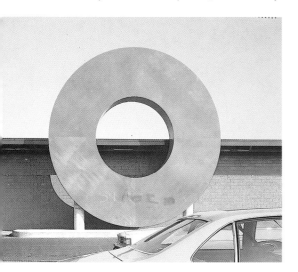

Basco, Inc. Showroom, a letter, 34 ft. high, Philadelphia, 1976

Yes, I think it is a better way for a creative person, although there is an important place for theory in the steps between induction and design. Yet there should not be all that strong a link between theory and practice. If you build a building to demonstrate a theory you achieve a dry building. In particular, if you try to impose too much theory on a small building the building becomes a cluster of bumps and carbuncles; it isn't in the end a work of art, it is a demonstration, a lesson. While designing, you may well fill up your mind with theory; but after that, get a good night's sleep, try to forget everything you were thinking, and start again with the problem at hand. When we do theoretical research and analysis, it's at the applied end. In order to design, you have to know enough about the specialist fields to ask questions. I've learned, in dealing with for example social theoreticians or urban sociologists, that they don't know enough about architecture to tell me directly what I need to know. I have to frame the questions to suit their field. I at least have a verbal skill I share with them; they don't have manual, graphic or visual skills, which means they cannot bridge to my field. I must be the bridge. I think people like me are needed to make bridges between disciplines and help theory pertain to architecture. I don't want to be a sociologist, but I want to use social imagination to help architectural imagination.

However, there is a difficulty: there aren't enough sociologists and sociologists today aren't interested in architecture. For this reason, I may sometimes have to be the sociologist on my project, suggesting, for example, the sequences and mixes of population groups that may live in certain sections of a city over the years. I assume the role of sociologist not because I want to be one, nor because I'm the best, but because I'll be better than none at all. But if anyone is to make social information useful for design, the architect must do it because the sociologist usually can't.

118

There are also areas of value judgement where social scientists can spell out implications, but others must make decisions. For example, certain people in the United States, particularly poor people, may want to bring the whole family, mother, grandmother and five kids, to a hospital when they visit, because there's no one at home to look after them. The sociologist can tell the hospital that. The value judgement about whether the hospital wants to deal with the four kids that are not sick is a matter of their policy. It's not mine as an architect, it's not the sociologist's, it's the hospital's. I can't plan spaces for the extended family because I think that's right, unless the hospital tells me to. **I'm trying to separate out the roles. I mustn't do what the hospital should do and I shouldn't do what the sociologist should do. I should do what is consistent with my role as an architect or urban planner.** I must be very straight with my client and say what the issue is. I could plan for the extra spaces and for the relation between spaces that fits the policy and tell my client that it would cost you *x* more, and you could use the extra space in this way. If *x* is $ 50 million, they probably won't do it; if it is $ 2.000 they may. The question is, should you plan according to your own values without informing your client. This is a question of morality and of understanding your role.

There could be a lot of money invested in air-conditioning, technical equipment, etcetera, while there is almost no money left for putting the hospital in its site, in the urban tissue. When do you say 'I will only make the building if there's more money for the façade', or 'I won't make much of the façade but will invest the money as much as possible in the programme itself'? What are your priorities?

We must be guided by our clients. We find our hospital clients are much concerned that their new buildings look auspicious. They are in a market situation, they have to attract people. Your clients' expectations are what you should be working with. As a human being I could say 'this hospital should take poor sick children and I don't think you should put marble on the front'. And I can argue quite lucidly about why you shouldn't. But we accept our clients' value system, and if we find their requests totally unacceptable we shouldn't accept the project.

What would you do if public needs were really in conflict with the client's values?

This is a complex question. On the one hand, the needs of the public are protected by laws and regulations that architects and clients must obey. Beyond that, the question arises of who defines public needs. The architect? The client? The politician? In reality there must be a debate between client and 'public', however defined, and some sort of negotiation must be attempted. In this the architect could (but rarely does) serve as a broker.

How?

Well, for example, when planning the Denver Civic Center Cultural Complex I worked specifically for the three public cultural institutions that hired me, not for the city – although I made recommendations for portions of the city, covering land use, transportation, parking, services, circulation, urban design and landscaping in neighbourhoods surrounding the Complex. I tried to make recommendations useful to the city as well as the institutions, so they would be accepted by both.

When people asked 'Well what did you learn from Las Vegas?' you once answered 'We learned to reassess the role of symbolism in architecture and this helped guide our search for an appropriate architecture for a Post-Modern period'. Coming from Europe, let us say interested in abstract principles and not starting from empiricism, one might ask what you think this Post-Modern period is about for which you are going to find an appropriate architecture.

You must know that we have disclaimed connection with the movement called Post-Modernism. Freud said he wasn't a Freudian and Marx said he was not a Marxist; and we are not Post-Modernists. We feel that we had a great deal to do with initiating a rethinking of Modern architecture, but what resulted wasn't what we intended. For me, a Post-Modern period has meaning separate from that rather bombastic style called Post-Modernism: it's a time when the tenets of early Modernism are no longer applicable. As a very young architect I went to Holland and photographed Duiker's Zonnestraal and the Van Nelle factory. I loved early Modern architecture and still love it; but, although it was wonderful, it is not for our time. Post-Modernism involves a loss of innocence. The people who adored machinery came mostly from peasant cultures. That love affair with machinery should not have survived the Holocaust, nor the war in Vietnam. Our loss of innocence about technology informs our critique of Modernism.

The social goals of the early Modern Movement were important and poignant. The Modernists seem to have assumed that governments would build all housing. That didn't happen anywhere and certainly not in the United States. And the housing that was built, people didn't like. People didn't like what architects thought they should like. Loss of innocence again. The architects, with their high aspirations and their certainty that people ought to live the way architects thought they should live, were accused by social planners in the sixties of causing urban social problems. Again, loss of innocence.

We were taught in the planning schools to be sceptical about our own certainties and to be cautious; to consider whether there could be anything bad about our recommendations for improvement, if our suggestions could have any unexpected consequences. All of this again brought loss of innocence, a Post-Modern condition. I think there is a theology of Post-Modernism that has the Holocaust in mind and talks of loss of innocence. This is more in line with our thinking. Today we architects have ideals that are tempered by irony. Irony is a gentle emotion, it isn't satire, it isn't harsh, in a way it is laughing at yourself. But the laughter is very serious.

Do you hope that the people who use or see the building will relate critically and consciously to what is happening in the building?

Modern architects felt that the people would come around to their way of thinking, that when revolution came the people would put aside their icons and recognise that factories are beautiful. We felt that the industrial symbolism in Modern architecture was not something we could put our hearts into and that the aesthetic rule-systems of Modernism had become socially harmful and aesthetically deadening. This brought us back to representation and symbolism. Looking at other people's views of allusion, symbolism and appearance would, we felt, make us more sensitive architects. We found Las Vegas aesthetically exciting partly because it did not follow the canons of Modernism but consistently broke the rules, introducing shocking allusions to historical architecture, solving architectural problems, often very directly, in ways that the academy said you should not do. When Bob Venturi and I first met we shared an enjoyment of such shocking solutions. I brought them from England and he had learned them in the United States and Italy. We went round finding things in real life that architects on juries told students you couldn't do. Those made us laugh, because they were supposed to be wrong. But we saw, too, the vitality of architecture you 'couldn't do' and its irony. How do you define irony? In the not matching, not meshing, of the elements of a building or group of buildings there is something funny. But not meshing in the social sphere can also induce irony; when conflicting values are juxtaposed to produce an untidy architecture that makes you laugh, there is irony in that too. I don't think you have to be a sophisticate to be ironic. Peasant and folk cultures use irony.

That's the old tradition of the irony of the buffoon. But now irony has to do more with sophisticated thought about aesthetics than with the intrinsic value of objects or the world itself. This is the romantic impetus defined by theoreticians like the Schlegel brothers, who said that after the end of the classical world-view and the start of the Romantic era there can be no art without irony. It seems architecture had to wait another 150 years to get that accepted. A few artists had already begun in the nineteenth century, and, if we look at Dada or the collage, art then had a much greater sense of the ironic than architecture. But do you think that ordinary people who see those ironic buildings are actually perceiving the ironic aspect?

Some do and some don't, that becomes a question of levels of communication. I see no reason why architects shouldn't have their own language and talk to each other separately from the public about a building, so long as this doesn't harm the public. But if architects do only this, which the Modernists tended to do, then they have not met the public need. I think a great institutional building should communicate on many levels, it should have something for everyone. I wrote an article, 'Architectural Taste in a Pluralistic Society', on this topic. It was in part a critique of *Popular Culture and High Culture* by the sociologist Herbert Gans. He felt that, given the variety of tastes in the United States, each 'taste culture' should have its own art and architecture provided by members of that culture. I think this is unlikely to happen. Artists

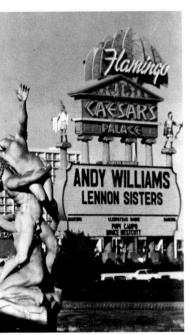

Caesar's Palace, Las Vegas, 1968

Still from 'All in the Family'

who rise within the class system are likely to flee the value system of their original class and choose another one. Certain television-comedies are loved by large numbers of people in the United States. *All in the Family* was one like that. If you were a sophisticate or if you were a simple person, there was something for you in it without its being condescending. Some great art has broad appeal, some does not. When we, as architectural artists, design institutional and civic buildings we ought to try for the former. Talking as I do with you now across a table, watching your reactions, I can build closely to your value system – though as a responsible professional I must warn you that, if your house is idiosyncratic, it may not sell; there are reality checks. But if I'm an urban designer I can't afford to build only what the mayor wants, I must consider what the people of the city want or are going to want. To do so I must take to the people's representatives questions that concern their constituencies and questions about the future.

The Sainsbury Wing of the National Gallery in London is a very interesting project for elaborating things we are talking about. As a commission it's very complicated because everything is in it, from the technical basics to social thought and highbrow aesthetics. So the question is 'How can you be ironic according to the programme of such a building?'

I think we were concerned with the place of the individual in the whole, and the place of the secular in the sacred – the equivalent of where the laundry hangs out in the *palazzo*. We wanted to make vivid architecture from these juxtapositions.

Caesar's Palace, Las Vegas, 1991

Pennsylvania Avenue Project, Western Plaza, Washington, 1980

And to show a kind of conflict without making a building which you can't use?

Seattle Art Museum, 1992, with sculpture of Jonathan Borofsky

In a large complex building not all spaces will be equally convenient to use, but those that people use most frequently or intensely should not be sacrificed for expressive aims. Another important juxtaposition is between light and dark. Our Seattle Art Museum has sheer blank walls because daylight is not wanted in the exhibition spaces. Also it has only two public entries, for security. Yet, contradictorily, we wanted the building to be open and inviting. There is a lot of glass at the ground level; here one sees the conflict between the desire for openness and the requirements of security. Upstairs, in a few spaces that are not galleries, you can look out at the city. In all our museums we draw the street into the building. The materials of the museum entrance and ground-floor lobby are hard and mostly stone, like the street. Wide stone stairs lead to the art, located, as in many museums today, on floors above the entry. Although the museum is only five storeys high, its scale must be larger than that of the high-rise buildings that will eventually surround it. We have employed scale relationships within the façades to suggest a civic scale. At the top of the building is a sign, big enough to represent the national importance of the museum. Where the striated limestone of the façade touches the glass face of the ground floor, we introduce a sinuous band of coloured stone and terracotta tiles. These modulate scale, from the very big sign to smaller and yet smaller elements, eventually to those at the scale of a person. Within the big scale stone walls have small windows that break the monumentality. Small accents of black and white syncopate the rhythms of the band of stones. At the base of the building, at the doorways, are small columns scaled to one person. Then a very big person, a Jonathan Borofsky silhouette figure in cut steel, stands near the doorway where the human-size person goes in. Having carefully set up the hierarchies of scale, we contradict them with a figure that's much too big. This is to keep the monumentality human. We try to mediate monumentality with irony or a little self-deprecation – the building laughs at itself or the architects, *not* at the client. The monumental is there, but the individual is placed within it to give it a human face. The big has the small set against it, the individual is set within the community.

Mostly in a museum you can't find out how the elements are organised. You don't know how the building itself works, especially in very traditional exhibition spaces. A simple trick is to let the people have a peep in the storerooms when they walk up to the exhibition so they see the difference between the rough material and the exhibition.

I think something else is happening in museums now. In the museums we designed we had to provide a great deal of non-museum space. Today's museum is part restaurant, part shop and part education department; it is full of lecture halls, conference rooms and computer spaces, where visitors can find information away from the paintings. Museums want to offer people different ways of knowing art. All this sits on the lower floors, yet people must be able to visit the art without their eyes being so assaulted by modern media that they can't look at Renaissance paintings or Native American masks. Our large stairways are in part a decompression chamber for the eyes, in part a build-up of expectation for the art.

We've tried to ease the complexity of today's experience of art by evolving floor plans that are so simple that people can retain them as ideograms in their minds and understand where they are. In the National Gallery and Seattle Art Museum the big stair rising up one side of the building, giving access to different levels, performs this function. If you can hold the idea of that stair in your mind, you can find your way in the building. We learned that from Walt Disney. Disneyland has a wagon-wheel organisation. Once you know that the Magic Mountain is in the middle and everything else forms the spokes and spaces of a wagon-wheel around it, you can find your way. In the National Gallery the rooms have been designed for the paintings there now – much more so than in the Seattle Art Museum, where the collection will change and grow. The National Gallery rooms need to be airy and light, which is difficult given the restrictive light standards for the conservation of paintings. A great deal of engineering was needed to make the lighting work. That's where technology is very important with us. But the rooms as perceived are like the rooms of a Renaissance palace, not exactly but vaguely. There is a chronological sequence to the display, but there are opportunities for choosing other sequences via numerous doorways. You can go east to west as well as north to south through the collection and from many galleries there are vistas to different eras (and from some to the city beyond). So we try not to be coercive, not to force an interpretation people don't want.

Is it true that when you go deeper into the building you are less involved with ironics and more with concentration? Do you mean that when you are concentrating on the paintings you don't need irony any more, you want to see the paintings as clearly as possible?

We give pride of place to the paintings; we make a space that is eloquent, I think, but not ironic. As you approach the Sainsbury Wing from the main gallery, there is a vista a block long, the length of the whole gallery. When you stand far back in the existing building and look down the vista, you don't know that there's a new building. You see the painting at the end of the vista as if it's in the existing building. Then as you enter the link between old and new you see a perspective of columns, just the architecture and one painting with, inside it, two windows. There's no irony here, but a bit of magic (it's actually a false perspective). In this spot the building is perhaps romantic, but in a very low-key way. This reflects our judgement of the needs of this particular building. In another, it would be different.

So style depends very much on the interpretation of the site and the programme?

Yes, 'style' or 'signature' are scorned words in architecture, but perhaps we cannot avoid them. Even fashion – defined as a way of doing things at a time – it is questionable whether designers can really avoid fashion, much as they may think they can.

Maybe there is something more than only fashion, there is also authorship. That is the reason why you can recognise over a span of several years a certain consistency in the work of this firm.

Some of our buildings look very different from each other; particularly among the houses, some are more romantic and others more formal. Yet there are many similarities too and I think they're all recognisable as ours, even though they adopt a vocabulary from their surroundings and are suited to their context. In the Sainsbury Wing our context was Classical and also honky-tonk, given that our most immediate neighbours were the existing National Gallery building, designed in 1837 by William Wilkins, and the tourist buses parked at the site immediately opposite our entrance. We picked up the Classical rhythms of the National Gallery, then syncopated them. Against this we juxtaposed the large openings of a world-scale attraction, which four million people will visit a year. There is irony in this, but there is also aesthetic enjoyment. We say the building is Palladio from east to west and Aalto from west to east. Where they meet, there is a dramatic clash of scales. Those 'Aalto' openings are very big. They're scaled to Trafalgar Square, and also to the munificence of the gift. The portico of the existing main building is very formal and lifted above the ground. Ours is at ground level and will take baby carriages, people in wheelchairs, and many others. During the 1991 demonstrations against the war in Iraq, people were all over Trafalgar Square with banners saying 'Peace now'. Our doorway rose magnificently over them, seeming to protect them and give them a setting. Our main façade does everything urban that we wanted, although it is also agonised in some way.

123

In a lot of your public buildings the entrance is behind the façade. It's put inside, more or less.

Yes. In this case large openings were created on the front and a skin behind. Functionally that gave us control, at the actual doorway, and shelter between the two skins for people waiting to come in. Urbanistically it gave us a means of defining the new wing and its entry at the scale of the square, and a means of enclosing the interior and providing a smaller opening at the scale of the individual. Philosophically the National Gallery is an ancient institution in a Classical building, yet right beside it is the highway that has gone through all our lives. There is a clash. The original building was intended for an élite, this building is designed for great numbers of people. The art is fantastically precious and yet on a Sunday afternoon people will walk through the galleries fifteen abreast, and each should feel welcome and able to establish a personal relationship with individual paintings. These are the conflicts the building represents.

Why is it then that so many critics of your work still stick to the idea that the consistency in the œuvre of this firm displays a certain lower-middle-class taste culture, whereas the method you describe implies that in every specific project or commission you are trying to embody all those different kinds of taste cultures?

Of course we admit that we are élitists, we don't argue with that; and as élitists we sometimes use popular culture themes symbolically. Also we try to be moral and responsible architects and, because we are urbanists as well, we know that we must satisfy a great many different tastes. It is all right for us to enjoy, for example, the tailing-off of columns and the windows that are partially there because they don't hurt anyone (except a few critics). But it would be very bad if we were to deny the educational aims of the museum, by saying, for example, that it's vulgar to use computers to describe art and that only art should describe art – the things high artists sometimes say.

The criticism just mentioned refers to the Pop element, which you so expressively staked two decades ago and which is still playing its role today as a ghost in whatever way one perceives your work. But it's also your use of the term 'what people want' that sets critics off. Reading your texts, the word 'people' comes up very often; the question is then 'What kind of people?'

National Art Gallery, Sainsbury Wing (extension), London, 1991

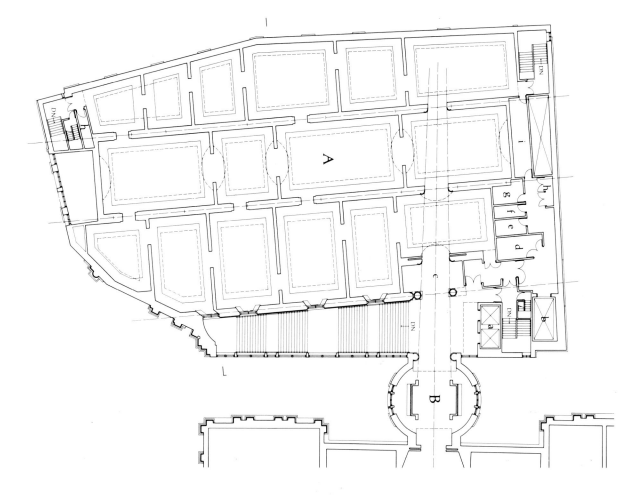

National Art Gallery, Sainsbury Wing (extension), London, 1991

I don't like it when architects say they are going to plan for 'the masses'. That's too global. We architects should understand the needs of small groups. We must consider taste cultures, lifestyles, market segmentation, we have to find ways of learning what groups want. When we design public housing, for example, we must simulate a community if we don't
have one and try to meet with its members face to face and in other ways. However, you can't design a courthouse for one market segment. Ideally, you should find ways to appeal to everyone.

Aren't you afraid that in the information society, in which people see a lot of signs all the time without perceiving a substantial meaning, without a link to reality, the building will only be seen as entertainment?

If we learn from Las Vegas and its signs, which are brash and interesting but send only superficial messages, does it mean our signs need to have superficial messages?

So you want to cut across the marketing segmentation of different lifestyles or taste cultures, to do something more? Are we right if we say that as a professional you respect what the client wants, and what the people who are going to use the building want, but you would also like to say something more about society? Are you an intellectual who can build?

Yes and no, that is we don't set out to say something about society. We set out to do our job. And we set out to follow the clients' values. For example, if they feel they have a world responsibility, we want to show that. I think there is some kind of social comment that comes out of our architecture, but we don't say 'Now I'm going to do social comment.' We may have arguments with the client as we go along, about details. There is always some element of negotiation with the client. You can also try to get the client to do something more than they had intended; you may succeed or you may not. And you may see comment in retrospect. Looking back on what you have done, you may see symbols, and metaphors, as I see the highway going through our work. And some agony. Picasso said of his *Maids of Avignon* that others would make it beautiful. For me that means other people, following later, using his inspiration will find ways to do beautiful paintings. I think our buildings have some of that quality. This makes it hard for us to find work because most clients would rather not have the anguish.

I imagine that apart from your professional skills, developing year after year, you also have a certain view of society as a citizen. Between us there can be a civic debate, and I guess that the talks you have with your client are not only talks between two professionals, for example the political professional and architectural professional, but also a talk between two citizens talking about a certain hidden agenda of what society should be and what architecture can contribute to it. Could you describe some moments in your past experience where it was possible to do something like that?

The intention of the National Gallery client group was to support and display a precious world resource and to find a way for the British nation to present that work to the world. That's the kind of motivation. Also they wanted to meet the needs of all the people and help them form a personal relationship with the art.
Now certainly it means trying to make a better society, but it is more specifically about the art. I think the vision of the Sainsburys, who gave the money for the gallery extension, is that their country needs help in the arts. There isn't the money any more for the government to do it. They have a duty now to help support and enrich this heritage.

There has been a basic need throughout all the different stages of human development: all people need idols. What seems to be lacking in your approach is a capacity to discriminate, to distinguish between what ought to be done and what should not be done. What ought to be idolised and what not. And if you take taste cultures or lifestyles as a point of departure, how would you position yourself, politically or ideologically: as an architect or as an intellectual who knows how to build?

When you say 'ought', the opposite is 'is', and the tension between ought and is ought to be part of a committed professional's lifestyle and work. If the oughts come too quickly, they may not be suitable and creative ones. Looking only at what is will not produce great art. But architects have at times been too quick to proclaim oughts, just as economists have at times been too quick to consider only what is. As a teacher, I told my students from economics 'You ought to express more norms and values', and my students from architecture 'Listen to what people are really telling you they want'. It seems that somewhere there is a good balance between is and ought. I was taught by urban social thinkers that **if you see something that is actually in existence, the presumption is it's probably needed or it wouldn't be there;** so at least be sceptical before you say 'This is bad, let's clear it away'. Yet at the same time judgement must be made and judgement ought to be explicated; you should say why you're making certain judgements. And if you are working for a client, the judgements ought to be made bearing in mind the values of the client. But of course I'm very involved with aesthetics and with trying to make something beautiful, though the beauty might be an agonised one if it is drawn out of the tension between is and ought.

The norm you just described has more to do with how to design, how the process should be organised, how long you will listen to clients, which people should be participating in the talks before you are going to design. But this doesn't say much about your world-view, your wish of how society should be. Your norm is more focused on the process than on the content isn't it?

How I feel society should be is not all that easy to translate specifically into a building, and besides I don't believe I can (or necessarily should) dictate social relationships through building design. We have resigned from some commissions because we thought things were happening that should not happen. We were hired to design an apartment building in a north-eastern United States city. Most of the housing was for upper-middle-income residents and twenty per cent of it was for moderate-income residents. We evolved

Along the road to the airport of Madras

plans we believed were right for that site, but the authorities turned them down and presented us with a silhouette and footprint of the building into which we were to fit the dwelling units. They were answering to political pressure from developers to have high buildings and from the community to have no buildings. We did what we were told. It meant a squat, bulky building where most apartments had poor light and, though the view was wonderful, most of them couldn't see it. Then we resigned. We did what the client needed us to do, to satisfy the authorities, then we resigned.

Is there any commission you wouldn't do at all?

I would not be very happy working on a prison. But if I had to keep my firm together and food on the table of the people working here, I might do it. There are many regimes I would not build for and some projects I would turn down for moral or aesthetic reasons. But for us, as well as for most architects, the dilemma is yearning to build, yet knowing that few prospects are good ones and that even fewer will become real projects. We must learn not to fall in love with a prospective commission without first considering whether we have any likelihood of obtaining it, and to say 'No' to invitations to enter competitions or be interviewed for projects where the chances of our being hired are low or non-existent.

The Need for Space as a Global Problem:
a Manifesto

Ernest Mandel

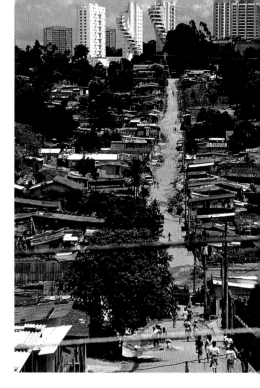

Sao Paulo

Of all elementary necessities, the protection of the smallest relevant social group against the elements of nature, and its isolation with respect to other human groups, is the one which leads to durable products: houses, homes. The most elementary need that this home has to answer to is that of *security against dangers*. Dangers are to a large extent, but not completely, socially and historically determined. Wolves or tigers no longer prowl around the big cities of today. Human dangers no longer refer to periodic attacks by enemy tribes. Technological dangers, on the other hand, are relatively recent. Fire hazard always existed, but not the danger of broken water, gas or electricity supplies, or of damage to drains. In order to provide for their sustenance, people continue to produce in a certain social relation that implies certain forms of communication with other people. The location and type of home depends on where and how production takes place.

128

Hong Kong

There is also an interaction between living space, organisation and extent of production on the one side, and production in relation to the scale of the inhabited area, on the other. Villagers do not need horses, carts, trams, buses or metros to move about within the village. City dwellers do have that need. These means of transport have to be produced, a process that radically alters the city: think of the construction of railways.

Housing is always living space. It satisfies more than just the need for security. Within the home people eat, drink and sleep, children are born and raised, people become sick and die. Size, partition and articulation of the domicile will facilitate or hinder all these forms of fulfilling needs.

Consumption and production were originally spatially integrated. Chickens and goats, if not the ox, the donkey and the pig, slept together with people in the same hut. The bed stood in the living room. The smithy was an annex of the home. Then came the separation. The stall, the studio, the factory meant a genuine architectural revolution. Nowadays a reversal is becoming apparent. Mainly because of the personal computer, a number of small producers are able to work at home, although, with the present state of technology, production still remains predominantly large-scale.

Living space is nonetheless never exclusively habitation. It always expands partly beyond the home.

The size and form of village and city influence living space and its content. Talking and shopping take place outside the home; meals are enjoyed, religious services are held. Originally all this happened within the cave dwelling. Children acquire more play and learning space outside the home. These collective forms of consumption were later institutionalised in particular buildings. Temples, schools, hospitals, shops, bars, libraries, museums and concert halls were built. Class divisions and the rise of the state led to the emergence of fossilised forms of wealth and power: palaces, barracks, prisons, gallows. All this grew together to become a city. Since then, cities were always polarised and therefore disintegrated or at least contain an element of disintegrating social coherence. Cities only surrender to total freedom of building after capitalistic society has become full-grown, resulting in total anarchy and deregulation.

Man's most valuable and scarce resource is time for living. Time for living always stands in relation to living space. Too restricted a living space leads to a loss of time. Gadgets have an emancipatory effect to the extent that they are really time-saving. In order for these gadgets to be used, the living space has to expand. If you're only allowed six square metres per person there is no room for your own stove, refrigerator, washing machine.

Why your own? The quantitative growth and diversification of needs is accompanied by a growing need for privacy, which can only be satisfied by larger homes. Once again, those who see the rebellion against lack of privacy as merely an expression of 'bourgeois individualism' lack any understanding of the misery that comes from a single stove having to be used by five families, or a WC that has to be shared by ten families. But, outside of socialism, living space as a means of satisfying the need for privacy is always in conflict with the need for sociability and harmony. Loneliness and insecurity are just as alienating as lack of privacy. The single-family dwelling survives as a space for consumption in order to prevent the total social isolation of the individual. But in the long term it cannot prevent the disintegrating influence of late-bourgeois society on human fellowship. Inevitably, the individual's attempt at pure self-realisation is most likely an initial reaction to sexism, patriarchy and authoritarianism, but it cannot hold back increasing isolation and thus alienation. That is why the reintegration of housing and

Man's most valuable and scarce resource is time for living.

129

Ernest Mandel

a greater space for living are the conditions for achieving a greater degree of well-being.

Small forms of group consumption demand other spaces than larger groups. This integration should not be purely economic or functional, i.e. cost-cutting in the short or medium to long term. It must allow an optimum satisfaction of a maximum of needs. People are not machines of consumption. Because of the way it was planned, Le Corbusier's technocratic idea of building 'living machines' was a reactionary Utopia. The loneliness of the inhabitants of the *grands ensembles* and the satellite cities is even greater than that of slum-dwellers. Many of the *grands ensembles* are in any case turning swiftly into slums.

Through the way it looks, greater space for living should also prolong and enrich time for living. Boring, straight, colourless streets and cold senseless rows of houses do not permit this. Cities without centres, such as certain 'car cities', increase frustration, boredom, loneliness. The street, the neighbourhood, the city should stimulate colour, fantasy, emotion, communication and harmony.

The purely quantitative growth in satisfying needs is necessary for a wider development of the human personality. But more is required. And the result of this hiatus is that of a growing demand for more quality of life.

To begin with, there are concrete material causes for this. Unbearable noise, the daily air pollution in cities like Los Angeles, Mexico City and Tokyo, with the periodic advice not to appear on the streets today, and catastrophes like Chernobyl, are forcing everyone to consider ecological issues. But the need for more quality of life is not just a question of physical survival. It is also emancipatory in a broader sense of the word. The gradual erosion of the so-called 'work ethic', particularly in the richest countries, makes this clear.

More quality of life demands more space. This space for life is being undermined by the mega-cities with their highways and concrete and glass canyons, even though some of these can sometimes be aesthetically attractive. The struggle for pedestrian zones, for large areas of green, for alternative energy supplies, for easily accessible and well-equipped schools and hospitals is also a struggle for participation, grass-roots democracy, self-control and the self-realisation of all. At the same time, the attempt to

Hong Kong

escape alienating space by returning to nature, in other words to small primitive village communes, is a romantic Utopia. In such a limited space the development of the full potential of rich inter-human relations is impossible. Marx's formula concerning the 'village idiot' remains more topical than ever.

The life-threatening results of contemporary technology and of the demographic explosion have to be solved in a different way than through regression to primitive forms of work, consumption and life: through the development of new techniques friendly to both man and nature. It is still possible, but it is becoming urgent.**?**

The quality of life is partly determined by the space for life. A humane society demands space for living, as well as architecture, housing and environmental planning that promote the optimum and as harmonious as possible development of all human possibilities.**?** To quote Marx and Engels, 'It is a society in which the free development of all depends on the free development of each individual.'

Alienating space

Of all forms of art, architecture is the most directly dependent on property relations, that is to say, on control over land, construction materials and building commission. The architect is an intermediary between client, contractor and user. He or she is dependent on various social forces. The law of supply and demand also applies here in every way. A few famous architects enjoy an exceptional freedom of choice and initiative, but they are indeed exceptions. That does not mean, of course, that the large majority of architects simply function as passive instruments of anonymous social forces or individual property owners and rulers. Cities long gone and those still existing would not be what they were and what they are today without the specific personality of a series of known and unknown architects. This only counts, however, to a limited degree. Housing and urban space are chiefly a function of socio-economic power relations.

The idea that cities in antiquity or in the middle ages formed organic communities, in which class divisions played no role, or only a marginal one, is founded on ignorance or self-deception. It is true that in

? There appears to be a remarkable incongruency between the good old 'five minutes to twelve' rhetoric of terminal cultural philosophy on the one hand, and the complete discrediting of comprehensive solutions which could put an end to need, on the other. Although a vision of the future is implicitly announced in your analysis, you are forced almost necessarily to revert to vague expressions concerning 'the development of new techniques'. The proposals for improvement remain vague. Besides, what value does your urgency still have now that thought has passed beyond redemption?

! My thinking is not past redemption, in so far as you mean by this a category of thought, but it is in so far as it refers to a concrete historical moment. The 'Post-Modern knowledge' which you are probably referring to is in any case, despite the notion of 'being after something', not at all new. It is a return to superstition, the pre-scientific (anti-scientific) superstition of the period before the Enlightenment, if not of the twelfth century. It is a non-religious version of the postulate of original sin. Irrespective of its scientific components, Marxism is also based on a moral choice. Marx expressed this concisely in the formula of the 'categorical imperative of abolishing all social situations in which man is an oppressed, exploited, alienated, humiliated being'. This means, among other things, that evil means can never lead to a sacred aim, as Marx said. Because of this, Marxism is free from all totalitarian temptation. Consistent Marxists can never condone degrading, inhumane practices, let alone apply them. This is ultimately a practical question. Practice shows whether people who call themselves Marxists really are Marxists.

130 *The quality of life is partly determined by the space for life. A humane society demands space for living, as well as architecture, housing and environmental planning that promote the optimum and as harmonious as possible development of all human possibilities.*

the medieval city there was no radical segregation between poor and wealthy neighbourhoods. But then the rich protected themselves from the periodic uprisings of the poor by giving their own houses the form of fortresses.

Since its inception, however, the capitalistic city was characterised by spatial segregation. The capitalists and the middle class did not want to live in the dirty, stinking districts of the poor. Nature itself determined the boundary between 'good' and 'bad' neighbourhoods: the direction of the wind, which blew factory fumes and the smoke from the trains away from the one towards the other. This was the origin of the classic division into 'West end' and 'East end' in London, Paris, Berlin and elsewhere. Later, in the USA people talked about the 'right' or 'wrong' side of the tracks.

But nature avenged itself on the greed of the ruling classes. Regardless of the direction of the wind, pathogenic organisms travelled from the poor to the rich neighbourhoods. Cholera and tuberculosis convinced the rich that a minimum in sanitary infrastructure for the whole city was in their own interests. The need to reduce the costs of moving, and the rise of electricity as the most important energy source, worked in the same way. The construction, improvement and maintenance of the urban infrastructure led to increasing environmental planning. Social segregation continued to exist. But poor and rich neighbourhoods were partially connected to each other through a common infrastructure. On the basis of this a new process of capital accumulation developed in the building sector. The building industry developed itself as an independent branch, although characterised by a much lower degree of mechanisation than other central industrial branches. It is a characteristic which has remained until after the Second World War. In Marxist jargon one speaks of a lower organic composition of capital, i.e. less machinery and more hand labour. Wages too are generally lower than in the large industries. Surplus and profit are thus above average. When landowner and building contractor coincide, the surplus profit will remain in that sector. Because of monopolies determined by the historical structural shortage of available land for building, the capital invested in land ownership and the construction industry

? Harmonious? Can you indicate what part criticism should play in such a humane society, when, in the nature of things, it harbours a moment of conflict?

! 'As harmonious as possible' does not mean without conflict. It has to do with a society in which conflicts do not lead to wars, civil wars, mass repression, hunger and exploitation. It is no 'paradise on earth'. But it is a qualitatively better society than the one that exists today, a society worth fighting for. The question is hypothetical. Let's first see what the role of criticism can be in the present.

increases faster than in the industrial or financial sectors. This process is further stimulated through the development of the urban infrastructure, which is financed by taxation and loans. Thanks to personal relations, corruption and pure fraud, the plundering of city finances by local landowners and construction industries fulfilled a role comparable with the plundering of the state treasury by army and navy suppliers during the original accumulation of mining and manufacturing capital.

A symbiosis was thus created between the rich, who control building land and public works, the local banks, the local political potentates and their representatives in the regional and national centres of power. These local power structures form the social basis and departure-point for the eventual power of big business.

The extent and the most pernicious consequences of corruption, fraud and criminalisation, to which the practices of some contractors in the building sector led, unleashed a reaction of local reform movements, usually through the agency of municipal elections, but with only modest results. This changed, however, with the conquest of the city administrations by the modern workers movement. Thus arose so-called 'municipal socialism', first in Vienna, Copenhagen, Stockholm and Amsterdam, and then in Liege, the 'red belts' around Paris, London, Bologna and various West German cities.

'Socialism in one city' is just as utopian, however, as 'socialism in one country'. The decades of economic expansion after the Second World War resulted in a radical migration to the cities and a permanent increase in the demand for cheap urban housing, which communal incomes and public subsidies are unable to keep pace with. A chronic housing shortage arose all over the world, even in the fortresses of municipal socialism.**?!**

Housing and its off-shoots such as the production of electric household equipment was actually one of the two most important driving forces of this long expansion; the car industry was the other. Timid attempts to respond to the housing shortage by stimulating the construction of cheap houses by means of higher taxes led to a massive exodus of the middle classes and the rich from the city, which meant less income for the city. Suburbia, with its single-family dwellings, expanded on a large scale. It became a vicious circle.

But the city of the twentieth century is not only exploding horizontally, but also vertically. City centres are more and more dominated by skyscrapers. The reason for this is chiefly speculative. When land at certain sites becomes expensive because of the imbalance between supply and demand, then it is obviously worthwhile, according to the criterium of maximum profit, to build ten times as many houses, offices, or both on the same area. High-rise architecture is the product of this. There have always been certain architects who seem to have been seized with a fever for height. Even the great Frank Lloyd Wright designed an absurd city in which 100.000 people would have had to live and work in a single tower 1.600 metres high. Fortunately it was never built.**?!**

The construction industry and the city planners are trapped in equations with many variable, if not unknown, factors: the price of land, building costs, rent levels, maintenance of houses and the urban infrastructure, municipal taxes, average interest rates determining mortgage credits, public subsidies, condition of public transport, removal costs and the time needed for travel between home and place of employment, the spread of shopping and recreation centres, and so on. The result goes without saying: irrational and inhuman cities are consciously being built, in the grip of short- and medium-term profit calculations. The evidence that most springs to mind is the systematic under-development of public transport in favour of the car and petrol cartels, with disastrous consequences as regards air pollution. It is irrational in a macro-economic sense as well. Private cars use proportionally much more energy than public transport. What's more, although only riding a few hours per day, these private cars clog the streets, and increase both the time and cost of movement. Just as bad are the consequences of the general spending restriction since the turnabout of the economic climate in the seventies. Savings are made on social housing, infrastructure, education and health care. Marginal poverty increases, and with it, a three-tier society. The permanent crisis of today's city is growing in proportion to poverty.

The numerous variables determining the profits of landowners and contractors endow the contemporary capitalistic city with a permanently instable and cyclical character.

A district, or a housing block even, can lose its status as a good neighbourhood from one month to the next. Prices of land, rents and property are falling. It is in the interests of property owners and speculators to encourage dilapidation and put a stop to maintenance work, sometimes with the complicity of

?! *The class nature of society was and still is a structural element of the city. Is this not essential, to the degree that a city without class systems would have to be called a spectre of amorphous agglutination and monotonous suburbanisation?*

Socialist housing districts in cities like Amsterdam, Hamburg and Vienna were the accomplishments of architects and city councils which on the one hand represented an established (segregated) minority, and on the other hand embodied to a large degree the ethos of an idealistic 'avant-garde' (Utopia). In this stage of capitalist production (the twenties and thirties) the reality of political and urban developments gave the lie to that same Marxism that the Socialists were still appealing to at that time; in Marx's model of development such housing districts would not even have been able to exist. What may we expect of socialism now, in our own historical age? Also in the light of the differences with 60 years ago:

- *In Western countries a large part of the principles of urban development have become standard government policy.*
- *The proletariat, the sustaining power of socialist politics, has changed into a heavily stratified body of 'employees', functionaries, and voters, and crumbled as well into a mass of consumers and television viewers.*
- *In Europe, zoning schemes, government monopolies and state and municipal regulations restrict the power that speculators and property developers wield through the production factor of land.*

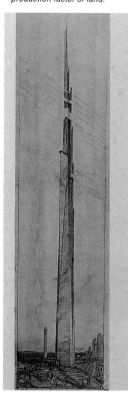

Frank Lloyd Wright, Mile High Skyscraper, 1956

Ernest Mandel

?! *You emphasise here the difference between supply and demand as the most important reason for high-rise buildings in the twentieth century. Do you mean that there is a shortage of land? This seems contrary to the facts. If you look at New York, the high-rise city par excellence, you see that the downtown and midtown high buildings all stand next to each other, while a few avenues further there are vacant lots. So there must be another reason for the vertical explosion, one that must also lie in the psyche of the speculator or client, an upward trend of thought as it were. This is especially true of office buildings. As far as housing goes, the high-rise solution seems to be mainly inspired by private property and the capitalistic need to maximise return, rather than a difference between supply and demand.*

the public administrations. As soon as the dilapidation exceeds a certain limit, the price for the land falls so that it becomes worthwhile to renovate and once again entice the middle class, despite the high selling price and/or rent. For the city centre offers advantages in terms of culture, health care, education and a diversity of consumer goods that are not to be found in suburbia.

Horizontal development of residential areas goes hand in hand with a new form of spatial segregation, just like that between luxury high-rise buildings and decaying *grands ensembles*. Between city and suburbia there are emerging satellite cities and new slum zones. This is particularly the case in the Third World, but also in the poorer metropolises. Whole districts are being created without any infrastructure, without a minimum of hygiene, with degrading conditions worse than those of nineteenth-century slums.

The symbol of this is the slums of Calcutta. The absolute bottom is reached when the homeless are forced by local *mafiosi* to pay 'rent' for a place to sleep on the street. The ultimate origin of 'rent' thus becomes crystal clear: instead of providing a 'service' for a tenant, money is extorted through monopolised control on access to land.

The population explosion which has led to the growth of mega-cities in the Third World is primarily of social-economic, rather than biological, origin. The surplus population shifts from the countryside to the city in the hope of improving its living conditions. This does not mean that its marginalisation is

Carel Weeber, social housing, The Hague, 1985

abolished. But the global consequences are catastrophic.

Cities like Mexico City, Cairo, Bombay and Jakarta will have up to 20 million inhabitants in the year 2000. They are literally in danger of suffocating in air and water pollution, noise and explosive violence, including mass murder of children.

The crisis of the contemporary city is as obvious as the crisis of bourgeois society. The building industry and city planning are determined not by fulfilling human needs but by the demands of capital accumulation. Alienated space becomes alienating space. Catastrophic socio-economic irrationality and catastrophic human frustration are the inevitable product of this.**?**

The liberation of space

In the nineteenth century, the housing shortage was discovered at the same time as the 'social issue'. Solutions were proposed and were also put into practice. The difference between advocates of moderate reforms and those who advocated radical projects is not one between realists (supporters of *Realpolitik*) and utopists. It is a question of the difference between improving the lot of a minority or that of the large majority. The advocates of radical changes take the view that, without humanly acceptable living

? *Apart from the glaring discrepancy between rich and poor, the negative moral implications of class distinctions were based on such analytical concepts as surplus value, exploitation, abjection, alienation. In the West, only alienation is left over. Your observations repeatedly deal with this alienation, with which, apart from the ideological meaning of the term, you seem to testify to philosophical essentialism. It is precisely this essentialism that is regarded by many contemporary philosophers as outdated, since it intrinsically attests to a totalising conception of knowledge that ultimately brings about the opposite of the emancipation that the idea of alienation had in mind. What you are envisaging, becoming master of one's own fate, is exactly that which your philosophic opponents dispute; not only because one's own fate does not have a nature that can be positively formulated, but also especially because the movement of thought necessary for this already bears within itself the seeds of its opposite. It is this epistemological doubt that seems to be lacking in your argument. Can you find terms with which you can parry the philosophical incommensurability between you and your critics.*

! It is the fashion today to deny the validity of Marxist economic theory. 'Marx is dead, look at the Eastern bloc'. But one cannot falsify a scientific theory in terms of the practice of certain political groupings that improperly appeal to it. It would be the same as condemning the scientific and medical discoveries that led to

Aldo Rossi, social housing, The Hague, 1992

inoculations against epidemic diseases because those inoculations were massively misused in the Nazi camps for torture and murder. In numerous writings we have attempted to prove that the notions of 'surplus labour', 'surplus value', 'exploitation', 'concentration and centralisation of capital', 'overproduction', 'crisis' and 'social polarisation' (decrease of the 'self-employed' in the total working population) are even more relevant today than in the nineteenth century. That is a judgement confirmed by empirical facts, not a dogmatic preconceived idea. One can only (attempt to) falsify that judgement with other empirical facts, not with pseudo-philosophical arguments. In all respects our thesis implies that these notions are accepted as objective facts and not as subjective states of awareness. Marxism is based on a combination of two elements, each of which possess their own autonomous, internal logic. Like every science, scientific socialism relies on constructive doubt. All knowledge is provisional and subject to revision. But this revision must be based on concrete facts. Whoever makes an absolute of doubt, or questions the scientific nature of particular labour hypotheses, without basing himself on such facts, is himself dogmatic, not a 'Post-Modernist critic of science'. The difference between the thesis that the sun revolves around the earth and the thesis that the earth revolves around the sun, does not correspond to an 'ideological choice'. With the facts that are

Ernest Mandel

available to us today, the first thesis is unprovable, the second proved.

The Marxist idea of alienation is indeed sometimes reproached for being based on 'philosophical essentialism', and for carrying itself to the point of absurdity. The abolition of alienation through people determining their own fate would assume a positive definition of that 'fate', which would be impossible. The process of thought which would be required in order to make this fate possible would itself undermine such (total) emancipation, if not make it impossible. This critique is not inherent to the Marxist vision, so it cannot reveal any supposed internal discrepancy that vision might contain. It stems from an imaginary, apologetic interpretation of history and society in the guise of a certain philosophical discourse.

In the first place it is static. It presupposes that the objective of 'abolishing alienation' from the beginning can only be seen as total. On the contrary, Marxists regard the dynamic nature of this self-emancipation as a process. It is a matter of successively abolishing concrete forms of alienation. It is not necessary to know exactly how labour will ultimately be organised in a classless society in order to understand that producers-consumers – whose activity is no longer determined by market laws, and therefore not by advertising either, nor by the pressure of money, nor state despotism, bureaucratic decrees, the dictate of experts – are people who to a large degree determine their own fate and are therefore involved in an encompassing process of emancipation. Producers who themselves decide what is to be produced and how, are qualitatively less alienated than producers for whom decisions are taken by others. Secondly, the 'Post-Modernist' critique of

space for all, even the favoured minority cannot free itself from the alienating results of alienated space for living and working. You cannot build harmonious districts within irrational and inhuman cities. The bourgeoisie and the well-to-do middle classes have nevertheless periodically attempted to do this, naturally without success. A succession of American architects have designed the 'house of the future'. Nothing of this has really influenced the day-to-day building industry. Even the Bauhaus can in part be judged accordingly. It will always be the case that the problem of liberated living space can only be solved in its totality.**?**

This presumes in the first place the abolition of private appropriation of land and a building industry dominated by the pursuit of profit. These areas should be put in charge of the community. This is what we call the socialist solution. A different wording essentially changes nothing as long as the given content remains the same. The formula of 'power of decision in the hands of the community' has by no means sufficient concrete contents. Which community decides and in what way? Each district? Each village and each town? Each region? Each country. Each federation or each continent? The answer points to an articulation of the power of decision between these various domains of space. In what relationship? Experience, that is to say the people themselves, will determine that. There is no ready-made answer to this question.

But the decisions ought in any case to be really democratic, including the possibility of choice between various projects. That presumes genuine pluralism. Trotsky predicted that competing parties of architects would arise, which the people could choose between after lengthy public debates.

That this power of decision by the majority must safeguard the rights of the minority as well as the freedom of choice of the individual (within the framework of the possible), and that it presupposes the ability of the majority to review its decisions on the grounds of experience, goes without saying.

For a long period, various generations at least, the issue of living and working space will revolve around the application of scarce resources. It is essential then to establish priorities. Socialists reject the despo-

The life-threatening results of contemporary technology and of the demographic explosion have to be solved in a different way than through regression to primitive forms of work, consumption and life: through the development of new techniques friendly to both man and nature. It is still possible, but it is becoming urgent.

Marxism is ideological (idealising) and thus itself subject to 'essentialism'. It assumes that thought processes are ultimately decisive for the content of processes of emancipation, if not for history. Marx states, on the other hand, that emancipation is an actual movement of people who are attempting to abolish actual abuses. The abolition of slavery, the elimination of the Inquisition and of absolute monarchy, are actual historical moves, an actual historical advancement. In every way, what came afterwards was not perfect, but anyone who assumes that such an assessment is sufficient to question the progressive nature of these changes is being inconsistent, if not hypocritical. Is it really a matter of indifference to him that he no longer ends up being burnt at the stake because of his ideas, that his children are no longer captured with a rope when they leave their home and sold as slaves? The real progress embodied in the above-mentioned stages of emancipation can be questioned even less. The actual process of emancipation does not depend on the people themselves determining their 'ultimate' fate in advance. It includes a growing determination of one's fate. That's exactly why it can be neutralised by no 'movement of thought' whatsoever. People who to an increasing degree decide their fate themselves can also be less and less ideologically manipulated and limited in their self-activity. What this self-emancipation will 'ultimately' lead to can only be partially predicted today. In other words, we reject any vision of an 'end of history'. Emancipation and determination of one's fate are processes of 'permanent creative revolution' which will never be fulfilled, a permanent revolution of thought included.

tism of the state, of experts, of the market and fortunes, in determining priorities. The power of decision must come from the people themselves. That does not mean, however, that government co-ordination, experts or the market can be totally and immediately excluded. In the long-term this would be unrealistic. But it does mean that the final decisions can be consciously taken by the masses themselves. It means that, in the final analysis, these same masses themselves choose between the major versions of long-term development. The progressive liberation of housing and living space for all people should be viewed in two successive phases. It is a lengthy process, with no immediate goal to be achieved. The first phase envisages achieving a minimum of humane housing for all inhabitants of the earth, while protecting the natural living environment. No one has the right to deny a minimum of welfare to hundreds of millions, if not billions of people, under the pretext of safeguarding the chances of survival of future generations. Anyhow, no one can predict what these chances of survival will be.**?**

Radical ecological despotism seems to be absurd, particularly when it concerns housing. It is an echo of the myth of original sin. Every form of building is always an intervention in nature. Every building alters the natural surroundings. If one wishes to avoid that then one has to return to the cave dwelling. And even there people altered nature, if only by means of their wall drawings. It is not a question of leaving nature unchanged. It is a question of implementing inevitable changes in such a way that the ecological balance is not disturbed. Changes that are scientifically sound and that respect nature should be sought after, not a subjection of mankind to dubious 'irrefutable laws of nature'.

Achieving a minimum of housing and living space for all the earth's inhabitants already raises gigantic problems, which will be even more aggravated when the world population soon reaches 10 billion. These problems can still be solved, but their solution demands, among other things, democratic planning and a crucial worldwide redistribution of resources. What is equally required is a combination of changes in the city and in the countryside.

In the Third World in particular, this would presuppose radical land reforms, linked to a radical reform of the city. The homeless must be housed. Those living in slums must have access to the technical, sanitary and cultural infrastructure. The slums must be replaced by liveable housing.

Recreational living space outside the city, in parks and woods, must be secured, restored and enlarged, without endangering the ecological balance. This assumes, among other things, large-scale re-forestation and the radical cleansing of rivers, streams, seas and oceans.

It is enough to sketch such a plan of action and to estimate its costs, if only approximately, to find that this first phase, which is still far removed from a harmoniously ideal solution, would take a very long time.

What does the harmonious solution, which we call the second phase, consist of? Trotsky described it with the phrase 'urban village'. Ultimately it goes back to Friedrich Engels, and refers to living communities that are capable of genuine self-determination. At the same time they must have easy access to a high standard of sanitary and cultural infrastructure, and to recreational space in open nature.

It is a question of 'green urban villages' embracing extensive – but not exhaustive –, small, technologically advanced industry and distribution centres, without undermining the quality of life and with a radically reduced burden of labour and time.

Sao Paulo, 1960

Hesitantly, very hesitantly, what we are aiming at can be defined as an urban village of 20-25.000 inhabitants, in 4 or 5 districts, divided into various 'belts', whether parallel or not. (Soviet urbanisation in the twenties envisaged 60.000 inhabitants.) Institutions such as high schools and optimally equipped hospitals can be shared by various of these urban villages.

Once again, all these figures and descriptions are nothing more than rough estimates and calculations. They will definitely need to be reviewed in the light of experience and of changed consciousness. But even as rough calculations they make the extent of the task clear once more. An expected world population of 10 billion people would involve the building of half a million urban villages.

Of course this cannot occur out of thin air. Many of the existing villages and cities at the beginning of the second phase could serve as a starting-point. The same goes for some of today's existing villages and small cities, as well as districts of larger cities.

Nevertheless, the task of ensuring such free communes for all the earth's inhabitants seems so sizeable that the question arises as to whether formulating such an aim is not just a game; can these ideas really be realised? I do not think so. A target to be aimed at is just what it says. Common sense teaches us that when someone doesn't know where he wants to go to, he won't arrive there either. (The reversal of the

134

? *A revisionist impulse is foreign to you. Ultimately, despite the extraordinary flexibility of the system, capitalist society will be destroyed through its own contradictions. This macro-economic vision, however, is shared by fewer people than ever. How can a situation become more urgent and the radicalisation of social tensions in a revolutionary moment come closer and closer, while at the same time the number of people supporting this theory steadily declines?*
That the masses themselves want a consensus is proven by numerous striking choices that these same masses make. For example, the recent introduction of the system of saving stamps in a supermarket chain, allowing people to save up for their own shares in the chain instead of the usual stamps. Everyone, even those on welfare, is becoming middle-class. How can you still motivate people in a world in which the problems of this world are no longer reflected in the lives of people who are able to do something about it?

! Someone who is under the economic pressure to sell his labour power is a wage labourer, even if he feels he belongs to the middle-class. That 'feeling' does not put him in a position to escape being periodically laid-off by the bosses. In the long term only practice will prove whether this experience leads him finally to change his consciousness or not. Thirty years – or even less! – is an insufficient length of time to answer this historical question; just think of the first half-century after the beginning of industrialisation.

? *The Stichting Milieudefensie [Environmental Protection Foundation] in Holland has published a report in which they introduced the notion of 'environmental usage space per head of the global population'. Inherent in this was of course the big issue of redistribution, which is in line with your emphasis on the right to living space. When you talk about 'a minimum of humane living space for all the earth's inhabitants', you are in fact talking about a world revolution. You think that the chances of survival of future generations should not serve as a pretext to leave the current status quo untouched. But the truth is that global lawlessness has no need at all of such a pretext. The above-mentioned report was simply received with derision by the 'realists'. How do you think you can ever convince these realists of another reality?*

! My argument implies in every respect a redistribution of resources on a global scale, a real 'world revolution', for which the political conditions have to be gradually created, including moral motivation. But not just this motivation. For the large majority of the inhabitants of the Western nations and Japan their own survival depends on helping solve the problem of the inhuman conditions in the Third World, at least on an elementary level, before they lead to the extension of barbarity on a global scale. I don't have to convince anyone with arguments. Reality will do it better.

means-end dialectic, for that matter, lies at the basis of all opportunistic politics. It is one of the keys to explaining the historic failure of Stalinism and reformist social-democracy.) If one really wishes to radically humanise housing and living space, then one has to constantly keep such a concrete aim in mind. Planned and realised projects then have to be tested against the question: have we come closer to our aim? Are we going in the right direction? **?**

Here we can clearly see a distinction between the first and the second phase. During the first phase the aim is to immediately reduce grinding human poverty and then to gradually eliminate it. It is not, therefore, a question of immediately creating ideal conditions. But for this very reason one should not stick false labels on these ad hoc solutions.

It is fashionable nowadays to throw mud at the October revolution and its immediate aftermath. In reality the twenties were high points of free creativity in all areas of science and art in the Soviet Union. These radiated far beyond the borders of Russia, particularly in the case of Soviet architecture, which is to a large degree the mother of all contemporary architecture, even though its projects usually just remained on paper owing to the lack of material means.

Soviet architecture was characterised by a combination of boldly experimental avant-gardism and deep social consciousness. Today, after sixty years of experience, we know that the transitional period and bureaucracy itself throw up specific problems concerning housing and living space. New forms of

? *On the other hand an all too explicit fondness for the target to be aimed at has often resulted in disdain for the present; a problem that you have already warned against with respect to the overlooking of the interests of those who are today without rights in favour of so-called future scenarios. How do you think you can avoid your goal being institutionalised into an historicist utopianism?*

! For me it is important not to simply abandon reforms that can be realised immediately, or even to disapprove of them, because of objections of this sort. The dialectic between reforms and revolution, between immediate realisation and goal to be aimed at, remains as relevant today as when Rosa Luxemburg engaged in a polemic about this with Bernstein at the turn of the century. But in judging reforms it should never be forgotten what the goal is: the gradual elimination of human misery. Reforms that lead to this misery being consolidated for large masses are questionable, to say the least. Reforms realised with the effect that the self-activity of the masses is restricted, if not repressed (through accepting a permanent consensus with the bourgeois party) are even more questionable.

On this map, the size of each country is in proportion to its wealth

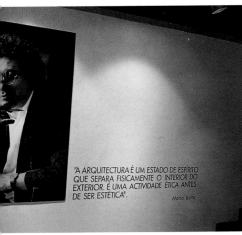

"A ARQUITECTURA É UM ESTADO DE ESPÍRITO QUE SEPARA FISICAMENTE O INTERIOR DO EXTERIOR. É UMA ACTIVIDADE ÉTICA ANTES DE SER ESTÉTICA".
Mario Botta

'Architecture is a state of mind which physically separates the inside from the outside. It is an ethical rather than an aesthetical activity.'

alienation spring up, combined with old ones. But tentative forms of real emancipation blossom as well. The culture park is a good example of this. The lengthy process of liberation from alienated and alienating space is thus actually a process of growing emancipation, that is to say, of man's self-determination. Becoming master over one's own living space means to become master over one's own life and one's own destiny.

The Swiss Mario Botta is one of today's most renowned architects. He calls himself a romantic and says that he is socially sensitive. He is inconsistent, in the sense that he mainly builds private houses for wealthy people. But, as he correctly says, 'We as people should be able to control our own environment. Otherwise we will lose our intelligence, our understanding.' (*Frankfurter Algemeine Zeitung Magazine*, 24 October 1986). Indeed; but all people should be able to do that, Mario; all people.

A Modern View, or a View on the Modern?

A Conversation with Richard Rogers

As an architect you have involved yourself in politics. Could you elaborate on the political responsibility and latitude in architecture? Do you really believe that architecture can influence the brief?

My involvement with politics over the last two years resulted primarily from my profound rejection of the Government's *laissez-faire* attitude towards the built environment and a frustration at the unproductive restrictions imposed by the planning system.

Architecture and the built environment play a significant role in the quality of life but in Britain it has been the subject of misunderstanding and neglect. The Government can and should involve itself by informing and consulting the public and setting an example through its own patronage.

We tried to focus on raising standards and awareness by introducing a formal competition system for government projects, adding the built environment as a subject for children in schools and seeking to involve ordinary people in the local planning process. At the larger scale we were pushing for an overall strategic body for London (which is the only major capital to lack a voice or governing authority) to coordinate transport and land use and to specifically protect the public realm of the city.

We live in an age of ecological threats. Architecture can contribute to a responsible approach to the environment by building more safely. But, as a medium for cultural reflection, is it able to contribute to a change of attitude?

Pompidou Centre, Paris, 1977

'The summit of the escalator system, suspended beyond the main structural framework. Not a remote monument but a people's place. Our competition report recommended that the Pompidou Centre be developed as a "love centre of information covering Paris and beyond (...) a cross between an information oriented computerised Times Square and the British Museum, with the stress on two-way participation between people and activities/exhibits".'

It must not be forgotten that cities are the single largest consumers of energy, polluters of the atmosphere and generators of waste. Our buildings consume 50% of our total energy requirement. Running, constructing and demolishing buildings inefficiently has contributed to the current environmental crisis. The architect can work on the building's performance making the building run more efficiently, consume less, emit less. Careful orientation, utilising safe and reusable materials and extending the life of the building by incorporating a high degree of flexibility all contribute to this.

However, architects should not focus entirely on the individual building project but look towards the relationships of the parts of the city to look at the global problem. In recent projects such as the commercial centre in Shanghai and the masterplan for Val d'Oise outside Paris we proposed an urban strategy based on creating a more ecologically sustainable environment. Energy consumption was reduced to 35% of that of conventional towns.

I do not see where the work of the architect ends and that of the urbanist or transport engineer starts, nor incidentally the structure or service engineer on the smaller scale. The architect has a unique training and experience and that is to challenge and to open possibilities. He is the generalist which in effect means that he must be capable of grasping the principles of most of the disciplines in order to guide them towards the broader goals.

'Architecture immortalises and glorifies something. Hence there can be no architecture where there is nothing to glorify.' Using this famous quote of Ludwig Wittgenstein as motto of your book A Modern View, *the fundamental question comes up: what is it architects could glorify and immortalise nowadays? How does this respectable motive relate to the wish to offer servant space? You once stated that architecture glorifies shelter. Has shelter any glory and if it does: is that all there is?*

If architecture can glorify it can also reflect the decay of a society in crisis. The last decade in Britain has witnessed the most staggering building boom. The motivation behind this transformation of our cities and urban peripheries has been profitability above all else. The result has been the evolution of a 'building product' – an enclosure of maximum efficiency, fast to erect, cheap to build and designed to last five years. The paucity of these buildings and the environments that surround them stand as memorials to the poverty of the ethics and ambitions of our society in that period.

Architecture is not created by architects alone but relies on its great patrons, great engineers, talented builders and shared visions. When the vision transcends the pure profit motive and looks towards improving the broader social picture then architecture is created, which indeed glorifies the ideals of that society. There is much to glorify in today's democratic world, just as there is much to lament. The architect and the patron are responsible for the significance of their building and that starts with the evolution of the brief, the manner in which it is built and its relationship to the public realm.

Tomigaya, I; Exhibition Building, Tokyo, 1992

'The design of the building is based on the principle of a simple shelf system. The two steel towers support the main floors with the flexibility to increase the area by adding temporary mezzanines which can be stored in a separate location. This creates a series of dynamic spaces which can be transformed to suit specific requirements. The tall building is shaped to utilise the power of the wind by means of a turbine. The aerodynamics of the building have been tuned so as to double the wind speed in the gap between the two towers. in this way a wind-driven generator can produce enough electricity to power the entire building.'

138

But how does this attitude relate to your philosophy of defining buildings into their served and servant components?

In the past we had Vitruvius and the proposition that a building could attain perfection through a complete control of its proportions and composition. The exercise of architecture was the exercise of creating a perfect and unchangeable object. This concept of built form related to the philosophy of a society wishing to define and fix relationships. The twentieth century has seen the transformation of philosophy away from static and hierarchical relationships (within society and between Man and God) to our present post-Einsteinian position where the philosophy of change now dominates thinking. This philosophical change has also motivated architecture and this shift in thinking has been accompanied by a complete transformation of the technology of building which has further undermined the principles of traditional architecture. Our own reaction to this situation is to seek an architecture that can accommodate the changing needs of the building's users and maximise the performance of the building by making best use of the new possibilities created by technology. One aspect is the manipulation of the floorspace of the building to create a greater flexibility of use and the other is to work with the servant elements of the building programme which today make up close to one third of the building in terms of both cost and space.

The framework of the building has a very long life whilst the servant spaces containing technologies which are continuously being updated, modified or replaced have a different role. We are trying to create a legible language of architecture. A language where each piece says what it is, what it means. **We have moved away from the purity of the Miesian block towards buildings which are responsive to their urban context, set into the city, legible to the passer-by, richer in their layering and texture and, most importantly, more able to absorb change, alteration and addition.** So we are looking for an order made out of construction systems, a legible hierarchy of systems which nonetheless try to keep pace and order the inevitable chaos of the constantly changing modern world.

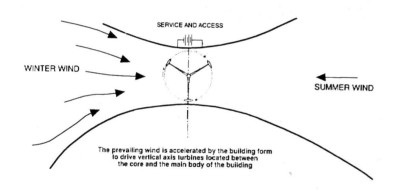

WINTER WIND

SERVICE AND ACCESS

SUMMER WIND

The prevailing wind is accelerated by the building form
to drive vertical axis turbines located between
the core and the main body of the building

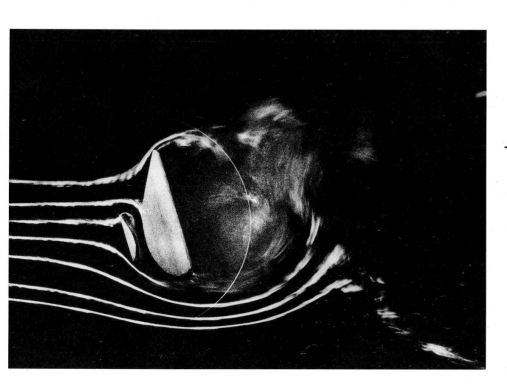

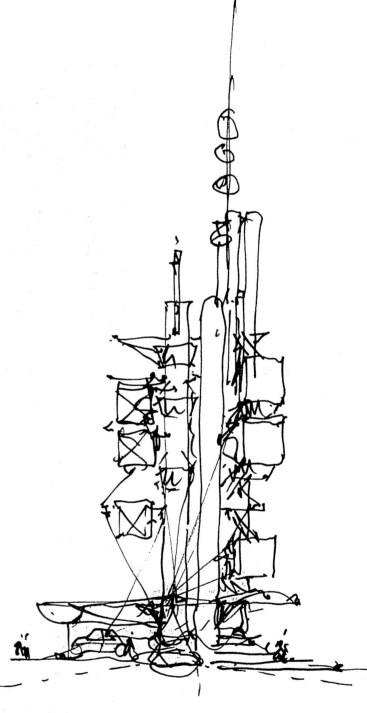

Tokyo International Forum Design Competition, 1989

'I believe in the rich potential of science and technology. Aesthetically one can do what one wants with technology, for it is a tool and not an end, but we ignore it at our peril, for without it we cannot achieve our potential. The Tokyo Forum is designed as a public meeting place. Modern technology has allowed us to develop a new range of spaces, experiences and activities expressed by new forms. Social concept, technology and form are inseparable.'

The dynamic architecture that you have produced wants to challenge the very conventions and norms of society and is indeed perceived as controversial. How does this seemingly revolutionary approach conform with the views of your conservative clients like Lloyd's who seek to rule out risk?

Lloyd's have actually had to build three purpose built headquarters this century alone. In the past they have been singularly unsuccessful in predicting their medium term needs and this has resulted in their buildings becoming rapidly obsolete. The main problem has been the huge increase in demand for underwriting space which has consistently outpaced their expectations. The key proposal of our building is that there is an interchangeability between market and office space so that the market can theoretically expand until it has filled the entire building. This is a concept which completely rejects the classical notion of static hierarchy which characterised all their previous buildings.

But the concept of interchangeability goes much further because an underwriting space has to cope with five to ten times more people than a normal office. This implies a quantum leap in demand for building services such as lifts, fire escapes, air-conditioning, toilets, power and telecommunications. The service zones are located outside the building so that they do not disrupt the market space and so that they can be easily accessed for maintenance, replacement or addition. The building is equipped with enough services to cope with medium term predictions. If this demand increases way beyond predictions, as it has done consistently throughout the century, then a substantial increase in lifts and fire stairs etcetera will need to be incorporated. The dynamic, asymmetrical form of the building is designed to take such additions without undermining the integrity of the architectural concept.

So, to answer your question, Lloyd's reacted extremely positively to a dynamic architectural concept as they appreciated that this was in fact a means to actually reduce their risk!

During your career you have shown a strong faith in technology. You once said:

'We are living through a period of enormous scientific and technical advance; perhaps a second industrial revolution. The computer, micro-chip, transputer, bio-technology or solid state chemistry should give us more time to work out our complex social and political problems'.

Here you pretend that technology is just a neutral tool which you can use for problems we are confronted with. But don't you think technology has its own dynamics, remodelling our perceptive framework in which we pose our problems? Social problems always seem technology-bound.

Zoofenster; Brau und Brunnen Building, Berlin, 1991

'The design responds to the pivotal points of the site, both as the centre of an important pedestrian circulation system and as a key landmark on the Berlin skyline. The proposal is currently the tallest building planned for Berlin, with a public viewing gallery on its uppermost floor.'

Red arrows flying over the pyramids, Egypt

'From pyramids to fighter jets – incredible advances in technology, today much of it squandered on armaments.'

Lloyd's of London Headquarters, 1986

'Architecture is teamwork in which the client plays a major role. Lloyd's reflects the dedication and sensitivity of the client just as much as the contribution of the architect. Lloyd's was designed so as to link together the somewhat oversimplified neighbouring blocks and the more articulated architecture of the past. From a distance the skyline is enriched by the servant towers which place the building within its context.

The brief demanded 'flexibility to meet changing needs well into the next century', implying no only easily adaptable interiors but a form organised so that parts could be added or removed without loss of design integrity. If one can access and change short-life parts of a building, its total lifespan can be extended. Lloyd's is clearly divided into a long-life central zone housing people and a short-life external zone containing technology.'

**Inland Revenue Headquarters,
Nottingham, Competition Entry, 1992**
'The Inland Revenue Headquarters represents an ecological approach to design. Low energy consumption and creation of a highly landscaped environment form a basis of the scheme. The twin administrative functions of the institution are disposed between two concentric half circles. The central linear garden enhances the quality of the accommodation and creates a curved roof-line which can harness the prevailing wind for natural ventilation.'

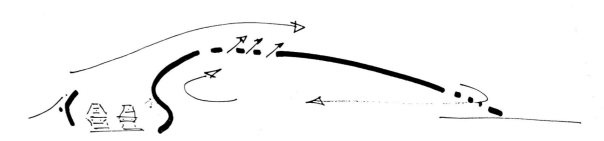

Today technology not only comes after a problem, but also precedes it. How do you succeed in dividing technology and 'the complex social and political problems'. In other words: isn't there a strange contradiction between your recognition of a pluralist society, and your faith in the linear progress of modern technology? If there isn't any straight line in history or culture left, why then do you still believe in the straightness of technology?

142

Technology is a tool which architects ignore to their loss. It is not that there exists a linearity in *the progress* of technology but there is and has always been a consistent and constant relationship between the ambitions of the architect and the possibilities provided by technology. Our Tokyo Forum project proposed giving the entire ground level of the site to public functions focused on open air spaces. This simple social ambition to create a large public space in the heart of a capital which has few such spaces led to the conferences spaces (the actual programme) being suspended like ships in giant cradles. Technology widens the possibilities of the architect's imagination, it serves man, it is not an end in itself.

The question remains: what to do if the possibilities provided by technology are exceeding the ambitions of man (i.e. the architect)?

I suppose your question precisely highlights my point. Technology is nothing but an enabler, a catalyst for cultural activity. The invention of the television led to the creation of a huge broadcasting culture. What was initially a purely scientific creation without meaning spawned a huge social and cultural development. Nor is this a particularly new concept. I doubt very much that primitive man set up a research programme to melt metal in order to produce better tools. Man's development through the ages is inextricably linked to his inventiveness in the face of his own discoveries. **Today's challenge is to use all our civility to guide our use of these discoveries and technologies.**

You have always had a major interest in the quality of public space, thus showing a strong sense of democracy. But what has public space to do with the public sphere in the electronic paradigm?

One of the phenomena of contemporary life is that the revolution in information technology has actually increased the need and usefulness of face to face contact. Today few developments, be they scientific, economic or cultural, are solitary activities. The city is still primarily the place where culture exists and by culture I mean the communication of people. The city is the glorification of all that is the public interaction: the street, the park, the square, the museums, theatres, cinemas.

The crisis of today is the lack of cohesion between the private and public realm, between the cultural needs of the citizen and the commercial criteria of the builders. Government has the crucial role in forging a meaningful relationship between these two forces.

***Shanghai Lu Jia Zui, Masterplan for a
New Commercial Centre, 1992***

'Urban design is a dynamic rather than static
process which focuses on establishing a robust
infrastructure (open spaces, circulation systems,
transportation network etc.), which forms a
framework for design and construction. The plan
for Lu Jia Zui is based on mixed rather than zoned
use to create a 24-hour city. An integrated
transportation strategy reduces dependence on
car travel to a minimum, thus lowering energy
consumption and pollution.'

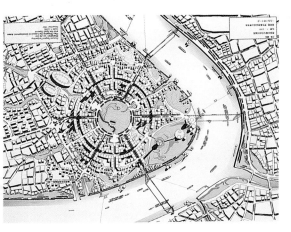

'Ruling out risks', Art in Ruins, Buying Time I, 1989

Visions' Unfolding:
Architecture in the Age
of Electronic Media

Peter Eisenman

During the fifty years since the Second World War, a paradigm shift has taken place that should have profoundly affected architecture: this is the shift from the mechanical paradigm to the electronic one. **?!** This change can be simply understood by comparing the impact of such primary modes of reproduction as the photograph and the fax on the role of the human subject; the photograph within the mechanical paradigm, the fax within the electronic one.

In photographic reproduction the subject still maintains a controlled interaction with the object. A photograph can be developed with more or less contrast, texture or clarity. The photograph can be said to remain in the control of human vision. The human subject thus retains its function as interpreter, as discursive function. With the fax, the subject is no longer called upon to interpret, for reproduction takes place without any control or adjustment. The fax also challenges the concept of originality. While in a photograph the original reproduction still retains a privileged value, in facsimile transmission the original remains intact but with no differentiating value, since it is no longer sent. The mutual devaluation of both original and copy is not the only transformation affected by the electronic paradigm. The entire nature of what we have come to know as the reality of our world has been called into question by the invasion of media into everyday life. For reality always demanded that our vision be interpretative.

How have these developments affected architecture? Since architecture has traditionally housed value as well as fact one would imagine that architecture would have been greatly transformed. But this is not the case, for architecture seems little changed at all. **?!** This in itself ought to warrant investigation, since architecture has traditionally been a bastion of what is considered to be the real. Metaphors such as house and home; bricks and mortar; foundations and shelter, attest to architecture's role in defining what we consider to be real. Clearly, a change in the everyday concepts of reality should have had some effect on architecture. It did not because the mechanical paradigm was the *sine qua non* of architecture; architecture was the visible manifestation of the overcoming of natural forces such as gravity and weather by mechanical means. Architecture not only overcame gravity, it was also the monument to that overcoming; it interpreted the value society placed on its vision. **?!** The electronic paradigm directs a powerful challenge to architecture because it defines reality in terms of media and simulation, it values appearance over existence, what can be seen over what is. Not the seen as we formerly knew it, but rather a seeing that can no longer interpret. Media introduce fundamental ambiguities into how and what we see. Architecture has resisted this question because, since the importation and absorption of perspective by architectural space in the fifteenth century, architecture has been dominated by the mechanics of vision. Thus architecture assumes sight to be pre-eminent and also in some way natural to its own processes, not a thing to be questioned. It is precisely this traditional concept of sight that the electronic paradigm questions.

Sight is traditionally understood in terms of vision. When I use the term 'vision' I mean that particular characteristic of sight which attaches seeing to thinking, the eye to the mind. In architecture, vision refers to a particular category of perception linked to monocular perspectival vision. The monocular vision of the subject in architecture allows for all projections of space to be resolved on a single planimetric surface. It is therefore not surprising that perspective, with its ability to define and reproduce the perception of depth on a two dimensional surface, should find architecture a waiting and wanting vehicle. Nor is it surprising that architecture soon began to conform itself to this monocular, rationalising vision – in its own body. Whatever the style, space was constituted as an understandable construct, organised around spatial elements such as axes, places, symmetries, etcetera. Perspective is even more virulent in architecture than in painting because of the imperious demands of the eye *and* the body to orient itself in architectural space through processes of rational perspectival ordering. It was thus not without cause that Brunelleschi's invention of one-point perspective should correspond to a time when there was a paradigm shift from the theological and theocentric to the anthropomorphic and anthro-

?! *Why do you say 'should have'? In* The Structure of Scientific Revolutions *Thomas Kuhn shows that knowledge is not simply and linearly accumulating towards a final truth, but that it evolves around paradigms, which encompass a corpus of knowledge till too many facts no longer correspond to its inner logic. Then a paradigm shift takes place, and the apocryphal facts help constitute a new paradigm. So it's an epistemological notion whereas you seem to regard it as a set of morals to go by lest you want to be included in the contemporary Zeitgeist. The shift you mention seems to be a historicistic view on the future in which any intellectual backwardness is moralised in the name of subjective definition of the present day.*

?! *Just as literature, or music, or ballet, etcetera, could change without losing their formal characters as words in a book, sounds in time or movements in space, architecture can lose its metaphorical capacity of the eternal meaning without becoming obsolete altogether. One cannot deny that architecture has already changed its narrative during the post-Nietzschean shift in social and philosophical thought, although it didn't change its basic characteristics, being shelter, meaning, fundament, occupation and so on. Since architecture is much more than art, science and language, it's not so vulnerable to the paradigm shifts you speak about. Being linked to the biological, anthropological and phenomenological dimensions of life, some aspects of it stay outside any cultural paradigm. Now, whereas classical thought annexed the supra cultural aspects of architecture, exactly because of their lasting qualities, and their rich potential to represent the classical world view, you seem to fight against a metaphor, and not against the intrinsic logic of a cultural medium itself.*

?! *Suppose we say: architecture was not only the monument of overcoming gravity, it really overcame it. Then we have another story. You seem to present architecture only as a medium of cultural reflection but it also is bricks and mortar. Maybe because of its wider meaning than only being art, it resisted your paradigm shift for so long. Because this shift took place in the modalities of culture, i.e. the modes of experience, and not so much in the daily life and the social structure. You seem to suggest that your paradigm shift is a 'fête accomplie' but if we dig into the structure of the social organisation, we find a lot of very lasting things, transcending personal lifetime. We understand your desire to give your existence a wider historical meaning, more or less stating that after the Holocaust and the Gulag, all survivors can 'simply' pass away, is unbearable But should that desire really moralise daily life?*

Wexner Center for the Visual Arts, Columbus Ohio, 1989

Nunotani Headquarters Building, Tokyo, 1992

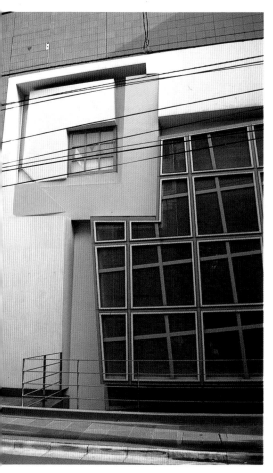

Koizumi Sangyo Building, Tokyo, 1989

pocentric views of the world. Perspective became the vehicle by which anthropocentric vision crystallised itself in the architecture that followed this shift.

Brunelleschi's projection system, however, was deeper in its effect than all subsequent stylistic change because it confirmed vision as the dominant discourse in architecture from the sixteenth century to the present. Thus, despite repeated changes in style from the Renaissance through Post-Modernism and despite many attempts to the contrary, the seeing human subject (monocular and anthropocentric) remains the primary discursive term of architecture.*?!*

The tradition of planimetric projection in architecture persisted unchallenged because it allowed the projection and hence, the understanding of a three-dimensional space in two dimensions. In other disciplines – perhaps since Leibniz and certainly since Sartre there has been a consistent attempt to demonstrate the problematic qualities inherent in vision, but in architecture the sight/mind construct has persisted as the dominant discourse.

In an essay entitled *Scopic Regimes of Modernity* Martin Jay notes that, 'Baroque visual experience has a strongly tactile or haptic quality, which prevents it from turning into the absolute ocular centrism of its Cartesian perspectivalist rival.' Norman Bryson in his article, *The Gaze in the expanded Field* introduces the idea of the gaze (*le regard*) as the looking back of the other. He discusses the gaze in terms of Sartre's intruder in *Being and Nothingness* or in terms of Lacan's concept of a darkness that cuts across the space of sight. Lacan also introduces the idea of a space looking back which he likens to a disturbance of the visual field of reason.

From time to time architecture has attempted to overcome its rationalising vision. If one takes for example the church of San Vitale in Ravenna one can explain the solitary column almost blocking the entry or the incomplete groin vaulting as an attempt to signal a change from a Pagan to a Christian architecture. Piranesi created similar effects with his architectural projections. He diffracted the

?! There is however an absolute difference between the perspective ordered by God Himself through the Platonic and Pythagorean rules in the world of the Anciens, and the post-Perraultian subjectivism from the eighteenth century onward. After the first introspective revolution, exemplified by the work of figures such as Jean-Jacques Rousseau, John Soane and Lawrence Stern, architecture and its perception never was derived again from eternal principles. The Moderns cried victory. From then on we see the rising preoccupation with space, and the movement of the individual in that space. To the Modern Movement this subjectively experienced space, notwithstanding Corbusian Purism, was the Leitmotiv of any architectural design with social pretensions. So, apart from the Benthamite monocularism, there is yet another pattern in history that reflects on you, whereas you present radical subjectivism as a real breakthrough.

The electronic paradigm directs a powerful challenge to architecture because it defines reality in terms of media and simulation, it values appearance over existence, what can be seen over what is. Not the seen as we formerly knew it, but rather a seeing that can no longer interpret. Media introduce fundamental ambiguities into how and what we see.

146

monocular subject by creating perspectival visions with multiple vanishing points so that there was no way of correlating what was seen into a unified whole. Equally, Cubism attempted to deflect the relationship between a monocular subject and the object. The subject could no longer put the painting into some meaningful structure through the use of perspective. Cubism used a non-monocular perspectival condition: it flattened objects to the edges, it upturned objects, it undermined the stability of the picture plane. Architecture attempted similar dislocations through Constructivism and its own, albeit normalising, version of Cubism – the International Style. But this work only looked cubistic and modern, the subject remained rooted in a profound anthropocentric stability, comfortably, upright and in place on a flat, tabular ground.

There was no shift in the relationship between the subject and the object. While the object looked different it failed to displace the viewing subject. Though the buildings were sometimes conceptualised, by axonometric or isometric projection rather than by perspective, no consistent deflection of the subject was carried out. Yet Modernist sculpture did in many cases effectuate such a displacement of the subject. These dislocations were fundamental to Minimalism: the early work of Robert Morris, Michael Heizer and Robert Smithson. This historical project, however, was never taken up in architecture. The question now begs to be asked: Why did architecture resist developments that were taking place in other disciplines? And further, why has the issue of vision never been properly problematised in architecture?*?!*

It might be said that architecture never adequately thought about the problem of vision because it remained within the concept of the subject and the four walls. Architecture, unlike any other discipline, concretised vision. The hierarchy inherent in all architectural space begins as a structure for the mind's eye. It is perhaps the idea of interiority as a hierarchy between inside and outside that causes architecture to conceptualise itself ever more comfortably and conservatively in vision. The interiority of architecture more than any other discourse defined a hierarchy of vision articulated by inside and outside. The fact that one is actually both inside and outside at architecture, unlike painting or music, required

Alteka Office Building, design, 1991

?! Because architecture is not only an art. Your thought seems quite exclusivist in the way that architecture as such is either willing to respond to or denying the contemporary cultural condition. But, whereas it responds in its narrative and metaphorical capacity, possibly it doesn't as a functional object or as a métier. As a consequence of your opinion, one could ask humankind why, after the debunking of the cognitive powers of Homo Sapiens, he still walks as a homo erectus. Your Alteka Tower reflects a wrong posed problem and emanates from a confusion of categories.

vision to conceptualise itself in this way. As long as architecture refuses to take up the problem of vision, it will remain within a Renaissance or Classical view of its discourse.

Now what would it mean for architecture to take up the problem of vision? Vision can be defined as essentially a way of organising space and elements in space. It is a way of 'looking at', and defines a relationship between a subject and an object. Traditional architecture is structured so that any position occupied by a subject provides the means for understanding that position in relation to a particular spatial typology, such as a rotunda, a transept crossing, an axis, an entry. Any number of these typological conditions deploy architecture as a screen for looking-at.

The idea of a 'looking-back' begins to displace the anthropocentric subject. Looking back does not require the object to become a subject, that is to anthropomorphosize the object. Looking back concerns the possibility of detaching the subject from the rationalisation of space. In other words to allow the subject to have a vision of space that no longer can be put together in the normalising, classicising or traditional construct of vision; an other space, where in fact the space 'looks back' at the subject. A possible first step in conceptualising this 'other' space, would be to detach what one sees from what one knows – the eye from the mind. A second step would be to inscribe space in such a way as to endow it with the possibility of looking back at the subject. All architecture can be said to be already inscribed. Windows, doors, beams and columns are a kind of inscription. These make architecture known, they reinforce vision. Since no space is uninscribed, we do not see a window without relating it to an idea of window, this kind of inscription seems not only natural but also necessary to architecture. In order to have a looking back, it is necessary to rethink the idea of inscription. In the Baroque and Rococo such an inscription was in the plaster decoration that began to obscure the traditional form of functional inscription. This kind of 'decorative' inscription was thought too excessive when undefined by function. Architecture tends to resist this form of excess in a way which is unique to the other arts, precisely because of the power and pervasive nature of functional inscription. The anomalous column at San Vitale inscribes space in a way that was at the time foreign to the eye. This is also true of the columns in the staircase at the Wexner Center. However most of such inscriptions are the result of design intention, the will of an authorial subjective expression which then only reconstitutes vision as before. To dislocate vision might require an inscription which is the result of an outside text which is neither overly determined by design expression or function. But how could such an inscription of an outside text translate into space? **?!**

Suppose for a moment that architecture could be conceptualised as a Moebius strip, with an unbroken continuity between interior and exterior. What would this mean for vision? Gilles Deleuze has proposed just such a possible continuity with his idea of the fold. For Deleuze, folded space articulates a new relationship between vertical and horizontal, figure and ground, inside and out – all structures articulated by traditional vision. Unlike the space of classical vision, the idea of folded space denies framing in favour of a temporal modulation. The fold no longer privileges planimetric projection; instead there is a variable curvature. Deleuze's idea of folding is more radical than origami, because it contains no narrative, linear sequence; rather, in terms of traditional vision, it contains a quality of the unseen.

Folding changes the traditional space of vision. That is, it can be considered to be effective; it functions, it shelters, it is meaningful, it frames, it is aesthetic. Folding also constitutes a move from effective to affective space. Folding is not another subject expressionism, a promiscuity, but rather unfolds in space alongside of its functioning and its meaning in space – it has what might be called an excessive condition or affect. Folding is a type of affective space which concerns those aspects that are not associated with the effective, that are more than reason, meaning and function.

In order to change the relationship of perspectival projection to three-dimensional space it is necessary to change the relationship between project drawing and real space. This would mean that one would no longer be able to draw with any level of meaningfulness the space that is being projected. For example, when it is no longer possible to draw a line that stands for some scale relationship to another line in space, it has nothing to do with reason, of the connection of the mind to the eye. The deflection from that line in space means that there no longer exists a one-to-one scale correspondence.

My folded projects are a primitive beginning. In them the subject understands that he or she can no longer conceptualise experience in space in the same way that he or she did in the gridded space. They attempt to provide this dislocation of the subject from effective space; an idea of presentness. Once the

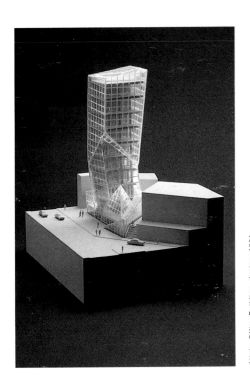

Peter Eisenman

Alteka Office Building, design, 1991

?! *Well, just wait for the real paradigm shift, instead of prescribe the phenomenon. If the mental equipment of men is simply correspondent to the new cultural condition you suggest, it will be very easy to dislocate vision. As a matter of fact, in the new paradigm there will be no more perspectival vision taken seriously. However, your very question implies all but a complete shift. (So architecture doesn't drag its feet.) Now, if we accept that yours is a historicistic (in Popperian terms) rather than a paradigmatic analysis, then your questions are valid. The problem still is that you try to project a metaphorical form, derived from culture, into architectural practice of the future again. This is reification. This is also the reason why a form that illustrates the so-called electronic paradigm is only entertaining for a moment, and should be updated all the time.*

Claude Gaçon, Objektive Weltsicht I, silk screen print, 1992

University of Cincinnati, College of Design, Architecture and Planning, design, 1991

environment becomes affective, inscribed with another logic or an ur-logic, one which is no longer translatable into the vision of the mind, then reason comes detached from vision. While we can still understand terms of its function, structure and aesthetic (we are still 'four walls') somehow reason becomes detached from the affective condition of the environment itself. This begins to produce an environment that 'looks back' that is, the environment has an order that we can perceive even though it does not seem to mean anything. It does not seek to be understood in the traditional way of architecture yet it possesses some sense of 'aura' logic which is the sense of something outside of our vision that is not another subjective expression. Folding is only one of perhaps many strategies for dislocating vision dislocating the hierarchy of interior and exterior that preempts vision.

The Alteka Tower project begins simultaneously with an 'el' shape drawn in both plan and section.

Here, a change in the relationship of perspectival projection to three) dimensional space changes the relationship between project drawing and real space. In this sense, these drawings would have little relationship to the space that is being projected. For example it is no longer possible to draw a line that stands for some scale relationship to another line in the space of the project, thus the drawn lines no longer have anything to do with reason, the connection of the mind to the eye. The drawn lines are folded with some ur) logic according to sections of a fold in René Thom's catastrophe theory. These folded sections in turn create an object, which is cut into from the ground floor to the top.

When the environment is inscribed or folded in such a way the individual no longer remains the discursive function; the individual is no longer required to understand or interpret space. Questions such as what the space means are no longer relevant. It is not just that the environment is detached from vision, but that it also presents its own vision, a vision that looks back at the individual. The inscription is no longer concerned with aesthetics or with meaning but with some other order. It is only necessary to perceive the fact that this other order exists; this perception alone dislocates the knowing subject.

The fold presents the possibility of an alternative to the gridded space of the Cartesian order. The fold produces a dislocation of the dialectical distinction between figure and ground; in the process it animates what Gilles Deleuze calls 'a smooth space'. Smooth space presents the possibility of overcoming

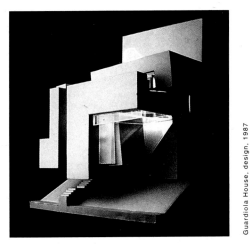

Guardiola House, design, 1987

Peter Eisenman

149

Folding changes the traditional space of vision. That is, it can be considered to be effective; it functions, it shelters, it is meaningful, it frames, it is aesthetic. Folding also constitutes a move from effective to affective space.

Jewellery (Ring), 1986

or exceeding the grid. The grid remains in place and the four walls will always exist but they are in fact overtaken by the folding of space. Here there is no longer one planimetric view which is then extruded to provide a sectional space. Instead it is no longer possible to relate a vision of space in a two-dimensional drawing to the three-dimensional reality of a folded space. Drawing no longer has any scale value relationship to the three-dimensional environment. This dislocation of the two-dimensional drawing from the three-dimensional reality also begins to dislocate vision, inscribed by this ur-logic. There are no longer grid datum planes for the upright individual.

Alteka is not merely a surface architecture or a surface folding. Rather, the folds create an affective space, a dimension in the space that dislocates the discursive function of the human subject and thus vision, and at the same moment creates a condition of time, of an event in which there is the possibility of the environment looking back at the subject, the possibility of the gaze.

The gaze according to Maurice Blanchot is that possibility of seeing which remains covered up by vision. The gaze opens the possibility of seeing what Blanchot calls the light lying within darkness. It is not the light of the dialectic of light/dark, but it is the light of an otherness, which lies hidden within presence. It is the capacity to see this otherness which is repressed by vision. The looking back, the gaze, exposes architecture to another light, one which could not have been seen before.

Architecture will continue to stand up, to deal with gravity, to have 'four walls'. But these four walls no longer need to be expressive of the mechanical paradigm. Rather the walls could deal with the possibility of these other discourses, the other effective senses of sound, touch and of that light lying within the darkness.

The Invisible in Architecture could be conceived as border. Without borders nothing can exist, or at least we cannot know of it. At the border, something ends and something else begins. Or *can* begin. A difference thus exists the moment we become aware of a border. Border creates order.

There are numerous shades of meaning in the 'border' concept. In its unmarked sense the term 'border' indicates a more or less humdrum, barely emphasised dividing line – something we can merely step over. We know there are differences between the domains on either side, but take no exception to this fact. Border controls have been abolished. The 'frontier' on the other hand is an evasive, mobile border, one we are forever about to reach but never quite reaching, something we still have to work towards. An unconstrained ambition pushes this frontier ever further even as we strain towards it. Frontiers are there to be advanced. Finally, there is the 'limit', an almost metaphysical boundary beyond which lies the eternally unknown. The limit is absolute, an impenetrable shell. Beyond the limit all is either sacrosanct or taboo.

These are the three variants of the concept that figure large in the current discourse on the border. This discourse has now become omnipresent. Wherever we raise our lantern, be it in culture, economy, biology or psychology, we stumble on not just the vocabulary but the symptoms of the borderline syndrome. Sometimes it seems as though an entire new branch of science has been created to tidy up the boundaries of identity and meaning. Its idiom swarms with terms like 'pataphysics', 'simulation', 'hyperreality', 'transgression', 'difference', 'semantic instability', 'deconstruction', 'disjunction', 'virtuality', 'decentring', 'fragmentation' and 'excess'. Were there no intrinsic coherence to be detected in this post-humanistic paradigm, we should think ourselves dissolving in some final entropy in which communication had become an a priori impossibility. Taking into account developments in transport, telematics, genetics and politics, we can hardly believe otherwise than that today's acute aware-

150 *Border*

ness of border is due to the fathomless crisis of the border itself (assuming the term crisis is still appropriate in this new paradigm).

The border is not only to be understood as the final station of the visible but also as the framework within which institutions and disciplines operate. Practice, training and even much criticism hamper discussion on that framework or moralise it into something dubious. It is acceptable to dress up the border or even discuss it in depth – but keep your hands off the social and economic actuality! In a world in which everything has become in-between, where there appear to be no borders, there are in fact certain vanishing points beyond which silence reigns. It is in the area past these vanishing points that micro-politics, macro-politics and possibilities of change have their domain. Our concern here is with the dominant mechanisms of repression, the invisible limits. By enthroning the border as the primordial subject of culture, we run the risk of losing sight of the differences that really matter; whereas our aim should be to throw some light on them.

The classical world view respected the border. The modernist world view ignored it. The post-modern world view has *problematised* it. We no longer face a border that surrounds us but carry the problem of the border within us. Our present culture is a borderline one, in which the border is simultaneously a problem everywhere and a philosophical imperative nowhere. The only border that receives collective support seems to be the one that is supposed to shield Western prosperity from interested parties elsewhere. Meanwhile, value judgements are becoming increasingly interchangeable. In the schizophrenetic border traffic between the true, the beautiful and the good and their respective counterparts, antinomies between irreconcilable extremes turn into related modalities. Standpoints vary effortlessly from hyperfuturism to the Club of Rome, from virtual reality

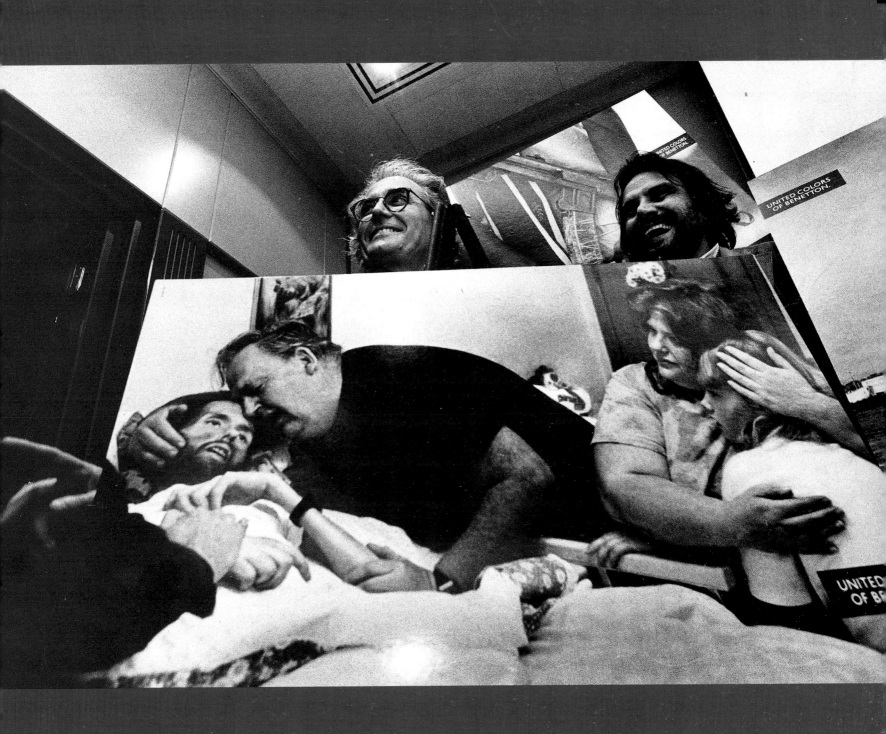

to the limits to growth. It is hardly surprising, in this situation, that the grotesque has become the most popular literary and visual device. He who is not grotesque is nothing, he simply no longer counts.

Our consciousness of border is supposed to have given us an eye for differences. But in as far as differences actually exist, they are chiefly prized for their form. United Colors of Benetton, for instance, glorifies purely outward diversity. Differences in mentality, calling or social class are smothered with a dense cosmetic layer. The tension between the actual and the possible is fudged into the superficial cliché of formal conciliation, a *promesse de bonheur* attenuated into a form which can conveniently be assimilated by production. At the same time, a homogenising ideology is propagated: consume and behave like us, or else... The result towards which this works is a pasteurised plurality in which people cease to take an interest in one another – the United Colors of Indifference. It thus becomes clear how form, as a critical intervention, allows itself to be sidelined and is forced to retreat behind the borders of its own domain. Form is emasculated as a means of creating and revealing boundaries. The borders are thereby reinstated with redoubled force. Material borders are growing indistinct, it is true: the Berlin Wall has fallen. But electronic, administrative and economic borders are continually being strengthened – borders that hinder unification, channel movement and help preserve countless forms of dependency. Borders tend to fade within the privileged cultural disciplines; here, distinction ceases to matter. Yet at the same time we disregard the borders that form the hidden preconditions for our privileged position.

In its role as shelter, habitation, construction and enclosure, architecture is concerned by definition with the problem of border: its major duties necessarily imply the demarcation of boundaries. Architecture must also invariably work within the limits created by the demands of usage. Moreover, it is a form of cultural speculation and as such participates in the crisis of border. And, precisely because it is itself border-creating by nature, it forms the ideal medium in which to tackle the problems of border. Usually this takes place in a mundane way, the issue being literally the border of the architecture, the boundary of the built mass. We then find ourselves at the level of the art form, which can delimit space in numerous conformations according to the standpoint one wishes to take: membrane, facade, interface, skin, mask, billboard etc. Merely the research into such interpretations of the physical border of a built object offers several footholds for the analysis of attitudes.

We can, furthermore, distinguish countless other manifestations of the border in architecture: production specialisms, functional differences in the programme, aesthetics, routing, physics, constructional joints, materials – every decision about these is also a statement about border. This all forms part of the architect's practical awareness of his *métier*.

There are, however, dimensions of the border experience that tend to be much less considered. This brings us to the institutional borders of architecture, to the economic bounds of yield and profit, to the restrictions of specified programmes. Surpassing even these constraints are those of a social configuration in which architecture has only a very limited sway, as a specialism of form within a mechanism that is further dominated by economic interests. It is illustrative of the reduction of the discipline to a specialism, that the debate about border is conducted purely in terms of craftsmanship. Rarely is an architect a participant in a cultural debate. All architecture can do is supply interesting 'events', i.e. one-off *tours de force* in form, which admittedly are formally capable of addressing the cultural problem of the border but nonetheless perpetuate the institutional constraints of architecture unaltered. This results in projects in which the architect has the freest possible rein in the surface and the circulation spaces but refrains from any direct involvement in the programme of requirements. The architectural object becomes principally a collage of *différends* which mark it out as a distinct work. Only after that claim has been satisfied can it return to being the declaration of a standpoint, and then only at an illustrative level e.g. of the dissolving borders that have developed into a leitmotif of culture. The question is whether, and how, this dilemma can play a role in the architect's practical work. While every border is being challenged, the architect is still expected to create borders. The more strongly he or she articulates this dilemma in design, the clearer it becomes that his or her position has been marginalised to that of a designer. It is in no small part due to this paradoxical situation that architecture is becoming increasingly a subject for cultural philosophy.

Three strategies and three architects Architects draw borders, whether they like (to believe) it or not. There are countless ways in which architecture can relate to the problem of border. We classify them as follows:

Archaism
The first strategy strives for the domestication of whatever lies beyond the frontier. Galí does not do this as part of an offensive process but by seeking the core of everything, an ultimate authenticity, and thereby constructing a defensive bulwark founded on the nature of things. An abstract interpretation of durability is concretised in a specific location with the spatial aid of tectonics, material, grid and path. This bulwark then stands in contrast to that modernity which rips up everything in its path. **Beth Galí** sees the border as an advancing front, with Design winning ground at the expense of Chaos, the *terra incognita* of the periphery. The border, whether between city and countryside, between private and public, between park and square or between footpath and road, is invariably designed with the greatest attention to detail. Nature is domesticated to the phenomenological level of the living room. The park becomes the outlet valve for the city.

Facadism
The second strategy sees the border as a mask that unambiguously represents an absolutised order. The form, both interior and exterior, refers to a redundant interpretation of the substance. The function is concealed behind a cogent image that defines its own laws. This façadism has elevated the border to a region, and restricts what the architecture has to say to that region. Memory is represented statically as a literal commonplace. **Rafael Moneo** treats his borders as a separate, discrete image with the aim of bringing the architectural object more than ever into the public arena. The border of the building is the facade, which is monumentally present and is to be experienced above all visually. Despite the powerful materiality, it is an image that 'sets the boundary' here. It is not just the border of the building but also a cultural boundary: a limit to the decline of the discipline or even of civilisation itself. A limit: so far and no further. Architecture, and *basta!*

Fascinism
The third strategy sees the border as something utterly flimsy if not materially dissolute. We can better speak of an interface, which indicates the aspiration to find the briefest possible transition between one thing and another. Identities fuse into a congestive maelstrom. Movement is the watchword. In architectural terms, this fascinist standpoint emerges chiefly as transparency. The building ceases to exist as mass. The impediment, whether in movement or in the view, is an outmoded idea. **Elisabeth Diller and Ricardo Scofidio** do all they can to exemplify and legitimise the porosity of categorical borders. They show that borders themselves depend on a consensus and that their transgression is thereby guaranteed in advance. The border of Diller and Scofidio is the border in its simplest sense; border traffic is now unimpeded. They show us the intermediary between man and machine. Architecture is a prosthesis – no, man is an appendage of the machine.

In our philosophy, a house can grow along with the needs of its occupants. The architecture of the future will be such that the building will envelop its occupants like a third skin – the first being our natural skin, our clothing the second.

Ton Alberts & Max van Huut

In the series of urban houses I have designed up to now, the walls were intended to question the nature of contemporary society. The exterior environment is invariably cut off, and a new, separate world is created inside. **Tadao Ando**

To configure space means to play with limits. Sometimes a building's frieze is the beginning of the limitless vault of heaven – limitless like the architect's profession.

Ricardo Bofill

One operates within the limits of architecture, one attempts at times to push the limit but always from inside. We are no longer interested in symbolisation. The great game of signs is no longer of any consequence. Architecture if it is to be at all must firstly be itself. It must know its own form. We prefer to articulate ourselves by placing objects in the world.

Julia Bolles & Peter Wilson

The laws of statics say that in the world of criticism certain things you can do and can't do. But the new moralists say there are things you shouldn't do. Why is it not permissible when it is possible? **Santiago Calatrava**

Think of an intermediary architecture on that edge between people's lives and the given city, a kind of city furniture poised to refurbish rather than rebuild... Build in fictional gestures and narrative side-steps, because peripheral ingredients can upgrade reality when thrown in with it.

Nigel Coates & Doug Branson

Precisely because it has limits, architecture speaks to us of what is excluded by the limits, of the mystery of life and death, of the mystery which gives us a significance as particular entities, as human beings. **Pietro Derossi**

The body as site cannot be detached from the body as situation. The body enters our work as content rather than source, preformed, and de-territorialised with matter and event. Ubiquitous and inert. **Elisabeth Diller & Ricardo Scofidio**

The excellent runway of over 3000m already at Stansted, is able to accommodate all the planned increase in traffic. The runway is well aligned. The terminal zone is situated at the south east end of the runway with enough land to expand from 8 million passengers per annum to 15 million passengers per annum. **Norman Foster**

The main access to the Parc de l'Escorxador, on axis with one of the streets of the Cerdá grid, divides the Joan Miró Library into two symmetrical wings – one for adults and one for children. Crossing through a narrow passage of parallel walls, one finally gains the open space of the park. **Beth Galí**

I had a funny notion that you could make architecture that you could bump into it before you realise it was architecture. **Frank Gehry**

...I'm sure it's true world-wide, the sculpture you're asking for – the depth of the façade, the chiaroscuro, requires a construction technique that allows for recession and advancement of the wall plane and, my dear, that is very expensive.

Michael Graves

Ultimately, my goal is to create a place that houses the world, to enclose within an apparently delimited space the universe. **Itsuko Hasegawa**

A conception of architecture which treats structure and dressing, material and space, as mutually independent categories appears to be the most adaptable to circumstances. But the playful, accidental moment which results from architectural unity dissolving into computerised data cannot be one-sidedly brought into play by architectural decorators. All interested civilians, civilian associations and associations of tenants should take part in this. Each building will then express a collective compromise, the specific taste of a restricted moment as experienced by both users and authorities.

Jacques Herzog & Pierre de Meuron

On the fringe of the modern city, displaced fragments sprout without intrinsic relationships to existing organisation, other than that of the camber and loops of the curvilinear
freeway. Here the 'thrown away' spreads itself outward like the nodal lines of a stone
tossed into a pond. The edge of a city is a philosophical region, where city and natural
landscape overlap, existing without choice or expectation. This zone calls for visions and
projections to delineate the boundary between the urban and the rural. Visions of a city's
future can be plotted on this partially spoiled land, liberating the remaining natural landscape, protecting the habitat of hundreds of species of animals and plants that are threatened with extinction. What remains of the wilderness can be preserved; defoliated territory can be restored. In the middle zone between landscape and city, there is hope for a new
synthesis of urban life and urban form. **Steven Holl**

Architects have to stop thinking in terms of building only.
Hans Hollein

Unless zoning ordinances, planning and building briefs are radically rewritten, architects
can do nothing but contribute to the ecological holocaust that is now underway.
Leon Krier

Despite the invention of bureaucracy and of its mechanical organisation at the beginning
of the twentieth century, architecture knows no bounds: its apparent limitations are rapidly dissolving. Only modern architects imprison themselves in their own pigeon holes.
Lucien Kroll

The term intermediary zone is useful when considering the symbiosis of interior and
exterior space. In Western culture, particularly in the currents of modern thought that
are based on rationalism, it is considered important to clearly differentiate between any
two distinct phenomena. But by dividing all of existence into either yes or no, interior or
exterior, mind or body, the warmth that lies at the border between the two extremes is
lost, sacrificed to rationality. **Kisho Kurokawa**

The Werf/G.D.H.-terrain is an uncompromising project which is becoming fantastic. It
scores so high because the client was prepared to invest in the materials, to choose
somewhat more expensive bricks and construct a new quay using the old stones from the
wharf. Everything has been designed, the layout does not stop at the front door.
Lucien Lafour & Rikkert Wijk

When one thinks back about the 1960s or 1950s and the more ideological prej-
udices of architecture, one sees how limited these people were, because they
didn't have access to certain materials, to certain architectures. They only
knew about rebuilding in certain patterns and certain clichés about world
order. I don't know any architect who believes these things any more. The pic-
ture is now more scattered and confusing and much more open, which I think
is good. There are more interesting things coming than might appear from
what is being built. **Daniel Libeskind**

Architecture arrives when our thoughts about it acquire the
real condition that only materials can provide. By accepting
and bargaining with limitations and restrictions, with the act
of construction, architecture becomes what it really is.
Rafael Moneo

If you want to follow architecture's first rule, break it.
Bernard Tschumi

A channel is a limit on two sides with the others left open for growth. Early Modern
architects perhaps channelled rather than limited their ideas on architecture, achieving
force through the narrowness of their definition. In the end, the limitations proved too
narrow for the breadth of problems faced and the tastes of the society. This does not
mean that limits and channels don't apply today. They must merely be sought in other
ways. Each architect brings to the task a multi-layered set of ideas, preoccupations, and
proclivities, as well as years of training; these condition a response. There is not a clear
slate at the beginning of the design; the question is whether the limits in application are
those that can help architects creatively channel their ideas. The sonnet form with its
limitations on length, rhythm, and rhyme, has been a vehicle for the highest expression
in poetry. For us, the limits have to do with questions of scale and appropriateness.
Owing to our studies of Las Vegas we have at times been accused of taking liberties or
producing libertine architecture, when we have merely been looking for new parameters,
new guidelines. We search for limits but for those arising from within the problem.
Robert Venturi & Denise Scott Brown

España Invertebrada Revisited

The edge of Barcelona. Llobregat. Behind the brow of Montjuïc. The sun is at its zenith. After a long search through the baking hot outskirts of Barcelona, we reach the goal of our journey: Fossar de la Pedrera, an old quarry where Franco had a group of Catalan anarchists machine-gunned in 1939. As well as being a mass grave and a memorial, the spot is now a park. We lie on an immaculately trimmed lawn, surrounded by a ridge of hills, recovering in the shade. The grass is lush and deliciously soft, and the coolness is sheer luxury. Not far away, two youths are flying kites. One of them climbs to the top of the hill and lets his kite soar to an immense height. Now and then groups of foreign tourists pass by. They are clearly not here to honour the dead, but to enjoy this lovely park with its distinctive atmosphere, which was designed by Beth Galí.

The tranquillity is suddenly and rudely broken. A helmet-clad police officer on a motorbike comes growling and bouncing up the path. His heavy, off-the-road machine surmounts the carefully placed obstacles with ease. He takes the final steps up to the lawn with a flamboyant leap. Turning off his engine, he beckons to us. He points to our camera. Didn't we know it was forbidden to photograph graves? Had we no respect for the dead? He is satisfied with our explanation that we are not photographing the tombstones but the park itself, a jewel of landscape architecture. We congratulate him on his working surroundings. Gratified, he takes off again, the rumble of his machine echoing long around the quarry walls.

Now the sun has moved on too. We leave the oasis. Walking along the ridge we find ourselves in an ill-defined outlying district spread out along the harbour. Our bus will stop here in twenty minutes. Suddenly, we are involved with the police again. Who are we, our passports please, what are we doing here. As they talk to us, a group of youths emerges from the shadows of a deserted warehouse and start making their way towards us. The officers get back in their car and drive off. Surely they must have seen this ominous-looking gang. In the park, the strong arm had been there to point out our errors; here, where we really need it, it is powerless. We are alone in the underworld. Moments later we peer into the barrel of a revolver. The youths, five of them, are testing our nerves. We hear their questions, but from their nature it is clear we need to play the innocent tourist. We do not understand a word, we know nothing and are just looking for nice places to visit. One of the boys slaps his dog and forces his snout in our direction. We try to explain how we think the grass of the Fossar de la Pedrera must be good for football. They have heard of our compatriots and football stars Johan Cruyff and Ronald Koeman, haven't they? We haul a few architecture magazines out of our bag to distract their attention. It works! Gradually the mood becomes more relaxed. The youths thumb through the magazines and visibly inflate on recognising pictures of Galí's designs. The dog, confused by its master's obvious teasing, starts looking more playful than murderous. The pistol disappears into a pocket. They begin to understand that we have come to visit their world. It is as though we were two of them. Of course they will not rob us. We made it. Thank you, Beth Galí!

Design as a Strategy of the Left

The following morning we visit the office of the city councillor for culture, Oriol Bohigas. He dismisses our account of yesterday's adventures with the laconic remark that there is always a chance of running into *marginales* in the outskirts of town. It's just the kind of thing they do, he says, relighting his cigar. Later in our conversation, he admits that

Montjuïc Cemetery, new access and new design of north façade, Barcelona, 1992

Et in Arcadia Ego

The treatment of the natural limits, left more or less untouched in the Beth Galí's Fossar de la Pedrera, transfers the issue of border on a different level: the limit we project becomes that between life and death, present and past. The strong physical quality of the surrounding rock cliffs gives this sacred place a special intimacy, while at the same time allowing a direct and exclusive contact with the sky. If the empty lawn is to be seen as a reflection of the sky above, then it also can be interpreted as infinite. It is only thanks to the absence of any architectural intervention on the vertical walls of the quarry, that the abstraction of the horizontal plane of the lawn can be achieved: the eye perceives a physical boundary which gives no temporal clues as the mountain was there since time immemorial. The very presence of the enclosure hints at the presence of something beyond.

Alessandra Dini

Wandering about on a land that we love is a liberating experience. The grasping and releasing of lush terrain, revelling in physical powers at their heights of play with the ground below, probing here and there with our footprints as we please, unfettered by instincts or mechanisms, brings on a primal freedom known only to man. The earthen passage carries us back to our origins, to the beginnings of the human adventure, renewing an urge to explore that can be traced to paleolithic times, even to hominid ventures out of the trees, as well as to the earliest gropings of infancy. The passage also gives rise to an exquisite mutation of being. Through fleeting moves people learn about and release their innermost selves by the simplest of means, expressing hidden traits about who they potentially are, from the many available, giving momentary form to their latent identity. And most urgently, every surge onward in space and time calls the body itself back to life, as impassioned flesh and bone, a figure struggling to be free of itself and burst out of its frame in a wave of being, resurrecting one's very existence in the world.

Henry Plummer

Parc del Migdia, Barcelona, 1992

given the chance he would domesticate the rougher inhabitants by offering them all a well-furnished plaza. By treating public space as though it were a bourgeois living room, he hopes to soothe the threats of social conflict by the benefice of public design. Earlier that week, during our local investigations of Galí's work, we had seen how that worked. Parc Joan Miró, designed by Beth Galí and others, has a pool with a Miró sculpture standing large as life in the middle; and there we encountered a couple of derelicts bathing in the fresh running water, art within grasp. Clearly, as far as they were concerned the park was an excellent public facility. At this commodious address, the internal strife of a rapidly modernising city can be smoothed over. Bathing is unofficially tolerated.

Barcelona has won worldwide admiration for this approach. Since the death of Franco, public space has been rehabilitated at countless locations in the city centre. After socialists gained control of local government, they started a programme of rehabilitating the city's social connective tissue. Their success can best be measured in terms of the enthusiastic use that is made of the new city squares. There was no longer the money, the ideology or, above all, the élan for all-out radical plans. The city sought its salvation in a moderate remedial policy, which eventually resulted in a striking visual rejuvenation. Barcelona has become a typical example of a successful transformation on the basis of modest expectations. The self-disillusionment of the Left as a social system has paradoxically produced a wonderful metamorphosis. But does that apply to the *whole* of Barcelona? Have the problems really been solved? Not for the kids in the harbour, certainly. And nearly not for us . . .

The city authorities are well aware that the job is not yet finished. This is why visual improvement is continuing all around the outskirts. Beth Galí is involved again. She has already received international attention for her graveyard design of 1986, mentioned above. But her Parc del Migdia and Sot del Migdia, on the other side of Montjuïc,

are at least as ambitious. There, she has restyled a complete landscape in accordance with the well-proved design method we met in her earlier projects.

In the Migdia project, Galí unwittingly reveals the limitations of Barcelona's environmental policies. We can see how the continued, self-satisfied administration of an ideologically disillusioned but socially highly successful Left has resulted in a practically religious faith in the persuasiveness of design. Design was once a means to achieving the impossible, the rebirth of Barcelona. The world gaped at Barcelona's feats in this area. But is that enough to secure the future of a city?

From *Memento Mori* to Picnic Site

Montjuïc used to be regarded as a holy mount, as the *Alter Barcelona*, as the negative of the city – literally so, because it was the location of the quarry that supplied the stone to build the city. It was also the place of the dead, and a place where city dwellers could go for a breath of fresh air. These alternative functions vanished when the world exhibition and the Olympic Games came to the mountain. Not even Galí's Parc del Migdia and Sot del Migdia could restore the old tranquillity. It is no longer an alternative for the city, but an extension of a certain kind of urbanity into the landscape. Galí called the chief route through her plan a *Rambla*, referring to the famous promenade below in the city. It is not nature that is 'designed' here, but the city using the means of nature.

Beth Galí demonstrates a perfect control of her craft in these plans. With consummate skill, she transforms fifteen years of Barcelona urban design experience into a marvellous rural *mise-en-scène*. Using the means at her disposal – shadows, paving, greenery etcetera – she traces the sweeping lines of her designs in the earth. Her manipulation of *chiaroscuro* is masterly. Like other celebrities in her field such as Dimitris Pikionis and Georges Descombes, she transfers ostensibly isolated signs from an iconographical plane onto a phenomenological one. The observer's experience is supremely activated by these places. Nature is the ink – or, rather, the B6 pencil – she uses to sketch the background for a carefree life. All kinds of natural elements, including different kinds of wood and inorganic materials, scents, shadows and shafts of light, form the colours of her palette. Natural materials and light are deployed in an almost typographical way, resulting in a park as a form of graphic art. Edges, canopies, pergolas, areas of glass and bandstands are scattered with feigned nonchalance, betraying an exceptional subtlety. Every distinct function of surface, route and point receives its own formal treatment in the design. Galí plays with scale, repetitions, interruptions, lines and profiles. The cross-section determines the landscape. She does not work from above, placing an oppressive grid over the terrain, but microscopically examines every ridge, convexity, prospect and soil variation. She works at ground level, taking a worm's eye view. Even the gravestones of the Fossar demarcate a horizon in the landscape. The view is from below – the viewpoint of the dead, we are tempted to say. Here, time stands still.

There is something else morbid about this place. For in spite of – or perhaps even because of – the refinement contained in this landscape, it is all too clean, too finished.

At this point we enter the universe of clichés. When Galí wishes to mark the transition to the graveyard, she does so by making a gateway like a house of cards. What a coincidence, life is like a house of cards too! Then, right along the length of the necropolis, she extends a semi-transparent screen, making the zone behind it into a realm of shadows. What an original idea! Design surpasses itself to become an analogue of the literary. Even the experience-heightening technique that has garnered such worldwide praise in the Barcelona method appears to lead all too easily here to little representational jokes. When we also consider the exceptionally fine lawns, we get the impression of a cloak of charity being drawn over death and the history (and hence also the future) of life in Barcelona. The cloak is ambiguous by definition. The *memento mori* has become a picnic site. Come and visit the dead, but not for purposes of contemplation. Death is not a part of life but of life-style. Even death is covered up by the social democratic politics of conciliation. Everything is brought down to a profane, mundane level, like an endless funeral tea.

In the park, every path has been laid out to encourage pauses and thus the enjoyment of the varied landscapes and the variety of materials. There is a repeated emphasis on experiencing the landscape as a whole *(the belvederes)* or a special physical detail

Fossar de la Pedrera, Barcelona, 1986

Ludger Gerdes, 'Dood' (Death), Floriade Park, Zoetermeer, 1992

Designer talent is so omnipresent that there is hardly any room left for spontaneity in social behaviour, conducted as it is along the prescribed routes and interrupted only by the equally obligatory belvederes. Meeting is fostered only by moments of visual awe: all you can say is 'Beautiful, isn't it?' In this place one can fly kites, seek cool repose, stroll. Taking it easy is the ultimate good. The Parc del Migdia is a paradise of civilised behaviour, an extension out to the periphery of the zones where *marginales* are tolerated. The leftist policy of small scale interventions and improving examples is inflated here into a full-blown paradigm.

(e.g. a subtle step). On the other hand, social encounter is something which is not allowed for in the programme. Just as strolling is something from which chance has been eliminated here, we are not expected to see one another as anything more than items in the pastoral decor. The urban park is here rather like a private garden. You come to rest, and for that purpose the park is perfect. However, it has thereby lost the character of an open-air theatre. Perambulation is revered as a Sunday fetish. (Admittedly, a free Sunday afternoon was never the right moment for a revolution). This park is a social democratic variant of the English romantic garden, with the

Library Joan Miro, Barcelona, 1990

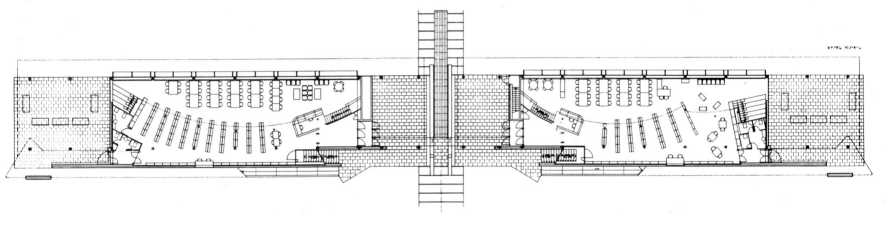

Fossar de la Pedrera, Barcelona, 1986

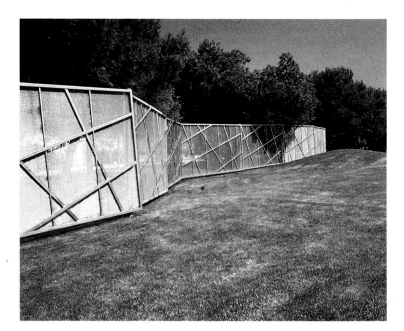

Parc del Migdia, Barcelona, 1992

emphasis no longer on the sublime experience, the simulated Chaos, but on the relaxing ramble. You will not find a speaker's corner in this park. And thus it accords with a tradition of comfortable apathy that has emerged in Spain since the definitive extirpation of the Franco legacy. However, all this is hopelessly insufficient for someone who has been privileged to stare down the barrel of a gun while walking down by the harbour. No doubt this applies to the owner of the weapon, as well.

Barcelona's programme of parks and plazas, of which this park is such an excellent example, concentrates entirely on promoting the existence of nice places to be in. Congeniality and direct solutions to concrete problems are primary. What characterises these locations is their strongly pacifying character. The designers have discovered that it is perfectly possible to achieve this end by taking an extremely sophisticated, tactilist approach. Urban problems prove manageable by means of a strictly autonomous, principally tectonic approach to the craft. The citizen must be brought into close, even haptic, contact with his city. But when that happens, the citizen no longer functions as such, but as the anthropological unit 'human being' who is presumed to have a uniform level of need for material identification with his environment. In a metropolitan environment the tactile experience is generally so strongly repressed that people are only too happy to agree with efforts to rehabilitate it. Nobody resists. Nobody wishes to be specific here, let alone angry. The daily need passes for a long-term goal. As a result, public space no longer forms part of the public ambience but has become a consumable commodity, drained of every political nuance. *Mañana* is the message. And is that so surprising? Even death has been banished from this life. Nothing may be allowed to remind us of the time when death was at the service of life. The heroes lie beneath the green sod, and thereby, unwittingly, this life has been placed at the service of death. Consciousness of the social situation has been downgraded to a topo-

graphical palliative. The senses are stimulated in order to dull the prick of moral awareness. A subtle game is played with pastorality and material boundaries, to save us having to think about the social boundaries. This totally depoliticised design is, however, far from value-free. It signifies the cultural condition that has overtaken many metropolises: the formal mitigation of stresses that are material in origin. Form, reinforced here by an architect of unimpeachable talent, acts as a distraction from the failure to solve social discords.

From Dissension to Diversion

José Ortega y Gasset wrote, in 1921, a famous essay called *España Invertebrada*, in which he accused his country of moral spinelessness. Spain was an impotent, incompetent also-ran. This image is still applicable, albeit in a slightly different sense. The triumph of topographical tectonics appears to have banished both the formulation of a political will and the programmatic and environmental articulation of such a will into a definitive background role. The retreat into phenomenology 'brackets' every criticism. As a design strategy, it begins from its materials and seeks the integrity of things. It is thus capable of constituting a relevant critique of the indifference of the metropolis. But after a while one gets the impression that the search for integrity is not only a necessary condition for critical resistance, but also a sufficient condition. At that point, the Heideggerian critique of civilisation starts sounding merely good-humoured. Things that should have been mute start babbling away again. The *España Invertebrada* of today is a bastion of the stylistic faith. The outward tactility no longer has anything to do with that resistance that some hoped to see in it, in their search for an answer to cultural globalisation. This is not an architecture of dissension but of diversion.

Sot del Migdia (open air auditorium)

Fossar de la Pedrera (memorial)

Parc del Migdia (belvedere)

The Fossar was originally a stone quarry with a common grave of people who fell victim to the Franco regime; now it is a memorial. The design of this space grows from within, to reach its natural borders without interfering with them. Thus it acquires an abstract lack of dimension that allows us to go beyond its limits: the limit we project becomes that between life and death, present and past.

If the Fossar de la Pedrera is the transformation of a natural place into a sacred precinct, the auditorium of the Sot del Migdia is its secular counterpoint. As in the Fossar de la Pedrera, the project nestles in the natural landscape which contains and defines its space, but whereas in the Fossar the only direct contact with the outside is through the sky, in the Sot the view of the whole city confronts the empty space and becomes the auditorium's backdrop. The effect plays on our subconscious memory of theatres whose space is delimited by a backdrop, which may create the illusion of depth but which we know to be only a thin plane. The city, seen in this context, loses all materiality and the limit of the auditorium flips back and forth between being infinite and two-dimensional.

Being a space which is occupied in its entirety, the point of contact with the vertical walls of the mountain

becomes particularly delicate. While in the Fossar the absence of construction on the far side of the 'sacred' lawn allows it to extend indefinitely, here, where the space had to have a limit, we encounter three sloping elements which contain the auditorium as theatre boxes. These platforms perform the transition from the built landscape to the natural one, at the same time counterbalancing the concrete bleachers on the theatre side. Thus, the central space is perceived as an intentional, rather than casual, depression in the landscape. Along the perimeter, the mountains become spectators, at the same time marking the border with the Migdia Park which extends along their side at a higher level, filling the landscape between the Fossar, the wall of the cemetery, and the auditorium. Seen from the park, the auditorium with its patterns of coloured asphalt becomes another piece of landscape and a logical continuation of the park itself. With its irregular shape and large scale, the park is organised and understood through the paths zigzagging its entire surface: whenever they reach a limit, they pierce it with a sharp, wedge-shaped balcony which seems to throw the visitor towards the city, seen in the distance. The aggressiveness of these balconies succeeds in stretching the virtual space of the park over the whole city. *Beth Galí*

▶

Location Montjuïc, Barcelona, Spain **Assistants** J. Arriola, J. Benavent, M. Quintana and others **Client** Municipality of Barcelona **Design** 1984-89 **Completion** 1984-92

Galí/Quintana Arquitectes *Cemetery and Memorial, Open-air Auditorium and Public Park*

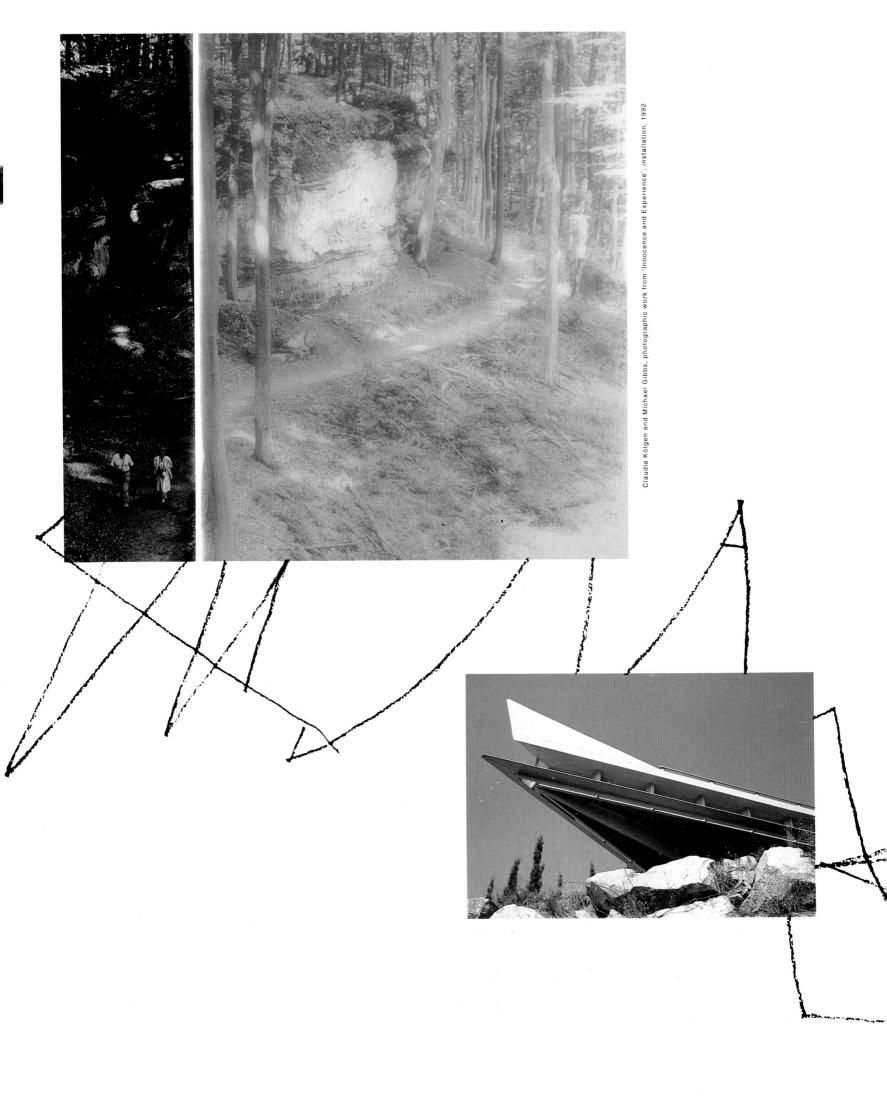

Claudia Kölgen and Michael Gibbs, photographic work from 'Innocence and Experience', installation, 1992

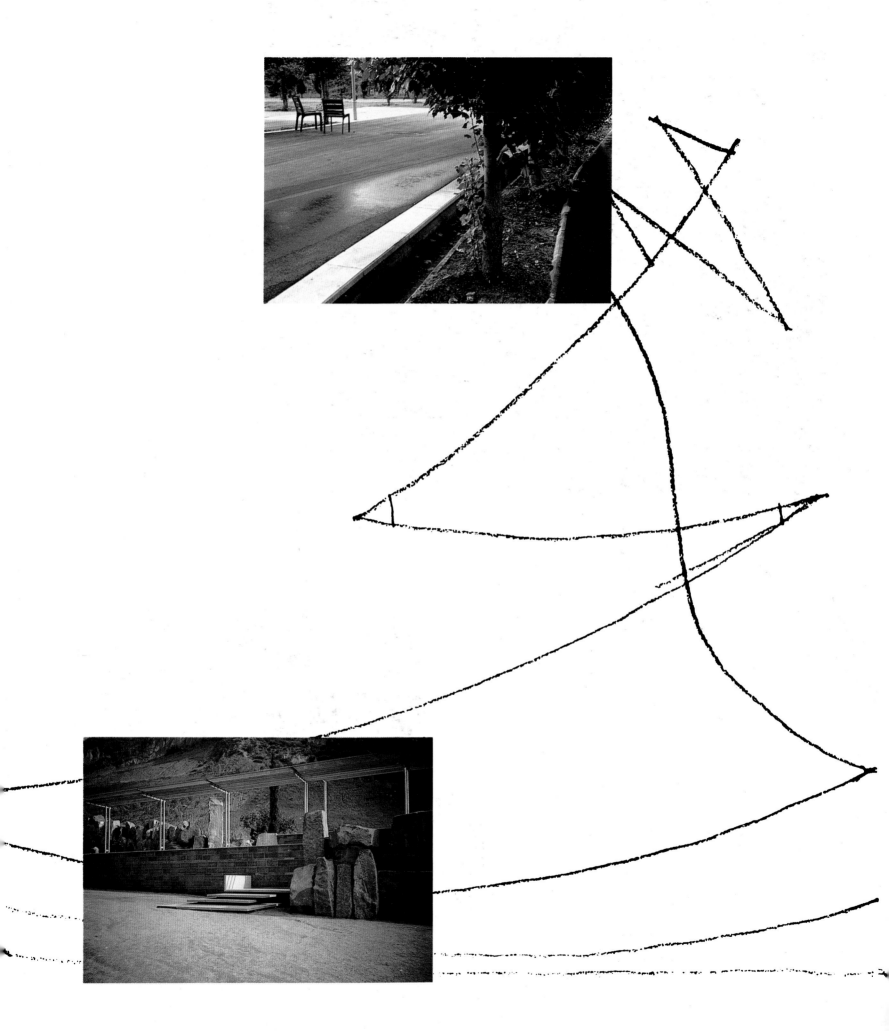

On the Work of Rafael Moneo
¡No Pasarán!
Moneomentality for our Times

What's in a name? First name Rafael alludes to a message from Up There. Surname Moneo is Latin for 'I remind' and also 'I admonish'. Seldom can an oeuvre fit its maker's name as well as this – at least, when we consider Rafael Moneo as a builder of monuments.

Adolf Loos considered tombs and memorials to be the only kinds of architecture that could be classed as art. In all other respects, the duty of architecture was to be useful. He took this standpoint because he wished to free architecture from the countless pseudo-artistic compulsions that obscured the true nature of the craft.

Measured against the bloodless functionalist rhetoric of the Modern Movement, the influence of Loos' ideas was overwhelming. In declaring war on Ornament, Architecture seemed to be saying goodbye to Art. To judge by their words, the members of the architectural community actually came to believe this was what they had done. But in retrospect, were they not deluding themselves? In its highly successful role as purveyor of universally lifeless slabs and boxes, Modernism looks not unlike a movement for the promotion of the necropolis. Its crowning product has been the dormitory suburb, with apartment blocks like serried ranks of tombstones, modular façades like neatly stacked funerary urns, and a population piled up as though already resting on the Far Side.

Parallel to the early Modern Movement, there were still some traditionalists who wilfully resorted to the monumental. Architects varying from the social democrat Berlage to the fascist Speer designed consciously monumental structures to express higher artistic principles. That was their job as artists, after all. And it was not long before some architects within the necropolistic ranks of Modernism became aware of a need for a similar, explicit monumentalisation of the anonymous slab. We can see traces as early as the forties. For Giedion et. al., the sober visual programme of the architectural gravediggers had become a little too successful. Post-Modernism has pursued this idea of the monument as a unique work of art, developing it into what urbanist Bernard Huet called 'a fist in the belly' of the contemporary city.

So this was architecture's aesthetic answer to the ethical plea of Adolf Loos (an answer Loos provided himself anyway by his own monumentality and his wish to express programmatic 'moods'). Loos warned architects that if they felt they had to make art, then they would find themselves restricted to those areas where image and function were identical (and where it also served as a physical and spiritual receptacle for the past), namely the tomb and the memorial. In that case 'architecture' would no longer be concerned with life and the world and would thus have abandoned its utilitarian function.

But in an age marked by extreme specialisation and social compartmentalisation, the role of the artist is a much more attractive one than servitude to utility. Only the artist is free – and you don't give up a position like that for an ethical revival, even if you do choose to suggest the opposite. Loos thought that having drawn his distinction, the

Rafael Moneo and Manuel de Solà Morales, Diagonal Block, Barcelona, 1993

conclusion was simple: live in truth. But subsequent generations of architects preferred to live in falsehood rather than give up being artists. Hence the necropolises and the monuments.

This view of Modernist architecture is admittedly a provocative one and we could obviously sketch a different, more flattering version of the history of twentieth century architectural utilitarianism (a version which has many more adherents). We could also define the role of the artistic calling in architecture differently. But if we can point to anyone whose preference for monumentalism fits our version of history, then it must be Rafael Moneo.

Construction, Moneomentality and Res Publica

Monuments are supposed to be greeted with respect and silence. The American architect Kevin Roche, referring to Moneo's Mérida Museum of Roman Art, once expressed it as follows: 'This is one of the examples where the building is convincing, but the explanation isn't... So it seems to me you would be much better off without the explanation. Give us the building.'

All right, here you are. The building arises from the context in as far as the materials, its relation to urban morphology and the historical significance of the site are concerned. It reacts both to the vernacular of the surroundings and to the Roman remains above which it stands. But in spite of these signs of adjustment there is no way in which it could be called modest. On the contrary it is primarily monumental, and for at least three reasons. Firstly, being built on top of an archaeological site with catacombs and all that, it has all the features of a Piranesian *mise en-scène*. Imposing an orthogonal grid on the old foundations creates an irregular pattern with an extremely evocative

Is architecture today no longer able to endure as it did in the past? In today's architecture does there exist the sensation that works are perishable? I think these questions must be answered affirmatively, and only in so doing will we be able to oppose such a tendency, by acknowledging the gratifying way in which buildings accepted their own lives in the past.
Rafael Moneo

If the past now includes the ordinary traces of old everyday life among its valued contents, there are different things to be said about the sense of uniqueness which hangs over the celebrated objects within its changing repertoire. This sense of uniqueness may indeed still characterise precious works of art, but in recent times it has drifted far from its old academic moorings and it can now be held in common by, say, a phrase of rhyming slang, an old piece of industrial machinery (preferably in situ), a hand-painted plate from the turn of the century and a cherished landscape or place. It is not merely official cultural policy which determines the meaning or the extent of the modern past. The uniqueness of heritage objects may indeed be pointed out in

official guidebooks, but it is far more powerfully expressed in the vernacular measures of everyday life, the unique heritage object has aura, and in this respect the national heritage seems to have a persistent connection with earlier traditions of bourgeois culture – a connection which may even be especially strong as the modern past reaches out to include not masterpieces but the modest objects of bygone everyday life in its repertoire.
Patrick Wright

When we build, let us think that we build forever.
John Ruskin

Cemetery, Granada

spatiality. Here the monumentality is psychological in nature. Secondly, the simple main form has a gigantic volume, giving it a monumentality reminiscent of Peter Behrens' attempts to reconcile industrial and historic architecture. Here, the monumentality is morphological. Finally, the building shares much of the character of the nineteenth-century museum in which historical glory had to be expressed in full. To achieve this, all the material, spatial and illumination registers are pulled open. In this respect, the monumentality is above all institutional.

The meaning of this monumentality is something we can readily analyse, but the Mérida Museum's mood of concentration and contemplation is a less tangible affair. Words would only sully this exalted atmosphere with the vanities and subjectivism of everyday language. To Moneo, the building is always the touchstone for the word. We never catch him uttering elaborate theories. His work must first and foremost speak for itself. As a representative of the Madrid school, his architecture is earnest and imperious. Allowing ourselves to be tempted into obvious geo-historical clichés, we could also link his work with the introversion and barren inhospitability of the *Meseta Central*. The Counter-reformation Catholicism of Castile, Philip II and his El Escorial spring to mind. This is the architecture of Madrid the power centre.

But although Moneo lets the spatial-historic context speak through his work, he speaks principally for himself. His special mixture of autonomous type and specific context gives his architecture the universally admired stature of a solid, sensible statement amid the incessant gabble of architectural utterances that threatens to deafen us. It is this impression of solidity that lasts. Moneo is not solely interested in claiming a status as an independent artist. He believes an artistically purified architecture is capable of fulfilling a public duty, to restore an age-old link between building and society which has fallen into neglect. The form of a building used to be largely determined by the method of construction. This could be seen in the building itself and thus gave the building a measure of transparency, general comprehensibility and authenticity. However, modern building technology has made form independent of its construction, which is now no longer evident from the appearance of the building. This partly explains the totally arbitrary exteriors produced by the architectural packaging industry. Architecture and building no longer necessarily go together.

> 'Today arbitrariness of form is evident in the buildings themselves, because construction has been dealt out of the game of design. When arbitrariness is so clearly visible in the buildings themselves, architecture is dead; what I understand as the most valuable attribute of architecture disappears.'★

This statement on the death of architecture and its loss of tectonic substance is not in the least exaggerated. On the contrary, Moneo regards exaggeration and irony as signs of the profession's decadence. It is specifically his lack of ironic distance from the métier that makes Moneo look more and more like a new hero, not afraid to take up arms against the pervasive exhaustion of meaning. He takes the means of the craft as his guide – the constructional technique, the typology and the properties of the material – with the aim of making a 'legible' public architecture. It is striking that he establishes his communication with the public not so much by the transparency of his construction as by the recognisability of forms and types, his monumentality and tactile proximity. And how could he do otherwise? Now that architecture has, in Moneo's words, 'lost its necessary contact with society and, as a result, has become a private world',★ a transparent structure can no longer really denote the *Res Publica*. It is now more critical than ever that we pose ourselves the Wittgensteinian question, 'Can there be architecture where there's nothing to glorify?'

★ Moneo, Rafael, 'The Solitude of Buildings', *Architecture and Urbanism* 8 (1989), pp. 36-37.

★ Moneo, Rafael, op. cit. p. 36.

Whom Should One Glorify?

This immediately brings us face to face with the present status of the monument, the device that Moneo has made into the *leitmotif* of his work. A monument is literally something that reminds. In Lewis Mumford's words, 'The monument is a declaration of love and admiration attached to the higher purposes men hold in common'; to which he adds, 'An age that has deflated its values and lost sight of its purposes will not produce convincing monuments.' Perhaps Moneo sees the monumental qualities of his buildings merely as an expression of permanence. But even if his intentions are this modest, the cultural implications of his monumentality remain precarious. Sigfried Giedion already perceived this problem in 1943 when he wrote, 'Monuments are (...) only possible in periods in which a unifying consciousness and unifying culture exists. Periods which exist for the moment have been unable to create lasting monuments.' Admittedly, in a direct reaction to Mumford, Giedion expressed the opinion that there really was a genuine modern monumentality which could be found in the work of Brancusi, Arp or Picasso; however, the public was not ready for it. The present-day public clearly is ready for these heroes of the historic avant-garde – but more for their heroism, at a safe historic distance, than for the undiminished monumental significance of their work.

It is questionable whether Giedion really would have been satisfied with Moneo's monumentalism. The problem is still unsolved: the monument is dead, long live the monument! Moneo lives and works in a period that lacks collective values to monumentalise.

I have the impression that buildings are going to last less well than they have in the past. There is a widespread yet largely unarticulated belief that buildings are going to disappear, and I share this sensation as well. Architecture is now prepared for being an ephemeral art. That is one of the reasons why architecture today so frequently appeals to the superficial image of its predecessors; todays society does not believe in the lasting

long life. My point of view, however, is that this durability – this condition of being built to last – is very powerful. One must still fight for that. It would be favourable to have more stable cities, more stable architecture, more durable and less ephemeral constructions. I realise that being against ephemerality is a very difficult issue, but that is the position which I have taken, with the awareness that I could be mistaken.

Rafael Moneo

We knew that [the task of architecture] was a question of truth; we tried to find out what truth really was. We were very delighted to find a definition of truth by St. Thomas Aquinas: *adequatio intellectus et rei*, or as a modern philosopher expresses it in the language of today: 'truth is the significance of fact'.

Ludwig Mies van der Rohe

Better the rudest work that tells a story or records a fact, than the richest without meaning.

John Ruskin

I would say that in other times, ideas were realised through the building itself. Now it seems that these ideas don't exist except in a description of the process, and that once the building has been completed, it doesn't

New San Pablo Airport Terminal, Sevilla, 1991

There is simply no 'unifying culture' or other effective public sphere in which values can be shared. How could such a public sphere be created? Would it be enough to court the public with a demagogic, monumental awesomeness, an impressionistic aggrandisement of something vaguely familiar? This awe-inspiring vagueness could be read as practically anything. There are quite a few things that people find awe-inspiring – among other things, the power of the establishment or of vested interests.

So what is the content of Moneo's monumentality? Somehow, whether deliberately or otherwise, his work never makes this clear. Is the monumentality a (perhaps unconscious) legitimising ploy, a piece of propaganda for something? Or does it appeal to a merely formal consensus? If the monumentality is meant to express some public meaning, does it also question this meaning? Is there any critical reserve? Or is the populism a conservative legitimisation that cuts both ways? Perhaps a modern-day monument largely celebrates the power under whose aegis it is built. And considering the architect-friendly institutionalism of the Spanish *colegios*, this presumably applies to Moneo too. Moneo's own statements, clear and strongly-worded though they may be, are also paradoxical. Anyone reading them carefully can only conclude that their condemnation of formal arbitrariness is irreconcilable with the entirely arbitrary decision about 'what I understand as the most valuable attribute of architecture'. It is this ambiguity that raises Moneo above the carnival of forms but at the same time makes him a major figure in it.

¡No Pasarán!

Moneo thus stands for himself and, as a result of his strong identification with it, for his craft. For Moneo, in both word and deed, it is literally a question of architecture and *basta!* Enough of placing the profession at the mercy of pure utilitarianism; enough of leaving architecture to rot in the bedlam of Megalopolis; enough of infiltration by semantic incongruities; enough of letting the social context nibble away at the ground plan; enough of arbitrary, autonomous façades that deny the construction; and enough of scorning tradition as an irrelevance. Like a present Popularis, Moneo proclaims a return to discipline, in form, in profession and in behaviour. In this work, the consul pronounces 'Me or chaos'. His architecture, with its sharp edges and its bulwark-like character, is a fortress built to defend the integrity of his profession, to hold off the ubiquitous compromise of the good, the true and the beautiful, with their opposites. The cosmic order, or whatever is left of it, needs protection. That is the purpose of the closed and self-possessed buildings of Rafael Moneo.

We might also mention here the views of Giorgio Grassi on the emasculation of architecture as a social project. According to Grassi, architecture can currently express nothing but itself, because all possible references have become obsolete. Meanings are no longer held in common. The only thing left for architecture is to restrict itself to its own, inherent properties. Architecture can survive only by objectivising its own means. This is Roland Barthes' theory of 'the death of the author' illustrated in practice: better a dead author than a dead architecture.

'Architecture implies the distance between our work and ourselves, so that in the end the work remains alone, self-supported, once it has acquired its physical consistency. Our pleasure lies in the experience of this distance, when we see our thought supported by a reality that no longer belongs to us. What is more, a work of architecture, if successful, may efface the architect.'★

Architecture should emerge with renewed strength   ★ Moneo, Rafael, op. cit. p. 40.
from this presumed self-effacement. It involves restoring an adequate sense of reality, and he believes this can be achieved by concentrating on the construction. Construction techniques now make it possible to be completely arbitrary, so the architect must consciously enforce the 'legibility' of his architecture. The professed farewell to the personal signature, and the concentration on the authenticity of the building and material, is meant to defeat the ephemerality with which architecture is presently stricken:

'Architecture is now prepared for being an ephemeral art. That is one of the reasons why architecture today so frequently appeals to the superficial image of its predecessors; today's society does not believe in the lasting condition of its own creations. The initial impact of the building is what counts, not its long life. My point of view, however, is that this durability – this condition of being built to last – is very powerful. One must still fight for that.'★

¡No pasarán! Accursed ephemerality, thou shalt not   ★ Moneo, Rafael, 'The Idea of Lasting',
pass these walls! Moneo's walls work as a boundary   *Perspecta* 24 (1988), p. 154.
between two worlds, and that is why they are so   ★ Colquhoun, Alan, 'Between Type and
                                                        Context', *A & V* 36 (1992), p. 9.
impenetrable and so massive. Their presence is prominent enough for them to 'constitute a third space of their own', as Alan Colquhoun puts it.★ The boundary is not just the instant of in-between but a region in its own right. It is not just a line of demarcation but stands for its own nature as a line of demarcation. The boundary has become an image.

Mérida Museum of Roman Art: Moneotony

Rafael Moneo's preoccupation with achieving a monumental air of reality is at its most explicit in this archaeological museum. Although built above the remains of an aqueduct and a basilica, it seems impervious to them in its autonomy. Moneo hopes to stay

In Moneo's work, 'concept' is never privileged. The elements must sustain themselves on the basis of their own integrity, not on the reflected prestige of an overarching idea structure. Architecture, for Moneo, both necessitates and exceeds its description as a field of theoretical inquiry. This is what gives the empty measure, the space of denial, its importance in his work.
Assemblage

The constructed world is our global heritage, our cultural and social topography, which is anything but artificial. Specifically addressing the situation in America, the newly transformed landscape, contrary to popular sentiment, deserves the same attention and respect as the one created by nature.
Rafael Moneo

Architects should accept techniques and use building systems for starting the process of the formal invention that ends in architecture. Even an architecture such as Le Corbusier's should be seen in the light of the

tionally implied being a builder; that is, explaining to others how to build. (...) It should appear as if the techniques imposed have come to accept forms boundaries, for it is the acknowledgement of these limits that renders so explicit the presence of building procedures in architecture. Paradoxically, it is technical flexibility that allows architects to forget the presence of technique. The flexibility of today's techniques has resulted in their disappearance, either in architecture itself or in the process of thinking about it. This is something new. Architects in the past were both architects and builders. Before the

Using the brick without a joint secures the *brickness* of the material, keeps the brick in a more pure state, and allows the wall to remain as an almost abstract architectural element. I believe the abstract use of materials depends on our attempts to keep their own identities alive, without dissolving them in the reality of the architectural element.
Rafael Moneo

Architecture arrives when our thoughts about it acquire the real condition that only materials can provide. By accepting and bargaining with limitations and restrictions, with the act

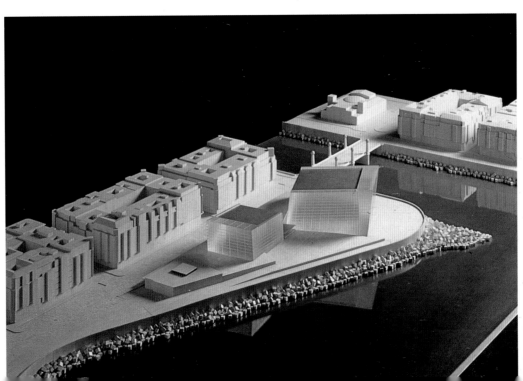

one step ahead of representation:

'The work alludes to Roman architecture, but naturally it isn't Roman. (...) the authenticity of the image is kept by the reality of the construction. This building is probably not far from what Roman architects would have done... I tried to go about making a Roman architecture in a direct and real way, not by means of representation but by means of strict reality. And for me the problem of realism is connected to construction, to the logic of building itself. It is one of the issues in which I am most interested.'

The architecture aims to be as 'real' as possible, but the representative photographs of this project tell us something else. Suppose we look at Didi Biggi's photo of the entrance. The arch formation, the niche with its interplay of light and shadow, the headless statue in the wet style and the spotless white of the two passing nuns, all blend to suggest a masterly *mise en-scène* of durability. Add to this the marble frieze (the only marble in the whole building) engraved with MVSEO, and we have all the ingredients for the representation of the unrepresentable. To put it another way, the appeal to pure, uncontaminated sensation makes for a glossy image... The building, with its monumental arches, its buttresses, its imperturbable materiality and its sumptuous calm, is so explicit that it constitutes a denial of itself. The new world order commands us to kneel before culture in the guise of a museum, and the first thing we see is a marble frieze with the word MVSEO on it. The irony that Moneo hates so intensely has forced its way in nonetheless. As a cultural manifesto, the absoluteness of an Architecture refined into pure Art has acquired a hyper-meaning. The interior spaces full of headless and handless statuary seem to celebrate the architect's abstention in thought and deed. Of course, that is one way to combat arbitrariness: treat the building as an *Unzeitgemäße Betrachtung*.

Congress Building and Auditorium, San Sebastian: Moneomania

168 In Moneo's design for the congress building and auditorium in San Sebastian, we once again see the simultaneous use of formal abstraction and personal theatricality. The latter is apparent in the way the building's two monolithic masses are marooned in their context. Moneo describes them graphically as 'stranded rocks', adding 'They do not belong to the city, they are part of the landscape'.★ That landscape is mainly determined by the sea wall of basalt blocks along the bay. Thus we can regard this cultural centre as a symbolic defence.

The most prominent features are the facades made of blocks of moulded glass; the choice of this material, with its immaterial effects, tempted critics to see this building as representing the start of a completely new chapter in Moneo's oeuvre. In daylight, the two volumes have a reflective, mysterious character. At night, with internal illumination, they look more like phosphorescent crystals. 'Undoubtedly', Moneo says of these, 'the moulded glass blocks will give the construction the abstract, remote quality that we are seeking'. Pierluigi Nicolin has described this project as 'an exploration of a boundary between art and architecture'.★ Again, Moneo has opted for Art. Moneo is the artist-architect who

★ Moneo, Rafael, 'San Sebastian', *Lotus International* 70 (1991), p. 60.
★ Nicolin Pierluigi, 'Minimal Architecture and Aesthetic Shock', *Lotus International* 70 (1991), p. 58.

National Museum of Roman Art, Mérida, 1984

bestows his glistening salt crystals on the city. It is precisely their immaterial effect that gives architecture yet another chance to prove its invincibility – as art, once again. Moneo has now himself achieved a quality he once admired in I.M. Pei's Hancock Tower, and without his having to abandon the fight for the realness of the building. Even more so than with the monumental materiality of the Museum in Mérida, the image can be reduced here to the minimal point at which it coincides with the object. The artist creates his image without external intervention, and without imposing a meaning on it. But in spite of that it remains... an image.

Überarchitektur, but 'Rafael is Abundantly O.K.'★

Moneo is in control of his craft to an exceptional degree. He sees it in such strict and ascetic terms that we could almost say his craft controls him. His passion for the métier has proved overwhelming and has brought him to a position of extreme essentialism. His search for the 'natural laws' of architecture and his formal teetotalism tempt him to produce what can best be described as *Überarchitektur*. The arbitrariness with which Moneo does battle is pandemic precisely in that nihilistic region 'beyond good and evil'.

★ Rowe, Colin, 'Moneo's Spain', *A&V* 36 (1992), p.4.

What is fascinating about Moneo's work is not the pure, minimalist structure but the way it satisfies the great need for strong images. Moneo is searching for an *essence* of architecture that can stay permanently free of the caprices of *existence*. In spite of his intentions he demonstrates that even the most uncompromising idiom cannot evade the clutches of representation. Even Moneo the Titan preserves only a formal image of the past, of the monument, and of a public meaning; he does not embody a public meaning in its own right. His ascetic strategy can as easily be interpreted as a simulation. Not only the cultural condition of the present is to blame for that, but Moneo himself – striving for the inescapable image. Mass-appeal masquerades as authenticity; a tune you can sing along with first time. It is his play of innocence that earns him worldwide acclaim. His mixing of image and truth into an appealing, evocative whole (Moneo described his Logroño city hall as 'suggesting an atmosphere in which the soul of the discipline resides') can only be applauded. In fact, applaud is about all we can do.

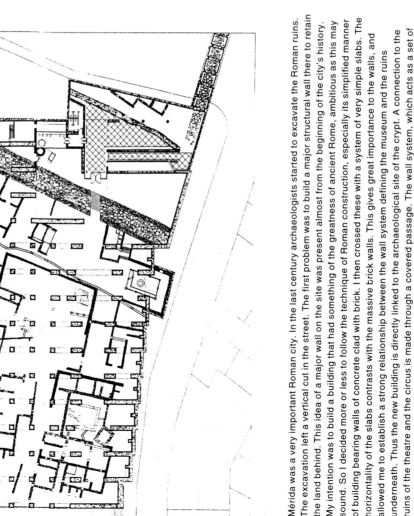

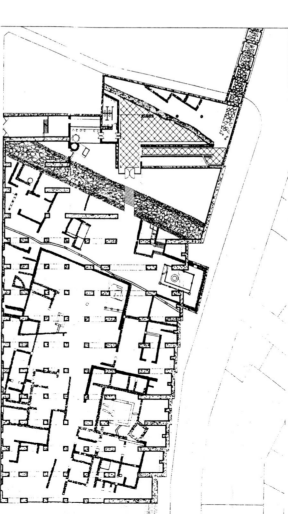

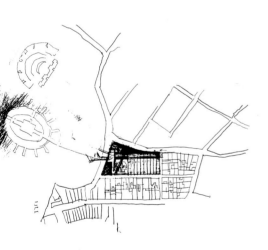

Mérida was a very important Roman city. In the last century archaeologists started to excavate the Roman ruins. The excavation left a vertical cut in the street. The first problem was to build a major structural wall there to retain the land behind. This idea of a major wall on the site was present almost from the beginning of the city's history. My intention was to build a building that had something of the greatness of ancient Rome, ambitious as this may sound. So I decided more or less to follow the technique of Roman construction, especially its simplified manner of building bearing walls of concrete clad with brick. I then crossed these with a system of very simple slabs. The horizontality of the slabs contrasts with the massive brick walls. This gives great importance to the walls, and allowed me to establish a strong relationship between the wall system defining the museum and the ruins underneath. Thus the new building is directly linked to the archaeological site of the crypt. A connection to the ruins of the theatre and the circus is made through a covered passage. The wall system, which acts as a set of buttresses to the vertical cut of the street caused by the excavations, was architecturally ordered through arched openings in which, however, frontality still dominates. The openings create a perspectival space in which, however, frontality still dominates. The

main gallery is the result. At the same time, the system of parallel arched walls provides an appropriate frame for containing the archaeological fragments in the museum's collection. The different levels defined by the corridors in the narrow galleries allow views of the fragments from different vantage points. There is also a workshop with a space for conservation of paper, mosaics, and bronzes. The brick cross-walls are lit in three ways. One is a skylight above the central space, allowing light to fall directly over the museum. A second is a north light, which reflects light off the walls and is good for lighting sculpture. The third, providing a kind of Baroque light, comes from an indirect source. The bays are twenty feet and the walls are two feet thick on the main level; underneath they are four feet. The height is fifteen metres. It is a rather dramatic space. I would like people visiting the museum to have the feeling that not only the crypt but also the new walls were 'found' by excavating, that the walls have been there since the third century after Christ and were uncovered in the process of building another building some centuries later. I like this kind of continuity between the old site and the new wall built on it, between the ruins and the new building. *Rafael Moneo*

▼

Location Mérida, Extremadura, Spain **Assistants** N. Laroche, J. J. Echeverría, E. de Teresa and others **Client** Spanish Ministry of Culture **Design** 1980 **Completion** 1986

José Rafael Moneo Arquitecto ***Mérida Museum of Roman Art***

LE PATRIMOINE

On the Work of Elisabeth Diller & Ricardo Scofidio
A Life to Machine in

In the Slow House in North Haven on Long Island, designed by Elisabeth Diller and Ricardo Scofidio, everything revolves around the panorama. Not a 'magnificent' panorama, but a corrupted, tormented, twisted one. It is not their intention that an observer should be able to look out from the living room, which is reached via a tortuous and deliberately frustrating *promenade architecturale*, and casually enjoy the sight of the beautiful Noyack Bay. On the contrary, the point is that the visitor is made conscious of the socio-historical conditions that have induced us to call such panoramas 'magnificent'; and of why that is no longer possible... The project is a manifesto of doubt about the dominant visual and cultural codes. It operates through a mechanism of postponed need-satisfying towards an experience of having pleasure in confusion. Simply enjoyment is kitsch. One must have pleasure at the correct intellectual level – the level at which uncertainties dance.

The most striking means the architects have employed to this end is the video monitor mounted above the living room fireplace. Using a video camera (supplied), the inhabitants can 'correct' the real view of the ocean to that of any desired season, for example by replaying a recording from six months earlier. The absolute autonomy of both seasons and climate is thereby annulled in one blow. Alternatively they may prefer to play a videotape by artist Jan Dibbets, showing a crackling open fire for hours at a stretch. In this way not only would the panorama be ridiculed, but also the experience of the interior. First the concept of the vista and then the clichés of intimacy and security are reduced to a game of codes.

The provocative approach to design taken by this New York duo of architect/artists who also make environments, installations and performances is heavily inspired by Marcel Duchamp. Since Duchamp all art has been conceptual. Diller and Scofidio set themselves up as perpetuating the halting tradition that Duchamp inaugurated, namely the decoding and deflation of 'civilised' experience. The Slow House itself makes an indirect reference to Duchamp's *Bicycle Wheel,* the first ready-made in the history of art. This wheel, a utilitarian object from the street unexpectedly promoted to art object, acquired its new status through the very act of displacement. (This stratagem was, of course, meant to undermine the idea of artistic status itself.) Duchamp, meanwhile, setting the wheel spinning in his studio, thought he could see in it... a flickering fire. 'It was a pleasure for me to look at, just as I enjoyed looking at the dancing flames in the hearth.' This subtle interweaving of banality and the sublime, of refuse and spirituality, ushered in modern art with a vengeance.

What the bicycle wheel was to Duchamp, the video is to Diller and Scofidio. On the one hand, the sublime experience of landscape is mocked in its own setting; and on the other hand, the sanctuary of the hearth and domesticated natural beauty are definitively relocated to the T.V. screen. It is conceptualism at its apogee. Although our sensibilities appear to be challenged by the prescribed scenario of experience in this house, everything is in fact attuned to a strictly cerebral programme in which countless notions

The American Mysteries, stage set, the mystery writer revealed at opening of scene one, New York, 1984

from literature, philosophy and art vie for our attention. It is not for nothing that this architectural work has been the subject of several solid, highly erudite critiques, each more hermetic than the other.

Man is a Dividual

Entirely in accordance with the avant-garde strategy of *épater le bourgeois*, Marcel Duchamp's purpose was to deride narrow-minded preconceptions about art. His critique was primarily psychological in nature, the butt being the art lover's tendency to adulate the 'beautiful' – the 'sublime' never having really caught on anyway. This psychological approach, which went well with the early Modernism in literature and art, is now difficult to uphold; for we live in a time in which psychology is making way for technobiology – or so it would seem, with science fiction scenarios continually crossing the line to scientific reality. For Duchamp, it was still a world *without* God. Diller and Scofidio live in a world *better* than God. More intricate conceptions are needed for this world than lifeless ready-made objects in whitewashed galleries. Now at least there has to be some movement of the subject – man is himself the ready-made. At the very point in history when man seems to have taken definitive charge of improving the Creation, he is increasingly losing touch with the carrier which made this possible, his own body. Logical, because as we all know if you turn into God you are no longer in need of a body.

But not everyone has taken note of this promotion of man to Olympian status, and by no means everyone is a party to this step up in the world. To enter heaven on earth, you have to be well heeled – and be of a speculative inclination. In fact what we are chiefly concerned with here are mental conceptions. And since every one of us is still limited to the confines of his or her own physical body – with a few cryobiological exceptions – we are obliged to get acquainted with these conceptions (which as yet exist only in the mind) through conventional means: art, architecture, education

---

Perhaps by heeding the words of Loos, that 'every work of art possesses such strong internal laws that it can only appear in its own form', Diller and Scofidio might have placed more importance on the integrity of architecture and its ability to affect change.

Brian McLaren

The object types of Diller and Scofidio neither serve nor dictate; they simply reveal.

Anthony Vidler

Diller and Scofidio equally operate in times when the architectural observer cannot be engaged by or take possession of a building through the ritualistic experience of its fixed and common iconography. They therefore deploy their paradoxical hinges as invitations to the observer for self-investiture, and to complete and take possession of the architecture. Their ambition perhaps is to establish an architecture where the hinges are not isolated events but pivots that activate a dense and continuous fabric of meaning, of forms and surfaces crowded with latent actions.

Architectural Review

Scofidio and Diller are involved with the idea of 'mask/masque' in a modern way. Their mask/masque covers stilled time, for its physicality has no past, no future... only present.

John Hejduk

etcetera. Our brains have long been elsewhere, but the brain's communication still takes place through the medium of printers and paper, oil and canvas, bricks and mortar. And videotape.

Sometimes this communication takes the form of an exhibition. According to curator Jeffrey Deitch, whose 'Post Human' show has been successfully touring America and Europe, our future definition of ourselves is based on the artificial. Instead of a permanent personality, we shall have to learn to rediscover ourselves continually. Deitch presumably means by this that the idea of the 'self' will ultimately disappear. However, we are not yet ripe for this kind of escape from our psychic pettiness. For the while we shall have to make do with our old personalities.

There is no point in recapitulating here every trend towards prosthetisation of the human body. The tenor of all those horror-drenched films, novels, paintings, theories and now (it seems) buildings is the observation that man and matter are becoming ever more compatible. The ultimate wish of every systems designer, the ultimate interface. Just a question of connecting up the synapses to the rest of the world. Everything in that world is transplantable. Although we have not yet reached that stage, the culture industry is working at full steam to soften us up for this operation by digitalising the analogue world view. As in hospital we have to be purged before the real cutting work can begin, i.e. we must first get rid of our preoccupations and illusions of individual autonomy. (The philosophical profession, already frustrated at its lack of social relevance, will be all too pleased to lend a hand. Surely supplying material for a theory of the end of sociality was the obvious course of action.)

The end of sociality also means getting rid of the body that was regarded as the medium of sociality. In our present culture, we can detect many different shades of acceptance of this loss. The most archaic are those who still try to stem the attack on the body, i.e. those who express their alarm at the dangers of pollution and of technology and plead for islands of resistance. More or less neutral are those who clinically diagnose the end of bodily integrity. We have had the *homo clausus*; the grotesque is the new master. There is not much we can do about the grotesque after all. (For example, the Brazilian artist Tunga incorporates such powerful magnets into a piece of his work that some viewers become nauseous. Ironically it is those art-lovers with a prosthetic pacemaker who are repelled by this work!) Finally, there are those who make a manifesto of this new condition and sometimes even seem to relish the prospect of it. Or at least, they do not varnish it over with mitigating circumstances. Unflinchingly, the mangled body is displayed. Consider the kind of art and photography that shows details of death, often monstrously enlarged, the corpses of victims of drowning, rape and chain saw murders. Take Andres Serrano, for instance. Nothing remains but a landscape of putrefaction. The idea of the body has been laid to rest. But where can this idea, with or without its wounds, still live if its former house is no more than a ruin of the flesh? Whichever way you look at it our body continues to be the only vehicle for thinking this broken idea, this meta-idea. This kind of art is thus its own conceptual implosion.

Baroque 'n Roll

Of course, Diller and Scofidio must always create bodies (architectural ones, that is) and make space for bodies (the users). But what distinguishes their work more than anything else is the way they tackle the issue of the vanishing frontier between mind and body through their (architectural) choreography. Not only in the Slow House, but also in their *withDrawing room* in San Francisco or in the stage set for *The American Mysteries*, they go further than the mere representation of the body *in statu demolendi*. In the new paradigm, too, the body will move – not as the designer of its environment (Da Vinci), nor as the centre of its environment (Soufflot), nor as an objectiviser of its environment (Schlemmer) but now as the passive plaything, a mere function, of its environment. The architecture of Diller and Scofidio is that of a human being who has made himself into a puppet. The 'user', in as far as we still can speak of one, is continually led along, deceived and manipulated. Sometimes you can look, and sometimes your view is suddenly interrupted. Logical routes do not exist and everything is subservient to a process of consciousness-raising, the conceptualisation of the conditions of experience.

These architectural environments bring the history of the spatial concept to a new milepost. For about three hundred years, since the *Querelle des Anciens et des Modernes*, architecture has been in the grip of subjectivism. No single (divine) order was still acceptable as the absolute criterion of the universe. Space, formerly identified with divine substance mediated by light, was declared profane and empty. Man had to find

The withDrawing room, installation 65 Capp Street, dining formation at virtual second level, San Francisco, 1988

173

Diller and Scofidio call our attention to the possibility of presence of something non-figural - the spatial structures that order our bodies. (...) Their method is descriptive rather than prescriptive, culturally analyti-

By confining their focus to a limited number of peculiar *spatial* relationships, Diller and Scofidio shift attention from the figural presence of the body acting within a world of objects, to the conditions under which the

Leonardo da Vinci and Schlemmer constructed two fundamentally two different models for the relationship between man and this world. As we slip further away from the model of Leonardo and that past of Schlemmer, into

From the outset, I should note that although Diller and Scofidio have somewhat disingenuously attempted to unify their projects to date by identifying them as 'bodybuildings', I find the work lacking the unitary character

his way in the new space. At first this undertaking was marked by great emancipatory optimism: in this space, man could become conscious. But when that quest failed over and over again, with Freud finally presiding over its bankruptcy, there was not much option left but to fetishise space itself. The Moderns made it an *absolutum inconcussum* and were forever putting off the question of *who* the space was actually for. Now that man at the centre of space is not only having a hard time of it, but has been literally handed over to the machine, it is no longer possible to preserve the illusion that that space is still for him. On the contrary, he is there for the benefit of space. The things in that space, too, are not there for us but we for them. To paraphrase Jean Baudrillard, the world is taking revenge on our pride.

Diller and Scofidio supply the *thinking space* for this new condition. Space has definitively mastered us. We have moved from the pretence of a 'machine to live in' to a 'life to machine in'. Now that architecture is no longer an extension of our body, the time-honoured basis of classical anthropomorphism, man can now become an extension of

Epater le Cyborg

All the same, we should note that this programme has now run its course. The self-styled agitators of today are agitators no longer because the glass houses they bombard with their artistic devices are no longer inhabited. Now that everyone tries to be astonishing, there are no longer enough of the good old bourgeoisie left to be shocked. The Duchampian project has been fulfilled and now suffers from the very thing Marcel Duchamp himself despised, repetitiousness. In other words, it has both succeeded and failed at the same time. Duchamp characterised Classical painting as masturbation of the sense of smell and gave a similar description to repetition in its own right: 'To me, repetition by an artist is equivalent to a form of onanism'. All the same, Duchamp realised that such repetition was an inevitable fate. *Ewige Wiederkehr* and the like. Thus we remain eternal bachelors who, in their longing for the unreachable bride, perpetually turn in the same tight little circle: longing, lust, onanism, frustration, longing... *ad infinitum.*

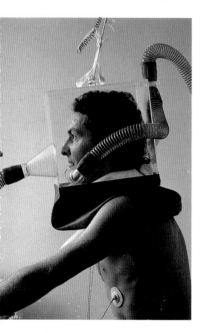

Athlete's breath monitored to determine metabolic rate

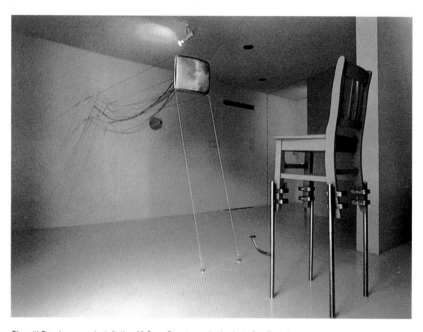

The withDrawing room, installation 65 Capp Street, prosthetic chair, San Francisco, 1988

Marcel Duchamp, The Large Glass / The Bride Stripped Bare by her Bachelors, Even, 1923

architecture. Architecture is no longer the serviceable forum for *homo faber*; instead, *homo cyberneticus* is subservient to those prostheses for our central nervous system, the computer, the modem and the video. Man no longer has to feel threatened by technique. Now he can unequivocally identify with it. Diller and Scofidio are the perfect illustration of this analysis. They show us the final consequences of the Post-Modern role-swap of man and space: man has become inert and space has become mobile. Literally mobile, in the sense that the Slow House overflows with hinges and mirrors – not as an aid to ergonomy but as a reflection on our pivoting world view. *Trompe l'oeil* is as nothing in comparison. Figuratively mobile, i.e. without locus: *trompe le corps*. That Baroque should triumph anew in this day and age...

Diller and Scofidio, too, show traces of this affliction. During a lecture titled 'A Delay in Glass', during which Duchamp's life work The Bride Stripped Bare by her Bachelors, Even was brought to life, Diller described this performance as follows: 'Everyone is in hot pursuit. The bride is in pursuit of her fall. The bachelor is in pursuit of his rise. The Oculist Witness is in pursuit of the vanishing point. The Juggler is in pursuit of the centre of gravity. And I am in pursuit of a conclusion'. But there was none.

With their bachelor machinations, they underscore our cultural condition all the more poignantly. No sooner was adolescence invented, we found ourselves condemned to eternal adolescence. The idea of presenting a urinal as art appears to have originated in Brussels. According to Duchamp's civilisation black book we have all become a sort

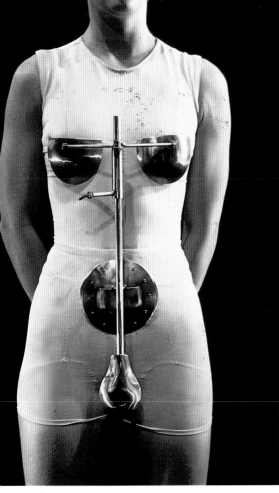

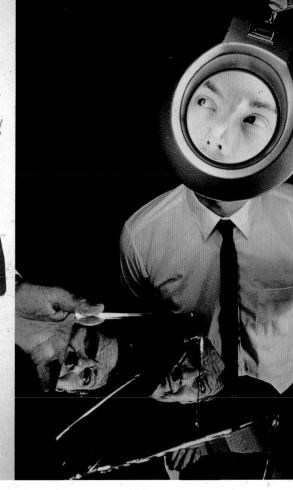

The Bride's armour

The Automarionette

The Oculist Witness

The Rotary Notary and his Hot Plate

The disembodied head of the Bachelor gives
commands to his beheaded body

Bachelor: I adore you.
Bride: I'm taboo for you.
Bachelor: I adore you.
Bride: I'm taboo for you.

The Bachelor longs for his object of desire

Tourisms: suitCase Studies, 50 Samsonite suitcases on the way to the airport

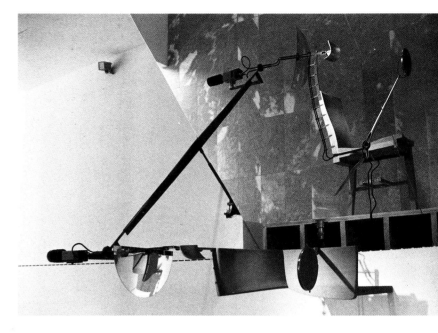

of *Manneke Pis*, urinating like awkward, oversexed youths on the tombstone of the classical world with its honourable, well-integrated personalities. Manneke Pis with borderline syndrome.

The venerable tradition of the shock of the new (Duchamp style) has become one massive, endless orgy of self-gratification. The work of Diller and Scofidio is still obsessed by Duchamp's nerve-jangling show. Art has rescued itself from its anarchists by stamping their anarchy as the paramount form of art.

But at the end of the day, perhaps, this work is principally interesting to those artists and architects who still feel entrapped within the frontiers of their trade. For anyone else, dispensing with the bourgeois concept of art has become an incomprehensible, futile meta-strategy. For architects, in particular, it is a *testimonium paupertatis* of those who are disappointed in their faith in Architecture. However, those who direct their faith not at an abandoned concept but at the politics of life itself have something better to do. Or so we thought. Duchamp, too, had a better idea – playing chess.

Infra-thin and Neo-Eleatism

Henri Bergson, the philosopher who in his theory of Creative Evolution defined *élan vital* as the fundamental principle of the cosmos, thought he had found the definitive solution to the famous paradox of Achilles and the tortoise which was devised by the pre-Socratic philosopher Zeno of Elea. Bergson observed that movement and distance, and thus time and space, were not mutually reducible. In the paradox, time is measured in spatial units; in Bergson's view movement is thereby incorrectly characterised as a succession of contingent moments of being, which are in fact totally alien to movement. In that way you can endlessly continue chopping up distance into smaller

portions without ever arriving at the core of the matter, fluid motion itself. By strict adherence to the categories, the error of the paradox was now unmasked. The tortoise would always be overtaken because movement is not a succession of tiny distances but a category in its own right.

However, for Bergson's contemporary, Duchamp, Zeno was still alive and kicking. What Zeno did to space – conceptually slice it into an endless number of tiny autonomous pieces – Duchamp did to time (see his painting *Nude Descending a Staircase*, for instance). '*The Large Glass* (*The Bride*...) is an inframince pulled out of a continuum,' Diller tells us. Duchamp set the scene, and here it is, visualised literally by Diller and Scofidio. The free movement of man in a neutral space such as the Moderns envisaged has been made obsolete by the digitalisation of humanity into a cyborg/cyberpunk. Man has become ever more definable as a collection of ones and zeroes, as flip-flops. The self, formerly one and indivisible, now falls into particles. Everything is compatible but only because everything is divided into discrete energy packets (the packets are interchangeable, not the person). And so we return to the world of Zeno and live our lives by the rule of neo-Eleatism, with our bodies animated by prosthetic souls. Achilles the epic hero is the loser again. We are all tortoises, slow but continually ahead. Ahead but always single. In our bachelor homes, under our armour, we remain bereft of one another. And still jogging...

Hence the name, Slow House.

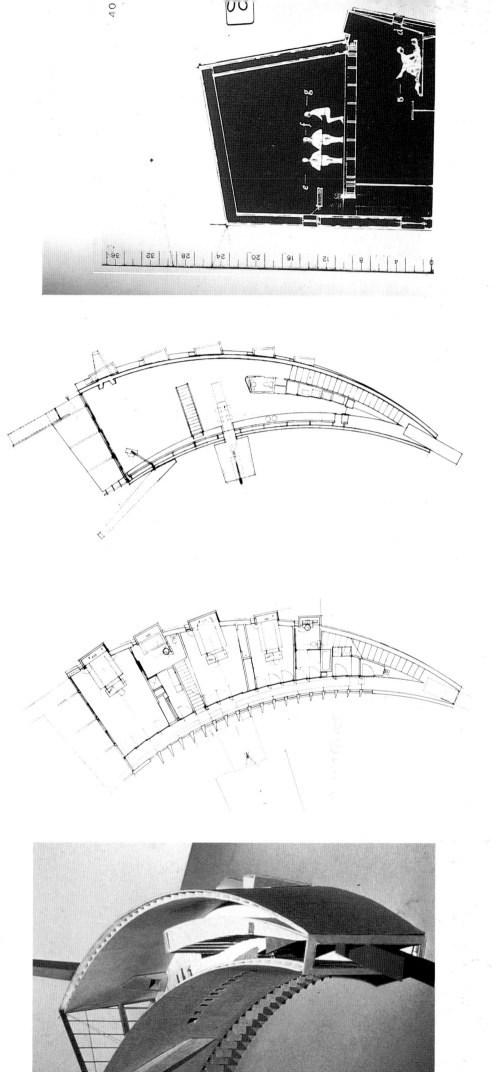

The Slow House is a vacation house currently under construction in a resort community near New York. For the vacation house, 'view' is the object of desire. The ocean view, in particular, is the most highly valued commodity; 'view' at its most reductive and most dramatic. In the unobstructed view to the horizon, vision is only limited by the frame of the 'picture window' and the falling away of the earth's curvature. It is precisely because there is nothing to see but the edge of the earth, that the observer's concurrent feelings of mastery and feebleness are evoked. The Slow House is conceived as a 'decelerating' passage to the view. Specifically, it is a door to a window, physical entry to optical departure. The passage through the house is anti-perspectival, the axis of vision is bent. The only direct view is withheld until the last moment. The fireplace and television, both domestic icons, create a

split focus around the picture window. Broadcast television can be switched to a closed circuit system in order to receive input from a video camera, mounted at a height of 40 feet and directed at the water view. The T.V. monitor, cantilevered before the actual view, offers an alternate picture window. The lamination of the two images of the view produces a disturbance, the horizon line will always be discontinuous. The view may be recorded and deferred. Day may be played back at night, fair weather played back in foul. The view is also portable; it can be transmitted to different locations in the house. The Slow House can be understood as a complex instrument of vision, employing mechanisms of desire and denial. 'Nature' and 'artifice', normally thought to be oppositional, are put into a fluid exchange. *Elisabeth Diller and Ricardo Scofidio*

Location North Haven, Long Island, New York, United States of America **Assistant** V. Wong **Client** withheld **Design** 1990 **Completion** 1994

Diller + Scofidio *Vacation Residence The Slow House*

▲

Between Omnipotence and Aluminosis

A Conversation with Oriol Bohigas

Oriol Bohigas, architect, writer, city-planner, politician, catalyst. There can be few cities that bear the stamp of the personality of their head of city planning to such an extent as Barcelona. Bohigas is famous for the splendour of his unobtrusive gestures, interventions in miniature (an unexpected little plaza, a beautiful piece of pavement, etcetera) to improve a neighbourhood, taking a single street block as an example of what can be done. He is not someone you associate with totalising or one-dimensional megaprojects, but rather with subjective and provisional statements whose aim is not to change the world radically but slightly.

During the eighties Bohigas worked on a massive rehabilitation project with the aim of restoring the old city after all the years of neglect under Franco. In his architectural approach it was not the overall plan but the object and the detail that were important. A strategy of 'seeding' was pursued that resulted in a series of unforgettable and exemplary sites that help heighten the citizen's sense of responsibility and make the city far more attractive for tourists. With this acupunctural approach to city planning Bohigas has helped Barcelona to join the select club of metropoles that are sufficiently interesting for capital to put down roots. He has been supported in this by the marvellous way in which the building industry is organised in Spain. The involvement of government in both the work of construction and in architectural education and the guild-like structure of the building trade, assisted by a building standards commission that has been an ideal mediator – all these factors have meant that Barcelona has so far been able to resist the anonymous activities of property developers and speculators. As a result its little squares have been transformed into islands of social life in a dynamic city model.

In the meantime Bohigas has become an important purveyor of culture in the new Spain. He has been appointed city councillor with special responsibility for cultural affairs; in this capacity he works on a programme for propagating culture and for opening a number of important cultural facilities that Barcelona has sorely needed for a long time. Now that the Olympic Games are over and Barcelona is less in the limelight, the prospects for culture look good and Bohigas is determined to strike again in his own inimitable fashion. Bohigas' cultural supremacy, however, is not entirely uncontested. On visiting a number of his projects to collect material for this interview, we heard that many of the actual residents were blaming Bohigas for the exceptionally poor state of the buildings. *Aluminosis,* a chemical reaction of aluminium on concrete is resulting in a gradual disintegration of the material. The residents live in the poorest areas of the city. They are fed up with Bohigas' prestige projects; all they want is proper living conditions. Like so many other architects of the fifties Bohigas could hardly have foreseen this development; his fame however makes him an easy target and he is personally held responsible for what is happening. *Bohigas, Oriol y Ayuntamiento que esperais que se hundan os cimientos.* Aluminosis. No administrator is all-powerful. Even someone like Bohigas can't do everything.

In a metropolis the misery of the inhabitants is the misery of anonymous people. The city has no time for them; the city can't wait. The pressure of outside capital is increasing and other demands than liveability make themselves felt. If Barcelona is not to lose its appeal, it will have to embark on a new sort of investment and devise still more ambitious plans in response to the increasingly powerful forces that are gaining control of the city. Instead of a policy for new buildings what is called for is a structural development plan. It is hard results that are needed, not a provisional policy.

Culture under Bohigas' direction will also have to take this expansion of scale into account. One result of the Olympic Games is that the infrastructure has largely been prepared; if all the publicity around Barcelona is to continue, the advantages that have already been booked will have to be subjected to proper management. This means bringing cultural provisions up to the required level. A city can only attract attention if there is a guarantee of a whole range of cultural activities.

While endorsing the mayor of Barcelona's plans for expansion, Bohigas himself owes his reputation to a purely architectural piecemeal approach to urban renewal. There's no point having grand schemes for a city when there isn't any genuine city life. If you take that as your starting point and encourage the creation of beautiful sites scattered throughout the city, this vision will be realised automatically. Bohigas' first consideration was not what was dictated by the pressure of events, but what was *feasible* in the given circumstances. So far, so good. What's more, until recently Barcelona seemed too small for a generalised urban

Oriol Bohigas i Guardiola

strategy, and Cerda's plan had already given it a solid frame. Now however it is the turn of the outskirts. The nineties will be crucial and choices will have to be made in response to phenomena far greater than any discussion about specific local sites. The provisional policy has been a success; now the time has come to stand up for values, certainly in the case of culture. Will the man who is famous for his pragmatic organisational skills also be able to meet this new challenge?

You are the councillor responsible for culture in the socialist-run city government of Barcelona.
What according to you is the direction the left is currently taking in Barcelona?

The left in Europe is not the left as we have known it. That's also the case with Barcelona. It is true that we have a left-wing coalition here between the Socialists and the Communists, but in practice our administration is social democratic. In that respect it strongly resembles the situation of the Italian and French Socialists: the government is nominally left-wing. That doesn't mean that there aren't distinct differences between the *gauchisme* that is in power here and the centrist-right wing approach. In my field for instance this can be seen in what matters get special attention. The left is interested in public space, the infrastructure, the problem of the neighbourhoods and the fate of the outskirts of the city. The left is also very sympathetic towards the public character of the institutions. The right on the other hand is primarily concerned with marketing the city, with culture and the status of the institutions.

You are 'left-wing' and at the same time you are responsible for culture. What contribution can you make in
that capacity?

There are only a few things that I can do. In the first place I spend a lot of time trying to explain to a great many people how economically important culture is. A flourishing culture has an impact on other areas of policy and can help solve problems there too. In the second place my task is to round off or improve the enormous public works of the last few years. In recent years the city has concentrated mainly on new squares and parks and that sort of thing, while cultural provisions have lagged behind. Take for instance our great National Museum. This museum has been closed for a long time due to a major renovation that is being carried out by the architect, Gae Aulenti. One of the most important museums in the world, with an unrivalled collection of medieval art is quite simply closed! The same is true of many other museums.

Another case in point is the opera, which is also a quite unique building. It is urgently due for restoration to meet with present-day requirements. And we need a new concert hall and a new city theatre. These are urgent priorities. To get it all off the ground it is of great importance that the social relevance of architecture be appreciated by everybody. That might sound simple, but it isn't. During recent years we have had any number of spectacular cultural events – festivities, festivals, open air theatre, but that doesn't mean that the number of people who go to the new cultural institutions has in fact increased. This brings me to my third important task, which is the democratising of culture. This is maybe the most left-wing aspect of my policy. It is important to build a new concert auditorium; more important still is that there is an orchestra good enough to play there. But the most important thing of all is that there actually is an audience. Call it cultural reeducation. That has to begin in the schools and that means that we have to collaborate with various departments, in particular that of education. Then the government of Catalonia and the central government will also have to be roped in, because the municipal administration can't do everything alone.

There are quite a lot of different parties involved. Isn't it hard to see that they all work together effectively?

It's true that it isn't easy to have an overview of the different cultural bodies that operate in a single city. Madrid, Catalonia and Barcelona all have their own officials. At this moment I don't know which body is responsible for what. In Barcelona this is particularly ill-defined, because the indecisiveness and opposition of central government have meant that the city has traditionally run a great many things by itself. I could give many examples of cultural autonomy being thrust on us. Schools, museums, cultural centres, all these organisations are paid for by Barcelona. This has to come to an end, but not in such a way that Barcelona loses its own character.

So you're going to need a lot of money, especially since you've announced that the emphasis is going to be on culture now that the Olympic Games are over. How do you propose to set about fund-raising?

First of all, it is much better to draft plans and put forward programmes even though there isn't yet any money for them, rather than do nothing because we don't have the means. The money will only come if we have projects. Up until 1992 we spent a lot of money on urban and infrastructural facilities. There are enough sports stadiums now and enough traffic problems have been sorted out. It's now time to siphon off some of that money into the cultural sector. After the urban explosion it is now time for a cultural explosion. My theory and that of the mayor is that for the next four years culture will be centre-stage.

In this connection Pasqual Maragall, the mayor, made an odd statement. He said: 'The day we bring Barcelona up to date with other cities I'm sure things will get better, but if we don't strive to achieve minimal conditions of infrastructure, people won't follow us, however much we preach'. And on the same occasion he said: 'What now is clearly needed is involvement of architects with general systems and I think in these and a few other places a more abstract view of the city will be much more important'. There would seem to be a sort of conflict here with your policy because your plans point to a great concreteness, while he is arguing for more attention to planning. Is there a conflict between your policy in the area of culture and Maragall's plans for the city?

Oriol Bohigas and Josep Martorell, housing project, Barcelona, 1959

No, because the fact that I occupy this office in the municipal department of cultural affairs means that I am completely in agreement with the mayor. The situation is like this: in recent years we have attempted to regain control over the city primarily through activity on the architectural front. We had the money and this enabled us to cope with the problem of city-planning. City-wide strategies weren't appropriate at the time. Our policy is an example for the whole of Europe; we have shown that an architectural approach can produce exceptional results. Of course I am exaggerating how it worked in practice because special solutions for specific sites would not have been enough if they hadn't been backed up by a general vision of the city. The result is that there are at least a number of new sites in the city that really belong to the people. Now we've reached the stage where we need to have a policy for the city as a whole; this means we will have to formulate our plans much more abstractly, because our aims are more complex. This isn't any alternative to what we did in the past but a direct consequence of it. My plans for culture are a good example. From a special approach to a specific site to a more general vision of how the city functions as a whole. I said that culture will be given priority, but I did not mean that the architectural approach to the city will be superseded; rather the gains we have already made in that area will have to be expanded into a general policy. The mayor's statement also means something else, something that has to do with the physical state of the city. I mean that the policy that has been pursued to date was mainly concerned with the city centre. In that area however the population is declining, while in the periphery it is growing. If we want, as a metropolis, to develop a strong relation with the cities in the region and if we don't want the outskirts to

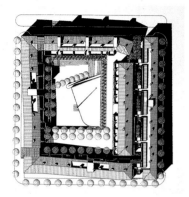

Josep Martorell / Oriol Bohigas / David Mackay, Mollet City Block, Barcelona, 1987

get lost in chaotic developments, a broader vision of urban renewal is needed. That's why the next four years have to be dedicated to cultural projects and to the metropolitan planning that Maragall was talking about, in order to keep pace with the enormous process of modernisation of Barcelona that itself is part of a much larger context.

What is the role of culture in all this?

183

I want to do roughly the same thing with culture as I did earlier with my city planning schemes. On the whole I don't believe in Utopian projects. I am someone who likes to start with whatever is most urgent. As I just said, my main aim now is to set up a number of cultural facilities and to work for a democratisation of culture. Only when we have completed these projects can we begin to think in terms of a cultural policy. With my city projects of the eighties it was the same. First of all a number of sites had to be created in the city, before we could talk about city planning. In matters like this it makes no sense to proceed from a general plan to the details. It has to work the other way round.

An outsider might think there was a clash between the aim of developing a general vision of the city as a large-scale organism and at the same time continuing the tradition you have described of starting with the details. Is there a conflict there?

No. The Olympic Games have brought about a whole new situation in our city. The result has been a breakneck expansion, even though our policy of taking a specific approach to each project remains unchanged. But now we have to start thinking of the future of the city as a whole: Barcelona has to consolidate the fame and position it has won. Within five or six years we will have to have implemented all the infrastructural advances in the areas of public services and culture. Our view is different from that of the former left. We see the future as being a constant process of change in the present and in present conditions.

Ten years ago there was a sort of natural connection between the poverty of the city and this concrete architectural approach to urban renewal. At that time any more ambitious idea was unthinkable. Now you are operating in a situation where you have to provide cultural facilities for a city that has become more wealthy. You may want to do that in the same specific pragmatic way; the old natural connection is no longer available, however. If I understand Maragall's words correctly, he wants a greater degree of predictability for investors, because he wants to attract companies to use Barcelona as a base for their operations; rehabilitating the old neighbourhoods is no longer a priority. The question is whether this predictability is possible, if you continue to employ the specific and detailed approach.

The call for predictability is in itself a means to persuade potential investors to believe that it is happening. It is more that a call like that generates confidence, than that we can say for certain what we are going to experience at some time in the future. Let's be frank about it, if you want to start four or five large-scale projects, then you know in advance that you will only really have the money for two of them. I don't believe in dreams. There is never any shortage of problems, but they must not be allowed to dominate the situation so that we no longer do anything at all. Right now there is no coherence; everybody does what he feels like. At the level of citywide culture standards of coherence will have to be created, because once the physical basis for the culture has been laid, then it's a matter of the content and quality of the things we manage to promote.

We'd imagine it was pretty difficult to promote the democratisation of culture while still trying to influence the ideological content of that culture.

So far that's not been a problem because we've succeeded in making a virtue of necessity; we are so far short of anything like an adequate situation that we've had to put all our energy into catching up instead of wasting time in discussions of content that don't lead anywhere. To take an example, we need music schools for every neighbourhood, plus the equipment they require. If we were to do nothing but bother about quantities, we could still believe we were doing the right thing.

So we will never know whether you will have the content to justify building these cultural establishments. But surely you'll need to see some quality first? For instance if you think back to the Olympic Games, presumably you have an opinion about that spectacle which has got in the way of any number of your plans?

Helio Piñon and Albert Viaplana, Plaça dels Països Catalans, Barcelona, 1983

Jaume Bach and Gabriel Mora, Plaça Virreina, Barcelona, 1985

I was totally against the Games and I think it was an absolute disaster for the culture of Barcelona. I think that it was a mistake of the first order to try and give Barcelona which is a monoculture a place among the great powers. We behave as though culture is flourishing in Barcelona but the opposite is the case. I think that in the long term the city will benefit far more from an easily accessible museum with an unrivalled collection, than it does from short-lasting spectacles. Events like that don't lead to anything that lasts unless you have the cultural conditions in the form of schools, theatres and cultural centres to guarantee a good aftermath. I am not against spectacles as such, but before you know it it's all over and you're back to square one. In the end the city benefits most from an increased participation in culture.

Ten years ago you could fall back on a strong consensus between city administrators, architects and city planners. That was because you all had the same goal of achieving an adequate level of urban renewal; and it was only a matter of reaching an agreement about the strategies to follow. If you want to do the same for culture, however, a consensus like that will of course be much harder to achieve, because culture cannot be so easily reduced to a specific goal. What's more you seem determined not to establish any priorities of content. How do you think you're going to escape conflicts of opinion?

It certainly will be a great deal more difficult, for two reasons. The first is that it is much easier to bring urban planning and urban design in line with each other. Whether it is a case of the spatial organisation of neighbourhoods or the improvement of social conditions, the means and ends are more or less the same. In cultural affairs none of this is so straightforward; on top of that, I'm by no means familiar with all the areas involved.

Daniel Freixas and Vicenç Miranda, Parc del Clot, Barcelona, 1986

Luis Peña and Francesc Rius, Parc de l'Espanya Industrial, Barcelona, 1985

The thing that makes it so much more complicated is that the people who work in the cultural sector are often difficult characters. Most of them haven't been educated at a university where they would have developed the notion of checking their ideas against the facts as a sort of reflex. In fact they are often downright crazy. If you aren't crazy you'll never become a good actor or artist. But the problem is that it is not possible to have a serious discussion with them about cultural policies. In the field of culture everyone is such a monomaniac, so totally self-involved, that you really need other, more impartial people to take the decisions in this sector. In fact the only weapon you have with them is your own power of persuasion. That and, of course, the budget, but that's not my decision. What I mean is, I know what my programme is, but I'm less clear about what my possibilities are.

Won't the Olympic Games work to your advantage in the long run as far as your budget is concerned?

That's certainly a possibility. Barcelona will be a more comfortable city to live in with a better infrastructure. Moreover the rest of the world is beginning to notice that after forty years of stagnation the city has got a completely new image. It is already something that people have actually heard of Barcelona.

We don't only want to talk about policy matters, but also about your views on architecture and urban development. As a sort of bridge between our discussion on culture and the question of urbanism, we'd like to ask you how you'd define the public domain.

Still from closing ceremony Olympic Games 1992, with mayor Pasqual Maragall

It is in its public space, its open spaces that the city really comes alive, not in its architectural volumes or its private spaces. This means that the designing of the public space, the squares, streets, parks is actually much more important for the city than the architecture. It is in the public spaces that one can actually have some impact on the city. That's why my policies for the city have always been policies for the outdoors. From the designer's point of view this means a reversal of traditional planning. Now we have to have some idea of what is likely to be going on outside, before we get down to actually building any buildings. Throughout history there has never in fact been any discussion of a genuinely public space. No matter whether it was the *haute bourgeoisie* or the aristocracy, the monarchy or the church, their activities have certainly created a public domain but only by a sort of superimposition; all these activities were in fact intended as private matters. In the twentieth century the public has had this space as it were dumped on it. When we design something new now however we have to ask straightaway what its social purpose is. This produces an impasse that is reinforced by the power of these historically charged places. While we are obliged to treat a square or a street as having a social function, what impresses the public is successful examples in the public domain and these are almost always monumental. I mean that we are landed with a monumental vocabulary for the public space that was in fact appropriate to the private. We have to aim for a social space without there being any tradition for it. We will have to find a middle road between the public space that is for everybody's use and the collective memory in which the old masterpieces still prevail.

We will have to create spaces that still manage to convey a representative picture of the collective identity while being ideal for everyday social activity. Representation and collective use, that's what it's all about. You have to get your identity from it and be able to play football there.

In the context of a recent music festival, a large orchestra gave a concert in the cathedral square. The orchestra played a series of musical arrangements of the greatest hits. All of this was subtly lit by enormous spotlights that seemed to set the cathedral ablaze. Above all this was a white dove that circled round the spires searching in vain for a place to rest. What did we see then? A concert of popular music transformed the square into a meeting place. The illuminated cathedral provided the monumental representation that you just described. Is this the marriage of opposites that you have in mind?

You can't always play Mozart, that's the problem with festivities like that. Still, I do think the cathedral square is a good example of what I mean. It is used for all kinds of social occasions and at the same time it has managed to preserve its sacred character.

We had the idea, to paraphrase Ortega y Gasset perversely, that what was involved there was a Rebelión de las Plazas. *These squares with their representative character get a sort of independence that hardly has anything to do with their history any more. Squares are sold as design. What you are offering isn't an experience of the city but a stage.*

That's not always true. With the Escorxador, the former slaughterhouse, for instance, the situation is completely different. In one part people can play games, in another it is green; further on there is an area for performances, but it is also possible just to stroll around. The thing is always to have a double appeal. You want to do more than just pass the time pleasantly and watch what's going on; it's also a part of your life.

But the main aim is to create an atmosphere. When the board of Quaderns *asks a number of photographers to take photos of bygone Barcelona, they all come up with poetic vistas. It continues to be extremely difficult for a designer or an administrator or a photographer to say something real about the programme that actually has some relevance for the lives of the citizens themselves. Do you think that as an administrator you will be able to accomplish anything on the programmatic level?*

I think that a good design for a public space always originates in a good programme, and that the reverse is also true that a good programme can originate in a good design. You will always have to work your programme out in advance, just as you do in architecture. But the best designs in the history of architecture are those where design and programme developed in tandem. I aim for that in my work too. The programme of course is the point of departure. But the reality of the programme only begins to emerge once one has begun to work on the design. A designer does not know what the users will be able to do with a given space before he really starts designing it. There is no such thing as a linear succession of programme and design either in architecture or in urban design or in planning. I think the design is the programme. The design is just the way you give concrete form to both programme and function. Form and function are precisely the same.

That's true, of course, but form is not the only instrument you have. There is also the question of the organisation of the space, of the spatial arrangements that you make. That has everything to do with your social commitment. Take the Plaza de Gracia by Bach and Mora. There is hardly any question of form there; what you do have are minimal means that in an almost natural way have a positive influence on social behaviour.

People should realise that this is also a result of the design. The programme means nothing beforehand. You can have a parking problem, but that doesn't mean you have a programme. For far too long people have been reluctant to think and talk about the city in terms of form. That's the fundamental problem, as I see it. A slight shift in the form of your public space or in the architecture, and life itself is changed. There are squares whose layout justifies the programme and others that don't. **I've found out that everything boils down to design: the programme, the collective aspirations, communality, all these things can only get off the ground if the design is there. We should discuss form, not what people call content; Form is content.**

If form is so important for you, do you still believe that it can still have an open structure? The way you talk about it, design would seem automatically to mean design that has already been carried out. The form of the squares in Barcelona is more or less without exception one that makes it pleasant to spend time in them. But what does a form like this have to offer to the angry masses? Your designs are mainly about creating a good atmosphere...

Designing definitely doesn't mean that all elements have to receive the same amount of attention; that would be superdesign. By design I mean the way that you give the form a structure; it is perfectly possible to do this while still making sure that you remain flexible for possible future activities. For a new neighbourhood, for instance, that might mean we'd make a general assessment of the scheduling and the allocation of space; then we'd ask a couple of architects to fill that in. After they have come up with a more complete breakdown you can call in a host of other architects to design details. In this process however the discussion about formal aspects remains intact. A functional discussion would be much too simplistic; you can't just delegate the process to any one person. For the Olympic Games, of course, we knew that we would need a certain number of hotels, flats, offices, sports facilities and things like that. The real problem however is how to give actual form to that programme. Life does not depend on what functions there are but on the choice of priorities with the functions: how do people cross the street, are the houses right for a square or do they belong to a street front, how is the landscape organised? The choice you make with questions like that can change life.

The fact that you pay such attention to social usefulness implies a desire for social reconciliation. The image one has of the many successful squares in Barcelona is one of children at play, and old people chatting to each other, people who are enjoying the sun or else the shadow of a well placed tree. All in all, the aim is to achieve a harmonious environment. The open design we are talking about doesn't relate to any

How to keep up the city? Oriol Bohigas / Josep Martorell / David Mackay, Parc de la Crueta del Coll, Barcelona, 1987

flexibility vis-à-vis the future, but to possible alternative uses in the present. If you had a different ideological attitude you might just as easily have come up with a confrontational space, in other words, a space that wouldn't put conflict in the straightjacket of a conformist form. Don't you think that architects ought to be able to make designs for both sorts, for both the hard and the soft kind of public space?

I believe that Barcelona needs harmonious spaces. I'm not against the other variety but we don't need them so much here. But I do admit that the form that a space has gives structure to social life. One example is the famed Plaza Real, a neo-Classical square that was a considerable problem neighbourhood in the seventies. When I was director of the City Planning Department we turned it into a pedestrian precinct. We also thought we were doing a good thing by making a genuine living room in the city with the use of concentric benches. Now, listen to this! **The square as a living room has become such an enormous success that it is mainly used by marginals. Every day they do things there we'd rather not have to see.**

You give a good example of the problematic aspect of the notion of harmonious design we were referring to. The idea of the square as a living room came about during the wave of social criticism at the end of the eighteenth century. Names such as Ferdinand Tönnies and Camillo Sitte come to mind. It was based on a notion of community current among the middle classes who were horrified by the anonymous abstract monumentality that was being imposed on the big cities in Europe. Instead they opted for the harmony of a fully fledged class society. This culturalist view of society as one large family is of course no longer acceptable in a multicultural society. The emergence of marginal groups has landed you with quite a bill to pay for this anachronism.

But of course you use the model of society as one large family because you hope that at a given moment it will actually also come about. It is also difficult to give the public a space that really suggests the problems of the city. You could hardly expect people to enjoy something like that. That is why we don't give people the space of existing society but the space of the society that we aspire towards. If we manage to teach people to accept marginal people in these places, then we're well on the way to bettering their situation. They're much better off there than in the isolated places in the city where they used to hang around until now. This process of improvement is a gradual one; if it means that these people become visible it can be easier to help them. The drawback however is that other people start avoiding the square just because of the marginals. It is a complicated problem and not one that can be formulated simply in terms of urban development. Primarily it is a social question and I am not a sociologist. The sociologists will also have to say where they stand.

You are a politician, however...

As a politician I think that the city should have as civilised a form as possible so that society itself becomes as civilised as possible. We can't go on wandering around in a city chaos if we set any store by a degree of social order. After forty years without collectivity having any meaning it is high time the city had a programme for creating an order like this. **The city, in my view, is an excellent scenario for civilising the population.**

What do you propose to do with the periphery, then? The periphery is currently virtually impossible to organise, let alone transform into a civilised order.

That is a problem. When I first took office as head of the City Planning Department (1980) we coined the slogan: 'Let's create more amenities in the city and more monuments on the outskirts'. The periphery is in fact not part of the city at all. It is the suburbs, not the *urbs*. Unlike the centre it doesn't have any cultural identity. It also doesn't have any centralised structure. It often doesn't have a single metropolitan network; there are no monuments there, no visual hierarchy. We wanted to remedy all that, once more with public spaces. It was a matter of creating the feeling of the centre. Making monuments, designing large open spaces that would make one think of those in the city centre. That's what we did in the Via Julia, for instance. It was a hideous space, in fact it was more a sort of empty patch with buildings on all sides. We designed a promenade and put up three pieces of monumental modern sculpture. The place really has acquired a character. It has become a focus for all kinds of social contact.

189

In 1952 a competition was held in London for a monument to the Unknown Political Prisoner. A huge number of artists took part. A furious debate ensued about what abstract art meant, because it was suddenly clear that the forms of Modernism did not permit any glorification of the collective. Abstraction might well be appropriate for a personal statement, but it offered no comfort to anyone looking for a communal meaning. Has that also been your experience as a patron of works of art?

Yes, definitely. My own preference is for monuments that have a historical signification. If a monument commemorates a person or an event, it can have much more collective meaning than when the form alone is monumental. Unfortunately we live in an age where paying homage to heroes in this way is no longer something that people do. Urban renewal therefore also cannot exploit it as a focus.

You yourself of course are part of this tendency. As a city councillor you are at the centre of this process of the increasing abstraction of power. In the meantime with Chillida's superb sculpture in the swimming bath of the Crueta del Coll you have at any rate shown that monumentalism has other possibilities. Apparently one can appeal to human beings' capacity for feeling awe by a much more direct route than historical iconography. The only thing that's a pity is that the pool that should reflect Chillida's primal knot is now dry.

Yes, we've been really fortunate in having the money to pay for the rehabilitation of so many city sites over the past decade. But we will be even more lucky if we can pay for the upkeep of all these sites. A monument is important, but its upkeep is much more important.

In Search of Ground

Kenneth Frampton

'The situation is hopeless, but it is not serious.' Karl Kraus (Viennese saying)

Byzantine chapel, Athens

The history of architecture over the past century and a half can be read as the history of its transformation under the impact of technology. A.W.N. Pugin's Contrasts of 1840 is prophetic in this regard since subject to the effects of the industrial revolution he already perceives the ultimate significance of this transformation not only in terms of architecture but also with regard to the mobilisation of the entire society in the service of applied technique and commodification. He patently regards this secular process as boundless and sees that all will fall grist to its mill in the fully administered Benthamite society of the future. At the same time he identifies architecture as the one site upon which the battle between value-free process and the spirit will come to be fought and this prophecy surely remains as valid today as in the mid-nineteenth century.

Since Pugin's time technology has penetrated deeply into the field of building production, not only in terms of the familiar innovations of reinforced concrete and steel frame construction but also in terms of mechanical services. Today some two thirds of the total budget of any large building is expended on mechanical and electrical provisions of one kind or another from air conditioning to piped information. Despite these inroads and the marked tendency to reduce architecture to nothing more than a fairly gratuitous aesthetic effect, that is to say to a marketing veil or 'decorated shed' drawn over the substance of processes that are exclusively economic, building remains an activity that still resists full commodification by virtue of its 'archaic' character. This intrinsic resistance arises out of a number of closely interre-

190 Despite the marked current tendency to reduce architecture to nothing more than a fairly gratuitous aesthetic effect, that is to say to a marketing veil or 'decorated shed' drawn over the substance of processes that are exclusively economic, building remains an awkward activity that still resists by its 'archaic' nature its full transformation into commodity form.

lated factors. First there is the unavoidably idiosyncratic character of its connection to the earth, which has been an important element in making it inimicable to on-line, automated factory production. One may think of this as a kind of irreducible topographic interface between culture and nature. Second there is the matter of its size and expense, that evidently makes it into an object that cannot be as rapidly amortised as the vast range of production goods that are constantly absorbed by the metabolism of the consumer society. Third, the relative permanence is evidently essential to the speculative exploitation of the value of the land on which the work stands and last but not least, built production has so far proved intractable to the organisation of large markets sufficient to justify the investment required to sustain the full organisation of production and consumption cycles, in respect of distribution, media control, planned obsolescence, et cetera.

Thus despite the erosion of its 'ground' on all sides, from the destruction of the city and the expansion of suburbia (universally advanced as a matter of automotive economic policy after the second World War) to the present attempt to simplify the architectural object through the superimposition of cybernetic processes and the further dispersal of control and responsibility through specialisation, architecture still remains as one of the last bastions of craft practice, wherein so-called high-tech elements and hand-worked forms may still becarefully assembled.**?**

To stress tectonic rather than scenographic values in the constitution of architectural form is evidently a strategy by which to stiffen the resistance of the field to its further dissolution through the instrumental maximisation of international capital. As I have already suggested, the various levels at which this resistance may be applied reinforce rather than diminish the intractability of tectonic form. In order to expand this potential we need to elaborate the various ways in which the confrontation between technology and the life world may be dialectically mediated through architecture. In some respects building finds itself in much the same position as other practices such as agriculture and medicine, wherein the

? *'The erosion of ground'; 'the last bastion of craft practice'; you tend to formulate your vision of history in a pessimistic manner, based on a strong feeling of a slow apocalypse. However, the disenchantment of the world, or the universal consumerism, also can be considered as a total pacification which at least diminishes the chance of a new holocaust. Could you give a clear moral criterium, which is obviously valid for our times, from which you derive your pejorative description of our destiny?*

! *My pejorative view, as you put it, has an ecological basis, but it also arises from a certain despair in face of the global crisis of the welfare state. I don't see how one can be so sure about total pacification given the ecological nemesis that threatens the planet. Tomas Maldonado put it already 20 years ago: 'It is not possible to make anything without waste but this is distinguishable from an ideology of waste'.*

? When Heidegger asked his pupil Victor Farias to translate Being and Time *into Spanish, Farias escaped from this awful job by saying that whoever wants to read Heidegger, has to read it in German. Heidegger is said to have been very satisfied with this answer. This short story shows the intrinsic connection between the criticism of universal civilisation and the Heideggerian version of* Kultur, *which as an opposition goes back to the eighteenth century (Goethe). You also want to resist the compatibilisation of architecture with the global village. Where does this culturalist momentum in your thought come from?*

! *Perhaps from my own agricultural past. What does the term global village mean, other than the fullest expansion possible for multi-national capitalism?*

application of maximising scientific technique has led to ecologically negative results, producing such undesirable consequences as world wide soil erosion and water pollution through the abuse of insecticides and artificial fertilisers or the equally deleterious side effects in allopathic medicine turning upon the overuse of antibiotics and high-tech surgery.

Despite the reactionary aspects of his thought there is perhaps no other thinker of the twentieth century who has responded more profoundly to the advent of 'technological mobilisation' than Martin Heidegger. In much of his writing, he seems to touch the very core of the modern predicament. As far as tectonic culture is concerned he has articulated a number of fundamental insights that warrant citing here in as much as they reveal the limits of the field in an ontological sense. **?**

Perhaps his most crucial insight pertains to the irreducibly topographic character of the bounded domain as opposed to the space endlessness of the megalopolis. This he first articulated as a generic opposition in his essay *Building, Dwelling, Thinking* of 1954:

Dom H. van der Laan, Chapel, monastery, Lemiers, 1986

'What the word for space Raum, Rum, designates is said by its ancient meaning. Raum means a placed cleared or freed for settlement and lodging. A 'space' is something that has been made room for, something that is cleared and free, namely within a boundary, Greek peras. A boundary is not that at which something stops, but, as the Greek recognised, the boundary is that from which something begins its presencing (...). Space is in essence that for which room has been made, that which is let into its bounds. That for which room is made is always granted and hence is joined, that is, gathered, by virtue of a location, (...). Accordingly spaces receive their being from locations and not from 'space' (...). The space that is thus made by positions is space of a peculiar sort. As 'distance' or stadion (in Greek) it is what the same word stadion means in Latin, a spatium, an intervening space of interval. Thus nearness or remoteness between men and things can become mere distance, mere intervals of intervening space (...). What is more the mere dimensions of height, breadth, and depth can be abstracted from space as intervals. What is so abstracted we represent as the pure manifold of the three dimensions. Yet the room made by this manifold is also no longer determined by distances; it is no longer a spatium, but now no more

Between home and heaven. Stuart Klipper, Road to Bonneville Raceway, Utah, 1990

Martin Heidegger

Alberto Campo Baeza, Carcia Marcos House, 1992

than extensio-extension. But from space as extensio a further abstraction can be made, to analytic-algebraic relations. What these relations make room for is the possibility of the purely mathematical construction of manifolds with an arbitrary number of dimensions. The space provided for in this mathematical manner may be called 'space', the 'one' space as such. But in this sense 'the' space, 'space' contains no spaces and no places.'

By 'place' Heidegger clearly intends a domain wherein it is possible to dwell in a permanent, caring and revealing sense, particularly as our life process is limited by the biosphere and by our psycho-biological character. The consequences of this for tectonic form are surely that the built domain has to be inscribed in such a way as to be able to stand against the rapacity of technological space-endlessness. For Heidegger the rootlessness of the modern world begins with the translation of the Greek experience into the administrative edicts of the Roman imperium as though the literal translation of Greek into Latin could be effected without having had the same experience. Against this misunderstanding, Heidegger seems to posit the presence of tectonic form and with it the materiality of things.

Ludwig Mies van der Rohe, Barcelona Pavilion, 1929

> *'That which gives things their constancy and pith but is also at the same time the source of their particular mode of sensuous pressure - coloured, resonant, hard, massive - is the matter in things. In this analysis of the thing as matter, form is already co-posited. What is constant in the thing, its consistency lies in the fact that matter stands together with a form. The thing is formed matter. This interpretation appeals to the immediate view with which the thing solicits us by its looks ...'*

This concept of things looking at us rather than vice versa seems to imply by way of contrast the implicitly dominating and distancing effect of the perspectival view-point.

Heidegger's aperspectival vision counterbalances our tendency to overemphasise the appearance of things rather than their substance. All of this turns on the paradoxical opacity of the retinal as opposed to the tactile revelatory character of the things in themselves. More critically it also implies an opposition to the domination of the panoptic viewpoint.

194 ***To stress tectonic rather than scenographic values in the constitution of architectural form is evidently a strategy by which to stiffen the resistance of the field to its further dissolution through the instrumental maximisation international capital.***

To the extent that architecture lies suspended today between world creation, (Arendt's 'the space of human appearance') and the maximising thrust of technology it must, try to save itself, by remaining committed to discriminating between different states and conditions, that is between the inertia of the thing and the instrumentality of equipment or between the worldliness of the institution and the unworldliness of the *domus*. The tectonic becomes an essential mode by which to embody, reveal and express these differences; the various conditions that is, under which different things appear and sustain themselves. Under this rubric different parts of a building may be rendered according to their ontological status. As Heidegger will put it in a later essay treating with *The Origin of the Work of Art*, architecture not only has the capacity to express the intrinsic character of the materials from which it is made but also to reveal the different instances and modes by which the world comes into being.

> *'In fabricating equipment (e.g. an axe) stone is used and used up. It disappears into usefulness. The material is all the better and more suitable the less it resists perishing in the equipmental being of equipment. By contrast the temple-work, in setting up a world does not cause the material to disappear, but rather causes it to come forth for the very first time and to come into the open of the work's world. The rock comes to bear and rest and so first becomes rock; metals come to glitter and shimmer, colours to glow, tones to sing, the word to speak. All of this comes forth as the work sets itself back into the massiveness and heaviness of stone, into the firmness and pliancy of wood, into the hardness and lustre of metal, into the lighting and darkening of colour, into the clang of tone and into the naming power of the word.'*

Two further insights from *The Origin of the Work of Art* seem particularly relevant to our understanding of the scope of the tectonic. The first of these turns on the conceptually related but etymologically distinct term *techne*, derived from the verb *tikto*, meaning to produce. However, according to Heidegger this term has further connotations. On the one hand, it means both art and craft, the Greeks failing to distinguish between the two. On the other, it implies knowledge, in the sense of apprehending

? *This disqualification of a critique that repeats verbally the language of post-modern architecture, seems in a way to correspond with the reluctance of giving the word too much influence in the strategy of authenticity. If the tectonic form is directly related to the experience of the body, and if this dimension of architecture is considered as an area of resistance, then criticism as such could be a mental tool which has long-lasting negative effects on the experience of the real. How do you estimate the role of criticism in the strategy you are opting for?*

! There is no such thing as a neutral mode of beholding and all writing, all thought must in some way or another affect our manner of experiencing the world. How could it be otherwise? There are I suppose almost as many different kinds of critique as creativity with the one fusing into the other and vice versa. Negative thought has its limits, since it is not only a negation of a negation, but it also tends towards a negative regression, in which everything, all life has to be postponed and nothing can be affirmatively asserted. Under such a purview reality cannot be brought into being; cannot be experienced.

Kenneth Frampton

? Topos and typos both transcend the individual capacities to enter a certain discussion, with rational arguments, on what architecture is all about. You tend to diminish the role of the individual to strengthen architecture as a category in a global erosion of meaning. How do you consider the individual, trying to transform the type as institution?

! I subscribe very much to Alvaro Siza's aphorism, 'Architects don't invent anything, they transform reality' and his insistence elsewhere that the architect who gives the people what they want is a demagogue. He goes on to say that 'the architect must learn from the people, but the people must learn from the architect.' Between these two aphorisms there is surely sufficient ground for individuals to transform the world as it is given including both types and institutions. The operative term however is trans-form and not the arbitrary repudiation of traditional form.

? Apparently the tactile quality of architecture seems a possible sign of resistance to the easy consumption of the architectural image. But even tactility has become a marketing technique. (See today's Sony designs for example where, contradictorily enough, the remote control is wrought into a very bodily shaped form. Or the display of Mario Botta's realness in tourist brochures of Tessin.) How do you consider this annexation of the body by a marketing representation?

! As Jean-François Lyotard, amongst others, has remarked, the body is no more immune to subjugation by techno-science and commodification than any other aspect of the life world. I find it interesting that your 'counter-examples' illustrating the co-option of the body, happen to be drawn from two particular areas: (1) consumer products and (2) tourist advertising. In neither case are we talking about the experiencing of architecture as such. The role played by second order cultural phenomena is certainly omnipresent in and around architecture but they are always one remove from the direct experience of the space and material from which the building is made. This applies as much to new work as to the experience of existing environments. It may be noted that the work of Peter Eisenman is at its best as a piece of graphic design or as a conceptual idea or as a mixture of both. The built Kozimi Building in Tokyo however is a far weaker proposition in reality than as a drawing or a photo. The same disappointing pheno menon may also be found in the work of Daniel Libeskind or even in the work of Rem Koolhaas and Zaha Hadid. All this architecture is better drawn than built and this almost proves de facto its lack of tactility.
This proposition can be put the other way round. The elevation of the Tugendhat House proudly displays the absence of a graphic aesthetic. It has to be built to come into being and the result is of a higher order than any drawing. In all this I am talking about acts of marginal resistance, not about any kind of total overcoming.

what is latent or present within the work; that is to say it implies the idea of *aletheia* in the sense of ontological revelation. Are we not close here to Gianbattista Vico's aphorism *verum, ipsum, factum;* that is to say to the fact that man can only finally know what he himself makes. In other words a work becomes an artwork through the manifestation of a made *factum*. Beauty in this sense is contingent on the emergence of what we may identify as an ontological ethic. All of this is distinct from connoisseurship where works of art are offered solely for aesthetic enjoyment or where later by virtue of preservation they are withdrawn from the world. Of this withdrawal Heidegger would write, 'World withdrawal and world decay can never be undone. The works are no longer the same as they once were. It is they themselves to be sure, that we encounter here, but themselves are gone by'. Elsewhere Heidegger asserts the necessary opposition between the culture of the world creating work and the nature of the earth; the one being dependent on the other and vice versa. 'Measure' and 'boundary' are the delimiting terms by which Heidegger articulates the interface between the world-work and the earthwork.

Heidegger's thinking in this regard combined with his later emphasis on 'dwelling, caring and letting-be (*Gelassenheit*)' have led a number of commentators to see him as a pioneer of eco-philosophy. Global technology was anathema to Heidegger in as much as it lacked insight into the intrinsic limits of things. Aside from the direct impact of such phenomena as acid rain or global warming, Heidegger thought that neither nature nor history would be able to withstand the unworldliness of technology if and when it would be fully applied at a planetary scale. As Michael Zimmerman has put it in his study, *Heidegger's Confrontation with Modernity*; 'Letting something be, taking its measure - these activities can occur only within a world. As we saw earlier, "world" names the historical clearing opened up by a work of art, of statesmanship or of thought.'

Amid the political, cultural and ideological depletions that have attended the last decade of this century, techno-science asserts its universal prowess as the one remaining discourse about which any kind of consensus can be reached, thereby always extending the reach of planetary mobilisation with all the disturbing ecological, cultural and ethical consequences that this would seem to entail. And while the fields of pure science and mathematics may have aporias of their own, these pale beside the 'loss of centre' that has affected architecture, as one superficially fashionable post-modern style has succeeded to another under the ever changing impact of the media, with its insatiable appetite for the fashionable. The same must unfortunately also be concluded about much of the theoretical elaborations that have accompanied these developments.**?**

How then should we begin to reclaim the 'ground' within which architecture might be reconstructed as a critical and creative discipline? I would like to advance here the model of a converging paradigm comprised of three strands, *topos, tectonic* and *type*, the topographic as the changing configuration of the site as given –, the position of the earth on which the work will stand; the tectonic as the substance of the built-work, as the irreducible thingness of its material, and finally the type as the constitution of the space of human appearance.

Thus the 'site' in the deepest meaning of the term needs to be recognised and defined at two different but necessarily interrelated levels; on the one hand, the topos or a transformed, transforming and transformable landscape/townscape and on the other the typos as the evolved, evolving and evolvable institution.**?**

In all this we are returned to the *political* and the phenomenological and hence to what I would like to call the *cantonal*; the *canton* that envelops both the idiosyncrasies of the site and the experience of the body. The ideological domination of techno-science tends to suppress the *inter subjective*, the one thing that by definition is never 'value-free'. I am of course alluding to the ideal of direct democracy, to the idea of the *canton* as the site within which the institution must be brought into being. This notion of canton returns us, I believe, to the notion of undistorted communication as posited by Jürgen Habermas; the still extant Enlightenment potential for the self-realisation of the species-being through discourse. This means that architecture must constantly strive to return itself to the concrete, if open-ended, space of human appearance, rather than to the maximisation of processal or biological functions as ends in themselves. As Hannah Arendt reminds us it is the aspiration of the human spirit rather than life itself that is ultimately the highest good. This aspiration can only be fulfilled through lived experience, through the politicised, phenomenological base of the *canton*. To identify and sustain such realms, in the face of global mobilisation, is, of course, extremely difficult. But once this aim out of passivity or opportunism is relinquished, the one remaining hope, the sign of the 'not yet', will be erased.**?**

Ecology: the Invisible Factor

Manfred Hegger

'He who is not yet dizzy, doesn't know better' (Peter Sloterdijk)

Spaceship Earth

Our civilisation is developing with a blind and frantic speed. This development demands urgent alternatives. Ecological building is an obvious alternative in a specific area.

Social Context

The basis for ecological building derives not from the architectural, but the environmental debate. Ecology relates to the world as a whole, the world we all inhabit; the 'global dwelling' understood as a multiply networked cybernetic system, in search of equilibrium. Ecological theory reveals the wider relationships between our basic existential needs, and creates insights into the long term effect of our own interventions. However, to attempt a comprehensive or definitive overview of those existential needs remains a hopelessly ambitious proposition, the issue being simply too complex. Environmental formulae, diagrams, equations, etcetera, in the manor of pre-ecological science, should be approached with caution.

In any case, ecology has allowed us to realise that incessant and ever quickening action against these 'natural' interrelationships threatens the very basis of our existence. We are cheerfully sawing the branch we sit on. Nevertheless, there are indications of changes in values. Optimists already see a fundamental new epoch on the horizon; the second enlightenment as the enlightenment of the first or even the very end of the scientific age. Whatever that may be, the threat of environmental collapse forces us to recognise the natural cause of regeneration and the limits of ecological systems; to respect them in our own social and technological systems and in planning our physical environment.

Even in economics the environment is now included, as a limited resource, along with traditional factors of labour, capital and land. Normative standards governing social behaviour and the relationship between man and nature are gradually changing. Within this process fundamentally different attitudes towards ecology can be discerned. One method of inquiry is *scientific.*

How does it work? What universally applicable laws lie behind this or that phenomenon? This approach, inherited from the nineteenth century, has developed within our own time into eco-system research. The object is no less than to comprehend the totality of living nature as a change of systems, and to discover the laws governing its interrelationships and equilibrium. Eco-system research is the basis for a comprehensive nature technology with man at the centre. Not without reason does this movement use the expressions 'environment' and 'environmental protection', with their implication that the problem lies outside the observer. This scientific methodology stands in contact to the *existential* method of inquiry: how do I live with and in, nature?

In this emphatically subjective approach one is less concerned with scientific principles and more with the acknowledgement of nature and one's personal responsibility. Here the ecological consideration is one component of an ethical system governing one's own life. The subject is contained within the same field of view – subject and object thus become one. Here the individual's own actions are all important. The radical nature of this position is therefore not manifested in words but in a correct life-style. The most important consequence of this is the renunciation of consumer behaviour.

Politicians rightly regard this attitude as naive. Social Scientists see the historical compulsion to maintain living standards as a significant obstacle. One also fears that these ecological demands can only be met at the cost of other, new social injustices. The technocrats among them have a more dynamic understanding of nature; it should be subject to manipulation, as a component of a project or experiment. Technology influences and accelerates these processes.

The neo-conservatives go further. They say: Why not let us create nature to meet our own needs? A functionally appropriate nature which does not limit economic growth; in other words, nature as an industrial product. Contrasted with this is the image of the fulfilled life in harmony with nature, as represented by the evangelical, emotionally committed ecologists. It appears by comparison romantic, expressing a tranquillity and peace alien both to society and nature itself. Here life stands still.

Nevertheless the ecological movement has set a great deal in motion within the structure of society, through crucial concepts such as 'think globally, act locally', self sufficiency and self-help. In the future rigid distinction between paid and unpaid work and between living and working will no longer be possible, with not only greater self-employment and self-sufficiency, but also the increasing trend to working at home. The technology available to our information-based society provides the necessary preconditions for these changes. Whether the associated risks can also be overcome remains to be seen (e.g. isolation at work, increasing stress from competition, automated work monitoring, loss of solidarity and support etcetera).

Post-materialistic values such as self-awareness, introspection, idealism, co-operation and holistic thinking are increasing in significance; essential among our concerns are community participation and self-realisation. These values apply primarily to the sphere of leisure and non-paid work, however, in the formal area of employment similar changes can be observed. Traditional virtues such as hard work, discipline, rigour and order are still in demand, but gentler qualities such as motivation, group identity etcetera are becoming more widespread.**?**

Sociology embraces this change in society's value system within the expression 'Post-Modern'. Similarly the Post-Modern relationship between man and the environment are determined by the head and the heart, requiring a more responsible attitude to nature and resources. Post-Modernism acknowledges this social change.

Ecological Architecture

It would, of course, be a mistake to assume that the architecture of post-modernism is the same as Post-Modern architecture since it is acknowledged that this term, has already been usurped. Postmodern architecture is characterised by a mixture of eclectic montage lifted from past styles and periods combined with the visual imagery of the fun fair; it is a formal and closed architectural style.

The changes of objectives and values, embodied in Post-Modernism, are far more aptly expressed in

**? ** *If these values are post-materialistic, they must have a different meaning than the ones in the implicated pre-materialistic era. One could argue that they are propagated to support a new kind of economical thought, in which human resource has become a very important topic in management techniques. Do you really think these notions are a critical answer to the materialistic world view of modern society, or could it be producing the same old conditions of production?*

**! ** Concern for the environment is being used as a new sales strategy. It seems to perpetuate our consumer society. Yet, at the same time it is carrying a strong notion of ethics. As a result, environmental arguments tend to be examined very critically. False promises increasingly often result in fatal sales problems (e.g. Daimler Benz, Duales System). On the other hand, reduced environmental impact of consumer action produces marked shifts (e.g. in packaging, in food). Ecological thinking seems to affect production and consumption increasingly.

Manfred Hegger

In its architectural manifestation ecological building has made practically no really effective contribution to any coherent urban design.

197

ecological building, which makes the essential issues of the environmental debate tangible. It has given them physical form and provided visual evidence.

Ecological architecture can be divided into two main categories: 1) buildings belonging to the technical/ecological infrastructure such as wind power and solar energy installations, and 2) buildings as architecture (close to environmental desiderata).

It is significant that only a small number of ecological projects have so far been carried out; many remain on the drawing board. Of the projects built, the majority are single houses on the urban fringe; groups of houses or estates form a far smaller proportion and apart from the occasional meeting hall there are practically no public buildings.

In German-speaking countries in particular, ecological architecture has developed out of the crisis in architecture of the seventies, and out of the criticism levelled at the barrenness of our cities, and their disregard for human needs. In addition recent medical evidence on diseases caused by asbestos or the use of timber preservatives have focused attention on the important role in our well-being that buildings play by providing our 'third skin'. Over and above these factors there is the widespread awareness of the mindless waste of both energy and resources, constituted by buildings, which could not be allowed to continue.

Like all new movements, ecological architecture has searched for its roots in the past and in the process discovered the remains of the vernacular building tradition. Norwegian log huts, Tessin mountain villages, Indian pueblos, along with other examples, have all been held up as examples of 'building in harmony with nature' and contrasted with Western imperialist architecture. This is, of course, a misrepresentation since it is these very buildings, constructed by the 'little man', which represent man's 'battle with nature' even if often built with very limited resources.

In its architectural manifestation ecological building has made practically no really effective contribution to any coherent urban design. In terms of design quality the few built examples lag far behind the garden suburbs built at the turn of the century. It is, however, only in this wider context that one can create an ecologically based relationship between man, building, infrastructure and nature.

By comparison ecological engineering has developed at a rapid pace; one only has to think, for example, of solar and wind powered generators. Systems such as these have an ability to fascinate; they are simple, innovative and extremely effective, demonstrating the economy and practicality of energy collection in an aesthetically attractive manner.

Like the ecological movement in general, the ecological design movement appears to be split in two directions; the one evangelical and emotionally based, the other technological. Currently the former position is mainly occupied by architects while the engineers tend towards the technical and reformist position.

The requirements of ecological design are exhaustively set out in the various manuals, pattern books and prescriptions (see table), but ecological action extends beyond such rule books and what is necessary is a matrix of principles which can be related to the individual problem, and an integrated application of the rules that exist. **?**

In ecological building individual decisions and actions must be made within a comprehensive framework. At the same time the changes in society, described above, need to be met, while also creating a structure for society's own relationship with both nature and the environment.

Monte Verità from the series *Freude in der Freiheit*, 1922

? Before building a brief should be written. What do you think the chances of an ecological approach could be in that phase of the process? It must be much more satisfying to design in an ecological manner with a brief which produces the right conditions for such a design.

! This is correct; the importance of a detailed brief with respect to the environment has been proved by a number of competition results and buildings. Ecology is not a style, nor an attribute of a building. It rather refers to a way of thinking. Therefore, ecological considerations need to come in at the very start of planning. They determine the end-product in many ways, in subtle rather than in obvious forms.

? If you speak about the 'innate relationship between man and nature', you seem to imply one of the pillars of ecological thought: the belief in a natural harmony. Even if you nuance this by stating that today's society needs a comprehensive conceptual framework, this basic notion remains. Then, of course, one can also speak of 'alienation'. However, this essentalism faces many objections from postmodern social theory, which renounces any functionalist thought of society as an organism. Could you argue why you still believe in the concept of alienation in a post-Marxist world?

! The term 'alienation' is not a Marxist invention. In a wider sense, it was used by Hegel to describe materialist ideas of nature and history, also describing the lost unity of man and his environment. Ecology is all about re-establishing this missing link.

A Short History of Ecological Design

The process of industrial urbanisation weakened the innate relationship between work and leisure, man and nature. In order to reverse this process of alienation there have been continuous attempts at reintegration. **?**

In mid-nineteenth century England there were the modern workers' estates with their communal gardens. Around the turn of the century they were succeeded by Ebenezer Howard's garden city movement, which attempted the reintegration of town and country. The entries for the competition *The Growing House* organised in 1932 by Berlin's City Planner, Martin Wagner, are of particular interest; the designs contain the first examples of conscious ecological design with entrants proposing conservatories and using the principles of solar energy and rainwater conservation. Although the concepts for the basic house types are extremely simple, they are designed to be extendible and are suitable for self-build. These beginnings allow us to guess at how modern architecture might have developed; instead they were distorted by the *Blut und Boden* movement in the Third Reich, to its own ends, and any promise of reform was completely extinguished.

Our consciousness of the unique and finite nature of the Earth has now been re-awakened by space travel, the energy crisis and incipient environmental problems. The first man on the moon surely recognised just how precious our resources of food, water and shelter must be. The view of the earth from the moon served to strengthen this awareness of the planet.

Air
Development in fresh air generating zones or lanes is to be avoided. In creating settlement and building layouts, main wind directions are to be considered. Overheating and lack of air exchange are to be avoided by appropriate density and building patterns. Inversion climate in public open spaces can be escaped by leaving air lanes and creating moderate roof surface temperatures (e.g. planted roofs). In areas with high wind speed, unwanted wind cooling effects may be avoided by appropriate building forms, good surface: volume ratios and wind screening (by buildings or plants).
Measures:
• no high rise building in delicate climate conditions,
• low air resistance building forms in relation to main direction of wind,
• wind screening vegetation in areas with high wind speed and danger of cooling thoroughly,
• planted roofs for low surface temperature and oxygen generation.

Energy
Non-renewable energy should be applied in a rational and economic way, environmentally harmful and toxic emissions are to be

Manfred Hegger

minimised. Energy loss (e.g. caused by transmission of energy) is to be reduced. Buildings ought to be constructed with high insulation standards and heat storage capacities. Wherever possible and feasible, renewable energy should be adopted.
Measures:
- use compact building forms and minimise cooling surfaces in order to reduce heat losses in moderate and cool climate zones,
- prefer natural ventilation and cooling means to technical ones wherever possible,
- arrange zoning and orientation of uses according to sun exposure and other conditions of climate,
- make use of ambient energy sources.

Water
Use of drinking water ought to be minimised, by water saving systems and by collecting and using rain water or waste water for inferior purposes (e.g. toilet flushing, watering gardens, laundering). Underground water may be fed by rain water. Roofs and other surfaces (except streets) ought to drained direct into soil. Waste water may be pre-cleaned or cleaned on site.
Measures:
- use water saving taps,
- collect rain water in water tanks, cisterns, or ponds, create wet biotops,
- clean and use rain water for toilet flushing, watering and laundering,
- reduce need for large scale and expensive rain water drainage, retention and purification systems,
- feed surplus rain water into underground water supply,
- pre-clean or clean waste water on site by biological means.

Materials
Buildings should be designed and built with regard to the use of natural resources for building materials, transport and construction. This includes the use of energy resources for production, transport and use/maintenance. Hazards originating from materials have to be reduced to a minimum for builders as well as inhabitants. The use of non-renewable resources is to be minimised.
Measures:
- use materials with low energy impact in production, transport, and use/maintenance,
- avoid materials containing hazardous chemicals harmful to builders and inhabitants,
- prefer materials produced from recycled materials and lending themselves to recycling after use,
- make use of long life materials and materials for easy repair.

Soil
Ground ought to be in used in an economic way. Recycling of spaces used previously is superior to reclamation of virginal land. Sealing of ground is to be minimised. All areas not used for traffic should be kept for vegetation. Subsoil water streams must not be interfered with in building processes.
Measures:
- confine building developments to recycled land or empty sites within built-up environments,
- use building patterns with minimal circulation spaces,
- choose socially acceptable housing densities,
- reduce traffic areas to a minimum
- arrange parking spaces with minimised circulation areas.

Waste
Waste is to be avoided in production and use. Unavoidable waste should be collected and prepared for recycling.
Measures:
- avoid waste by introducing composting for organic remainders,
- collect recyclable materials separately, create appropriate spaces and facilities.

Experiences such as these have led to the rediscovery and revaluation of much that had been previously either buried or destroyed: • the alternative buildings of the Hower children and drop-outs created from the refuse of consumer society, or from what nature provides free, • anonymous, climate dictated buildings, convincingly published by Bernard Rudolfsky, • energy saving initiatives to cope with the first energy crisis, • experiments with passive and active solar energy and other 'renewables', and • the concept of 'building biology' and its contribution to health conscious design. Building biology attempts the integration of many of these principles. However, it frequently fails as a result of the complexity of the problems involved.

Dilemmas and Traps in Ecological Architecture

In ecological design the same contradictions occur as in the environmental debate at large; in both, different kinds of questions are posed; there are (as well as in the other factions), both fundamental and technological movements. Translated into built form the dogmas and principles of those groups produce a paucity of architecture and, according to the philosopher Jürgen Habermas, suffer from 'under-complexity'. This applies to the eco-technocrats, whose rigorous optimisation, applied with cold logic, would inevitably produce a new Functionalism. In urban design, for example, most would be a rigid architecture of long, narrow fronted blocks with uniformly correct orientation.

'Under-complexity' is also a danger to the fundamentalist group with their highly subjective ethical

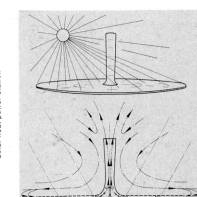

Solar heat power station

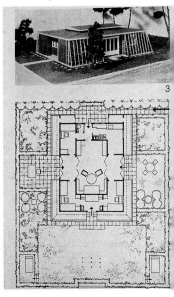

Martin Wagner, The Growing House, competition entry, 1932

system. The esoteric aura surrounding them creates barriers against the outside world. In contrast to the technological ecologist, the movement demands adherence to the correct life-style. This, and the appropriate rituals in behaviour, make the individual either a member or an outsider.

However, truly consistent ecological behaviour generally presents a conflict with the well insulated economic status enjoyed by the typical 'eco-house' dweller and society's most efficient contribution to ecological reform would be a simple reduction in consumption. Since this sort of self-imposed limitation is uncommon, the ethical principles of this group generally descend into a trivial 'green consumerism'. Even the Old Left and the Greens look after themselves quite comfortably in the face of apparent ecological catastrophe. A conformity to ethical principles is affected which has little substance in reality, or which is otherwise compromised by concern for their own well-being. They live apparently agreeable and healthy lives without having to pay much regard to the more complex aspects of the environment.

The creation of 'one-dimensional' rules prevents the very variety and openness needed if ecological principles are to be applied into buildings on a more comprehensive scale. This will not encourage the creation of a new, everyday building culture on environmental lines. Ecological design may only achieve a break-through when it is able to demonstrate good examples and evolve an appropriate architecture.

Architects continually create traps for themselves by translating simplistic one-dimensional rules into built form:

1) *The Regionalism Trap*: the retrospective search for vernacular or regional architecture as a reaction against the apparent uniformity and banality of modern architecture. Regionalism assumes that all the traditional built forms provide the optimal response to local environmental conditions and are therefore an automatic guarantee of ecologically sound architecture.

However, 'Mickey Mouse architecture' and romanticised provincialism are often the response. The result is a collection of 'film sets' carried out in an international provincial style derived from anonymous and rustic buildings. It imitates rather than innovates; nevertheless the style apparently provides reassurance allowing us to enjoy the benefits of progress and to avoid the sufferings of change. Ecological Regionalism is both retrograde and addicted to harmony.

2) *The Building-Biology Trap*: this is an anthropocentric concept, placing man (in this case the potential user) firmly at the centre. Its adherents allege quite simply, that the modern house makes us sick. 'Healthy living' is the key expression for this group, and also the title of one of their specialist magazines. This can be achieved only if one follows their comparatively simple rules, for example natural materials are good, whereas plastic is bad. Similarly concrete is carcinogenic, but because one cannot dispense with it entirely a distinction is drawn between the good 'bio-concrete' and the internal electrical-field producing 'old-fashioned' concrete. The theory equals the effect on health of quite disparate phenomena such as certain timber preservative treatments, the alleged effects of electrical ring circuits and even the electro-magnetic field supposedly spread like a net over the whole globe. The primary concern of building biology is individual well-being of the building user. The ecological side effects are seldom properly considered, (damaging interventions in natural and social systems, such as the over exploitation of cork oak, transport expenditure on exotic materials like cocos fibre and the limited durability of many materials). Natural materials are employed as if there were no naturally occurring poisons. Building biologists claim that they alone build in harmony with nature. This, of course, is a misconception: building has always been a struggle against nature, often carried out within regional traditions and with extremely limited means.

3) *The High-tech Trap*: the adherents of this movement maintain that all problems, including environmental ones, can be solved by the rational application of science and technology. This is raised to the level of architecture, even if only emblematically. While it is no doubt correct that in the future we will use more rather than less, technology to solve environmental problems, High-tech equates the use of means with architecture itself. This is done through imagery, such as the use of over-dimensional conservationists, large areas of solar wall or the expression of eco-technical system and plants by means of deconstruction. 'Eco-tech' may produce interesting solutions in individual buildings and be appropriate to pilot projects and prototypes, but there is a danger that employed in the wider context it could be over-prescriptive; for example it might dictate that groups of houses should all be uniformly oriented in order to achieve optimum solar gain; this would be inimical to create user-friendly social spaces. This application of new technology may be environmentally friendly, but it diverts attention from indeed essential issues such as social interaction and may lead to the postponement of decisive action in more crucial areas.

4) *The Alternative Trap*: ecological design like many other aspects of ecological thinking was initially developed within the 'alternative movement'. From this it has been possible to campaign on rational issues such as simplicity of life-style, modesty, recycling as source of building materials and solar energy. They have been put into practice in a number of imaginative ways using glasshouses, domes, mud structures, *'pueblo' dustings* along with a variety of other architectural fantasies. Although there are numerous fascinating structures and spaces, their image has remained esoteric – even bizarre. The occupant's desire for self-expression is often manifested in extreme forms which have virtually no common ground with the needs of the average European householder. Often self-built, these structures are usually crudely constructed, with little regard for conventional comfort and technical performance and of limited life-expectancy. This awkward ideology and the buildings devised from it, have played an important role in initiating the debate and extending horizons. However, ecology is now too important an issue to be left neglected in its niche of the alternative ghetto.

With all these particular movements the suspicion arises that there is a deliberate attempt to make ecological architecture as visible and deliberate as possible. In the case of prototypes or exhibition buildings this no doubt has its place but ecological architecture cannot simply be achieved by the use of grass roofs, or 'green' façades, cladding or conservatories. The sum of the parts of the genuine ecological components should not be obvious or force its presence on the observer. In the majority of cases the rule should be: *ecology is invisible*. The above instances also demonstrate the fact that design principles are generally over simplified and one-dimensional. They too easily filter out the complex reality of society and exclude the potential for real diversity.

Themes for Ecology in Architecture

Complexity and Simplicity The morals of ecology imply a comparison between simplicity (holism) and diversity (of life-forms). The comparison of the two concepts appears at first sight to bring a contradiction. Great diversity implies the opposite of simplicity, namely obscurity and heterogeneity. In contrast to simplicity, diversity is a new concept introduced into the debate by the ecology movement. The model of natural equilibrium which exists in human society can be ascribed to diversity to a degree that puts it at the other end of the scale to the traditional political goal of equality.

A literal transference of ecological diversity contains an element of arbitrariness, even danger. Is it, for example, correct to interpret savage nature as natural harmony? Should natural cycles, with their inevitably amoral, but highly complex evolutionary rules, serve as models for human society? Or is a pacific nature – a controlled complexity – implied here?

Manfred Hegger / Doris Hegger-Luhnen / Gernot Minke / Günter Schleif, Ecological settlement Kassel-Frasenweg, 1987

? *Complexity has become one of the main topics of postmodern theory but from an interested point of view one often perceives complexity as the cosiness of our time, in which everything has its particular place, but no values are valid to discriminate. What is terribly difficult is to develop a critical macrosocial theory that provides you with arguments for a public debate on social objectives, and at the same time to respect complexity. Could you elaborate on the link between ecology and critical theory? How do you consider the fate of dialectics anyway?*

! *If critical theory is about a reasonable society, about man liberated to experience a new sensuality, this carries strong relationships with the idea of human ecology. It needs an appropriate way of thinking to understand ecological networks, and to find ways of economising on our environment. Dialectics may be a basis for this; not in a Marxist way, but simply as the old art of creating new ideas by logical operations and controversial thinking.*

Simplicity is, in comparison, an established ideal associated with modesty, curtailment and even asceticism, and thereby also with ethical and social values. The definition can also embrace balance, holism and integrity; concepts which for centuries have distinguished philosophy, the arts and other manifestations of the intellect. Their elementary principles are over-simplification of the complex processes involved in the reality of society and nature. This applies equally to the ecological principles described above; integrity and uniformity infer safety. But to quote Gustav Landauer: 'In mankind, and especially in nature there are no perfect forms, nothing rounded or complete. Only words, pictures, gestures and fantasies are rounded and perfect. Reality is in the movement'. At best simplicity can be distilled out of complexity by concentrating on just one point. For example the entries for the Growing House competition (described above) exemplify the characteristics of simple solutions, explored on several levels. Although a scheme of this sort has never been carried out, simplicity appears to dominate over complexity. Simplicity and complexity can be treated as opposites in a dialectal process, which may lead us to a new and complex quality in everyday architecture.**?**

Ecology at different scales The degree of ecological/technical input and the complexity of the problem are set out below:

Individual dwellings/house groups Here, where simplicity and modesty are the principal criteria, the fundamental approach is properly justified. The houses are relatively small and require only limited site area; the surface area of the enclosing structure should be a minimum. A simple basic form can be completed or altered incrementally over a period of time. A degree of self-expression is appropriate both to building function and the architecture. There should therefore be no restriction on the use of symbolism if it derives from the inhabitants' own desire for self-expression and a fairly loose planning framework should allow for the occasional excesses.

City/region For the city or region the situation is very different; in general an ecological/technological approach will be appropriate. It is unlikely that many will respond to calls for voluntary reduction in consumption. We cannot therefore assume that large, new fundamentalist eco-communities will develop with reduced consumerism as a widely accepted ethos (or even as an inconvenient necessity). One of the principal ecological requirements will be to decentralise these administrative systems. It would be feasible to promote a rational system of local government on ecological lines at communal or regional level, perhaps based on the model of Davis/California. Despite this, many systems will not be able to reduce consumption below a certain sensible economic threshold. Important decisions will continue to be made by central authorities; among them will be the most critical for environmental development – namely the legislative one.
We anticipate a positive development of an eco/technological organisation, which will become increasingly complex. Depending on circumstances this administrative organisation will have to be expanded.

Community/Estate/Neighbourhood The estate and neighbourhood establish and intermediate scale between individual, house and city; at this level the eco/technological and fundamental approach can complement each other. This is actually the context in which the complexity of the over-

House on Ohayo Mountain, Woodstock, 1948-71

Like the ecological movement in general, the ecological design movement appears to be split in two directions; the one evangelical and emotionally based, the other technological. Currently the former position is mainly occupied by architects while the engineers tend towards the technical and reformist position.

202

riding requirements of society and community and the simplicity appropriate to house building, can be synthesised into architectural form. Here also, public space for different kinds of social groups can be overlaid with spaces for individual and private initiatives. Sensible ecological measures in the community would establish fairly loosely defined limits within which residents could operate, developing their own interests freely without the restrictions of group pressure. The individual can make his/her own ecological contribution outside the general consensus. At this scale it is also possible to develop an eco/technological infrastructure which would ensure a largely autonomous provision of energy, on the basis of the example pioneered by Vester in Denmark.**?**
Environmentally conscious urban renewal can also be considered at this level. This would be a logical development, since by not building afresh but refurbishing the existing stock, resources could be conserved. Selective demolition the opening out of congested spaces, re-routing of traffic and the energetic remodelling of the existing built fabric would all be appropriate measures. This process should not however, threaten the social ecology at neighbourhood level. If over ambitious or one-dimensional strategies are employed environmental problems could be exacerbated rather than relieved. The Frankfurt research group, Social Ecology, have warned of the dangers of creating 'highly toxic packages'. The ecological question is always enmeshed within the social fabric, human behaviour patterns, spatial interrelationships etcetera, these are all subject to continuous change. Ecological architecture must be part of a new culture of everyday building.

A View of an Ecological Architecture with Complex Characteristics
All too often architecture fails as a consequence of the complexity of the total problem. The parameters set by technology and the social demands are extraordinarily diverse. Despite his best endeavours the architect runs the risk, of responding to them in an over-simplistic, or under-complex, manner. In their totality they create a tension and polarity between the social and formal, the real and utopian, the col-

? *The re-use of existing stock resources is of course very important but will require enormous social measures to accomplish the moral and economical shift. How do you think to get rid of speculation, the capitalist wish to shorten the turn-over time, the need for flexibility, etcetera. Who do you think is going to take these measures?*

! In the past years, we have lost a political alternative. If capitalism alone cannot manage to bring about change to save our living fundamentals, we may experience the development of new alternatives with an ecological bias. Environmental measures need strong political action on an overall basis, complemented by an individual attitude based on strong beliefs. Policies are needed to reach both levels.

lective and the individual. These are tensions which one should not attempt to smooth away; whenever one succeeds in maintaining them projects derive a particular quality – a dual character. This implies accepting things simultaneously, which at first sight might appear to be mutually exclusive. The usual compromise between these opposites is, however, often neither feasible nor desirable and only opposites which remain intact – the one informing or questioning the other – provide the correct degree of complexity and animation.

Ecological architecture is not concerned with the harmonious design of fashionable eco-stage sets on its own; even ecologically well considered architecture is not a panacea. The really important ecological decisions and actions take place outside the sphere of architecture entirely.

However, the environmental dimension creates another dynamic in architecture. The many layered fabric of arguments, ideas and actions directed towards a more careful use of our resources, will also fundamentally change our houses, our cities and the way we live together. It is therefore indispensable that ecological design will free itself from its esoteric or technological one-dimensionability and grow out of its niche position. It will affect all levels of house design from the construction of the individual house, to large scale planning and urban renewal. Here its integration alongside other disciplines, in the complex decision making process, will be of critical importance. Besides ecology social issues, time-scale, space and technical problems will all require proper consideration. However, it is to be hoped

Manfred Hegger

Architecture without architects

203

Gunnar Daan, T. de Vries, House with studio, Langezwaag, 1988

that the many layers involved in such a planning process can produce simple solutions; the product could be a functional, lively architecture – an expression of the user as much as the designer.

A new form of building could emerge; complex in its conception but simple in its realisation. Modest and inconspicuous, it should be incomplete, offering scope for future developments. Reflecting the nature of our society, it would embody dual qualities: formal, vigorous but simple and perhaps elementary basic structures, accommodating a varied and informal 'fit-out'. Initial structures and spaces which stimulate the imagination, allowing space for varied and lively additions. In urban design terms it could have quite simple objectives such as spatial containment, the definition of ownership and zoning, whilst the basic built elements might comprise simple enclosures, enable cores and 'street frontage' buildings. In some instances the basic provision might just be the facade or structural system. These basic elements would allow completion and extensions to take place in discreet stages, within an overall planning strategy. In this way a new and vital architecture will develop, never either complete or self-contained, and evolved within defined parameters. Ecology would set the pace for a different, human architecture; one which both creates form and allows it to be created. A way of building which will make the learning process, passage of time and moods visible; giving expression the use and the users but containing the potential chaos, within an overall concept. The formal language of this dynamic architecture is ordered chaos, contained spontaneity, structural variety and complex simplicity.

Desperately Seeking Siza

A Conversation with Alvaro Siza Vieira

There is not much that is *definitivos* about Alvaro Siza except for his favourite brand of Portuguese cigarettes. After a career to date of four decades of unbroken activity, he is now among the select group of most acclaimed master builders of our time; yet he has always remained remarkably modest both in his pronouncements about architecture and in the claims he makes for himself. While nobody would deny his extraordinary professional skill and while the ease he displays in projects of every scale is universally admired, Siza remains someone who does not put on airs about how unique he is. On the contrary, in his numerous interviews he continues to define his role emphatically as being that of someone who does no more than transform something that already exists. To quote his own words, 'Architects don't invent anything; they transform reality. They work continuously with models which they transform in response to the problems which they encounter'. The critical role in international architectural practice that is attributed to him is not expressed in any stated programme; his appeal lies more in his subtle approach to the trade, to his materials and to the social context of his work. One feature that is always present is a notion of frozen conflict. In practice this means a process in which all the elements, architectural and otherwise, are allotted their place in all their integrity, almost always in 'innocent' white or in the natural colour of the surrounding environment. This is true of the Bouça dwellings in Oporto where the little aisle that is so typical of the normal working class housing in Oporto is preserved with its proportions unchanged while at the same time a transformation has been introduced that makes the flats a pleasure to live in. The same goes for the apartment building that Siza designed in the Kreuzberg neighbourhood in Berlin where a typical gloomy tenement block has been turned into a once-off statement by the foreign 'author' and is imbued with his charisma. No matter what the project, Siza concentrates both on ensuring that the paradoxes inherent in the commission are given free play, while at the same time highlighting the frozen semblance of a consensus based on the local conventions he is confronted with. When these conventions suit him so, as for instance in the Punt en Komma project in The Hague, the result is small-scale context-based works that always seem to say 'yes' to the conditions that gave rise to them. In Berlin, however, the context and the point of departure have a negative historical content: here Siza's architecture would seem to say 'no', however much as a designer he would rather not admit it. Modernism functions here as a mask to express an infinite sadness, something that graffiti artists have in fact immortalised in the façade: *bonjour tristesse*.

Those who have not had the chance to visit any of Siza's buildings, or who have only seen a few of them, will have to make do with Siza the critic if they want to come to a proper assessment of his critical approach. Siza himself will in any case not be of much help, concerned as he is with seeing that fine craftsmanship gets maximum play. Concern about what people think of his work has no place here. To put it concretely, Siza's concrete architecture is all that Siza cares about; Siza's echo is the domain of his admirers. If you want the architect, you'll come across him in the endearing interiors of the prospective occupants of his buildings, sometimes caught off his guard as he draws a Corbusier-type sketch; or else you'll see him travelling somewhere between here and eternity. But you'll rarely, if ever, see him in the frontline of his own exegesis.

All the same, we cannot say that Siza refuses to have anything at all to do with his fans. He has already given many interviews; in the lounge of a Maastricht hotel, enveloped in a cloud of *schlager* music, he was pleased to pass the time of night with us and to talk about the work of the architect and the role of criticism. We did not understand how so pragmatic a person as Siza, who takes the world as he sees it, could at the same time be such a great artist. He reminds one of Picasso who once said with apparent nonchalance, 'I don't seek, I find'. In the meantime he continues to astonish his public with these apparently random works. Right from the start we have to admit it: we are still none the wiser.

You have become quite famous in recent years and many people are thinking about your work, even people who haven't actually visited your buildings. Are you satisfied with the current discourse?

In people's criticism of my work I often recognise the mental process that I have gone through myself during the design stage. When that's the case, I'm delighted to have been understood, of course. It can also happen that critics notice things that on the whole I was not aware of myself when I was designing a building, but which with hindsight are very plausible. These are the criticisms that I learn the most from. But it happens just as often that I read pieces that seem to use my work only as a pretext to write something.

Your projects have been effusively described in masses of publications throughout the world. Your work is

Alvaro Siza Vieira

fairly often used as a sort of touchstone by critics who praise your approach as being exemplary. They discuss your work, your reputation, your method and your personal signature; doesn't this machinery of criticism have some impact on you?

No. Of course I keep up with it, that's just part of my work. But that doesn't mean that it is all of equal importance for my real work which is designing. A good example of this is Kenneth Frampton's criticism. I can use it a lot because he is very open to my way of working. That means that he goes to the cultural heart of the matter and doesn't get lost in a mass of details. In fact he is interested in my work because of its bearing on his own; it is therefore no distraction from his own preoccupations. It is rather the incomplete criticism of those critics who are determined to link my name with a notion of critical regionalism; I hate to say it, but one step further and you get something as suspect as regionalism. One mistake leads to another. Anyone who reads Kenneth Frampton's work properly and takes a proper look at my work, won't see any influence of a conservative regionalism on our methods. What we are trying to do is to look into the creative possibilities inherent in the tradition, but we often get put in the same pigeonhole as the conservative body of thought that for a lot of people has a sort of copyright on the word 'tradition'. Tradition is important when it contains moments of change, when it is not just outward form and when it also implies an idea of what goes on inside a building, of conflicts and a potential for innovation. Otherwise tradition just means being stuck in a rut.

We are particularly interested in how criticism invests certain sorts of architecture with cultural relevance. The reason we are asking you how you are affected by the interest in your work is because we are also curious to know how an architect responds to this process by which his/her architecture is generalised into a cultural value that transcends the concrete object. Are you really able to use the insights produced by criticism in your actual designs?

Never directly. Although as a profession we are not isolated, there are still enormous gulfs between the different areas of knowledge in our society. All we can do is to read literature, listen to music, look at art and so forth. In the same way we also read criticism as a part of the contacts we need to survive in this world. Architectural criticism does not have any special status as a conveyor of ideas and I don't ever see myself reading a piece of criticism and using it as a point of departure for a new project. My task is to solve practical problems. There is of course a partial relation between these problems and the views of the critics, but they relate just as much to the views of many, many other people.

Are you saying that you are a pragmatist?

My attitude towards ideals is pragmatic. I belong to a critical movement that has become firmly established in Portugal since the Revolution of 1974. At the time I was really excited by the idea of social change. That does not however have to lead to a dogmatic architectural programme, or even to a working method that is based on a theory. I am a firm believer in praxis, and I don't have much time for the idea of the loner of genius who does everything all by himself. You need other people as well, at every level.

You've often said that. You don't invent anything; all you do is combine and transform something that exists already.

That's right. I work with provisional models that are constantly altered by force of circumstances. My designs as a whole comprise an experimental research programme that can never be planned in advance. I don't work within any theoretical framework nor do I offer a key as to how you should understand my work. What I am interested in is projects that anticipate new developments that one hardly has a name for yet and which exploit the potential of a specific place, the culture that prevails there and the resulting tensions and conflicts. I look for proposals that go beyond any passive notion of just giving material form to an idea, that, by trying to grasp all the facets simultaneously, refuse to impose limits on reality. The point, then, is always to avoid static images and a linear development in time. With every design you need to make a serious attempt to capture one concrete moment of a fleeting image in all its aspects. In concrete terms that means that a project begins for me as soon as I assess the situation on the site itself. That's when I try and size up the scope of the programme. I let all kinds of elements work on me; they may be vague but that doesn't mean they are any less important.

We detect quite a contradiction between this combination of Siza the architect with his unique style and Siza's modest working practice that resists being placed in any theoretical or ideological pigeonhole.

I've learnt to stop treating architecture as consisting of privileged forms and materials; that's the hallmark of the strictly disciplinary approach. I think it is more realistic to start with the problems of the people and their environment. About these, it's extremely difficult to make any generalisations. I work independently

206

and at the same time I talk with the people I'm working for, particularly the occupants. Sometimes you have a difference of opinion; then you look for a solution together. I'd much rather do my utmost to incorporate the complexity of everyday life in my plans than to offer ready-made solutions and then pack my bags and go. And that remains true, regardless of the scale of the project. Whether you're dealing with a small dwelling, or a part of a city, there is no difference in its importance, nor in the quality of the experience; nor can there be any difference in method. Everyday life is equally complex at all levels. It is a matter of innumerable fragments that attract your attention to a greater or lesser degree. As an architect I want to design a space that captures these fragments.

Even so you are and continue to be a specialist who is called in to help. You are also what people call a top architect and, if only because your career has been such a success, you acquire the status of an authority and this makes it difficult to communicate on an equal footing with your clients during the design process. On top of that you are also under pressure from the laws of the market which means that you are constantly working against the clock. How do you deal with that?

It's true that the current system of financing projects only allows for an extremely short period to think about both the commission and the programme. The investors have for a long time been aware of the fact that communication costs money. Add to that the computerisation of our profession; the computer has made an enormous contribution to the ideology of efficiency, without it always being so obvious that this claim is justified in practice. But no matter what machinery you devise there are quite simply no short cuts one can take in the process of finding solutions for architectural problems. Not only that but in our age it is more essential than ever to insist on having that time. Social, technological and economic developments occur so fast that to give anything like an adequate answer to architectural questions one needs all the time and energy at one's disposal. The architect needs this period of time not so much to produce a design, but much more for the almost unconscious analysis of all the facets of the commission. Every commission needs ideas to bring it to life and ideas take time to ripen. It's as simple as that. The wealth of mutual relations between all the different aspects, for instance, the precise articulation of the spaces, that's something that doesn't just happen by itself. When money plays too big a role what you get is a poverty in these relations. ***A good architect works slowly.***

207

The way you put it makes it sound very anonymous: you never seem to feel the need to point out where Siza, the artist leaves his mark and why and when he does so. You describe an extremely complex process requiring so much sorting out that one might think you were a cog in a wheel rather than a really brilliant designer. 'Desperately seeking Siza!' Where's the symbolic dimension, where's the architect who's got his own tale to tell?

The same is true here too, either a symbolic dimension emerges of its own course or it doesn't come at all. In some situations you have an opportunity to develop a symbolic level and in others you don't. And I have to admit that the symbolic dimension is something I really don't bother about at all.

Okay, with that attitude you can maybe make your small contribution to tradition, but you seem unwilling to admit the fact that you also have your own signature, that you are both artist and architect. It's not that your heart's not in the conversation, but when you come to talk about your work you seem to underestimate your position enormously. How do you view the ambiguity on the one hand of your position as a modest participant in a lengthy process and on the other your role as a unique designer who is capable of presenting us with an architectural event of the first order?

Once again the answer lies in the method. Although I work with existing conditions, I'm apparently also the person who has the sensitivity to add something to them that is exceptional. It is of course not a case of a mechanical reproduction of something that's already there, but of transforming it so subtly that it becomes quite literally a unique construct. What I am able to do is to seize hold of something that's already in the air, and which requires concerted efforts to crystallise into a theme I can actually make something of. You may succeed in catching it, but your work doesn't end there; you will constantly have to measure your basic assumptions up against the place and moment in time you are working in. What I mean by this is that understanding duration is not a matter of scientific knowledge nor of history; it requires a great many other faculties that are by no means so easy to define.

How can you do that if you're thinking about the future of a building? The way you talk about your working method you seem acutely sensitive to the present use of a project, but when it comes to imagining what your building might be like in fifty years' time, one would think a vision of the future based on pure daring would be more to the point than one based on sensitivity.

Boa Nova Tea House, Leça da Palmeira, 1963

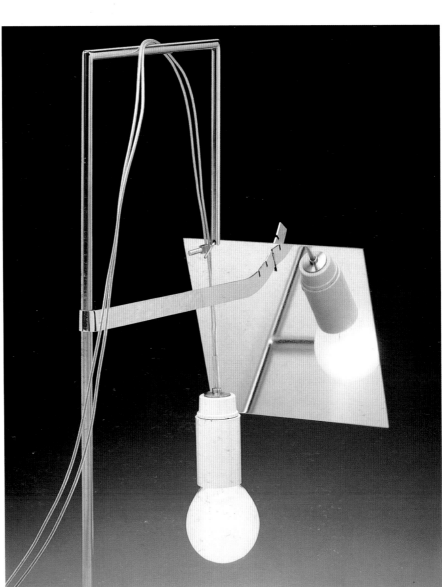

Table lamp, 1992

Swimming pool, Quinta da Conceição, 1965

Bouça Housing, Porto, 1977

Housing in Schilderswijk Ward, The Hague, 1986   Two Houses in Van der Venne Park, The Hague, 1986

If we have to solve a problem, then today's needs are obviously much more important than those of tomorrow. All architecture that assumes the opposite is insensitive. All the same, I still need to do all I can to situate the building in a context of change and not treat it as something static. Knowledge and information are not enough; intuition also plays a role. That fits in very well with the notion of the architect as a creative artist. You have to try and obtain as precise a picture as possible of all the facets of your project, so that your solution is also as flexible as possible. Taking a couple of variables and coming up with a static solution is not the right way to do things. Precision requires an interdisciplinary approach on many fronts; no work is ever autonomous, if you think how many matters are involved. That's also why time is so indispensable; the less time you allow yourself the more your solutions are oversimplified.

A strange ambiguity also seems to emerge in your line of argument. On one hand you talk about the sensitivity a designer needs and the importance of intuition and on the other hand you appear to want to emphasise the aspect of scientific knowledge.

They are two sides of the same coin. When I'm working on a project in a city I am unfamiliar with, my own experience is not enough. I will have to make a deeper exploration of construction methods, technology, the future use of the buildings and goodness knows what else. So I need plenty of facts. That's the aspect of acquiring knowledge, then. Equally important, however, is a good appreciation of the culture and atmosphere of a situation. One's analytical equipment is hopelessly inadequate for such a task. Once again it's sensitivity that counts. One's handling of the different aspects of a commission has then itself a multifaceted character. It is not enough to have all the facts at one's disposal. The first impression is just as important, not in any self-indulgent sense, but already with a view to a potential building. The basic outline comes very quickly; then one has to fill it in with concrete information.

Let's link up your notions about the architect's approach to his work with your ideas about the status of architecture. According to your working method as you've just described it, your architecture can never not be 'of its time', seeing that you take the present moment and the context as your points of departure. On the other hand your architecture can hardly be described as belonging to this time. It is not without reason that it has frequently been regarded as having a sort of immunity to time. It is architecture as it really is, that is simply there; it is an architecture of presence. In that respect it does not belong to this time, which is one of ephemeral materials, of speed and the conquest of physical space by virtual space. Is there a contradiction there?

There is always a conflict and that even increases as I get older. I have to be on my guard not to oversimplify things, but you can hardly deny that architecture *is* physical presence. There is of course a conflict between modernity and the stillness of my buildings, but there is no contradiction there. Architecture that is still has a definite potential for incorporating a historical dynamic. Only not at the level of illustration. It's hard however for me to point out what this attitude towards architecture consists of, because the dynamic I'm talking about is very difficult to capture in a static description. But the fact that I may have difficulties defining my position doesn't justify the frequent charge that creative architects like myself don't have the first clue what is going on in the world. In my view it is a question of developing a sort of knowledge that participates in the numerous forms of knowledge that are possible in our time.

You certainly pay some attention to dynamics but on top of that you talk more about the evolutionary aspects of a specific culture than about revolutionary developments in economics, technology, management expertise etcetera. In the world of these developments things no longer revolve around a concrete context or a historical situation but round an extra-contextual, extra-historical situation that changes so rapidly that you can no longer employ concepts such as continuity, tradition and evolution to describe it. You call the architecture that exploits this idea 'illustrative', but couldn't you imagine an architecture that might in fact be a more interesting commentary on just this phenomenon?

Yes, my own architecture. I think that the greater the speed of the process of modernisation, the more gradual and more motionless architecture will have to be.

Why?

I feel like saying 'because'. That seems like the proper way to explain an idea like this.

Why do you think that the greater the speed the more important it becomes to stand still? To get peace and quiet?

No, that's not what I'm talking about. What I mean is that there are roughly two real attitudes one can adopt in the present situation. The first produces an architecture that appears to be inescapably caught up in the process of change. That is the ephemeral architecture I mentioned. The other attitude is one that produces a stable architecture. **What I'm interested in is a stability that gives**

one the possibility of reflection, even of participating in change without immediately turning into a comet that whirls around randomly in the universe. As far as I'm concerned, when I think of architecture, I think primarily of stability, serenity and presence. You can't just plunge into the giddy whirl of events and still expect to have an architecture that is stable and motionless. You have to define your position in the midst of this glut of information. The more information I can assimilate, the more serene my architecture becomes. I think that most architecture is not sufficiently motionless, because we aren't able to assimilate enough information. I mean that between the presence of things and the rapid changes taking place in the world there is a great deal of interaction. They aren't opposites.

What do you mean by that concretely? In New York, for instance, which is the realm of speed and change par excellence, would you erect a completely still building that would contrast with the speed of everything around it?

New York is proof of what I'm saying. Most of the buildings in Manhattan are extremely stable. There are few cities where the buildings at street level are so solidly and massively anchored. The frenzy in New York does not lie in the architecture, but in the intersections between the buildings, the traffic, the innumerable things going on, the mixture of cultures. The architecture forms a solid and static foundation for all that speed. The tops of the skyscrapers are narrow and fantastic, but lower down they are sturdy and unambiguous.

Is this a good example of what you mean by 'still' architecture?

Why not? These buildings have got something that makes them one with the ground; they are tight, they are consistent and they have their own autonomy. They are independent of each other. Their outlines are completely separate but that is just what makes them fascinating as a whole. The absence of any attempt to try and find some kind of urbanistic relationship is what gives the whole a very high degree of integrity. I don't see much future for architecture that deliberately tries to express the dynamics of modern life.

So you admire New York? But if we compare your solutions with those of New York – a pretty odd comparison from the point of view of function – it's difficult to understand what your admiration is based on.

It's okay in New York!

Is New York really okay? That's the question. You surely can't understand the stability of a specific architecture without immediately thinking of the social conditions where this stability occurs? Wouldn't it be a less forced comparison if you pictured New York as a neutral frame, a sort of basis for the frenzy of modern life and the grid system as a sort of silent matrix where money consumer goods and information can continue to flow with as little interruption as possible? Your architecture would seem to contain an implicit criticism of a world order like that, since your buildings suggest a feeling for materials, for space and for human proportions. Your caution is really amazing. Surely you're not afraid of saying what you think about cultural questions? In the seventies you even worked for the SAAL, a highly critical programme of architectural renewal in Portugal. By taking a stand both verbally and in your architecture, you've made a crucial contribution to the cultural debate. Something like that is just what is lacking in the architecture of the big investors and speculators we think of when we think of Manhattan. If your architecture is used, with your tacit consent at least, as a model of one form of cultural resistance, or is at any rate described as a means of increasing people's sensitivity to architecture, you can hardly start eulogising the isotropic space of New York architecture and urban design, with its neutral uninterrupted floor areas.

Well, maybe I'm referring to other buildings. There are so many buildings in New York.

Surely we were talking specifically about the 'upward trend of thought', about downtown and midtown Manhattan?

That is only a partial and biased notion of New York.

Okay then, let's talk about the New York grid system then. That's something you find everywhere. The grid is the condition for a serene and autonomous architecture which is what you admire. But at the same time the grid is a model for an emphatically economically-based way of thinking. How can I maximise the profits I can make from my plot of land? In terms of logistics and infrastructure, how can I organise my affairs most advantageously? The architecture that pushes its way upward to the sky is therefore not devoid of economic aspirations, and the cultural aspirations that pertain to them. There is surely sufficient evidence there for you to form a judgement about what is wrong with this city.

The grid pattern may well be a good one for the economic order, but you also get it in ancient Egypt and in many other cultures as well. So I would never think of it as being synonymous with capitalist management. It's much more than that.

Rem Koolhaas with Zoe Zenghelis, The City of the Captive Globe, 1977

Faculty of Architecture, Porto University, 1993

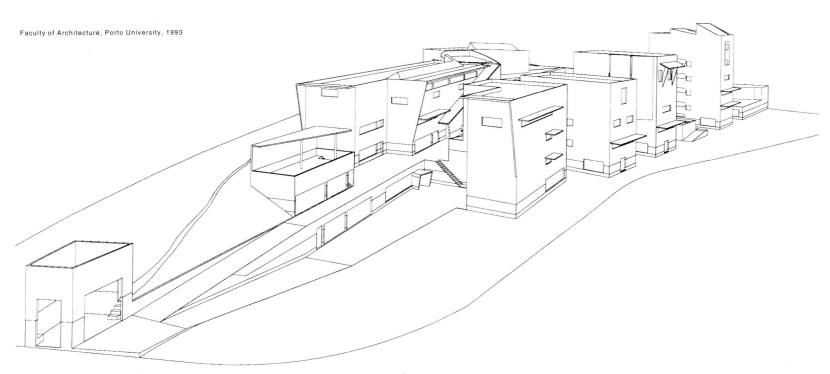

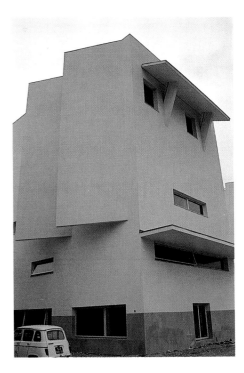

So you view everything in its specific context. New York has a tradition of profiteering. Portugal has other traditions again. You argue that you must check out what the main themes are in each situation in order to exploit them. The question remains, how do you propose to propagate a tradition like that and still maintain your critical attitude?

I respond to the tradition in a way that is dynamic, every bit as dynamic as the tradition itself is. If I want to capture the feeling of a city then I really do mean the whole city. And that also means the influence on the city of its history. In my case it's not just a case of looking for the roots but also for how all the trends that developed from these roots also converge. Ergo: cosmopolitanism is contained within the tradition.

But at what point, then, can your architecture function as an instrument of criticism? In the course of working out your programme? If your architecture tends towards stillness, how can that stillness be interpreted as cultural criticism when at the same time you state that every place has to be appreciated on its own terms? Or to put it more concretely, if you were asked to build a prison in a country that had an extremely repressive tradition in designing prison cells, what would you do? Or to take a less emotionally charged example, a law court?

Probably I wouldn't build a prison at all. I very much like working on projects where plenty of participation is involved, but I'd sooner not even begin on something like that. Even though there are growing demands for making prisons more humane by giving them a new character, it remains an impossible commission. A prison's purpose remains that of housing criminals, not ordinary people. That's not something I want to have anything to do with. It is true that there are prisons whose typology is extremely interesting but the commission to design a prison is always so tied up with the functional requirement of controlling people that it becomes a monstrosity. The only function that actually plays a role there is that of control; every building that has only one function is in fact a monstrosity. The relation of a building to its function needs to be much less schematic and formal if you want to produce good architecture. A law court building offers more possibilities, but there too, speaking personally, I think there is too strict a link with function. The power of the law is invariably obliged to inspire a sense of awe in people and a specific typology goes with it. If you really want to break with that, you shouldn't take on the commission in the first place. That's why I really like designing dwellings, because there isn't such a high degree of specialisation of the spaces with them. If you have an idea of history as changing very rapidly, you will go to great lengths in your detailing to ascribe specific functions to specific spaces. But if you have more respect for time, you can afford to be much less specialised and still give the spaces an appropriate character. That's how it has been done in European cities through the ages, with countless houses from previous centuries still being lived in. It's the relation between the function, the character and the representation of the institution that interests me. I don't feel so comfortable with too strict a definition of function.

What sort of possibilities do you have if you are reluctant to be too tied down by functions?

There was a time when architects worked hard to redefine the programme. In the sixties and seventies they tried to expand their area of action. Just as in recent years architects have become much less concerned with the life *inside* their buildings, so less and less attention is being paid to the rewriting of the programme. The concern for materials and for the process of construction is also on the decline. Or else the mode of construction often seems to have been chosen completely arbitrarily. I think that this faith in the treatment of form in complete isolation is one of the worst things in the design process at the present time. Equally bad is the almost triumphant acceptance of the separating out of the different areas of knowledge. **This total specialisation in all areas of our work creates a void that explains much of the emptiness you find in present-day architecture.**

Can architecture escape this trend?

That won't be easy. The whole system of production is based on it. Architecture doesn't have many weapons to deal with it. You can of course produce isolated projects and these can serve as an example. But in general architectural design is powerless to do anything against it. The problem is much too big.

Now you are accepting specialisation as something inevitable; as though you are confirming the very thing that you criticise. Surely you're something more than just a specialist?

Yes, you have a responsibility to take a stand there. It is a cultural question that everybody has to deal with in his or her own field of activity. Architecture too can adopt a critical position in this respect. You can look for a certain kind of work or else you can refuse it; you can stop collaborating with certain architects. With other people and in other areas that are not strictly professional all kinds of things are possible. I think there are some grounds for hope there.

213

The Invisible in Architecture could be conceived as topos. But isn't a place visible? No, a place, a topos, is something you just feel. Perception of place operates through all the senses and depends on the memory too. Place is directly related to the subject of Being. In this, it is the human scale, the body, that matters. Or conversely, only that which we can directly experience can be a place. Place only arises in the mind of the person who is there. Under this conception, space, time and action merge. Place is a rooting in the ground, an existence that has become an essence.

The landsman has his own microcosm which is stationary in the universe, and this can give rise to the idea that the universe rotates around him. His place is the anchor of all identity and gives everything else its connotation. But the sedentary life is in decline and hence also the significance of place. The land, for millennia the bedrock of a belief in a Self, is now dominated by machinery. The enormous harvests are gathered without sweat or blood being shed. Few labourers are needed on the land, and even these travel from location to location, by car or by air. In the rest of the world, either the soil is so eroded or the small plots have become so untenable that the inhabitants are forced to move on or away: the land has too little to offer them. Thus there are two kinds of nomad – the wealthy, whose idiosyncratic home (or perhaps *Heimat*) is located in the individual brain, surrounded by communications equipment in office or living room, whose life consists of transfers of person or data by motorway, aircraft, television or fax; and the utterly destitute, whose place is in the shanty town or the immigrant boat, and whose life is a permanent hunt for the basic means of existence.

The dual nomadism, the universal diaspora, forms part of our 'global metropolis'. Between these contrasting caravans there is a *peau de chagrin*, a zone that is inhabitable but continually further degraded by the disruptive effect of the two nomadisms; crumbling suburbs where migrants on the way up, with a place to call their own at last, clash explosively with earlier cohorts

Topos

who have failed to find a place among the richer nomads. And then there is naturally still a forgotten canton here and there, untouched by modernity, which, once discovered, survives for a little while as a focus of nostalgia and hopeless resistance. Finally, there is the place as a historic relic, protected and smartened up by monument committees and CNNed to our TV screens as animated wallpaper.

The place cradles the function, weaves it into the existing fabric. But, whatever Post-Modernism would have us think, this fabric is exhaustively monofunctional; the function tends to instigate the place, which thereby loses many of its qualities. When we study the zoning plan of this world, we see that only now the Athens Charter of Le Corbusier's CIAM is globally paramount. We can pick out a) recuperative places, b) production places and c) recreational places. To these we must add d) places for storing information, e) infrastructure f) 'nature', and g) places for dumping the inevitable waste. If we are to believe the popular future scenarios, countless objectivised spots such as these are likely to be brought into line by computer technology. Living, working and recreation can then take place largely at home in a mainly virtual space: the 'electronic cottage' (Alvin Toffler). Whatever the case, this modernisation and functionalisation of the place has a number of far-reaching consequences.

In the West, the communal place has been banished from the city. The collective topos is being replaced increasingly by media that allow reception by but not communication between people of flesh and blood. The source of authority has shifted from the public physical space to the communicative media (especially television). The physical place is thus arguably dead, i.e. it no longer has a visible presence among our repertoire of life-determining forces. Accordingly, the physical place is losing its relevance to the social definition of the individual.

The less significant the place becomes as public domain, the more we see an adulation of the place as *sanctus sanctorum*. It has become a spiritual entity. Broadly speaking, this has become the most widespread notion of place among those who are seriously concerned about the consequences of modernity. Around the globe, in their vision, there is being drawn a fine-meshed network which eliminates all obstacles and delays, and which reduces every place to an A or a B between which the straight line is the shortest path. Thus the world will soon be flat after all. They wish to use place to bring the juggernaut of civilisation to a halt and create an island of resistance in which exemplary alternatives are possible. In these places, the ground can still be cherished, and a direct, tactile experience is still possible. The place can be restored to its former glory – a rehabilitation of authenticity amid the universal atopia of simulation and virtual reality. Thus the name-giving path appears in opposition to the anonymous grid, the depth of a trace to the flatness of the map, the centripetal topos of Frank Lloyd Wright's Robie House to the isotropic space of Le Corbusier's Maison Domino. The abstraction of rationalism is challenged by the concreteness of phenomenology. Finally, this reaction to atopia can result in the celebration of the body, the only really autonomous place still left to us. The body is everyone's ark in the deluge of information.

Architecture is, by necessity, the creation of a place, even when the latter is delimited by nothing more than transparent curtain walls. The place is where the building touches the ground and comes literally into contact with mankind and the history of the location. The materiality of the built object is, a priori, an obstacle to modernity; it is an act of resistance against the modernistic passion for clearing away every physical and psychological barrier. The solidity of the foundations exacerbates this opposition. Nonetheless, the 'critical' attributes of architecture fall all too easily prey to modernity – if not as a demolition site, then as museum piece. This is because it has abandoned its competence to guide and critically interpret the act (architecture's legitimacy!) and has thereby become a willing victim of the dissolution of place. The action has been expelled to the private domain and to the electronic 'places' of the new media. The architectural place has thus become little more than an artificially preserved habitat. No wonder this predilection for topography is nowhere so clearly at the cost of action as in architecture. What is more, in as far as a social critique has actually been formulated in architecture in recent years, its touchstone has been the ideal topos rather than the sphere of human actions.

In this criticism, it is stressed that having a somatic identity will help us recreate a relationship between man and his built environment, a relationship with the material world around him. Architecture, by offering a helping hand in the reinstatement of somatic identity, comes to play a part once more in the development of man's capacity to either adapt to or distinguish himself from his environment. It is precisely the interplay of attraction and detachment that gives us a sense of place.

Still, this architectural strategy can never really become an alternative. After all, such things are only possible on remote, idyllic islands, and there are few of those left nowadays. Thus tectonic, place-defining tours de force are inclined to have more an air of provincialism about them, if not of nostalgia. The place that architecture thus offers does no more than distract attention from the fact that the destruction continues uninterrupted in other parts of the world. Moreover, this architecture becomes a tourist attraction even before the paint is dry. No sooner has a place been discovered than it is annexed by the wealthy nomads with their passion to perpetuate and fossilise the place in photos and videos. They re-experience the realness later, in the comfort of their homes.

Three strategies and three architects Architecture, by its nature as a delimiter and as a provider of habitation, creates place, but the extent to which this forms part of a conscious strategy varies. In this respect, we distinguish the following three strategies:

Archaism The first strategy presupposes a need to reinforce the place explicitly. It attempts to rediscover the genius loci; it cherishes the relationship between design and surroundings; it celebrates the materiality and the tectonics of the built object; it aims to respect the life-world of the users; and it appeals to the sense of touch as a medium for experiencing place. The place comes alive through a _promenade architecturale_. The body is respatialised by the creation of a place that stimulates the tactile sense. The place is a 'niche' for the human being, a sheltered spot in an overwhelmingly dynamic world. **_Santiago Calatrava_** never wavers from his belief in this notion of place. In designs whose function is mobility, in particular his bridges, he creates pauses where man and construction meet. In his designs for static programmes, his work is principally about the absoluteness and aura of the pure object.

Façadism The second strategy attempts, despite the phenomenological nature of the place experience, to create a topos by means of representative images. The relationship to the place develops largely through an iconography. Thus while Facadism can induce recognition, it is incapable of invoking direct perception, let alone supporting the growth of a somatic identity. Since the visual cortex has the sole responsibility here for the processing of impressions, the experience retains strongly discursive and verbal attributes. Perhaps language offers a house to live in but not a home. **_Pietro Derossi_** denotes place by means of a narrative image. Topos is for him an interplay of linguistic elements, a field of polysemic alternatives, a network of interpretations. Due to the indirectness of this approach, any statement it makes about place can only be narrative. The space is dominated by a treatment of the surface.

Fascinism The third strategy takes cognisance of the bankruptcy of the topos and prefers to become involved in the creation of non-place, often termed the periphery. Now that the place-experience is falling prey to speed, there is no alternative but simply to fall in with this historical tendency. Thus it seeks no _stabilitas loci_, nor a _corpus integritas_, but the furnishing of the atopia of the Now.

Julia Bolles and Peter Wilson accept the loss of the topos but are not prepared just to ignore the false re-enactment that has come in its stead. Therefore they operate with a kind of double morality in which references to the environment go hand in hand with ark-like constructions, vehicles of exile. They thereby create an autonomous topos in which a universal, atopic message is propagated. It is not the content but the form of things that determine the chance of survival in the maelstrom: 'the simple massing of autonomous objects'.

I want to be grounded. Therefore my buildings are somewhat larger on ground level. They are steadily standing. They want to be bound to the earth. I'm keen on having everything related to Mother Earth. **Ton Alberts & Max van Huut**

I want to create an architecture that is in harmony with the climate and other natural conditions of the land and is based on the character of place but at the same time is made self-sufficient by a rigorous logic of its own. **Tadao Ando**

We want to create spaces that make a person passing through them feel like an actor. He will straighten up and play. **Ricardo Bofill**

Architecture is both particular, because it is grounded, and universalisable, because it is a subject for memory and media. To deny place and experience is irresponsible, to resist universalisation impossible. **Julia Bolles & Peter Wilson**

In my work, the structural, tectonic device is most important, thus, I insist so much on the section. And for this reason the section plays such an important role, and not so much the plan. **Santiago Calatrava**

In the initial stages I try to visualise the building as a place after it is built. I think of the people in it and the way they will look at it – find the sources in that. I use the sketchbook as a catalyst. I love the irrationality of drawing – just to draw a line and see what happens. It's not quite automatic drawing, but it's starting with something you know, such as the outline of a site. You draw it and very often it develops into something else and it's that development which you can't do simply by sitting down and analysing something and redrawing it using the usual logical processes of design. I much prefer a process which uses sequential operations to allow the unpredictable element to emerge. It's a conversation between the mind and the paper. **Nigel Coates & Doug Branson**

It is the specificity of the project, in the place, here and now, that opens us to reflection regarding the universal, the free vastness of the land. **Pietro Derossi**

Consider the body stripped, stripped of cultural fixity, of gender codes, of ethnic and political codes... de-signed, the body as site: a primary surface for signification like the surface of the earth or a blank page. The body is a surface vulnerable to a surplus of meanings, constantly being rewritten... The body is a site for transient texts of the marketplace. **Elisabeth Diller & Ricardo Scofidio**

I myself am very fond of running, driving and flying. But if all buildings were designed to be seen from a moving car, the result would be nightmarish. Our buildings are usually always centred, set on an axis – very traditional in fact. **Norman Foster**

In the interior of the Joan Miró Library, the reading room, defined by radial bookshelves placed along a curve, opens itself towards the park, yet maintaining a certain distance from it thanks to the sheet of water reflecting pool lying between the trees and the building. Here as well the natural light gets reflected by the water and filtered through the wide eaves. **Beth Galí**

I am interested in finishing work, but I am interested in the work's not appearing finished, with every hair in place, every piece of furniture in its spot ready for photographs. I prefer the sketch quality, the tentativeness (...) rather than the presumption of total resolution and finality. **Frank Gehry**

There is in any language, and certainly in architecture, a general language. At the same time, there must be a specific language. The Humana Building, for example, would be very awkwardly placed in any other location in that city. There are five or six-storey Victorian storefronts adjacent to the building and because of that, I've employed a reference to a loggia or colonnade in the building and on the face of the building, and hoped that the point will be caught that there is a similarity. Though one might find another site for those various references and activities, they do become more specific to Louisville and that particular site than to somewhere else. So there's where my 'take' on architecture becomes localised to the site. **Michael Graves**

Trying to incorporate in the Shonandai project all that had been excluded by modern planning, I discovered I was designing not so much a work of architecture as a topography. (...) My intention was to bury 'modern' architecture underground and to create above it 'topographical' spaces continuous with the site. **Itsuko Hasegawa**

Topos is constantly misunderstood and seen in a traditional way, not as the awareness of our own body, the awareness of being alive...
Jacques Herzog & Pierre de Meuron

Architecture is bound to situation. Unlike music, painting, sculpture, film, and literature, a construction (non-mobile) is intertwined with the experience of a place. The site of a building is more than a mere ingredient in its conception. It is its physical and metaphysical foundation. The resolution of the functional aspects of site and building, the vistas, sun angles, circulation, and access, are the 'physics' that demand the 'metaphysics' of architecture. Through a link, an extended motive, a building is more than something merely fashioned for the site. **Steven Holl**

Architecture is not necessarily either a shelter or a monument. But one of its principal distinctions consists in the fact that a building is constructed or produced by whatever means are appropriate. A cave is not architecture, neither is a tree, whereas every sheet of steel erected in the desert is architecture. Architecture is a creation of space, created by men and for men. **Hans Hollein**

Build in such a way that you and your loved ones can find pleasure at any time in using your buildings, looking at them, living, working, holidaying and growing old in them.
Leon Krier

We should never start inventing! When rationalists invented houses arranged in lines along a street plan, they robbed the inhabitants of all the reptilian habits that prevailed in the old urban spaces and in their articulations. When they thought up the tree model for functionally stacked dwellings, they robbed the inhabitants of their equally reptilian patrimony of old-style house plans that paraphrased the human body.
Let's get subjective, right now! **Lucien Kroll**

Positive efforts to create intermediate zones is a way to rediscover and reclaim the valuable elements and mode of being that were excluded by Western dualism and binomial opposition. This is the reason that topos, regionalism, and the 'noise' of minor cultures have once again become the themes of architecture. A forced compromise between the two opposing elements of dualism does not create a new rapport (of symbiosis). Symbiosis involves the mutual inclusivity of at least some aspect of two opposing elements, and the creation of a dynamic stability. Such a dynamic, or symbiotic, relationship is achieved through the tentative establishment of an ambivalent, multivalent intermediate zone between the two elements. **Kisho Kurokawa**

Town planning is just making places, places where people can sit in the shade or where children can play properly, protected. **Lucien Lafour & Rikkert Wijk**

The city is an historical product which will also disappear into history, as it appeared in history. I'm often perplexed when people get so obsessed with the notion of the city as if it was the final and ultimate development of architecture. One should think of other things, not only of cities. Of a world without cities for instance. A world where cities are no longer the controlling power centres of society and culture. Where culture is independent of place. **Daniel Libeskind**

The constructed world is our global heritage, our cultural and social topography, which is anything but artificial. Specifically addressing the situation in America, the newly transformed landscape, contrary to popular sentiment, deserves the same attention and respect as the one created by nature. I would venture that in the modern world the species of landscape that ecologists courageously struggle to preserve has the same value and deserves the same respect and attention as the environment that mankind has elected to create. **Rafael Moneo**

It is not the clash between fragments of architecture that counts, but the invisible movement between them. This invisible movement is neither a part of language nor of structure. This movement is nothing but a constant and mobile relationship inside language itself. **Bernard Tschumi**

In a building or city, universal elements can be combined in unique ways to meet the needs of a specific project or site. The unique may be suggested within the universal by symbolism. Symbolic allusion for today should, we believe, be representational. This is the essence of our notion of the decorated shed: you use the going building conventions of the society to produce the decorated shed, and on the front use representation to make the building unique.
The problem at its most extreme could be posed as: How would you design a McDonalds for the Piazza del Popolo? Is the only answer that one shouldn't do it?
Robert Venturi & Denise Scott Brown

Gothic After the Death of God

When we look at the work of Santiago Calatrava, we see lively urban scenes, incomparable constructions and elegant details. The bridges and canopies to which he generally applies himself look like an unrestrained game with the basic concepts of statics, a pure manipulation of natural laws. But take note: this is a *plastically* articulated manipulation, determined not only by the constraints of physics but by a subjective preference for forms derived from animal skeletons. Calatrava's monumental images are reminiscent of the gigantic rib-cages, vertebrae and whalebones in a natural history museum.

In Calatrava's best projects this skeleton is a thing of great autonomous beauty. The bones shine through the complex living tissue as in an X-ray. He orchestrates the slumbering potential of an infrastructural node with great virtuosity. The place becomes a memorable experience, a stage in an ordinary journey which is elevated to the status of ritual.

Calatrava clearly finds himself in good historical company, with Viollet-le-Duc, Antoni Gaudí, Robert Maillart, Pier Luigi Nervi and Felix Candela. Like them, Calatrava makes poetry out of the kind of civil engineering usually treated as just a prosaic business of applied mathematics. As art approaches science, science turns irresistibly back to art. Calatrava's zoomorphic structures of concrete and steel, his technical precision and his fabulous *mis en-scène* (descended from that of Gaudí) make his architecture into compelling *Gesamtkunstwerke*. At times it approaches the grace of the Gothic.

Calatrava is not especially concerned with designing a novel ground plan, but with investigating the spatial and tectonic character of the structure. This obtains its distinctive quality through a design method based on cross-sections and three-dimensional models. Calatrava takes the programme for what it is and concentrates on staging an overwhelming experience. Now that Calatrava's soaring international fame is bringing him a growing and increasingly varied stream of commissions, the fine, generative added value of his architecture is coming under pressure. His X-ray bone structures are undiminished in their beauty, but what of the flesh and blood? Does the social tissue really benefit from continual exposure to this penetrating radiation?

Bridging the Historical Pillars of Modern Architecture

Calatrava's architecture is characterised by a fusion of civil engineering and sculpture. Extreme abstraction materialises as a figurative image, and the end result of a complex series of calculations turns out to be art. No wonder he reaps boundless admiration and seldom more than muted criticism. For critics, Calatrava's work is a puzzle but at the same time it offers a potential way out of the trap that has hampered them since the Enlightenment: the disciplinary dichotomy between architectural design and technical construction. The Modern Movement of the first half of this century did its best to rise above the historic split between Beaux-Arts and Polytechnique, but it continued to be true and is now more so than ever that the architect is concerned largely with design while the engineer (and the investor) determine the underlying structure. This long-

BCE Place, gallery and heritage square, Toronto, 1992   Salisbury Cathedral, 1220

established split has deprived everyone of the capacity to think about meaning and structure simultaneously. In this light, Calatrava's genial inventions seem to offer deliverance from the institutional impediments. The artist can appear in the guise of the engineer (and vice versa) and expression and structure prove perfectly compatible. *Poiesis* and *techne*, having degenerated as the result of a misunderstanding to become the opposing poles of architecture, find their reconciliation in Calatrava's work. But because the strict dividing line between the areas of competence has also seriously clouded the perceptive powers of the critic, this work is seen by many critics as being no more than a mythic synthesis that is inevitably unique to Calatrava. Calatrava himself never places the institutional conditioning of the profession in jeopardy. By virtue of the intense power of the image his work presents, he avoids this danger and even adds to the strength of the métier.

The Phenomenology of the Dynamic Structure

Calatrava's civic works have an almost indescribable charisma that leaves few passers-by or users untouched. What holds our attention is the phenomenology of the dynamic structure: a pronounced organic presence that expresses the power of natural forces in materials. When this captivating quality coincides with a programme of infrastructural development in town or country, the architect succeeds in blending everything into a virtuoso expression of social traffic, physical sensation, architectural insight and the laws of bending moments.

At the core of all Calatrava's designs is a movement curbed, a restrained force that gives the impression of being about to break into motion; and this is present in every work down to the level of the finest particulars. His control over that movement is subtly exerted by a perfectly detailed interplay of contrasts – light and shadow, convex and concave, weightless and heavy.

Another noteworthy aspect, observable for instance in the façade of the distribution

When searching in the library of the ETH in Zürich under the lemma Gaudi, I found a little book which I looked through. It had astonishing beautiful drawings, carefully put together. It had chain-models, constructed in a simple way, economically too, but I thought it highly important. I looked it through again and again and studied it. The interesting thing is that it was made in that university, and also in other places far from Spain there are people who are interested in Gaudi. I like that very much. My relation to Gaudi is pure admiration for his work. The direct Modernism of his work, I think it is a tremendous experience. What fascinates me enormously in Gaudi's work is the human dimension behind it, and also the whole circumstances under which these buildings were made. How they are tremendous engagement, as for example the canopy of the cathedral in Mallorca, which is for the people who know it a wonder of Modern art.

Santiago Calatrava

It is interesting to ask oneself if architecture or engineering can be art. It is a question I asked myself more than once, and I think it is connected with the work of one person and with his development. I do not think that any of my buildings can make the claim of being a work of art, not even a *Gesamtkunstwerk*. So I think my work must be seen as an evolutionary unity, and I think I have at least tried to indicate my curiosity for several things with this miscellenea of subjects, projects, or interests.

Santiago Calatrava

The modern engineer has two things I like very much. One is an empirical understanding of nature. Engineers look at phenomena and try to describe them, for example taking a slope and its movement and modelling these in terms of, say, shear forces. The second is pure creativity. The conceptual work in devising forces which cope with the problem. And I think that is why the evolution of respect for the landscape can be achieved more successfully by the engineer than by the architect.

Santiago Calatrava

The connection between a projected work and the urban context is of great importance. First of all any architectural or engineering work has a technical or practical purpose, for example to span a river, to cross an obstacle. From that stage onwards, the task of the architect consists in learning, educating, in urbanising, in practising urbanness with the design.

Santiago Calatrava

Drawing and architecture are two different things. Architecture is a phenomenon in itself. It comes more from the world of ideas directly applied to the materials used in building. Graphics intervene: they have now become almost a hindrance.

Santiago Calatrava

centre in Coesfeld-Lette (1983) and the Stadelhofenstation in Zürich (1984), is that however daringly the construction may be exposed to view it is never used to convey the technocratic message that is typical of so much high-tech architecture. There is no technicist mask that exalts technology as an end in itself. Calatrava opts for a formal vocabulary derived from biology and thus distances himself from the explicit glorification of technology. Moreover, he treats the social, urban and topographical elements that underlie his commission with great care. In his early work, especially, Calatrava shows much respect for the public space. His concern for a social meaning of the place is illustrated by the separation of pedestrian and motorised traffic, and by the *belvederes* and little *piazzas* which produce a momentary pause in the circulation so strongly suggested by the structure, allowing people calmly to take over. Especially in his bridges, these points of rest are linked by lines, for example in the form of staircases or linear elements of the basic structure. He thus clarifies the inner logic of the architectural object as a whole and enhances its relationship to the landscape.

The everyday movements of the public and the specificity of the landscape interact with the plasticity of the architecture. At the same time, the structure functions as an imposing urban monument. In his recent work this monumentality, which is an essential constituent of Calatrava's fame, seems to be gaining greater autonomy. A powerful architectural vitality is emerging independently of local and social context. This vitality does not so much generate force as represent it. The hidden potential of the place is no longer mobilised as the source of the image. The rationalist approach of the construction is becoming ever more clearly revealed by a subjective preference for skeletal anatomy. Thus the architecture loses in social meaning, but gains in force and autonomy. It seems to do more good than bad for the popularity of this work.

Autarchitecture

However self-referent and autonomous the finished result may be, the ideological choice shows through. By means of its ontological treatment of the material and construction, the work aims to stimulate a genuine communication that is not yet sullied by the mediatised, touristic habit of vision. With Calatrava, architecture is not a cultural metaphor but a modest platform, a possible basis for regaining a kind of moral integrity. In his structures, this need is condensed and furnished with an ostensibly pure image. It becomes a kind of manifesto of the unrepresentable. An essential feature of Calatrava is the non-cerebral way he communicates this manifesto. That is why Alejandro Zaera connected Calatrava's work to Robert Vischer's aesthetic theory of the symbolic empathy (*Einfühlung*) in which the architect imparts his building with an *anima* that cannot be deduced logically or grasped in conventional linguistic terms, but which can be felt through an almost mystical relationship with the material, a relationship that is somewhere halfway between animism and pantheism.★ Material, space, light, proportions and construction come together at an unconscious level to form a meaning that can scarcely be reduced to rational terms. Calatrava's zoomorphic skeletons seem to

★ Zaera, Alexander, 'The Living Structure', *El Croquis* 43 (1990), p. 174.

appeal to this kind of perception. It is not the radicalised distinction between beauty and utility that is at issue here, as it was in the aesthetics of the avant-garde, but the healing force of the pre-conscious experience: in other words, the region in which we are all equal. Thus Calatrava's bridges are also bridges in a spiritual sense, bridges leading the way from an overheated sign system to an unsullied world. The principle of symbolic empathy produces, in Zaera's words, 'a subjective action capable of impregnating with emotion the process of creating objects'. We might call it 'autarchitecture', architecture that is self-sufficient. Man is offered a framework, but is confined by that framework at the same time. Escape from this 'theology of the beautiful' is possible only in a physical sense.

Ultimately Calatrava's organic architecture can offer no more than a temporary way out of the malaise of meaning. Nature provides the images of vitalism, but the annexation of these images by architecture does not produce vital architecture of its own accord.

Horizontal Gothic

Analysis of the architectonic components of Calatrava's work produces inevitable reminiscences of the Gothic – but as a horizontalist construction between mortals rather than a verticalist building style of the divine. The architecture manifests itself in the interaction of structure and light. The actual circumscription of space is postponed; space is not delineated by walls so much as by openings. Calatrava creates a diaphanous structure which makes the incident light critical to the architectural experience (this works at night too, with artificial light). Similar correspondences with Gothic architecture are present in the skeletal structure with its web of constructive ribs, the alternating system, the penetration of light into even the smallest of internal spaces,

Bach de Roda – Felipe II Bridge, Barcelona, 1987

Rather than the reflection of an *idea* (which never can be grasped as such), Heidegger understands the thing as the 'gathering of a world'. The meaning of a thing or form thus consists in what it gathers. As examples he analyses nameable things such as 'jug' and 'bridge'. (...) Heidegger intends 'gathering' in a very concrete sense. The description or 'saying' of a thing is possible because it has a name which belongs to language. Language 'contains' the world, and is called by Heidegger the 'House of Being'. It serves to reveal things as they are, to interpret something that remains in relation to the here and now.

Christian Norberg-Schulz

Calatrava escapes from the tautological construction of abstract language to introduce relations that are external to the project's reality. In the analogy, which is the subjective perspective that animates the object, the totality of the project is absorbed without any waste. (...) The projects made by Calatrava cannot be interpreted as either abstract creations or mimetic interventions with reality, that reject the utopia as well as the contextualist adaptation, in search of an individual identity for the organisms that he builds.

Alejandro Zaera

It is a question of having the spectator participate in our own artistic or inner experiences. Abstraction allows this possibility because it

replaces objective truth with one's own subjective interpretation.

C. Th. Dreyer

I understand the rules of the architect - just as a *maestro di opera* understands his. You have to feel responsible for every person on site. I like to be with the work force because the human component in buildings is hugely important.

Santiago Calatrava

It is my intention to produce buildings that are built for their environment and which seek a relationship with their surroundings. The aim is to reach once again an understanding between engineering and architec-

ture in the sense of the creation of static, formal and plastic possibilities of the respective materials. Behind all this stands the search for a unity between the art of architecture and the art of engineering.

Santiago Calatrava

There are no rules, absolutely no given truths in any of the arts. There is only the sensation of a marvellous freedom, of an unlimited possibility to explore, of an unlimited past of great examples of architecture from history to enjoy (...) Structural honesty for me is one of those infantile nightmares from which we will have to free ourselves as soon as possible.

Philip Johnson

Neothomists who hoped to prove, around the same time as Robert Vischer invented symbolic empathy at the end of the nineteenth century, that modern science could coexist with medieval mysticism.

'Why is it not Permissible when it is Possible?'

The great attractiveness of Santiago Calatrava's work resides in the compelling overall image that results from his virtuoso elusion of the countless commandments and taboos that prevail in the discipline of architecture. The work escapes the dichotomy of technology and design. It escapes the fragmenting character of the avant-garde while having a similar intention to unite art and life. It escapes the linguistic codes of iconography but succeeds at the same time in telling a story, audible by *Einfühlung*, taking advantage of the expressiveness of the architecture as autonomous object. But perhaps the greatest secret of this work lies in the rebirth of the Gothic, now no longer as a verticalist building style in the name of God, but as a horizontalist construction between people. Especially when public commissions are involved, the work of Santiago Calatrava always contributes considerably to the liveability of the place. Qualities that we continually encounter in Calatrava's oeuvre are the separation of pedestrian and motorised traffic, an anchoring in the location that gives the structure a great unaffectedness but also makes possible a positive experience of the place, an

★ Frampton, Kenneth, 'Look No Hands: Santiago Calatrava and the Well-Tempered Reconstruction', in *Santiago Calatrava Engineering Architecture*, Basel .

Railway Station at Satolas Airport, Lyon, 1993

the pointed arch form present in many of the roof constructions, the translation of divinity into structural integrity, and the predominating stress on the emotional effect that the architecture is intended to invoke. There are Gothic associations too in the way the work is carried out: a guild-like band, the master mason and his mates. However, in contrast to the medieval way of doing things, the *maestro di opera* is here anything but anonymous.

222

The soaring spans of the Gothic were once meant as a flyover to God. Now the bond is broken, and Calatrava makes a bridge between people. That does not necessarily imply the end of the Gothic, as his civil-artistic achievements show us. But the architecture is not about the verticality of the relationship with Deus Pater nor about experiencing a Platonic mysticism of light, but about a spiritual environment for here and now, a place under a meaningful constellation. Calatrava does not use walls to convey a cultural message but resorts to the autonomous strength of the skeletal structure. It is precisely because Calatrava prefers to function as an adjunct to a natural order (a divine whisper in the ear) rather than an independent voice in a cultural debate, that the wall is not the natural medium for him. The wall, as a face or a mask, is inclined to suggest an iconographic potential that could conceivably threaten the autonomy of the structure. An architect who steers clear of the cultural debate will always place the highest value on that construction, the unconscious of architecture (Giedion). Thus the space is not sharply compartmented as it would be by walls. Calatrava always postpones the joint in a 'displacement of the point of bearing', ★ in a graceful, fluid motion.

God is dead but the Gothic lives on. This is reminiscent of the mental gymnastics of the

The laws of statics say that in the world of criticism certain things you can do and can't do. But the new moralists say there are things you *shouldn't* do. Why is it not permissible when it is possible? If you asked me why, for example, I designed columns in the shape of my hand, I would say because it is possible. And that is what engineering is: the art of the possible.

Santiago Calatrava

My interest is centred on introducing a new vocabulary of forms of a Surrealist character somewhat in tune with the times (even though I do not much believe in my time). In Spanish we call concrete *Hormigón* which comes from - to form. That is the most beauti-

ful quality of concrete: its ability to take on any form. You have an incredible freedom when working with it.

Santiago Calatrava

I influence the form to the extent that I make it approximately what I want. I mean, my forms were not given. I have influenced them in the way my feeling dictated me on that moment. My feeling told me to design an arch in a perpendicular form, and of concrete, but then I made it out of steel because of building-technical reasons. There are many technical demands. That is quite universal, I suppose that everyone works that way. The important thing is that in my case, cornering a certain arch, a number of para-

meters is possible. It is basically a free choice. For example, I could have made a buttress-bridge or perhaps a simple ledger, or something like a continuous layer. But yet I made arches, and that was a fundamental choice.

Santiago Calatrava

I think the feeling of lightness, floating and flying, is just like the feeling of for example illumination, always a reference to something. It is something like knowing that light exists, because the dark does too. This means that you can estimate the contrast when there is light, because light and darkness are opposites, and some parts start to shine. That is what happens when you paint, and when you

are looking for the most light, the most illuminated spots. The most light you can get is when the paint correlates with the whiteness of the paper; you cannot go further than that. You can accentuate the white by putting spots of dark next to it, so this white is much whiter than the paper as a sheet. And what is valid for paintings is so too for other things. A light weight can be obtained by putting a heavy one opposite. That is the way you make this feeling, it is this contrast which communicates the feeling of lightness.

Santiago Calatrava

It is a quality that enables him to achieve a plastic assembly of revealed ligaments that serve to transform the *techne* of structures

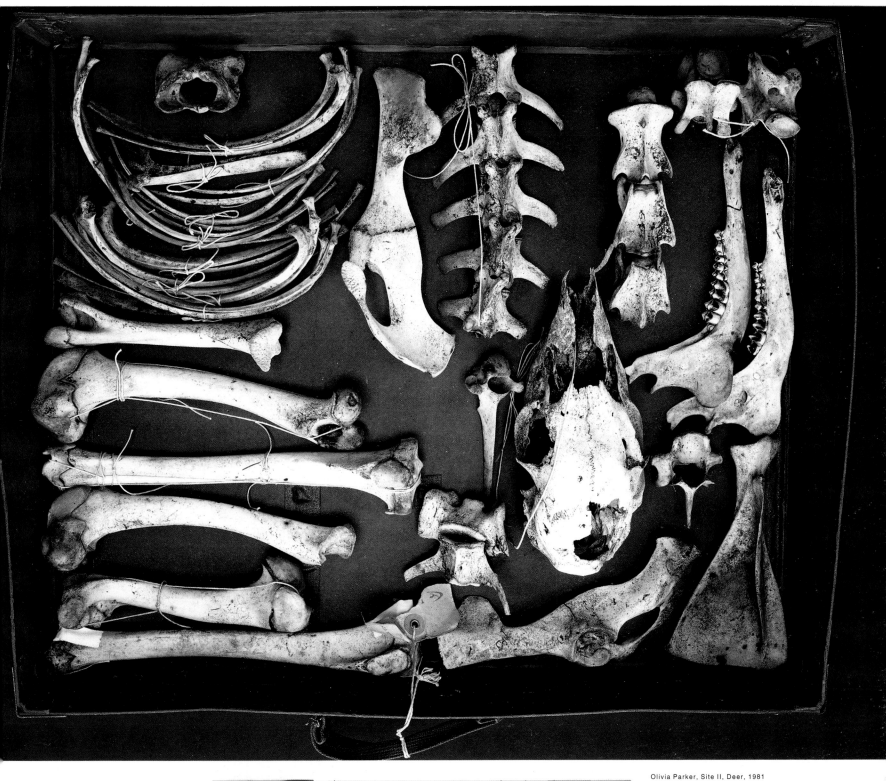

Olivia Parker, Site II, Deer, 1981

Draftsman checks custom designed implant to be
used in patient w/bone tumour

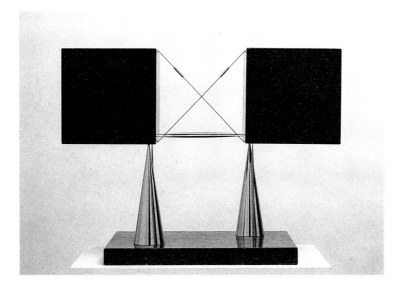

Toros, 1985

alternation of movement and rest, and a drawing of attention to the surrounding landscape combined with a place for encounter. The transparency of his construction and the reticent colours of his materials demonstrate Calatrava's sympathy towards his public.

Still, it looks as though a functional programme that can enjoy these benefits can be no more than a simple one. In the case of his bridges, roof structures, canopies and suchlike structure, the strongly autonomous image can be an immense relief after all the soulless 'solutions' that we pass by every day. However, when the function implies a somewhat longer stay, these brilliant, unapproachable structures with their evident autonomy can get in the way of the social texture. It then emerges that this autonomy does not evoke an experience but ends up referring to itself in an endless process of self-congratulation. The Other suddenly seems to get alarmingly little space. The space is no longer a podium for the possible but just a physical consequence of an approach that strives for the realisation of what is possible within the discipline of building.

> 'A current problem is that in the world of criticism certain people are developing moral criteria about engineering. The laws of statics say that in the world of criticism there are certain things you can do and can't do. But the new moralists say there are things you shouldn't do. (...) Why is it not permissible when it's possible? If you asked me why, for example, I designed columns in the shape of my hand, I would say because it is possible. And that is what engineering is: the art of the possible.'★

This narrowing down of the socially possible to the technically possible is yet another proof of the reduction of architecture to a specialism of design and technology. That Calatrava unites these two aspects is a fine thing, but the fact that this is accompanied by a lessened interest in the potential of everyday life, something

★ Quoted in Lyall, Sutherland, 'A Colloquy; Some Things About Santiago Calatrava', in *Santiago Calatrava, Dynamic Equilibrium*, Zürich 1991.

that has become visible in recent work, strikes us as a serious loss. It is as though we are left with *no more* than the X-ray photo. Of the living tissue, hardly a trace remains.

224

Telecommunication Tower for the Olympic Games, Barcelona, 1992

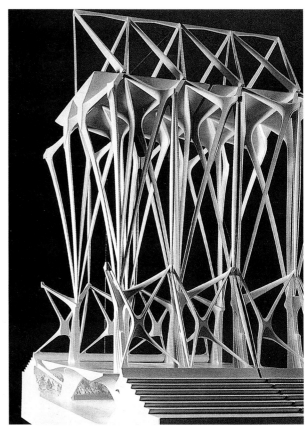

St. John The Divine, New York Cathedral, competition entry for completion, 1991

into the *poesis* of dynamic form.
Kenneth Frampton

Working as an architect or engineer naturally requires a source of inspiration. But because engineering and architecture are professional practices, nature cannot be the only source. My relationship with the so-called anatomical schemes has to do with the solution, by means of models, of certain structural problems which are closely related to nature. For example, a cantilever is the simplest engineering representation of a tree. The restraint is represented by the roots of the tree. Both obey certain laws of bending moments. So however most engineers think about it, I believe that the professional activi-

ty of an engineer lies mainly in the development of analytical models which describe nature in a realistic way. Working with isostatic structures almost inevitably leads one to sketching nature. When, for example a dog stands on his four legs it constitutes an isostatic body. The load is divided by the number of legs, there are no other forces present other than those supplied by the muscles.
Santiago Calatrava

Architecture and nature are joined in a metaphysics of place.
Steven Holl

I am especially interested in the idea of kinematics. Strength both in architecture and in mechanics is equal to mass by acceleration. Mass is an abstract universal unit. So this means that mobility is implicit in the concept of strength. A simple way of translating all that is to say strength is like crystallised movement.
Santiago Calatrava

The word aseptic has an association which is not necessarily connected with bacteria, but with the aseptic connection between work and hand. This is important to me. Once I experimented with sculptures which were not only designed on a plan, but could also be ordered by telephone. So that the relation

between my work and my hands would remain more anonymous.
When I say by telephone it simply means I have to control the elements of the figure in such a way, in its material and dimensional being, that I can only pass it on by a codification into words. Just like I speak of a cube, of an edge and of a way to work on an edge, I speak of a certain material too, and I speak of cones of certain proportions; and in that sense, and only codified in words, I pass it on by telephone, and it is constructed as I want it.
Santiago Calatrava

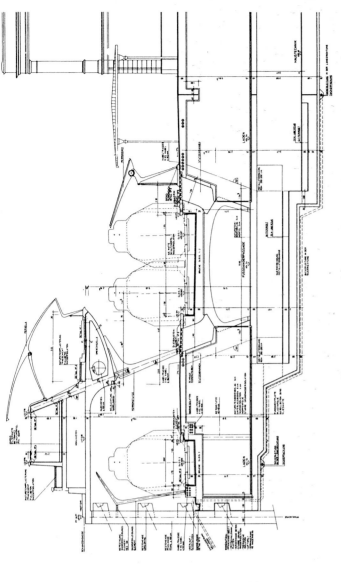

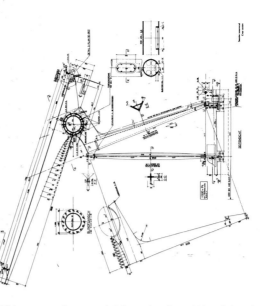

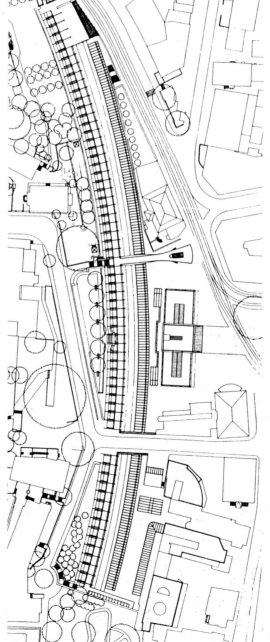

The project for the Stadelhofen station concerned the construction of a station above ground in a largely underground railway linking the suburbs of Zurich with the centre. The scheme affected an area of about 270 by 40 metres located at the edge of the old fortifications in the centre of modern Zurich. The site is characterised by two adjacent zones: a hill contour and a plain. The design method could be typified as 'design by section': the cross-section, which is split up into three levels, remains almost identical throughout the 270 metres that the slightly curved plan extends, following the layout of the tracks. The station is characterised at platform level by the portico that covers platform number three and the central platform of the station. The upper part of the portico picks up the foot of the slope, marking a sharp line that runs along the whole upper side of the station. The curved line is interrupted four times by bridges, each one different from the others. The bridges link the project to the existing road system. The steel pillars of the portico support the concrete caisson of the roof at four

points arranged in the shape of a cross. The pillars have a single base on the ground. They have a box steel structure with an H-shaped cross-section and are made up of two parts: the actual pillar with two transverse supports and an equaliser set on top of the pillar, forming the two longitudinal supports. The trellis that covers the promenade on the upper level of the station is formed out of a steel structure made up of vertical supports similar to those of the station canopy, supporting a steel tube that runs along the entire length of the promenade. The underground layer contains a road, lined at both sides with shops. This road is located under the tracks: the various subways link up here. Its roof is characterised by the concrete arches that support the train tracks. The gap between supporting arches is closed in a longitudinal direction by a sloping wall, along which filters light from the concrete-framed glass blocks set into the platforms. *Santiago Calatrava*

Location Zürich, Switzerland **Assistants** A. Amsler, W. Rueger **Client** Swiss Federal Railways **Design** 1982-84 **Completion** 1990

▼

Santiago Calatrava Valls S.A. *Stadelhofen Railway Station and Mall*

BRANDY
OSBORNE VETERANO

- *Un poco macho un poco ángel* -

Pietro Derossi
'The Risk of Interpretation':
Being Realo in Architecture

Is there such a thing as asymptotic thinking, a way of thought that keeps approaching the heart of the matter but always pulls back just before reaching it for fear of repercussions? Are there ideas which aspire to being definite, but only if there are no consequences? Yes, such thinking and such ideas do exist – in the head of Pietro Derossi. He is an architect who never lets himself be pinned down; he is far more concerned about what he does not do, about what he fails to notice or even deliberately excludes, than about what he actually does.

He demonstrates that existentialist engagement lives on even though its spiritual father is dead, even though the political system it once supported now exists only as a fossil somewhere in the Gulf of Mexico, and even though people have become wary of those who suit the action to the word. Derossi's philosophy is a throwback to the pre-Socratic wisdom of never stepping twice in the same river (not even once, actually). Moreover, he has preserved the anti-authoritarianism of the sixties. Engagement without authority, that's what it's all about. Self-evidently, when such an approach is taken in architecture only the projects speak the (casuist) truth. The projects are always 'provisional', 'experimental', faintly 'anarchistic' or 'open to change'. They are also 'centrifugal' by nature, a 'mix of styles and references', lacking a coherent aspect, 'openly composed' as a 'system of episodes', and 'circumstantial' in conception. Thus this architecture does not attempt to rehabilitate itself as an institution but to provide favourable material for discussion. We could alternatively say that it is an attempt to anticipate as many variables as possible. Hence it is not meant for the critics but for the user, that ambivalent creature called mankind. The human being is inconsequential. Architecture must be human. Therefore architecture must be inconsequential, QED. For the inconsequential buildings of Pietro Derossi, we refer you to the illustrations and your local travel agency. As for the theory of inconsequentiality, we present you with the architect's own reactions on the eight themes of this book. He met our request with great assiduousness. Derossi does not see himself as an author; he has no wish to ordain a definitive meaning for his architecture with his seal and signature. So what good would interpretation do us? Everything has been left open, after all. The architect has used the scholarly structure of this book as a framework for bolstering his relativism with additional arguments. In the editors' view, these arguments should be allowed to speak for themselves. We give the floor to Pietro Derossi under the following heading:

228

Durée

Heidegger, harking back to the words of Hölderlin, tells us that the words of the poet endure. But I think that this type of duration has little to do with stability and permanence. The duration of poetry comes from its openness to change. Its polysemy leaves it open to an infinity of interpretations. Architecture, when it is capable of becoming poetry, is revolutionary in the sense that it deconstructs the metaphysical obsession of objectivity, of the definitive solution, of the foundational message. The pursuit of duration as permanence is not a posture of humility. It is a posture of violence which seeks to exclude risk from life by replacing it with the identification and repetition of types. The idea of permanence excludes and sterilises the growth of language. It is the development of language which gives reality form, and this becoming is not simulation, it is actual reality. The opposition between reality and simulation proposed by Baudrillard is a naive thought: it assumes that reality, now and in the past, can be closed in its objectivity; it assumes that simulation is an act of will (avant-gardistic), a stepping back from reality. The path toward reality is the path toward language. It is the duration of a voyage, it has the quality of nomadism. Language manoeuvres between intention to speak and seduction in order to convince, and seduction is often quite willing to simulate. The duration of architecture has little to do with its physical life. Architecture changes under the attentive scrutiny of our gaze, and opens itself to new interpretations. It is the duration of continuous change.

Context

What is the difference between place and context? The term place (or topos) begins with a body and moves toward dialogue. The term context begins with dialogue and moves toward a body. Dialogue, in the hermeneutic sense, is an interactive process rapport between demand and response. It is an intrigue (as Ricoeur would put it) of demand and response in action in the city, perhaps more legible in its parts. The context, as a dialogue in progress, has the character of spectacle and narrative. An infinite narrative, in movement. The architectural project inserts itself in this intrigue, placing a story within the more general story of the context. The formal choice of the design presents itself as the stopping point of an investigation determined by an operative necessity, and not by the achievement of an essentiality, a cogency. In the specified form which temporarily closes itself in a narrative all that which the choice has excluded hovers. The narrative, surreptitiously, also speaks of what it leaves unsaid, of that which in the process of figuration has only been glimpsed, that we have been able to arrest. Paradoxically, this limitation of the responses to the demands of the context brings what is left unsaid into play, and opens toward the vastness of possible worlds. And this vastness, to which the work of architecture alludes, introduces the work into life, in the sense that it legitimises its openness to successive interpretations. The context is an intrigue of dialogues in different languages: that of physical forms, of history, economy, politics or love. They speak, removing themselves from other situations and other contexts, or from that which differs from them. By making its difference explicit, the context appears as a temporary piece of the world, suspended, waiting. The architectural project can tell a good story.

Border

Death is the limit. That which limits me and on which I reflect. And it is this reflection that gives a sense to my life. Death speaks to me of the temporary, of the transience of all I can know. To make architecture is to know, to know in the temporary. The Utopia of Modernism wanted to transcend the limits. To constitute a new world order, definitive and therefore immune to vital processes and the contingencies of the worldly. Architecture as a definitive solution presents itself as a 'work', an 'opera', and a true work is timeless, classical. The origin of classical thought in the Egyptian world was aimed at exorcising death with the force of an essential monumentality. The classical work (perhaps misunderstood) has no conceptual or physical limits. It is eternal and it is everywhere. In a hermeneutic approach the problem of the limit is present in all actions, not as a deprivation or a lack but as a destiny, a single chance for survival. The presence of the limit offers us the possibility of reality. We could say: it is the condition which enables me to act without first acquiring general orders which are designed to cancel out all limits. In architectural design, the limits are physical and conceptual, but two limits mingle and confront one another. In giving form to a thought and a thing (a thought within a thing and vice versa) the design, on the one hand, obeys its limits while, on the other, precisely by accepting limitation it places it in discussion, open to interpretation. Precisely because it has limits, architecture speaks to us of what is excluded by the limits, of the mystery of life and death, of the mystery which

Biffi Scala, Restaurant, Milan, 1988

gives us a significance as particular entities, as human beings. The limit delimits and displays its temporary nature. The uncertainty and doubt of the temporary can be the force of poetics, the strength of placing oneself in discussion and of accepting, without subjective presumption, the risk of interpretation.

Topos

The topos is an occasion, and has the consistency of a body. It is the opportunity to make the intention of design explicit, in its state, in a time. Here and now. Things are located in the place, a multiplicity of things that display their singularity and their relations. We say things, and not objects, to bring out the fact that we are not dealing with presences external to the observing subject (in contrast to the subject), but with sensible figures that involve things amidst existing ones: things which, modifying the place, make new functions, new uses possible, communicating new messages (or reproposing old ones). The topos is delimited by walls, ceilings, floors, poles, or by rows of trees, canals, paths, profiles, etcetera. But these limitations are not a secondary part of an overall design: even the limits have the sense of an opportunity. On the one hand, they exercise the violence of a closure, on the other, thanks to their occasional nature (and the temporary nature of the here and now), they raise questions for all of the things they exclude. Design, if located in the topos, with its intentions and programs is conditioned by the finite nature of the occasion, but this finite quality is that which 'tells us that there is always an infinity of meaning to develop and interpret'. It is the specificity of the project, in the place, here and now, that opens us to reflection regarding the universal, the free vastness of the land.

Programme

Often by programme we mean a plan (town planning) which comes before a project. The task of the design project is that of giving a finite form to the specifications of the programme. This dependency of the project on the plan has led to very poor results. The plan defines abstract objectives which are not verified and the project, excluded

229

Biffi Scala, Restaurant, Milan, 1988

rience of the world; and time makes space relative, revealing the temporary nature of its presence. To design and to construct means arranging things in a place: but it also means entrusting those things to the course of time, which will lead them to assume an infinity of meanings. We might say, like Gadamer, that architecture is an art which makes space both in the physical sense of offering an opportunity for other forms to penetrate it, use it, modify it, and in the more general sense of subjecting itself to future interpretations. Thus every architectural space presents itself as an event in waiting. Space thus understood does not call for an abstract contemplation, but rather for immediate use: it wants to be the container of living phenomena. In calling for use it provokes the poetic message and specifies its qualities. For example, we are not interested in a monumental space, but rather in a space which induces us to reflect on the idea of monumentality. Space and time, with their uncanny interweaving, are inscribed in the language of architecture. Their reciprocal relativisation keeps its distance from the great 'recits', and deconstructs (metaphysical) attempts to form a 'style' within the continuing pursuit of meaning in living.

from the objectives, seeks legitimacy in self-referentiality. We have to reconstruct a direct dialogue between plan and project. A necessary strategy in the present situation, heir to a strong credibility granted to the plan/programme, might be to invert the hierarchy: beginning with the project/programme, considering the project not just as a proposal of solutions, but also as a tool for study and reflection. The project is a thought which approaches things in their presence and represents them to us, in the sense that it presents them to us (re-presents). The presence speaks to us of time and suggests the relative nature of our activity. The relativity of the here and now. The project is a limited programme: it does not seek general rules as the basis of an absolute legitimacy. It appears, instead, as a strategy to extricate ourselves from the complexity of the appeals in progress in a place. The appeals are political, functional and economic in nature, and come from the history of the place and that of the designer. The project is the temporary representation of a mediation in the midst of the pluralism of the appeals. The occasional nature of the commissioning agent (the client, but not only the client – we could also say of the civil society) must not be considered as an obstacle and an annoyance, but as an essential nutrient of the project. The project/programme does not have an autonomous quality, a priori, which can be imposed. The quality comes from the specific dialogue of the occasion: it is the narrative of the factors and events which have accompanied the unfolding of the dialogue, of agreements and hostilities. The project/programme reveals the plurality of the appeals and proposes a possible solution through a work of mediation. In presenting itself in a form which offers a view of its temporary character, the result of mediation, the project speaks of the complexity of the world and of the earth. That is, it can wear the language of poetry.

Space

It is the time of life which makes the measure, poses the issue of finiteness. But time is not an abstract category, above things. It is the decline, the ending of men and things that introduces us to the specifics and enables us to feel time. Time is the time of designing (finite), of being, therefore it unfolds and manifests itself in a proximity which has to do, first of all, with space. Space makes time relative, it introduces it to the expe-

Identity

It is well know that identity, in Aristotelian terms, means that things are identical if the definition of their substance is identical, and that substance is that which exists by virtue of an internal necessity. If this is the definition of identity, the Modern Movement and, in particular, its transformation into an international style has had the definition of its identity as its principal objective, or the recognisability of its objects as belonging to an already defined substance (or, we could say, idea). The architectural criticism of today which condemns the Modern Movement for 'a loss of identity' paradoxically attributes the term identity with the meaning of difference, without making a profound investigation of the meaning of this substitution. A hermeneutic knowledge which attributes the pursuit of truth to a process of dialogue views the problem of identity with

Biffi Scala, Restaurant, Milan, 1988

230

BIFFI SCALA

...ICATO AL LIMONCELLO   18000

...AL POMODORO FRESCO

...E AL PESTO

...NE

...NA

***

...ACEI CON SALSA PESTO

...ALLO ZAFFERANO

...O E RUCOLA

...O ALLA MILANESE

...LLA VENETA

***

...O ALLE ERBE   28000

FILETTI DI SOGLIOLA MIMOSA E CAPPERI   30000

COSTOLETTA DI VITELLO ALLE ERBE   30000

TOURNEDOS DI MANZO RADICCHIO E BASILICO   30000

CARPACCIO SCOTTATO ALLA SCAMORZA E RUCOLA   28000

***

COPERTO 10000   SERVIZIO 15%

BIFFI SCALA s.r.l. - 20121 MILANO - PIAZZA DELLA SCALA - TEL. 02/866651 r.a.

Biffi Scala, Restaurant, 1988

suspicion precisely inasmuch as identity implies the objectivity and stability of substance: in architectural terms, we might say that it implies a stable reference model. If by identity, in a transgression with respect to its literal meaning, we mean the capacity to be recognisable for the quality and specificity of the message within a complex accumulation of communications, then we are talking about the evidence of a difference. A work of architecture expresses its difference when, in describing of narrating itself, it establishes a dialogue with all that is different from itself. We return to the problem of the context, the physical and mental environment, starting with which architecture attempts to provoke an event of communication. Difference thus understood is the denial and dismissal of presence; or, better, the breakdown of any pretence of the definitive quality of presence (Vattimo). In the place of identity, we could speak of the authenticity of architecture. Authenticity is the condition which is born of the deconstruction of universal models, of the acceptance of the finite nature of experience and of its precarious nature. It is the authenticity of the existence of habitation.

Representation

For Hegel, art is dead because it speaks in an obscure manner, in its sensible form, of a concept which is better expressed by the language of philosophy. Art, for Hegel, represents in a reductive manner a meaning which can be better represented with another messenger, one capable of guaranteeing the evidence of truth. We can rediscover art (and architecture as art) as we accept the temporal and spatial relativity of truth. Representation, therefore, does not mean giving a sensible form to truth, but rather seeks to speak of the truth, of the constant pursuit of its occurrences: we could say that

representation gives form not to a completed occurrence, but to an expectation. Representation reveals itself through an activity of symbolism. But what is the symbol if not a shard of pottery (the so-called *tessera hospitalis*) given as a souvenir to a friend and guest, in the expectation of a future meeting? Representation is a 'fragment of being' which speaks of ancient, secret rapports with the world, but which wants to reconcile itself with the world, wants to be understood by the world. Representation does not refer to another meaning, but is itself the meaning of this expectation. The representation of a work of architecture can change the world because it, in itself, is a fragment of the world which offers itself to reality, participating in the play of differences. It does not represent change. It is (in the exposure of its language) the change. If we take this 'function' of representation into account, architecture is urged on toward its primary pragmatic role. Its truth or, better, its occurrence of truth, knows the uncertainty of circumstances: its role is not to stop but rather to produce movement. And this task can be achieved at a variety of levels: the tactile, physical, institutional level, etcetera. And it can be aimed at many categories of users. The choice of reference points, on the one hand, is part of a process of manifestation of an intention to establish a dialogue with the world (with the context) and, on the other, it is precisely the contact with these references which reveals, due to its finite nature, the possibilities which have remained hidden. Even criticism, if it is to follow the process of representation 'in its dual quality of discovering, revealing, manifesting on the one hand, and of hiding and secrecy on the other' (Gadamer), must get closer to things. Criticism, which from afar launches curses or consecrates heroes diving into the murky sea of obsolete ideologies could, and must, finally abandon the field.

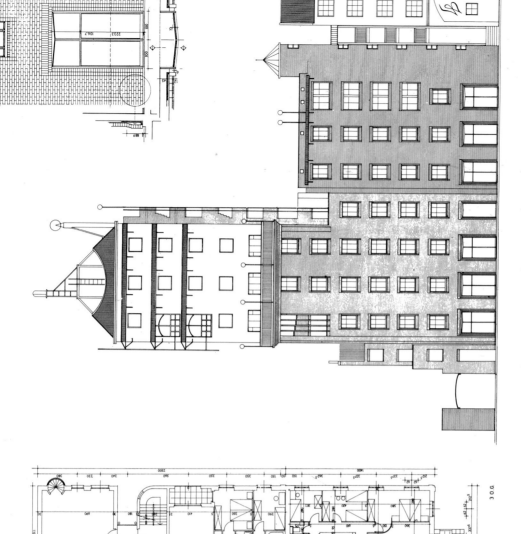

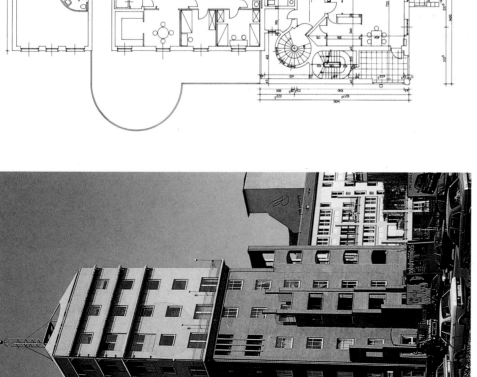

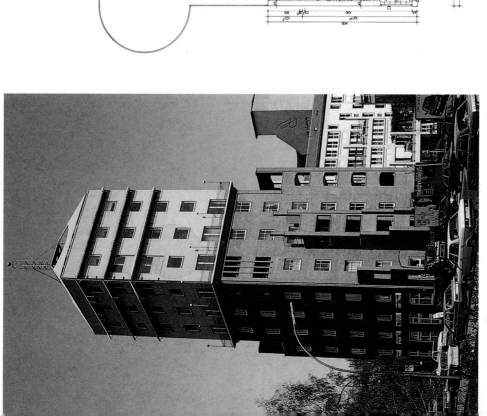

The project for the tower block and adjoining building on the former site of the Luderitz and Bauer bookbinders has been conceived as a completion of the city plan drawn up by the architect Tarrago. As an overall concept we have adopted the suggestion of a division of Tarrago's ninth block into separate parts, assigning greater importance to the internal road on which our tower block is located. For this reason the point where Wilhelmstraße and the internal road meet should be regarded as a true junction between two roads and is reminiscent of the typology of the classic 'Berlin street corner', a feature still to be found in many parts of the southern Friedrichstadt. Thus our building has been conceived as if it were made up of two superimposed parts. Up until the sixth floor we have carried out a reconstruction of the historic corner of the block with a brick building, with regular openings, extending along Wilhelmstraße; its ground floor can be used to house stores. This building terminates in a coping, or cornice, that marks the start of the second part, the tower proper. The tower will be

plastered or faced with a uniform material to distinguish it from the base, and it will have a different form of window together with enclosed loggias. The tower is partially covered by a roof that opens to reveal a structure rising toward the sky. We envisage setting a solar lamp on top that will project a luminous spot onto the blank wall in front, on which a sundial will be marked out. The round terraces, providing a link with the fire escapes on the north-west side and the loggias on the south-east side, mark a diagonal twist that should impart a sense of rotation to the tower. Thus while the lower six floors of the building hold a dialogue with the memory of the past and form a street front, the tower holds a dialogue with other towers, campaniles, or obelisks that stand out against the sky in the distance, protruding above the average height of buildings in Berlin. This superimposition proposes a complex and differentiated interpretation of the city and attempts to suggest a reflection on the relationship between high rise buildings and life in the streets. *Pietro Derossi*

▶

Location Wilhelmstraße, Berlin, Germany **Assistants** S. Caffaro Rore, F. Lattes, F. di Suni and others **Client** IBA and H. Klammt **Design** 1983 **Completion** 1987

Pietro Derossi Architetto *Apartment Building with Tower*

'Comrades! Today a friend of mine died; he had renounced life. But I want to speak to you about life not about death. The goal of every man, as recorded in some constitutions, is the search for happiness. One might argue that individualism like this is the consequence of May '68, a date that already belongs to the past. No, it is older than that.'

'In 1821 Leopardi wrote: up till now we have employed the politics and science of nations rather than of individuals, their progress and their happiness. And yet we know that we should live justly.
I am here today to talk to you about a personal problem. Comments... murmurs...'

I will address the meeting in the form of a question. People ask questions in order to know something... Primo, is it forbidden for an old comrade like myself to feel love as though I were 18? For it is true, I love a woman whom, because she is married, I shall refer to as G.T.

Stills from La Terrazza, movie by Ettore Scola.

'Secondo, would it be lawful for me to live with this woman and leave the woman who has been my companion for 35 years? Who has grown old along with me, forgiving me, even consoling me for a certain reserve that I felt in the bosom of the party? But let us not talk about that now...'

'Tertio, can this hypothetical and painful undertaking be reconciled with my wife's right to happiness? Here too I am indulging in paternalistic nonsense, as though the personality of a woman was dependent solely on her married state. Even so I ask myself the question,... I ask you: is it reconcilable with the equal sharing of responsibilities?'

'And with the defence of pluralism against individualism, with our ideals for a better society, consisting of free and equal human beings. In short,... is one permitted to be happy if this happiness causes unhappiness to someone else? I am asking you to tell me: 'yes' or 'no'. Thank you. The meeting is silent, ... dumbfounded'

On the Work of Julia Bolles & Peter Wilson
Ark-itecture

'Man is at the same time subject to two movements: one of terror, which rejects, and one of attraction, which commands fascinated respect. Interdiction and transgression correspond to these two contradictory movements.'

This statement by Georges Bataille is eminently applicable to the ideas and work of Architekturbüro Bolles Wilson. The firm's architecture has a Janus head. Sometimes the buildings and drawings seem to evince an attempt to repel the waves of modernity; and at other times they seem to accept these waves as a *fait accompli* and even to take pleasure in them. The work is simultaneously rejecting and attracting. It commands respect for the built object, yet at the same time it blends effortlessly into the metropolitan flux that has rendered helpless everything of value.

Until now, Julia Bolles, Peter Wilson and their partner Eberhard Kleffner have had to realise their ambitions in small or unexecuted projects. Many of their ideas have reached us in word and seductive image without having had to pass the test of feasibility. But the building of the New City Library, Münster, makes it possible for us to measure the extraordinary ideas underlying this work on and at an appropriate scale, against the built reality. This reality refuses, however, to conform to any univalent criterion and takes a variety of forms. Their work is a protean insertion into an existing context.

Emptiness Transcended

When we speak of reality, we inevitably come up against the philosophical problems of Post-Modernity. In Peter Wilson's case, however, there is a concrete and perhaps existentially determined reason to concern oneself with a possible bankruptcy of the *Realitätsprinzip*. As an Australian immigrant, he has himself had a dual experience of emptiness.

Not only must he be aware of the real emptiness of the desert landscape, but his position as migrant must have confronted him with the Other in no uncertain terms. The literary topos of meeting versus isolation is something we all know and care about, but the fact of a major geographical displacement and the concrete experience of a new environment must make itself felt in a profession concerned with physical anchoring in the ground. The mental relationship between the emptiness of a landscape and the existential emptiness, and what actions to take in this context, is accordingly a central theme of the work of Wilson and his firm.

Wilson sought the climate where this kind of alienation is radicalised *in extremis* of his own accord. During his training and subsequent lectureship at the Architectural Association, he demonstrated his affinity for the ideas of architects like Bernard Tschumi and Nigel Coates.★ Preoccupied by the consequences of living in an electronic metropolis, they investigate, each in his own way, what is to become of such an archaic discipline as architecture.

★ It is surprising how far the architectural movement that has devoted itself to designing a world of 'exploded thought' has found its major inspiration in specific *schools*: Cooper Union (John Hejduk) and the Architectural Association (Alvin Boyarski).

'Now the post-McLuhan media, electronic, communication revolution has led us to a new trauma… We are all participants in the new perception – television slicing together disconnected fragments, slicing time. What characterises this new perception? A constant state of flux (video clips, mass transport), a dematerialisation of objects (surface is no longer absolute, interior and exterior no longer opposites), an absence of appropriate or absolute hierarchies of scale (grand narratives become micronarratives, a chair is as significant as a city), information itself is no longer the property of the book (it is electronic, invisible). What is the result? The horizon, the certainties of Cartesian geometry, the cone of perspective geometry focused on the viewer – all these have in a short space of time ceased to be our measure of the real. This radical transformation will be seen to characterise the end of the twentieth century as the discovery of optical perspective characterised the early Renaissance.' ★

★ Levene, R. & F. Cecilia, 'Interview with Peter Wilson', *El Croquis* 47 (1991), p. 15.

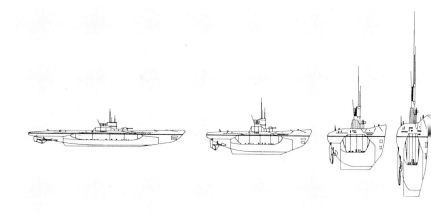

An autonomous hermetic environment

Bolles and Wilson, who became acquainted at the AA, are fascinated by mankind's drifting. The vagrant character of human culture, a consequence of the brave new world described above, recurs frequently in their projects. Their work symbolises the wanderings, but the means of transport are themselves also halting points. You don't just *go* somewhere, you *are* somewhere. This interchangeability of journey and destination occurs over and over again. A large measure of ambiguity prevails at a philosophical level, too. On the one hand, physical and existential emptiness is presented as an architectural concept; on the other hand, this takes place in a universe that has become too full. The emptiness is a virtual one which is always on the point of filling up with *events*, no, with minor factualities, no, with electronic impulses. But the emptiness is reconfirmed precisely through this tendency to pointlessness. Emptiness transcended! This Baudrillardian implosive thinking sometimes makes their architecture into an exercise of impossible mental gymnastics.

Function follows Form.
Peter Wilson

The tradition of Functionalism, the great singular typologies of the nineteenth century (station, hotel, department store) and the twentieth century (airport, supermarket, parkhouse etcetera) have become increasingly inappropriate as contemporary opera-

Public man, it now appears, is no more susceptible to brusque rational treatment than anyone else: he too has aspirations, likes old things as well as new, and wants to have everything nice. He is no longer a cipher, he has become a client. As the professional assurance of the sixties encountered the uncertainties of the seventies, a period of adjustment set in. This had little to do with the moral attributes of the various styles and

take over the Functionalist credo intact, continuing to justify everything by reference to the programme with the difference that the program was no longer reductive but now included anything that could be deemed to affect the satisfaction of the user. This change from didactic to opportunistic motivation in the professionals is in itself a conformation of the shift in public opinion.

Robert Maxwell

If architecture's only purpose is to reflect function, to become visible and have form only to the degree that it transparently reveals the programme, composition becomes impossible. But it can be recuperated if some space can be inserted between form and function. This has been done. Primarily through the use of abstract form, a secret programme can be put to place and subjective values added on top of the empiri-

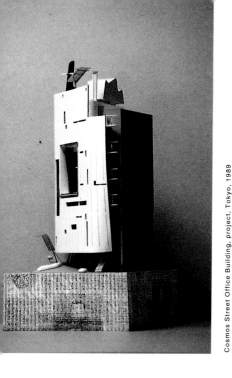

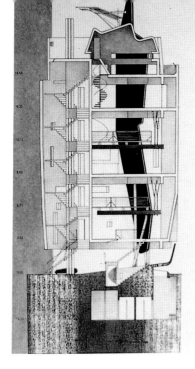

Cosmos Street Office Building, project, Tokyo, 1989

'How to Intervene?'

Bolles and Wilson have a joint stock of personal experience that typifies exactly the fate of architecture in the metropolis, a fate that is not generally presented to us in such a pure form. In Tokyo, they were invited to design a building for the Cosmos Street project without further programme details being specified (1989). The client could be sure of later finding a commercial user, in accordance with the laws of property speculation. As Kazuo Shinohara once wrote 'In the West meaning is put into things, in Japan it is taken out'.

At first sight it seems to be a splendid thing for architecture to have such autonomy. However, the assignment is already an indication that the client was reckoning on the self-censure concealed in the architect's practical spirit. It was supposed to be a building, after all, not some piece of sculpture. Apparently the separation of form-specialism from economic content has become so marked that it no longer even matters who begins the job. The architect is so unambiguously constrained by the laws of the market that he can do all his work in advance. The market is then pliant enough to go along with him whatever he designs.

But what cultural significance can architecture have if the building is *on offer* regardless of function? The speculator strengthens his position not only with flexible architecture but with the names Bolles and Wilson. The architects, confronted by a bewildering lack of strings, opted for a literal homologue of the layout of a newspaper cutting that the client gave to Wilson about himself.

The fascination for the ultimate flux in Japan as a whole, and the Tokyo commission in particular, have landed Bolles and Wilson in their latest paradox. How can one intervene as an architect in a world that, through an anonymous stream of undefinable particles, has made intervention as such into a futility? In Wilson's words:

'A relevant contemporary urbanism must learn a mode of perception that recognises the patterns, modes and intervals of everyday experience. The next question and one that we must all address ourselves to is how to intervene? What effect will the forces and voids of the new field have on the architectural object?' ★ In other words, how can one be a drifter in a global village, with its global village pump, idiot and community?

★ Levene, R. and F. Cecilia, op. cit. p. 18.

Membrane Architecture

An important aspect of Bolles' and Wilson's work is that they do not place thought before subjective action. Their concern is with conducting the profession of architect. Although they make no secret of their intellectual interests, the building itself continues to function as a stimulant. Theory forms an outer membrane, as it were. The transpiration though the intellectual skin activates thought and action emanating from the architectural object. Accordingly, there is little sense in performing an integral analysis of their oeuvre in order to understand it better. Since they experience reality as a succession of things without any higher order, we can make do with a simple summary of their intellectual and architectonic *topoi*.

The architecture of Bolles and Wilson has been characterised as an interplay of *con*-ceived and *per*-ceived space.★ Both a phenomenological and an intellectualist thread are playfully woven into the series of projects, and play is made of this too. The object forms a bridge between the ritual or social act, and the subjective experience of the space itself. It is practically as though their method corresponds to the desired effect of their buildings: on the one hand, an autonomous, physically conceived space; and on the other hand, the perceived space that stimulates thought. The intellectual level is thus determined almost entirely empirically and derives from the action itself.

★ See Dollens, Dennis, 'Ninja Architecture as seen from New York', *El Croquis* 47 (1991), pp. 79–88.

When we are obliged to continually change scale, perspective and modality, both spatially and morally, and we can no longer fall back on a common denominator that reduces everything to the criterion of the recognisable, the *interface* concept becomes tremendously important. The interface as an architectural phenomenon keeps pace with the view that the traditional wall, whether clad or not, has lost its power to impart identity. With the identity problem (a univalent meaning is no longer sufficient), the wall loses its traditional utilitarian function as a carrier of identity. We need membranes, as it were, which on the one hand demarcate spaces and concepts so that separate experience and thereby communication remain possible, while on the other hand they are thin enough to respect the flux of things and ideas. However, Bolles and Wilson do not associate these interfaces, these zones of physical and mental interchange, with transparency, as we see in the work of Jean Nouvel. The interfaces have the double action of a skin and are opaque but porous. The façades and internal partitions are always an intermedium that can be experienced as such. Bolles and Wilson work with mass, and this does effectively stipulate a boundary. However this mass *suggests*, by means of incisions, embrasures and penetrations, that 'other' on the far side. This duality, the simultaneous demarcation and blurring of identity, is something we encounter repeatedly in their work.

237

A directly related notion is that of zoning. Zoning results from the inclusion of elements that somehow enclose or intervene in the space. The user walks a zoned route which is articulated by means of the above-mentioned interfaces. The mind becomes conscious of this articulation as the body moves. As one enters and passes through the space one becomes aware at the same time of its various (programmatic/philosophical/ritual) constituents.

The suggestion of the Other is achieved by the provision of screens, which function as masks. The mask is used as a means of evoking expectations of what lies behind it. This is suggestive of a kind of architectural psychoanalysis, in which signs occur in an endless chain of associations, which can be investigated more and more deeply and exhaustively. The building is a unit; it ends somewhere and defines a place, as the skin does for the body and the subject. But meanwhile the process of signification never ends – an associative chain is set in operation, and this generates new knowledge ad infinitum. So we have yet another paradox: the building is unified entity, but it leaves room for the ultimate plurality, the subconscious.

Bolles' and Wilson's montage technique, with membranes as permeable separators, results in a *Raum ohne Eigenschaften* – not in the emancipatory sense that Siegried Ebeling gave the term,★ but as a space that does justice to the Baudrillardian implosion of meaning and the associated existential emptiness. It is not the Kantian condition of the possible that is involved, but rather the *condition des faits accomplis*.

★ In *Der Raum als Membran* (1926), Siegfried Ebeling argued for a negative space that 'only affords the physiological precondition' for real life.

Conceived and perceived space, interface, zoning, masks and collage all offer material for what Wilson calls the *extra-functional* in architecture. Now that the programme has become completely banal (with the Cosmos Street assignment as apogee), it is important to restore architecture to its poetic strength. This is no longer to be found in traditional representational devices, but in the manipulation of the ostensibly neutral means at the disposal of the architect.

Exhibition pavilion for the 1990 Osaka Expo of Gardens and Greenery

A Hybrid of 'Motion' and 'Place'

Alongside the artistic principles and concepts, we can recognise a highly characteristic iconography in the work of Bolles and Wilson. The bridge and the ship have been constantly recurring motifs since the mid eighties. Both signify simultaneously 'motion' and 'place'. A good illustration of the *bridge* concept is the plan for the Berlin Kulturforum, which was revealed in the very appropriately titled exhibition *Berlin: Denkmal oder Denkmodell?* (1988). The site, on the periphery of the Potzdamerplatz, is one scorched by history. Nowhere is the term 'crossing' as unpalatable as in this location, the former *Todesstreifen* (and we haven't even gone into the highly-charged name *Kulturforum* yet). In their design, *The Forum of Sand*, Bolles and Wilson proposed leaving the Kulturforum definitively incomplete while still giving the space a highly specific character by constructing a circular platform of sand. This raised circle is to be populated by various fragments: the Pfennig Brücke is to be transported here and have two cafes situated on it; and there are four multi-storey car parks and a tower-block library. Furthermore, the project consists of a broad avenue of grass and a few other structural elements. Naturally, the essential feature is the sand platform, which embodies the 'aesthetics of disappearance' (Virilio) in both a spatial and a material sense. All that fits here, where Berlin has so long lacked a heart and where the Kulturforum is overburdened with the physical consequences of the excessively long and earnestly held belief in *Kultur*, is the metaphorical material of the yawning emptiness, the essence of the desert, the ground of the wilderness. Bolles and Wilson extrapolate the geological substrate of the city to a cultural sign. *The Forum of Sand* is the absolute non-place, the totally delegitimised residue of *lebensraum* politics. Cynically, none other than the former NSDAP sponsor Daimler-Benz is to form the nearby bridge between East and West, to the sundering of which it so actively contributed sixty years ago.

The bridge of Bolles and Wilson goes from nowhere to nowhere and hence confirms that emptiness does not necessarily have to be compensated by an architectural extravaganza, but can also be 'architecturally legitimised'.★ The bridge gives this non-place a very clear distinguishing feature and memorialises a terrible past. At the same time, it underlines the futility of a simple denial of that past. Thus it bridges not only space but time. It does not serve for the conciliation between two banks but between two eras.

★ Neumeyer, Fritz, 'Weerzien met een brug', *Archis* 6 (1990), p. 49.

An exemplar of the *ship* concept is the Münster city library. The building, in which we can recognise nautical metaphors, is severed by a fissure that functions as an internal pedestrian street, the *Büchereigasse*. This results in two separate volumes, the 'slab' and the 'ship'. The division of the building corresponds to the symbolic and physical separation of the organising structure. One wing, the ship, houses the traditional printed media; the other, the slab, houses the electronic media. The internal street also serves as an urban connection to the surroundings, and is aligned towards the nearby Lamberti church. The strong division underlines the above cultural analysis of Bolles and Wilson.

Once again they take an object-oriented approach, which can be seen not only in the whole (the ship) but at a smaller scale too, resulting in a collage-like composition.

238

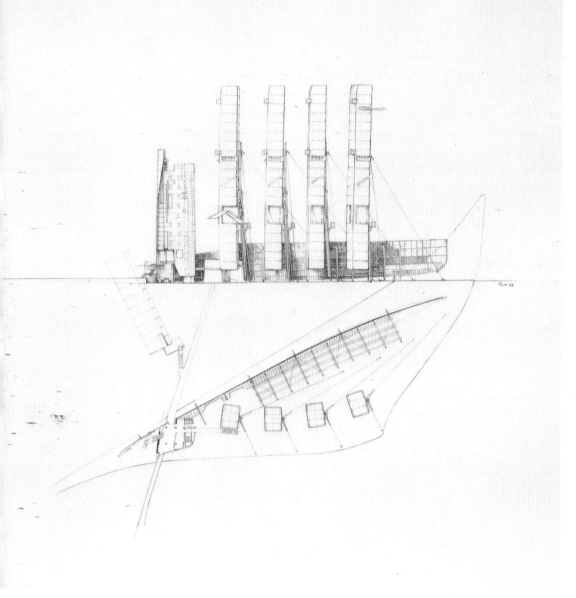

Forum of Sand, competition entry for Kulturforum, Berlin, 1988

Inside, there is an interplay of numerous separate volumes. This results in residual spaces which are used for the access means such as stairways and bridges. The exterior is fairly closed but, being a membrane, it repeatedly offers suggestions of the interior. It is not a smooth shell, but a skin. The treatment of its surface does not so much reflect as generate the contents. A notable feature in this respect is the use of copper cladding along the internal street. This refers in part to elements of the urban context such as the roof of the cathedral or the surface of the local cobblestones. From this point of view, the use of copper is a confirmation of the topos. But there is also an abstract metaphor at work here, of tradition stored in the books. This relates the topos to the type. In Henry Labrouste's Bibliothèque Sainte Geneviève in Paris, the architect represented the content of the books by the names of the authors. Of course, those names were neither tied to the building nor necessarily to the book as an object. The library was a house of learning, where universal knowledge could be acquired. In the case of Bolles Wilson, the metaphor relates specifically to the book as an object; the copper refers to the materiality of the *carrier* of knowledge and its historical wearing away, not to knowledge as such. Hence the ship takes on the physical character of the *place* of storage. The main thing is the place where knowledge resides. At the same time, however, the question of the evanescence of knowledge is raised. It is precisely because of the separate character given to the electronic media building that one becomes aware of the status of the knowledge those media convey. Names are reduced to data. It is not the carriers of the information that matter (ones and zeros have little grandeur) but the death of the author in the post-McLuhan world. Owing to the explicit duality of their message, we can say that Bolles and Wilson simultaneously illustrate and block the *Zeitgeist* of the 'super-present'. The world is a flux but still has places to offer. Their work is both tactile and virtual at the same time.

The concepts of bridge and ship fuse in the idea of the ark, a recurrent theme in the oeuvre of these architects. On the one hand, the ark is the ship that withstands the Deluge, and the refuge for God's selected survivors. On the other hand, it is the bridge that carries humanity over to the clean-washed world. The ark is not just a means of weathering the storm but also a rite of passage. 'Arkitecture' functions as refuge and vehicle to the new era, the Post-Modern world of the electronic paradigm. Or, to put it the other way round, every endtime has its Ark.

Suppose the Ark Were to Leave Without Us...

The work of Bolles and Wilson repeatedly shows us a remarkable mixture of nostalgia and affirmation. They bring to their work the considerable professional skill needed to make a complex zoning system function well. This is manifested especially in their firm control of spatial design. Since they fit multiple functions into a few elementary principle forms, they have to work out their design down to the minutest details. The neutral box has made way for bodily forms. Consequently the flexibility of their design can only function by virtue of the independent forces evoked by the location. Meanwhile they are continually incorporating intellectual notions into the architecture in a way that rises above the simple, metaphorical interpretation.

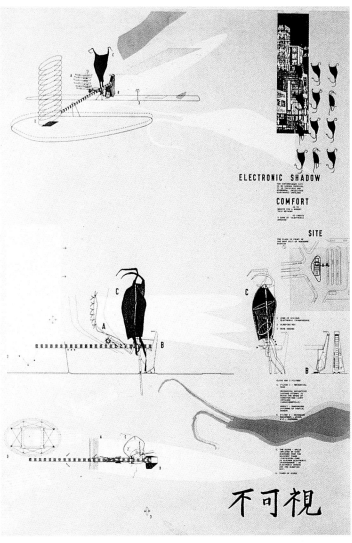

The Ninja House, competition entry, 1988

But their subtle treatment, both physical and psychological, of the world as they find it today, demands a continual renewal process. The train of thought from the copper roof of the nearby cathedral, via the metaphor of the carriers of knowledge, to the idea of tradition can turn out to be a trap for them. The new paradigm, which acquires its monument in the form of the electronics slab next to the ark in Münster, is exceedingly hard to swallow as a *fait accompli*. What do these architects really think about it, apart from the fact that things have become very complex in the new world. Such questions are raised but not always considered satisfactorily, let alone answered. What does the storage of knowledge mean as an idea in a world where we communicate through an interface? Is that knowledge potential or virtual? What is to happen to all those who fail to make it into the ark? These questions, above all, are broached by the work of Bolles and Wilson. Despite the merits of their architecture, it is painfully clear that we are stuck for answers.

Only skyscrapers under construction show the daring constructive ideas. The impression of high rise steel skeletons is massive.
Ludwig Mies van der Rohe

Only completed buildings can talk about architecture.
Louis Kahn

Now the post McLuhan media, electronic, communication revolution has lead us to a new trauma, today Baudrillard writes 'the real exists only as that which can be simulated'. We are all participants in the new perception - television slicing together disconnected fragments, slicing time. What characterises this new perception? A constant state of flux (videoclips, mass transport), a dematerialisation of objects (surface is no longer absolute, interior and exterior no longer opposites), an absence of appropriate or absolute hierarchies of scale (grand narratives become micronarratives, a chair is as

significant as a city), information itself is no longer the property of the book (it is electronic, invisible). What is the result? The horizon, the certainties of Cartesian geometry, the cone of perspective geometry focused on the viewer - all these have in a short space of time ceased to be our measure of the real. This radical transformation will be seen to characterise the end of the twentieth century as the discovery of optical perspective characterised the early Renaissance.
Peter Wilson

Creative invention of programme is now often the true subject of architectural competitions (clients must produce, but what?). Simultaneously familiar programmes have suffered an exhaustion of content. (The large office is reduced to square metres and underfloor media channels. A formula which alone does not dignify the lives of its users or the city in which it lands.) Architecture must provide more, it must learn to take up the responsibility for its own prescription. To do this it is necessary to identify and even to isolate extra-functional qualities. The pre-functional and the extra-functional in architecture move into the realm traditionally

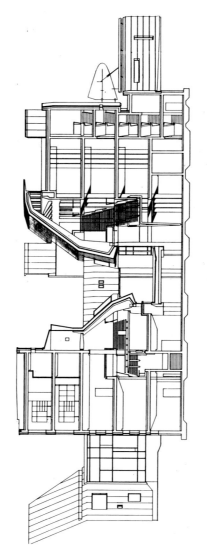

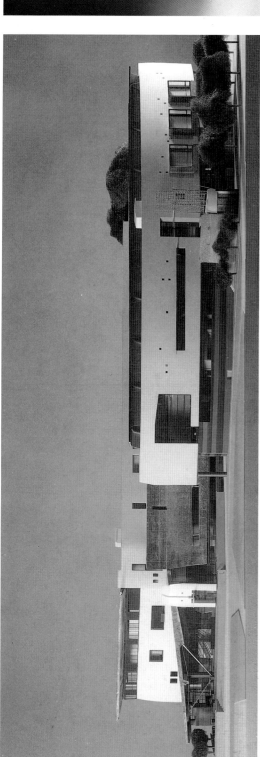

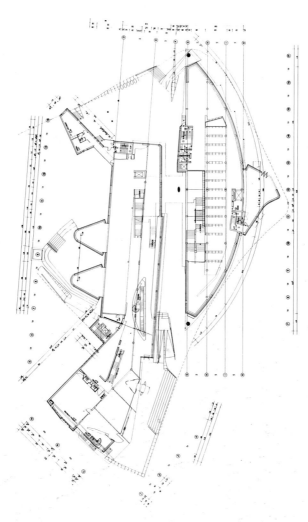

The medieval pattern of Münster is still today preserved in legal boundaries. The sensibility of Modernism infiltrates this pattern in the 1956 theatre, but also, as in every city, more pervasively as the spaces of the automobile, channels of movement and permanent voids (car parks). It is in one of these forty year old voids that the new library is to be inserted. The first element of the library, a slab, forms in collaboration with existing houses a triangular block. The second element, a ship-like solitaire, forms an outer and more solid perimeter to the block. The library is cut in two by a new pedestrian street, the Büchereigasse [Bookery Alley] which presents the latent axis of the nearby Lamberti-Church. This division is also programmatic. Short, unconcluded axes are a characteristic of Münster's baroque insertions. This library is the first in Germany to tackle in its formulation the question of the changing status of information. The result is the three zone library, with near, middle and far zones). The far zone is long term storage with no public access. The middle zone is that with which we are most familiar, the lending library, the realm of the book (knowledge as object). The plan registers this as a clear form, a segment of a circle (ship floating within the city – the circle today must be incomplete). This zone is quiet, books

line its large curved wall. What is new in Münster is the near zone, a zone of pure information, the library as a supermarket of information. On the ground level of the slab, just within the secure realm of the library, is the unprecedented, active information centre, the Medienstraße [Media Street] of the near zone, with Infotheque, Literatheque, Novitheque, Glossotheque, Hobbytheque, Phonotheque, Münstertheque and Lusotheque. It is divided from the middle zone by the Büchereigasse. Connection between the two is via the first floor bridge on which is situated the main information desk (common to both slab and ship). Connection also occurs in the basement (sound library) where the two buildings become one.

Café, exhibition space and newspaper reading salon are in the uncontrolled area at the entrance end of the slab; above in the slab are two floors of offices. Where the building is cut in two by the Büchereigasse the open façades are re-enclosed by two large sloping copper walls. These are the *leitmotiv* of the library, staircases are situated under them in both slab and ship, light falls down their internal face. Glass strips below these walls expose the entire ground level to the passer-by. *Peter Wilson*

▶

Location Alter Steinweg, Münster, Germany **Assistants** F. Haas, M. Schlüter, A. Kimmel **Client** City of Münster **Design** 1987-90 **Completion** 1993

Architekturbüro Bolles - Wilson und Partner *Stadtbücherei Münster Municipal Library*

Visitor of Simon Wiesenthal Museum of Tolerance, Los Angeles, 1993, looks at one of many exhibits dealing with racism and prejudice

Myth and the Fate of Secularisation

Gianni Vattimo

Myth today

Philosophical thought about the presence of myth in the contemporary world cannot be founded upon an essential or metaphysical definition of myth. This is due in part to the fact that the dream of philosophy as a rigorous science has been definitively *ausgetraumt*. More specifically, though, it is due to the fact that the theme of myth itself appears to us today in an uncertain light.

No satisfactory theory of myth – one that would define its nature and its connection with other forms of relationship to the world – exists in contemporary philosophy. Nevertheless, the term and the concept of myth, even if not carefully defined, have wide currency in our culture today. At least since the appearance of Roland Barthes' *Mythologies*, mass culture and its by-products generally have been analysed in terms of mythology; and the presence and place of myth in political thought have generally been conceived in terms of the now distant but still important work of Georges Sorel, *Reflexions sur la violence*, in which myth appears as the sole agent capable of moving the masses to action.

Even Claude Lévi-Strauss, who approaches myth from a specialised anthropological point of view, states in *Anthropologie structurale* that 'nothing resembles mythic thought today more than political ideology. In contemporary society the latter has in a certain sense replaced the former'.★ Although Lévi-Strauss cannot be accused of making only vague use of the term 'myth', a claim such as the one made here – that is,

★ Lévi-Strauss, C., *Anthropologie Structurale*, Paris 1958, p. 231.

that political ideology has replaced mythic thought for us today – depends in the last analysis upon a rather stereotypical understanding of the term. Indeed, in the later *Mythologica*, when Lévi-Strauss applies a more precise and specific concept of myth to the question of its possible survival in the contemporary world, he makes reference instead to music and literature as the elements of experience in which myth – in no matter how faded a form – endures today.★ The presence of myth in our culture, however, generally is not considered in terms of this rather technical and restricted understanding of the notion of

★ See especially the final chapter of *L'homme nu* (Mythologica IV), Paris 1971, and the 'Ouverture' of *Le cru et le cuit* (Mythologica I), Paris 1964.

'myth'. Instead, it is usually dealt with in a much more general sense, where it is understood as any combination of the following: as the opposite of scientific thought; as the opposite of demonstrative or analytic thought; as narrative or as the fantastic; as a locus of affect; as having little or no pretence to objectivity; as having to do with religion, art, ritual, and magic; or, finally, as the target of scientific demythisation and disenchantment (in the sense of Weber's *Entzauberung* of the World). Rational knowledge about reality,

> 'wherever it seeks to constitute itself as a theoretical consideration and explanation of the world, finds itself in opposition not as much to immediate phenomenal reality as to the mythical transfiguration of that reality. Long before the world presents itself to consciousness as a complex of empirical "things" and empirical properties, it has already presented itself as a complex of mythical powers and actions.' ★

This quotation from Cassirer's classic work of 1923, which is perhaps the last great philosophical theory of myth in our century, contains an element that is implicit and fundamental in the modern theory of myth – that is, the idea that myth is a kind of 'prescientific' knowledge, at once ancient and immature, identifiable

★ Cassirer, E., *Philosophie der symbolischen Formen* (1923), vol. 11, Darmstadt, Wissenschaftliche Buchgesellschaft, 1958.

with the childhood or adolescence of the history of the human mind. Even Lévi-Strauss, who certainly does not have a crudely evolutionistic concept of human development from mythos to logos, and who in fact sees himself as radically antihistoricist, considers mythic thought as the 'past' of our culture (inasmuch as he tries to locate its contemporary surrogate in the guise of political ideology, or its residual traces in music and literature).

Yet the idea implicit in the respective positions of Cassirer and Lévi-Strauss – to say nothing of Weber – is one that today makes us feel uneasy. No one would now accept the thesis, for instance, that myth is the specific form of thought of the primitive mind alone, or that civilisation is a process of demythisation in which the mythic world view is gradually abandoned for the scientific one. At the root of this uneasiness is the fact that the modern philosophical theory of myth – right up until that of Cassirer – has always found its articulation within the framework of a metaphysical and evolutionistic idea of history. It is this very framework of a philosophy of history that can no longer be recuperated today. As a result, even a philosophical theory of myth can no longer be precisely defined, and the common use of the term 'myth' registers and expresses a theoretical confusion. On the one hand, the term continues to refer to a form of thought no longer current and often considered more primitive than our own, in any case to one characterised by a lesser degree of objectivity – or of technological efficacy – than that ascribed to scientific knowledge. On the other hand, the concept of myth as primitive thought appears unsustainable in the wake of the crisis of the evolutionistic metaphysics of history (along with the very idea of scientific rationality), as well as in the light of less theoretical motivations linked to recent and current political events. This confusion can be understood through a brief survey of the principal attitudes that most influence our thinking about myth – attitudes I will describe on the basis of certain 'ideal types'. These are not explicitly articulated at a theoretical or practical level, but are nonetheless present and representative of the cultural situation we find ourselves in. These 'ideal types' can be called *archaism, cultural relativism*, and *limited rationality*. All three are characterised by incoherence and self-contradiction chiefly the result of having left unresolved the problem of the philosophy of history, the source of every concept of myth. All three are borne of a rejection of the metaphysics of history that sustained the 'modern' theory of myth, yet fail to formulate their position in theoretically satisfactory terms because they lack a new philosophical concept of history: they have simply set the problem aside.

Tendencies of archaism in The Netherlands, Wiel Arets, Academy of Arts and Architecture, Maastricht, 1993

Gianni Vattimo

Archaism

I would describe archaism as an attitude that, to use a term Derrida employs to describe an analogous state of things, could be called 'apocalyptic'. It is typified by the widespread contemporary distrust of Western scientific and technological culture, seen as a way of life that violates and destroys man's authentic relationship with both himself and nature, and which is inextricably bound to the capitalist system of exploitation and its imperialistic tendencies. The early-twentieth-century avant-garde artists'

Archaism, cultural relativism and limited rationality do not state where they themselves stand as theoretical positions.

fascination with African masks can be understood as a sign of the prophetic function that art has often had, as is the case here, in regard to the general direction of a culture and of a society. What was, for the early-twentieth-century avant-garde, principally an interest in modes of representation of the real that were uncontaminated by the long tradition of inherited artistic languages and genres – freely combined, especially in Expressionism and Surrealism, with a programmatic polemic against bourgeois culture – has today become a widely held attitude. The bad conscience of the liberal intelligentsia toward the so-called Third World can certainly be found in its approach to myth as well. Without the backdrop provided by such a sweeping political perspective it would be impossible to explain either the popularity that cultural anthropology has enjoyed in the last decades as an intellectual fashion or indeed the spread of 'structuralism' (not just in anthropology) as a left-wing theoretical position during the years of its greatest diffusion at a mass level. At the basis of all this there was originally the idea that both a purely structural study of 'primitive' myths and cultures and a general reconsideration of man in nonhistoristic terms (as exemplified by Lévi-Strauss's statement, in his polemic against Sartre, that 'we should study men as if they were ants') would destroy the Western myth of progress and its imperialistic and colonialistic implications. This was to be done in the name of a mode of thought that would recuperate the 'authentic' values of a relationship between man and nature unmediated by scientific objectivisation,

Archaism hopes to discover a possible way out of the errors and contradictions of current scientific and technological civilisation.

which was seen as strictly linked to the capitalist organisation of labour – as both the critical philosophy of the Frankfurt School and the Lukács of *History and Class Consciousness* had shown.**?!** Both this critique and a sense of bad conscience about imperialism and neo-colonialism have more recently been combined with ecological concerns about the devastating consequences that science, technology, capi-

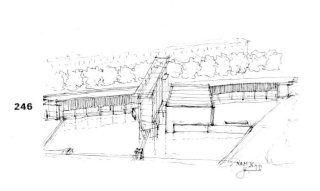

Tendencies of archaism in The Netherlands, Jo Coenen, Dutch Architectural Institute, Rotterdam, 1993

talist exploitation, and the arms race have had on both nature and the physical nature of man himself. Archaism is the sum of all these factors. In this perspective, myth appears not only as not being an essentially overcome phase of our cultural history but precisely as a more authentic form of knowledge, one that precedes the destructive mentality of objectivising, quantitative modern science, technology and capitalism. From a renewed contact with myth, archaism hopes to discover a possible way out of the errors and contradictions of current scientific and technological civilisation. This renewed contact with myth takes the form of either an analysis of the myths of 'other' cultures (those studied by anthropologists working among existing primitive peoples) or a reading of the ancient myths of our own Western tradition (as is the case for the Greek myths, re-examined with anthropological methods and mind-sets by philologists and historians of the structuralist school). Much of Nietzsche's and Heidegger's recent popularity in continental European culture seems to be related to these tendencies (even if based upon misinterpretations that I will not discuss here). Nietzsche's critique of Socratic thought and of decadence, as well as his concept of the nihilistic direction of Western culture, and Heidegger's *Seinsvergessenheit* (with all that it implies), are interpreted as appeals for the recovery of a premetaphysical (prelogical) attitude toward reality, which is largely identifiable with a return to myth. The critique of scientific and technological civilisation, as well as the renewed interest in archaic thought – both of which are found, in different forms, in Nietzsche and Heidegger – are taken as a point of departure for the recuperation of myth, even if neither Nietzsche nor, least of all, Heidegger justifies

?! *Pushing this Frankfurter's train of thought into today's station, one could conceive capitalism as a source of archaism. Since consumption replaces production as the guiding principle, the myth of progress is bound to yield to myth of a different kind. Consequently, archaism might serve extremely well as the ideology of non-critical submission to the late-capitalist system, and to consumption-ideology. Suppose we're on the right track, would archaism be a reaction to the myth of progress, or rather a subtle continuation of the same? Like a kind of sophisticated tuning job disguised as its own negation?*

an undertaking such as this. It would be difficult, however, to point to philosophical positions or cultural projects that explicitly propose a return to mythic knowledge.

The single exception is, at present, the so-called New Right movement in France and Italy, which takes up the anticapitalist polemic of Fascism and Nazism and combines it with themes from the 1968 student revolt. As is the case for the two other 'ideal' approaches to myth that we will discuss shortly, though, archaism does not articulate a complete doctrinal position. This, as I have already suggested, is a consequence of the failure of archaism to propose an alternative to the crisis of metaphysical historicism of which it is itself a product. Thus it is destined to remain theoretically mute, or in any case not to define a precise position for itself. **?!** Archaism, when it does not turn to the restoration of traditional cultural values and consequently to right-wing politics, may also elaborate an 'utopian' critique of scientific and technological civilisation and capitalism (as is the case for some of the liberal European thought). Such a critique openly admits that it is not only pointless but politically dangerous and unacceptable to try to restore the 'traditional' values of European culture. At the same time, though, it appeals to mythic knowledge – uncontaminated by Western capitalist rationality – as the foundation for its rejection of modernity and its errors. In this critical perspective, currently popular in continental 'left-wing' circles, authors like Nietzsche and Heidegger are joined together with the more radical members of the Frankfurt School, such as Walter Benjamin and his intellectual precursor Rosenzweig. Yet here too –

?! *Although probably theoretically mute, archaism is the talk of the town. In studios of architects, artist and movie makers alike, in meditation-centres and on holidays in Tuscany, you name it, archaism is the It-word. Even if the creed is an individual one, shouldn't we define archaism as a movement, even if it lacks statutes?*

Gianni Vattimo

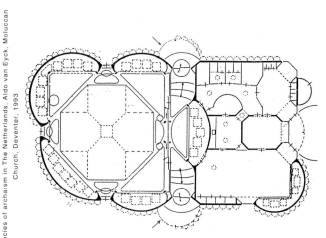

Tendencies of archaism in The Netherlands, Aldo van Eyck, Moluccan Church, Deventer, 1993

247

often on the basis of rather arbitrary readings – myth is understood as the kind of thought that is closest to that original or sacred language theorised by Benjamin and supposed to be outside of the rational knowledge of Western science and philosophy.

Cultural relativism

The second approach that, in our present-day attitudes, conditions and qualifies the presence of myth is

Limited rationality describes that ensemble of cultural attitudes that treats mythic knowledge, understood as narrative, as a more adequate form of thought for certain fields of experience.

cultural relativism. According to this position, the fundamental principles and axioms that define rationality, the criteria of truth, ethics, and the experience of a historical humanity in general, are not the object of rational knowledge or demonstration insofar as the very possibility of demonstration invariably depends upon these same principles and axioms. Thomas Kuhn's theory of paradigms, for instance, at least in its original form, could be considered as representative of this approach (which has proven to be extremely popular in the epistemological debate of the last few years). Heideggerian hermeneutics often is taken to be a theory of this type, even if there are good reasons to think that this is not necessarily the case. In cultural relativism any thought of an univocal rationality, thanks to which we could call certain forms of knowledge 'mythic', has been banished. Moreover, the idea that the first principles upon which a specific cultural universe constitutes itself are in fact not the object of rational and demonstrative knowledge opens the way to our seeing them also as the object of a kind of mythic knowledge. Even scientific rationality, long the guiding value for European culture, finally reveals itself to be a myth: not more than a shared belief on the basis of which our culture has been organised. Thus, as Odo Marquard has pointed out, the very idea that the history of Western reason is the history of a progressive abandonment of myth (or

★ See Marquardt, O., *Abschied vom Prinzipiellen,* Stuttgart 1981, p. 93.

Cultural relativism ignores both (a) the effective context in which the thesis of the irreducible plurality of cultural worlds is put into place, and (b) the effective impossibility of isolating one cultural world from another.

Entmythologisierung) is itself a myth, a central belief that is neither proven nor provable.★

As opposed to archaism, cultural relativism does not ascribe any sort of (mythical) superiority to mythical knowledge in regard to modern scientific knowledge. It only refuses to place these two modes of knowledge in opposition to each other, since both are founded on fundamental assumptions that

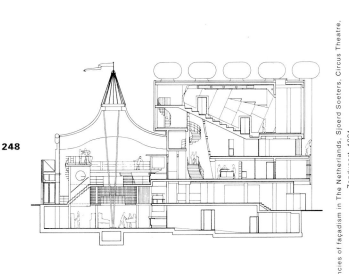

Tendencies of façadism in The Netherlands, Sjoerd Soeters, Circus Theatre, Zandvoort, 1991

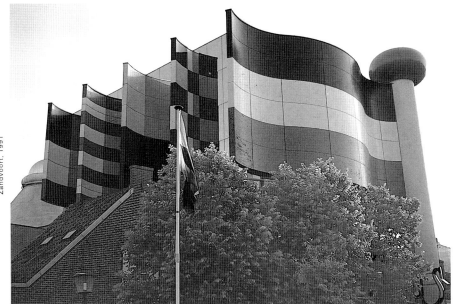

share the characteristics of myth – that is, they are based on beliefs that form a part of lived experience and are not susceptible to scientific proof. These beliefs, which lie at the basis of every cultural universe, are not always called 'myths' (as Marquard chooses to call them).**?!** Nevertheless, cultural relativism's interest in myth is every bit as vital as that of archaism – not because it tries to uncover in myth a more authentic form of knowledge, but because in the study of the myths of other civilisations it seeks a more revealing method for studying our own, in the conviction that our civilisation too has a fundamentally mythic structure. Such a presupposition (even if never made explicit) can be shown to be present, for instance, in Roland Barthes's 'mythological' approach to mass culture. As in Marquard's use of the term, 'myth' in this case stands for a non-demonstrable and immediately lived knowledge. Thus its meaning is still, in the last analysis, highly conditioned by its strict opposition to the characteristics of scientific knowledge.

?! *If this kind of thinking implies the equivalent of myth and axiomatic clarity, aren't we on the brink of obscurantism? Does this obscurantism involve Derrida's enunciation, 'there is nothing outside the text'? Maybe you envision an ethical moment that prevents this slide, but where?*

Limited rationality

The third contemporary attitude toward myth I call *tempered irrationalism* or the theory of limited rationality. Here the term myth instead is assigned to a specific meaning, one linked to the original etymological significance of the word – for 'myth' means 'narration'. In this form it sets itself in opposition to, or distinguishes itself from, scientific knowledge: it accomplishes this, however, not through a simple reversal of the latter's characteristics – such as demonstrativeness and objectivity – but through the working of a positive element of its own, *narrative structure*. Limited rationality describes that ensemble of cultural attitudes that treats mythic knowledge, understood as narrative, as a more adequate form of thought for certain fields of experience. Yet at the same time it does not challenge or explicitly call into question the validity of scientific or positive knowledge for other fields of experience. We can find examples of limited rationality in at least three disciplines:

1) In psychoanalysis, where psychic life tends to be considered as structured in terms of narration (both in its everyday functioning and in the therapeutic situation). In the case of Jungian psychoanalysis and its variants, this same psychic life is seen as necessarily expressing certain basic themes and archetypal myths, which in turn structure it not as abstract principles nor as an interplay of forces but as 'stories' that cannot be reduced to underlying structural patterns for which they would serve as mere surface manifestations (Hillman speaks of 'polytheism' in this same sense).

2) In contemporary theories of historiography, where the narrative hypostasis has shown itself to be increasingly important as a model. Narrative analysis not only reveals the rhetorical models on which historiography is constructed, but – above all else – also points, in revelation of the essential multiplicity of these very models, to a basis for negating the unity of history. It recognises the irreducible *plurality* of history itself, a history ever more difficult to distinguish from myth (insofar as it no longer reflects

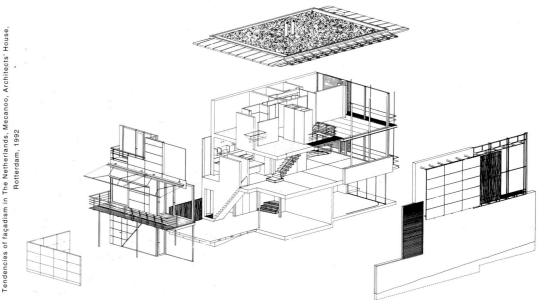

Tendencies of façadism in The Netherlands, Mecanoo, Architects' House, Rotterdam, 1992

?! *In* Erfahrung und Armut *Walter Benjamin describes modern times in which narration is virtually extinct. Recently, 'limited rationality' seems to imply the eminence of narration. Are we confronted with a kind of Benjaminian problem? Your examples speak clear language: they indicate far-reaching formalisation of narration. Clearly, Roland Barthes sanctions this condition by means of his theory on 'the death of the author', doesn't he?*

?! *Your concept of 'limited rationality' seems to have an analogical sympathy in architecture: for the figurative and ornamental. 'The story' is being told in the façade and by the façade, by the surface at large. (Pietro Derossi comes to mind. Allow us to recall your admiration.) Do you believe there could be a more abstract narrative? For instance, a story looming up from the montage, in the 'between'? As opposed to the operative monopoly of pre-programmed symbolism of psychoanalysis and mass media?*

the norms of reality).

3) In the sociology of the mass media, which has substituted Sorel's original application of the notion of myth to (revolutionary) mass movements with an analysis, in mythological terms, of the contents and images of the world produced and distributed by film, television, literature, and other mass-market media.**?!**

These various ways of thinking about myth – taken as a term that can be applied to numerous fields of experience – can be called theories of limited rationality for the following reason: all three have in common the idea (which goes back to Plato and Aristotle; see, for instance, *Timaeus 19d*) that certain fields of experience cannot be understood through the use of demonstrative reason or the scientific method, but require instead a kind of knowledge that can only be described as 'mythic'.**?!**

The limits of myth

As I said at the outset, the different attitudes (which generate markedly different positions in regard to myth, but which nonetheless all share an intensive interest in it) have resulted from the dissolution of the various metaphysical philosophies of history. Yet, at the same time, all three have failed to take the fact of that dissolution sufficiently into account. Precisely for this reason they cannot avoid the errors and contradictions that render them unsatisfactory from a theoretical standpoint. *Archaism* clearly does not tackle the problem of history, insofar as it is powerless – when confronted with the modern world – to produce a viable position, that is anything other than a call for the restoration of 'traditional' culture (from, significantly enough, a 'right-wing' perspective). Right-wing traditionalism, representing the only apparent political program of archaism, reveals the latter's theoretical weakness pushing to an extreme degree. That weakness consists in simply reversing the myth of progress into a myth of origins, which simply as such are supposed to be more authentically human; they are therefore supposedly worthy of serving as the goal of a political revolution or, at the very least, as the touchstone for a critique of modernity.

The idealisation of origins, though, is just as empty as the idealisation of the future for its own sake (which is what the secularised ideal of progress and development has always done, and continues to do). Furthermore, we have a relationship today with our origins only through the mediation of a process that is, in the last analysis, derived from those same origins. This process – the context in which origins are given to us – both separates us from them and connects us to them. Archaism would simply put aside the problem that this process presents, for if the condition of alienation and dehumanisation in which we find ourselves today is derived from our origins (as their *Wirkung*), why would anyone wish to return to those origins? Problems of this type – which are problems of the philosophy of history – are precisely what archaism tries to put aside without having really addressed. Yet these same problems are still urgently contemporary ones, even if metaphysical and evolutionistic philosophies of history

Tendencies of facadism in The Netherlands, Leo Heijdenrijk, 'Ruins', social housing, Amersfoort, 1992

have been definitively abandoned.

The same could be said for *cultural relativism*, except that in this case it is evident that the problem of historicity has been neither raised nor resolved, but merely 'skipped'. Cultural relativism ignores both (a) the effective context in which the thesis of the irreducible plurality of cultural worlds is put into place, and (b) the effective impossibility of isolating one cultural world from another (and not only from our own universe). The problem that anthropologists working 'in the field' must often confront – what is the relationship between themselves, as representatives of a strong and often colonialist culture, and their native sources of information? – presents only one aspect of the broader hermeneutic dilemma with which cultural relativism does not deal. The study of 'other' cultures always occurs in a context in which the pretence that these 'other' cultures are (or can be) represented as distinct and separate objects of enquiry must appear as utterly false and impossible. They are instead like speakers in a dialogue; but, once we recognise this, the question must then be raised of the common horizon on which the dialogue itself takes place. Such a question, obviously, invalidates from the first any project – like that of cultural relativism – to represent 'other' cultures as isolated objects. This common horizon is the problem of the philosophy of history itself, and cannot be so easily done away with.

Finally, the theory of *limited rationality* also attempts to skirt the problem of its own historical position. Recall that limited rationality depends upon the idea, found in a number of different forms, that myth is a kind of narrative knowledge that is supposed to be suited to certain fields of experience (mass culture, psychic life, historiography). Limited rationality does not recognise, though, that it is founded on a tacit acceptance of the distinction between *Natur-* and *Geisteswissenschaften*. Yet this same distinction has become ever more problematic and tenuous in recent years. The notion that even exact science is a social enterprise has become widespread; the objectifying methods of the natural sciences are now seen as a moment within a social context, and this realisation thus returns us once again to the field of historical and social 'sciences'. It is an antihistorical illusion to think that the two fields – history, psychic life, and so on, on the one hand, and experimental science on the other – can possibly be kept apart. Both the hermeneutic developments of historicism, and the recent epistemological studies of the *Naturwissenschaften* (here I am thinking of Kuhn, Feyerabend, Lakatos, et al.), point toward a breaking down and an elimination of this distinction.

In varying degrees, and in different forms, then, the three contemporary attitudes toward myth – all of which deserve more consideration than can be given here – put aside much too quickly the problem of their *own* historical contextualisation. They do not state where they themselves stand as theoretical positions.**?!** Archaism proposes a return to origins and to mythic knowledge without asking what the 'intermediary' period (or meantime) between today's world and its beginnings might be. Cultural relativism speaks of separate and autonomous cultural universes, but does not say which of these universes is the domain of relativistic theory itself. Limited rationality does not have an explicit theory about the

Gianni Vattimo

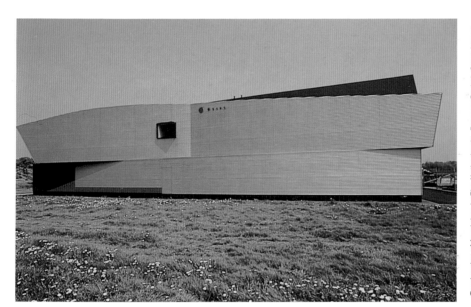

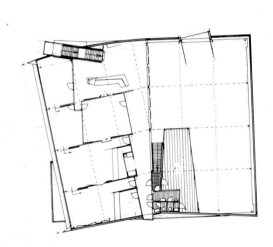

Tendencies of fascinism in The Netherlands, Ben van Berkel, Store house, office space, Amersfoort, 1992

251

possibility of distinguishing fields reserved for mythic knowledge from fields reserved for scientific rationality. The idealist or positivist version of the metaphysics of history had an answer for all of these problems: it conceived of history as a single progressive process of *Aufklärung* and emancipation of reason. The process of emancipation of reason, however, went far beyond the expectations of both idealism and positivism. A vast number of peoples and cultures spoke up on the world's stage, and it gradually became impossible to believe that history was an unitary process with a continuous development toward a *telos*. The coming true of the universality of history made universal history impossible.**?!**
Even the idea that the historical process could conceive of itself as *Aufklärung* – as the liberation of reason from the shadows of mythic knowledge – lost its legitimacy, and demythisation was recognised as being itself a myth.

Myth and the Post-Modern
Since the discovery of the mythic nature of demythisation fails, then, to legitimise the three approaches to myth we have described, it follows that to demythise demythisation does not mean to restore the privileges of myth – if only because, among the myths whose validity we must recognise, there is the myth of reason and its progress in history. Demythisation, or the idea of history as a process of emancipation of reason, is not something that can be exorcised so easily. Nietzsche already demonstrated that,

when the value of truth itself is shown to be a belief founded on vital needs (and is therefore an 'error'), previous errors are not simply restored to their former position. As he says in *The Gay Science* (aphorism no. 54), to go on dreaming with the knowledge that you are dreaming is not the same thing as pure and simple dreaming. The same can be said for demythisation: if we want to be faithful to our historical experience, we must realise that our relationship with myth, once demythisation itself has been proven to be a myth, will not be restored to its original state, but will remain marked by this very experience. A theory of the presence of myth in contemporary culture must take this as its point of departure.**?!** Nietzsche's remark in *The Gay Science* is not just a philosophical paradox; it is the expression of one of

?! 'Maintenant je sais; je sais qu'on sais jamais?' *(Jean Gabin)*

When even demythisation is unmasked as myth, myth itself recovers its legitimacy, but only within the framework of a generalised, weakened experience of truth.

the fundamental aspects of the destiny of our culture, one that could also be called 'secularisation'. In this term we find the two elements of Nietzsche's paradox – to know that one is dreaming and yet to continue dreaming. The secularisation of the European spirit over the last few centuries is the result not only of the discovery and demystification of the 'errors' of religion, but also of the survival of those errors in different, and in a certain sense degraded, forms. A secularised culture is not a culture that has

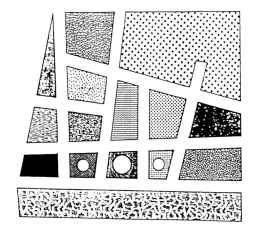

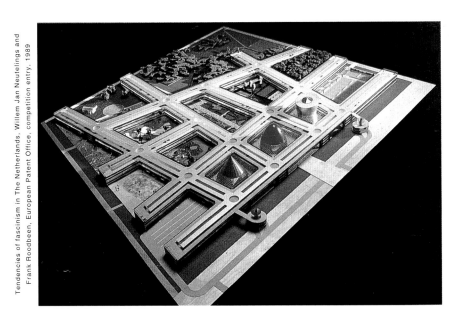

Tendencies of fascinism in The Netherlands. Willem Jan Neutelings and Frank Roodbeen, European Patent Office, competition entry, 1989

Myth and the Fate of Secularisation

simply left behind the religious contents of its tradition; it is one that continues to live them as traces, as models that are hidden and disfigured but nonetheless profoundly present.**?!** These ideas are seen clearly in the works of Max Weber. Modern capitalism does not create itself out of a rejection of the Christian medieval tradition, but instead becomes its 'transformed' application. Löwith's research on modern historicism leads in the same essential direction: the various metaphysics of history, up until Hegel, Marx, and Comte, are only 'interpretations' (deprived of the original theological context) of the Hebraic-Christian theology of history.★**?!** Not so much in Löwith as in Weber, though, or as in Tönnies's opposition between 'community' and 'society', we find that gain and loss are inseparably bound together in the process by which modernity (understood as industrial capitalism in Weber, or, in Tönnies, as a society no longer based on organic relations) detaches itself from its original religious foundations. Modernisation does not occur because tradition is abandoned, but rather because of the appearance of a sort of ironic interpretation of it, or distortion. Heidegger speaks, in a somewhat similar sense, of *Verwindung*.★ The latter preserves tradition but also, to a degree, deprives it of its content. Both Norbert Elias's argument about the history of European civilisation, and Rene Girard's thesis about violence and the sacred (and about Christianity as a process of desacralisation), appear to be quite close to this notion of secularisation.★

★ See Loewith, K., *Meaning in History*, Chicago 1949.
★ On the notion of Verwindung, see especially Heidegger, M., *Überwindung der Metaphysik*, in *Vortrage und Aufsätze*, Pfullingen l954.
★ See especially Elias.,N., *Über den Prozess der Zivilisation* (1937) vol. 1, 1969: vol. 11, 1980, Girard, R., *Des choses cachées depuis la fondation du monde*, Paris 1978. It is hardly necessary to add that neither Elias nor, especially, Girard drew the same conclusions from their work that we try to draw here.

?! So, secularisation *isn't the right word, since we keep detecting a metaphysical dimension. However, human consciousness might develop to the point that the myth becomes obsolete, might it not? Couldn't the pacification and mitigation of various polarities eventually create a condition in which* Artificial Intelligence *manages the world, ushering human kind into an endless era of ennui. Wouldn't that be the one and only real* secularisation? The one *already suggested by the term since its coining.*

?! One might state that capitalism is absolutely indifferent to this tradition. Disregarding the metaphysical dimension, it elects and applies the profitable aspects only. Hence, capitalism could be declared the destroyer of fundamental (religious, metaphysical, even ideological truths. So capitalism is not about presence or absence of religion or philosophical certainty of some kind; it lives of its created interchangeability of any value. Wouldn't it be more adequate to say that the disrooting nature of capitalism turned its historical roots in tradition into an irrelevancy, a neglectable quantity?*

Gianni Vattimo

For Elias the modern process of civilisation develops when power and the use of force are concentrated first in the figure of the sovereign, then in the absolute state, and finally in the constitutional state. In the succession of these phases, the collective consciousness undergoes a radical transformation: the individual subject, in all social classes, internalises the 'good manners' of the courtier, who had been the first to renounce the use of force in favour of the sovereign. Passions are no longer as strong and open as they were in past periods. Although existence has lost some of its liveliness and colour, however, it has acquired a greater degree of security and formalisation. Here as well we see that progress is accompanied by a lesser degree of intensity of experience, or by a sort of emptying-out or dilution of experience.

?! Girard is concerned instead with civilisation in general. According to him, its path goes from the birth of the sacred – which exorcises universal human violence by concentrating it on the sacrificial victim, but nonetheless allows it to survive as the basis of all institutions – to its demystification by the Old Testament and Jesus Christ. Christ shows that the sacred is violence, and opens the way to a new human history that can be called 'secularised' (even if this goes against Girard's own terminology). Modern European culture is tied to its own religious and mythical past, not only by a relationship of overcoming and emancipation, but also, inseparably, by a relationship of preservation-distortion-dilution. Progress has a sort of nostalgic nature, as classicism and romanticism have taught us. The meaning of this nostalgia becomes manifest only when the experience of demythisation is pursued as far as possi-

?! *George Simmel links this phenomenon with the rise of mass society in the metropolis; and with the inherent blasé attitude needed for survival, along with the impact of money on the notion of quality. In your opinion, certain phenomena might change their appearance, however remaining intrinsically the same. But how does one reconcile this with the irreversible processes of urbanisation and quantification of existence, monetary units, i.e. dollars?*

Tendencies of fascinism in The Netherlands. Koen van Velsen. State Academy of Fine Arts, Amsterdam, 1992

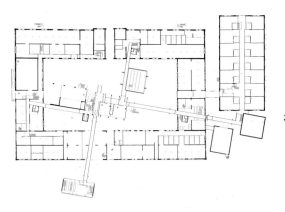

253

ble. When even demythisation is unmasked as myth, myth itself recovers its legitimacy, but only within the framework of a generalised, 'weakened' experience of truth. The presence of myth in contemporary culture does not stand in opposition to modernisation; it is instead a consequence of modernisation, and should be seen as modernisation's ultimate point of arrival, at least up until now. Moreover, the moment of the demythisation of demythisation can be considered the true and proper moment of transition from the modern to the post-modern. It is in Nietzsche that this transition takes place in its most explicit philosophical form. After Nietzsche, and after radical demythisation, the experience of truth simply can no longer be the same as before, for there is no longer any apodictic evidence of the kind in which thinkers, during the era of metaphysics, sought to find a *fundamentum absolutum et inconcussum*. The Post-Modern subject, when it turns toward itself and searches its consciousness, is confronted not by the certainty of the Cartesian *cogito*, but by the *intermittences du coeur* described by Proust, the *récits* produced by the mass media, or the *mythologies* rediscovered by psychoanalysis.

It is precisely this experience that the 'return' of myth in our culture and in our language tries to capture, certainly not that of a mythical primitive culture uncontaminated by modernisation and rationalism. Only in this sense – through a weakening of the notion of truth – can myth be understood to point toward the overcoming of the opposition between rationalism and irrationalism, and to open a possible new direction for contemporary thought. **?!**

?! *Risking a deep sigh of yours: you give ample evidence of awareness pertaining to shortcomings of philosophical system construction. In order to uphold the system, the constructors need to delete many a valuable issue/aspects. On the other hand, wouldn't one say that a counsel's speech on 'weak thought' diminishes the incentives for strong action?*

Architecture, Development, Memory

Hal Foster

I am not an architectural historian. I say this partly as an excuse and partly to be permitted to write speculatively – in a way that people schooled in a professional language do not often write. Cultural critics often regard contemporary architecture as if it were somehow isomorphic to economic forces. Although I, too, will sometimes treat it here as a simple inert object, what in fact interests me is its discursive complexity.

The Russian Revolution confronted artists with the potential anachronism of the category Art. So now, in a very different way, advanced capitalism confronts architects with the possible obsolescence of the category Architecture. But one can read this development otherwise – as a mandate to think the 'refunctioning' of the discipline. The first part of my text touches on the present conditions of such a refunctioning; the second part of the text concerns the emblematic role of architecture in historicist models of history.

I want to begin with a general remark about criticism that is especially important for architectural discourse. For me the concept of criticism is bound up with the concept of the public sphere. Now whether one regards this sphere as historical or heuristic, criticism depends on it. In certain ways the two forms, the institution of criticism and the notion of the public, are coeval aspects of the same bourgeois cultural revolution. Of course, this revolution was stopped short when other groups – initially other classes – demanded that the rights and representations of the bourgeoisie be made truly public, truly open to all. This demand continues in different ways, and it is only in this form, in the many counter-publics of the present, that one can speak of a public sphere at all (for the most part, the old public sphere has gone the way of spectacle – to the point of our corporate-state-media sphere). Yet,

254

When architecture is received as an activity of public concern, this public is rarely captured in its condition of conflict and contestation; it is seen instead as a supine statistic. As a result, architecture and public become disjunct.

institutionally, criticism has not proven very able to sustain these counterpublics, to articulate residual and/or emergent interests alternative to dominant ones. Nor has it proven very able to pressure architecture, its institutional support, to do so. By and large it has accepted its own default – even embraced its erosion as a site of analysis and alternative. Too many architectural critics are bagmen for the boys downtown. If this sounds reactive at best, paranoid at worst, it is. And that is my second general point about criticism today. Critical culture depends on political culture, and our political culture is reactive in its anxiety about the present; the mainstream is pledged against the innovative, the other. **?!** In such a climate criticism cannot help but be reactive too, and it is; when it is not simple ratification, criticism is steeped in resentment, trapped in negation, severed from affirmation. And I mean affirmation that is critical, not celebratory, of the status quo – affirmation that releases new modes of thought and action as well as rescuing repressed modes in cultural, social, and political life. There is a great atrophy of this annunciatory criticism today, and practice atrophies with it.

What does all this mean for contemporary architecture? For one thing, it is rarely received as a practice of public concern. How often do the journals present architecture as a civic issue of civic participation? And how often, when it is so discussed, does the subject involve everyday building – and not this designer-design or that architect-personality? When architecture is received as an activity of public concern, this public is rarely captured in its condition of conflict and contestation; it is seen instead as a supine statistic. As a result, architecture and public become disjunct; one effect is that the public aspects of architecture are treated as reified quotients. Relegated to categories like *ersatz* atriums and puny plazas, meaningless monuments and monster malls, these public quotients of architecture are compensatory; they serve, like most public art, as pathetic substitutes for spaces of public appearance (at least such nineteenth-century precedents as the department store and the grand boulevard possessed a phantasmagorical wonder that provoked a reflexive, Baudelairean subculture; so far the malls have given us 'Dawn of the Dead'). **?!** A nuisance to powers that be, they are used only by the homeless, who are harassed there (the rest of us are merely surveyed).

?! *You represent the situation as an accomplished fact. On the one hand you suggest a certain margin for political involvement in architecture, which could manifest itself also in criticism; on the other hand this criticism doesn't amount to much because of its present reactive nature. This ambiguity appears to be the main origin of your trust in small-scale solutions, for instance when you refer to architects such as Aalto and Siza. However, these architects are known to have connections with local structures of power, be it that they appear less dangerous in periphery Finland or Portugal than in Manhattan. What, if any, possibilities do you envision for politically articulated positions in the centre of power?*

?! *Two decades ago Manfredo Tafuri described in his* Project and Utopia *how Modern architecture, aspiring to manifest itself outside its confinements, to become a political movement, had failed. As a result, at the close of the seventies strong sentiments against architecture becoming a sociological issue arose. Its autonomy was proclaimed. The question is: could the professional architect still be identified as such, while following your advice?*

Venice Biennial, Fifth International Exhibition of Architecture, 1991

Ville Nouvelle, Marne la Vallée, Paris, 1984

Battery Park, New York City, 1987

Another corollary effect of this discursive separation of architecture and public is that architecture is regarded primarily as an individual practice – again, in terms of this design by that architect-personality or this project by that megalomaniac-developer.

Not much critical consideration is given to the social complexity of architecture (e.g., the impact of an office building on the community of its site or the psyches of its users) or even to the actual practice of building: not just grand projects like the mini-city spectacles of a Baltimore waterfront, but the worka-day architecture of new urban villages, office parks, and governmental buildings. As far as I can tell, such activities are rarely acknowledged by architectural discourse; they are shunted into other cate-gories (Business, Real Estate, Arts and Leisure). And this, I submit, is an extraordinary mystification in which architectural criticism, theory, and education all generally participate. The powers that be (the Philip Johnsons, Donald Trumps or local administrators) could not devise a more perfect ideological mask than the one we produce and reproduce daily in the course of our own practices as architects, crit-ics, and teachers – even (or especially) when we think we are at our most theoretically subversive (my tone may suggest that these developments are new, but in fact they comprise the present state of an his-torical process – the architectural/urban vision of state capitalism – punctuated by such famous figures as Baron Haussmann and Otto Wagner, Albert Speer and Robert Moses, Philip Johnson and John Portman).

On this score, architectural criticism is an easy target, but it is not my only one. Architecture in the academy also participates in this mystification. It does so simply when it excludes or neglects certain mundane architectures, political processes, or social groups. In my limited exposure to architectural conferences and academic critiques (the first often gladiatorial, the second always sadistic), these things are often held to be beneath contempt or at least beneath interest. Again, I speak as a layman, and for the layman two figures have come to dominate the field: the *developer-architect* and the *academic architect*. According to this view, architecture has become subsumed by development, on the one hand; on the other hand, it has become rarefied in the academy. This is cynical, perhaps overly so, for there are points of resistance and renewal in both arenas. But this process of reification and rarefaction in architecture cannot be denied. How is this located historically? Does it begin with the split between architecture and engineering – a split that rarefies the practice of the former as it allows the logic of the latter to dominate? Does it derive from the ambiguous position of architecture, as the most practical or worldly of the arts, in the Modernist projection of formal autonomy? This will to autonomy was also part of the bourgeois cultural revolution, but to a great extent its critical charge is now void. Indeed, to a great extent this will to autonomy allowed the rarefaction of architecture in the academy that in turn abetted its reification in development. In any case, exactly how this happened, exactly how the developer-architect and the academic-architect were produced, I cannot say. I can say, however, that one way to respond to these twin figures is to produce another dialectical pair: as opposed to the *developer-architect*, the *political architect*; and as opposed to the *academic-architect*, the *counter-disciplinary architect*.

Now what might this first creature, the political architect, be today? For example, rather than develop homeless shelters as part of a zoning variation or a building deal (as a developer might), an architect could work to expose the architectural preconditions of homelessness – maybe not in building, maybe not in drawing, maybe outside the discipline as it exists today. But to present schematic shelters to the homeless or to reimagine the house type altogether – the first as a conscientious salve, the second as a compensatory vision of grandeur – is not enough. Instead an architect might reveal the production of homelessness as an effect not only of certain policies (regarding welfare, housing funds, and so forth) but also of certain architectural/urban assumptions. Now, perhaps, I sound naive rather than cynical, for what happens then to architecture? Might it not just become politics or economics or sociology?

In part. But what is architecture now, what has it ever been? Such an analysis is not irrelevant to sophisticated discourse. Deconstructivist architects argue that both Pre-Modern and Modern architecture are mired in a metaphysics of presence – of the shelter, of the home. If this is true, an antifoundational critique of such architecture might make the homeless its subject. So, too, it might consider the *unheimlich*, the uncanny. Both these terms exist at the limit of architecture. Architecture enframes. Abjected, the homeless are pushed outside the frame – and so challenge it. The same is true of the uncanny: architecture rarely allows for sensual intuitions of space and structure; what might happen if it entertained unconscious ones? Indeed, what might a psychoanalytical architecture be?

What about the figure of the counter-disciplinary architect? I pose this figure in opposition to the rarefied academic-architect, and here I appeal to a post-structuralism that is not so active in architectural discussion today, at least as this discussion centres on deconstructivist architecture. We can argue whether deconstructivist architecture is truly deconstructive of architecture, or true to the methodology of deconstruction; clearly architecture is an important site for an inquiry. But at some point we must ask where such architecture stands in relation to the general rarefaction-reification of the discipline today. For example, it may well address the metaphysical assumptions, the humanist subject-positions, of architecture in a Derridean sense. But does it engage the aspects of the discipline in the Foucauldean sense? Unless it does, I am not sure how fully critical, even deconstructive, it can be. I mention Foucault to suggest one way that a counter-disciplinary architecture might proceed to think the disciplinary aspects of architecture. I use 'disciplinary' in the sense of how architecture constructs its authorial subjects and trains its practitioners as architects (in relation to other discourses and practices, of course, but also in the university, even in apparently nondisciplinary curricula and projects); and disciplinary in the sense of how architecture constructs its recipient subjects, trains our spatialities and temporalities, our bodies and minds, our conscious and unconscious activities. In short, the point is not so much to contrive (say) anti-panoptical projects, but to consider whether or not architecture can be thought outside a system of a surveyed space, outside a regime of a disciplinary gaze, outside an order of regimented

John Portman in the interior of the Marriott Marquis Hotel

256

bodies, outside a time-space of compelled circulation (the flow of people, goods, information, money) – in short, to think architecture in terms of its technical, microphysical effects on our bodies and minds.

A question here in passing: for Foucault the gaze historically produced in different architectures and inscribed in different subjects is sexually indifferent. Is this so? Can a critical architecture today afford to think that it is so? And a personal aside as well: recently, I have become interested in typological developments. Some time ago (1988) I was in Seattle, my hometown, for an architecture conference. As if to compensate for its evermore dense downtown, there is a spacious new mall, and it struck me as a weird inversion: an initially urban type, the department store, first developed into a suburban type, the shopping centre, now returned to an urban setting. This inversion – it has happened elsewhere too – is troublesome, because the suburban mall is presented as a primary form of public urban space. It is accepted as a space of public memory, too, which makes it even more problematic, for in such spaces the history of place is consumed as spectacle. In Seattle, this means the use of a North-west Coast Indian design abstracted as a general logo for the mall.

A few weeks later I was in San Francisco, where I saw a further development of the mall type called the San Francisco Emporium. Here not only is the suburban mall transplanted to the city, but the horizontality of the shopping centre is rotated back to the verticality of the department store. Picture a structure that is a spiral à la Guggenheim: the floors appear as bands around a central abyss. On every floor, one is forced to stop, to walk by stores, and to pick up each escalator. Granted, I was there in the Christmas frenzy, but I have never experienced such architectural delirium; it is beyond the vertigo registered by Fredric Jameson in the Portman Bonaventure Hotel in Los Angeles. Apart from the subjective effects, people are positioned in this emporium as particles in a wave chart, surveyed and directed strictly in terms of flow (do men and women, children and adults, inhabit this flow differently? Do designers account for such differences?). Meanwhile, the stores, long eroded within by the protean commodity, are now eroded without by the demands of circulation. There is minimal definition of each store; in fact, the structure has an almost televisual transparency that attests to the present transformation of architecture in our social regime of spectacle surveillance (indeed, a primary architectural experience today is an image of your own body in a monitored space – an elevator, an apartment lobby, a museum, etcetera. The limits of architecture are continually extended, dissolved, redefined in this way – caught between the inertia of our bodies and the acceleration of everything else).

For architecture to be critical in the counter-disciplinary sense that I want to develop it must reflect on its own role in techniques of power. I am confident that such investigations are underway. Here, however, rather than speculate, it might be useful to consider, albeit abstractly, the premises of critical programmes already in place. Often such programmes are conceived in terms of an oppositional architecture. This immediately raises the famous question of Aldo van Eyck: 'How to pose an architectural counterform in an urban society without form?' I used to think this was a provocative paradox, but it now strikes me as a misbegotten opposition, one that may debilitate more than support a critical practice. For the notion of a 'counterform' suggests that there is only an outside or inside to our social dynamic, a dynamic that the notion of 'a society without form' suggests we cannot really know. But our capitalist social dynamic can be known; it may be difficult to represent, let alone resist, but this is not a priori an impossibility, at least as long as one does not oppose an outside to an inside. This opposition is now deconstructed – less by Derrida or Deleuze, Peter Eisenman or Bernard Tschumi (though they help us to think it) than by advanced capitalism. And yet it still seems operative in critical thought, in architectural thought, where it is reproduced in such a way as to constrain theory and practice to one of two positions: either an inside position, such as the model of a 'collage city,' which is often interpreted as a curatorial, even commemorative approach to modern development, or an outside position, from which one can only impose a more or less utopian model onto the city. (this latter position often takes the form of a will-to-monumentality in Modernism and a will-to-marginality today). In the inside position, one tends to 'relate to the forces of the Großstadt like a surfer to a wave' (as Rem Koolhaas has put it); and in the outside position, one seeks to transform the city according to some totalist logic or some private dream. When such a transformation was partially possible, it tended to tear up the city – to fragment it all the more. And now, when it is much less possible, it serves to reinforce the marginality of the architect, a marginality that many architects today fetishistically embrace as if architecture were now only sustained authentically through tokens of its 'loss' or 'impossibility'.

My point here is not that the notion of an oppositional architecture should be surrendered, but that its

Michael Belenky, photograph of old West Side Highway, New York City, with Intrepid sea Air Space Museum in the background, 1988

257

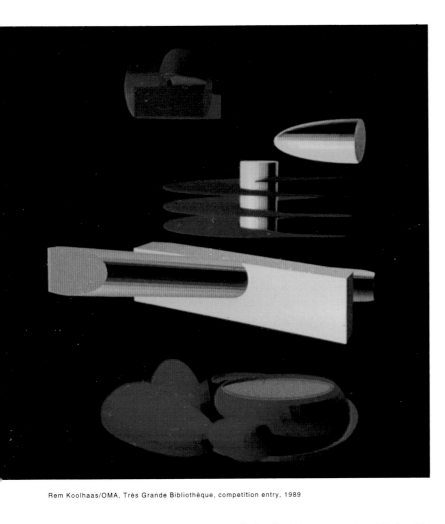

Rem Koolhaas/OMA, Très Grande Bibliothèque, competition entry, 1989

Zaha Hadid, Moon Soon restaurant and bar, Sapporo, 1990

258   terms must be rethought. It might be that the notion of a critical architecture is problematic too, but for the opposite reason: not because it projects a mythical outside to the social field (an outside that is then either heroically overcome or whimsically embraced), but because it assumes too much the field that it seeks to transform. By this assumption it becomes closed to the very historical changes, to the very innovations in spatialities and subjectivities that it might otherwise articulate to radical effect. Such articulation, by the way, is my ideal: an architecture that, rather than discipline spaces and subjects to a synchronic calculus of design and technique, recovers residual spatialities and subjectivities and articulates emergent ones – an architecture that would, in effect, set architecture in motion in a way sensitive to the nonsynchronous nature of our historical experience.

How is such a model different from an architecture of resistance? Maybe this is to hypostatise another term (as perhaps I did above with the notions of 'oppositional' and 'critical' architectures), but 'resistance' seems to stake a defensive posture; that is, it tends to forfeit the annunciatory possibilities of practice. In short, like 'opposition,' 'resistance' must also be rethought; what this might mean can be suggested by a very important model of an architecture of resistance, the model of 'critical regionalism' proposed by Kenneth Frampton.★

Frampton begins with an opposition of universal civilization (rationalist, 'technophilic', capitalist) and regional culture; the first is pledged to appropriative expansion, the second to cultural difference. Rather than trust in the innovative aspects of new capital or in the traditional aspects of old cultures, he advocates a dialectical engagement of the one by the other, whereby each in effect crit-

★ In his article 'Toward a Critical Regionalism: Six Points for an Architecture of Resistance', in Hal Foster (ed.), *The Anti-Aesthetic: Essays on Postmodern Culture*, Washington 1983.

icises and corrects the other. It is a strong concept, one that, articulated in the work of his cited designers (Alvar Aalto, Jørn Utzon, and Mario Botta), can approximate the sort of architecture I advocated above – an architecture sensitive to the complexities of residual and emergent spatialities and subjectivities. But unless one lives in a relatively homogeneous society (as did or does the Finn Aalto, the Dane Utzon, and the Swiss Botta), it may be difficult to act upon today. For the principle of 'critical regionalism' is tied to a problem that may not still be our own, not entirely anyway. A primary theoretical source for the notion of 'critical regionalism' is a 1961 essay called *Universal Civilization and National Cultures* by the philosopher Paul Ricoeur. In 1961 – after the liberation wars of the fifties and before the neocolonial conquests of the sixties and seventies (that is, before the First World's re-penetration of the Third World to supply its labour fund and marketplace) – Ricoeur could still look to the new post-colonial configuration of the world with optimism. In such a moment of release it was possible to project a genuine 'dialogue' between worlds, to insist on the resistance of the regional; twenty-eight years later it has become much more difficult. This is not to say that mono-civilisation is an accomplished fact, that capitalism has penetrated everywhere. (I have less and less sympathy for the apocalyptic models of contemporary cultural criticism that speak of a universal West or a hyperrealistic world; often such criticism is simply another refusal of differences.) But it is to say that relations of global and regional, centre and periphery, are much more complex today. As the Vietnamese filmmaker and writer Trin T. Minh-ha says, there are First Worlds in every Third World and Third Worlds in every First World, to say nothing of Second and Fourth Worlds. What does this complexity and contradiction do to the model of 'critical regionalism', which again seems to rely on homogeneous local cultures for its articulation? How might it be complicated in its turn?**?!** Perhaps it can be complicated along the lines of the model of 'cognitive mapping' proposed by Fredric Jameson.★ In this model Jameson relates the relative inability to map a phenomenological position in the megapolis –

★ Jameson, Fredric, 'Cognitive Mapping', in Nelson, C. and L. Grossberg (eds.), *Marxism and the Interpretation of Cultures*, Urbana/Chicago, 1988.

as demonstrated by Kevin Lynch and colleagues in the 1961 *The Image of the City* – to the relative inability to map international class relations in advanced capitalism. In so doing, he extrapolates the concept of cognitive mapping in Althusserian terms. And yet, though he complicates it greatly, the principle of a 'map-in-the-head' seems to contradict his own diagnoses of the Post-Modern condition of schizoid subjectivities and deterritorialised spaces. This said, one can fully support the project – to think the renewal of sited political communities that can act locally and think globally.

If my discussion seems contradictory, it may well be. I am not sure of my own position among these discourses. But I can point to a general problem that any contemporary critical practice must confront. This is not a problem strictly located 'beyond' architecture; in fact, contemporary architecture sometimes addresses and sometimes abets it. The problem involves the principal ideologeme of the discourse of postmodernism: the atrophy of the historical sense and of the utopian imagination; more precisely,

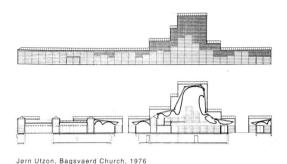

Jørn Utzon, Bagsvaerd Church, 1976

?! *In the meantime it developed far beyond this point. The confusion caused by the notion of regionalism led us to deep six this entire critical regionalism. The architects allegedly sailing under this flag, however, sometimes developed an awesome respect for the phenomenology of architecture, which at times shows neo-animistic traces.*

Hal Foster

259

'The past as picture, history as stage.' Thomas Cole, The Architect's Dream, 1840

the inability to grasp the past except scenographically as a series of pictures or tableaux and to project the future except in terms of entropy or apocalypse, according to scenarios of slow capitalist contamination or sudden technological catastrophe. Obviously, this inability circumscribes any practice that seeks to develop the contradictions of the present into a critical conscious-

★ Foster, Hal, 'Neofuturism: Architecture and Technology', *A.A. Files* 14, (Spring 1987).

ness of past formations and future possibilities. In the space remaining, I want to touch on a few of its implications. I have discussed the problem of the future seen in terms of an autonomous technology in another place.★ Here I want to focus on the problem of the past seen as a picture. Though invalidated a long time ago, this model remains operative in many ways.

We tend to cherish our faculty of memory even as its activity remains obscure to us. Yet, its institutional determinations are historically problematic. In Antiquity, for example, memory was an aspect of rhetoric, part of a system of persuasion and power; in scholasticism, memory was an aspect of ethics, part of a regimen of obedience and order. Of specific interest here is that from its institutional beginnings memory was often conceived in architectural terms as a mnemonic of place and image: in rhetoric the orator would devise an architecture of elements to which were assigned specific ideas, even words, to be recalled in the course of argument.★ Now this particular art of mem-

★ See Yates, Frances, *The Art of Memory*.

ory may seem innocuous, but it sets up a persistent cultural pattern that is not innocuous: the tendency to think of memory in terms of space, in effect to spatialise time, to pictorialise history. This has many ramifications: our tendency to consider knowledge in terms of visual sites (like topics, tables, taxonomies); more importantly, our tendency to reduce the past (personal and collective) to so many tableaux for aesthetic contemplation, which, as we know, is so often melancholic, nostalgic, passive. It is in this way, in part, that we restrict our historical apprehension, that we effectively repress many histories by our symptomatic representation of a few dominant ones. This, of course, is an old Freudian problem. In a famous early passage in *The Interpretation of Dreams*, Freud relates the dream to the rebus in order to suggest the folly of a pictorial reading as opposed to a linguis-

260 *My ideal: an architecture that, rather than disciplines spaces and subjects to a synchronic calculus of design and technique, recovers residual spatialities and subjectivities and articulates emergent ones – an architecture that would, in effect, set architecture in motion in a way sensitive to the nonsynchronous nature of our historical experience.*

tic interpretation. And in a famous late passage in *Civilization and its Discontents*, he suggests that it is misbegotten to see the individual unconscious in terms of space. There he draws the analogy of a ruinous Rome – of a Rome whose levels and fragments obscure one another. But the unconscious, he argues, does not work in this way; it is formed in a process of repression, not ruination. The same is true of our collective unconsciousness, of our tribal histories – or so I would argue. They cannot be spatialised, they should not be pictorialised.*?!* And yet this is how, at many levels of historical awareness, we still grasp the past – as a sequence of pictures, a series of monuments.

There is a painting in which this ideology is stated bluntly because confidently: *The Architect's Dream* (1840) by the American, Thomas Cole. There is much one might say about this picture. What, for example, is the mythical origin, the vanishing point, at which the architect gazes? Is this figure not, in some sense, a naive avatar of the *Angelus Novus* of Paul Klee and Walter Benjamin, who, caught up in the storm called progress that propels him backward into the future, sees nothing but ruins amass before him? Here, I invoke the painting simply as a diagram of the dynastic or imperial model of history. It is a model in which the architectural – the monumental – stands in for the historical. This fetishism of the monument serves two purposes – both to commemorate and to disavow historical change: to commemorate the ascendant (American) bourgeoisie as the self-proclaimed epitome of history, to commemorate its claim to a post-historical position from which history is simply collected as so many pictures or styles, and to disavow this history, to disavow that it, the bourgeoisie, is involved in historicity. Traditional art history is riven by this same contradictory ideology; architecture is too. In fact, the still dominant model of art history – that of Wölfflin – tells its narrative as a continuous reinterpretation of past works, and this model is based – explicitly for Wölfflin – on the paradigm of architecture. It quickly became structural to the pedagogy of art history, especially when, with the technology of the photograph, the concept of transcendental style could be contrived and the method of abstract comparison established. To our eyes, the Cole painting might seem a parody before the fact of this art-

?! Would this be a pronunciation with objective claims, or do we detect residues of iconoclast tradition in which a picture is not necessarily true? Like your recommended source of inspiration, Foucault, you are preoccupied with oppression, suppression and repression. But, keeping the means and purpose of education in mind, one is likely to advocate an expressed representation of our history.

historical model of opposed cyclical styles, but this is still dominant pedagogical practice. And that is my point, or rather my question: as crude, as obvious, as this ideology of the historical appears to us, I wonder if we have truly surpassed it. I do not mean simply its dynastic or linear aspects. I mean its fetishistic aspect, its selective-suppressive aspect. I mean the model of the past as picture, of history as stage (as in the Cole painting) and as rhetorical theatre of exclusive memory performed strictly for us. For all the many critiques of historicism, most of us, I think, remain members of this modern cult of monuments.

Of course, my critique of the-past-as-picture is directed, in part, at so-called Post-Modern architecture, but it extends to many other practices as well. In two famous essays, *The Age of the World Picture* and *The Question Concerning Technology*, Heidegger considered this problem. In the first essay, written before World War II, the-world-as-representation and the-individual-as-subject of-this-representation are seen to be coeval. In the second essay written after the war, both the-world-as-picture and the-individual-as-subjected-subject are seen to be produced out of a fundamental instrumentality that has become second nature to modern man. And here the crucial term is the past not only as picture but also, in this perspectival array, as 'standing-reserve' – there as a repository to be used as we wish. This instrumentality is linked by Heidegger to a pervasive technology, and it is this technology that he rails against. Has architecture broken with any of this – with this model of the past as picture and standing-reserve, with this instrumentality and technology? Can it? If we want to develop a relationship to the past that is redemptive and not fetishistic, and a relationship to the future that is responsive and not destructive, I think it must. (There is also an historical question to ask in passing: What is the relation between the establishment of Architecture with a capital A and the instantiation of perspective? Was Architecture thus set up in perspectival opposition to the subject at its very beginning?)

By way of a conclusion, I want briefly to think about this problematic art of memory, this pictorial fetishism of history, as it is inscribed in our museum architecture and our museal culture in general. I want to do so by reference to a 1985 Louise Lawler photograph of a storage space in the Rude Museum in Dijon. (Rude is best known as the sculptor of the emblem of French patriotism, *La Marseillaise*, of 1833-36, part of a cast of which is seen in the centre of the Lawler image.)

The caption given to the photo reads in part: 'The Art of Memory – the restriction and placement, its deposition in material form with extreme emphasis on presentation, selects a limited number of acceptable issues with limited ways to speak.' Now this old art of memory lives on, of course, not only in architecture, but also in the museum. Indeed, the typical museum is a theatre of memory where works of art as pictures of the past serve fetishistically to occlude more than to clarify historical practices. But this theatre of memory does not begin or end there. It is endemic to our museal culture: it may be one reason why we still tend to think time in terms of inert stages or phases rather than, say, dialectically or in difference (again, I would argue, architecture is emblematic of this history of periods and pictures). This spatialisation of time has an important corollary no less endemic to our museal culture: the tendency to temporalise space, so that different peoples are said to inhabit different times, so that 'further away' comes to mean 'more primitive'. As Johannes Fabian argues in *Time and the Other: How Anthropology Makes Its Object* (1983), this is largely how we construct our others; if we do not deny them historical time altogether, we freeze them in the past. That is, either we assign them to different developmental moments in our own history, or we judge them according to an imposed criterion of authenticity whereby they only really existed – genuinely, purely – in the past. This pastoral myth of cultural loss seems sweet if sad, but its effects are insidious, for it positions other cultures as mere ruins that must be saved by us and stored in our own theatres of memory – in our texts, museums, architecture. This murderous myth not only permits the continued appropriation of the past of other cultures, but also blocks any constructive engagement with the 'present-becoming-future' (*James Clifford*) of these cultures. In any case, one sees the effects not only of this pictorialising of our own past but also this plundering of other cultures everywhere in our culture today, and in many ways architecture has propounded this phantasmagoria more than any other cultural practice.

'The-world-as-representation.' Toraja *tonkonan* style on the roof of a modern villa, Rantepao, Sulawesi

The Invisible in Architecture could be conceived as programme. A programme is implicit in every act, be it mental or physical. It is often said that we know a man, and what he stands for, through his actions. The action discloses an underlying programmatic logic, which binds that action with presentation and representation to form a seamless whole.

But, in architecture, because the programme transmits the functional, instrumental and rational demands of a project, it simultaneously conveys an order that hopes to prolong itself in, and by means of, that project. The programme is thus also the vehicle of an ideology. There are special, perhaps political, interests involved; there are hidden agendas and psychological pre-occupations. This kind of programme is an invisible one. It manifests itself through everyone's immanent, involuntary enmeshment in the social and cultural order in which they live. And it is a programme no-one may depart from, we are forced to continue accepting that order as normality.

It is precisely through this invisibility that action slips into stylised representation and quick fixes for utilitarian problems. A consequence of this is that the programme concealed in the action becomes visible principally at the level of cliché. Hence the programme can no longer be a subject of public dispute; instead, it becomes a *fait accompli*. This state of affairs is exacerbated nowadays by the great ease with which we can pour ridicule on historic programmes with utopian goals. After all, in practice, these programmes were fixated far too naively and mechanically on their goals. We now know how much harm they did. The result is that we are less inclined than ever before to tackle the all too evident problems by taking a programmatic approach. Our aim is no longer to actualise a utopia, but to stem the dialectic side-effects of a utopia. These problematic side-effects have taken over the central role that was once the preserve of a utopian purpose.

Our own times, when form predominates and content goes unrepresented, do not provide a climate that favours an under-

Programme

standing of the programme. We have a poor view of the reasons and motives behind the form. The importance of the 'programme' vector is that, when we are aware of it, it places us in a position to trace the commodity structure – the ingrained practice of daily life that invisibly reproduces the functional position of the dominant ideology – in theory, politics and art.

Who still believes in the programme as a plan for the future couched in positive terms? Since the fall of the Berlin Wall and the end of the bipolar world order, the political programme seems to have lost its solidity as a formula for people to hold onto. That old programme was based on a certainty about the right way ahead. This certainty has vanished. All we know now is that many ways ahead are wrong. Whatever remains of social concern concentrates on staving off the most alarming threats: the greenhouse effect, large-scale deforestation, ozone layer depletion, wars, famines and epidemics. These matters are seldom placed in a political perspective by those who can really do anything about them. Involvement with such phenomena goes no further than a system of indulgences, donations, development aid percentages and awareness campaigns. In other words, the problems of this world have become apolitical. The programme of Late Capitalism is accepted as being an 'impartial' mechanism. It goes together with a fundamentally new mentality, and moreover with a new conception of the programme. Instead of a notion of the will, it becomes a deterministic fact.

Here, at last, is the moment at which the disassociation of form and substance, about which people have been complaining for so long, can finally and unreservedly take place. And as far as the vector 'programme' is concerned, what better illustration could there be than the fate suffered by the public domain. That domain is now no longer a necessary consequence of public action, but is a problem of form that precedes public action – to such an extent, that the problem of form overwhelms the public problem. It produces a situation in which people are no longer concerned with politics but with the face of politics.

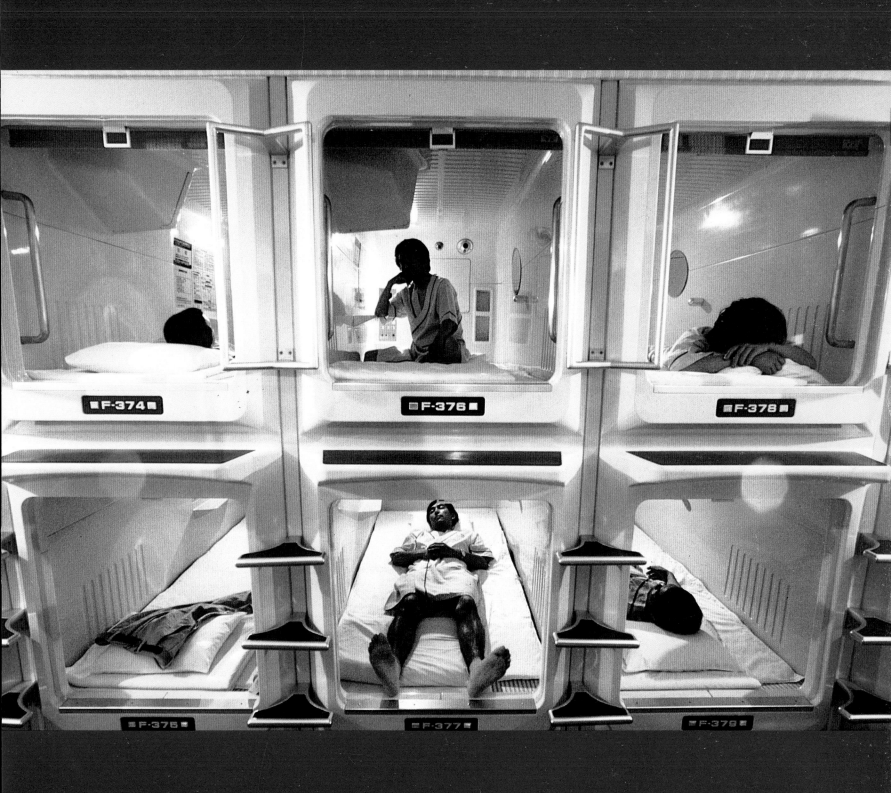

Our contemporary public domain knows no 'natural' locus, and this leads to a loss of community. We no longer congregate to engage in the public clash of interests. Individually, we have plenty to say, to criticise and to protest about; but there is no obvious domain in which we can convert our words and dissatisfactions into actions. There are no addresses. We are thrown helplessly on our own devices. The treatment of the programme reflects this development in that it is becoming more and more the dominion of the starring personality. This individual objectives his own subjective position – in the literal sense, too, of materialising it as a physical object. When the object rules the roost, it is hardly surprising that the image is everything. Our interest can go no further than the prestige of the image, and understanding can go no further than that which is allowed by the limited framework of our own, familiar discipline. Exposure and confrontation on the grounds of super-disciplinary criteria has become practically impossible.

A direct consequence of the widespread distrust in any positively-couched political programme is the flagging programmatic ambition of architecture. Since everyone wishes to or has to formulate his own micro-narrative, doing it by means of a programme is becoming a rare thing indeed. The outcome is that the economic capital of the function is becoming detached from the intellectual capital of the design. Now that justification on programmatic grounds has lost its credibility, architecture tends to strand in self-legitimising craftsmanship. Neither will architecture find salvation by binding on its shoulders the wings of art, as long as that art remains one that distances itself from any political programme.

Certainly now that architecture has to resign itself to increasing marginalisation as a craft of formal design and packaging, it seldom probes the possibility of guiding or influencing action. The bulk of building comes about as a pragmatic answer to functional programmatic requirements. In such architecture, the programme, conceived though it may be in purely utilitarian terms as a required number of square metres, is practically the *raison d'être*. But even in those few scraps of architecture that aspire to being more than just an efficient husk, the ideological programme remains concealed behind the representational programme, behind the 'luminous' architecture's own narrative.

Architecture's neglect of the programme is rooted deep in the past. In the early days of modernism's radical utilitarianisation of society, the progressive wing of the architectural fraternity became increasingly dissatisfied with the aestheticism of antiquated neo-styles. These architects were fired with a desire to contribute to the modern project, and accordingly supplied the neutral platform it demanded. But in doing so, they abandoned the critical faculties of their craft and reduced it to no more than a tool. The programme was narrowed down to the immediate utility of the project, and ultimately to a dutiful parallelism with the (concealed) programme of the status quo.

When architects woke up to this state of affairs during the sixties, it was already too late. Many of their tasks had already devolved into the hands of engineers, bureaucrats, managers and environmental artists. The architects still had one speciality with which to fight back, their skill as designers. Thus, not long afterwards, they proclaimed the autonomy of their craft. But it turned out to be the craft of the packaging expert. Within that craft, the programme of requirements and the ideological programme manifest themselves mainly in the form of unique artistic and autonomous acts. The programme is welcomed in as a frame to prop up the teetering edifice of free-standing design. That this course of action has now become an integral part of building practice will be clear from the immense resistance that the architect meets when he or she wishes to become involved with the deeper content of the programme. Such involvement is generally seen either as involving an exorbitant cost, or as implying that the project will remain limited to a folly, a fun thing to brighten up a public space but without serious social import.

Three strategies and three architects Most architects waste few words about the programme. Nonetheless, in their designs, we can read the whole functional and representational programme of their target group and their clients. In the respect of manipulation of the programme, we distinguish the following attitudes:

Archaism Archaism is effectively an anthropological interpretation of the programme, as the totality of mankind's unchanging practical needs. Because our everyday needs are recognised by one and all, this architectural tendency is fundamentally apolitical. The programme refers here to largely unconscious 'universal' premises of our existence, to somatic identity and to needs for security and identification. The programme aims to offer *everyone* a foothold, and it therefore manifests itself in the architecture as a relatively neutral and subtle game of spaces and volumes. This modest approach has undeniable political consequences, in the sense of its being an example of resistance to the unrelenting march of modernism. But, at the same time and through its very nature, it is incapable of proffering a programme of change; for, after all, it concentrates on what is, or is supposed to be, permanent. As far as propagating an intellectual programme is concerned, **Lucien Lafour & Rikkert Wijk** have tuned their ambitions to a very low pitch. They reveal themselves, by principle, as master builders in restraint. The programme is seen here in the most basic possible terms: Lafour and Wijk create an open space for the less well-off, a space that gives people a feeling of belonging to a community. At the same time, meeting and privacy, accessibility and parity, are on offer to all.

Façadism For the façadist, the programme is not so much a problem as a fact that has to be represented in (consumable) signs. For this purpose, Design is the method *par excellence*. Design gives everything distinction in form without perceptible differences in content. Although this approach clearly pursues the linking of programme and form, it rarely rises above the level of a recognisable, figurative palliative. It raises no questions but offers an unbroken stream of (at least ostensible) solutions. The 'slowness' of content is concealed behind the 'speed' of sign. The design is a masquerade, an aesthetisation of the poverty of experience. The museum is not merely **Hans Hollein's** preferred kind of project; he makes everything into a museum. In other words, he prefers to strip his programmes of their public significance as the locus of confrontation. He likes to offer us togetherness with atmosphere. In his buildings, we - that is to say, the well-heeled public - can take pleasure in a digression. Art is no longer a call to action but a decoration of spare time. This is accompanied by a theatrical *mise-en-scène* that, in Hollein's work, goes far deeper than the building's skin. The façade concept is expanded to become a metonym for consumable, static information.

Fascinism Fascinism aims to enrich the given programme with post-historical (i.e. post-programmatic) insights, and create an atmosphere that evokes not a sense of recognition but the ecstasy of alienation. The human subject is not expected to simply enjoy what he is offered, but to be overwhelmed by a sublime fascination for the hyper-present. Although the frequently sharp-witted inspiration of this intellectualistic strategy is seductive, it produces spaces that are practically 'unmanageable'. Indeed, in these surroundings, history is no longer written; on the contrary, the liberal ideology of the end of history is proclaimed. The highly sophisticated, abstract conception of form does not refer to the substance but to the *atmosphere* of a programme. **Bernard Tschumi** does everything possible to avoid static images. He even professes a desire to manipulate the programme to the level at which architecture can escape its own aesthetic straitjacket. But neither does Tschumi effectuate an expansion of the discipline's expressive means: they are and, as ever, remain confined to form. The action is not influenced. Thus Tschumi is at his best when making programme-free follies. These provide the perfect illustration to accompany an intellectual culture that has let the object of its criticism slip through its fingers.

Architecture can have a liberating effect on mankind. It will develop and guide us in life. Society will have a soul again, which of course requires new creative energy if it wants to be realised as an integral human perfection... **Ton Alberts & Max van Huut**

The creation of architecture must be a criticism of problems of today. It must resist existing conditions. It is only when one faces up to today's problems that one can really begin to deal with architecture. **Tadao Ando**

Programme and use do not coincide with form, even though they converse with it. **Ricardo Bofill**

The programme is a transitory invention that cannot be ignored. Most programmes are banal, it is the overcoming of this banality that injects life into buildings, the object. The process of drawing up a programme is an attempt to give objective and numerical value to transitory needs, desires and habits. The writing of the rules of a puzzle which must be both questioned and solved with absolute seriousness. It is only at a moment that the object comes into focus that the programme is authenticated. Julia Bolles & Peter Wilson

Any architectural or engineering work has a technical or practical purpose, for example to span a river, to cross an obstacle. The task of the architect consists in learning, educating, in urbanising, in practising urbanness with the design. **Santiago Calatrava**

We wanted our designing to become forthright and expressive, for the distortions of the mind to be thrown out onto the buildings so that once built, they would throw some of the same feeling back. If architecture really were to have more than a guest/host relationship with the people that filled it, it would have to anticipate the way experience constructs its own narratives, constantly superimposing logic and emotion. Architecture, we said, should define an anthropomorphic field which constantly parallels and opposes experience itself. Nigel Coates & Doug Branson

The project is a limited programme: it does not seek general rules as the basis of an absolute legitimacy. It appears, instead, as a strategy to extricate ourselves from the complexity of the appeals in progress in a place. The appeals are political, functional and economic in nature, and come from the history of the place and that of the designer. The project is the temporary representation of a mediation in the midst of the pluralism of the appeals. Pietro Derossi

How can the 'revised' body re-enter architectural discourse and put into question our assumptions about space and about program particularly at a time in which architecture has irrevocably broken away from anthropocentrism? Elisabeth Diller & Ricardo Scofidio

At the risk of over-simplification, the designer's task could be summed up as analysing set problems in the widest sense and organising the best available resources to achieve the highest performance solution in the most economical manner. Norman Foster

One could see a park in the city as a window on the past or on the future, a recollection of what was there before or a hypothesis as to what might be there after, a subtraction or a superposition of a few layers of history, or an operation that makes them selectively transparent. **Beth Galí**

I try so much to fight the programme as to re-order the priorities. And then I take great pleasure in being able to get the thing to function in conventional terms and to have a certain visual character – all within a budget: what I like to do is develop a project's potentials. Frank Gehry

It is crucial that we re-establish the thematic associations invented by our culture in order fully to allow the culture of architecture to represent the mythic and ritual aspirations of society. **Michael Graves**

One of my aims is to reconsider architecture of the past, which was adapted to the climate and the land, and to see human beings and architecture as part of the earth's ecosystem. This includes a challenge to propose new design connected with new science and technology. Itsuko Hasegawa

I think we are trying to make a piece of reality which can be taken apart, which works rationally. Since we are surrounded by so many things and events which we cannot clarify at all, to which we have no access, we make an object which offers a language all of its own. This offering of language is an expression of hope. To some extent this attitude is clearly utopian, because the enlightening is always utopian, not resigned. And this attitude is certainly far from being affirmative. **Jacques Herzog & Pierre de Meuron**

General theories of architecture are constrained by a central problem; that is to say if a particular theory is true, then all other theories are false. Pluralism on the other hand leads to an empirical architecture. A third direction is the adoption of a limited concept. Time, culture, programmatic circumstance, and site are specific factors from which an organising idea can be formed. A specific concept may be developed as a precise order, irrespective of the universal claims of any particular ideology. **Steven Holl**

All building is ritual. Hans Hollein

Modern barbarism can only be defeated by bringing urban civilisation into the suburb, i.e. by building true urban centres in the suburban desert. Not expanding the cities but expanding the public realm by redeveloping the suburbs is, I believe, the main goal of civilisation. Even though commerce is a constitutive part of it, the establishment of a public realm is not and cannot just be a by-product of commerce; it is primordially a matter of public interest, of building communities. The urban master planner needs the independence of the legislator, his loyalty being to the 'public interest' of the community and not to the private interests of the shareholders. **Leon Krier**

Of course a solid programme is necessary to build something that will stand up to the test of utility. The question is, though, how is this programme implemented in practice? Is it the architect's fate to always follow the schizophrenic wishes of the specifier of the brief? Or is it the brief-writer who must expect the architects to come up with ideas that will give their precise, regimented schemes life and blood, body and clothing? **Lucien Kroll**

Since human beings live in contradictory ways, it is only natural that societies and cities too should contain mutually contradictory, opposing elements. As might be expected, however, the analytical approach strives to eliminate from architecture and cities the intermediate spaces and vagueness that formerly existed harmoniously there. In doing away with these things, they decrease ambiguity and diversity in human beings as well. I do think we should glean and pick up again the things – intermediary zones and vagueness – that the Functionalists have cast away. Oriental philosophy and Japanese culture provide an excellent groundwork on which to do this gleaning. **Kisho Kurokawa**

We like to work on the very simple things that closely affect people. The programme of course is the most important, but that goes without saying. We do not design North-facing living rooms if it can be avoided, because on the few days of the year the sun shines people want to enjoy it. I think it is very important we believe we are building for people. **Lucien Lafour & Rikkert Wijk**

Every architecture programme requires a response that can not only be seen as a physical or objective: its response comes from elsewhere, and therefore does not lie in the realm of proposition of knowledge. It has to be revealed in the process of thinking about a project. Now, one may want something to be revealed, but that doesn't mean it will reveal itself. In my own work I would never want the methodological issue to obscure the first place of madness which is involved in the spiritual quest for an adequate response to the architectural programme. **Daniel Libeskind**

I see architecture as always addressing the same questions throughout history. Each generation will try to answer the question of meaning in the work of architecture in its own way. For some, this reality will be found in the interpretation of programme or in the investigation of typology. For others still, the reality of the building will be sought in its lasting tangible presence, which speaks about the architectural principles behind its construction. That is where I would like to be. **Rafael Moneo**

If writers could manipulate the structure of stories, words, and grammar, couldn't architects manipulate the programme? If architects could use such devices as repetition, distortion, or juxtaposition in the formal elaboration of walls, couldn't they do the same thing in terms of activities that occurred within those walls? **Bernard Tschumi**

The social vision of the client should guide the programming process and help direct the vision of the architecture. In our experience clients are not ignorant of their own business, but there may be countervailing forces within their group and, if they cannot mediate for themselves, we must do it for them. In programming the architect has the right to state a personal value position but no right to secretly manipulate the programme or design in directions different from what the client wants. If the architect cannot accept the client's value system then this is not a project to accept. On the other hand, the need to allow for future changes of programme over the years, or to think of the next director and users and indeed the next community, should certainly be brought up by the architect. It is not the architect who should make decisions for the future, but possibly a combination of elected representatives and artists should – those deputed democratically to make such decisions and those who have an ability to intuit the future, without self indulgence but with extra sensitivity. **Robert Venturi & Denise Scott Brown**

On the Work of Lucien Lafour & Rikkert Wijk
Quality for Ordinary People

In his *History of Western Philosophy*, Bertrand Russell analyses the ideas of Friedrich Nietzsche by imagining a conversation between the German philosopher and Buddha. Both have been invited by God the Creator to give their advice prior to the creation of the world. In the course of the discussion that unravels between these opposites, life is reduced to two fundamental principles: compassion, and the urge to destroy. Nietzsche practically blows his top every time he is obliged to hear Buddha's unctuous words. The latter talks of a world full of fellow-feeling and involvement, of tolerance and mercy. For Nietzsche, these are all inventions that give the weak an excuse for staying that way. His tale of Zarathustra descending the mountain demonstrated that Christian love of one's neighbour was not a timeless ethical principle but a device that served an evident interest – namely that of the highest common denominator, the man in the street interested solely in maintaining the status quo. Only the lazy, the inflexible and the superficial benefited from this clammy, comfortable universe. But the man who could face up to the naked truth of existence had no need of such a creation. So lay on the lash, the lash of struggle, of truth, of honesty; and, above all, of a language purged of all its metaphysical assumptions.

However great the distance between these two standpoints, a synthesis has become possible in our own time. In the work of Lucien Lafour and Rikkert Wijk, the vocabulary of Modernism, with its connotations of dehumanisation and its farewell to all that is 'definitive', proves capable of coexisting with a sincere involvement with the lot of ordinary people. Partly because of their individual backgrounds, the cooperation of these two architects is marked by a blend of tropical intimacy and metropolitan aloofness. Perhaps it is this combination of qualities that puts them in a position to rehabilitate the language of Modernism while retaining the critical, anthropological consciousness introduced into architecture by Team 10. The style that went along with the shock of the new thus turns out now to be applicable to the eternal constants of existence.

But when we look a little deeper, can we really still see a synthesis? The social housing of Lafour and Wijk is a product of a social democracy which, in the crisis of the welfare state, has become a victim of its own accomplishments. Revisionist socialism has defeated both revolutionary socialism and liberalism. Much has been achieved and consolidated in the form of a consumerist consensus, but new problems such as the environment, the increasing streams of refugees, the concentration of power in the hands of transnational enterprises etc. demand new solutions. Meanwhile, the present political configuration prefers to sweep these issues under the carpet.

It is seldom that architecture lends itself to an investigation of these questions as well as that of Lafour and Wijk.

The Architecture of the Post-Marxist Left

If there is a social democratic architecture that simultaneously reveals the enthusiasm and the dilemma of leftist housing ideology, then it must be that of Lafour and Wijk.

Their work is still strongly reminiscent of the idea of society being something that can be fabricated. But it also shows all the signs of the kind of disillusion that has produced the slogan 'think globally, act locally'. Lafour and Wijk clearly go along with a critical tradition which achieved prominence in the Netherlands from the late fifties onwards, in circles around Jaap Bakema and Aldo van Eyck. Their aim was to temper the univalent functionalism of CIAM. In the European context, Team 10 inevitably springs to mind here. Team 10 aimed to defy the sterile architecture of post-war reconstruction by paying more attention to the social and urban context; but they also attacked the guiding principles of architectural Modernism itself, in which life was reduced to a number of measurable functions (light, ventilation, space, habitation, work, recreation and transport), to which the design strategy merely had to conform in order to be considered a success. The consequence of this was a technocratic abstraction of real life which, when applied in practice, resulted in an architecture that totally failed to answer the human need for identification with the surroundings. Team 10 and its Dutch members opted for an architecture in which life was approached from a more complex, anti-hierarchical viewpoint.

'Our hierarchy of associations is woven into a modulated continuum representing the true complexity of human associations. (...) We must evolve an architecture from the fabric of life itself, an equivalent of the complexity of our way of thought, of our passion for the natural world and our belief in the ability of man.' ★

Although this riposte to Modernism undeniably implied a correction to the poverty of the functional idiom, the design philosophy remained metaphorical in character. No longer was the machine or the product of industry the perfect metaphor for the house, but 'nature' or 'life' as seen from an anthropological viewpoint. This aspect of architecture, which implied the opening of the field to the consideration of issues other than purely architectural ones, never formed an explicit part of the programme. Perhaps it was inevitable that the anthropological concern remained largely metaphorical, in the light of the utopian thinking that still pervaded Team 10.

★ Alison Smithson, quoted in Agrest, Diana, *Architecture from Without*, Cambridge, Mass. 1991, p. 47.

'Team 10 is Utopian, but Utopian about the present. Thus their aim is not to theorise but to build, for only through construction can an Utopia of the present be realised. For them "to build" has a special meaning in that the architect's responsibility, towards the individual or groups he builds for and towards the cohesion and convenience of the collective structure to which they belong, is taken as being an absolute responsibility. No abstract Master Plan stands between him and what he has to do, only the "human facts" and the logistics of the situation.' ★

What Team 10 were saying was that the break with global legitimisation was definitive. But – and in this they showed themselves to be preeminently social-democratic – this was not necessarily at the cost of their Utopia. Utopia, and thus the metaphor, remained. Utopia shook off its teleological accent, however, and

★ 'The Aim of Team 10', statement in Team 10 Primer, quoted in Smithson, Alison (ed.), *Team 10 Meetings*, Delft 1991, p. 8.

For years now architects have been providing outside instead of inside, but that is not their job at all; their job is to provide inside even if it happens to be outside.
Aldo van Eyck

When I say, make a welcome of each door and a countenance of each window: make of each a place, because man's home-realm is the in-between realm – the realm architecture sets out to articulate, – the intention is again to unmask false meaning of size with what right-size implies!
Aldo van Eyck

Space has no room, time not a moment for man. He is excluded.
In order to 'include' him – help is homecoming – he must be gathered into their meaning. (Man is the subject as well as the object of architecture.)
Whatever space and time mean, place and occasion mean more.
For space in the image of man is place, and time in the image of man is occasion.
Today space and what it should coincide with in order to become 'space' – man at home with himself – are lost. Both search for the same place, but cannot find it. Provide that place.
Aldo van Eyck

Architecture need do no more, nor should it ever do less, than assist man's homecoming.
Aldo van Eyck

What is happening here therefore cannot be called revolutionary, but a superior simplicity is achieved that is a delight for both the resident and the casual passer-by, easier to experience than to write about. The dwellings have been placed on either side of a central traffic axis: rows of medium-rise buildings across the axis and low-rise buildings along it. It could hardly be simpler, and a closer look shows that it does not need to be more complicated. Taken together, the variety in building heights and roof forms, the spacious entrances and the round balconies, the lay out, which ensures no two blocks are completely identical, the transparent stairways, the galleries, the roof terraces and the use of colour, all ensure the blocks, which in

Marica house, Paramaribo, 1974

Burmanstraat social housing, 11 dwellings,
Amsterdam, 1983

Holland Inc., Country of Feasibility Studies

Since the eighties, the no-nonsense politics of the Netherlands have effectively converted the country into a corporation. Holland Inc. has manufactured its social Utopia, at least wherever it has proved 'feasible'. Feasibility is the country's highest good. Everything else that was once an ingredient of the social Utopia – solidarity, equality and a belief in the inherent goodness of mankind – has dissolved into the mass consensus of the social middle ground: play streets and doggy toilets as palliatives for man's evil streak. And since practically everyone belongs to that middle ground, there are few objectors.

A physical consequence of this median society is a deadly uniformity of the urban landscape. Apart from the exceptional museum pieces, all city centres have come to look alike in their pedestrianised consumerism. Around them lie the universally identical dormitory suburbs and overspill towns, themselves centreless, where the primary model of harmony is invariably the solidly nuclear family, and the only cohesive forces are the shared communal facilities. If Fukuyama's 'era of boredom' has set in anywhere, then it is here. Holland is a country where the urban landscape and the housing for all (middle) classes reached an admirable level of quality within the bounds of the bureaucratic possibilities. That nice little house in the suburbs is now within everyone's reach. All the same, projects of outstanding quality are few and far between. In the bulk of social housing construction projects, architectural meanings play a subsidiary role. The main aim is to be certain of finding tenants and to keep down maintenance costs; in other words, to build inexpensive and liveable houses to attract an eager market and give the landlord as few problems as possible. In the case of houses built for the private market, a quick and risk-free sale is primary.

The architect is in a weak position. His ideological and political role is ever more confined. Architects occupy politically influential positions seldom if at all. Everyone is concerned about his own patch. The city councillor wants prestige and another term of office, the client wants a return on his investment and minimum maintenance costs, and the architect wants future contracts and/or a further shove along the road to stardom. Clients demand seductive architectural images and are no longer interested in a conception of humanity. It is something of a miracle that Lafour and Wijk, together with the very occasional 'good' client, have succeeded in swimming against this maelstrom to realise a modest architectural oeuvre that tries to escape the widely perceived ideological vacuum and makes a stand for a less anonymous existence.

269

Architecture of Human Interest

The urban planning of Lafour & Wijk lacks a centripetal force. They give the district a transparent dynamic structure by using a system of multiple lines of sight along the built volumes and visual openings between them, without ignoring the individual characters of the buildings themselves. The district acquires a personality of its own through its frequent distinctive orientation points and its richness in public facilities. We find a real concentration of vision only in the identity of the volume and the dwelling. But that is not to say that the architects' have not considered the urban context here

became a 'motivation' or an 'energy' that operated here and now. It is this inflation of Utopia that is also recognisable, and to an even greater extent, in the work of Lafour and Wijk. Particularly when Lafour says, 'We have no vision of the future. It is all happening so quickly. A vision of the future is outdated as soon as it is expressed. All we can keep thinking and keep saying is that we can all build much more beautiful buildings.' ★

More beautiful buildings bring more happiness: 'I think it is very important we believe we are building for people. That the buildings, therefore, and the surroundings are made in the first place for the people who are going to live there.'

But these architects also go a step further. The work of Lafour and Wijk is still open to Team 10's critique of Modernism. All the same, it shakes off the constraints of Team 10's biological and anthropological metaphors. They are receptive to all kinds of cultural and formal references, from tropical typologies to the *Plan Zuid*

★ Lucien Lafour, 'Interview IV', in Kloos, Maarten (ed.), *Lafour & Wijk Architects*, Arcam pocket 2, Amsterdam 1991, p. 86.

of Berlage. These are particularly noticeable in their social housing. They reevaluate the urban element, at the larger scale of street and public square, without losing sight of the individual experience. No longer is the 'structuralist articulation' of the separate units the guiding principle, as is visibly the case in much of the work of the Forum group. Now people are more concerned about the visual coherence of the urban image. Architecturally, they have taken an immense step forward. What a pity that the word 'forward' has become ideologically meaningless!

Ellen Health Centre, Mariënberg, 1975

too. The façade is never conceived only from the dwelling outwards. It also has a character that derives from the urban structure. The smallness of scale and the articulation of the block/main volume work together and reinforce each other. The façade often undulates due to local constrictions, and these are directly related to the differentiation of dwellings, to external views and insulation, and to access and/or balconies. Access to the dwellings is via porches and short walkways, a feature which fosters social contacts between residents. They exclude the possibility of alienation, and this is also the intention of the deliberate difference between front and rear, the angles, the jumps, the use of gables and the classical proportions of the façade. All this is achieved by a highly intelligent use of seriality in the construction of the dwellings. There is diversity in spite of the use of prefabricated elements, and this is due in part to the cheerful use of pastel tints in stucco and/or brickwork, giving their work a distinctive mediterranean character. From the point of view of urbanism and the articulation of the ground plan and façade, the dwellings are reminiscent of the work of Hans Scharoun (for example, the residential block in Zabel-Krügerdamm, Berlin, 1966-70, and the housing scheme Charlottenburg-Nord, Berlin, 1956-61). As with Scharoun, the symmetry is frequently deformed in accordance with the organic principle of destabilising the viewer's *Standort*, his confidence in his own perception. Unexpected openings and lines of sight abound. Naturally, we can also pick up reminiscences of their teacher Aldo van Eyck. The work of Lafour and Wijk is characterised by an admirable alertness to the urban structure and the horizon of the inhabitant. This architecture is meant for people and their everyday wonts. In no case does the visual order reflect a social hierarchy. There is a mediocrity in the non-pejorative sense of the word, an architecture without extremes, acceptable to everyone. There is only one thing that matters in this architecture: the satisfaction of what people need. 'We like to work on the very simple things that closely affect people' say the architects. 'The programme of course is the most

270

important, but that goes without saying.' Or, as Izak Salomons puts it, 'It is their ability to bridge the chasm between the isolated élite of architectural mandarins and the man in the street and their ability to transform the ordinariness of daily life into a well-balanced and elegant humane environment that make the architecture of Lafour and Wijk a standard for the future.' ★

What makes this work into something more than an illustration of social pacification as purveyed by Holland Inc., is that the initial impulse of Utopia remains recognisable. Lafour and Wijk confront us with the dilemma of the achieved Utopia in which someone like Francis Fukuyama, with his 'endist' theory, can celebrate worldwide triumph. The design-stage of the Netherlands is finished; and in spite of the resulting digestible but unexceptional sliced-bread architecture, at least it is still about people. Humanity – whatever Foucault may think – is still unfinished; and this architecture, whatever its socially affirmative character, also helps us see the technocratic post-history ideology in perspective.

★ Salomons, Izak, 'Elegant Ordinariness', in *Lafour & Wijk Architects*, Arcam pocket 2, Amsterdam

Social Democracy as Fatality

Lafour and Wijk understand people because they recognise themselves in them. They do not gather their knowledge of the needs of the man in the street by abstract cross-cultural surveys, but by a sort of feeling for the daily joys and woes of their public.

'We do not design north-facing living rooms if it can be avoided, because on the few days of the year the sun shines people want to enjoy it.' ★

Their modesty emerges not only in their perception of their role, but also in their forms. There are no efforts to force some or other 'meaning' onto the public. *Their* manifesto is not to have a manifesto, not to aim too high, not to unveil yet another architectural theory screaming

★ Rikkert Wijk, 'Interview II', in Kloos, Maarten (ed.), op. cit. p. 29.

Urban Plan, Olympisch Stadion area, Amsterdam, 1992

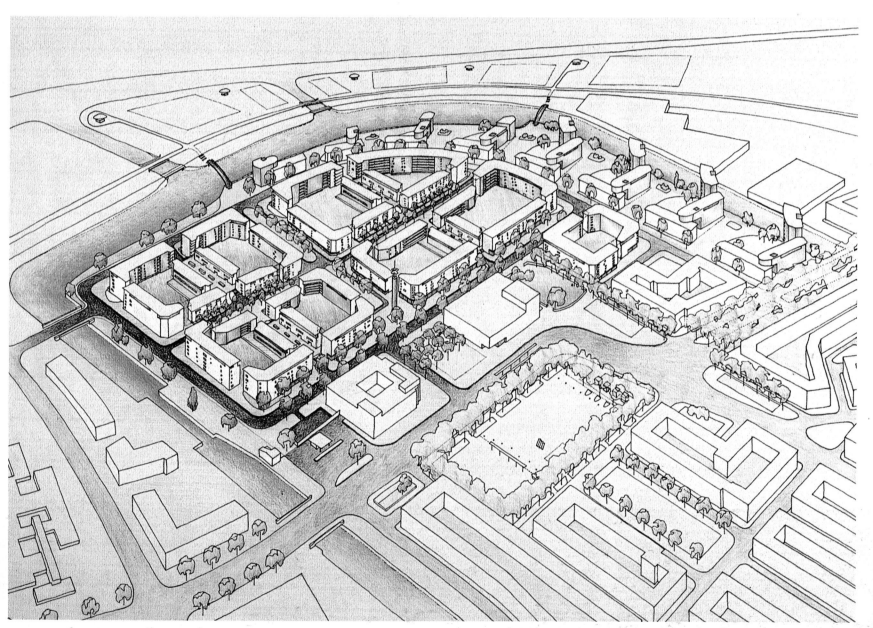

School, extension, Galibi, 1978

for attention. People still have to make their own Utopia, just as in the high days of the Modern Movement. But the events of recent history have given the self-made Utopia a rather more subtle form. Heroes and pioneers no longer exist. Utopia is here now, and we have to learn to like it. The key principles are now adaptation to, and acceptance of, the human condition. After all, it is now clear enough that mankind is fundamentally bad, but since everybody accepts the fact it no longer leads to blood and mayhem.

This diverse, cheerful and comfortable architecture, in as far as it represents a view on the state of the world and how it ought to look, is an ambiguous statement. It is not an illustration to accompany the pedagogical and philanthropic visions of a social democracy. On the contrary, its Modernist connotations are instrumental in making us acutely conscious of that ideology. It is the ever self-confirming social democracy that aims to mitigate social tensions by the satisfaction of daily needs. Everything is provided for – sleeping, eating, living, relaxation. By dint of the media, the satisfied consumer is 'involved' in everything that goes on, but in the passivity of his easy chair he is galactically remote from any real social intervention. Buddha's timeless plea for a society of give and take, of live and let live, has been implemented just a bit too literally.

Both culturally and architecturally, the ambivalent politics of communal discipline *plus* individual emancipation can be recognised in the social democracy of old. The time-honoured striving of the Left, the condition of *communitas,* remains unattainable so all the effort goes into achieving the precondition of *communitas*: the emancipation of the individual. We are all prepared to stand together for a cause, be it the nation, the *Gemeinschaft*, the language or now perhaps 'Europe'. On the other hand, the individual has to develop his own capacities and, above all, distinguish himself from the herd. To get by in this paradoxical situation, the only system possible is what Hans Magnus Enzensberger termed 'mediocrity and delusion'. In this culture, the difference between one person and another – which is minimal from the point of view of social distinction, political choice and economic importance – is stage-managed. Everyone is just sufficiently different from his neighbour to allow him to retain a sense of individuality, but at the same time sufficiently similar for the idea of a community to persist. It is the kind of culture that we would expect under the hegemony of the middle class, one in which all conflicts are resolved by means of 'reasoned dialogue'. As is known, the integrative

capacity of this structure has exceeded all expectations. Ideological fanaticism, utopias and plans that smack of totalitarianism are thrown out. There is no *Verelendung*, no large-scale impoverishment. In the guise of uniformity, almost everything is levelled out.

Between Acceptance and Resistance

The architecture of Lafour and Wijk also falls into line with this cultural 'ideal'. Against the background of a comfortably neutral urban environment, the good citizen can continue to feel unique in his or her own home with its own ground plan and distinctive detailing. Unity in modest diversity. And everyone who wants to can work on shaping his private needs or can enjoy his well-earned rest. It speaks for itself that criticism has little foothold in this situation. Although this architecture can be read as a reproach to the tasteless and impoverished mass-production prevalent in the trade as a whole, it is really a conciliatory one. It is more inclined to legitimise the limitations within which architecture has allowed itself to be forced than to pillory them as over-restrictive. The world may change a little, but, as Nietzsche observed long ago, this attitude simply fails to get us anywhere and merely serves as an excuse for the status quo. In fact it is an attempt to enhance life by means of a fixation on the *preconditions* for that life.

On the other hand, Lafour and Wijk take their duty to build 'for the people' seriously. So much so, that their subtle handling of the 'quotidian programme' raises questions about the cultural substance of that programme. Where social democracy has allowed its concern for the community and for emancipation to decay into sterile categories, these architects remind us what it was all about in the first place. Thus they reinstate the utopian motive while criticising the all too passive enjoyment of the achieved Utopia; and they do this by the roundabout method of modestly manipulating the programme.

Perhaps this work achieves as much as architecture ever can achieve towards unmasking the hidden defects of a consensus society, without thereby attacking the profession, the occupants or social democracy's predominant achievements. These, according to the architects, must always be protected from the material consequences of social criticism. They show a great aversion to every intellectual endeavour that contradicts the pragmatic aspects. The work raises questions only within the available solution space; and even these questions are difficult to recognise because they are blotted out by the equation of the horizon of experience with the horizon of expectation, and by the soothing of every social discontent with commonplace comforts. Thus this architecture does not seem to make much of a contribution to the revival of the Left so long sought by its architects and their kindred spirits in the social democratic quarter.

P.S. More and more reports are reaching us from the political front about the demolition of the welfare state. If and when social housing also falls prey to the non-interventionist state of tomorrow, please regard the above *Neue Unübersichtlichkeit* as not having been written. Old-style polarisation will then be in fashion again. Let Lafour and Wijk build the barricades!

The tendency to deny limits, never using the one solution or the other but, if possible, both, explains their fascination with situations of transition: for the interior and the exterior as two complementary notions in both architecture and urbanism, for entrances and stairways, for the stone step not only as a connection between inside and outside, but also as a world between sun and shadow. And for the juxtaposition of cultural differences: the use of colours from tropical world in the sober context of the Netherlands, and, in the beginning of their careers, plain Dutch Modernism adapted to the climate of a country still deeply rooted in its traditionalism.

Maarten Kloos

We have no vision of the future. It is all happening so quickly. A vision of the future is outdated as soon as it is expressed. We can only keep thinking and keep saying it can all be much more beautiful buildings.

Lucien Lafour

In lifestyle and architecture Lafour has developed characteristics that are uncommon in the normally severe, well-ordered culture of the Netherlands. He might be described as an ebullient gentleman-architect with a cheerful yet elegant style, who combines proud self-confidence with a gentle interest in people. (...) And since good architecture can be seen as a self-portrait of its creator, one can hardly be amazed that Lafour's architecture shows the same traits as his personality: sensitive to essentials in life, colourful and careful with details.

Izak Salomons

Lucien Lafour has given an impulse that can be carried further: test empirically, observe, improve – do! again and again, until it becomes possible to say, 'Look, that's how we do it here – how we function well in what we build'.

Aldo van Eyck

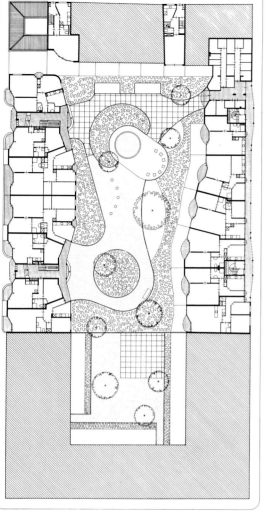

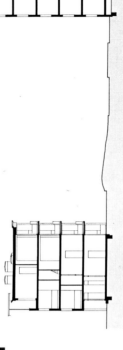

The project on the Realeneiland consists of two blocks (in which 65 dwellings of various sizes have been realised) built between existing warehouses and dwellings. This situation was the starting point of the design. In order to create a gradual transition from the broad warehouses of 12.5 metres to the narrower dwellings of eight metres on the other side, undulating façades for the inner court have been employed. The unity of the whole is retained by using prefabricated components like balconies, bays and stairs in the outer walls. An important principle in the design is that the dwellings should receive as much sun as possible. All the dwellings are oriented towards the south, which results in the walls of the inner court having various functions. On the north side there are living rooms and balconies, on the south side kitchens and galleries. South elevations are relatively open with tall windows and animated by cheerful colours and the curves of projecting balconies. On the north elevations, stairs and access galleries are designed so that comings and goings on them provide some enlivening theatre to these sunless façades. For the benefit of the view from the other side, this façade was made special by designing it very

bright and transparent. Lafour: 'The façade is designed as a diamond with cut facets. Because of this the façade has light and shadow.' Colour also plays an important role in the design. And again, the situation was the starting point. The salmon pink on the Realengracht façade fits in the reddish brown bricks of the warehouses. The stucco at the inner court is yellow so it fits with the grey-white of the warehouses at the inner court. By tilting the ground floor somewhat above street level, the residents have an unrestricted view over the cars. In order to retain a view of the water from the inner court, the block on the Realeneiland is shorter. This open corner gives the inhabitants the feeling not to live in a hermetically sealed area. The inner court, which is laid out as a communal garden, can be reached through two other gateways. All the dwellings are reached by an intermediate form of portico and short gallery. *Based on: Lafour & Wijk Architects, Arcam pocket 2, Amsterdam 1991, pp. 56-57; and: Liesbeth Melis, 'Situatie als uitgangspunt voor de architectuur', De Architect, April 1989, pp. 47-51.*

Location Realengracht and Vierwindenstraat, Amsterdam, The Netherlands **Assistants** T. Konijn, I. Liem **Client** Foundation Lieven de Key, Amsterdam **Design** 1985 **Completion** 1987-89

Architectenbureau L. Lafour & R. Wijk **Realeneiland Housing**

▶

Wien bleibt Fort Europe bleibt Wien

When a profession is socially in retreat, when other trades are invading its field of competence, there always remains the Napoleonic option – attack as the best defence. So when architecture is in peril of being gobbled up by mass production, anonymisation and spiritual impoverishment, and when this cultural medium par excellence seems to be losing its historic status as the mother of all arts, there is still always the possibility of designating *everything* as architecture. Frustration with architecture's marginalised position evaporates like snow in summer. This is exactly the trick Hans Hollein pulled off in his manifesto *Alles ist Architektur* (1966) in which he neatly inverted the customary roles. It was not a case of society winning ground at the expense of autonomous architecture but architecture expanding its territory by proclamation:

'Everything is architecture. Architects should leave off thinking of everything in terms of buildings. Architecture is a medium for communication. Man creates artificial situations. That is architecture. He expands himself and his body. He communicates himself. Chased from paradise by an irate God he wants to create his own paradise.' ★

In other words if architecture no longer carries any weight as an art form you simply declare it almighty. Architecture is no longer a term for specific (built) objects but for anything that functions as a medium – and thus for every possible facet of reality. Curtailment of the *task* of architecture is countered by an inflation of the *concept* of architecture.

★ Quoted in Lootsma, Bart, 'Hans Hollein', in Brand J. (ed.), *Architecture and Imagination*, Zwolle 1989, p. 205.

of life, and Hollein as a contribution to the survival of his craft – and thereby, indirectly, also to the quality of life. That element of directness or indirectness is critical to the appreciation of both their work.

Homo Quasi-universalis as Chameleon

Since his manifesto, Hans Hollein has made the best possible use of the space he has created for himself. He has built up a career in which practically anything has been possible. For 35 years, he has been moving through the fields of culture as an all-round talent – architect, artist, exhibition designer, writer of articles and manifestos, organiser, jewellery designer. While his fame as a stylist has now reached international proportions, the changefulness of his apparel rivals that of the chameleon.

Still, Hollein's work is nowhere near as inconspicuous as the average chameleon. His oeuvre includes few offices, houses or utility buildings, such assignments being restrained as they are by standard typologies and cost analyses. When what you want is architecture which bears an outward resemblance to any other architecture, Hollein is not the right person to ask. He is *la différence* in person and so is his work. Hollein's architecture is a pattern book of original and unique forms, a kaleidoscope of idiosyncrasies and variations. The assignments Hollein accepts always call for exactly what he is best at – distinctiveness of form. At the same time, in a moral respect, he adapts

Retti Candle Shop, Vienna, 1965

Jewellery Store Schullin I, Vienna, 1974

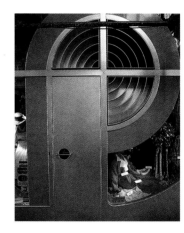

CM Boutique, Vienna, 1967

276

As it happened there were other ways in which people were working hard for an aesthetic revival in the same period. Not that everything was art (or architecture), but that everyone was an artist – an important difference. Joseph Beuys democratised art, as opposed to attributing the elitist status of art to everything else. His aim was to restore self-respect not to art but to humanity – and to do that by means of art. So it was not a little ironic that at the opening of Hollein's *magnum opus*, the Städtisches Museum Abteiberg in Mönchengladbach (1983), the first thing the visitor saw in the central hall at the start of an aesthetic route were Beuys' *Blocks of Fat*. Both Hollein and Beuys wished to preserve an aesthetic domain: Beuys explicitly in the interests of the quality

chameleon-like to the vicissitudes of a prodigal society. He operates in a situation which calls for standing out without dominating, for exception without charisma. In other words, what matters is being noticed without really being noticed. Hollein is the ideal designer for this milieu. His work radiates glamour without moralising. The message is that everything is in flux but nothing really changes.

Architecture for the Honest Burgher

That Hollein's breakthrough as an architect came through designing shop interiors is no mere coincidence. Architecture is the most explosive art and it has to stand up to

Hollein covers a region of visualised thoughts which starts from Vienna, and after many journeys, departures and verifications, goes back to Vienna, '... the big head-brain-city left over from an empire which is now, on a national level, wisely recalled more in irony than an impotent regret. The city itself and its inhabitants seem relatively immune from the frenzy of "progress", from the will to economic and consumer expansion, almost as though they had already been through it and, in a state of decelerated metabolism, looked on as others burnt themselves out in the lucid folly governing the mythology of the great metropolis'.

Gianni Pettena / F. Raggi

As for me, I want first to have precise ideas about architecture, then I can start to consider the specific project.

Hans Hollein

You dig a hole.
Pile up some rocks.
Put up a pole.
Architecture comes into being.

Hans Hollein

Architecture
is in exile now
on the moon
or at the north pole
while people are building

houses	houses
houses	houses
houses	houses
houses	houses
houses	houses
houses	houses
houses	houses

Hans Hollein

Through thousands of years, artificial transformation and determination of mans world, as well as sheltering from weather and climate was done by means of building. The building was the essential manifestation and expression of man.
The development of science and technology, as well as the changing society and her needs and demands confront us with entirely different realities. Other and new media of environment determination emerge. There is a change as to the importance of 'meaning' and 'effect'. Architecture affects. The way how I take possession of an object, how I use it, becomes important. A building can become entirely an information - its message could may be rather experienced through the

Preliminary School, Vienna, 1979

the assaults of climate. Even in an age of Post-Modernism the exterior is necessarily less susceptible to the whims of fashion than the interior, which can change as often as the owner wishes. If we examine the Retti candle shop (1965) and the Schullin jewellery shop (1974), it is clear that an architect of bourgeois distinction like Hollein feels perfectly at home with such briefs. He is more interested in creating an intimate atmosphere to suit the wishes of his client than in giving permanent expression to a public issue. Hollein's work is private even in his public buildings. He upholds the style of a historical process, the rise of the bourgeoisie, which has elevated the private domain into a principle of life and placed it on the agenda of an age. The middle-class, the historical category that brought the individual to the centre stage of culture, is also the inventor of the public domain as an arena in which individuals can act. At the same time it is the destroyer of that arena; for paradoxically the rise of the individual was associated with the technical, economic and political marginalisation of the subject, the *conditio sine qua non* of the individual. The definition of the individual entailed its own negation, and hence also the negation of public debate as a means of settling issues between individuals. Sort that one out!

Hollein's work is admittedly public or semi-public, but it is above all a region for hyper-individual bourgeois fantasies. Whether we consider the shops as backgrounds for ritualised private transactions or the museums with their emphasis on contemplative wandering through the rooms, Hollein offers freedom of movement to the most subjective feelings of the visitor. By this he reveals the hidden agenda of his own conception of culture.

Even though the public domain is in crisis as a cultural category, the meanings carried by the façade will remain vulnerable to the forces that dominate public space for as long as the street remains part of that public space. These forces leave little room for introspection, and personal perceptions are subordinate, not least owing to the advancing role of architecture as a publicity medium. Introspection and personal experience are nonetheless essential to bourgeois culture. Hollein's projects supply the places where, against the odds, these bourgeois desiderata are satisfied.

With a little goodwill, the shop projects can be put down to historical coincidence. Following the forced contraction of Austria after the First World War, Vienna was by no means a centre of growth. For several decades little in the way of new architecture was commissioned. The work of Hollein's early period still shows unmistakable signs of these straitened circumstances. With his museum in Mönchengladbach, however, and to an even greater degree with his plan for the future Guggenheim Museum in Salzburg, Hollein has made his evident preference for the *Raumplan* into a veritable *Leitmotif*. Hollein does not wish to circumscribe, but to hollow out. His guiding principle in this is not so much a Cartesian coordinate system as pure fantasy. Hollein's work appeals to the imagination, not to some functionalist principle. That makes it rather difficult to evaluate his work objectively – you simply have to *experience* this architecture. Unless you talk about it at a meta-level: there is a specific intention behind Hollein's unique design style and we shall now attempt to probe it more deeply.

The Museum taken up into the Underworld

Subterranean building is gaining ground... In an age of internationalisation and rising mobility, with an unstoppable flood of consumer goods, the roads are becoming congested, the railways overloaded and more and more people are harassed by pollution and delays. That is why much research is taking place into transferring traffic to extensive underground networks.

The advantages of such a transfer are clear. Ideally, if the bulk of transportation were to take place underground and the many environmentally damaging and anti-aesthetic activities of industry were to be hidden from view, it should be possible to create a park-like landscape, a reserve for nature and culture, at ground level. That would be a further step in the process of modernisation. Not only would it mean the colonisation of a new region (after the earth's surface, the water and the air) in accordance with the capitalist law of expansion, but the separation of Modernity and Post-Modernity would become a physical reality. Modernisation can thunder on at full tilt underground, while on the surface we go on professing the end of history. With impeccable prospects and healthy lungs, the leisured public would make its way towards the museum and the sculpture garden, which would be waiting to absorb them in droves.

Meanwhile, the new Hollein museum in Salzburg opts for an inversion of this strategy. This projected European branch of the Guggenheim Corporation is to be tunnelled into the rock of the city. Whereas Hollein's ancestors were miners and thus specialised in digging up nature's heritage, Hollein aims to bury our cultural heritage. Just as with the shops, where he was able to set the greater part of the scenario himself without being inhibited by the possible insensitivity of the neighbours, he can have things entirely his own way when underground. This is façadeless, contextless architecture. The designer can focus all his energy on intensifying the inward-directed experience, as a preparation for the individual meeting with Art. The site is freely manipulable in all three dimensions. Thus Hollein has extracted the maximum possible freedom of action. He is not prepared to wait for the removal of the tare of society from the inhabited world. Culture will just have to live underground for the while.

---

means of information (Press, T.V, etcetera). As a matter of fact, it is of almost no importance if e.g. the Acropolis or the pyramids exist in physical reality, as most people are aware of them through other media anyway, and not through an experience of ones own. Yes, indeed their importance - the role they play - is based on this effect of information. Thus buildings might be simulated only.
Hans Hollein

Limited and traditional definitions of architecture and her means have lost their validity. Today, the environment as a whole is the goal of our activities - and all the media of its determination. T.V. or artificial climate

tion or shelter. The extension of the human sphere - and the means of its determination - go far beyond a built statement. Today, everything becomes architecture. 'Architecture' is just one of many means, is just a possibility. Man creates artificial conditions. This is Architecture.
Physically and psychically man repeats, transforms, expands his physical and psychical sphere. He determines 'environment' in its widest sense. According to his needs and wishes he uses the means necessary to satisfy this needs and to fulfil his dreams. He expands his body and his mind. He communicates. Architecture is a medium of communication

Architecture is spiritual order realised by building. Architecture - an idea built into infinite space, manifesting man's spiritual strength and power, material form and expression of his destiny, his life. From its origin to this day, essence and meaning of architecture have not changed. Building is one of man's basic needs. Its first manifestations were not roofs put up for shelter but the erection of sacred structures, the marking of focal points of human activities - the beginning of the town. All building is ritual. Architecture - expression of man himself - flesh and spirit at the same time. Architecture is elemental, sensual, primitive, brutal, terrible, mighty, dominating.

subtle emotions, sensitive recording of the slightest excitations, materialisation of the spiritual.
Hans Hollein

The shape of a building does not develop out of the material condition of its purpose. A building shall not show its use. It is not an expression of structure and construction, it is not enclosure or refuge. A building is itself. Architecture is without purpose. What we build will find its usefulness. Form does not follow function. Form does not originate by itself. It is the great decision of man to make a building into a cube, a pyramid or a sphere. Form in architecture is form determined

'Vanity', dressing table and mirror, M.I.D., 1982

Neues Haas Haus, commercial building, Vienna, 1992

The Hollein Museum

The space in a Hollein-designed museum is a curious additive chain of separate rooms, achieved with the aid of visual apertures and a labyrinthine *promenade archi-tecturale*. The many residual spaces this technique produces are places where formal oppositions are given expression. The main route is always a rising or descending path through the interior of the building, with bands of light streaming in from unexpected angles and enhancing the dramatic quality. The visitor can often see into adjacent rooms without necessarily being able to enter them directly. There is never any sense of a closed box.

278 The Hollein museum, composed as a small, polymorphic city, brings the observer into a state of slight disarray. But at the same time something happens that has become impossible outside the museum: the observer experiences the confusing sequence of differentiated rooms under the influence of an integrating, harmonising aesthetic regime. This regime makes the variations tangible not as interruptions but as a continuity. Instead of drawing attention to inconsistencies, the optical disorientation induces sensations of perfection and aesthetic allure that whet the appetite to see more. It is the artistically designed space that tends to impress, not the art on display. Hollein wants to gratify and seduce. He tries to manoeuvre the visitor along ostensibly uncoerced routes through the museum, but meanwhile his museum pits itself against the exhibited work, enveloping it as a *Gesamtkunstwerk*. The architect manipulates all the dimensions of perception. Whatever direction you walk or look in, the movement and the gaze are always captured. All chance has been banned from experiencing the space, and is allowed only in the circulation pattern. Locomotion is free, in short, but not the aesthetic framing of reality.

There is always a conceptual layer in Hollein's work. He invariably enters into a dialogue with his assignment, and the dialogue achieves expression in an iconographic form. In the Retti candle shop, there are visual allusions to the candle. The Austrian Travel Agency (1978) hints at journeys to far off places. In the museum, sure enough, there are reminders of the work of art. But there is never any subjective gesture which leads to a reading relating to the 'other', to an understanding of this work as a critical statement.

Musealisation of the World View

With art prices soaring and accordingly scrupulous conservation of collections, there is a tendency to shut out the yellowing light of day. The principle of hanging on to what you have implies the all-out exclusion of every ravage of time due to climatic inconstancy, daylight or the corrosive breath of visitors. The new Guggenheim Museum has no more than two skylights, and these are meant to make the interior of the rock visible (with the support of artificial lighting) and to reassure the claustrophobic visitor.

But art is conserved not only in the technical sense but also morally. It may seem paradoxical, but time is increasingly shut out of the contemporary museum. The fascination with the concrete products of the past amounts to a reduction of historicity to consumerism and entertainment. Hollein's work can be seen as a model of this kind of musealisation. Despite his museums' lack of chronology or nineteenth-century style monumentality, and their undeniable compliance with the social democratic demand for lowered thresholds, they remain temples of bourgeois culture. The reason is that the programme of the museum is not significantly altered. With Hollein, the programme still underwrites the exaltation of individual genius, without the least attempt to illuminate the consequences of such genius in a broader context. Thus the museum becomes a place where genius is neutralised, exalted to death. It makes no waves; on the contrary, it aims to calm them. Each work of art is an absolutely unique entity whose effect derives entirely from itself and which imparts itself principally through

AFTER A SUCCESSFUL COLONIZATION

THE MOTHER SHIP LANDS

The Guggenheim Museum Salzburg, competition entry, 1990

absolute form. And although all art has become conceptual in a certain sense since the advent of Concept Art, the ideology of the original remains entirely unimpaired.

The museum is no platform for a critical debate that generates social alternatives, but an oasis of quiet in which art can present itself to the enjoying citizen. The art and art historical objects distract attention from social tendencies, and reaction to current historical processes is postponed. (In Hollein's museums, moreover, every response to a work of art is absurd *a priori*, for the art is merely an embellishment of the architecture.) The museumification of culture is thus the end point of the bourgeois dream. The historical self-legitimisation is complete and the middle-class is no longer a social/historical category but the finale of a civilisation.

Hollein's self-enclosed aesthetic system, with its subterranean compensation for a major cultural loss, is a masterly allusion to a culture that is becoming more and more isolated from any critical social programme. This culture merely puts on a show of social involvement; the mechanisms of repression, discipline and exclusion can continue unimpeded. The task of the museum's accumulation of ostensibly correctly illuminated and untouchable objects is to give a suggestion of substantial accessibility. But the closeness of the selective reality inside the museum simultaneously implies the inaccessibility of the total reality outside. Hence it is clear that we have become complete outsiders. That is also why we are forever being 'initiated', as it were – into the 'bad news' on television and into the 'good news' in the museum. This situation was once known as repressive tolerance, but now it no longer even has a name. Whether the museum is a tourist temple, a supermarket, an institution of further education or an archive, it is now more than ever also the bourgeois trophy cupboard. Ideas are not exchanged but merely showcased. There is a taboo on discussion. What remains is the adulation of the lone genius in search of personal immortality.

Hollein's work is a perfect actualisation of this cultural programme. In the first instance
280 it rises above its *raison d'être* and becomes autonomous aesthetics. But on a closer look, it is clearly the autonomy which is exactly to the taste of the bourgeois *reservatio mentalis*. As a result of its perfect execution, the restricted programme of a museum of

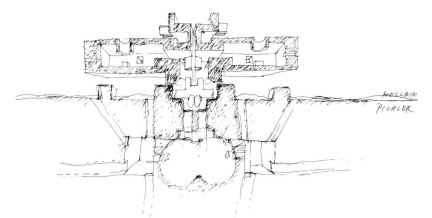

Hans Hollein and Walter Pichler, Valley City, 1963

fine art becomes redefined at a universal level. ★ A visit to one of Hollein's museums is not merely a day out but a confirmation of the museumification that affects us all.

Vienna as a Bastion of Fort Europe

For centuries, Vienna was to many people the last halt before the wilderness. It was a bastion of Europe as an idea, the continent where Graeco-Christian civilisation has triumphed. Three times the Turks had stood at the gates, and three times they were repelled. Vienna was seen as the deliverer of European culture from the threat of (supposed) barbarism. As late as 1815, at the Congress of Vienna, Von Metternich aimed to underline the gravity of his responsibility with the words 'Asia begins at my back door'.

★ See also Bekaert, Geert, 'Museum Abteiberg Mönchengladbach', *Wonen TA/BK* 21 (1983), p. 11.

Less than a century later, the very same Vienna had become the 'laboratory of world dissolution', as Karl Kraus put it. It was the theatre of a comprehensive failure of every attempt to unite modernity with tradition. Practically all known preoccupations and literary topoi of twentieth-century Western bourgeois culture found their origins and most intense synopsis here: Freud, Wittgenstein, Von Hoffmansthal, Herzl, Lüger, Kokoschka, Otto Wagner and so on. After Vienna's role as protector of Europe was played out, it suddenly proved to articulate the foundering of the idea of Europe.

After yet another hundred years or so, this idea of Europe or whatever is left of it is suffering from out-and-out museumification. In the process, the museum is no longer associated with the heroic, it is no longer the tangible result of a European triumph. Now it is the reserve of the status quo, which in the absence of a historical project continues to reproduce itself. Europe has thus become a perpetuated version of Vienna's heyday. Better, Europe is now the end of Vienna! How ironic it is that now that the 'Turks' stand once again before the gates of Vienna and before all those other gates of Fort Europe, the museum is becoming the new metaphor for a society that shuts itself off, a society that no longer offers the Other a place in its museum (there is such a plentiful supply of 'others', after all), but leaves them to perish outside as 'illegal immigrants' or 'economic refugees'. *Wien bleibt Wien*, now that all Europe can recognise itself in Vienna. How apt that a Viennese architect should offer us the most suitable images for this situation!

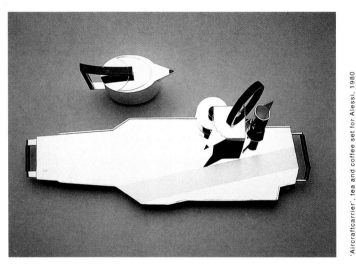

'Aircraftcarrier', tea and coffee set for Alessi, 1980

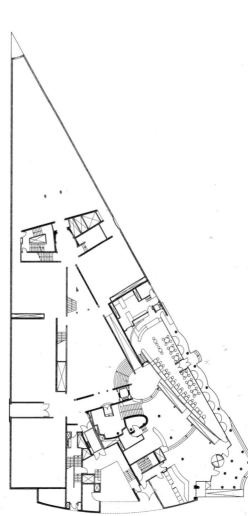

The draft is the result of two premises: firstly, considerations in terms of municipal planning, urbanity and urban character as well as the conditions of the building site and its specific layout; secondly, the programme, its functional consequences and the necessities of presentation of fine art objects to a public of different educational background. The eastern end of the insular area is an important landmark in the approach to the historic core of the city characterised by a marked triangular shape. The apex of the triangle is conceived as a succinct solitaire, although integrated into the building proper. Visibility from long distances and noticeability of the design media are significant prerequisites. In order that the building communicates optimally with the historical town centre it was consistent to strive to place the main entrance at that point. This superimposition of an asymmetrical, diagonally oriented area of access on a symmetrical structure puts the building into complex interrelationships. In the interior, it seemed important to continue access by penetrating into and climbing up to various levels of event. A significant feature was to elevate the main action area of the entrance hall from a direct relationship to the street outside and also from the secondary functions like reception desk and cloakroom. The entrance hall proper is therefore about 1.5 metres above the entrance level, whereby the feeling of participating in an event is

intensified and disturbances from the secondary functions are minimised. From the central hall, the various departments and storeys of the museum are disclosed directly, in terms of both visual surveyability and physical accessibility. In addition to the doorkeeper's cabin, administration and library areas are also accessible both from the entrance hall and directly from outside. From these rooms there is visual contact with the museum rooms themselves. The café is, on the one hand, close to the entrance and the museum area; on the other, it is an independent element which should animate the street in front, the fabric of which is reshaped by the new museum. The collections are accessed from the large entrance hall. We avoided doing this only via lifts or high (psychologically inhibiting) vertical staircase shafts but endeavoured to achieve it by an experiential diagonal penetration of the building. Many roundwalks are possible; the desired outlooks are frequently broken down into zones serving communication. The roof areas have been planned so that the intentionally shaped roof structure – the result of necessary superstructures for air conditioning and light access – has an aesthetic effect and builds upon a clear moulding line on the main building mass. The silhouette has been articulated because of its significance in the cityscape. *Hans Hollein*

Location Domstraße 10, Frankfurt am Main, Germany **Assistants** R. Burgard, F. Madl, S. Eto and others **Client** City of Frankfurt am Main **Design** 1983-85 **Completion** 1987-91

Hans Hollein Architekt *Museum of Modern Art*

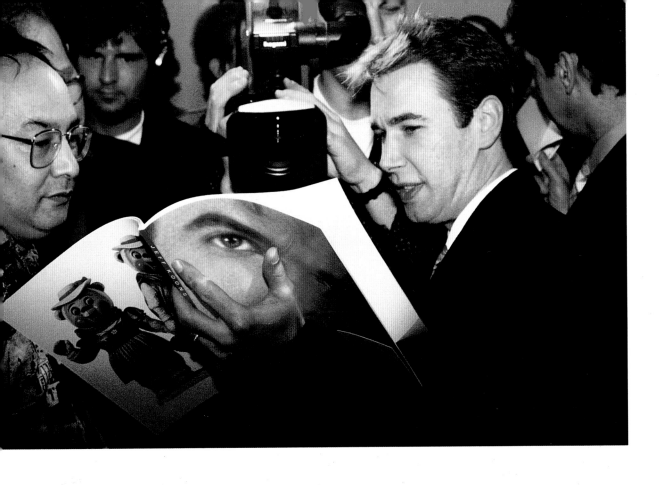

Jeff Koons, Made in Heaven, installation, 1991

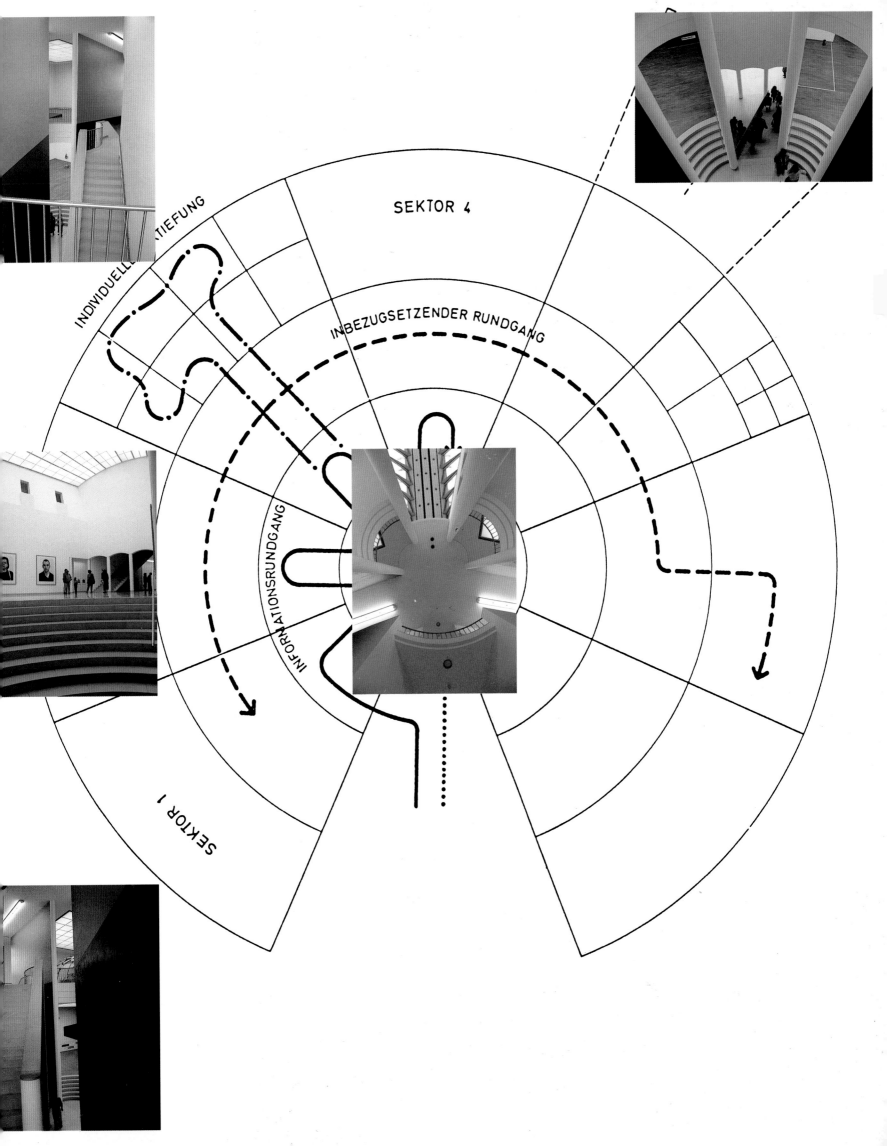

SEKTOR 4

INDIVIDUELLE VERTIEFUNG

INBEZUGSETZENDER RUNDGANG

INFORMATIONSRUNDGANG

SEKTOR 1

On the Work of Bernard Tschumi
The Concept of a Tschumi does not Transgress

Where Do You Stand? Part I

Where do you stand when you are acutely conscious of 'the paradox of architecture', which means you cannot think about it and experience it at the same time? Where, too, if you tirelessly ponder and publish about the historically-grown moral domination of thought over subjective experience which makes everything so abstract? Where, too, if all these things are so much on your mind that you have developed a vocabulary in which you can say it all so beautifully that you have become totally dependant on it? And as a result of all this you have become further than ever estranged from pure experience? So that you *propagate transgression*, sing the praises of sensory and somatic pleasure in architecture as an abstraction, making experience into a philosophical category? So that your theory becomes a burden precisely where it ought to have become superfluous?

'The Concept of Space is not in Space'

According to Bernard Tschumi, the above paradox is 'about the impossibility of questioning the nature of space and at the same time making or experiencing a real space'.★ In other words as soon as you start thinking, it gets in the way of your own experience. This idea of our intellectual capacity as a burden with the implicit glorification of uncompromised experience is laden with philosophical preconceptions. In this train of thought the 'concept of architecture' is an obstruction.

★ Tschumi, Bernard. *Questions of Space*, London 1991, p. 27.

'Architecture constitutes the reality of experience while this reality gets in the way of the overall vision. Architecture consists of the abstraction of absolute truth, while this very truth gets in the way of feeling. We cannot both experience and think that we experience. "The concept of dog does not bark"; the concept of space is not in space.'

For someone who is inclined to see the world in such problematic terms, discovering the above-mentioned paradox of architecture must be enough to give a sensation of transgression all on its own. In a profession that, ever since Vitruvius, has been in the habit of codifying itself in tractates and leaving the experiencing of its products to other people, it is an act of salvation to posit *experience* as the polar opposite of *understanding*. Bernard Tschumi has scrutinised this dialectic opposition in exceptional depth. It has brought him world fame as an intellectual who builds. Or, we may perhaps say, a builder who has a theory into the bargain. Tschumi the avant-gardist has seen that the world is no more than a construct of subjective thought and at the same time has succeeded in overcoming this mental stumbling-block by going into action. The kind of salon intellectual who, seated at a desk in his attic or ivory tower, understood the world but was incapable of changing it seems to have become finally outmoded in the light of Bernard Tschumi's career. His work seems to be an actual bridging of the gulf between art and life, and hence the ultimate fulfilment of the avant-garde wish. Just consider

this: his *magnum opus*, the Parc de la Villette in Paris, was generally applauded as a breakthrough in both architecture and in cultural politics. The intellectual world was gratified by the long-awaited practical triumph of high-class thinking. The practical world, the world of architecture and politics, was euphoric over a design that appeared capable of carrying off the official approval of the vanguard of thought. Thought in Paris, naturally.

How does the Occasionally Built Reality of Tschumi look? Tenuous

Having excelled for years in the formulation of controversial theories of architecture, and blessed with a sophisticated graphic technique, Tschumi found an opportunity in the commission for Parc de la Villette to show that a complex architectonic organisation is possible without the aid of traditional means such as composition, hierarchy, order or balance. The park thus shows no traces of a synthesis. The brief was 'deconstructed' by Tschumi into three elementary principles: movement, meeting points and events. During the design process, this trinity was formalised with the concepts of lines, points and surfaces, which remain separate and autonomous. The design involves the repeated opposition of dynamics and points of rest. The architectural object obtains its identity through an interplay of mass and motion. Where the public is meant to take possession of the project there are expressive circulation structures (walkways, staircases etc.) which often float in front of the main volume. This movement is strongly accentuated by exuberant structures that remind us of Russian Constructivism. For Tschumi, strict adherence to the brief is not cardinal; the architect must comply with it, and that is all. But what the brief can do is inspire an idea which can legitimise a logistic (grammatical) invention – as in the New National Theatre,

To really appreciate architecture, you may even need to commit a murder.

Architecture is defined by the actions it witnesses as much as by the enclosure of its walls. Murder in the Street differs from Murder in the Cathedral in the same way as love in the street differs from the Street of Love. Radically.

Bernard Tschumi, Advertisement for Architecture, 1976

Architecture is the ultimate erotic act. Carry it to excess and it will reveal both the traces of reason and the sensual experience of space. Simultaneously.
Bernard Tschumi

The game of architecture is an intricate play with rules that you may break or accept. These rules, like so many knots that cannot be untied, have the erotic significance of bondage: the more numerous and sophisticated the restraints, the greater the pleasure.
Bernard Tschumi

Transgression. An exquisitely perverse act that never lasts. And like a caress is almost impossible to resist.
Bernard Tschumi

Architecture only exists through the world in which it locates itself. If this world implies dissociation and destroys unity, architecture will inevitably reflect these phenomena.
Bernard Tschumi

La Villette's 'programmatic deconstruction', its insistence on intertextuality over contextuality, its indeterminate textual systems, its combinative *folie* production, and its insistence on the contamination of architecture by film, psychoanalysis, philosophy, and literary theory - all subvert and rewrite Modernism's post-fordist ideology of the plan and the programme, and thus their inherently conservative distinction between architectural theory and architectural practice.
Michael Speaks

Hailed as 'A Park of the twenty-first Century,' La Villette is truly an 'architectural thinking' which has become detached from all referents, as the future present, dissolving itself, like Hans Haacke's productions, precisely as part of the circuitry and modulation of contemporary capital. Tschumi has thus remarked of La Villette and architecture in general that 'Architectural is not about the spatial illustration of theoretical or philosophical propositions at any one time; rather it participates in them, accelerates and intensifies them. With La Villette, then, we are no longer in a situation in which there is an architectural theory, in the form of the plan, or the programme, juxtaposed to a practice as realised built form; no longer a situation of an inside where complex models based on philosophical concepts are devel-

284

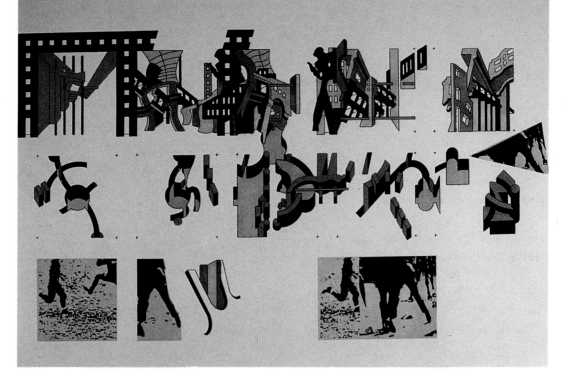

Manhattan Transcripts, Part 4, excerpt, 1981

Tokyo (1986), where the need to accommodate musical activities gave Tschumi the idea of structuring the building in analogy to the lines of notation in a musical score which can represent every kind of tone, melody and rhythm. To Tschumi, all functional spaces are essentially interchangeable and fulfil specific functions only in the given configuration. Tschumi stages the ground plan and the main volume of a design at a conceptual level and barely attends to the actual programmatic function. At points where the function involves movement, he surprises us with a flourish of expressive Constructivism. His real interest is in the dynamics of the moving subject and in the mass and articulation of the plan. In the designs for both the Très Grande Bibliothèque (Paris, 1989) and the station in Kyoto (1991) we can see how Tschumi confiscates the circulation spaces even before starting on the allocation of the main functional areas.

A central issue for Tschumi is the recognition of the imagination as a coequal element in the designing and experiencing of architecture. In his view this aspect has been chronically undervalued in Western architecture since the Renaissance. Thinking was marked by principles such as order, harmony, demarcation and purpose. It was always insight and practical knowledge that were responsible for the unity of the plan. Every question that fell outside the limits of comprehension was out of order. Architecture was invariably made the alibi for totalising thought and was thus never itself. It was at the service of a metaphysical system, either divine or rational.

Since the imagination was not to be trusted, it was invariably worsted by truth, understanding or common sense. The imagination was volatile, unbounded, imponderable and was hence seen as a perturbation of the rational process that led up to a building: from the clearly defined programme without any white areas, via the planned design process, to the defined use and agreed meaning. But for Tschumi, attention to what falls outside the rational process, the absent and implicit, the neglected and the repressed, is precisely what will save architecture.

Metonymic Tschumi

The unprecedented debate around Parc de la Villette arose from an interplay of social forces for which the architect found an intriguing form at exactly the right moment. The site on which this multifunctional leisure park was established, alongside the Boulevard Péripherique, was previously the location of the abattoir. It thus automatically occupied a place in the widespread discussions on the reallocation of industrial and semi-industrial zones. Moreover, it formed part of the universally resurgent interest in the city periphery as an ostensibly chaotic but no less important location for building projects. Further, with Tschumi as the chosen architect, the project complied with the flourishing trend of granting commissions to internationally active architects, thereby further boosting the maverick's star status. Finally, here was an opportunity for architecture to come forward with a cultural standpoint of the first order. Architecture figured visibly in both the sociopolitical and philosophical discourses and hence accrued an enormous social prestige. Parc de la Villette is a sign of the rebirth of architecture as a constituent of society after years of a languishing existence as a function of economy. Tschumi has become a metonym for the revival of architecture. But pioneering architecture is no longer the precursor of a new society, as the Modernists preached. This time architecture is deployed as a mask for a society that frantically puts up a show of change while in fact largely disabled by massive stasis. The forms may well recall the revolutionary élan of the Russian Revolution, but the content is drawn from an apolitical theory of deconstruction.

285

---

oped, and an outside where they are implemented. Instead, via *folie La Villette*, a whole series of 'architectural thinkings' become possible - Jameson's cognitive maps, Baudrillard's simulation scenarios, Foucault's heterotopias, Deleuze's smooth spaces, Derrida's aporias. No longer to be understood as mediatory spaces invested as Althusser's 'post-stations' in the empty space between theoretical principles and the concrete, nor as occupational sites between 'architectural thinking' and architecture, between theory and practice, these 'thinkings' are *folies* - in this, *my* La Villette - heterotopian sites, to be read, written and abandoned in a constant negotiation.

Michael Speaks

To a certain extent, Tschumi remains faithful to his early research. Heterogeneity and resistance are still dominant themes in his work, although their early activist political edge has today given way to fragments of French antihumanist philosophy. In proclaiming the end of utopias, Tschumi seemed to adopt Tafuri's project of demystification. Like so many other aspects of his work, however, this is only a façade; for Tschumi's ascension in the academic and professional worlds of architecture may be attributed to

his ability to play on the most persistent of contemporary myths. Perceived as a European intellectual by Americans and as an American architect by the French, Tschumi has profited from both the prestige of French theory in America and the legend of American pragmatism in France. Judging Tschumi by his actions rather than his rhetorics, one discovers that the eroticism of the borders is not just a playful game.

Louis Martin

When an architect invents a new theorem, or an architectural culture invents a new theorem, it is a very important moment in architecture.

Bernard Tschumi

I'm more interested in the mechanisms of film than in the movie itself.

Bernard Tschumi

It was in this precarious situation that Tschumi set to work. Heavily over-conscious of the social and philosophical determinants that limited him, he produced a design that above all else was about 'the event'. But what event? And why?

The real paradox lies not in the architecture but in Tschumi's own programme. It is the paradox of the avant-garde. Realising that life can be understood backwards but only lived forwards, Tschumi has to choose between thinking and doing. If he thinks, then he is bound to get bogged down on the periphery of the world stage. If he does something, then he runs the risk of being totally irrelevant on the world stage. For an architect with the intellectual standard of Tschumi, the paradox of architecture is an inevitable fate. But once you look deeper than the pretty things this has achieved for philosophy and architecture, there remain the following questions to be answered:

Where Do You Stand? Part II

Where do you stand if, as an architect, you wish to jettison the principles of order, balance and harmony? If you wish to throw over functional planning and the unity of content and form in favour of a game of fragments played with brittle signs with no agreed meanings? If you want all these things while you have a concrete commission, a programme and a goal? And while you will ultimately have to commit yourself to a design that will travel the world on computer screens and in four colour printing, a design of which countless people get no more than a fleeting impression? While there are so many people eagerly looking forward to the completion of your project?

What is the role of the architect if you no longer believe in pioneering projects by pioneering architects, nor in heroes who intervene in history? If you wish to debunk that whole idea? If you no longer believe in charismatic personalities, in individuals who achieve things by strength of will, but in a world dictated by signification systems? If you no longer believe in the present but in the absent, in that which is forever unstated and remains between the lines, which resists capturing in language: the imagination, the experience, the unconscious? If you lose your faith in all that at the very moment you are elevated to the gallery of honour of architecture, the moment you are appreciated for your perspicacity and become a public figure?

What are you if formal and programmatic conflict constitutes the *Leitmotif* of your work? If you have had your fill of harmonising your work with mankind, the environment, the commission and ideology? If you prefer to be vague, undefined, uncoordinated and inconsistent, just as imagination is? If you can only see the opposites of these, order, fixity of purpose and efficiency, as the attributes of repression, and if you find ideological consensus nauseating? If you then feel yourself to be suffocating in that soft blanket of pluralism, in the democratic gum where everyone sticks to his opinions but nobody knows what grounds there might still be for stating them? And if you then observe that conflict and complexity are a comfortable pose in a world full of opinions that nobody listens to?

286

Kyoto Station, competition entry, 1991

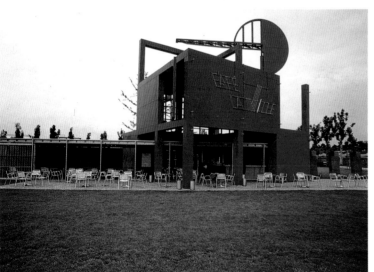

Parc de la Villette, Paris, 1987

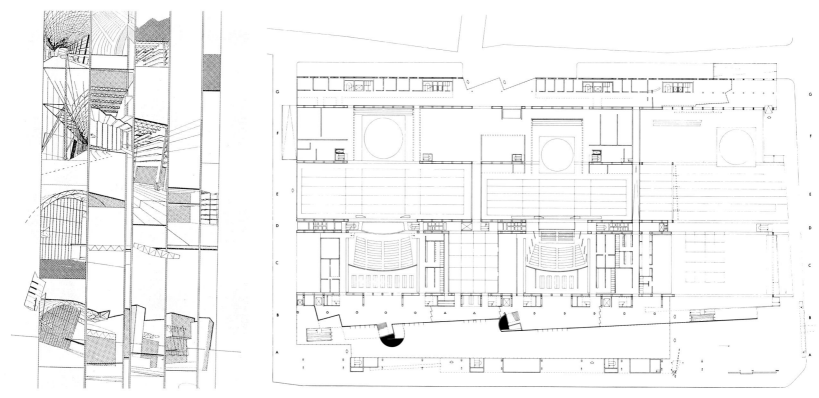

New National Theatre Tokyo, competition entry, 1987

What do you do if you imagine that by your subversive ideas you are crossing swords with the dominant power, which relies as ever on control, repression and the mental straitjacket of unitary meanings? If you think that your inverted world, that cunningly contrived carnival, really gives the authorities their comeuppance? That you are engaged in a guerrilla war against the totalitarian temptation? If you are convinced of this while prominent officials, presidents and city councillors, bureaucrats and technocrats – that whole herd of independent spirits – support your plans, while the powers that be are mightily satisfied with you?

What has got into you if you sincerely believe you are dismantling the worn-out clichés of the architectural discipline? If you do not flinch at smashing taboos, and want to reinstate simple pleasure. If you seek immoderation, rising above your functional brief in order to give ecstasy a chance again? And if you then observe not the expected resistance, repression and isolation but thundering applause?

What do you achieve if you see your designs as scenarios that offer a continuous sequence of experiential incidents? If you intervene in your brief by inserting unexpected confrontations with the historic conditions in which the users of your projects are located? And if you are then forced to admit that experience has been overtaken as a historical fact by spectacle, by simulation? That the inspiration you draw from a filmic syntax is insufficient for the staging of a significant experience? And if you are forced to accept that architectural dramaturgy does not necessarily produce drama?

What do you cause, finally, if your striving towards a decentring of the subject, your wish to create a heterotopia, a centrifugal network of non-hierarchically performed interventions, turns out to attract masses of fans, dignitaries in search of 'socialist' environmental planning, an amiable sunday public with a well-defined longing for relaxation? And your 'dis-place' turns into a touristic monument?

What are you, then? You are your own *'concept Tschumi'*. You feel in your element and take the credit for the most prestigious project of 'the park for the twenty-first century' and beyond.

Transgression by assignation, tomorrow in the park; forever professing the unexpected while at the same time having to work for years on a single project; basing yourself on intertextuality and becoming a superstar; being an acclaimed 'anarchist'; breaking new ground in an art form that, philosophically speaking, is only just beginning to discover the disenchanted world; staging spatial and filmic happenings while the end of history is being declared; becoming a world famous architect just when architecture has relinquished its revolutionary force; etcetera. All this is the fate of a tragic hero, lost in a *fin de millennium*. The concepts of Tschumi do not bark. Nor do they really bite, alas.

This is a new type of library combining the pursuit of modernity with the pursuit of knowledge; the athlete with the scholar. Opening simultaneously onto the Seine, Paris, Europe and the rest of the world, it enjoys at the same time internal 'circuits' of library culture. The building will act as an urban generator of a new area of the city. Inside there are multi-media 'circuits' for the public, circuits for the books and visible architectural circuits of the most up-to-date information technology. A main 'circuit' offering both excitement and architectural permanence is combined with reading 'trays' offering maximum flexibility. The fact that the library is not located in the historical centre of Paris is considered to be an important and positive factor. Its very eccentricity allows it to break away from static concepts of libraries. It is not a frozen monument, but must instead be turned into an event. Hence the concept of open circuit, where the endless pursuit of knowledge is matched by the pleasure of physical effort. Locating a running track over the library is more than a dynamic convenience. It embodies the library's complex role as the generator of a new urban strategy (the open circuit). Within the new library, five interrelated sets of circuits can be identified: the visitors' and administrators' circuits, the book circuits, the electronic circuits and the mechanical circuits. While each circuit has its own logic and its own set of rules, the circuits interact constantly at strategic locations. In order to comply with the inevitable evolution of the programme, first during the planning stages, then over many years of use, we have devised a free and flexible system of 'trays'. By placing public circulation on one side and storerooms on the other, we have obtained the free space on the 'trays' only rhythmed by the grid of the structural columns and the grid of stairs. Throughout the history of architecture, some of the most significant works have been library programmes, for example those of Boullée, Labrouste, Carrère and Hastings, Asplund and others. The new library should be compared to such illustrious precedents even though nostalgia for outdated spatial forms should be avoided. We have therefore displaced the traditional central reading room towards the exterior. The space of the Great Hall inside, and the Esplanade outside, is the revolving circuit of the project. The architects have searched for dynamic circuits of the future, whereby the concept of library revolves around movement: movement of people and movement of ideas. *Bernard Tschumi*

Location Paris, France **Assistant** L. Merlini **Client** President François Mitterrand **Design** 1989 **Completion** unbuilt project

Bernard Tschumi Architects *Très Grande Bibliothèque*

▶

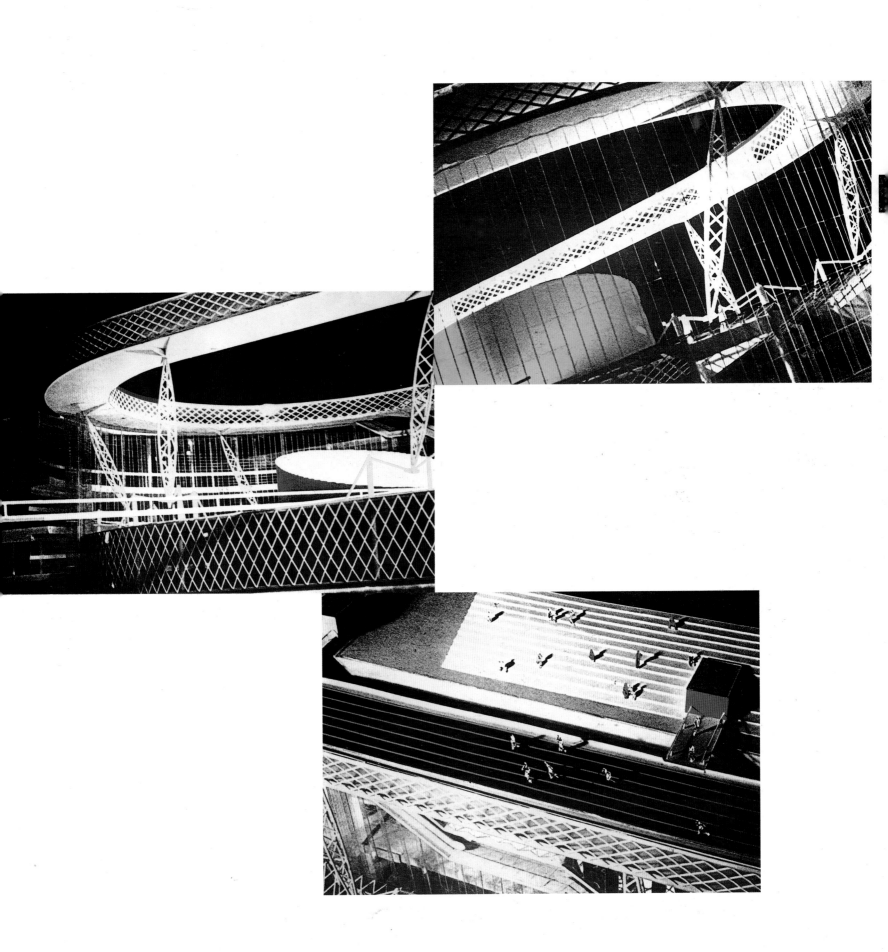

Rye Bread Architecture

A Conversation with Herman Hertzberger

Herman Hertzberger once described his work as 'rye bread architecture', contrasting it with the flashy architecture of deconstructivism. Maybe that does not sound very appealing but with this approach he has in fact succeeded in producing an oeuvre of major importance that is both consistent and widely respected. Hertzberger's achievement has been to continue nothing less than the humanism of Forum and Team 10 into the present day. He began his career in the intellectual circle around Aldo van Eyck and the importance of collectivity and of the 'encounter' have continued to remain primary for him. His work does not contain any isolated artistic *tours de force* in the middle of nowhere; what you do get is a large number of (partially) public buildings, including schools, cultural institutions and one government ministry complex. The public domain has always been a crucial concern for Hertzberger, despite the fact that architecture has become a specialised designers' discipline and despite the depoliticising that architecture suffered from in the eighties.

According to Hertzberger, in our current concern with the public domain we have everything to learn from spatial organisation in primitive, close-knit societies. Hertzberger is at his best when he is commissioned to create spaces for children, that is, for a group where there is supposedly plenty of interaction. Just as in non-Western cultures where individualism plays a smaller role, the play of children does not yet admit of the extreme individualisation that adult citizens in our social-democratic society set such store by. Children have not yet developed any clearly defined identity and are much more capable of being genuinely open to each other. Hertzberger's architectural stages form the ideal theatre for that process of socialisation and his work has an appeal for anyone who appreciates the timeless importance of social intercourse.

But the neutrality of this notion leaves the content of this intercourse undefined and this also leads to a problem of differentiation. Contact between adults often proceeds in an extremely complicated fashion; anthropological commonplaces are simply not enough. It is true that anthropology as it is propagated by Team 10 provides a welcome change from the alienating idiom of Modernism, but it does not help one to make one's choices of content at a cultural and institutional level. Even in Hertzberger's domestic architecture, which one would think was the terrain *par excellence* for the values of family and for individualism, we get the same emphasis on collectivity. Photos of his work show not so much isolated objects, as humans in their capacity of social beings involved in some interaction or other against an architectural backdrop. It is rare that the individual in all his/her uniqueness is given any priority. This architecture is based on a fatherly concern with the vicissitudes of human beings, who are never allowed to be really autonomous. Too bad for an individual who would rather not have anything to do with the group. The problematic of the big city dwellers, their 'anonymity elevated to monumentality', to quote Otto Wagner, and their wish, based on self-preservation, to be left alone, remains a sore point in Hertzberger's work.

The great power that is nevertheless inherent in this oeuvre is to a great extent the result of his rewriting of the programme. His concern for the public domain means that the list of functional requirements is often complemented with a meticulous treatment of the marginal areas, that part of the design that is not yet entirely bureaucratised by programmatic demands, the in-between areas, connecting zones, and openings. It is there that the architect can claim to have a role in the construction and organisation of the building as well. His extraordinary preoccupation with the public domain can be seen everywhere; the result is that every detail becomes a public issue. In the end, in the view of the critic Kenneth Frampton, even something as specialised as the articulation of a structural joint, is treated as a matter for public concern.

Your former office in Amsterdam looked out on Rem Koolhaas' Byzantium building. Do you miss the view?

As a building I think Byzantium is really not at all bad, only it doesn't live up to its pretentions. I have to watch what I'm saying, however, because it's forbidden to make negative comments about colleagues in public. I even once received an official reprimand on the note paper of the Royal Institute of Dutch Architects in which their lawyers gave me a shot across the bows for my publicly expressed disapproval of the proposed demolition of Aldo van Eyck's orphanage. Apparently you are only allowed to say that sort of thing in a closed panel discussion. It is a shame that architects all too often treat critical comments as an attempt to harm their business interests.

Herman Hertzberger

*In other words there are numerous mechanisms in your profession that get in the way of any serious dis-
cussion on content. Don't you think it strange that on the one hand you have won great acclaim for an
architecture that is based on a critical approach, while on the other hand, as an individual architect, you
have to play the game according to the rules of the trade?*

De Drie Hoven, Nursing home, Amsterdam, 1975

All it is, in my view, is that colleagues are afraid that negative criticism will lose them commissions.
This anxiety gets in the way of any discussion about the cultural importance of architecture. To return to
Byzantium, you might think this fear was entirely unfounded. People's criticism of Byzantium hasn't
harmed Koolhaas at all. It's true however that you can go too far with the freedom you have. The authorities also have some responsibility here. An administration with a feeling for culture should be prepared to
take controversy in its stride and should be fully aware how vital it is that good architects like Van Eyck and
Koolhaas are given the chance to design a couple of public buildings. In the quarrel around the preservation of Van Eyck's orphanage we are beginning to see something like a rehabilitation. Everyone who visits
the Berlage Institute now says that it is extremely suitable for public events. Architecture means daring to
take risks and if there is anyone who doesn't dare take risks it is the Dutch. I have been allowed to make a
fair number of public buildings and I regard this as a sign that the authorities appreciate my work. I was
given the commission for the Muziekcentrum in Utrecht, and have designed any number of schools and
one ministry building.

Are you saying that you don't take any real risks?

Of course I am not completely without a feeling for strategy. In Holland I feel like a fish in water. I am aware
of the limitations but on the whole I can live with them. Even so I take Rem Koolhaas seriously when he
states that you have to be prepared to take more risks. An architect is someone who, as it were, builds
strong legs for tables, while an artist does just the opposite; he saws the legs away from under you. Van
Eyck and Koolhaas are the only two architects in Holland who try to do both. That's the way for an architect
to make a greater contribution to culture and that's also where the notion of the architect as an artist really
begins to mean something.

*Do you also employ your strategic sense during the design phase, so that you get the chance to deploy
your artistic skills?*

If you get a flash of inspiration about urban development and the city planner in charge is against you, you
can forget it. Unless you still manage to get your way by a back-door, by lobbying in the city council, for
instance. But that's not something I really enjoy. Some people come into their own in conflict situations.
They work best with daggers drawn; that means they often win, but they also lose sometimes. I sometimes
make a concession to maintain a friendly atmosphere. I am dependent on my clients and that means I can't
afford to have a quarrel with them. I also want them to be able to identify with the project. Being open-minded is the best policy for me; it certainly seems to have brought me good results.

*It must be very difficult on the one hand to proclaim that 'being open-minded is the best policy' and on the
other hand to state that you are the artist, that this is how you see things and that's how they have to be, in
other words an extremely personal expression of an extremely personal attitude.*

If a city planner tells me that I have to put an accent at the end of the street, I won't straightaway say I can't.
But I have of course built up a certain amount of experience and that means that I'm now prepared to risk
being awkward sometimes; this gives me a basis where I feel a little freer and that means perhaps that
I even dare do a few things I wouldn't have done previously.

But on the whole your basic point of departure is harmony?

No, I really don't agree with you there. Look at the photos I've had made all these years; you'll often see a
great contrast between the social situation and the architectural context. What's more, my rather rough-
and-ready architecture has often put a question mark after the prevailing optimism. Or take the Vredenburg
Muziekcentrum in Utrecht: that's probably been my most controversial building. I managed to make a place
like that more accessible to the public. What couldn't be done by making the tickets cheaper was achieved
by an architectural device that literally made the building more accessible by exploiting the fact that it was
part of a shopping centre complex. I've done everything I could to eliminate anything too solemn. At the
time it was a very effective statement and it contributed a lot to my reputation. I don't think you can do that
sort of thing any more. A theatre or a public building doesn't need to feel particularly accessible any more.
That battle has been won. What buildings like that need to express now is a festive spirit. All those grey
materials don't feel right any more. In that sense the times have quite simply changed.

Do your buildings easily become dated?

Even though you always try and make your buildings effective for as long as possible they remain tied to the time they were made. In the Centraal Beheer insurance company building that time-tiedness is itself clearly stated. At a certain moment people stopped wearing jeans and wore two-piece suits to go to work. People started conforming again. That had a lot to do with high unemployment; people wanted to pass unnoticed. That whole festive atmosphere around the Centraal Beheer building with all those plants and other slightly weird features has simply vanished. Then they called in an interior decorator and spent millions of guilders just on making the building look respectable again. Apparently the operation was more or less successful. Now I get people coming and telling me that my building been completely ruined. In a sense the Centraal Beheer building has been spoilt but in another sense it is a triumph for me because the narrative of the structure has been able to bridge such a long span of time. I'm really delighted when the basic structure of a building lasts for a long time while the details have a short life.

In addition to changing notions about decoration, the design of the supporting frame also implies a cultural prise de position and is bound to show pronounced anthropological preferences. No matter what cultural questions your architecture raises, at the level of the basic structure what you offer is a form that is 'inviting' to Humanity, with a capital H. Isn't that so?

I am not likely to change my point of departure, but different accents are always a possibility, and I'm not necessarily the one who provides them. The Drie Hoven old people's home, for instance, had an enormous 'public' area. Currently more and more of that area is being turned into private space, which is a tendency

that I personally find quite disturbing. And the structure makes this possible, because it consists of nothing but pillars and you can build a wall wherever you like. All this is completely in line with the increasing trend towards individualisation. In every primitive culture you see a great emphasis on community and on a good balance between the public and the private. In the sixties and early seventies the balance even roughly tipped back again towards more public space, but that trend has now been completely reversed; in my opinion that is definitely a step backwards.

Measured by what standards?

By anthropological standards, the standards of primitive cultures. It is an article of belief for me that in a well functioning society there is a balance between public and private.

But does that separation between public and private always need to be seen spatially? You could also say that the public domain is more a mental concept.

Maybe. You could argue that people are constantly in touch with each other via their computers, or via television. But in a spatial sense – architecture is my profession after all – things are going very badly.

But does that also mean that things are going very badly with humanity from an anthropological point of view?

Certainly at the level of architecture and urban design. No matter how much my opinions and my approach to design changes, I will always continue to fight for improvements. I have three main themes which are also incidentally the titles of my lectures: *A Public Domain; Making Space, Leaving Space;* and *Inviting*

'Making space, leaving space', Apollo Schools, Amsterdam, 1983

'Inviting form', Batjan School, Amsterdam, 1986

Form. These three subjects remain crucial for me; the only other thing I would like to get across to people is that you don't always have to say things in the same language. I am not convinced that the language I used in the sixties and seventies was the most appropriate language for what I wanted to say then. I would like to spend some time now investigating whether I can't say things in a completely different way. Spatially, of course, but also in terms of materials. Maybe I have always made things too easy for myself; perhaps I told myself that if I stopped fussing about materials and just used a clearly defined kit, everything would all work out okay. I would now like to take on the challenge of trying other ways of creating space. The rise of graffiti is the umpteenth proof that the old approach no longer works. At the time I literally said that I thought it was important for people to be able to write what they felt on the walls, and that therefore it made more sense to work in concrete than in brick. But now I've seen the result, I've had to eat my words. What I'd like now would be to make a building out of marble. That would be a challenge, to see how I could use expensive materials to make something that would still be accessible to people. In fact that isn't a contradiction at all. The real contradiction is that buildings made of inferior materials have become inaccessible simply because people don't have any respect for them.

In addition to materials, figurative and narrative elements also play a role. There is always a sort of abstraction and neutrality in your buildings; they do not make any very specific statement so that symbolism has quite a modest role in them. In fact representation also doesn't play any part in your work. Wouldn't something that is figurative be just that inviting element you are talking about?

The whole area of symbolism in architecture is something that I have felt an aversion for; a friend of mine, however, Johan van der Keuken, a film director who has actually made photos of my work, structures his films with a whole series of connotations and associations. I can't offer any argument against the suggestion that I could or should do something like that too. But I'm not ready for it.

People like Nouvel and Tschumi try to find a metaphor for contemporary society. They make façades which are a statement and an abstraction at the same time and which work as an image of present day society.

It's not so much the façades as the metaphor that's often transparent; it is a bit superficial. But if you were to ask me who I think are the greatest architects at present, I would certainly include Nouvel in my list. Even so I think that what he does is all a bit too hasty. I get the feeling you could demolish what Nouvel has to say with a couple of cobblestones in half an hour. A building like that, you can literally knock it to pieces.

That's actually what the metaphor is saying. What Nouvel is saying is that there aren't any cobblestones, cornerstones, coping stones or facing stones any more. There aren't even any touchstones. In fact there aren't any stones any longer. All we have is sensations, in his view.

I think that's too superficial a picture; it's perfectly clear that there still are stones. **The real skill lies in constructing a frame that you can put the life of the building inside of.** Then you can change it around later on, if you want. I think that with both Tschumi and Nouvel nothing at all is left of the building. After a couple of years you'll have to get rid of it all. Either it will have rusted or it'll be falling to bits or else there just won't be anything left of it. My main complaint is that there won't be any frame either where you'll be able to add something else later on.

The architects we're talking about start with an analysis of society and end up in architecture, but they could just as well have made a good film. They are more interested in speculation than in the discipline. You on the other hand make the frame your ultimate criterion, and that means that you stick with the discipline. Presumably you rate it higher than speculation?

Yes, though I should add that I like it very much when the frame is flexible enough both to assimilate and reject various periods. My design for the Media Park in Cologne does have those formal bits of frame, but, if you want a metaphor, it also has a sort of non-place in the middle.

That's the void of course, something that's very much in at the moment. An empty centre as a metaphor of the Verlust der Mitte, *to quote the title of Hans Sedlmayr's famous book.*

The question is can you make a place that does not just consist of the elements it contains. Perhaps that's where a sort of metaphor still creeps in. You can either highlight this metaphor or else you can shove it into a corner. The structural frame that you just described as supporting the metaphor is, as it happens, treated by a critic like Kenneth Frampton as being a metaphor itself: it is a matter not so much of the representation of the metaphor, but of making architecture itself present, as solid as can be, material and tectonic. A theory like that would be like a licence to continue on the same road, but with my Media Park project I have burnt my bridges behind me. What I have to do now is rediscover myself. I am no longer able to come up with a set of solutions that when put together would make up a complete story. It's a very difficult moment for me right now. The thing that I regard as particularly important is to avoid being too specific. The less you define things the more people's own creativity is stimulated. It's strange, but that idea worked best in the Drie Hoven building, because there the structure was used literally as a neutral grid. I believe I have far more metaphors in my work than I've dared to admit, but they aren't metaphors that refer directly to society. I think that I will continue to be reticent in my symbolism, and that I will leave it to my viewers to interpret it as they please.

In the Montessori teaching method that you value so highly a certain structure is also provided within which one develops according to one's own abilities. It is a question of the individual coming into contact with the collective in the way that suits him or her best. But while the performance of the individual is facilitated an important aspect is overlooked and that is the attention that needs to be paid to the role played in one's development by strict isolated concentration. In the Montessori philosophy great stress is laid on the possibility of encounter, but almost none on the problem of the encounter. Loners and the more introverted children don't get on so well in that system.

That's obvious enough and there are a lot of people who have to get along as best as they can in that system. I've always been told that there's nothing more infuriating than being expected to finish off your house by yourself. There is certainly a germ of truth in that. It's the price you pay for the Montessori philosophy. I've also often been accused of making too great a demand on people's own inventiveness.

If we now look at the problem from an architectural point of view, doesn't your attempt to achieve a neutral structure come from a passion for space as a stage where social behaviour can have free play?

I used to think that space was a such a vague notion that nobody knew what it really meant. But I've changed my mind now. Space is the ideal concept, perhaps just because you can't define it. Spatial organisation, the idea that things are well placed vis-à-vis each other, that you have achieved the right perspectives, the right distances, the right measurements, and that within them you correctly expressed the needs of the group of people who will work in that building, the longer I work the more that becomes a definite principle. If I say space, I already mean public space and public space is the place where changes can take place. I once said that the street is the space for revolution. Revolution can't take place without the street. The street is a public living room; it is where people change the situation *together*. But the mass media have largely taken over the street now.

What about your famous indoor streets; is there something that needs changing there?

You do of course wonder what it means to talk about the public domain inside a building. I am of course entirely aware of the fact that life in the city consists of more than just borrowing sugar from your neighbour. It makes no sense to try and turn an indoor street into a sort of village. But a covered walkway in a block of flats can mean that people don't lie dead in their flats for weeks, without their neighbours noticing. You can look after each other's kids or borrow coffee or sugar. There's nothing so special about that, and I am also well aware of the dangers of too much social control. But I do think that a city that is entirely based on anonymity works less well a) because you don't borrow sugar from each other and b) because it is more dangerous. All those places where you are free to be anonymous are also places where you can get mugged or raped.

One big problem at the moment is the notion of public space in the city. Currently an enormous confusion prevails on this subject; you won't find anyone who'll give you a definition of the public domain that goes beyond public facilities or public security. Architecture or city planning should at least be able to do something about that. But that still leaves untouched an enormous area of what in a social, political and aesthetic sense might be thought of as the public domain. How is it that nobody talks about that any more, when you'd think that from the point of view of intellectual debate it would be the most interesting aspect?

The failure of socially committed architecture was bread and butter for the next generation of architects. It was stated that architects had no influence whatsoever on human behaviour. What they really meant was: let architecture just confine itself to building pretty objects in between all the other objects. Of course that is a dreadfully defeatist attitude, but if you open your mouth and say that architects can do something more, then they ask you to give them some examples. Maybe I'm a special case, but I actually can offer some examples, for instance the amphitheatre-like inner areas of the Apollo primary schools in Amsterdam. Currently, however, it is not fashionable to mention something like that. I think that architects at present are simply disillusioned and just leave it at that. They are all incredibly worried that their colleagues will laugh at them. They are afraid of being thought of as being too cosy, a fear that was fostered by people like Carel Weeber. He had a powerful argument there. But cosiness in fact is nothing more than

'Public domain', Montessori School, Amsterdam, 1983

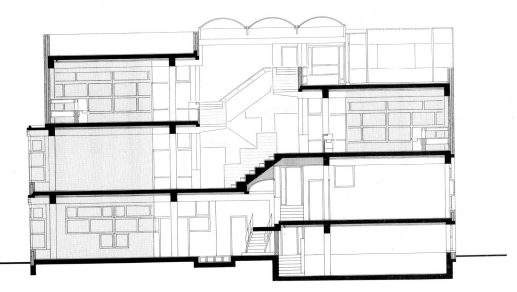

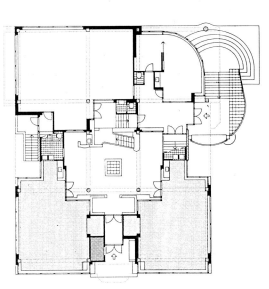

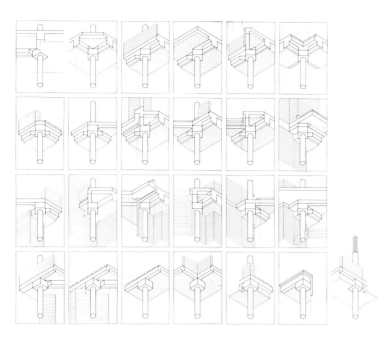

Ministry of Social Affairs and Employment, The Hague, 1991

300

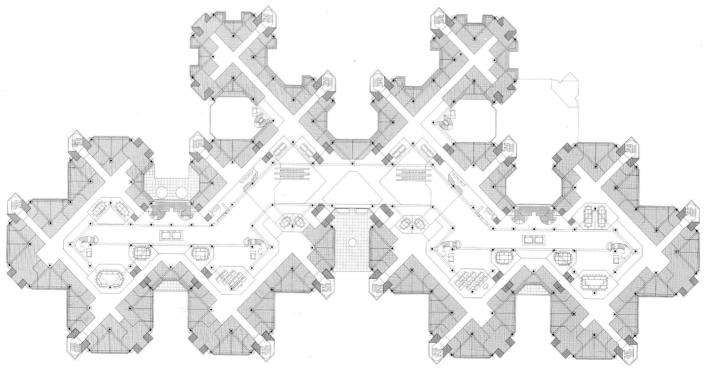

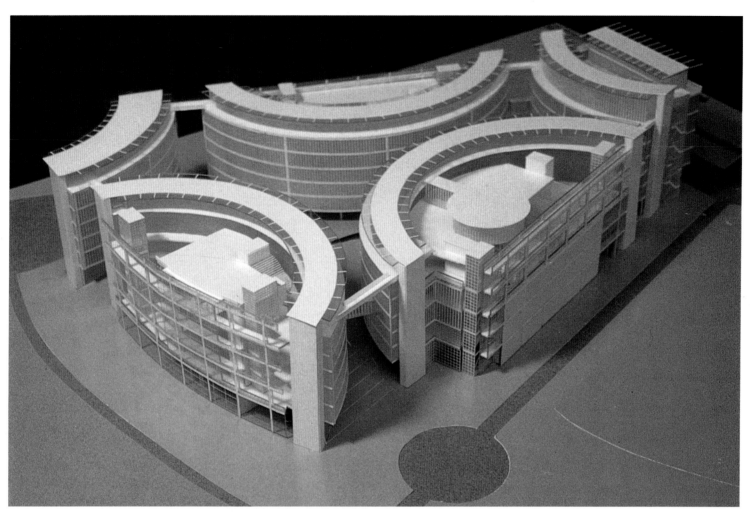

Media Park Cologne, competition entry, 1991

Sony Tower, competition entry, Berlin, 1993

the Dutch spirit that found its supreme expression in the Delft school and that has always existed everywhere. In that respect Carel Weeber has made a number of pretty demagogic statements so making sure that the whole matter acquired negative associations. The fact that you make road humps and try and build better play areas is now enough to earn you the reputation of being petty bourgeois. **What used to be called a sense of social concern is now regarded as paternalism** with the result that a good quality has suddenly become something negative, even though of course there definitely is a moment when social concern does turn into paternalism. But every attempt at social intervention has become suspect through a fear of being thought paternalistic and that's why nobody dares to burn his fingers any more by bothering about the question of public space.

You are now talking about how public space should be used, but there is also something that quite literally towers above all that, and that is the façade that partially determines the image of the city and that is an important function. In the Employment Ministry building the (bureaucratic) labyrinth of the ministry is expressed in the public areas through the metaphorical power of the façade. But you don't seem to bother so much about the urban context that is, after all, the recipient of that message.

Centraal Beheer, office space, Apeldoorn, 1972

With the Ministry of Employment building, I was given a remote place where there was hardly any suggestion of a street. That was why I put the street inside the building. As a result the street cannot fully be called a public space, but when 2000 people walk around in it, it becomes a public area in a way. Other people are allowed to use it; they are fairly open-minded as far as that goes. Even so this street is not entirely successful. There are features that are small and medium-sized, but I have omitted to include anything that is large-scale. I have now realised that I also wanted to include something really large-scale. That would have given it a monumental effect, not for the sake of being monumental but rather to get rid of the dichotomy between large and small. These only become really interesting concepts at the point when both large and small are absent. But in a building or a part of the city where both small and large measurements are well represented, it makes no sense at all to use terms such as large-scale or small; they don't mean anything then. To return to the main question of how it is that the designing of public space is no longer a theme that we are currently interested in: my view is that that's because we've got nothing to celebrate, unlike, say, Oriol Bohigas, with his project for new city squares after the death of Franco. There is something else that we can learn from Barcelona and that is that where everything is organised in a comparatively authoritarian way, the space for non-authoritarian structures can be designed in an authoritarian way. In our situation where everything is anti-authoritarian but is often also terribly bureaucratised, it's no longer possible actually to make anything new. We need people who are capable of exercising authority and of giving a lead in building beautiful public spaces.

Barcelona is a good example of a government policy that gives priority to the notion of harmonious open spaces being public living rooms. But in the work of Libeskind or Koolhaas you see that the notion of the public domain itself becomes a theme in terms of its fragmentation and because it no longer has any clear place within the paradigm of the democratic exchange of ideas. They employ another means to get out of the impasse, a method that gives pride of place to what is fragmentary and random. This could be another way of escaping the current malaise in urban design, and also one that is perhaps easier for the individual designer to achieve, if we agree that there's nothing to celebrate.

If urban design no longer has as its hallmark the principles of consensus, that doesn't mean it has automatically to be conceived of in so narrow a way; I have to admit I am suspicious of this tendency. As far as Koolhaas is concerned I haven't yet noticed deviations of this sort in his practice; just think of the IJ-Plein in North Amsterdam, that is in fact quite perfectly organised.

Libeskind is of course a completely different type. Even though he makes intellectual leaps that you lose track of, as a person he is easy to understand. I get the idea with Libeskind that he landed in this world as a nomad, that he has never had any roots, does not know where he belongs, and that means he is first and foremost a cosmopolitan. Our great strength – which is also a weakness – is that we have our roots in a country that is highly – perhaps too highly – organised, and which is wealthy enough to give everyone an opportunity. With the result of course as far as that goes that we inevitably end up being placed in a certain mental category.

But apart from the fact that his personality is so fascinating and intriguing, he also wants to deduce general conclusions from his cosmopolitanism. He claims that his view of the world, his theory are valid for everybody in the West, for humanity that has been uprooted ever since the holocaust.

That's just his projection. There isn't any consensus on that and to say that there is is repressive. The fact that he wants to impose a consensus on us comes of course from the fact that he is a moralist and wants to convince us of his point of view; as an artist too he feels obliged to bear witness.

That's not so idiosyncratic; after all, he has allies among the philosophers, Levinas, for instance, and among the architects, someone like Eisenman.

I see what you're getting at! Van Eyck's 'between' and the 'between' of Eisenman. I'm not much of an intellectual but I think that I shouldn't have much problem explaining the similarities and the differences between them. Theoretically speaking the differences are not so great; they're both concerned with an area where various things overlap, only Van Eyck of course gives it a human content while Eisenman certainly doesn't. He borrows a lot from Jacques Derrida. I'm not such an expert on Derrida but, as I understand him, Libeskind's concept of being *displaced* tallies perfectly with his notion that no single point can be seen as the centre. But to suggest that you can use this to make a public space that no longer has anything to do with democracy but only with the fragmentation of society, I've yet to be convinced of that.

And Eisenman's generalisation about the Jewish Diaspora, in which deconstructivist architecture is a reflection of the fate that is in store for all of us, don't you see anything in that?

It doesn't make any sense to me, architecture having that level of meaning. What I'd like to know is how Libeskind is actually going to make a real building. If he takes himself seriously he'd maybe better do just that. Because once he starts to make a building, he will have to think about its foundations whether he likes it or not. You can't duck the need for foundations! He also has the idea of designing the void. According to me you can't design the void; what you design is always space; the most you can do is to build it in a shaky or inadequate fashion and then it will indeed look more like a void than like a space.

Your space is something you can enter. It is a stage where activity can take place, while Libeskind's emptiness is something that you can quarrel with. In his extension to the Berlin Museum for instance, what you get is a structural line consisting of voids, a negative space that is a component part of the whole building. Where these voids and the main route intersect, you bump into something that isn't there.

In my view he is completely wrong when he says that his spaces are based on the ratios of Schönberg's *Moses and Aaron*. That just doesn't make sense! You can't compare these things with each other and the fact that he's working on something like that is proof for me that when he comes to carry out his project he'll be faced with enormous conflicts. What you often see right now is a confusion between the representation of the space, the models and drawings, with the space itself. The representation becomes an end in itself, a sort of art form that can be so fantastically beautiful that it undercuts its own market, because in reality it can't ever be built that perfectly. You would do far better to keep your presentation a little businesslike so that when the thing is built people don't feel let down by the reality. I'm afraid that the direction people are heading now is just the opposite. It'll take a real architect to realise in practice the picture you get in that fantastic presentation. After everything he has said, Libeskind runs a great risk that we'll end up asking if that was all he meant.

With Koolhaas you could say that what he eventually builds is a little disappointing, after the fantastic concepts that he's come up with, but I think that he manages to pull the fat out of the fire. The Danstheater in The Hague is surely the perfect example of how, despite a limited budget and other considerable obstacles, one can succeed in making a genuinely surprising space in which the reality contains a vision that tallies with the original design. Koolhaas does not just write splendid scenarios; he is enough of an architect to see them through in practice.

But whether Libeskind will succeed I'm not sure. That's why I think that everybody who claims to have something to say and who also claims to be an architect, should straightaway be given the chance to build something. **For me the built result has primacy over the theory.**

I don't say that the philosophical theory should amount to less than a number of stones piled on top of each other, but **at a certain point I think that people who philosophise about architecture ought to try piling stones on top of each other instead of just words.**

303

Forest of Wallers, spectators waiting for cyclists in Paris-Roubaix

Our Culture is in Need of an Art of Exposure

Richard Sennett

One difference between the Greek past and the present is that whereas the ancients could use their eyes in the city to think about political, religious, and erotic experiences, modern culture suffers from a divide between the inside and the outside. It is a divide between subjective and worldly experience, self and city. Moreover, our culture is marked by hard struggle whenever people seek to make inner life concrete. This sets us off not just from our own origins but also from non-European cultures nearer in time whose masks, dances, ceremonials, shrines, sacred grounds, and cosmologies connect subjective life to physical things.

This divide between inner, subjective experience and outer, physical life expresses in fact a great fear which our civilisation has refused to admit, much less to reckon. The spaces full of people in the modern city are either spaces limited to and carefully orchestrating consumption, like the shopping mall, or spaces limited to and carefully orchestrating the experience of tourism. This reduction and trivialising of the city as a stage of life is no accident. Beyond all the economic and demographic reasons for the neutralised city there exists a profound, indeed 'spiritual' reason why people are willing to tolerate such a bland scene for their lives. The way cities look reflects a great, unreckoned fear of exposure. 'Exposure' more connotes the likelihood of being hurt than of being stimulated. The fear of exposure is in one way a militarised conception of everyday experience, as though attack-and-defence is as apt a model of subjective life as it is of warfare. What is characteristic of our city-building is to wall off the differences between people, assuming that these differences are more likely to be mutually threatening than mutually stimulating. What we make in the urban realm are therefore bland, neutralising spaces, spaces which remove the threat of social contact: street walls faced in sheets of plate glass, highways that cut off poor neighbourhoods from the rest of the city, dormitory housing developments.

304 *Our culture is in need of an art of exposure; this art will not make us one another's victims, rather more balanced adults, capable of coping with and learning from complexity.*

The wall between inner and outer life arose in part from our religious history: Christianity set Western culture upon the course that built a wall between the inner and outer experience. The shadows cast by that wall continue to darken secular society. Moreover, attempts to unify the inner and outer dimensions simply by tearing down the wall, making the inner and outer one organic whole, have not proved successful; unity can be gained only at the price of complexity.

The exposed, outer life of the city cannot be simply a reflection of inner life. Exposure occurs in crowds and among strangers. The cultural problem of the modern city is how to make this impersonal milieu speak, how to relieve its current blandness, its neutrality, whose origin can be traced back to the belief that the outside world of things is unreal. Our urban problem is how to revive the reality of the outside as a dimension of human experience.

Our culture is in need of an art of exposure; this art will not make us one another's victims, rather more balanced adults, capable of coping with and learning from complexity.

A city ought to be a school for learning how to lead a centred life. Through exposure to others, we might learn how to weigh what is important and what is not. We need to see differences on the streets or in other people neither as threats nor as sentimental invitations, rather as necessary visions. They are necessary for us to learn how to navigate life with balance, both individually and collectively.

The belief that the interior is the true scene for inner life is a legacy, in secular society, of an older Christian ideal. But now this interior space of the soul has become a space for a new kind of inner life. The home has come to seem so necessary a refuge because of the modern secular idea of human character: that it is malleable, and that its most significant moulding moments happen early in the life cycle. To mould a young human being, you must protect it from destructive outside influences. This belief, self-evident to us, was not at all self-evident to earlier ages, who practised what would seem to us a shocking disregard of the young. The fact that so many children died in the *ancien regime* before reaching adulthood had tended to mute intense feelings about them. With improvements in child care and through

Richard Sennett

medical advances like vaccination, it became less emotionally dangerous to care intensely about one's children. And economics dictated that one do so. In ages governed by the inheritance of property and place, bloodlines are how the family relations are impressed upon property, position, and power. Ruskin's was an age in which inheritance of social position and property had cracked apart; it was instead animated by entrepreneurial striving; the formation of that strength of aggressive, tough character in the male child was an urgent matter. Moreover, the length of time that both boys and girls seemed to need in order to develop themselves stretched out from ten years to twenty. The time of childhood was divided, like the space of the house, ever more elaborately. All the stages of human development seemed, by the time Freud wrote, to proceed in a gradual unfolding, physical, mental and psychological, each step consequent for the future.

The notion that character develops and reveals itself in an interior marked by the division of labour spoke logically in the nineteenth century from the new importance placed on childhood development; partitioned shelter was necessary for this prolonged, difficult, perilous process. By contrast, the mixed confusions of a crowd, a street, a smoke-filled bar, seemed no place for the protracted process of developing a baby into an adult. The stimulations of the street lacked the sequential order of the rooms of a house. Self-development and the exposure to the city's differences thus became opposed in visual terms: the linear, interior order of unfolding, distinct scenes as in a railroad flat, versus the outside chaos, the

street like a collage; the shelter of the sequential versus exposure to the synchronous. We still see in terms of these oppositions. In sum, the *émigration intérieure* was a voluntary withdrawal dictated by dislike of a shoddy, materialistic society.

Rockefeller Center does not prompt the word that comes easily to mind in looking at much modern architecture. Rockefeller Center is not 'inhuman.' It is not experienced as a space of domination, it is not perceived by New Yorkers as a space of power. This much-loved ensemble instead arouses a sense of comfort. It is by walking from the deadly stillness of Rockefeller Center's side streets at midnight into the noise and hustle of Sixth Avenue that one feels suddenly exposed and vulnerable, even though the dark side streets are in fact more dangerous than the swarming open spaces around the nearby bars and hotels. What is most important about this space is that it is empty. This visual emptiness arouses a peculiar sensation of authority.

The space of authority, in Western culture, has developed as a space of precision: that is the guidance it gives to others. In the Christian cities were to be found the root of the desire for legibility that Kevin Lynch celebrated. Those who have dreamed Ruskin's dream or followed in the path of the first *émigrés intérieure* sought for this legibility in a domestic interior. Its sequence of spaces was to provide moral orientation: in a home, adults were to be disciplined in the same way as children in their rooms, trained how and where to separate the functioning of their bodies from contact with other people; how to make

?! *This reasoning might still serve modern architecture, but it doesn't seem to apply to the abundance of forms in the language of post-modern architecture. Here we might draw a parallel with the weakening of Protestant tradition, since the economy of production with the highly valued thrift has been replaced by a consumption society with inherent prodigality. Protestant economy pertaining to money and imagery turns into the rebirth of the carnival. In contemporary (European) cities we see excessive tendencies toward the realm of the museum; the narrative, so much valued by you, is being staged for the sake of (tourist) sales only. So, narrative space, advocated by you, becomes an instrument of power as well.*

love in the silence and darkness of a room furnished to that end; how to behave when received into a parlour as opposed to a more informal sitting room. It might be said that those who sought to interiorise attempted to build a space of authority for themselves, and they failed.

Sacred interiors were spaces of the Word, of confession and prayer, of submission to God, who would, as Augustine first promised, protect his children. Precision and charity, definition and refuge were indissoluble. Today the secular space of authority is empty; it looks like the side streets of Rockefeller Center. The visual forms of legibility in urban designs or space no longer suggest much about subjective life or heal the wounds of those in need. The sanctuary of the Christian city has been reduced to a sense of comfort in well-designed places where other people do not intrude. Safe because empty; safe because clearly marked. Authority is divorced from community; this is the conundrum of sanctuary as it has evolved in the city. Any New Yorker looks at this conundrum when passing the city's most famous landmark, across from Rockefeller Center. The cultural problems of the city are conventionally taken to be its impersonality, its alienating scale, its coldness. There is no more in these charges than is first apparent. *Impersonality*, *coldness*, and *emptiness* are essential words in the Protestant language of environment; they express a desire to see outside as null, lacking value. They are words that express a certain interest in seeing; the perception of outer emptiness reinforces the value of turning within. But that old unhappiness has left its residue as a certain practice of visual denial, as the acceptance of sensory denial in everyday life to be normal. More than normal – reassuring. Nothing as important as the inner struggle to account. Therefore, one can deal with the outside in purely instrumental, manipulative terms, since nothing outside 'really' matters. In this modulated form, neutrality becomes an instrument of power.**?!**

There is, today, a disturbing sign that the organic, enlightened attitudes do not lead to embracing complexity. We find this in the very fact that many modern planners who subscribe to the organic ideal in cultural terms have given up on visual planning. These planners perceive that architects are absorbed in making signature buildings like designer clothes; they detest modern architects who often put more emphasis on stunning forms than flexible forms adapted to human uses. These planners point out that parts of New York are beginning to look like a fashion parade of styles in glass shirts, brick shoes, and steel hats. In the same way making mega-plans for mega-buildings seems antisocial, this tyranny of definition (whose roots go back to the medieval city) involved in planning on a grand scale. Therefore these planners focus on 'communication'.

The substitution of verbal communication for visual definition echoes with an eighteenth-century ideal of unity. The planners who focus on making people talk about goals, mutual difficulties, and everyday frustrations seek to create communal solidarity. Their hope is that a sense of unity and common resolve will appear among people who have undergone endless nights of talk in rooms furnished with plastic furniture and lit with strong fluorescent light, the participants having drunk too much watery coffee out of papers cups and struggled to keep awake when it is not their turn to talk. Few planners who have pursued this path in the last generation would want to argue that 'the people' best know their own needs; whether or not that is true, it is beside the point. In a society threatened by passivity and withdrawal, to encourage ordinary citizens to talk about social realities is to make the speakers care about one another, or so it is hoped. The old educators would have recognised in this new attitude to 'communication' their values of cultivation and *Bildung*. The point of this verbally-oriented planning is also organic: to achieve solidarity through talk.

The wholeness the Enlightened man looked for he too sought to hear; he believed in the beneficent powers of freely flowing discourse; his coffeehouse (these places were only for men) was where he sought to hear unity. There was a reason for this talk. People came to find out what was happening in the city; a Londoner or Parisian in search of news went in search of coffee. Any stranger had the right to sit and join in the talk, the room awash in tobacco smoke but not in alcohol fumes, as 'libations' were thought to slow the tongue rather than loosen it. The coffeehouses of the Enlightenment were the places where political parties met; these chatting rooms were the original seats of insurance companies like Lloyd's of London, whose members needed to know everything to calculate their risks. Planners of 'communication' are in search of some kind of modern replacement for the coffeehouse.

The Christian city put great value on the inside – on shelter within buildings as on inner experiences.

The Enlightenment city sought to take people outside but on to fields and forests rather than streets filled with jostling crowds. If the Christian pilgrim had difficulty relating his faith in God to the parade of human differences on a street, so the Enlightened planner found it difficult to reconcile his faith in nature with an urban crowd. The reason the polarities matter today is because of what lies in between. Our society is subject to enormously varied and complex stimuli in economic, political, and erotic life. Yet both the codes of inwardness and unity which have shaped our culture make it difficult to cope with the facts of diversity. We have trouble understanding the experience of difference as a positive human value.

This general difficulty is particularly urgent among those who are engaged in urban and architectural design. The planners who have devoted themselves to Enlightened forms of 'communication' work are experts in *Gemeinschaft*. In the face of larger differences in the city they tend to withdraw to the local, intimate, communal scale. Those who work visually and at a larger scale find it as difficult to organise diverse urban scenes as did the younger John Wood. The modern planner lacks visual precepts for how races might be mixed in public places, or how to orchestrate the zoning and design of streets so that economically mixed uses work well. It is equally obscure how to design house projects and schools that mix races, classes, or ages. Human diversity seems something beyond the powers of human design.

The Enlightenment bequeathed a peculiar, indeed surprising legacy to the modern world which has compounded this difficulty. The Enlightened ideal of wholeness has passed into the modern definition of the integrity of well-made things. Thus a conflict has arisen between buildings and people; the value of a building as a form is at odds with the value of a building in use. This conflict appears in some simple ways. It seems wrong to alter or change an old building with an addition at the side or new windows, because these changes seem to destroy the 'integrity' of the original object. Changing historical needs are seen as threats to the integrity of the original form, as though time were a source of impurity. Groups dedicated to urban preservation sometimes speak, indeed, of a city as though it ought to be a museum of buildings, rather than a site for the necessarily messy business of living.

308 *Both the codes of inwardness and unity which have shaped our culture make it difficult to cope with the facts of diversity. We have trouble understanding the experience of difference as a positive human value.*

The way buildings are constructed now contributes to this conflict. Buildings now are much less flexible in form than the rows, crescents, and blocks of the past. The life span of a modern skyscraper is meant to be forty or fifty years, though steel skeletons could stand much longer; service stacks, wiring, and plumbing are planned so that a building is serviceable only in terms of what it was originally intended for. It is much harder to convert a modern office tower to mixed uses of offices and apartments than it is to convert a nineteenth-century factory or eighteenth-century row-block to these uses. In this shortened time frame, the 'integrity of form' acquires a special meaning. The original programme for a building controls its brief lifetime of use. The physical urban fabric has thus become more rigid and brittle.

Our eighteenth-century ancestors never meant to bring a world of brittle buildings into being; nor, in the making of buildings, as in the making of constitutions, did they believe there was anything sacred about original intentions and first forms. They wanted, instead, the open window to arouse the public's enthusiasm. But in time the enthusiasm aroused by experiences of unity between inside and outside subsided; 'unity' came to refer to what objects were in *themselves*. The Enlightenment bequeathed to us the anti-social building, its visual values expected uses and changing needs. This is the unexpected consequence of the search for organic unity of form.***?!***

The architecture that Sigfried Giedion celebrated, for example, is embedded in a tragic irony. The pursuit of the whole has revived the religious break between the spiritual and the worldly. The art of Mies van der Rohe is an art marking this divorce, and it is great art, greater certainly than the work of architects who have made a more conscious effort to reckon with their surroundings. It is forged from the architect's power to see coherence, to create unities, but these powers have passed across the fatal divide in our culture in which the whole becomes the self-sufficient, in which it achieves its integrity through becoming a thing unto itself. They arouse in others an intimate of absence, of untouchableness. This is our experience of the sublime. This religion of art is a faith fatal to those who design environments. For

?! *If you really want design to express this diversity, design indeed fails. But, regarding design as a means to absorb diversity, contemporary metropolitan environment might just as well be deemed a success. In the cacophony of opinions, design needs to be non-specific lest nobody feels excluded. In terms of Edward Hall, this implies the necessity of distemic space, supported even by socio-biological arguments. To you, the mix in public space is a need; to others it is a horror. Does your criticism of the integrity of closed buildings relate to the socio-cultural necessity of distemy?*

?! Just briefly, why do we need to appreciate the experience of difference? Doesn't knowledge of difference suffice?

the consequence of this faith is an even greater indifference to the everyday needs of people using buildings, an indifference to use equal to the negligence of Christian otherworldliness. The integrity of an object conflicts with the needs of generation after generation who must somehow contrive to live in it. The story the work of Mies van der Rohe tells, at its most troubling, is that what makes for great art no longer makes for conscience. Unity has lost its moral meaning.

New York should be the ideal city of exposure to the outside. It grasps the imagination because it is a city of differences par excellence, a city collecting its population from all over the world. Yet it is here that the passion of the Parisian poet – that desire for enhancement of stimulation and release from self – seems contravened. By walking in the middle of New York one is immersed in the differences of this most diverse of cities, but precisely because the scenes are disengaged they seem unlikely to offer themselves as significant encounters in the sense of a vivid stimulus, a telling moment of talking or touching or connection. The leather fetishist and spice merchant are protected by disengagement; the admirable women who have made lives for themselves near Gramercy Park are also disengaged, not those needy sort of Americans who feel they must tell you the entire story of their lives in the next five minutes; the junkies doing business are seldom in a mood to chat. All the more is this true – more largely – of the races, who live segregated lives close together, and of social classes, who mix but do not socialise. Nor are the chameleon virtues of the Chicago urbanists much in evidence: people do not take on the colours of their surroundings, the light-hued colours of otherness. A walk in New York reveals instead that difference from and indifference to others are a related, unhappy pair. The eye sees differences to which it reacts with indifference. **?!** This reaction of disengagement when immersed in difference is the result of the forces that have created a disjunction between inner and outer life. These forces have annihilated the humane value of complexity, even in a city where differences are an overwhelming sociological fact. Sheer exposure to difference is no corrective to the Christian ills of inwardness. There is withdrawal

What is characteristic of our city-building is to wall off the differences between people, assuming that these differences are more likely to be mutually threatening than mutually stimulating. What we make in the urban realm are therefore bland, neutralising spaces, spaces which remove the threat of social contact: street walls faced in sheets of plate glass, highways that cut off poor neighbourhoods from the rest of the city, dormitory housing developments.

and fear of exposure, as though all differences are potentially as explosive as those between a drug dealer and an ordinary citizen. There is neutralisation: if something begins to disturb or touch me, I need only keep walking to stop feeling. Moreover, I suffer from abundance, the promised remedy of the Enlightenment. My senses are flooded by images, but the difference in value between one image and another becomes as fleeting as my own movement; difference becomes a mere parade of variety. This display of difference on the street obeys the same visual logic, moreover, that ruled the construction of the first Modern interiors. These scenes are sequential and linear displays of differences, like the rooms in a railroad flat. Linear, sequential distinctions are no more arousing outside than they were inside. A New York street resembles the studio of a painter who has assembled in it all the paints, books of other artists, and sketches he will need for a grand triptych that will crown his career; then the painter has unaccountably left town.

Writers like Hannah Arendt and James Baldwin represent two poles of response to indifference. At one pole the subjective world is shunted aside so that people can speak to each other directly, resolutely, politically. At the other pole subjective life undergoes a transformation so that a person turns outward, is aroused by the presence of strangers and arouses them. That transformation requires the mobilising of certain artistic energies in everyday life.

The Renaissance man and woman literally saw time take shape in everyday life in the city; these shapes corroded human effort, as in the clock and clock-labour, or threatened the city, as in the cannon and its relation to the safety offered by the city's walls. The people who lived through the advent of these inventions deduced a new force beyond their control: *Fortuna*. Their lives came to be a struggle against the machine goddess of time. More than the forms of the star-shape city or the empty volume of the square in which a public clock has been placed, it is the character of their struggle that speaks to the present. If Le Corbusier's celebration of gleaming machines was foolish, a more humane kind of form-making – one like Leger's – has to acknowledge that in using and fragmenting and pasting together forms, the maker of them is engaged in a spiritual struggle against him or herself. It is a struggle against the human power to annihilate through regulatory order, to be sure; but if and when one wins this struggle, a person makes things of no permanent value, no ultimate worth, only present meaning. This humane, limited value occupies, as it were, only a small corner of our imaginative and intellectual powers – the humane construction is a small building in a larger city of beliefs, truths, regularities, clarities, and guarantees. The humane is so much less than what people are capable of. That is what we are struggling for – not fulfillment but to be less than we could be. **?!** Against the regulation of time in space, I will therefore propose another form for time in space, which I shall call narrative space – a more limited relation of time and space than the grand unity Sigfried Giedion sought, but one capable of guiding more humane urban design. Spaces can become full of time when they permit certain properties of narratives to operate in everyday life. I will try to show how the narrative properties of space give value to two elements in the city, walls and borders. The experiencing of these elements as narrative scenes is not very satisfying, not very fulfilling, yet embodies humane cultural values.

How, then, to return to the original question about invention and discovery, does a planner invent ambiguity and the possibility of surprise? He or she needs to think in terms of what visually will make for a narrative beginning. To create the sense of beginning, a radical change will have to occur in the framework of urban design. The change must take two forms: a change in the way urban open space is dealt with and a change in the way buildings are made. The open space issue is a matter of boundaries. A boundary cannot serve as wall, because this kind of enclosure is literally deadly: the life of the enclosed place ends when the designer lays down his or her pen. Time begins to do the work of giving places character when the places are not used as they were meant to be. For instance, just as children make the loading docks serve as playgrounds, adults on Fourteenth Street appropriate parking strips for sociable spaces. For the person who engages in this unanticipated use, something 'begins' in a narrative sense. To permit space to become thus encoded with time, the urbanist has to design weak borders rather than strong walls. For instance, a planner hoping to encourage the narrative use of places would seek to lift the burden of fixed zoning from the city as much as possible, zoning lines between work and residential districts, or between industrial and office workplaces. An architect seeking to create a building possessed on narrative power would seek one whose forms were capable of serving many programmes. This means spaces whose construction is simple enough to permit constant alteration; walls of brick are such weak boundaries, walls of plate glass are not. In a novel the beginning erases and effaces; space also comes to life in the present tense by being used to erase and efface – by acts of displacement. **?!** Faced with the fact of social hostility in the city, the planner's impulse in the real world is to seal off conflicting or dissonant sides, to build internal walls rather than permeable borders. Highways and automobile traffic, for instance, are used to subdivide different social territories in the city; the river of racing machines is so swift and thick that crossing from one territory to the other becomes virtually impossible. Similarly, functional disaggregation has become a technique for sealing borders; the shopping mall that is far from tracts of housing, the school on its own campus, the factory hidden in an industrial park. These techniques, which originated in the garden city planning movement to create a peaceful, orderly suburb, are now increasingly used in the city centre to remove the threat of classes or races touching, to create a city of secure inner walls.

The borders in fiction show what is lost in urban planning of open space by treating borders as though they were walls. People who live in sealed communities are diminished in their development. The wounds of past experience, the stereotypes which have become rooted in memory, are not confronted. Recognition scenes that might occur at borders are the only chance people have to confront fixed, sociological pictures routinised in time. It is only in crossing a boundary when people can see others as if for the first time. This experience of displacement and resistance we have in art and lack in urban design. The legacy of the Renaissance experience of time and space is an unexpected one: the humanism of the Renaissance suggests that the sense of 'natality' of which Hannah Arendt speaks, that same desire for present-tense life appearing in the designs of Le Corbusier and Leger, depends upon understanding the relation between places and events as in a narrative, a narrative fashioned around transgression and recognition, a narrative which evolves as people cross borders. The planner of a modern, humane city will overlay differences rather than segment them, and for the same reason. Overlays are also a way to

?! Don't you take it too far? The narrative you advocate seems to be restricted to space and the demarcation of that space. Wouldn't the narrative be more profound if the architect himself manipulates the programmes; especially since you feel that architecture should embrace the programme as flexible as possible? In other words: could your proposal transcend the domain of representation and deal with the content of its programme directly?

?! When a culture is swamped by 'awareness-campaigns' (Environment, Racism, Aids, Sexual harassment, The Other at large), one experiences a growing desire to transform this awareness into a sense of meaning: a condition in which the various 'awarenesses' stop the infighting for the public's goodwill in order to provide this awareness with a certain ring of self-evidence. How can we transform your plea from a sacrosanct endeavour into a naturally operational notion of the other?

A. Bonnema, Headquarters Nationale Nederlanden insurance company, Rotterdam, 1992

PI de Bruijn, House of Parliament, The Hague, 1992

form complex, open borders. Displacement rather than linearity is a humane prescription. This connection between the visual and the social focuses on the experience of limits; it is not, however, an ethos of weakness. Rather, Hannah Arendt's affirmation of the virtue of impersonality, the frustrations of catharsis and identity which appear in James Baldwin's essay *The Fire Next Time*, Serlio's invention of a scene of tragic limits, Leger's painting of the limits of how long things last, the restlessness of the outdoor pilgrimage planned by Sixtus V – all these point to a certain form that life can take in the dimension of the outside, an engagement with difference, an acceptance of impermanence and chance. The Christian dimensions must today be reversed in their value. The inside has come to be a destructive dimension; to flee within, in search of the permanent, the precise, and the guaranteed, is destructive. The outside could be the constructive dimension, as Baudelaire hoped. What the humanist tradition makes clear is that something like a tragic space will give the outside its constructive life, rather than this life coming from the relieving, urbane pleasures sketched by Constantin Guys, or the pleasures of leafy wholeness which animated the age of Thomas Jefferson. Against the expression of the permanent and the precise, the immediate and the imperfect: a contrast between sacred and secular vision. This secular vision implies as well a certain way of making the things which are to be exposed.

The artistic creations of ambiguity challenge what seems a humane idea of relationship in urban design, the idea of designing in context. A design made in the context of other designs seems a sociable creation; it refers to the buildings around it. Quite modest acts of design can make this friendly gesture. In renovating a row of townhouses, for instance, one might keep the doors that were originally used while changing the windows that give directly onto the street, since ground floors work differently now than three or four generations ago. In adding new buildings, one might keep to the height of old ones, even though one does not keep to the same register of floor heights or windows. Such designing in context is like the work that goes on in a live street, a matter of negotiating and balancing. Its principle is change by mutation. In the awareness of differences of time expressed in space, in the respect for what others have done, *context* seems the key word in thinking of how to design a city of difference. Yet spaces regulated according to these gentle principles are not arousing the way an Avedon photograph or Ashbery poem is. Life on the modern street involves the capacity to provoke uncertainty, as well as to account gently the presence of others. This is the art of exposure.

I have used the words 'tragic' and 'humane' to evoke certain qualities of experience. These qualities have to do with the relations people sense among themselves once they are no longer protected, once they are outside. The life of a street is the urban scene par excellence for this exposure, it becomes a humane scene simply when people begin to look around and adjust their behaviour in terms of what they see – a scene of mutual awareness. **?!** But this awareness can have, as we have traced it, a deeper structure. Turning outward implies a renunciation of certain impulses to wholeness and completion in oneself. Turning outward visually can also lead to renouncing wholeness and completion, or lead instead to another order of probing, restless vision; this is the story first told in the Renaissance when perspectival vision was applied to the making of streets. Turning outward can lead to ways of seeing which make of the fragmented and the discontinuous a moral condition. The attractions of wholeness which are nearest us in time are those of the Enlightenment, but the pleasures of this age seem today much more distant, more foreign, than the sufferings of a much more ancient religious culture. All that is left of Enlightenment wholeness is the affirmation of the integrity of artistic objects, these plans and buildings which have acquired rights against those who must use and inhabit them.

Action without the need of completion, action without domination and mastery: these are the ideals of a humane culture. In the very rejection of the cathartic event; the moment of fulfilment, these ideals might seem to lack an essential dimension of tragedy, which is its heroic scale. Heroic tragedy appears in the Greek dramatists, in Shakespeare or Dostoevsky. The limits on a person's control of the world stand revealed in this struggle. Tragedy can also be experienced as something 'far less grand and mythic but more pervasive immediate and intimate'.★ John Keats defined the more immediate experience of tragic vision, in a letter to his brother, as 'negative capability': 'when a man is capable of being in uncertainties, mysteries, doubts, without any irritable reaching after fact and reason.' On a heroic scale, tragedy consists in knowledge of self-limits gained searingly and in great pain; on Keats's more immediate scale, it implies knowledge that comes not through defeat, but rather in paying attention, contemplating differences.

★ Shoben, Edward Joseph Jr., *Lionel Trilling*, New York 1981, p. 216.

311

Tomorrow Can take Care of Itself

A Conversation with Jean Nouvel

Sören Kierkegaard once said:

'It is true what the philosophers tell us, that life can only be understood in retrospect. But they generally forget another law: that it can only be lived in a forward direction. It will be clear to anyone who thinks about this that life can never really be understood in the context of time, quite simply because I don't have a single moment of the peace I need to understand life in retrospect.'

With this statement he laid the foundations of Existentialism that would later be such a decisive influence on the philosophy of the twentieth century. In the end the only things that count are one's acts. In this respect Jean Nouvel – who usually wears black – has proved himself a genuine Parisian. Few architects at present have been so eager to play the role of committed intellectual in the ongoing cultural debate, even if Nouvel's commitment is distinctly depoliticised. As an architect Nouvel is capable of talking back to the culture, and of presenting his work as something more than just an illustration of the culture. The high quality of Nouvel's discourse makes it a part of a cultural debate that is way above the normal level one gets in a highly specialised discipline like architecture. (Nouvel does however have the sense to realise that as an architect you had better not put on too many airs if only for reasons of tact and tactics.)

One of the subjects that Nouvel has repeatedly discussed is the supposed immaterialisation of architecture. That process, in his view, would not stop at Modernist achievements such as screen façades and structural steelwork but has continued through to the level of the meaning of the building itself which would eventually be no more than a climate regulating shell around the otherwise autonomous processes that go on inside. The front, once thought of as the boundary of the architectural object, is reduced to an interface between different modes of existence. There is no longer any inside and outside; in fact all the previous functions of the front have ceased to exist. We are in a permanent state of transition and the interface will limit any interruption in this flux to a minimum. In addition to his defence of this approach to the profession, Nouvel has also become involved in the discussion around the problem of the specialist in a culture that is undergoing the virtualisation of reality through modern technological media such as television, video, fax-machines, modems, etcetera, which lead to space and time shrinking till they eventually merge in an ultimate simultaneity. This development has enormous implications for architecture that has traditionally been understood as being the bringing together of space and materials in the context of time. In order to establish its position in this process it will have to give an explicit account of itself. A simple rejection is not the correct answer in Nouvel's view. This time of 'afterwards' demands a more subtle attitude. It is still a matter of thinking in stone (or in Nouvel's case, glass, that according to Jean-Jacques Rousseau is the most innocent of all stones). 'In a broad sense my audience is the public of my time; it has the same cultural background as I do, and I appeal to its spirit. I don't appeal to its eyes; that isn't interesting at all, but much more directly to its culture, to the realm of connotation in other words, to encourage it to ask questions about things.'

It follows that the virtualising of reality also has enormous implications for how we experience reality. It is no longer a hierarchical series of impressions registered by our eyes that gives a structure to our perceptions, but a continuous process of things which merge with each other or overlap, without one being able to deduce any moral from it. Architects are in a sense responsible for the environment and Nouvel regards his task as being to do justice to the new character of our experience of it. Nouvel's treatment of the entrance to a building is also distinctly culturally determined; he lays as little stress as possible on the physical transition between inside and outside, between public and private. Entirely in keeping with the relativising of every hierarchy, you never know precisely where you are as you follow your route through the building; nor, from an institutional point of view, do you know what you are. You are caught up in Nouvel's circulation. In the end you come up against the problem of identity: in this virtual reality you no longer know who you are.

The thing that is striking about all these examples is not so much the programmatic will to change, or a directly institutional commentary within a specific project, but above all Nouvel's urge to create a specific post-historical atmosphere. Even though his architectural objects are often hard, even reticent, they have an aura that negates this hardness and reticence. They do not function as objects but as pieces of machinery, like Duchamp's bachelors' machines. What Nouvel is particularly concerned with is the aesthetic

Institut du Monde Arabe, Paris, 1988

Jean Nouvel

experience, the creation of a cinematic ecstasy in which space is reduced to pure emotion, prised loose from Cartesian geometry with its rational purposiveness, its soulless dimensions of length, width and height. Nouvel does not just want to manipulate these three dimensions; he wants to give people a scenario in the cinematic sense of the word that enables them to experience this compression of time. By doing this Nouvel has turned his fear of not being in tune with the times into a positive approach. To quote his own words: 'I get in a state of panic at the thought that I am not making good use of the possibilities of my time'.

This brings us back to the necessity for the act. With his increasing emphasis on practice Nouvel has chosen for a reconquest of innocence. His aim is to heal the Cartesian fissure. The dichotomy between subject and world, between words and things, a divide that modern French philosophers have presented with some emphasis as being unavoidable, can only be overcome by the existential act of life dirtying its own hands. The hyperconscious Nouvel would be only too pleased to lose some of his understanding of life.

Let's get straight to the point. If one leafs through any article about contemporary architecture, or goes to any symposium on the subject, the name Jean Nouvel is bound to crop up. How do you feel about that?

That's not my problem, though of course you function better when you know that a majority of people approve of what you're doing. I can't complain about that. People's reactions are fairly predictable: in the first phase the word provocation comes up. People don't understand what I am doing and accuse me of seeking a confrontation. Then there is a phase where I have to explain things to important discussion partners such as clients, administrators and politicians. Once the work of construction is completed you get another set of heated reactions; but the building hopefully will be its own best advocate.

I am certainly not looking for everyone's approval. My architecture is committed in the sense that it argues for a certain attitude towards the present. I expect to get reactions to this attitude, ideological ones and more directly sensory responses; I don't have any problem with them because the majority of them are favourable. The worst thing would be if there were no reactions at all; but I am not trying to elicit them. There is no sense in which I organise or orchestrate them. They usually come of their own accord; and that's something that I can feel satisfied about.

Who goes to make up your public?

Everyone, but above all the users, the people for instance who in the general way of things make use of the Institut du Monde Arabe or the Institut National de la Recherche Scientifique as visitors or to work in these institutions. You don't choose a public like this; it is a *fait accompli*. Lovers of architecture form an additional public, but they are of secondary importance. Depending on the purpose of the building, there is bound to be a public. Everything else is secondary.

One of the most important themes of your writings, your interviews and, for that matter, your buildings is the need for architecture to be 'up to date', to keep abreast, that is, of current cultural developments. Why do you give this quality such a priority?

Because I think that architecture is not an autonomous discipline and that it is bound to reflect the culture of a period. It is the visible evidence of its own time and of the preoccupations and aspirations of its own generation. We can never do much more than bear witness to everything that stimulates, excites and gives pleasure to our own generation. I often think that we wouldn't understand anything about the Greeks or the Middle Ages if we didn't have their buildings. That is why I always try to keep up with what is going on. Not from day to day as in fashion, nor in terms of decades that the notion of 'design' seems so dependent on, but in the sense of responding to all the aesthetic and emotional values of a given moment.

But that also means that you have to be able to give a diagnosis of a period or a situation?

Yes, that's true; it means one must have a capacity for synthesis; you need both to be aware of what's going on and to be able to distance yourself. An architect, like a film-maker, should know how to take the correct distance, to survey the whole and be able to analyse the details. But isn't this true of all kinds of activity? What does a good rugby or soccer player do if not place himself above the field in order to survey the situation?

The difference is that you don't just survey the situation, you also offer a pathology. Your work contains a certain view of historical destiny, a mixture of fantasy and apocalyptic elements.

The greatest difficulty is always first and foremost how you deal with historical destiny. There are certain facts that you can't get around, such as your historical and geographical circumstances. These are things that neither the will of a single person nor a local political decision can ignore. In our time, for instance, there is no longer any point in grumbling about the environmental chaos caused by the explosive growth of so many cities and suburbs. What's the point of complaining? That's just how things are. Nobody is going to pull everything down and erect, say, an eighteenth-century city all over again. What I'm interested in is to try and see something positive in what is happening at the moment. **Being an architect means choosing to be realistic.** Otherwise you're not an architect at all; at best you can make nice designs for abstractions such as Human Beings and Ideal Space. They may even be very beautiful, but being an architect means that you have to be capable of building something in a given situation at a given point in time; you must be prepared to do this in the world that is what it is, with all its political, financial and technological limitations. That's always been my aim. When I see what is going on today, I tell myself: I have to make sure I'm operating in this context and that I'm making something that gives a meaning to that context. That is much more important than the building in itself. I think that an architecture that genuinely deserves to be called interesting always reveals the context, letting it be seen, rather than exploiting it so as to appear more important than it is. I think that this is a greater achievement than designing something that is in itself good but which completely ignores its surroundings. Once again I believe that the philosophy of architecture is a constructive and realistic one. As architects it is our job to make the world more liveable; a little more lucid and beautiful than it was before. This means *practice*.

Do you think that people can become freer as a result of their architectural surroundings; is there an architecture that can enable us to think more clearly?

It's my conviction that the only really worthwhile gift you can give anyone is the joy and pleasure that you communicate. If someone feels good in a building and thinks it is beautiful and wants to stay there or return to it and talks about it with his friends, then something is going on that is of real importance, something that can change people's experiences and ideas. One can speak of architecture as being real if by means of something tangible something is influenced in the mental realm. And I remain convinced that you can distinguish a true architect from a false as easily as anything: the true one is the one whose finished project is always more interesting than his drawings and models. With the false one the reverse is true. He lets himself be carried away at the drawing board by all kinds of bright ideas, ideas that vanish as quickly as they appeared or else they fall flat as soon as they are tested against reality. A good building is always a hundred times more interesting than the photos and drawings.

If you talk about architecture having the power to change people's experiences and ideas, that suggests you are very optimistic. Do you agree?

In eternity all we are is little atoms and an architect's buildings only last a little bit longer than we do. The only hope an architect can have in my view is to make something permanent out of a set of emotions that belong to a very short-lived moment. **The capacity for capturing or freezing the values concealed in a specific moment, that is the power of architecture.** I love the fragility you get when something extremely fleeting is petrified. That is why I always work very hard at the different varieties of light in which my work can be seen: by daylight, in the evening, when it is raining or when the sun is shining, from a distance and close to, etcetera. Architecture for me is a not a sort of cold geometrical object that you only allow to affect your reason. That's a complete mistake. The way you experience a building in these different situations is far more important. A building changes according to the weather. In Chartres when a ray of sunlight falls right through the arched windows or the rose window, the cathedral becomes ten times more alive. It's so simple: buildings are intended for certain moments, like the signs in a musical composition. Certain places were designed for certain events. Churches, for instance, are for spectacle, for theatre and choral singing. Every building should be the ideal place at least for some people in some situations at some moments in time. This is the fundamental nature of architecture that has any quality.

You're interested both in the direct sensations linked to a specific moment, and in an intellectual analysis of present day society. Which comes first with you?

This opposition is no secret. In my work I am an advocate of making use of every opportunity and every pretext. This means that I don't believe in any generalisation, especially if it is a political one. Of course there is a larger context, but even so what you basically have to do is to forget every notion of a model to be followed, every trace of a conformist attitude. In my view this goes not just for architecture but for every profession, even politics. It is my view that we often have to prise ourselves loose from so-called political necessities. Fate is something that is over and above politics. Sometimes it can seem for a while as though it is political in character, but there are much stronger, more ineluctable bonds such as one's historical inheritance, technological development, etcetera, that weigh more. It isn't the architecture that makes a new world. Godard once said that he didn't have any idea of making a good film; he just wanted to make a film. This means that there is a moment when you just have to practice your profession and you cannot let all kinds of other considerations get in the way of it.

Isn't that being a bit naive?

Again it isn't a question of naiveté but of fate. At a certain moment you get into a situation where you need some kind of general perspective in order to know that right here and now there is only one thing that you can do. In any case the idea that you might be able to change the world with a film, a building, etcetera, is pretty ridiculous. You have to be aware of how much influence you have and above all what its limits are.

Isn't there such a thing as being too aware?

No, that's never a disadvantage. You always need to have as much awareness as possible. What is a mistake is to expect too much because you have too optimistic an estimate of the situation: yes, that's something that can have serious consequences, because it leads to being ridiculous, to pretentiousness, to something that no longer has anything to do with architecture. I repeat, the architect has a very simple problem. Nothing that I build is equal to how I imagined it, I'd be the first to admit that. As soon as I start, I put one foot carefully in front of the other till suddenly I feel the ground fall away. With one leg I'm still standing on solid ground. It's when you're in this position, with one foot on the ground and the other in empty space, that you're being a good architect. Sometimes you put both feet in space; that means the

Tour sans Fin, La Defense, Paris, project, 1989

Tomorrow Can take Care of Itself

Constantin Brancusi, Endless Columns, 1925-28

Media Park, Block I, project, Cologne, 1991

building won't be built. You fall flat on your face. A fiasco like that means your idea was too radical, too subversive, incomprehensible. Architecture continues to be the art form that depends on the greatest possible consensus. Perhaps the same goes for films. But compare this with a writer, a painter, a photographer. They do what they like! If we do what we like, we make a little drawing on a piece of paper, but that isn't architecture. In the same way a filmmaker can dash off a scenario but that doesn't mean he's made a film!

So far we have looked at your métier from the point of view of the artist. Can you also describe it from the institutional point of view of the commission that has to be realised?

The least you can expect from an architect who has his head screwed on is that he will respect the commission. Architecture has suffered a lot from things being produced that went right against any kind of reality, that had nothing to do with the world as it actually exists, as we experience it everyday. I don't think it's an insurmountable problem if some buildings have elements that don't quite make sense, for instance with regards to their upkeep. But they have to make sense for the people who have to live in them. I pay a great deal of attention to this. As far as participation is concerned I am an heir of May '68. The questions raised by the assignment should be discussed democratically. On the other hand I don't believe in creativity by referendum. That doesn't work.

How does something of outstanding quality come about? Is it the result of a series of brilliant decisions on the part of the architect?

I don't have a scrap of faith in intuition. I stick with the reality as long as possible before taking what I would call the creative leap. I also don't believe in inborn talent. Nobody is born with some fabulous gift or other. Maybe Mozart. Weren't the fairies supposed to have hovered round his cradle? Still less do I believe in brilliant scribbles that can conjure up something sublime. As though sublimity was something that could suddenly appear just like magic. What I do believe in is the possibility of the convergence of exceptional circumstances and a certain group of people. This can result in a crystallisation that is interesting because it bears witness to an age, to a specific sensibility, and also to the fleeting quality of the life that existed at that point in time. That is not very much, but it is also a very great deal!

Jean-François Lyotard said that we live in a society where sensitivity has taken the place of intelligence. Does your architecture relate more to this sensitivity than to intelligence?

I don't see any contradiction. You can be as sensitive as you want but the first condition for sensitivity is surely intellectual doubt. A person who never feels any doubt and never asks questions about anything, who thinks that everything will just land in his lap without any effort, what kind of sensitivity is that? Don't ask me. For me the acquisition of knowledge provides the material that enables sensitivity to emerge. I believe strongly, not so much in humility maybe, but at any rate in a sort of caution because in a craft like ours this is indispensable if you are to be able to stand up to reality. To me the word 'intuition' does not suggest hypersensitivity but rather a sort of undirected voluntarism.

Let's return to your analysis of society. You have given a full description of your own views. What do you think however about the possibility of achieving an ecological and social balance?

I hardly need to tell you that we live in a situation of balances that are constantly being upset. This is called dynamics. I don't have any belief whatsoever in restoring the balance by going back in time. What I do believe in is a permanent lack of balance while we search of something that lies *ahead* of us. As long as we put one foot in front of the other and don't fall flat on our faces. What's more, I am not particularly interested in all these ideologies that appear on the stage one after the other, the present ecological ideology, for instance, three-quarters of which consists of a somewhat suspect nostalgia. I have great faith in the future, but not in the sense of having unlimited time at your disposal or as a system of predictions. I never allow myself to forget that I am not building for tomorrow, but for today; even though I would love to live 5000 years later. That's just my nostalgia for the future.

You argued that a process of dematerialisation is taking place...

Yes, I have already been talking for fifteen years about dematerialisation in architecture. This also has to do with the development of new technologies, and the circumstances in which architects work. Right from the start people have tried to build as lightly and as simply as possible to shelter themselves against wind, cold and rain.

Seeing that gravity exists whether we like it or not, the architect's job is always to use the means at his disposal to make a structure that is as satisfying as possible, both in the relation between inside and outside and in terms of light. At one moment people want everything lit up and the next they want no light from outside to enter in. You can't have it both ways. It's my view that our possibilities have increased considerably this century. At the same time I think that modernity is a living concept whose content is in evolution. And I think that a building where the only idea is to show the structural reality will first and foremost be a boring building. I think that if a structure only invites you to say things like 'Oh, what a beautiful pillar! oh, what a beautiful beam!', it is saying very little. As far as I am concerned I try to use less obvious means to make buildings that are thought-provoking or emotionally inspiring: symbolism, for instance, or the incidence of light, through their tangibility, how the rooms follow on from each other, the setting. For me these are the terms that belong to today and today's emotions.

But this concern with today's terms surely originates in a historical vision that also takes into account what is implicit in the present and where that is leading us. What's going to happen tomorrow?

In this sense the future is simply a dream about something that we can't possibly know for certain. I don't allow myself to imagine what I will think about my buildings in 30 years time. Time doesn't interest me, only the present moment. Every time people fancied that they were building for the future, they ended up with a flop. The same goes for all those plans for cities and neighbourhoods for 15 or 20 years time. I just said it a moment ago: we would do better to know what our limitations are. I do not think of my buildings as belonging to the future but as being as intelligent as possible and appealing to people's senses and feelings as effectively as is possible *now*. 'Tomorrow' can take care of itself. I can't possibly know what they will discover tomorrow, what wars will take place, what the social developments will be in the neighbourhood for which I am making this building. Its greatest chance of survival will be if I make it as relevant and meaningful as possible for *now*. Then maybe people will allow it to remain as a piece of evidence and they will even feel affection for it. That is all I can do. I have nothing to say about what will come after our time. I am not clairvoyant; if you want a fortune teller you should go to the fairground.

You were clairvoyant enough to foresee that 'the future of architecture will no longer be architectural'.

That's something I'm convinced about. I made nine tenths of all the architects in France furious when I said that, all the professors of architecture, whole schools of them! They think that architecture is buried away somewhere in the genes of the profession, in other words in its whole history. And they think they can guess what the next phase will be because they know the entire history from Babylon to Louis Kahn. They couldn't be more wrong if they tried! Because the most important factor in the next phase is not the whole history of architecture but everything that is going on in the world at the precise moment when a new architecture is produced. It's fine by me if people know everything about history with the idea of actually using it! But it isn't the most important thing. What you need to get a grip on is the fact that in our time with its enormous production of images and its technological processes, people are exposed to a bombardment of information. The result of all this is a new notion of the whole visible reality. It should be clear then that the architecture of the future will hardly be influenced at all by what we have now. The thing that interests me is the poetry of a situation and finding a meaning in a context of plurality. I am not someone who loves what is pure to the exclusion of what is impure; I love them both. **I love everything.**

I make conceptual architecture. Architecture has to be conceptual. In our office we don't make the drawings first; the first two weeks we have discussions and these, of course, take the form of words. If we could say in words what we wanted to make then the project would in fact already be finished. Do you see what I am getting at?

On the other hand, the piece of architecture may start with words, but the words are the first thing that gets forgotten. What remains is the architecture. The most irritating thing in my view is to talk too much about architecture, because words have a very arbitrary relationship with architecture. You need to forget the words because the architecture will say it with other means. For me words are part of a personal way of working, that isn't interesting to anyone and isn't interesting for architecture either. All it is is the material momentum of my thought processes.

While we are on this subject, what do you think about the heteronymy of the ideas that go to make up the design of a building and the faits accomplis *that modern society presents us with? The dissolution of what was intended in the actual result?*

This brings us to a highly philosophical discussion about the historical and economical inevitability of buildings, their affective content and their discourse which can totally be wiped out by events. I think myself that architecture must have, will have to have, a transcendent dimension over and above all that. It will have to be able to adapt to the greatest and most catastrophic changes, even if only in its references. It is a good thing if you can picture your building as it would be in a situation of neglect or mutilation, of violence being done to it, of an extreme alienation from its goal. Buildings to which the most terrible things have happened

Hotel - Restaurant Amat, Bouliac, 1989

Cartier Façade Interdica, Fribourg, 1989

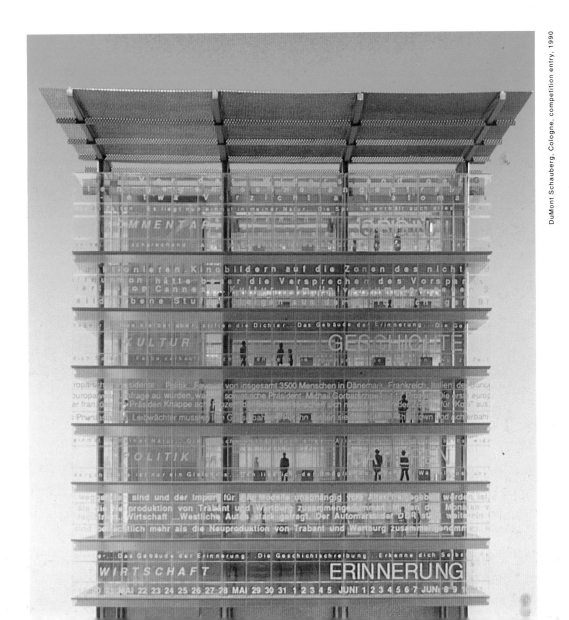

DuMont Schauberg, Cologne, competition entry, 1990

can be just as astonishing and emotionally charged as an architecture that has always been perfectly maintained and cared for. We have to accept the whole paradoxical relation between the partially unfulfilled aspirations of a building and what actually happens to it in reality.

Like a singer who never knows precisely how his voice sounds?

Yes, that's it; it's the relation between what is intended and the actual result, the proportion of what was not achieved to the element that was fundamental. Is that all you can do, taking small steps or avoiding risks? Architecture is in any case so much a form of applied art that for that reason if for none other you cannot avoid the necessity of costing your building according to social and functional requirements. And with these requirements all kinds of other aims and messages creep in, some of them recognised but others that are often hidden. But there are also elements in the design that the architect can turn at his own discretion into a hidden sign or message, that can only be decoded by his equals. The architect's own ideas may be quite shocking or subversive, as long as they are not expressed openly. The architect writes a sort of text consisting of different levels and the most personal of these can only be read between the lines.

If you look at the filmic quality of architecture, what sort of film do you think of?

I see the contemporary film director as a sort of architect. He has to put forward a draft plan that may or may not be accepted. There are administrative, financial, technical and organisational considerations. In a short period of time he has to bring a large team of people together in one place. But there are other similarities as well. In what I call the architectural substratum we experience the influence on time and space of the filmic aspect. The camera moves through a series of tableaus, puts a frame round the action, sheds various sorts of light on it. All this helps me in designing a building, when I am thinking of how one enters it and moves from one room to another, the meetings that take place and how one leaves it. This 'scenography' of the building is more than just the decor; it is a sort of play in itself. Take the IMA, for instance, for me this was a design based entirely on the idea of movement *forward*. As far as the 'editing' of the textures is concerned, if it isn't film, it is in any case video. In this respect architecture stands at the cross-roads of a whole variety of influences.

Can architecture ever be have such a potential for subversion as, for instance, the films of Godard?

Not to the same extent. Because a film by Godard usually doesn't cost very much and has no difficulty in reaching a large group of admirers. Godard is widely known as a *gosse d'art*, as the naughty boy of film. And once a film like that is finished and shown to the public, then it does at any rate exist. But a building, this has first of all to go through the whole social procedure. It has to be built, and then it needs to be used. Buildings where the conditions of the commission are eccentric are actually highly exceptional. Some of Gaudi's projects are a good example of this: they are subversive, provocative even crazy.

It is your aim to be subversive?

No, but I do aim to be dynamic. The only thing I want is to crystallise a single moment in all its diversity in a single place. As an architect you can never turn everything upside-down; at any rate, that's true of my way of working.

Even so, by using the currently popular Baroque means of architecture, you would seem to want to comment on the institutional aspect of the relation between design and programme. For instance in the Media Park in Cologne.

The Media Park is reasonably accessible as a project and can definitely not be described as heroic. It was actually a 'faster' project than most of the other projects I have worked on. The aim was to conceive of a programme that would be just as readable by night as by day. This was possible with the aid of various devices, amongst them the Potemkin screen, but with holes in them.

Broadly speaking the idea of a programmed building that you can see the life going on in and in which the typical images give you a clue as to what the whole building is like, this idea is typical of the average business quarter at the present day. The difference in my case is that I work a little faster than those people who all pay more attention to their 'image'. The Media Park is more a way of crystallising those aesthetic experiences that are connected with reading a computer screen; these can be beautiful without, for instance, it being possible to take photos of them. It is a question then of recreating a completely different scale, an aspect of architecture that is extremely illuminating and dynamic and that corresponds to one of the typical visual pleasures of today's world. That is why it is a good thing to design something of that sort.

Could you say something more about that?

They are projects that employ a number of means that are not yet very popular but which can profoundly affect the poetry of the city. If there are many buildings of this sort in a single street then they would after a while have a somewhat disturbing effect. That is obvious enough. But if the whole city was like that, then of course the character of the city itself would change and so, in the long term, would one's perception of what a city is.

That means that if your work is repeated often enough it can have a profound influence on one's perceptual equipment. What is left then of that uncritical fascination with fate? Is there anything left that is lasting?

What I've just been describing is an important element in my work but not the only one. The blueprint for the Tour sans Fin in La Défense, for example, is a another kind altogether. There you can find more lasting and metaphysical aspects and not just the element of fragility that I mentioned earlier on. But in my architecture the idea of something lasting is not expressed by the form but by the mentality. That's what it's all about. You see, I am very fond of buildings that reveal their fragility and their makeshift character.

The thing that preoccupies me is that all buildings can actually be protected only in one way. Not by using granite or reinforced concrete; something like that will at most make a difference of a few years. It is not a matter of civilisation surviving. A building must above all be a step in the architectural history of a specific moment of civilisation. Only then will it represent something; only then can people feel love for it and that is the basic requirement for permanence. The Katsura architecture in Japan, the Eiffel Tower, however unstable buildings like that are, remain standing because people love them. It is not really important for the walls to be a metre thick. One can of course think up other formulas for success; all I can say is that they're not mine. What I mean by this is that the more institutional a building is, the more it embodies something has to do with the culture, the more it will have an aesthetic value; and whatever the structural state of a building like that, it will be preserved. It should also be fairly obvious that things like that no longer have anything to do with architecture as such.

With an approach like that you disqualify a great number of your colleagues who give priority to autonomous professionalism. You must have many enemies.

That's true. In France, if you aren't a historicist, or a neo-Modernist and if you're not a supporter of architecture as an autonomous academic discipline, then you already have two-thirds of the nation against you.

Isn't it strange, however, that an architect who passes for a notorious eclecticist, who always reacts to the specific context, has so many enemies. You might think that an eclecticist would be everybody's friend...

The opposite proves to be the case. Because I have no intention of ever building a historicising or purely Modernist building, my architectural handwriting will never easily be accepted by a large group of people, no matter how carefully I respond to the specific character of a site. You see, people are fondest of things that recur all the time. Just think how many followers people have who always make the same things; it is not a coincidence that they get the opportunity to do just that. With my work people generally feel a little ill at ease because in each case they feel forced to adopt a different attitude.

If we apply to your concrete work this question of the difficulty people experience in accepting what you do, the aspect of boundaries or limits is perhaps a good way to begin. It is in fact there that you get the possibility of breaking through the standard patterns of historicism and Modernism with their all too familiar physical framework.

It is a matter of how you land in a certain situation. As far as I am concerned I think the most interesting thing is if someone can end up somewhere without having to make a whole series of moves first. Academic architecture always lets you know that you are approaching something somewhere a kilometre in advance. And, sure enough, in the end you do end up somewhere. As for myself I'd like to be inside somewhere immediately. This also brings us to the notion of an interface; all one has to do is to go through a screen. The boundary has become virtual and that also has something to do with being tactile. My plan for a Tour sans Fin in La Défense has something to do with that, but only lengthwise. The project on the Boulevard Raspail is another case in point. You simply cannot tell where the building begins and where it ends; you can see the sky through it. Inside you see trees growing. It is difficult to decide which is the real entrance because you enter the building at least three or four times. At one time you go through the screens; then you pass through an eight-metre high glass door. Meanwhile you still think you are outside. And suddenly you are in the lift; once again this is made of glass. You don't even know that you are in a lift, until it starts to move. What I mean to say by this is that the whole problem of boundaries is actually first and foremost a problem of interference. It is a question of the deeper meaning of a building or a space, of the whole way in which one perceives the structure and routes that with the help of the interface can be eliminated.

This means that the boundary becomes increasingly virtual. In many of my projects you enter from below like a space ship. The door in the sense of a door-tool is physically eliminated. You take an escalator and suddenly disappear. There is no more door, only flowing movements.

Fondation Cartier, project, Paris, 1991

Les Galeries Lafayette, project, Berlin, 1991

There is yet another dimension that is important and that is ubiquity, being everywhere at once; this has to do with the wonder one feels for the faculty of perception as a function of speed. In the project in Nogent sur Marne, for a nightclub, this is very relevant because an extensive video system has been installed there. Inside and outside are simultaneously present; what is more, our eyes see both the reality and the film. In the end you no longer know where you are. The space has become virtual because all that one sees is in fact a space which people imagine they have made their own. It is still of course a matter of the layout of the terrain and the interconnections, but no longer of the space in the mathematical sense of the word. Or rather, the whole aesthetic system of the building is a system that exists outside the boundary. Then, of course, there is the question of how the building is seen from outside, from a car or a plane, by daytime or at night. And if one thinks about these matters of perception, one will have to admit that the meaning of architecture changes. These are questions that have everything to do with present cultural and technological developments. I do not relate to the idea of an actual apocalypse, but I am definitely fascinated by visions like that of Baudrillard about the fatality of things having us in its power. That's also why, despite all attempts at devising a context and a programme, I think that you still have to hold onto the autonomous power of something that continues to make sense, even in a situation where the context is totally subverted so that the opposite happens from what one had planned. This field of tension can be seen very clearly in the IMA where because of a lack of financial resources the building hasn't been cleaned for four years even though a million visitors have passed through it. I could never have dreamed of something like that. The thing that is so interesting about this is that despite all the objective evidence of decay, the building continues to have a certain dignity and appeal.

Isn't it actually much more interesting to speculate on the field of tension between your own cultural relativism on the one hand and Arab absolutism on the other that still apparently manage to be reconciled in your architecture? If architecture wishes to participate in the cultural debate, this sort of tension is a rewarding theme, because it is something like this that enables us to see that architecture belongs within the realm of culture and not outside it. What is more, when you look at it from the architect's point of view, he or she is also just another ordinary citizen and as such is a potential participant in the democratic discussion about the options, the possibilities and the specific needs of our society.

No, as an architect I can't answer that. As an architect you can't carry the problems of the human race, or all the international problems on your own shoulders. It's simply more than I can bear! Of course as an ordinary citizen I'll be only too pleased to talk about these things at the bar of the Café de Commerce, but as an architect that's not my problem. Political questions like racism and integration, economic and financial matters, in as much as they have any relevance to my work, are more than I can be expected to cope with. And that's just as well. We are only just beginning to put the period behind us when we were all traumatised by architects who wanted to explain the world and to lay down sets of rules for achieving Utopia. I'm for architects having a completely different role. Every cultural attitude is potentially a critical one, although I believe that there have been times when that made more sense than it does in our time. At present in my opinion it's a question first and foremost of the *hope* that the political attitude essentially implied. I mean hope in a broad sense and not in the sense of some notion of progress. I've got nothing against a situation where a number of architects get directly involved with politics out of a desire for change. I am also delighted when more people come up with a principled attitude to their city or to architecture that invests them with a certain authority to influence decisions. It's also a good thing when architecture gives voice to its own point of view from its privileged position as a social intersection of interests. All that's well and good. But when all is said and done, your influence as an architect lies in the power of your proposals and your designs. Or even in a statement that is in some sense poetic in character. When a building has actually been erected and is provocative through the simple fact that it continues to remain standing, it begins to engage in a form of criticism that is much more effective than any story on paper whatsoever. There is a power in reality and people realise this all too little. The architects who have the most to tell are the ones who actually build.

The Invisible in Architecture could be conceived as space. Literally, as that which is encompassed by walls and is experienced there. And figuratively, as the region to which meaning is given by those who make use of it. This space can be approached either phenomenologically or ideologically. Every activity takes place in space but it also 'produces' a spatial ordering. People consume and produce space at one and the same time. These users of space now exist, moreover, in a cultural situation in which space has become an existential and moral problem. Implicitly and explicitly, it sets the tone for every cultural debate of recent years.

What kind of space is at issue? Visual, physical, psychological or behaviour space? Interior space, urban space or peripheral space? Space as the mould of things, as negative substance, or as a 'thing' in itself? And, if it is a thing, an independent entity, could it also be a dimension of thought, a notion? And can it, despite being present in itself, also be representative of something else? Is space more than the container in which an act occurs? Can space itself have a meaning as an atmosphere, an ambience? How, finally, can we characterise various spaces? What concepts do we need? Global space? Global village space? Hyperspace? Virtual space? You name it. And why do we attach different values to 'space', 'void' and 'emptiness'?

These are questions that crop up repeatedly. When culture was dominated by the ideology of an elite, there was some consensus about these matters. They were thus not yet a 'problem'. Now that pluralism has itself become an ideology, now that the individual, the fragment and the fragmented individual have been put on a pedestal, the question of space is dogged by a global Babel. Not that this impedes the debate in any way. On the contrary, the problematic nature of space tends to be stressed more and more frequently. 'The anxiety of our era has to do fundamentally with space, no doubt a great deal more than with time', wrote Foucault back in 1967. He thereby set the tone for a cultural period in which all metaphysical and transcendental

Space

conceptions of time were to be dismantled, to make way for a more immanent way of looking at things. Thinking turned towards the Other, instead of the Higher and the Utopia. We became aware of the world *alongside* us at the precise point where the price of believing in the world *ahead* of us started becoming so horribly clear. Time, the chief component of the ideology of Modernism and the basic stuff of the modernisation process, went out of fashion. Space became the vital ingredient of Post-Modern thinking. Not space as three-dimensionality, as a physical entity, but as a category. 'That new spatiality implicit in the Post-Modern' (Fredric Jameson). 'It is space not time that hides consequences for us' (John Berger). What consequences? Perhaps that, as John Urry puts it, 'it is space rather than time which is the distinctively significant dimension of contemporary capitalism.'

Here we conceive space as a microcosm of a certain mentality. Space is not only part of the physical and spiritual universe, but also an expression of it. It shows the relative order of things, the vertical stratification from profane to sacred and the horizontal stratification of social structure, cultural and economic entity, and geographic place.

The physical category of space has been a widespread topic of interest since the early days of scientific speculation. Space is a philosophical determinant of place, a *Satz vom Grunde* that makes the universe thinkable and intelligible. In the course of history, many thinkers have pondered the concept of space and attempted to capture its essence. In both physics and philosophy, space was and is one of the pillars of knowledge and hence a topic of critical reflection.

Still, space was never a point of discussion. As long as man saw himself as having an organic connection with the heavenly order, space was identical to the divine substance. After the eighteenth century, however, following the rise of individual sub-

jectivism, the departure from the classical paradigm and the accompanying secularisation, space became the theatre in which man was obliged to find his own place. Space was what remained when doubts about God went beyond a certain point. For centuries, space had been a modality of existence. Immanuel Kant believed he could provide unquestioned beliefs such as this with a philosophical underpinning, and described space as a logical category a priori. But the consequence of this objectivisation turned out to be the loss of every ontological foothold. Man was confronted with space because he was confronted with himself. Only after the conceptualisation, after the conscious awareness, of the preconditions of existence, did it become clear how arbitrary this existence was. And thus space changed from being a self-evident fact into a problem area in which the human subject had to manifest himself.

Nowadays, philosophers are concerned with mobility and circulation; architects have thrown out the Modernist dogmas but remain no less preoccupied with 'spatial effects'; sociologists study space as a social construct; artists make space-specific work; and ecologists proclaim the limits of growth. Add to this list the enormous expansion of migratory movements, the universalisation of the diaspora; add, too, the tearing down of the Iron Curtain, and the rapid developments in virtual reality techniques and spatial simulations; and it becomes clear why there has been an explosion in the jargon of space.

Not until now, in this time of unprecedented mobility and virtualisation, has the idea, the concept, of space really got through to us. An actual space or spatial experience becomes less and less necessary, owing to the many techniques for projecting (free) space such as telecommunications, television, fax, data links etc. Home becomes a place of work as well as a place to live and sleep. Yet we displace ourselves physically more and further than ever, through spaces that come to resemble one another more and more closely. We impress our own culture on that of others through the agency of transnational capitalism and tourism. We have already been conditioned before we go somewhere: we experience space not as a process but as a *diktat* of the tour guide. We visit tourist attractions (including nature), but avoid the spots where the social realities are all too obvious.

In the end, space loses its three-dimensionality by reduction to an image. Even though we live in three-dimensional space, we no longer experience it until we see the videos or the photos afterwards. Physical, geographical space is no longer a source of identity. This situation has come about through a whole series of activities that are not linked to space by necessity. The reality of an experience is no longer required to be synchronous with the event.

At first sight, the problem of space looks like the *primus inter pares* of all architectural problems. After all, it is the creation of space that gives architecture its *raison d'être* alongside sculpture. And who, on seeing the architecture of Borromini or Soufflot, would dare deny that a highly developed consciousness of space is at work there. Nonetheless, space has did not become a conscious architectonic *concept* until the end of the nineteenth century. Theorists such as August Schmarsow and Adolf Hildebrandt were among the first to formulate an explicit theory of space in architecture. Space came rapidly to be seen as the 'prime matter' of the architectural design. It was not long before architects such as Loos, Berlage, Schlemmer, Maholy Nagy, Mies van der Rohe, Scharoun and many others, officially proclaimed space as the precept and goal of their work. For one it was the poetic motion through space, for another the ergonomics, for yet another the need for optical transparency; all known architectonic means such as mass, construction, cladding, light etc. were deployed in order to create a desired space.

After the Second World War, this optimistic interpretation of space as a platform for human action declined. Space gradually came to be described as a decor of disillusion, the end of the meta-narrative or even as the end of History itself. Space has become the domain in which we think of the other as Other, a kind of socio-ecological consciousness. Space is no longer the region of the free will that tries to subjugate the world, but the region in which the blind will still has to be held somewhat in check. Although architecture unavoidably continues seeing itself largely as 'spatial designing', it has abandoned its high-flown emancipatory ambitions. Architecture no longer claims to rescue tomorrow from the straitjacket of the future, but at most to offer a solution for the problem of today.

It is a great pity that the professional discussion shows few signs of recognising these transformations in the cultural dimension of the space concept. Apart from a few avant-garde circles, the majority of architects show no interest in the relation between the conception of space and the Post-Modern condition. And this brings us once again to the invisible in architecture. The 'monopolists of space', as Geoffrey Scott once so aptly characterised them, pay barely any attention to the consequences of the disenchantment of the world for their own profession. Only a few architects have welcomed author Herman Broch's *Wertvakuum*, by definition a spatial idea, as an architectural theme, and this only in the last few years. Space is thus not only literally invisible, but it also appears to be missed all too easily as a cultural dimension.

Three strategies and three architects Although rare, there are now a few architects who have the courage to propagate their conceptions of space as a contribution to the cultural debate. They react against the isotropic, neutral space that Modernism saw as an instrument of emancipation. We distinguish the following:

Archaism Archaism answers isotropy with stereotomy. Its space is a place, a point of rest in a hectic world. It offers shelter and certainty through its strong tactility. The view of the horizon is framed in. The individual finds himself in a reassuring enclosure. **Ton Alberts and Max van Huut** wish to create an antiserum for Post-Modernity by building spaces that offer a stereognostic experience and have implications of spirituality. Moreover, they foster interpersonal meeting. Everything rotates around 'contact'. By falling back on anthroposophic principles, they aim for an architecture that is 'human' once more, in which the person can find 'his place' again. Their spaces are thus more likely to be references to Mother Earth than to engage with the actions that are performed on that Earth.

Façadism Façadism has no conscious spatial politics. It leaves the Modernist space more or less intact, but enriches it visually with a wealth of signs. The alienating character of functionalism is compensated by all kinds of iconographic identification points. At the same time, programmatic identities are softened by the creation of transitional zones. The space thus becomes an illustration of accompanying a formal view of the world. In **Kisho Kurokawa's** spaces, he aims to let everything melt into everything else, without hierarchical, moralising connections. The space is the common denominator for all cultures and an arena for the ultimate reconciliation. Nothing is left empty, and the *horror vacui* turns into a glittering feast of signs. It is a synthetic space that absorbs oppositions, a façade for a peaceful atmosphere.

Fascinism Fascinism regards space as the area in which everything has gone wrong, where Utopia and the hope of progress have failed. All that remains is a fascinating autonomous game that is more inclined to create a (moral) void than to fill a space. Architecture can do no more than offer apt illustrations of this historical process and therefore aspires to underline the alienation. **Daniel Libeskind's** approach is to reproduce chunks of historical reference, without creating any new coherent meaning. His spaces are an illustration for the Post-Modern realisation of the pointlessness of every historical project; in that sense, they are truly empty.

Irregularly shaped spaces advance the faculty of intuition.

Ton Alberts & Max van Huut

My approach to the person who will use these spaces amounts to acting as an intermediary in a deep dialogue between him and architecture, because my spaces transcend theory and appeal to the deepest levels. In other words, my spaces relate to the fundamental aspects of humanity. **Tadao Ando**

Architecture defines space. Architecture is space. Emptiness does not exist; space does.
Ricardo Bofill

Space and perceptual modes are inseparable. Today we must explore the new space of our changing perspective dimensions. Emptiness is the key. Emptiness is the essential and dominant quality of the city today. The emptiness of traffic spaces while the light is red, the weekend emptiness of business zones, the emptiness of the tourist attraction in bad weather. It is the flux between imcompletable patterns of built fabric, between good, bad, large, small and indifferent architecture. Emptiness is a field awaiting the invention of appropriate codes of use. The first step is not to resist the sublime qualities of emptiness, to explore its scales, its frequencies, its grains. Then comes the possibility of interruption (stones thrown in the pond), permanent objects, stoppages that give measure to this geography of absence.
Julia Bolles & Peter Wilson

In the design for a new bridge at Merida, Spain (1991), we proposed an arch spanning 200 metres in the middle. It was a great architectural gesture and, strictly speaking, totally unnecessary. So unnecessary that I didn't bother to rescale the foundations on which it is based. Yet I think this arch is one of the finest aspects of the project.
Santiago Calatrava

What was always more interesting to me was how to essentialise the nature of a spatial experience and then transfer it to the viewer. So it was always more an exercise in architectural communication than in making an observation about the nature of architecture as a thing separate from yourself.
Nigel Coates & Doug Branson

Every architectural space presents itself as an event in waiting.
Pietro Derossi

Our work maps out strategies for 'contractual space', that is, the unspoken social contract between encoded bodies and encoded programmes, in which architecture can bypass its typical role of complicity to perform critically. Situated between 'inscription' and 'prescription', this architecture of 'description' is concerned primarily with the hyper-present. Though description is commonly understood to be recapitulation, passive and uncritical, we employ it actively, as intervention. By articulating the culturally loaded spaces of and between surfaces and for grounding their relations, those relations inevitably become disrupted. **Elisabeth Diller & Ricardo Scofidio**

If the spaces that we create do not move the heart and mind then they are surely only addressing one part of their function? **Norman Foster**

The walls along the narrow passage through the Joan Miró Library are blank screens on which the sunlight gets reflected, giving a transparent brightness to the two porches. As foyers before the entrance to the interior of the building, these porches become a space where one can pause: only the sound of water spouts marks the entrance to a place where silence is compelled. **Beth Galí**

I approach each building as a sculptural object, a spatial container, a space with light and air. The manipulation of the inside of the container is for me an independent sculptural problem and no less interesting than the design of the container itself. **Frank Gehry**

While certain monuments of the Modern Movement have introduced new spatial configurations, the cumulative effect of non-figurative architecture is the dismemberment of our former cultural language of architecture. **Michael Graves**

In creating spaces we must recognise that human beings are a part of nature. Architecture must be responsive to the ecosystem as all of human existence is ultimately encompassed by nature. **Itsuko Hasegawa**

The perception of our architectures does not happen through the perspectival image, through photography or video, but through the reality of the exhibition space itself. We annexate and transform this space, make it part of our architecture, and then expose the observer to this transformed space. In this way the observer can experience our architecture in a spatial manner, can live through it in an almost physical sense.

Jacques Herzog & Pierre de Meuron

Psychological space is at the core of spatial experience. It is intertwined with the subjective impression of actual spatial geometry and born in the imagination. The absolute side of rational planning is in a contrapuntal relationship with the pathological nature of the human soul. It is in this mix, at its architectonic conception, that the spatial spirit of a work of architecture is determined. **Steven Holl**

Architecture dominates spaces, it soars upwards, it penetrates the earth, it stands out against landscapes, it spreads in all directions, it dominates space with its mass and void, it dominates space through space itself. Hans Hollein

The harder we search the more we find that the fundamental types of spaces and construction have been known for a long while. They remain relevant exactly because they are timeless. Leon Krier

Everything in its proper place – that is a fundamental tenet of the bourgeoisie, and it generates a very particular form of city. Later that form was termed 'hygienic' and was used to design working-class districts and then entire social complexes. Some people have ascribed the 'hygienic' regimentation to the use of prefab architecture. But prefab is in fact merely a convenient extension of the same formal principles. We, on the other hand, seek to foster the development of self-organising social autonomies out of disorder. Is that an ideology too? The times have changed, at least. **Lucien Kroll**

Modern Architecture was constructed on the paradigm of clear divisions of space – interior from exterior, environment from building, private from public, historic from contemporary – a strict order based on dichotomy. Yet what was lost to such dualistic articulation were the 'in-between' multivalent ambiguities, that is to say, the human qualities harboured in fringe and median environments. I seek a new symbiotic architectural space, to reintroduce symbiotic spaces between exterior and interior, symbiotic ambivalences between nature and architecture, symbiotic multivalences between contradictory elements. Kisho Kurokawa

We want to give the people a space that is poetic and as interesting as possible. You can organise it all and provide a space in a very ordinary way, but we are also looking to some extent for an interesting space, for the most beautiful cross-section possible, for the most spatial space possible. That is the beauty we have in mind.
Lucien Lafour & Rikkert Wijk

Emptiness is not a pure minus – not a deficiency as the idealists thought – but a play of new curvatures, curvatures eternally misadjusted to each other's hollowness. Daniel Libeskind

Distance – or if you prefer, the sensation of closeness – depends on material.
Rafael Moneo

Spaces are qualified by actions just as actions are qualified by spaces. One does not trigger the other; they exist independently. Only when they intersect do they affect one another. Bernard Tschumi

You have called space primus inter pares, we have more irreverently said that for Modern architecture space was God. We suggested that this was a deviation from tradition and that, in the emphasis on space, other aspects of architecture, primarily symbolism, were suppressed (although not eliminated) by the Modern Movement.
Different cultures have different conceptions of space and architects have for years analysed them. Films, from Jacques Tati to Woody Allen, are a good source of wry comment on the symbolic meaning of architectural and urban space. 'Death of God'? You tell me. Empty space? I like the definition of space as opportunity for something to happen.
The American city has the democracy of the grid, where the mayor's house and the gasoline station can be (almost) next to each other.
Robert Venturi & Denise Scott Brown

On the Work of Ton Alberts & Max van Huut
Consolation or Exorcism; a Healthy Mind in a Healthy Building

In Amsterdam's Bijlmermeer, the functionalist high-rise district of the sixties whose subsequent deterioration and bad reputation caused it to be euphemistically renamed 'Amsterdam South-East', there stands one of the most intriguing products of contemporary architecture. It is the headquarters of the transnational ING Bank designed by Ton Alberts and Max van Huut. This building is a clear case of *architecture autre*. The bank, known locally by the irreverent name of the 'monkey rock', has none of the technocratic clarity of the honeycomb tower-block flats in its vicinity. Nor does it bear any relation to the later low-rise additions, which were intended as a counterweight and a means of 'revitalisation'. The bank is a relic from the tradition of organic building that we identify with the 1910s and 20s with movements such as the *Gläserne Kette* and names like Hugo Häring, Bruno Taut and Hans Scharoun. It calls to mind the architecture of forced optimism whose products sprouted here and there like defiant weeds from the ruins of a shattered Europe after the First World War. Sixty or more years later, with our knowledge of the totalitarian temptations of this kind of architecture, and in the context of Western Europe's economic prosperity, we may sense a dated quality about this building. Yet at the same time it is like a breath of fresh air. It is not enough to dismiss this miniature city of social and monetary traffic as yet another formal variant of proliferating Post-Modernism. This building is intendedly the product of a social programme, of a well thought-out standpoint on the moral content of contemporary architecture. Ton Alberts and Max van Huut are architects who do not eagerly bow to the overpowering restrictions of the market which force architecture to become a veneer for commerce and speculation. They aspire to create buildings that are salutary, a prescription of hallowed space and purified material to cure mankind of his soulless condition – a remarkable objective, seeing that the architectural discipline has long consigned the building principle of the perfectibility of society to the waste-paper bin.

Amoral Dealings in Moral Architecture

Architectural criticism directed at the buildings of Alberts and Van Huut cannot avoid the following dilemma. What are we to think of an organic, even moralistic, architecture that allows itself to be taken in by a programme like that of the ING Bank, the preeminent operator among speculators in third-world debt? But then, how can we fail to be impressed by the treatment of the many programmatic levels in a way that respects not only the interests of the client, but also those of the user (here personified by the employee)? This architecture invites scathing criticism because of the very idea of the client. But in spite of the client, we could argue that the architecture succeeds marvellously in creating a perfect environment for people. It seems that the key to understanding this dilemma is the fact that the client's interests have come to coincide with those of the personnel. Not only is the bank delivered from the pangs of the sick building syndrome that dogged the previous headquarters, causing productivity to tumble;

De Waal Residence, Utrecht, 1980

but now the highly lucrative idea of the bank as one big family has much more chance of catching on than in the bloodless atmosphere of a Modernist tower of glass. And, we all know, you can always turn to your family... The 'problem' seems to have solved itself. We are clearly faced with a revival of corporatism, and just as in the early days of the present century this goes hand in hand with the vocabulary of organic architecture. Moreover, the directorship of this bank has shown a long-standing affinity for anthroposophy, which places people at the centre. Not a bad idea when those people are earning lots of money for you.

A Built Manifesto

The ING Bank building sums up many, if not all, of Alberts' and Van Huut's sensitivities and preoccupations. With the ample budget that was at their disposal, they were able to give vent to their thinking at every imaginable level. An ideology has come to full expression in this building. It is a metaphor for the modern way of doing business, a metonym for anthroposophical thinking and a synecdoche for a vision of humanity and the world we live in. It sums up ideas that the architects have been working out over a long period, notably in a number of villas, and which they have recently taken further in a number of similar commercial projects. The programmatic complexity, budget and in-depth involvement of the client combine to form an impressive cultural manifesto.

Our culture understands the geometric centre as special and as the place of primary human occupation. We would not typically divide the rectangular room into two halves, but rather, more appropriately, would tend to place ourselves in the centre, thereby precluding any reading of the room as a diptych. In analysing room configurations, we sense a cultural bias to certain basic geometrics. We habitually see ourselves, if not at the centre of our 'universe', at least at the centre of the spaces we occupy. This assumption colours our understanding of the differences between centre and edge.
Michael Graves

What is the ING building if not a morphological allusion to a castle or an artificial rock? The articulation of the building follows the structure of the bank's organisation. The project as a whole forms an expressionist ensemble of ten separate volumes, which are linked together by an elongated walkway. Arranged along this artery are the facilities of a more general, public character, such as catering services, large conference rooms, office gardens and entrance lobbies. Although the layout of the building is extrovert, the backward-leaning brick façades give it an air of introversion. As to its urban context, it is like an island adrift among the neighbouring commercial developments and standardised housing.

The building as a whole is segmented into ten tower-like structures. On each floor of each tower, there are separate offices for the management and meeting rooms, plus a flexibly-structured compartmentalised *Bürolandschaft* providing work units for eight people. The intention here is the same as that behind the division of the building as a whole into ten smaller masses, namely to reduce the scale to a more human level. The character of the interior is strongly determined by the organisation of space, the choice of materials, the design of details, the sculptures and 'natural' elements such as water and vegetation. These give the building an intimacy that is unprecedented among modern office buildings; and this, it appears, is also prized by the employees who work in the building.

Although there are countless plausible practical reasons (noise nuisance, outside views, problems of access, energy economy etcetera) for the peculiarities of this building, they can clearly mostly be put down to the architects' will to form. Alberts and Van Huut have repeatedly defended their design with such slogans as 'the person is central', 'small is beautiful', 'creation of identity' etcetera. However vague these sentiments may be, they are expressed in the bank building as practical solutions, such as the continuous semi-public space, the dimensions, the use of high-quality materials and the use of brick infill for the concrete skeleton. The design is geared to the experiential world of the user. The employee's identification with his or her work is largely conditioned by the surroundings in which it takes place, not by the content of the work itself. The idea that architectural devices thus serve as a means of functional representation will presumably not be a problem for the actual user.

Anthropos and Sophia

Because of the many potential misunderstandings, Alberts prefers not to term his work anthroposophic. All the same, it is clear that an anthroposophically inclined agenda operates in the building. The link to the earth is effectuated by the building's broad footing; environment and energy-conscious materials show respect for nature; the absence of right angles is a criticism of the functional rationality of the Modernist box; and the zigzag of the traffic zone points to a desire to make movement into an adventure instead of a predictable progress from A to B. Earth and nature, intuition and harmony, are the issues here. In this sense, the architecture aligns itself with the long tradition of criticism of modernity that has shadowed the bulk of opportunistic building since the end of the eighteenth century. 'The building', says Ton Alberts, 'is ordered

rationally both inside and outside, but there are also spiritual forces such as beauty present. Beauty is love in concrete form. All things considered, beauty is a rational entity. Without beauty, we can not live. (...) That is no "normal" rationality but a kind of super-rationality, and that is something we have introduced into the building. That is exactly what we mean by "organic".' ★

Anthroposophy has no style of its own, since it has no unique vision or thought which is to be expressed but aims only to create the conditions for the free formation of judgements. The architecture of Alberts and Van Huut is an expression of their ideas on the kind of atmosphere that will foster this process of judgement-formation. The bank building must first and foremost tell the user that he is 'somebody'. In contrast to the majority of Modernist boxes in which the international financial fraternity has tucked itself away, this building continually reassures the user that he is warmly welcome. Feel the touch of the banister that also serves as a stream; let your gaze drift around the magnificent hanging plants in the sacral open voids; throw open the window and enjoy the fresh air. Within the bounds of its competence, this architecture does everything possible to make you feel at home. This politics of identity has personal development, experience, quality and harmony as its watchwords. It is a kind of super-humanism that works as a remedy for the psychic chaos that has reigned since, say, Nietzsche and Freud.

★ Alberts, Ton, *Een Organisch Bouwwerk, Architectuur en Spiritualiteit*, Utrecht/Antwerp 1990, pp. 124 -125.

Leistungsform, Organwerk, Sinngehalt... and Profit

Since the ideas of anthroposophism are greeted with widespread scepticism and often drift off into a cloying nebulosity, Alberts has termed his architecture *organic*. This immediately brings to mind the idiom of German Expressionism in the form that emerged shortly after the First World War. This movement was fond of resounding phrases on the mystic powers of craftsmanship, the healing effect of the *Gesamt-kunstwerk* and the redeeming potential that architecture can have for a leader or a society. The Great War had effectively sanctioned a universal godlessness, but in spite of this, architecture was still capable of marshalling the sacrality needed to invoke an ethical reawakening in mankind. Organic building, traditionally situated within the established history of architecture as a kind of aberration of the Modern Movement, was characterised by a search for the *innerste Wesen* of the programme. In the words of Hugo Häring,

'We would like to approach things gently and let them determine their own form. We do not wish to thrust a form on them, to determine their form from the outside, to impose some or other abstract regularity, to do them violence.'

Organic building was concerned not so much with the *Ausdrucksform* as the *Leistungsform*, not the *Gestaltwerk* but the *Organwerk*. That is to say, the architect must actually sacrifice expression of his personality and let the organism of a building speak for itself. This strategy was entirely a product of the great yearning for a new harmony in a violated world. Not surprisingly, the original proponents of organic architecture invoked nature as the main source of inspiration. So does Alberts: 'When there is a bond between a building and the primeval fabric from which it is made, the beauty

333

of nature is reflected in architecture'.★ It is striking that the concept of nature to which organic building appeals has only been possible since the Enlightenment. Nature was subjected, but the new civilisation in which people found themselves aroused such disquietude that they found it necessary to appeal to nature as their healer. Organic building shows the same paradoxical character as the patient who yearns for a return to the circumstances that originally caused his disease; or as the dialectician who, now that the synthesis displeases him, hankers after the thesis.

★ Kloos, Maarten (ed.), *Architecture Now*, Amsterdam 1991, p. 14.

The essentialism that permeates the idealised picture of nature is, however, contradicted by the subjective experience of space. To quote Hans Scharoun:

'Through the perceptual experience that a space provides, a meaning determined by the architect is transmitted to the spectator and influences his behaviour and way of being in that space. The meaning of the space and the person's behaviour and way of being in that space are thus intimately connected. Therefore space does not have an autonomous, arbitrary meaning.' ★

★ Janofske, Eckehard, *Architektur-Räume, Idee und Gestalt bei Hans Scharoun*, Berlin 1985, p. 114.

Scharoun himself conceived completely asymmetrical ground-plans for his interior spaces, offering countless perspectives and viewpoints in order to stimulate the indi-

At Last, Here it is: Capitalism with a Human Face

Alberts' identification of innovation as a desirable result of organic building brings us to the point of the functional programme, for which this architecture is stripped of its social utopianism and given a new task as the head office of a transnational enterprise. There is not much to be said against innovation as such. But the kind of innovation intended here is part of the holy trinity of capitalism, the other components of which are 'expansion' and 'surplus value'. As known, there are many possible objections to this threesome, just as capitalism in general contains several severe internal contradictions. Alberts is not himself afraid of these contradictions, seeing his remark that 'we are in favour of an economic synthesis (...) in which the free economy is allowed to stay in existence'.★ Although there are several respects in which Alberts and Van Huut draw inspiration from brick-built Expressionism, the missionary zeal of the earlier organic building is foreign to them. They are fully prepared to accommodate to the material demands of the present: a Post-Modern bank does not keep vaults full of money, unlike the Doric monoliths of the past. Now that the National Banks are dumping even gold, the final bastion of eternal value, a bank has to preserve no more than hard-disk backups and documents. A bank need have no fear of living in a glass box in which everything is open to view. All the money is hidden away

★ Ton Alberts, op. cit. p. 14.

Dutch Gaz Utilities Headquarters, Groningen, 1993

Dutch Pavilion, Sevilla Expo '92, competition entry, 1989

vidual observer's active involvement in the experience of the space. Alberts, on the other hand, avoids right angles for other reasons.

'Non-rectangular spaces foster the development of intuition. Evolution goes one step further as a result. That is why it is important for a company to work in differently shaped spaces, because people who work in such spaces will tend to think in a different way. At least, they advance a step further in their personal development, and this is what organic architecture encourages. Organic architecture stimulates people to see through things more quickly and to step over thresholds more readily. In fact organic architecture is a precondition for innovation.' ★

★ Ton Alberts, op. cit. p. 112.

in the digital packets of the inter-bank data networks. But at the same time, management is gaining growing insight into the importance of the human resource. The staff may no longer be treated as obedient automatons, carrying out a dull, repetitive routine. Under conditions of flexible accumulation, the hardware is subject to capitalistic innovation – but the wetware in the heads of the employees needs continuous updating too. The people have to be offered something more than bare filing cabinets and uniform open-plan offices. They need a solid footing.

Organic architecture gives them that footing. In the ING bank the satisfaction of this need is expressed particularly well in the continuous pedestrian route through the building, designed to aid social contact, and in the high voids in every tower, designed

Shaping the Past and Present
The rectangle was, as it were, made a present to man. That is why we can see that approximately in the Greek era the intellectual powers are beginning to be developed. Great initiators like Pythagoras, for example, put energy into this. I am thinking in this respect of Pythagoras' theory, which made it possible to lay off a right angle. That is why we can see that approximately in the Greek era the intellectual powers are beginning to be developed. As the straight angle was developed in building, thinking powers were the powers of intellect, of logical thinking. Since it was rectangular forms that shaped our thinking powers, we may see these forms as a great gift. This is the very reason we have

now arrived at a material phase that increases our insight in the nature of the material world. Without this development we would not know the universal laws of the material world and we would not have any technical aids.
However, we have now arrived at a point where the 90 degree angle is used at all times and seasons as if there were not any other possibilities. It may seem feasible that by constantly applying rigid building forms built-up from right angles, we are over stimulating our capability to think and will undergo a process of crystallisation. We may indeed now find that we are growing more rational and material, because at present we ignorantly abuse the right angle we once

received as a reward for our development. We seem only to be able to make our built environment one that is ever growing more cold, hard, intensive, businesslike and poorer. The result is a lifeless world.

Roels Hifi, showroom, Wevelgem, 1993

Marina Abramovic, Shoes for Departure, 1992

Roels Hifi, showroom, Wevelgem, 1993

to elevate the spirit. People are inspired to become self-aware individuals who are nonetheless capable of responding maturely to collectivity. The only problem is that in the system within which this architectural space functions, the straightforward opposition between the individual and the crowd became irrelevant long ago. Individuality has become something of a lost cause, leaving the present day person to merge comfortably into the crowd. The crowd, in turn, lets itself be manipulated as one entity. This all-devouring herd longs for nothing but the global Big Mac. And the whole world is potential grazing for the beef.

The ING Banking corporation, known for Third World debt conversion (by which countries can get out of debt by selling off their sovereignty) and for megamergers in the financial sector, takes a direct hand in the compression of time and space in the global village and the corresponding transformation of the mentality of space. From that point of view, both the sacral voids and the socialisation route through the building are outdated concepts. Only Mammon can inspire awe in those towering spaces, and casual meetings are good only for exchanging consumer tips about market segments. The conclusion: the instant architecture wins back something of its archaic opacity in the architecture of organic building, the heads of its occupants become completely transparent. The temptation of vitalism to enjoy the fullness of life boils down to a primitive hunger for more of the same.

Archaistic Appeasement

In their architecture, Ton Alberts and Max van Huut opt unwaveringly to express a spiritual programme. By this, they place themselves outside the order of contemporary pluralism, in which high and low culture, and values and conditions, have become interchangeable. Their architecture offers a remarkable confirmation of how far it is possible to convert ideas into matter. At the same time it offers enchanting spaces which are delightfully finished. Moreover, their experiment in energy economy is only to be warmly appreciated in this ecologically dislocated world. But the ING bank building is intended to be more than these things. It is also meant to be a monument to humanity; and, indeed, it forms a wonderful background for the perspex trophies that the managers award their staff for exceptional performance. In other words, the humanity referred to is of an unusually limited kind.

General human dealings are at the centre. The architecture does not revolve around the occupant's highly individual quest for personal fulfilment. It concerns, rather, the stimulation of a balanced interchange between the individual and the collective in an endless game of give and take. The only exception to this rule is the architect, who has promoted himself to umpire. In the spatial articulation, every reference to hierarchy, programmatic contrast, inequality and intellectual doubt is carefully smoothed away in a all-embracing, pacifying atmosphere. Horizontally, the routing and the sequence of pleasant work-zones are dominant. Vertically, the visitor can lose himself in a vague, mystical atmosphere, bathing in filtered light. This is an architecture that preaches peace and harmony in a world where these two commodities are hard to find (except in the ideology of the end of history, of course). Because everything is directed towards

creating a congenial atmosphere and fostering social intercourse, the architecture can make no appeal to a critical consciousness, let alone to a willingness to do something about the less desirable aspects of the status quo. The built environment is purely placatory and in the long run that is no real philanthropy. For even the client knows better than anyone that stagnation is tantamount to decline, and that there is no time for criticism in a capitalist order. The dilemma showcased here in a heightened form is that a mild, sensitive answer to the observed dehumanisation will ultimately only strengthen the forces that make for that dehumanisation. Through its sharp stress on haptic proximity, the architecture loses the capacity for critical distance that is required by the programme. The higher the institutional level of the commission – and a transnational bank such as the ING is an extreme example as far as that is concerned – the more strongly is architecture subject to this dilemma. Through their anthropological approach and their exaggerated emphasis on the physical body, the organic builders (and their fellow spirits from the camp of architectural Structuralism) create a distrac-

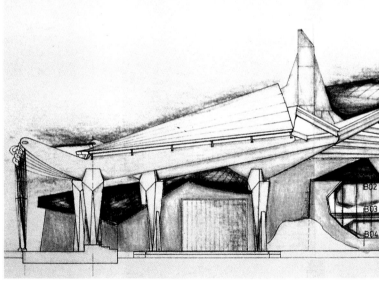

De Scheg, ice track and swimming pool, Deventer, 1993

tion. Thus we can charge this archaism with the same error as it accuses Modernism of: a disregard for the machinations of production that aim to mask divide-and-rule strategies by means of neutralising interventions. In Modernism, this neutrality consists of the transparent box. In archaism, it consists of the massage of the depoliticised body. In the vitalist variant of this archaism, namely organic building, everything is reduced to an indifferent life-energy, the Schopenhauerian acceptance of the world as 'will' and 'representation', to which every politics of change finally succumbs.

336

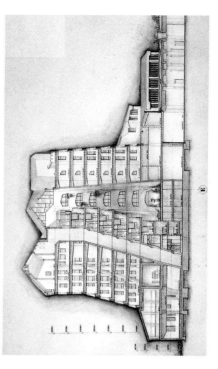

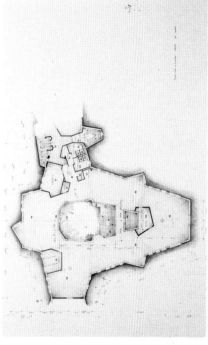

The building's appearance is determined by ten towers of varying heights. The walls of these towers are slightly sloping, reflecting noise upwards. The towers have pentagonal sun collectors on top: the building opens itself toward the crown of a tree. The relatively large external wall surface is made up nearly entirely of prefabricated concrete units, clad with handlayed bricks. Together, the towers form a capricious 'S' which winds its way through the shops, houses and flats of Amsterdam-Zuidoost. A quarter of the façade is formed by the windows, creating a favourable balance between heat loss and the admission of daylight. In each tower daylight also enters through a dome illuminating an internal void. Light art in the void provides additional light in the indoor walkway which connects the towers. Long hanging plants inside the void create curtains of green. The central facilities such as reception, four restaurants, library, film theatre and conference rooms are located on the indoor walkway. This walkway contains art that is not only beautiful, but sometimes functional as well. An example of the latter are the flow forms. They channel rainwater through the building in sinus-like movements, cleaning and oxygenating it. The channel is open so that the air gets humidified and the murmur of the water is audible. This enriched water is given to the plants that contribute to the natural atmospheric humidity. The walkway should give

its user a feeling of walking in the woods, or rather walking through organic architecture. Alberts & Van Huut desired a building that positively influences the user, thus creating optimal efficiency in the workplace. Combining this demand with those of the programme, they concluded that no large areas of office space were to be created, but rather smaller units appropriate for eight people. Such units, or 'cells' should then be flexible to grow to a size able to accommodate about forty people. Following the example of a biological organism, or a 'cell structure', the offices were then grouped into 'clusters'. Because the workstations are located within six metres of the exterior walls, individuals are encouraged to manually control the amount of air, light and heat supplied. Great attention has been paid to the building's energy efficiency. Its construction and the materials used inhibit rapid cooling and heating. The sloping walls and the solar collectors in the top of the towers make the greatest possible use of the sun as an energy source. In addition, a ceramic energy retrieval wheel draws heat from the extracted air. This heat is used to raise fresh air to the right temperature. *Based on: Domus 714, March 1990; and: ING Communications Department, Building with a difference, Amsterdam 1992.*

Location Bijlmerplein 888, Amsterdam, The Netherlands **Client** ING Banking Corporation **Design** 1978 **Completion** 1986

Architectenbureau Alberts & Van Huut *ING Head Office Building*

▶

C R E A T I O N

BRICK. THE ONLY LIMITATION IS YOUR IMAGINATION

Accept the challenge. Build with brick and discover
new dimensions of creativity. Be original. Be inventive.
But most of all let brick be your inspiration.

For further information about The Brick Development
Association contact Bob Lloyd-Jones, Director General,
at The Brick Development Association, Woodside House,
Winkfield, Windsor, Berkshire SL4 2DX. Tel: (0344) 885651.

BUILD
BETT
LIFE W
BRIC

uiry card

'Accept the challenge. Build with brick and discover new dimensions of creativity. Be original. Be inventive. But most of all, let brick be your inspiration.'

On the Work of Kisho Kurokawa
The Winning Coach is Always Right

Disneyland Japan, 1991

Dear Coach,

There is nothing we could possibly say against you. Inclusion in a book about architecture is a mere incident in a career such as yours. You are a *homo universalis* with guaranteed success in everything you do. Your buildings are being built all over the world. Your order portfolio is worth billions. Your media coverage is overwhelming. Yet these are no more than minor details in an oeuvre that stretches much wider than building alone. You are also a town and country planner, a philosopher, an engaged intellectual, a politician and a media personality. Moreover you are a prophet, guiding us towards a future that only you have glimpsed in all its glory. Your work is one great prefiguration of a world that will come some day. We, poor sublunaries, can only follow that road. We can only submit to the visions of Kurokawa the seer, who possesses knowledge of the spirit of the age to come. You are our leader, our omniscient coach. And as we all know, the winning coach is always right. Gainsay is foreign to you. Not only are you God in the deepest of your thoughts, but also in your office, where a perfectly oiled machine hums away to spread your message.

Anyone who wishes to portray you can count on the full cooperation of your disciples. When we contacted your office about material for this chapter, we received everything we asked for literally by return of post. It included a packet of press cuttings about the Kurokawa phenomenon, carefully selected with an eye to our local interests. Later, when we phoned to ask for additional pictorial material, we were treated to unsolicited advice about replacing our fax and computer equipment. Your office is not only faultless in protecting the interests of its master, but it is impeccable in promoting the kind of world he favours: a world in which the machine is totally at the service of a society which is itself so thoroughly perfected that it resembles... a machine. We cannot challenge you with counter-arguments, only with paradoxes in your thinking. We already know the historic price we shall have to pay for that: the eternal reserve bench. As reserves on your winning team, not much else remains to us but to splutter a few remarks about your symbiotic programme. We know that these words will cost us a place in the next match. But we can no longer stay silent; we too want to enjoy a bit of action, while our will is still unbroken.

You call your work 'the most representative expression of the spirit of the twenty-first century'. Who are we to question that?

Symbiosis

What will the next century, the next millennium, bring us? In your opinion, 'symbiosis', a concept which you see as suffusing the world of tomorrow. Hierarchy and discrimination will no longer dominate that world, but a fundamental equality of all cultures of all times, in all places. In this, you have laid the emphasis on the semi-public space, the intermediate zone, as the perfect vehicle for expressing your symbiosis theory. Bringing the street into the confines of your buildings can, in your view, add an 'Asiatic'

principle to Western Modernism. This will help the world regain a 'human' and 'organic' integrity. You have said, 'I seek a new symbiotic architectural space, to reintroduce symbiotic spaces *between* exterior and interior, symbiotic ambivalences between nature and architecture, symbiotic multivalences *between* contradictory elements.'★

In this, you would be breaking with the modernist 'paradigm of clear divisions of space – interior from exterior, environment from building, private from public, historic from contemporary – a strict order based on dichotomy'. The purpose of all this is 'to contain in the self the absolute Other that has hitherto ruled it'. You are engaged in decoding an oppressive society. From this point of view, your work is not only a reflection of a certain cultural configuration, but a prefiguration of a new culture. In the culture of the next century, logocentrism, eurocentrism and phallocentrism will be things of the past. The political and cultural domination of the Occident will be passé, and an ideologically indifferent 'intercultural' network will embrace the earth. From an 'age of power', whose chief motif has been the economy, we are on the way to an 'age of authority' in which moral principles count again.

Your architecture gives us a foretaste of how this new world will look in practical terms:

★ Kurokawa, Kisho, *Rediscovering Japanese Space*, New York 1988, p. 30.

There was a need to deconstruct time in order to reconstruct it in a new way that permitted the symbiosis of history with the present and future: in the same way, space had to be deconstructed, too. When the pyramid that placed Western civilisation at the top was dismantled, the cultures of different locales became freefloating units or particles that possessed their own independent values. Once this was achieved, it became possible to assemble or group the many different cultures of the world in any variety of forms.
Kisho Kurokawa

Science in its totality is built upon the distinction between the contingent and the neces-

between accident and structure. The qualities required for its birth are precisely those that do not form part of vital experience, that remain exterior as if they were independent of phenomena. The characteristic distinctive trait of mythic thought, like a bricolage over the practical plane, is that it builds structures not directly based on other structures, but rather using the residues and debris of phenomena; in English, odd and ends, in French, *des bribes et des morceaux*, the fossil testimony of the history of an individual or a society. Consequently, the relation between diachronic and the synchronic is in a certain sense inverted (...) mythic thought, a bricoleur, builds structures on the basis of

phenomena, while science, functioning simply in virtue of its own being, creates its own form of phenomena, its own means and results, thanks to structures that it elaborates constantly, and which are its theories and hypotheses.
Claude Lévi-Strauss

Diachronicity is, of course, the symbiosis of past, present, and future. One of the basic methods of Metabolism is to overlap and overlay time that is quite clearly and definitely past with the present and the future. (...) I came to strongly advocate the need for Modern Architecture to make contact with the culture and history of its region. Our

false, Western-skewed 'International Style' but by incorporating our history - and our respective histories - into the most advanced contemporary technology, into life in modern society.
Kisho Kurokawa

The second principle of Metabolism is the synchronicity of space. Before the advent of Claude Lévi-Strauss and his structuralism, the various cultures of the world were regarded as occupying different levels of development... If culture is viewed in a similar fashion, gradually developing until it approaches that of the West, modernisation must be interpreted by the developing nations as

like a barrel full of contradictions being self-confidently emptied over us. Your work, for instance, is inclusivist only in an iconographic sense. It has no tactility, and the buildings remain hard. Intuitively, we are told to keep out. We also recall the frequent use of Rikyu Grey, a greyish green that in twilight can be perceived as any colour. We recall the Japanese garden on the roof of the Pacific Tower at La Défense, Paris; your own house that conceals a traditional Japanese tearoom in its capsule forms; your building in Melbourne's City Centre, where you placed a gigantic glass dome over an existing brick building; and your Hiroshima City Museum of Contemporary Art, with its brickwork base, tiled middle layer and metal top layer as references to the integration of past, present and future. If we are to believe Charles Jencks, the empty central zone of that museum points to 'a functional entrance, a mushroom cloud, a sign of community and a conventional view of the heavens'. Figuration, ornament and mimesis have been granted a new lease of life only now that abstraction has achieved its definitive triumph. As you once said yourself, 'When attempting to transmit history through material objects, first history must be deconstructed into   ★ Kurokawa, Kisho, op. cit. p. 23. symbols and signs, and these fragments, endowed with a new meaning, must be incorporated into the work as bits of memory.' ★

Honjin Memorial Museum of Art, Komatsu, 1989

We can thus extend your theory about temporal diachronicity and cultural simultaneity by an overall semantic anarchy. You have taken Roland Barthes' analysis of Japan as *The Empire of Signs* as your new point of departure – and that in a worldwide practice. Now that the clickety-clack of Japanese shutters has echoed countless times through the universe, substance has disappeared altogether. All that remains is pure image. It is precisely through this lack of substance that syncretism becomes possible. Once again, the winning coach is always right.

Are You Right or Are You Right?

To start with, you have some criticisms of the Modernist-rationalist system of which you yourself make willing intellectual and moral use. Moreover, that system has itself always held the promise of that symbiosis which you now propose as the alternative. In other words, by stripping Modernism of its dream and attacking only the instrumentality of the Modern, and on top of that reserving exactly that dream to figure as your alternative, you leave your argument open to the suspicion of fraud. Perhaps this thought lends a colour to the following argument. Our apologies in advance.

What we so admire in you is your readiness to interpret the profession of architect in such a broad way that your built work represents only a small part of your programme. You have been unwilling to restrict your visions to an institutional discipline. Your work comprises far more than building alone. Your *ars combinatoria* brings you, and hence us too, into contact with politics, philosophy and the mass media. You are trying to take us somewhere ...

To you, the holistic cultural condition of the twenty-first century is inevitable. We are heading irrevocably towards a new, inclusivist culture in which the 'Asiatic' component will be at least as important as the Cartesian thinking that you spurn. Better still, Kurokawa will take over from Descartes. At the same time you see it as your duty to help bring about this age of humanity and mutual respect. Thus you see yourself in the midwife role that we already know so well from the gospel of progress. Thus you are both prophet and redeemer. You predict things and you make them happen too. You herald a new age, and meanwhile you have already made a start on it.

For us, the heirs of rationalism, it is either one or the other. Either you uphold a historicist view of history in which we shall live according to your predictions whether we like it or not; or we listen to your advice and get down to work. Thus we either have free will or we don't.

You have said, 'Modern Architecture's pretensions to universality were little more than a global scheme of Western cultural conquest in disguise.' But exactly the same argument could apply to your own Japanism. Heterogeneity can also be described as a mask for the homogenising processes of Modernism. Hence the ostensibly a-historical is actually as historical as it could possibly be. Just like Fukuyama. Everything is solved within the paradigm of liberalism.

You will no doubt say that objections like these are precisely the kind of weakness you have been fighting for so long, and that the symbiosis concept leaves all that behind it. But then we fail to understand why you still find it necessary to articulate any legitimisa-

West, and this is in fact the route that many developing countries, including Japan, began to march along.
Kisho Kurokawa

Technology and humanity may have been at odds in the West, but in Japan technology became an extension of humanity to be integrated and internalised, just as material things were considered extensions of the spirit and part of the same undifferentiated existence. In Edo-period Japan, the 'workings' (Karakuri) of technology were not set apart from humanity, but rather humanised as something intrinsically mystical.
Kisho Kurokawa

The search for possible exits from the alienating abstraction and reductionist strategy of Modernism has generally resulted in an even more alienating superficial variety and in the ideologically manipulated yet finally empty rhetoric of largely commercially oriented Post-Modern architecture. This reactionary neo-conservative movement repudiates not only the faults and mistakes, but also the achievements and originally critical attitude of avant-garde Modernism. Instead it propagates pastiche, pop or pseudohistorical forms, often only as dress over optimised and utilitarian structures that have been engineered strictly according to the dictates of efficient production and operation.

We are no longer a part of the drama of alienation; we live in an ecstasy of communication. And this ecstasy is obscene.
Jean Baudrillard

Architecture and urban planning must serve to facilitate not only function, but meaning, too. (...) Clusters of signifiers divorced from meaning now produce *simulacres* of meaning or pseudo-meanings, which colour and humanise spaces with humour, wit, speculation, and conviviality. The metamorphosis of free-floating signifiers and *simulacres* creates realms of 'atmosphere' or 'mood'. These poetic spaces open up not through the recombination of signs, but in stretching ambigui-

the ambivalent interplay of diverse *simulacres.*
Kisho Kurokawa

The discrepancy between theory and practice, between the way people say to have structured their life and their actual practice, belongs to the human deficiency. Japan stands out in this common practice, not only because of the huge width of this discrepancy, but also because it doesn't seem to bother the people. A certain contradistinction between formal and substantial reality exists everywhere, but the contrast in Japan is so much bigger than in the West, that we can postulate a fundamental difference. In Japan

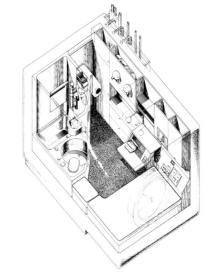

Nakagin Capsule Tower, Tokyo, 1970

Tradition and innovation in Japan

342

tion for your work at all. There is actually no need for you to convince anyone, yet your built, written and spoken achievements all amount to one huge effort to convince. So it seems you have a will, after all, although it wants something we can not oppose with the best will in the world. That way anyone could will something and always be right too. There is nothing we could possibly say against you.

As though you were a devout Modernist, you also believe that the architect's duty is to express the 'spirit of the age'. Just as the Modern Movement gave expression to the machine age, you wish to do so for the coming 'age of life', the era of symbiosis between man and machine. One thing never changes: supporters of the idea of a *Zeitgeist* with a style of its own are invariably optimists. There is no room in your vocabulary for a critical attitude towards the spirit of the times. Affirmation is the watchword.

At the same time, you make it look as though a radical move from a Modernist to a symbiotic paradigm must take place if we are to cope with the twenty-first century. That will be quite an undertaking, considering the world-wide dominance of Western ideas which you yourself recognize. In short, you now affirm what there *must be* tomorrow.

You criticise today on the grounds of what there *will be* tomorrow. To us, this looks like a case of category confusion.

Moreover, you are a revolutionary with a theory that excludes revolution by definition. You predict, or alternatively call for, a radical change. But in symbiosis theory as you apply it, every kind of radicalism is anathema. Are we to interpret your historical perspective as the final convulsion of a world view that thereafter will no longer exist? Must we accept your view of history *ex negativo*?

We found a similar kind of paradox in your implicit claim that you are capable of representing a holistic world. Here, too, we detect your presence simultaneously in and out of your own world view. There is a respectable, holistic world view. But that view, once achieved, resists all further deliberate representation. Propaganda for holism is a self-contradiction. As long as there is some pro-holist visual programme, there is no holism. The same objection could be applied in an even more extreme form to the symbiosis idea. One cannot be a proponent of universal symbiosis and part of it at the same time. Supporting an idea demands a certain analytical capacity, which you undoubtedly possess, but it cannot be reconciled with an organic, 'immediate' world. Abstract thinking,

be. Moreover, the gap between formal and substantial reality became institutionalised for the wielding of power in Japan.

K. G. van Wolferen

My aim to create an architecture that is philosophy, is literature, is not unrelated to the Japanese cultural tradition, which has always valued the invisible, the imagination. From that point of view, I do not regard the design of architecture - the realisation of material objects - as my sole task. Writing is also an extremely important part of my work.

Kisho Kurokawa

In a world which no longer consists of distinct domains and traditions, language becomes our rescue.

Christian Norberg-Schulz

When attempting to transmit history through material objects, first history must be deconstructed into symbols and signs, and these fragments, endowed with a new meaning, must be incorporated into the work as bits of memory. (...) Another method of achieving symbiosis between past and present is to incorporate the atmosphere or mood of the past - Japanese Buddhist thought or traditional Japanese aesthetics, or philosophy, or patterns of living, or arrangements of space -

past that we are trying to incorporate is invisible, a spiritual legacy, and our intellectual task is to discover a way to make this spirit come alive in Modern Architecture in a sophisticated form.

Kisho Kurokawa

Pluralism acknowledges the multiplicity of human experience and in so doing - as opposed both to the culturally destructive universalisation and uniformity of the International Style and also to the senseless fragmentation and superficial variety (the illusion of individuality) of the reactionary Post-Modernism - favours meaningful and liberating diversification; diversification

without deterministic hierarchy. In its best examples it achieves this by aiming at the cultivation and reproduction of sensitively differentiated yet commonly shared value systems within a given culture. In architecture, these value systems are rooted in and represented by the quality and spirit of actual human *places*.

Botond Bognar

Modern Architecture's pretensions to universality were little more than a global scheme of Western cultural conquest in disguise. And with what thoroughness was that successfully achieved in Japan! Even today, these assumptions unconsciously colour the vision

Fukuoka Seaside Momocha, commercial centre, 1988

which is necessary for your cultural programme, is simultaneously a stumbling block for the effectuation of that very programme. One cannot abstract in order to get rid of abstraction, or think in order to get rid of thinking.

Thus this is the origin of your ambiguity when it comes to the question of whether the world of the twenty-first century will exist in spite of us or thanks to us. On the one hand, we are supposed to put our weight actively behind it; on the other hand, we must transcend our own capacity for abstraction so as to become part and parcel of it. You give us the impression that we must make an active contribution to the abolition of our own activism. You won't be offended if we decline, will you?

This brings us once again to the legitimacy question. Who is served by symbiotic homilies such as those of Zen master Suzuki Daisetz, who wrote 'A is not A, that is why it is called A'? Who is served by the idea that we can save ourselves as a society by capitulating as individuals? The individual or the society? Perhaps the society. But what you propose as being an epistemological liberation from a rationalist and dualist straitjacket, can just as easily pass for the attempt to smooth over the enormous gap between formal and substantial reality which is so characteristic of Japan. It looks as though you deliberately plead the retention of that gap as a way of prolonging the exertion of power by those who have it.

So one more thing, Coach. When you announce to us the departure of the machine as such, and the start of a renewed respect for life in a symbiotic bond between man and machine, it remains very much a question whether that state of grace will really be so liberating and emancipating. You are right when you say that the machine was an oppressive metaphor of Modernism. Your criticism in this area affects us all. But when you propose replacing it by the new metaphor of 'life', we ourselves become metaphor. And this 'life' has all the features of a machine! It is easy enough to make that kind of link between man and technology. In this symbiosis, all our individual hopes of social improvement lapse, and we can do no more than accept the history of the future as laid out for us, with you as its advocate.

True, you succeed in creating an immense moral space with your views. But, in your biomatic universe, that space is filled only with impotent cogs. Your symbiosis is the symbiosis of the global village, the community of world nomads. People no longer communicate with one another there, but have become a function of communication.

Nostra Culpa

We look forward to the remedial training sessions you undoubtedly have in mind for us. We remain at your disposal, naturally, even if you relegate us to the reserve team.

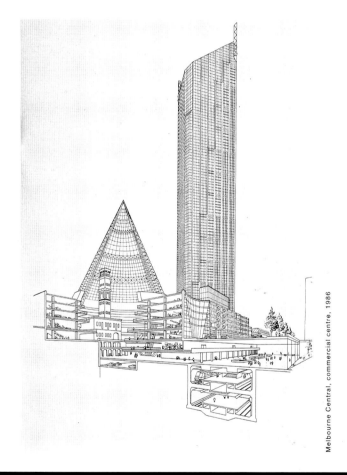

344

Melbourne Central, commercial centre, 1986

Kyoju-so villa and Ritsumei-an tea ceremony house, Tokyo, 1979

much that their own tradition of architecture has faded, grown obscure and even opaque to them. (...) In the modernisation-cum-Westernisation scheme of things, in which the standard conception of Westernisation was universal industrialisation, technological and economic assistance to developing countries were build-in adjuncts to industrialisation. From the very outset, Western cultural values stood matter-of-factly as the only valid paradigm for modernisation.
Kisho Kurokawa

Another nature will come into being when ideas of the global environment, traditional modes of thought and the 'feminine' concept are married to today's technology.
Itsuko Hasegawa

Metabolism is a philosophy of symbiosis between humankind and technology. In Western philosophy, which is the basis on which Modern Architecture is built, humanity and technology, religion and technology, art and science are regarded as fundamentally opposed to each other. (...) The philosophy of Metabolism, in contrast, sought to transcend the Western opposition between man and technology and to do that began from the assumption that man and machine could live in symbiosis.
Kisho Kurokawa

Modern Architecture and urban planning ended up exchanging success in achieving a certain type of industrial and administrative efficiency by isolating the various sectors of society according to function for a critical loss of organic integrity and humanity. Peripheral areas and intermediating zones, places where no clear divisions can be drawn between opposing elements or distinct functions - such ambiguous spaces are ultimately the most human. Sometimes such spaces may act as catalysts to meld and harmonise opposites, whether personal, social, or economic. Modern Architecture gives them no importance; in fact, they are anathema to its fundamental principles of function and efficiency.
Kisho Kurokawa

Since human beings live in contradictory ways, it is only natural that societies and cities too should contain mutually contradictory, opposing elements. As might be expected, however, the analytical approach strives to eliminate from architecture and cities the intermediate spaces and vagueness that formerly existed harmoniously there. In doing away with these things, they decrease ambiguity and diversity in human beings as well. I do think we should glean and pick up again the things - intermediary zones and vagueness - that the functionalists have cast away. Oriental philosophy and Japanese culture provide an excellent groundwork on which to do this gleaning.
Kisho Kurokawa

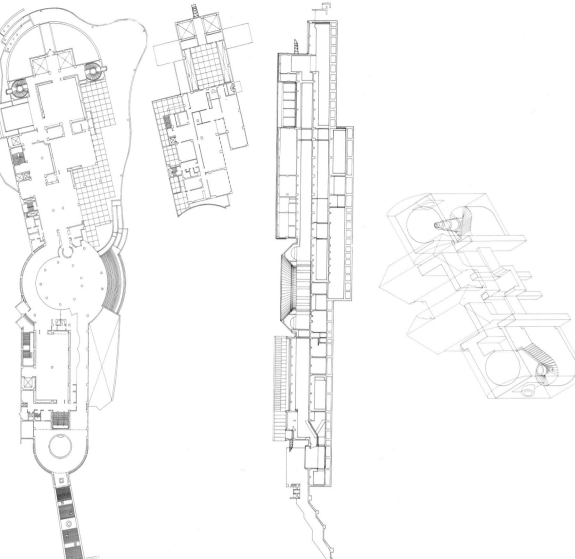

This museum officially announced to advocate 'contemporary age' as the first public museum in Japan. The word implies the wish of having a city identity after devastation by the atomic bomb. The master plan of Hijiyama Art Park, the site of the museum, was done by Kurokawa. A library had already been completed, and a natural museum was also scheduled. The 29-hectare hill of was to be transformed into a park with an artistic atmosphere. The Hiroshima City Museum of Contemporary Art was carefully situated on the ridge of the hill to preserve as much of the wooden areas on the slopes of the hill as possible. Some sixty per cent of the total floor space is below ground level. Many intermediary zones between the work of architecture and its natural setting have been incorporated into the building's exterior – a central approach plaza, a patio, a corridor, a stone garden, a stairway – facilitating the symbiosis of architecture and nature, interior and exterior. The materials used on the exterior also evolve gradually, from the natural stone foundation upward to roughly finished stone, polished stone, tile and aluminium; from earth to sky, from ground to universe, from the past to the future – all are in symbiosis. The overall shape of the museum is a linked series of gable roofs. It is segmented, a village, a group of dwellings.

This has permitted the museum to achieve a scale that does not dominate its natural setting. The gable roofs are a quotation of Edo-period storehouses, but the use of the contemporary material aluminium transforms the historical sign and imbues it with ambiguity. The approach plaza is a quotation of a Western city, yet there is no fountain or work of sculpture, indicating an empty centre. The roof of the colonnade that rings the central plaza is cut away at the front, in the direction that faces the city centre, connoting the site of the atomic bombing, and the pillars of the colonnade rise from stone exposed by the blast. Like the *roji* entrance-way garden leading to a tea room, this approach plaza has no particular function, yet it is an important area in the evocation of the meanings of the symbiosis of history and the present, and of heterogeneous cultures. A Henry Moore arch is set in the outdoor sculpture garden opposite the approach plaza, and from the cut-away section of the plaza, it suggests a gun sight that automatically leads the eye to the site of the atomic blast. *Based on: Kisho Kurokawa 1978-1989*, Japan 1989, pp. 34-35; *and: Kisho Kurokawa, Intercultural Architecture. The Philosophy of Symbiosis*, London 1991, pp. 170-172.

Location Hiroshima, Japan **Assistants** N. Abe, T. Ohta **Client** City of Hiroshima **Design** 1984-86 **Completion** 1988

▶

Kisho Kurokawa Architect & Associates **Hiroshima Museum of Contemporary Art**

Erro, Gemini Twins, 1976

About the Anti-Semitism of a Wall

This is an impossible story. It is the story of an architect who has to recognise his own failure at the point of transition from idea to building.

Elsewhere in this book, Herman Hertzberger explains that he finds architectural theorising practically worthless if its author has never seen anything of his own realised in bricks and mortar. This idea played a role for Hertzberger when he was on the competition jury for the extension of the Berlin Museum with a Jewish Museum, and he recommended Libeskind as the winner (1989). Libeskind had excelled only in building models and installations in which countless literary, historical and philosophical notions have been interwoven in exceedingly complex networks. Although he was seen in architectural circles and promoted himself as a designer with pretensions of realising his plans, Libeskind remained primarily a thinker. The laurels of the Berlin Museum competition gave him the chance to prove himself as a doer too. For Hertzberger it was in any case an excellent opportunity to put all Libeskind's fine words to the test against what he is so good at himself, namely architectural handicraft. Libeskind had to behave like a realist for once – then we would soon find out how well all those beautiful ideas stood up in practice.

The ideas remained beautiful; the design proved feasible and is being built, although with countless worrying delays. Hertzberger has at least had his way. But along with the building of Libeskind's first major work, it is very much the question whether the architect himself is at all happy about it. He is now doing justice to his qualification as an architect in practice, but it is becoming clearer and clearer that there is a strange tension between Libeskind's *Symbolbedürftigkeit*, his urge to metaphor, and the realisation of an architectural product. What is more, that tension is actually a paradox in which the architect becomes embroiled. Success looks like failure. Or worse still, it is failure masquerading as success. How did this come about?

Before success laid hands on him, Libeskind was a *Wunderkind* of Polish-Jewish ancestry, patently talented and versatile, who astonished the world with marvellous studies. Architecture looked like a suitable vehicle for ideas again. No other architect was as good as Libeskind at transforming philosophical reflections into exciting images. The material reversal of the philosophical concept of Presence was his speciality. He worked on projects such as the Pit of Babel for the Potzdamerplatz, and designed an '*Über den Linden*'. Time and time again, he demonstrated that architecture could serve as a vehicle for the intellect and hence capture the historical moment in form and matter. Nowadays the *ex positivo* approach to philosophy is practically obsolete and in Libeskind's view we should seek a conceptual framework that is a match for the void into which the twentieth century, and in particular the Holocaust, has cast us.

With his probing of the relationship between the physical void of architecture and the moral void of historical experience, Libeskind emerged during the eighties as the intellectual conscience among architects – someone who did not himself build but who

348

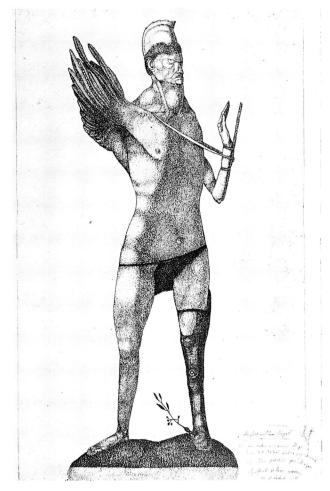

Paul Klee, The hero with the wing, 1905-38

enriched the profession with a depth of insight rarely achieved in this self-enclosed discipline. For example, Libeskind asks whether it is still possible for the architect to play a public role in an age when, for a variety of reasons, such a self-confident posture has become questionable. But nobody can place himself outside the situation; and as a result the debate has become marked by a kind of automatism, with little content. With respect to architecture, he showed that this situation led to a heavy preoccupation with the architectural vocabulary, while the expressiveness of this language was non-existent. The public was hereby simply seduced by form and failed to notice the historic loss of content.★ It was in the light of this *Mene Tekel* that Libeskind won his biggest assignment.

★ Libeskind, Daniel, 'Personal Statement', *A+U* 8 (1988), p. 131.

Not in size but in symbolic value, it was an assignment considered by some to be the most demanding project of the century. Let's wait and see...

Post-Holocaust Architecture as QED

The Jewish Museum, notably enough merely an extension to the Berlin Historical Museum, is an architectural programme with a heavily loaded significance. The task is extremely complex and has become all the more difficult now that the Wall has fallen

I don't want to be understood like I was advocating retirement. My issue is postponement in order to act: *epoche* as Husserl puts it. One should postpone the influence of [certain] factors on ones awareness, such as to put their power and intensity at stake. That's the only way to criticise them. However, I am convinced that one should be involved in the action.
Daniel Libeskind

In our times one can only think in the emptiness of vanished man. This emptiness does not excavate a shortage, nor does it prescribe us to fill a hole. It is nothing more or less than the opening of a space in which it is finally possible to think again.
Michel Foucault

How does one bring back the urgency, the immediacy which must have existed at some point of time, that violence that has to do with breathlessness? Where is the breathlessness in architecture? Why is everybody so confident? Why are people not breathless? Or why are they so out of breath for the wrong reason, running from one office to another and coordinating imbecilic data?
Daniel Libeskind

The architect must have some idea of immortality to do his work. After all, history doesn't exist.
Daniel Libeskind

and Germany is faced with internal embarrassments. In the light of increasingly overt anti-semitism, Libeskind's museum will draw all the more attention. How do you design a building for a piece of history that was almost totally eradicated by the Nazis, in a city that was itself practically wiped off the map, and on a rubble-strewn plain that was subsequently artificially built up by grace of the cultural compensation policy of the *Internationale Bau Austellung (IBA)*? The character of such a building must be almost entirely determined by things that no longer exist. Libeskind once described the Berlin Jewish cemetery, which still contains blank gravestones of Jews who had already reserved their final resting place. They form a silent but macabre testimony to their deported owners, for whom the 'final resting place' will ever remain a forlorn expectation. The empty faces of those tombstones tell us more than any other memorial could. Here it is the absence of a name that articulates the history of Berlin.

Over and above Herman Hertzberger's grounds, there was much more to be said for inviting Libeskind to take this commission, for of all architects Libeskind is the one who goes furthest in the building of nothingness. It is even his *Leitmotif*. The building is like a frozen bolt of lightning cast down alongside the old Classicist Berlin Museum. The new building can be accessed only via the old, so that the visitor is forced, as it were, to take cognisance of the radical break in the history of Berlin Jewry. This strategy of interweaving (*Durchdringung*) aims to give the Jews back a place that was taken from them by their persecutors. One might also term it compulsory correction through education, but that way of thinking would be a profanity here.

Besides the elaborate ground plan which suggests a ripped-up Star of David, both the façade and the spatial arrangement are likely to disconcert the all too naive German visitor. In the design, the external walls lean slightly outwards, display surgical incisions and are clad with gleaming metal. These features are intended to deprive the building of its substantiality. The interior space is characterised by absolute 'voided void'. A straight visual path – a 'structural rib' – cuts right through the zigzagging plan, and is accentuated at every intersection by a void. It is noteworthy that these voids operate as a kind of obstruction in the museum visitor's route. They are separated from the rest of the museum by glass walls on which thousands of names from the *Totenbücher* are engraved. Nothingness is an obstacle here; thus these voids symbolise the vanished Jewish life of Berlin. In a historical sense, too, you encounter this absence over and over again. 'Through the special emphasis on the accommodation of the Jewish Museum', Libeskind explains, 'it is an attempt to give a voice to a collective fate'. The problem is that this Jewish collectivity was one that was forced on them by the exclusion strategies which the Nazis devised as a way of coping with their own projected anxiety. The iconography of the museum, although intended for exhibition of living Jewish culture, is shaped by the history of its destruction.

However, Libeskind takes his imagery a step further. This commentary in space is not only on Jewish culture at its most distressed hour, but on our common fate that is presumably prefigured by Jewish history. 'The idea of the Berlin Museum is a model for the contemporary psyche, the state of the soul.'★ Libeskind believes that the Holocaust has made every illusion of rootedness and the associated claim to *Raum* impossible to uphold. And, indeed, it is not for nothing that *Raum* is listed in the *Wörterbuch des Unmenschen*.★ The museum as monument, as Heideggerian 'thing in the world', with its collection (memory) and its historical narrative (interpretation), is a totally obsolete concept in a culture that was, in Libeskind's own words, 'cremated in its own history'. When asked about his own Jewish consciousness, Libeskind replied 'Naturally, as a Jew there is nowhere I really belong'. In as far as his building is a commentary on culture as a whole, he seems to be saying that nobody – and certainly not the inhabitants of Berlin – belongs anywhere any more. That just falls short of implying that figuratively we have all become Jews, but it does suggest that in a philosophical sense *goyim* no longer exist. And that, of all things, in relation to the accommodation of the Jewish Museum, which, whatever way you look at it, is an attempt to give Jewish culture houseroom in Berlin again. Libeskind's building writes a full stop into history at a point where there is no more history. It attempts to focus a Jewish culture in this period when the Diaspora has become a universal condition. The building topographises the impossibility of a topography.

349

★ Libeskind, Daniel, 'Daniel Libeskind, Daniel Libeskind, Daniel Libeskind etc.', in Gevers, Ine (ed.), *The Borderline*, Maastricht 1991, p. 76.
★ Sternberger, D., *Wörterbuch des Unmenschen* ['Dictionary of Unpeople'], Munich 1970.

Ruins of the Holland House Library, Kensington, London, 1940, used in advertisement

Marking of the City Boundary, Groningen, 1990

Laying a Foundation Stone in a Moral Vacuum

Is it still really a matter of accommodation? Of a house for a fixed, coherent programme? Of bricks and mortar? When architecture becomes as intensely metaphorical as that of Libeskind, is it not likely that its metaphorical strength could overwhelm even the eternal meanings of structure, occupation and presence? The foundation, which is anchored in the ground, is in just as much trouble as is philosophical fundamentalism in its present state of deconstruction. Architecture may thus have reached the end of the line as the imagery of system builders, and might make a new start as semiosis without end. It would at least be appropriate close to the fallen Wall. Since 9 November 1989, inside and outside, the One and the Other, and good and evil have no longer been what they used to be.

The design of the Jewish Museum, with its zig-zag ground plan without logical termination, can also be understood as a reference to the Jewish tradition of endless analysis of the Talmud. The holy law must be forever interpreted and expounded. This cultural motif of endlessness recurs in countless later cultural expressions. An example is the never completed process of psychoanalysis, in which the ultimate core of the soul is never bared. Another is the process of deconstruction as propounded by Jacques Derrida, which centres specifically around the negation of the idea of an ultimate meaning. And the new incarnation of this old pattern, morbid though it may be, is the effect of the Holocaust. The latter has ensured the definitive unreachability of an ultimate dogma from which everything could be deduced and the failure of every interpretation. To round off this grisly line of thought, the *Endlösung* turns out to have produced a cultural universalisation of endless analysis. The result of the Holocaust was a tragic

perpetuation of the Jewish tradition. Architectural metaphors soon go out of date. But not this time. This is because the museum is, in a figurative sense, about a historic event which in a certain sense has ended history, the Holocaust. After the excesses of history, history in the guise of the course of civilisation cannot just carry on regardless. The *Endlösung* was a programme to relieve the history of Europe of the Jews. But with the modest distance of time that we now enjoy, we could say that the Jews were thereby relieved of the historic problem of Europe: the idea that mankind was capable of taking control of his own fate. Through those very excesses, we cannot go back to the world before Auschwitz. 'After the absolute zero-point', Libeskind said,

'after the Holocaust, everybody is a survivor. (...) Actually surviving means that you can't die. So those beyond the borderline, they died, they were murdered. But those who survived cannot die. They can pass away, they can have a heart attack, but they can not die.' ★

So how appropriate it is that Libeskind refers to failure as a sign of intellectual quality. 'I am not interested in those who succeed in stabilising the image and giving the final answer. I am interested precisely in those who teeter on the edge of failure or in those who actually fail. I believe that all great architects have failed. It is as failure that their work sets us an example.'

It is always the seeking, explaining and interpreting of things that excites Libeskind. That is probably what appeals to him so strongly in Paul Klee, whose work often provided themes for projects in Berlin. In his painting ★ See Gevers, Ine (ed.), op. cit. p. 81. *Hero with Wing*, Klee provided a parameter for twentieth-century historical awareness. His hero is no longer the demiurge who succeeds in forcing the world into submission,

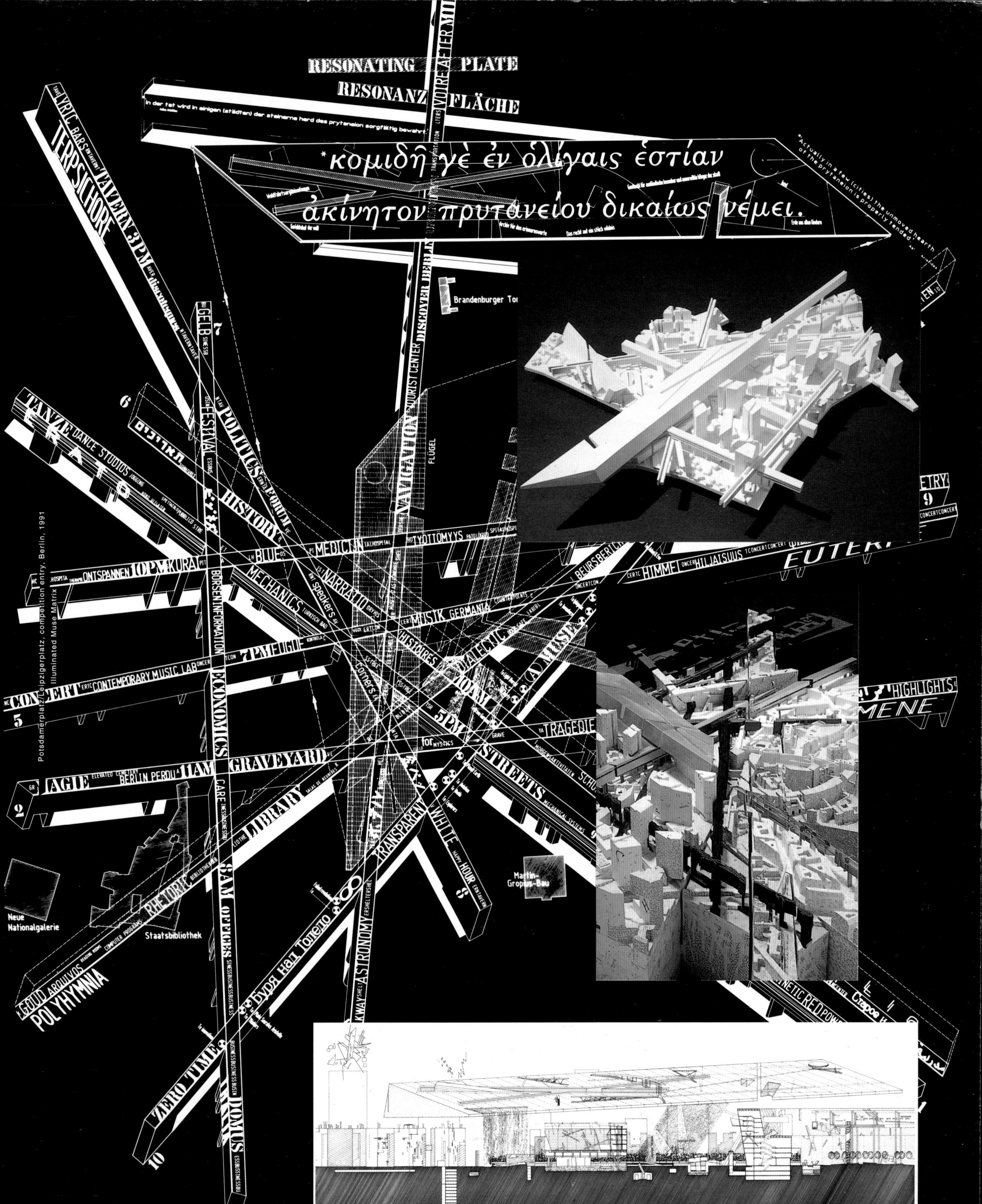

RESONATING PLATE
RESONANZ FLÄCHE

*κομιδῇ γέ ἐν ὀλίγαις ἑστίαν

ἀκίνητον πρυτανείου δικαίως νέμει.

Brandenburger Tor

Neue Nationalgalerie

Staatsbibliothek

Martin-Gropius-Bau

POLYHYMNIA

TERPSICHORE

ERATO

EUTERPE

Potsdamer Platz/Leipzigerplatz, competition entry, Berlin, 1991
Illuminated Muse Matrix

Section of Leipzigerplatz

but (in Hans Magnus Enzensberger's phrase) a 'hero of the retreat'. Pulling back before events take a tragic turn is what Libeskind admires most.

In the meantime, we have a nagging sense of doubt. The 9th November, now three years later, was the day of the museum's *Grundsteinlegung*. But how can we talk about foundation stones in connection with a philosophical manifesto of disintegrating foundations? Ground, stone... what are we worrying about? Time appears to trudge on in spite of all the philosophical speculations about the end of history, and the real seems to be winning ground; inevitably, the architect must strike while the iron is hot. Time actualises even Libeskind's ideas.

An Architectural Office as Shadow of the Promethean Process

Libeskind is showing no signs of retreating at present – on the contrary. In this respect he has failed once again, but in a different, much more literal sense. For it now looks as though he really is going to get a building built, in spite of countless setbacks. We are not referring to his adjustments to the plan. That kind of failure is usually the result of miserliness. In the present case the failure lies deeper. Libeskind has himself described his new career as a master builder as living in the shadow of the Promethean process. In that shadow, the feverish heat of the creative process is reduced to the clichés that lie within the potential of realisable architecture. This brings him back to the 'reality principle' that he was so anxious to avoid. The architectural object, the 'thing' in Heidegger's terms, must after all carry the cultural meaning, and that almost immediately brings us back into the phenomenology that underlies this 'work'. Libeskind turns out to be capable of piling up bricks – really, just like Hertzberger – and as a result he now gets some real recognition at last.

But there is yet more failure in this work, whether by choice or otherwise. By being elected winner of this competition, Daniel Libeskind has lost his Jewish identity in a philosophical sense. Now he is obliged to *represent* world (dis)order. Someone who aims to build as a way of expressing every existential, philosophical and ethnic uprooting, ultimately builds the transgression of his own (second) commandment and thereby his own repression. A coherent museum programme, with the pretence of telling us about the ways of the world, is also a prison; an architectural structure, on solid foundations, is like a barbed-wire fence; a wall, with the pretence of defining an identity, of separating here from there, the One from the Other, is thus anti-semitic.

On this point, the metaphor has gone too far. Has some Tom Thumb perhaps scattered pebbles on the serpentine lobes from which this absurd conclusion springs? Can we turn back? Or can we go forward? Where to, then? To questions like these, Libeskind's museum has no answer. Through the stress on the absolute 'zero point' of history as a universally dominant morality, every option, every perspective becomes futile. We can no longer die, let alone die for something. Life is over. We can only survive. Not in concrete (Alexander Mitscherlich) but in the metaphor of the slaughter of our forefathers. The organised introduction to Jewish culture on offer in Berlin can only take place in a funereal mood. But surely that wasn't the intention, was it?

Über den Linden, competition entry, Berlin, 1990

When everything is aggressively made to signify something, the whole cannot possibly mean anything.
Kurt Forster

I think architecture is a dialogue between the existing and contradictory forms, spaces, and functions, which immediately surround a building. The particular mission of building is to discover identity in the contradictions between decision and history.
Daniel Libeskind

Genius is the ability to conceive of imaginary objects as one would of real ones, and to treat them the same way.
Novalis

Since he let go of his love for divine *episteme* in favor of an opinion, the architect became a propagator of opinion: he lost his participation in 'Sophia' -that mysterious dimension of architecture called celestial by Alberti. Architecture becomes the territory of everybody (managers, renovation, interior designers, town planners - a 'fine profession') and of nobody at the same time.
Daniel Libeskind

Architecture, that divine luxury of faith, that highest crystallisation of the material freedom of mankind, its imaginative and mental power, should never yield to the status of being the degenerate product of necessity, delivered by the specialist of educational and monetary utopias.
Daniel Libeskind

The ideological derailment that architecture can actually put an end to experience and provide a final resting place or solution to a human desire is the cliché of architecture. But as the mother of arts it is the most important metaphor we have for stabilising and thus subverting human existence, a place in the world, the city, the crossroads, the temple.
Daniel Libeskind

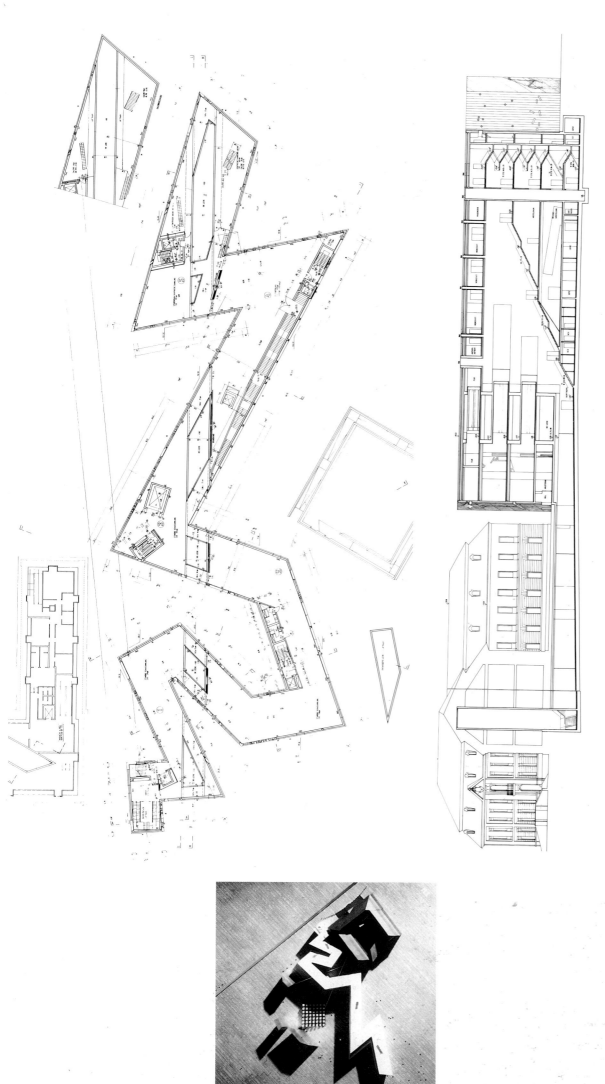

The extension of the Berlin Museum, with special emphasis on housing the Jewish Museum Department, is an attempt to give voice to a common fate: common both to what is *being* and to what is *other* than being.

The past fatality of the German–Jewish cultural relation in Berlin is enacted now in the realm of the invisible. It is this invisibility which must be brought to visibility in order to give rise to a new hope and to a shared inner vision.

Thus this project seeks to reconnect Berlin to its own history which must never be forgotten. The new extension is conceived as an emblem wherein the invisible has made itself apparent as the Void, as the Invisible.

Void/Invisible: these structural features have been gathered in this space of the city and laid bare in an architecture where the unnamed remains in the name which keeps still. Like Berlin and its Jews, the common burden – the insupportable, immeasurable, unshareable burden – is outlined in the exchanges between two architectures and forms which are not reciprocal, which cannot be exchanged for each other.

The urban, architectural and functional paradox of closed/open, stable/added, Classical/Modern, museum/a muse, is no longer reconcilable through some theoretical utopia and can no longer presuppose the fictitious stability of State, Power and Organisation. In contrast, the paradox presupposes the unchanging, i.e. change proceeding directly out of that which would exclude changing attitudes and unchanging opinions alike. What all

this amounts to is two lines: one straight but broken into fragments, the other tortuous but continuing into infinity. As the lines develop themselves through this limited-infinite 'dialectic', they also fall apart – become disengaged – and show themselves as separated so that the void, centrally running through what is continuous, materialises itself outside as ruined, or rather as the solid residue of the independent structure, i.e. as a voided-void. Fragmentation and splintering mark the coherence of the ensemble because it has come undone in order to become accessible (both functionally and intellectually). The torn shards both inside and out never pre-existed as a whole (neither in the ideal Berlin or in the real one) nor can they be put together again in some hypothetical future. The fragmentation is the spacing, the separation brought about by the history of Berlin which can only be experienced as the absence of time and as time fulfilment of what is no longer there.

The *absolute* event of history – the Holocaust, the burnout of meaningful development of Berlin and of humanity – shatters the place while at the same time bestowing a gift of that which cannot be given: the preservation of the sacrifice, the offering, the guardian night-watch over absent and future meaning. And out of the disaster of the too late there arises what is early: out of what is too far, the near. *Daniel Libeskind*

Location Lindenstraße, Berlin-Kreuzberg, Germany **Assistants** B. von Hammerstein, D. Bates, A. Terragui and others **Client** Senate of Berlin **Design** 1989-92 **Completion** 1993-96

Daniel Libeskind *Jewish Museum*
▶

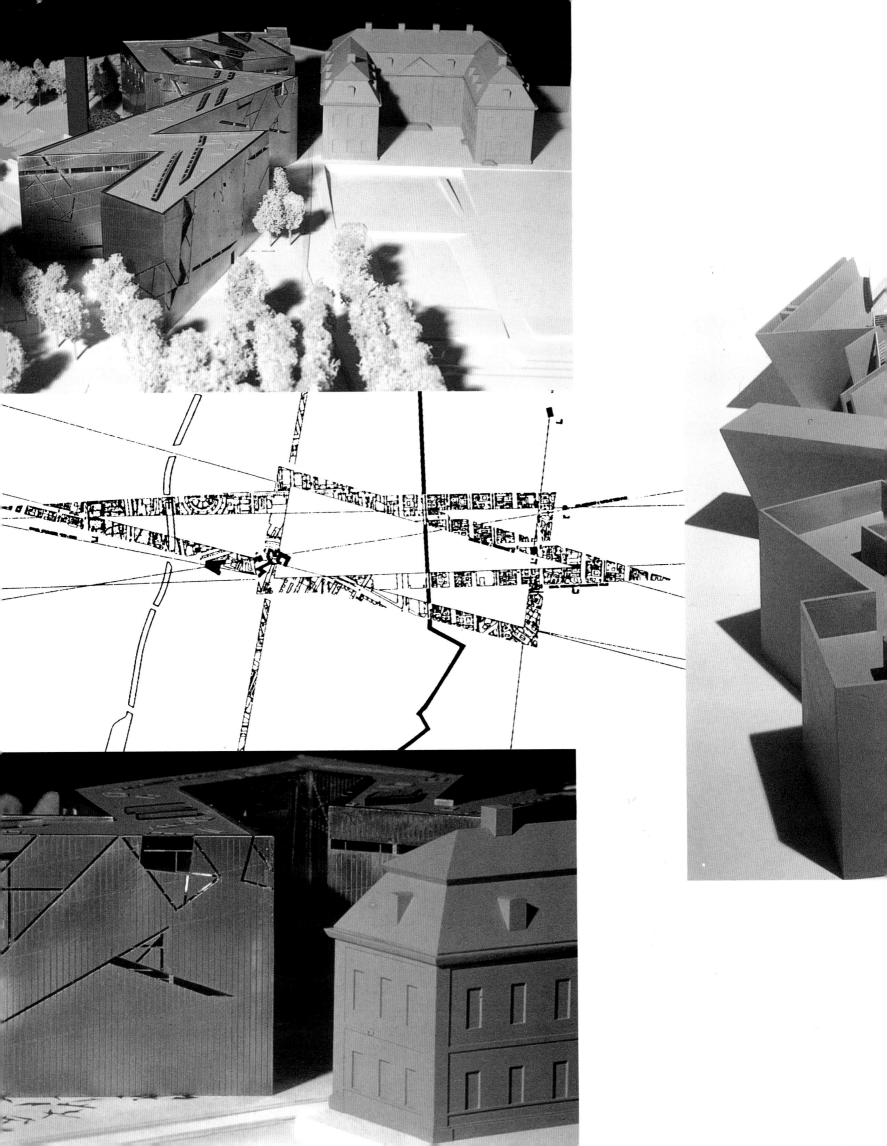

Hans Haacke, Die Freiheit wird jetzt einfach gesponsert – aus der Portokasse, contribution to site-specific art project 'Die Endlichkeit der Freiheit', Berlin, 1990

„Kunst
bleibt
Kunst."

The Reason I Laugh or:

The Topsy-Turvydom of Post-Modern Architectural Ethics

A Conversation with Charles Jencks

If there is anyone from the world of architecture who knows how to mobilise the press and television for his ideas (and to tailor his ideas to suit the media), then it is certainly the architect/writer/critic Charles Jencks. With an unremitting stream of books, articles, guest editorships, panel discussions, lectures and television appearances, he has grown into a provocateur of world repute, an *enfant terrible* among architects. His name seems to be forever connected with Post-Modernism, since the publication in 1977 of his book *The Language of Post-Modern Architecture,* in which he applied the term originally used for some time in literary theory to architecture. According to Jencks, Post-Modernism meant radical eclecticism.

Jencks is above all radically eclectic himself, having at his disposal an enormous reservoir of theories, labels and flexible contents, which he freely draws on. His strongest point is the incorporating of new movements and trends into historical frameworks of development, in a way that suggests that Jencks has seen things coming. Rather than surprise, one invariably gets the feeling in reading his texts that the new was inevitably about to arrive. Jencks himself is not so much a prophet, however, as a chronicler of history. It is as though he continually manages to keep pace with the merry-go-round known as pluralism. Jencks is journalist par excellence of pluralism, a man who, in the words of Stig Dagerman, 'practises the art of being late as early as possible'.

The journalist always reacts secondarily, living from the facts of others. He or she chases reality, which, because of the nature of time, is always running on ahead. This is why articles and news items constantly show signs of short-windedness and forgetfulness, giving rise to a situation in which intellectual topoi or metaphors are deployed in a cliché'd way, and prevailing prejudices are reinforced. What's more, the journalist, simply through his function, is a part of a mechanism that not only represents reality but also actually produces it. There has to be news to sell, and what news sells the best? Ultimately the only thing to be called news will be what offers 'infotainment'. Journalism in fact stands at the birthplace of *The Society of the Spectacle* and it is this society itself which is the sole fact that journalism itself is responsible for. It is actually a meta-fact.

But Charles Jencks is more than just a journalist, he is also a critic. He does not go in for continual changes of subject, he is not a victim of the issues of the day. Criticism means testing and in this sense it is just as primary. Although secondary as a medium, it will create a space of its own, which in its turn can then be occupied by (in this case) architecture. For Jencks and his work, semiology is apparently the ideal entry to every imaginable type of architecture. Having begun in the sixties as an advocate of the democratising of architecture, Jencks saw in semiology the path to a notion of architecture supportable for years to come: the theory of *'double coding'.* If architecture is communication, then try as architect to communicate with everyone. It is this view that has guided him through all sorts of architecture and provided him with the criteria for architectural criticism, the only constant being a plea for architecture that is in dialogue with the public, whatever that might precisely mean for Jencks. A critique which is also fed, of course, by a great passion for the building industry itself, as well as for art and literature.

Even though Jencks is a prime example of the adolescent who is unable to really decide on something, he is certainly persistent in his method. In 1986 appeared *Post-Modernism, the New Classicism in Art and Architecture.* Jencks' aim is to have done with the tendency to call Post-Modernist everything that deviates from the fossilised modernist standard (steel skeletons covered by a membrane of glass). Holding the patent on the term as an architectural notion, he defines it further: the movement that, from the Modernism of Baudelaire through to Baudrillard, attempts to form a bridge to time-honoured humanism. He argues for the rehabilitation of the Classical canon as this was the only thing able to suggest a harmony, 'even if it's not there at all'. This ironic addition is obviously the pivot on which everything turns. It's no longer necessary for there to be a meaning for his method, the method itself has to be heroically maintained. For Jencks, 'Free Style Classicism' is the field where this irony can remain recognisable.

Charles Jencks, the David Attenborough of architecture, tireless observer of the species that populate the world of building, and moreover futurologist, accountant, mastermind, show-off. Finally: critic, author of many a book of the month. A 'free style' mental gymnast talking about the last days of mankind and what's simply going to happen afterwards. 'Here he is: Mister Charles Jencks!'

Charles Jencks

Klaus Staeck, Es röhrt zum Himmel, 1974

357

In the first chapter of your book The New Moderns, From Late to Neo-Modernism *(London, 1990, p. 20)*
you write:

> **'In the final analysis Modernism is the ideology and style of modernisation and both will last until**
> **the Second and Third Worlds are fully industrialised and the problems of modernisation are so**
> **acute everywhere that the Post-Modern paradigm is adopted by the whole world. At that point**
> **ecology and semiology, not economy and materialism, will be the leading modes of thought.'**

Could you explain why this shift will take place?

From a materialistic angle industrialisation in the Second and Third Worlds is going to create such tremendous pollution that it will also create eco-catastrophes. No one is yet politically willing to do much about it,
so we are on a collision course. People will not solve their problems until they have to, or even until after
they had to. I think that's typical of the way cultures react. They react to crisis, when it becomes unthinkable not to react. I predict that we'll continue to pollute the world and eventually we'll use up most of its
resources because of modernisation: no one wants to abandon production. In that sense we are still Young

Moderns. Especially the Second and Third Worlders, who want to modernise. All these people are skating on ever-thinner ice. But the shift of thought will emerge when people are forced to change because of the ecological contradictions.

Ecology is a prerequisite of survival. But what about semiology? There you enter the cultural field.

Culture does not consist primarily of material goods, although material goods provide a certain basis for culture. We still live in a materialistic culture, but we will move back to the larger Western paradigm which is the *Graeco*-Gothic ideal of culture. When you ask me what is the measure of mankind, I answer it is culture. What is culture? Culture is meanings, information, words, and all the texts. That's not destructive to the eco-sphere and it's ultimately why people enjoy living. This understanding will dawn on people just because it's good for them or because it's true. Because there is still a pursuit of material ends and there is still a pursuit of control and power over those material ends, we will continue to be on this collision course. And morally it's indefensible to say that the Second and Third World cannot enjoy material goods as long as we are enjoying them. But if we are not going to give them up, we are all going to pollute the world till the eco-crash comes.

You describe it as a kind of confrontation between the material world-view and the semiological world-view. But one could also say that the semiological world-view sustains the materialistic world-view in a more subtle way, since nowadays semiology is paramount in many cultural fields. For example in architecture. Every architect once in a while speaks about 'using signs'.

Exactly, just as they are speaking about ecology. Both ecology and semiotics have permeated mass culture. It's true. But the fact that things are debased and vulgarised doesn't make them less true, or any less important. We have a whole lot of green products but they make no difference to the destruction of the eco-system. Nevertheless people are happy if they buy them, and that is part of the culture of going green. It is one of the paradoxes of mass culture.

If we may suggest the opposite: that in the Brave New World materialistic multinational power could make use of semiology as a kind of tranquilliser. Could that be true?

It definitely is true. Advertisers like Saatchi & Saatchi are capitalising on it. It's a powerful truth. But the fact that it can be exploited doesn't change the main point. Maybe you are Baudrillardians who are obsessed by the pollutant qualities of the information age, but it is not the only level.

What should be the subject of architecture, according to this multilayering of culture?

I think you can't generalise about the subject of architecture for all time. One could say that for all of us there are subjects such as the human body, the relation to nature (two of the great classical themes), the relation to construction and the relation to place. There are a whole lot of answers to your question, none of which is the answer. If you ask me what is the universe, as seen from a Post-Modern perspective, I think you can represent that. In a way my house is an attempt at an open ended Post-Modern text. We never knew exactly what the overall text was, but there is a double limitation; one is the form, a kind of 'Free Style Classicism' out of wood, and the other is the limitation to certain themes about the cosmos and about time.

You have to show the conflicts as well as the coherence. The problem with deconstruction is that it fetishises conflict, as does a certain kind of Post-Modernism. Always showing conflicts becomes another kind of essentialism.

Why are you so anxious to define the deconstructivists?

Because you have to see how typically Modern, with all it's deficiencies, the deconstructivists are. You can step back and ask why are they doing this to us. It's once again the producer's control over the consumer. To gain control over the client and creative autonomy. In the nineteenth century the Modernists fought for autonomy. They didn't want to be a subservient tailor, but rather a doctor, or politician, or the prophet belonging to the Modern Movement in art and architecture. In the 1820s Saint-Simon and others gave the avant-garde its prophetical role; they would lead society and produce what they wanted. In a sense that artistic autonomy is what Modernism and its continual revolutions are about. They say 'the public be damned, client be damned and consumer be damned, we are going to give you what we want'. They are carving out a free space for themselves. I should emphasise that the key idea on the Post-Modern agenda is to give equal power to producers and consumers, and this leads to its typical eclectic style and double-coding.

David Kolb in his book Post-Modern Sophistications, Philosophy, Architecture and Tradition, *(Chicago, 1990, p. 105) reproaches your eclecticism for being as modern as the Modern exclusivism of the twenties.*

He says:

'If we would escape the modern, we must avoid the temptation of saying that after the complete barrier between the architect and history we now have a complete freedom with history. To flip from no access to total access is to stay within the Modern. Perhaps we need to envision more carefully what would be truly beyond the Modern: the switch from "all or none" to "some".'

I understand why Kolb is critical of an absolute freedom and the idea that all styles 'may be played with'; of course that often trivialises style and history. But the point is that today all styles are equally open to adaptation and transformation, and it depends on the local context, the client, the function and several other concerns, including the architect's desire, which style or styles are in fact used. We are not in a nineteenth-century position which argued for the revival of one as against another, because now all are accessible. And the radical eclecticism consists in choosing the 'correct style or styles for the job' based on the many factors I have just mentioned. This is the positive kind of freedom we have. In that sense it already is the switch Kolb asks for, from 'all or none' to 'some'. Look at Venturi's recently completed extension to the National Gallery – a new classicism, a new black Miesian façade, new vernacular at the back, and on the inside new Tuscan – only 'some' styles, all relevant to the job.

But the problem is that there is no qualitative difference between the Modern anti-style and the Post-Modern embrace of all styles. What stays the same is 'the distance due to self-awareness'.

AJM & BLR, Landeszentralbank, Frankfurt

It's true that the 'Post-Modern' stands with the 'Moderns' in recognising our distance from historical models, a 'distance due to self-awareness' and the interruption of cultural continuity by modernism, industrialisation and the materialist interpretation of life. This indeed makes monoculture impossible and irony necessary – if hardly sufficient. Too much irony, or predictable irony, is as boring as naive or dumb or straightforward functionalism. The eighties saw the acceptance of pluralism and an irony which signals distance: these attainments can now be taken for granted, as new goals on the Post-Modern agenda are set. Look at the greening of the city and big business, at the Landeszentralbank in Frankfurt. The roofscape and six gardens of that building show one important goal of the future movement.

Even if you succeed in making clear the difference between late Modern deconstructivism and Post-Modern eclecticism, your analysis of deconstructivism will remain a sociological one; you look to their practice from the outside. But from the inside they see themselves in a more philosophical way. They don't see themselves as producers because the category of production is not valid any more, it's a term of a mechanistic world-view. Deconstructivists see their own products as text. There is a very substantial difference between text and product because there is no producer behind text.

For them you mean, but that's just pure ideology. Because there is always a producer and in this case it is them.

Robert Venturi and Denise Scott Brown, National
Gallery, Sainsbury wing
(extension), London, 1991

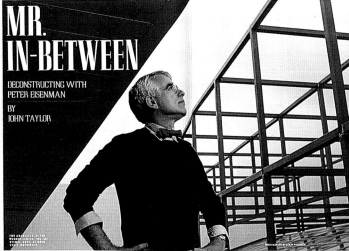

The architect Peter Eisenman at the Wexner Center
for the Visual Arts, Columbus, Ohio, 1989

Philip Johnson (commissioner),
Peter Eisenman and Frank Gehry
(architects selected to represent the United States
in the Venice Biennial 1991) at the Four Seasons,
New York, 1991

If they describe themselves as post Classical, while you describe them in terms of a Classical Modern position, we'll have a Babel. Of course they understand you perfectly if you are analysing them in that way, but they don't really want to communicate in those terms. How can you construct a framework for communication with people you don't want to understand on their terms, and who don't want to accept yours?

Basically there are three choices. You can say they are right, or wrong, or half-right and half-wrong. What I'm saying is that they are wrong, by and large, when they deny that they are producers; they produce buildings, artefacts, and texts. They may have learnt those texts from someone else, they may give them some intertextuality, but the role of the author still exists. They are authors and have responsibility; to deny it is just unadulterated ideology. **It's interesting that the greatest egotists of our century have been those who denied the role of personality in creativity.** Eisenman, whom I love dearly, is the greatest egotist in architecture, and he denies his ego – which is no surprise. Because by externalising his process and getting an *Archimedean* point outside culture, he tries to say this is just intertextuality and that he is not responsible for it. Eisenman's is an extreme form of controlling the discourse. He is unassailable, because he has got the code. This is an old trick which goes back to the Greeks, if not further. You usually get caught at this trick, politically. So it's quite funny and that's why I'm laughing, because he knows he is getting caught.

But you are still looking at it from the outside. How do you put your finger on it in such a way that he will accept the consequences and engage in a dialogue?

Peter Eisenman will not accept the consequences, but we still have a dialogue. We have a lot of conversations.

There is a human being on one side of the line, and there is another one on the other side, so in a mechanical way there is a dialogue; but is there, philosophically?

Sure, because negation is a form of dialogue and his negation, his wrapping up the whole Classical world including everybody but himself and Derrida, is an egomaniacal reading of history. He wants to impose it on the reader and on the rest of society too, to exaggerate his own importance. You can deal with that through dialogue and through conversation and see how it relates to the past and how it relates to the present. He still has to negotiate, he still has to enter into discourse with others; and that is the importance of dialogue. My metaphysic is different from his; his of three years ago, because he is now denying Derrida and deconstruction. The Pope must keep moving, the Pope of the New must never get trapped in a pigeonhole. The New Moderns, the violated perfectionists, have a certain attitude towards society in general which is characteristic of the Modern Movement of the last 200 years. I think that their world-view is coming to an end. Of course, world-views take 400, 500 years to come to an end and they can produce wonderful things in the meantime. I think that's happening with Modernism and late Modernism. Foster's Hong Kong and Shanghai Bank is an incredible piece of idiotic overdesign which legitimates the profession. From the Hong Kong banker's point of view it signifies brute, economic and material power.

They feel like they have a very efficient mental phallus. On the other hand the profession is flattered because the building has been designed all the way through truthfully, from beginning to end. Every single nut and bolt is designed and looks good too. What's more, fourteen entire issues of architectural magazines have been devoted to that building. It has never happened in the history of the architectural profession. Even the Eiffel Tower did not get that many magazine features. Peter Eisenman and his Wexner Visual Arts Center, Ohio, have been given red carpet treatment in ten international issues. What does that tell you? It's telling you that the design world wants to hear the message of Sir Norman and Peter Eisenman. Professional fame tells you about professional ideology, the reception tells you their message wants to be heard. But their message is deeply nihilistic, something of which they are not fully aware. Norman Foster would deny it, the bank would deny it. The message is nihilistic in the sense that Nietzsche – and with him the nineteenth century – understood: technology as an end in itself generates meaninglessness. Of course the people and the profession do not understand this, but since I'm not a nihilist I can laugh at it. And yet because it represents an important trend in the profession it has to be taken seriously. I live in this culture, these are Anglophones and I can see that they are the professional dominants. They may like to think of themselves as recessive, but Sir Norman as the knighted Modernist no longer can, and neither can Eisenman as the Crown Prince of Philip Johnson. So we basically have Sir Norman and Peter Eisenman, setting two Anglophonic discourses on architecture. I would rather have a more benign philosophy and benign people dominating the architectural culture, but I realise it's a pluralist Post-Modern world, and they are, for the moment, leaders.

Norman Foster, Hongkong and Shanghai Banking Corporation Headquarters, 1986

This pluralist Post-Modern world could still be monolithic. In the phrase quoted above you allude to an agenda that could subvert this. How can we escape from the pluralist situation in which we accept that you are making a few converts, that Peter Eisenman, Norman Foster and the others are making a few converts, each of you with a couple of propaganda magazines at his disposal, towards the major shift within a few decades?

You can't predict the future, it's unpredictable by nature. Nevertheless, we have to formulate a 'surprise-free world' that is an extrapolation of all trends to discipline our thoughts about what is possible. Because we are all engaged in shaping the way we want it to be. If there are no surprises and things continue to develop in the way they are going, the situation in 2050 will be eco-catastrophe and semiotic glut. Those two things will force a new world-view in so far as, in Marxist terms, the substructure forces the superstructure to develop in certain ways. I'm not a determinist, but I do believe there are relations between the deep structure of society and culture. It's not a bad prediction that – as the Second and Third Worlds industrialise and post-industrialise – they will adopt a world-view which is already here today, and is the right one. I'm also slightly sanguine about it, because I'm convinced we won't shift without catastrophes.

It's paradoxical that from a macroscopic, apocalyptic point of view you see disaster coming, you foresee a situation of limitation, of narrowing down, of think globally and act locally. But how can you act locally if you think globally? The other paradox is that evidence is on your side, but at the same time you cannot escape from the fact that in the cultural field everything is accepted; all the paradigms are living peacefully together. You are the person who has evidence on your side, but you cannot convince anybody any more because there is this cacophony of private opinions.

Klaus Staeck, Nord-Süd Konferenz, 1979

Yes, in the First World, not in the Second and Third Worlds. The party is quite localised. I'm not against the party going on. The point of having a 'surprise-free world' is a set of baselines, a paradigm so you and I can talk. A set of assumptions means that we can talk about how we ought to act, assuming this hypothetical world is going to come. It has catastrophic aspects to it, but there is also hope; how do we orientate ourselves? At the same time, and again this makes me laugh, there is likely to be something from outer space, as it were, that just hits us from the side, which will enable us to throw off these assumptions. But until it does, we must use these assumptions. First of all, the feast of paradigms. They are conflicting, aren't they? Conflict can actually be a form of engagement as well as disengagement. This is one of the things of which I recently became aware. Curiously enough the system is now working 'conflictually', to use that horrible word, and quite positively it has created a space of tension between paradigms which creates the illusion of a centred culture. In other words, the tension set up between those different paradigms establishes meaning, and that gives coherence to their conflict. Or are you saying the paradigms don't talk to each other?

They need each other because only together they form the discourse, but there are no consequences of the discussions. You hear a few arguments, then you go home and you think about those arguments and use them to strengthen your own arguments. That's normal, but you also get exhausted by it, because you aren't enriched by a new situation, a new level at which you both have a short-time consensus. There is no consensus. It is not focused on consensus. It is focused on 'take what you can get and stay put, being backed up by your own subgroup'. It's reasoning without levelling.

You are talking about dissent. It can lead to a devolutionary spiral. It's not so bad for the producers, but for the consumers you get more and more fragmented, isolated environments, a whole lot of good deconstruction here, Post-Modernism there, and Classicism elsewhere, and no one is responsible for the system as a whole. I agree, there is a necessity for these hardened positions to speak with each other and have a true dialogue. I come back to dialogue as a key concept – a dialogue is positive because it is open and doesn't know where it's going. The dialogue is creative whereas a dispute is a fixing of positions in which not much is learned – except the fact that you hold a position and that it is validated by your opponents who occupy an equally stupid one. That is a good description of the Cold War of Architecture, a situation we are in, and that's not good. **The only good thing is that pluralism reigns. Pluralism is allowed to reign within the tense oppositional system, which allows new positions to have room for manoeuvre.** Think of how awful the system used to be, where you only had a monolithic discourse. Of course I'm exaggerating, but basically from the fifties to the sixties you could learn Modernism and that was it. Now you can learn Modernism and a little something else in the architectural schools; so we do have more room to breathe in the West. Modernism isn't the only dominant now, it's contested.

But if you look at an office-building by Eisenman, or one by Michael Graves, or whatever kind of office, actually the layout of the plan is almost the same, so that on the economic level and on the programmatic level there is no debate. They just copy the ingredients of the system. In 'Against Pluralism' (Recodings, Art, Spectacle, Cultural Politics, Washington 1985) Hal Foster made a powerful point: pluralism tends to absorb argument. Is that what you want?

Pluralism absorbs argument, that's the point of dialogue; to hear all the arguments and move on from your dogmatic position to a new one. It is wrong if one doesn't arrive at a decision, or if it is not clear what the decision is. Foster is probably attacking pluralism as a form of avoiding decisions: just airing the subjects and then leaving them unresolved. Pluralism has been a form of pseudo-engagement in our culture, which doesn't mean, as Foster may imply, that it's a bad thing. It means that you haven't faced the results of the dialogue. If you follow Foster's position, you would end up in a dogmatic system where only someone knows the truth and imposes it. Then you would get action, from his point of view. I agree that liberal demo-cratic pluralism has often ended up in talk-talk-talk. But what happened in Iraq was act-act-act and you can see what the consequences are. I really believe in a new world-view. We are at the beginning of it, not in the middle. It has been formulated by scientists, theologians, historians, but it's interestingly coherent. There are lots of area's not filled in, but you know I'm a kind of optimist.

There are at least two major tendencies in your words. First, you condemn the present-day social situation by saying we are on a collision course. Second, you accept the present-day cultural situation by saying pluralism is a good thing. After all, could pluralism be a possible sign of our ability to avoid this collision course, or could it be just a symptom of it?

Pluralism is both the precondition for resisting further degradation of the environment and a problem in its own right. Unless different cultures have the power and willpower to assert their differences, there is little chance that the effort will be made to clean up the environment. Did you ever see a multinational agency act responsibly out of good will when it wasn't forced to? The UN, EC, Group of Seven, ASEAN, etcetera, are no different. Since all important problems are now global, there have to be global agencies to deal with them, but their responsibilities will always be pushed and monitored by nations, regions, cities and individ-uals. And for their activity to be effective, pluralism is the *sine qua non* (which guarantees nothing). On the other hand, pluralism does create its own problems of competition, disagreement and dissent, and there-fore its own form of waste. But it is a price that has to be paid for the freedoms we enjoy. The doomsday scenario for 2050 holds that eco-catastrophe will force a world dictatorship. Let's hope it's wrong.

363

We think one of the main characteristics of pluralism is the dissolving of traditional borderlines in the endist universe of Francis Fukuyama. If you accept a pluralist model, you have to debunk your own border, both morally and formally. You have spoken of your house as a representation of a new Post-Modern world-view. Could you give an example of architecture which represents the dissolution of that border?

Let's take the work of Frank Gehry. Gehry dissolves his own furniture in his rooms, his funny spongy furni-ture made out of corrugated paper. He has used it in the insides of one of his animals rooms: it's a warm environment which has nice acoustic properties. It gives an extraordinary lift of space, as the sky comes down from the top, it's almost a sacred space with a new sound – you can hear your heart beat.

Could you find a new identity in that space?

It's just amusing, it breaks down the border between furniture, ceiling, wall and what you are sitting on. It crosses the borders between high art and low art and those between furniture and architecture and rep-resentation and detail. Most important is that Gehry managed to invent 'detail-less architecture'; there are no real joints. How do you make a mistake in this? You can't! I find it a very exciting and extremely interest-ing form of the Post-Modernism that we were talking about in the early seventies-ad-hocism. On the other hand (I'm sorry to get into categories and to erect borders, but you have to erect them in order to break them down, in order to think) the reason Frank isn't altogether a Post-Modernist is his disdain of context and of a dialectical relation to adjoining buildings. He will often do the knife-edge juxtaposition; something that is completely surreal, like the Surrealists' discontinuous *exquisite corpse*. Just slam his buildings next to an existing one. I tried to persuade him, saying 'Your buildings are great but why assault the buildings next to you? They have as much right to exist as yours have'. He says that he can't do it well. That's inter-esting! Why do so many people make deconstructivist architecture? Because it seems easier and they can't do 'good architecture' or 'competent architecture'. Let me ask you a question. How do you sue Frank Gehry, how are you going to find a failure in this kind of architecture? Previously you knew when you had a mistake; there were clear borders.

Frank Gehry, State of California Aerospace Museum, Santa Monica, 1984

Charles Jencks and Terry Farrell, Thematic House, London, 1985

WIE SIE WURDEN
WAS SIE SIND

Bernard Prinz, Wie Sie wurden, was Sie sind, installation, 1982

Charles Jencks and Terry Farrell, Thematic House, London, 1985

'The book of stone, so solid and so durable, would give way to the book of paper, even more solid and more durable.' (Victor Hugo)
David Mach, Here to Stay, installation Glasgow, 1990 (Twelve giant columns consisting of 100 tons of magazines and newspapers)

You can attack him; on the level of the programme for instance. We have to dig in the programme of the building itself to see if he has found the right solution or not. Many of Gehry's buildings are fragmented. But should he use the same kind of fragmentarism and the same kind of structure for every kind of building? It depends very much on what kind of building it is and where the building is located. Gehry is used to a certain kind of style, he knows it very well but it is only linguistic professionality for him. It seems to be very difficult for architects to invent another kind of form each and every time. Don't you think it's very important to interpret the programme and then try to find a kind of form to use?

I agree. I would certainly suggest that for working in different styles, it is a necessity to be radically eclectic. You can't assume that Frank Gehry's style will work well for more than five or six things. It happens to work very well for small block planning, in the Loyola Law School and in the Aerospace Museum, both in Los Angeles. The feeling of flying, machinery and dynamism on the inside is wonderful and the outside it's fine. It's not successful around the back, however, because the previously existing brick building comes up and he slams into it – assaults it. It's the avant-garde beating, a kind of a dullard, which creates a great tension. So, funnily it's on scale with Los Angeles, it's an urban building; but around the back it's a Modernist bully. I would advocate some joint to show that a transplant is possible between his language and the neighbour's. The difficulty is how to teach an architect to master four languages and to be original and good enough – whatever these words mean.

Let's look at it from the public's point of view. You think people should have the capacity to be critical and when they have an increased awareness they can be critical. Can architecture make people more conscious, does it help them to reflect on society?

I don't think architecture usually makes us reflect on society unless we are told that this is an architecture that should make you reflect on society. The point is, everything is a sign of something else. And everything is interpreted by another sign and we are all of us 'interpretants' in the Peircian semiotic sense. That is, everything you think and everything I think, all this conversation, is a series of signs from other interpretants. The Modernist position of Richard Meier, Norman Foster and the classical position of Quinlan Terry are not trying to make us conscious of the contradictions of signs. They want to repress consciousness of difference. They want to pretend their approach is natural, integral and consistent, so they won't enter into this kind of debate. My feeling is that the architect in an open society should design an open structure. Perhaps to build a building within a building. When I first wrote about Post-Modernists in 1975, I said that architects are hopeless at designing interiors and understanding what normal people want. Therefore, let the architect design his spaces, structures and abstractions, which he does well, but afterwards let an interior designer, or someone else, add the missing meaning on another level. If architects can't do it and interior designers can, why not? We are a free culture. I hire you because you do nice spaces. Okay? And then I get rid of you. I get someone else to finish it, to do what I want. That leads to double design, double coding, producer and consumer oriented.

Aren't there talents who can do both?

There are, certainly. But they are marginalised because our culture does not really regard them as professionals. As our culture says divide and conquer, they all hire another profession. Architects do not know how to design fabric – things that people touch, and the software. We still live in a Modern era, where to produce the hardware is the basic name of the game, whereas we ought to be designing symbolic programmes and meanings as well.

Your analysis leads to the conclusion that there are two poles: on the one hand the absolutely programmed space which you mentioned in Stirling's Staatsgalerie for example, which implies a kind of coverage of art in a very sequenced, ordered and traditional way. The other pole, which is more based on El Lissitzky, was a heroic effort to let people act themselves. This refers to the whole Modern programme of transparent architecture, to withdraw as a specialist and give the occupant a wide berth for action.

Like Gropius, by whom I was trained. Gropius said provide an abstract structure and after a while people will be forced to act. They are like humus which grows like some kind of fungus. The object will force them. And then everything will be okay in fifty years. But **if you really want to make a pearl, you have to put some grit in an oyster. I don't give the oyster an abstract box and say 'make a pearl'.** That is why Gropius' American period did not produce great things.

In the twentieth century there is an odd opposition between the architecture that offers the people a stage for action, and the absence of integrated personalities who really know what they want in a fragmented

366

world. There used to be quite a few fragmented people around, who wanted to be helped, not being posi-
tioned on a neutral stage. So architecture offered something to people who could not understand the offer;
it was an offer for people who didn't see what this offer was all about. They were in need of symbols, signs,
they wanted a narrative.

The architect's view of the perfect noble savage is an intellectual like themselves, who will be provoked by an open structure to do something. By contrast, I think you have to give a structure for people to react to, a catalyst. If you are designing a museum, you need a symbolic programme, and the ability to design art-specific spaces, whereas museum curators want an abstract background. So they force architects into the Richard Meier mould, as at Frankfurt. This furniture museum has a set of white rooms in the International Style, where light dances around quite nicely. But this decontextualises art and leads to great historical anomalies. When you enter, you go up the ramp, and you arrive in the twentieth century; then you move to the fifteenth century, and then to the eighteenth century and then finally to Turkey and Islam. It's like Disneyland, except there is no comprehensible sequence and art-specific design. There is no attempt to articulate a sequence of different cultures, to explain and enhance different experience. It is outrageous that we do this. You can design highly specific spaces from time to time, even in a randomised, open structure. That's why I have criticised Richard Rogers' Centre Pompidou, with all its openness. After ten years they had Gae Aulenti redesign some interiors and define particular places. That is where I come back to the oyster and the grit. You need a symbolic programme and you derive this from the function, the context and the client.

But in negative terms then, you end up designing for people who are lost.

An open work has two separate meanings. First, as with Shakespeare, you have great works of art, which are capable of offering an unlimited number of interpretations. Second, the work that has not been finished, and the perceiver creates the closure. These are two quite different meanings of openness, both necessary. If I supply you with a lot of symbols in this house, as an architect I allow you to put them together to make your own narrative, or to make your own interpretation. If I tried it with none, you would not be interested, you would not be engaged. You have to give people something to chew on.

But, referring to your remarks about the ironic symbolisation of the programme. What if the programme is
too serious and too clogged with historical meaning?

There isn't anything too serious. A sign is always ambiguous, even a single sign, such as a cross. This can be interpreted either by someone who is not a Christian, or it can be interpreted by someone who is in a rebellious mood. All you have to do is decontextualise the sign or recontextualise it, or alter it in some way, so it immediately suggests that it is contesting the very thing it is upholding. I suppose that is, again, a Post-Modern position. In Post-Modern literature it is the complicity with the power structure and the subversion of its ends. You go along with the system of power, to a degree, in order to bend its direction, or change its meaning. Because otherwise it won't listen to you. And even in direct opposition, you are still honouring its existence. When you engage a culture you either oppose it, or try to subvert it from within. Subverting it from within is probably the more interesting. But then you have to be conscious of what sort of subversion you are attempting. You have to be a sociologist and a psychoanalyst as well as an architect. You have to get in there and find out what are the forces of the moment and the eternal forces, and mediate between them. That is why I respect Michael Graves and Philip Johnson – and also their attempts to engage mass culture. I think it is an important part of the Post-Modern agenda to break through and communicate with society. But very few people, and certainly not Johnson and Graves, can do it without end up losing direction, and losing what they want to communicate.

Are you the exception?

I am not arguing for a Post-Modern position exclusively. I am arguing for pluralism, and believe that the meaning of Post-Modernism is only within a spectrum of other positions. It is important to see the structure of tensions being created by different positions in confrontation. I believe there is nothing outside of the system. To a certain degree then upholding the system is important – so pluralism and meaning can exist. You have an obligation to the system of meaning quite apart from the position you cut within it. I owe something to my enemies, because without them my position would be undefined. If I were to win I would lose. If they were to win I would lose. The whole system of meaning depends on oppositions.

367

Interpretation, Mediation,
Narrative in Architecture

Pietro Derossi

The word city, in the sense of a unity of intents and form, does not correspond to any of the contemporary conurbations which have exploded in a thousand different directions, under the influence of a proliferation of relations and tensions; the word city has been replaced by the word metropolis (or megalopolis) which opens disturbing perspectives and excludes reassuring orders and recompositions. The great *récit* of the Modern Movement has broken down, and we find ourselves immersed in the maelstrom of fragments and differences. Together with that of the linguistic metaphor of the city, there also has been a breakdown of the legitimisation of civil behaviour and the sense of human activity; work and production are propagated without credible objectives, driven by rules of trade and finance. This overall condition creates a scenario of nihilism, in which the motivations of life are dispersed and in which all moral and political values are shattered.

At the turn of the century nihilism played an important role as an influence on art forms.**?** Art, inasmuch as it is an intention to communicate, loses all motivation when faced with the profound conviction of the emptiness of existence. The response of the avant-gardes in the field of the figurative arts was particularly explicit and radical. Paradoxically, the protagonists of these movements found themselves committed to communicating the impossibility of communication. The field in which the destructive effects were felt was that of language.**?** Language was denied its right to convey meanings and, thus, weakened, was reduced to the level of a provocatory game of nonsensical manipulation of meanings. This voyage away from reality for the purpose of throwing light on the decline of meaning in all social

? *Would this be the same nihilism as the nihilism of the megalopolis? Then an attitude emanating from a highly intelligent observation, now appearing as a normalised condition: a mere social outcome of a dated prophecy?*

! Citing Wittgenstein, we can think of language as a city, and the city as a language. The megalopolis speaks a disturbing language, suggesting the vanity of existence, opening the way for nihilist thought. Nihilism is not 'intelligent observation', it is existential temptation. The artist is a metropolitan man who narrates his experiences, speaks of his life. To speak, as an artist, of nihilism appears to be a paradox. This speech is possible to the extent that nihilism is not identified with the absolute. A small peephole remains, through which to shout our suffering, our stupor, our nostalgia. A moment before the silence falls.

368

The choice of figuration, the choice of giving form to the object and therefore of arresting the complex process of thought in its investigation of context, history, architecture, subjectivity (including of course, my own history), is a troubling act because it includes the awareness of an exclusion.

relations passed from Cubism, Surrealism, Abstraction to Pop Art and finished, we might say, with Conceptual Art, whose aim is to affirm the tautological destiny of any type of expression. A voyage and a defence, as Vattimo points out in *Poesia e ontologia*, a defence against the frustration caused by the loss of motivation to produce a discourse aimed at founding new social relationships. Having acknowledged the impossibility of art to promote a meaning for society, the only salvation is escape to a place protected from the practical demands of the world: a place in which one is permitted to play with the indistinct variations of language without having to deal with the disintegration of the forms and values of the metropolitan process. The posture produces and reinforces the idea of the autonomy of artistic action, an autonomy which is explicitly declared and pursued with continuous dislocations, shifts, digressions, ruptures (interesting parallels could be drawn with the Romantic Spirit, which had already announced the demise of art). This interpretation of the avant-garde in terms of nihilistic escape does not describe the entire scenario of artistic activity during the first part of our century: there were also utopian propositional efforts, but in order to examine this other scenario it is necessary to leave the field of the figurative arts and look at the field of architecture.

Architecture, in fact, took a different sort of voyage in temporal space. Contemporary to the works of Duchamp, from the followers of Art Nouveau to the great Expressionist revolution, the proto-rationalism born in Germany and in England led, through the initiatives of the Werkbund and later the Bauhaus, to the great propositions of the Modern. The Modern Movement, which from the twenties on transmitted its message to the entire Western world (with many, complex differences, from Functionalism to organicism and neoplasticism, etc.) presented itself as a great force to replace the bourgeois world of the nineteenth century. It is also a rather delirious force which, with a great sense of drama, as Giulio Carlo Argan has pointed out, defines precise lines of renewal subsumed in a new, general formalisation.

But we can also point out that beneath the propositional Utopia of the Modern we can glimpse the

? *Wouldn't it be more appropriate to say that language constitutes the domain in which these effects came to light? The effects however have been felt outside that domain. Linguistics at least could find consolation in the thought of having conducted research into a biological instrument for survival in evolution (Fritz Mauthner). Art and ethics however were left (out) in the cold.*

! I find it difficult to distinguish between language and its effects. We might ask if language speaks of art, or is the art itself. I lean in the direction of the latter. Concepts and things (including works of architecture) exist when they take form, when they express themselves as language. Furthermore – can an ethics exist which is not expressed, not communicated through its form, its language?

spectre of nihilism. To the extent in which one seeks to respond to an overall ideological crisis produced by a real situation of social transformation with a drastic breaking away from processes in progress in favour of the harmonious dream of a radical alternative, all references to history will be annulled, and with them the possibility of establishing a dialogue with the human experiences of the present and the past. Nihilism has to do with Utopia in the sense that it uses Utopia to give credibility, through hope, to the acceptance of a constituent negativity.

While this may be a simplified scenario (overlooking all of the crossover positions and contaminations between these two extreme positions) of the avant-garde movements of the early twentieth century, we can also note that today a transformation has occurred, almost an exchange of positions. While in the figurative arts there has been a softening of the destructive afflatus and a move in the direction of dialogue, or even narrative (consider the German neo-Expressionist movements or the Trans-avant-garde, or the most recent works of conceptual artists like Kosuth or Paolini), the architecture of the seventies

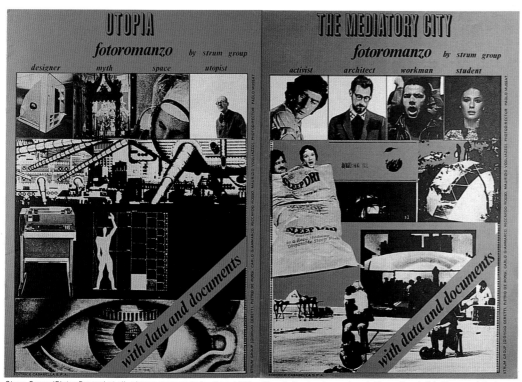

Strum Group (Pietro Derossi et al), picture story made for the exhibition 'New Italian Landscape (special issue *Casabella*), Museum of Modern Art, New York, 1972

'Pratone', a 'natural' armchair in polyurethane (with Gorgio Ceretti and Riccardo Rosso), 1966

? *There was also a trend that abandoned utopian schemes, wasn't there, not because of their inner philosophical logic, but because of the disastrous effects on the quality of daily life? Simply because hopes weren't realised. Architects such as De Carlo, Hertzberger, Erskine etcetera implemented a scaling-down, preserving the spirit of hope at the same time. What space/place do you allocate this tradition in your historical perspective? Don't these architects matter, really?*

! Nietzsche, inviting us to 'return to things', is inviting us to recompose philosophic thinking on the basis of experience. This does not mean that thought must become real: it means that thought must be based on reality. This is both its limit and its strength. Reality is full of hopes and desires. Of the three architects mentioned, Erskine is the one I find most interesting. I have always followed his work with attention. I like his experimentalism, his pragmatic stance, his ability to enter into the specifics of a time and place. What, at times, distances me from Erskine is the excess of signs, the disruptive expressivity which surreptitiously claims an autonomous role: an internal quality which is pleased with its own excellence, at the expense of communication. In any case, he is a great master.

has abandoned all of its utopian pretences, full of references and commitment to a process of reinvention of urban life, reproposing itself as an autonomous discipline, selfreferential, which takes place in situations which are sheltered from the chaos of social events; or, in any case, it is the architecture which operates in this scenario which has been successful both in terms of criticism and of public attention. The most important protagonists of this approach on the part of architecture to the issues of the figurative avant-garde is, as is well known, Aldo Rossi.**?** With a penetrating, precise critique of the simplificatory degenerations of the descendants of the Modern, Rossi shifts our attention toward the specific language of the discipline in order to reveal its historical genesis, internal rules, permanent features, analogies. With this approach, his works present themselves as essential, nearly sacred objects, expressing an enchantment far from the complex business of living. This is a surreptitious return to the sort of nihilism which declares, although nostalgically, that all is in vain and destined to die.

There are also other tendencies in today's architecture which are a part of this neo-avant-garde scenario. So-called high-tech architecture, for example, extracts from the complexity of the reflections on the role of technical progress in society (one thinks of Heidegger's essay *The Question of Technique*, in which technique is considered as the concrete expression of the realisation of the metaphysical, and therefore also becomes the central theme for a revision/distancing from idealistic philosophies); extracts, we were saying, a partial, perhaps banal, aspect: the possibility of reducing an edifice to an assemblage of structural elements. The quality of high-tech architecture is identified with the celebration of those technical inventions which exalt the excellence of construction procedures. Once again, the complexity of the metropolis is excluded from the design, its disturbing presence is ignored. Another very similar operation is that of the 'deconstructors': having accepted, in the same manner as Rossi's argument, the possibility of treating the linguistic specificities of architecture in an autonomous way, the deconstructors dismember language into a sequence of signs (those typical of the Modern) and the activity of the architect becomes that of manipulating the compositional rules which traditionally correspond to these signs.

It is legitimate to recognise, in these three predominant trends in contemporary architecture, a common matrix which is that of the rediscovery of the postures of the historical avant-gardes: an exclusion of the idea of any responsibility, on the part of architecture, for the concrete problems of habitation, and of any temptation to enter into a dialogue with the reality of the metropolis. But this escape into the manipulation of references no longer has the destructive force of the classical avant-gardes, which at least could recognise an enemy to be destroyed: the positivist optimism of the end of the nineteenth century. The manipulation of signs, their reduction to the level of symbols which communicate the impossibility of communication, today becomes an accepted paradox, strategically useful to passively respond to the demands of professional activity. The neo-avant-garde does not create ruptures or dismay; it becomes academic, standard operating procedure. It is within the open space of critical reflection on the self-referential involution of the Modern that the seduction of hermeneutic thought has taken hold.

Hermeneutics has suggested the possibility of not attempting to respond to the nihilism intrinsic to the explosion of the metropolitan condition, to which the decline of the credibility of strong, unitary thought corresponds, neither with a resistance to the frailty of the ideals of the *'polis'*, defending the utopian tradition of the Modern, nor by accepting the repression of any rapport with the 'living tissue', seeking refuge in the abstract sign of a language reduced to the level of an accumulation of demotivated symbols. Beyond this radical set of alternatives, hermeneutics opens up the possibility of mediation.

? You don't wish to allay complexity by means of artificial and simplistic order. Nor will you accept complexity as an accomplished fact which annuls our influence. You are active 'somewhere in between', halfway between God and Chaos. What is it like? Do you really conceive of this position as a 'between'? Or is it an alternative: a third position?

! My position aims at remaining 'between', but not between Chaos and God (which are the same, being disorder and absolute order). The 'between' I am seeking (I yearn for) is that of the circularity of thought between the part and the whole, the hermeneutic circle. The part is the opportunity for the design, in the here and now; the whole is the mystery of the metropolis, the 'free vastness of the land'. Two complexities which relate to one another in an endless process. The creative act, the design, is a mediation which does not permit itself general orders, absolute rules, great negations. Mediation is an assumption of responsibility, avoiding the temptation of reassuring simplifications.

370 *In deconstructive action nihilism and utopia lose their destructive force and reveal their impotence. Nihilism and utopia are a luxury we can no longer afford, or which is no longer permitted.*

The dizzying dispersion of the metropolis – and of the theories on the destiny of the city – can be seen as a condition of the present which is full of seductive possibilities. The first step is that of accepting the impossibility of compressing the entire metropolis into a unitary framework: of compressing it into an absolute negativity, or of celebrating it as the realisation of the overall dispersion of events in an abstract triumph of pluralism. It is precisely this 'impossibility' that reveals the indications which can open the way for an operative path which takes into account, with all of its problems, the rapport between the parts and the whole. If we accept the fact that the occasional nature of a part does not exclude the presence/absence of the whole, we can define this open, disturbing partiality as the context of the project; attributing a literary sense to the term context, that which is found in the text (fabric, narrative, specificity, language) of the city.*?*

In order to make this approach to architecture explicit we can outline an imaginary design process. The request of the client, which constitutes the opportunity or occasion, is to design the completion, the restructuring, the improvement of a portion of the city. The first operation for the architect is to 'visit' the place (not any place, but *the* place) which displays its characteristics, some of them explicit, others latent, others indecipherable. A cognitive itinerary begins which opens a thousand queries: the history, the functions, the social customs, the predominant formal factors, the rhythms of the fabric, etcetera. Certain themes (few) finish in the place, others reach out into a network of connections: the history of the place into the history of the city; the architectural forms into the other similar situations located in nearby or faraway places; the functions into discussions which examine or seek to transform attitudes and behaviours; the economic pressures into the politics of the city, etcetera. The place, with its character and its reference, is the context of the project, a context in which, and from which, the place opens out toward a pluralism of relations which propel it into the entire city, into thought. A network of tensions, desires, thoughts expands out of the place into the world of life. The architect, a subject engulfed by the objectivity of the context, places his conditioned subjectivity in play. The condition of the project takes the form, even if there is attention paid to history and tradition, of a conflict, a difficulty, a

Theatre complex, Turin, 1990

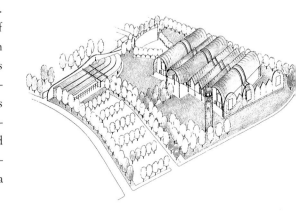

Pietro Derossi

? The narrative, the story can only start after the observation, the study, the research, very much like you stated. That is: after the experience. But what is there left to tell, when this experience has been stipulated by demolition, by periphery wastelands, by short-lived experience due to prevailing culture? Can and will you hang on to the narrative, actively, when all recounting is miscounting, when telling is selling, when tale has become retail, when we don't relate any more to the unrelatable?

! This question is the result of a misunderstanding, perhaps an imprecision in my text.
The narrative approach does not begin after experience. In my text I wrote 'A breaking down of the approach to the place into two successive moments – first I observe, study, investigate, then I narrate – would be false and inadequate'. Still I would like to respond. The existing city, the context in which I operate, manifests itself as a story: a story which is not an objective description, but an interpretation, one of many possible interpretations. The interpretation of a place requires intent, and the intention of the architect is that of transforming a place with a function, a form, in short through a work of architecture: the architecture which I must create, which will be a new story.
How can a careful, profound interpretation avoid the 'evils of the earth'? Not only will it not avoid them, it will even utilise them as nutrients (however bitter) for the design.
The 'objective' analysis, the abstract declaration of intent, the great artistic gesture avoid the evils of the earth, overlooking the intrigues of the world.

? We could add Lawrence Stern's Tristram Shandy *to the list. The book always trails the life of the author. The grammatical 'perfect' doesn't coincide with the actual 'complete': life cannot be described. Of course, this lucid intercourse with narrative and time in eighteenth century tradition should be distinguished from present day language games. To objectify the structure and space of a text, then an extraordinary discovery, is now all too often a cliché. We yield to the overwhelming amount of narrations which discuss themselves. How would you update the values recognised in the work of Diderot and Cervantes?*

! The examples of Diderot and Cervantes can be useful to reveal the procedures of the construction of a work of intelligence. Let us assume that the task of intelligence is to promote an opening of the field of reflection through an exposition of the play, relative as it is, of possibilities. The stance of those who wish to explain, predict, put things in order for us, is not interesting. In Diderot and in Cervantes the exposition of the hypothetical character of the work takes place through constituted semantic bodies. Their approach is different from that of contemporary authors, who have attempted to produce a deconstruction of language by working with signs, at the level of semiology (in architecture the example is Peter Eisenman). This theme is interesting and complex.
A fundamental reference for a development of this discussion is the text The Living Metaphor *by Paul Ricoeur.*

doubt, rather than of an organic continuity with that which exists. But here a question arises: in what manner does the interference take place between a condition of presence (active abandon) in a context and the genesis of a word, of a language, of an architecture? The impossibility of accepting unitary and general frames of reference does not permit us to lead the fluctuating and indefinite complexities of the context into a subsystem of a general structure. If the beginning of a design is there in what I see, in the reminders of vastness produced by the place, this is the condition which I can express, and this expression takes the form of a narrative. The context cannot but take the form of a story, just as a story cannot but find its form in the limits of a context.

A clarification is necessary. A breaking down of the approach to the place in two successive moments would be false and inadequate: first I observe, study, investigate, then I narrate. *?* The interpretative observation of the place already expresses itself as a story – that is, it already contains relativity, partiality, singularity – and the narrative, because it is influenced by initial requests of the client, contains the act of designing. The story design is a narrative which inserts itself within the more general narrative of the context and, in doing so, modifies it, putting it back into the interpretative cycle with new 'fuel'. If we think of Cervantes and his *Don Quixote*, a possible analogy emerges. In *Don Quixote* there is a principal story, that of the voyage of the knight and his faithful squire. During the voyage, the protagonists encounter many strange personages who enter the overall narrative with their fantastic tales, stories which do not seem to play a coherent part in the general plan of the novel. They are like heteronomies, and they introduce themselves as temptations. Cervantes often digresses from the main story line and, captured by the seduction of the unexpected guest, introduces a new narrative alongside the general itinerary. These stories are sometimes so interesting that it is difficult for Cervantes and also for the reader to abandon them and return to the 'main road' of the voyage of Don Quixote. We find a much more radical form of this type of open-mindedness in Diderot. In his *Jacques le fataliste*, he makes explicit in a direct manner that which Cervantes did surreptitiously. He confronts the reader with the problem of the structure of the story. Within the main narrative, which tells of the love affairs of Jacques, he inserts several lateral novellas, each a more profound treatment of a theme, a character. At a certain point these novellas stop and the author, Diderot, asks the reader: how would you like me to proceed? Should I continue to develop this new theme, or should I return to the original story? In this way Diderot induces the reader to reflect on the procedures with which one constructs the design of a novel. The design doesn't say what it already knows; rather it is a succession of attempts which develop, unravelling in a sequence of alternatives. Cervantes and Diderot, although in different eras, between Mannerism and Enlightenment, suggest a possible interpretation of the act of designing, an action which assumes and expounds its own relative nature. *?* The choice of figuration or refiguration, as Ricoeur says, in which one remarks the connection between the new and the density of the past, the choice of giving form to the object and therefore of arresting the complex process of thought in its investigation of context, history, architecture, subjectivity including of course, my own history, is a troubling act because it includes the awareness of an exclusion. In the established form, which is temporarily closed in a story, all that is excluded from my story hovers. The story surreptitiously speaks of all that it does not say, of that which, in the process of figuration, has only been glimpsed, all that we have not been capable of stopping. Paradoxically, this exclusion, which brings what is unsaid into play, opens out toward the vastness of possible worlds. An exclusion which opens. The refiguration, which has the nature of a narrative, is there, wavering between that which we have, in some way, fixed and the complexity of the contexts of which the work alludes, introduces the work into life, in the sense that it legitimises its openness to successive interpretations.

This condition of the design project permits us to make sense of the Heideggerian metaphor of the dual presence of the World and the Earth. To give definition to an architectural narrative means accepting the need to make the world, but in hazarding the action of design the infinite mystery of the Earth appears in the background, an impregnable vastness which, painfully, hides, excludes itself. It is worth specifying the fact that the Earth does not evoke only the mystery of its origin, the indecipherable *archè* of the genesis a possible reading of the meaning of the Earth in Heidegger's thought, but also the complex tangle of transformations in the continuous play of opening and exclusion. Design, in making the world, accepts and emphasises the presence of this alterity. An architectural project can live in this aleatory condition of presenting and negating itself, of declaring in order to speak of the unspeakable. But, always, it is speech, a waiting to be spoken, and thus never proposing the ecstasy of silence. Silence

372 'Garibaldi' area project, competition entry, Milan, 1991

Row houses on the Turinese Hill, 1974

? Your words imply a vivid preoccupation with 'exclusion'. Mentally and materially, the excluded issues rival the included ones in the process of designing. The layman might expect the designer to be proud of incorporating the foremost important issues in his design. Thinking beforehand of the process of exclusion, you foster all sorts of doubts, sans gêne, for that matter. You won't advocate the Übermensch's escape from nihilism, you would rather restrain yourself, supported by menschliches alzumenschliches daily life. Hardly a life in splendour, would you say, even when your pride climaxes now and then. If – at all – you do want to be remembered: by what token?

! A choice emerges from a thousand exclusions. This Yes, that No, and the Nos are infinite in number. In a schematic way, we can say that metaphysical thought has sought to avoid the dramatic nature of the choice with 'grand recits'. The Nos were excluded, before the fact! Contemporary hermeneutic thought proposed a pragmatic approach which brings choice back, in the everyday project of living, to things. Choice, fragmented in the complexity of life, rediscovers its hypothetical character and reopens the confines of knowledge.
This is a triumph of knowledge, not a repression. I would feel repressed if I had to take on the task of proposing a definitive truth: I would be repressed by the awareness of my stupidity and my hypocrisy. The splendour of a communicative act consists in opening the discourse to new interpretations. Designing, or selecting the figuration of a work of architecture, prepares us to become involved in the interweaving of discourses: discourses which deal with choices and conclusions. We await this involvement with trepidation. I hope that I will be remembered for having promoted reflection on architecture, not for having invented a style.

can only be the offering of the void or of absolute truth.**?** Designing within the fluctuating alternation of the World and the Earth can be said to have a deconstructive intent; or, perhaps, not an intent but a destiny for us, disenchanted hermeneutics, victims of the relativity of interpretation. Thus an acceptable meaning for the word deconstruction is revealed a word much abused today to indicate an ingenuous attempt to found a style based on the decomposition of semiologically classified elements in architecture. What is deconstructed is not the structure of the language but rather the remembrances of the metaphysical beliefs of architecture; a procedure which is more closely linked to a necessity than to a decision or an ingenuous will to transgress. The deconstructive process comes to life if it develops within the pragmatic procedure of making architecture. It can be seen in the intentions of the designer which manifest themselves simultaneously as will and commitment to choice and as painful doubt and ironic second thoughts: but it is important to understand that the sense of transience permeates the act of choice does not exclude passion, but rather exasperates it, exposing it 'without a safety net' to the unpredictable play of interpretations. In this activity there is a weakening of the subject. The subject gives up the presumption of legitimisation to escape from the viscous burden of objectivity to evaluate, freely, according to his own aesthetic conscience, rediscovering a function as interlocutor with the dense consistency of reality. In so doing he deconstructs perhaps with nostalgia every illusion of being able to seek refuge in a place which is external to compromise with the physical nature of things, in the gratifying world of metaphysics.

Nursery school (with Gorgio Ceretti), Turin, 1982

? You advocate the kind of pragmatism that conceptually ranges from opportunism to the most profound wisdom. Your approach attests a great sense of responsibility, but how would you define the criteria that constitute this responsibility? When do you draw the line – for instance in the nature of the commission, in the time span allocated to research and the beginning of the narrative, etcetera?

! If making architecture means responding to the needs of a client, if it means having the opportunity to resolve a real problem, it seems to me that there is a direct question of responsibility. This is the responsibility of communicating one's own point of view, of taking the risk of an interpretation. Architecture becomes irresponsible when it illudes itself that it has the right to close itself off, in its development, within the affable sphere of aesthetic consciousness. If we view design as a dialogue with a context, the problem of ethics appears every step of the way.

The deconstructive process also manifests itself in the things encountered by the project: the techniques, the materials, the functions become troubling words, each balanced between a possible relevance to the present and thousands of remembrances. Even the rapport with the clientele as context but also as a real professional opportunity opens a dialogue which does not lead to security and which places the very bases upon which the roles are founded in doubt. Deconstruction, seen as an opening and a breakthrough with respect to all preconstituted propaedeutics, can appear as the space and the time of a profane transcendence which does not hover 'high in the sky', but releases its energy in pragmatic action, in our case that of designing and building. A transcendence which cannot be monumental, but which reveals the fluctuating weave of memories and therefore brings back into play the mysterious afflatus of the monumental.**?**

Just as hermeneutics cannot be defined as a new philosophy, but as a response to the present condition of thought after the decline of the great metaphysical récits, thus the deconstructionist temptations emerge, as a necessity, in the conditions of metropolitan living. In deconstructive action nihilism and Utopia lose their destructive force and reveal their impotence. Nihilism and Utopia are a luxury we can no longer afford, or which is no longer permitted. Deconstruction seen as the product of a mediation distances us from the radicality of the avant-garde movements and proposes, in a new light, the process of anamnesis which they contain.

Afterthoughts on Architectural Cynicism

Henri Raymond

Just as there is an architectural triumphalism, so there is also a triumph of architecture: the purportedly universal urge to build, extending from silos to cathedrals and incorporating as it were the visible world. This triumph is also that of a profession whose practitioners until recently numbered in the hundreds, and presently in the hundreds of thousands, if only as a result of population increases. Yet, if we talk about the triumph of architecture, it is no longer so clear nowadays what this is meant to refer to: to the wondrous proliferation of architectural designs? To the emergence of more and more colossal architectural objects? To the universal competence of the architects?

The notion of 'architecture' is being stretched so far that it no longer means very much, and in several cases gaps are left that have to be filled with great difficulty: ambitious housing development projects that go wrong, areas of conflict between engineers and architects, planning that presupposes radical social changes and sinks into monstrosities (as in Ceausescu's Romania certainly, but what a lesson this contains for us!). In addition there is the enormous gulf that yawns between the public and architecture.

Nobody is able to adequately explain why the Opéra Bastille is a failure, although everybody agrees that it is. Von Spreckelsen's La Grande Arche in Paris La Défense is praised in the same way without valid arguments. It's a question of a crisis in architecture criticism which seems to have forgotten its relationship with a public, even with the sophisticated sector. At its best this criticism is an explanation of the most monumental errors; somewhat as though one were to replace music theory by Mozart's musical jokes which merely show the mistakes without referring to the rudiments of composition theory. The loss of a critique grounded in the rules of art is initially seen as a liberation from academicism. This issue is not to be dealt with hastily, but it has to be acknowledged that, with the abolition of the rule as an intervening factor, architecture can only measure its results against an immanent efficiency modelled on technology's 'Knowledge is Power'. To be sure, this commitment to results is particularly connected with projects initiated by the government or other bureaucratic organisations; yet even then, albeit less and less, it is possible to speak of a relation between commission and project. Nevertheless, even in this relation the influence of techno-bureaucratic structures makes itself felt, especially when it comes to regulations, which in their turn are governed by the commitment to results.

Efficiency versus Art

With the development of functionalism, what we call efficiency has acquired two sides. On the one hand the architect is obliged to achieve results that express a utopian goal. This is what happens with the big collective apartment blocks, where a way of life is made into a project, but it also happens when a building is adapted to the continuous progress of medical science. On the other hand, since the beginning of the Modern Movement, efficiency has partly been seen as the architect's duty to respect certain rules that are not of an aesthetic nature but are meant to have a specific immanent effect.★ Instead of the rules that have to be observed in order to ensure order and beauty, what we have are just the building's appearance and, nowadays in particular, its media-effect, which is now given the task of making a particular impression, one that may well still be rooted in a number of few rules but which can just as well be based on no clear rule whatsoever.

★ On the 'rule' its origin, its function, see Epron, J.P., *l'Edifice idéal et la règle constructive*, Nancy, 1980.

The flight into efficiency has a second, more far-reaching cause, namely the rejection of the Romantic distinction between Nature and Art. The aesthetic that Romanticism imposed upon the natural subsumes Nature into Art, with the side effect that objects belonging to another world than that of the rules of art nevertheless acquire an artistic meaning.

The Modern Movement in architecture, which opposed academicism, turns spontaneous architectural forms into Art (one is reminded of Le Corbusier's photos of silos). It extends the concept of 'architecture' to natural objects such as crystals, or sees New York skyscrapers as metaphors. Thus there arises in architecture aesthetics, just as in the other arts, a confusion between the artistic and the picturesque. We saw an example of this recently when the Grande Arche was universally proclaimed as 'beautiful'; of course, like all natural arches, it is beautiful, but it is meaningless, both from the viewpoint of artistic rules, and in the sense of what may be expected from architecture as artistic activity.

After the rejection of academicisms came the period of formal efficiency, of the effect of mass and colour, derived from an erroneous image of man and from an outdated psychology. It is all to do with

? What you see as the confusion of categories between Nature and Art assumes that these are categories. Against this we could say the following: even though there may have been a time when these categories corresponded to reality, we have gradually had to reach the conclusion that this opposition has been bridged by the artificial. Nature and Art have been reconciled through the artificiality of everything imaginable. On what grounds do you continue to adhere to a duality reminiscent of the eighteenth century?

! I used the term 'nature' in a monolithic sense of an object that 'falls from the sky', in other words an object that lacks meaning (like Mont Blanc, for example). I distinguish this 'natural' architecture from architecture with a rule. It is true that I passed over Boullée, who conferred patents of nobility on this Natura Artificialis by introducing pyramids, spheres and other so-called 'primary' forms in architecture schools. It is thus a question of a dualism within architecture. But one would do well to see skyscrapers, for example, or the Tour Montparnasse as objects with an intentional form rather than as actually made things. Henri Lefebvre spoke in this connection of mimesis as opposed to poiesis.

Henri Raymond

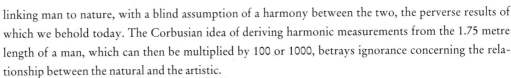

Cynicism in architecture, monumental mis-culture, are the elements in a mediatisation of architecture which addresses itself directly to the public, speculating on the pulverisation of values and conventions and on the swift disappearance of a 'system of fine art' whose future home is the world of postcards.

375

?! Who is this 'everyone'? There are also many people who, precisely on the grounds of an analysis such as yours, are looking for an alternative, not in rhetoric but in a phenomenological experience.

J.O. von Spreckelsen, La Grande Arche, Paris, 1989

linking man to nature, with a blind assumption of a harmony between the two, the perverse results of which we behold today. The Corbusian idea of deriving harmonic measurements from the 1.75 metre length of a man, which can then be multiplied by 100 or 1000, betrays ignorance concerning the relationship between the natural and the artistic.

The skyline of Manhattan, when it looks in the twilight like a mountainous horizon, can perhaps be compared with the Ecrin mountain range in the Alps – but can this sort of thing be made a basis of architecture? It is an amusing thought that, referring to completely secularised Platonic volumes, a first-class 'unculture' is being formed which wants to ground architectural certainty on rough and often chaotic effects, while Greek thought at least had the merit of having gone for advice to the gods, who were able to tame these effects and the shock that went with it.*?*

Cynicism and Architectural Rhetoric

From this one can thus specify the features of an architectural cynicism, in the sense indicated by Peter Sloterdijk's *Critique of Cynical Reason* a cynicism where two aspects can be discerned. The unkept promises of the Modern Project's Utopia have degenerated into a rhetoric which everyone excuses by saying that it belongs to the obligatory 'discourse' of the technostructure and therefore conforms to the expectations concomitant with an entity of measures aimed at results.*?!*

In a certain sense we could say that the trimming down of architecture is being compensated for by the flowery words used to win over the major clients. What in Le Corbusier's time could still pass for a lyric illusion connected with the splendour of 'pure' forms, has now become a cumbersome linguistic exercise, part of the professional stiffness which no longer misleads anyone. But all this is cynical, because a utopian discourse is once again being sold to the people like a sort of basket full of good intentions, but you can't bring in anything oppositional, on pain of being suspected of malevolence.

It can be expected that this implicit shamelessness will last just as long as the institutions that are content with it and promote it further. Yet a few recent examples indicate that it is dangerous to speculate on the 'radiant future' that Zinoviev talks about.

The second aspect of architectural cynicism tends to reduce the architectural to media effects, in other words to rely on the absence of architectural judgement on the part of the public. With the aid of procedures that are largely propagandistic in nature, attempts are made to mislead the public through all manner of publicity campaigns. 'Events' are created around monuments that stand for themselves, outside of any context and in the absence of any rule. When Bernard Huet defines in this way an architecture 'against the city',★ he is alluding to this succession of 'punchy campaigns' that have no correlation and are contrary to all the rules. This

★ Huet, Bernard, 'l'Architecture contre la ville', in *AMC* 14, December 1986.

aspect is particularly strong in Paris where the megalomania of those in power has expressed itself in a shambles of arbitrarily scattered objects (the Opéra Bastille, the Grande Bibliothèque, and the Ministère des Finances), so that urban space is strewn with monuments that have no reference at all to any communally-held culture and therefore should be called a-cultural.

Cynicism in architecture, monumental mis-culture, are the elements in a mediatisation of architecture which addresses itself directly to the public, speculating on the pulverisation of values and conventions and on the swift disappearance of a 'system of fine art' whose future home is the world of postcards.

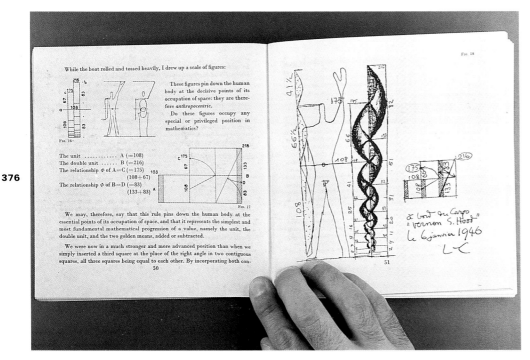

Le Corbusier, Double page from *The Modulor* (or. ed. 1948)

Le Corbusier, page from *Towards a New Architecture* (or. ed. 1923)

Indeed, those who reply to architectural surveys often lack a well-developed stylistic judgement; but it would be too hazardous to draw from this the conclusion that all information concerning architecture can henceforth be limited to the language of the elite on the one hand and the silent, stupefied passivity of the television viewer on the other hand.

Metaphors as Refuge for Absurdity

We can now understand why metaphorising is completely accepted in architecture at the moment; it is no longer a violation of the rules but a way of working aimed at an immediate effect. Rather than an effect of aristocratic irony (as in Bomarzo), it is more an attempt to suggest a connection based on nothing other than an easy allusion. Looking at recent work by Simounet (an apartment block at St Denis), one sees that even in a design group that is not without talent, the architecture supports promotional references to the feudal past of St Denis. That this reference is meaningless from the inhabitants' point of view, as well as from the viewpoint of urban planning, is of no importance for it is simply a matter of giving a pseudo-historical name to a media-image. Even though we have to repeat that it is still a talented piece of work.**?**

As we have described it, cynicism in architecture should be able to boast excellent prospects. In the

? *You were talking about renouncing an immanent rule. The architecture you are condemning, however, is also based on a rule. When Ricardo Bofill builds a 'Versailles for the ordinary citizen' in Saint-Quentin-en-Yvelines, he is appealing to a rather elementary urge for distinction on the part of the future inhabitants. The system of fine arts that you see parked in the world of postcards, makes its return in a prestigious, commercial scenography. It could be argued, then, that the world of postcards is coming into our very homes. Would it not be better to say that the rule has been turned into money, rather than having been abandoned?*

! These days an architect cannot sell because he knows how to apply the Rules. He sells because his product is mediated by the application of rules as regards familiarity, repute, prominence. His product does not bear the stamp of competence 'in accordance with the rules', but just his signature: 'Chemetov', 'Nouvel' or 'Bofill'. Knowing the rule is as Johann Sebastian Bach said, 'Anyone who does his best, like I do, can accomplish the same.'

most developed and most bureaucratic countries the connection between architecture and techno-structure seems to be a guarantee against all too radical aesthetic and social intervention; just as the cynical standpoint involves a succession of fashions, the replacement of Post-Modernism by high-tech with a little bit of cultural sauce carries no risk at all. And yet, by paying attention to such risks in this essay, it has been our intention to shift the perspective and to make a number of openings.

To shift the perspective is also for us a return to the historical, but by this we do not mean a propaganda machine focused, as in the Renaissance, on traditions which can be identified with the straightjacket of a shaken moral order. What we envisage is a return to a knowledge of the connections between architecture and society; not in the sense that Arnold Hauser gave to this, but rather in the way that Pierre Francastel has sketched it.

In this way we hope to recover something of the past that is still rooted in the memory of those who are the users of buildings and who realise that there is no such thing as a modernity without its subjects; and that this subject of aesthetics, which must govern the power of judgement, is slowly but surely becoming detached from the deceit of the media and, swimming against the stream, is rediscovering its true sources.**?**

Henri Raymond

Paul Chemetov and Borja Huidobro, Ministère de l'Economie et des Finances, Paris, 1988

Dominique Perrault, Très Grande Bibliothèque, competition entry, Paris, 1989

The Invisible Rule

Rules – which enable architectural judgement and thus a choice to be made – do exist and are based on aesthetic criteria; but they no longer have a legitimacy, at least in the world of the profession itself which has always leaned on the same rules in order to ensure its power! However, that lack of judgemental capacities is only to be found within the profession. Behold an interesting paradox, not on the part of the architects who, by dismantling the Academy, have sawn off the branch they were sitting on, but because this dismantling has in fact not been complete: it leaves a large area of questions and contradictions open within the profession, the Bofill phenomenon being good evidence of this. We can also visit Tokyo in order to observe that behind a few 'stars' who carry out their publicity campaigns in Europe there exist qualified architects with projects that would not have been rejected by the Prix de Rome jury in pre-war France. The paradox is that this domain, dominated as it is by the rule and even by a certain academicism, is not only a concession to the clientele left behind; it is an *internal* paradox: the same architects who produce so-called pure spaces for the propertyless classes and who nowadays think of filling these spaces with Post-Modern transparency, turn out in private to be 'normal' citizens able to take care of their own spaces with common sense. Very revealing in this respect was a special issue of *Architecture d'Aujourd'hui* devoted to the houses architects live in. Essentially, what this issue

Bernard Huet, rehabilitation Place de Stalingrad and Rotonde de
la Villette, Paris, 1988

Charles Vandenhove, social housing 'De Liefde', Amsterdam, 1993

Yoshikuni Kamichika, Takekuni Ikeda, Silman Herweijer, Pieter Bakker, Ted van Keulen, Jan Heeling,

Fred Hofman, Simon Levie, City Huis Ten Bosch, Holland Village, Nagasaki, 1992

showed was that hiding behind the representatives of established Modernism was often the amiable simplicity of ordinary daily life. The reader might well think that this is quite a normal thing: the commission is one thing and the architect's own house another. But can you imagine Michelangelo decorating his private quarters with Madonna's by Raphael? Where is the artist and where is the Art? But we do not want to show the architect-technocrat by means of his inconsistencies; what interests us is the way the architect's contradictions are connected with an aesthetic consensus which is much stronger and more important than he himself can imagine. Le Corbusier, with his diabolical media dexterity, thought he could make use of this inconsistency by calling out to his opponents, 'We are the new Classics!' He forgot that the Classicism prize is only awarded after at least two centuries. He didn't think of this because, for the sake of the purists, he added that genuine, original Classicism can appear in the guise of barbarity. And even to this day the Parthenon is sometimes kept in a number of French Academies wrapped up in a shoebox in order to certify the Modern Movement.

Nowadays computers have taught us that everything can be transformed into everything: the Empire State Building into a pencil, for example, or the Temple of Angkor into an Oldsmobile; which proves absolutely nothing. The invisible rule is elsewhere, not in the showing off of computers; the invisible rule is the survival, for both the public and the technocrats, of the principles that ensure that an object is made by art, for art and, besides a good deal of other judgements, demands an aesthetic judgement. **?**

Architectures and their domains

Nature and pseudo-nature The natural art of building did not arise from nature. It arose from the real or imaginary overpowering of natural objects (caves, crystals, vaults); it can therefore only emerge from a deliberate will to create one's own domain. Some mistakenly see this as part of human nature, which is totally fanciful (or rather erroneous) since this overpowering has to do with culture and is in no way indebted to an anthropological deduction, to man in his natural state or to cave dwellers. That is why it is also misleading when Heidegger makes his Temple arise from a landscape.

380 *Rules – which enable architectural judgement and thus a choice to be made – do exist and are based on aesthetic criteria; but they longer have a legitimacy, at least in the world of the profession itself which has always leaned on the same rules in order to ensure its power.*

The Temple rises up from it, but it is not landscape, it sets itself *against* landscape: its intention is to infinitely expand the sacred and, as is often said, to erase Nature. But this does not mean to say that people do not recreate it. That's why Le Corbusier is ecstatic about crystals and why we stupidly continue to admire his glass vaults, these insignificant objects, reflections of… nothing.

Metaphor as criticism In my opinion the best analysis of this has been provided by Tafuri: because of its metaphorical potential architecture is becoming a domain of criticism. Tafuri has demonstrated this as far as the Post-Modern derailment of the Baroque goes; but the same could just as well be said of an architect like Venturi, whose work made Post-Modernism accepted. On rereading *Contradiction and Complexity in Architecture* (1966) one notices that a domain of architecture is formed in connection with the incapacity of the Modern Movement to express anything other than its own modernity.

But in itself a metaphorical building is not architecture; otherwise a shoe enlarged 100 times as a signboard would also be architecture. At a certain moment then it should be obvious that metaphorical architecture does nothing other than derive its rules from something else: in the most favourable case – that of Bofill – it is a question of referring to another architecture, a solution that obviously refers to History.

Rule and its residue The best that can be said about the Rule is that it defines Art and offers a protection both to the client, who is assured of orderly work, and to the Artist, who is formed according to the rules, applies them, and thus finds protection in his own profession on account of the fact that he is schooled in the Rule. The work of J.P. Epron has shown how important it is not to confuse the Rule with Academicism, as the followers of the Modern Movement attempted to do. **?**

? You make it seem as though, on the subject of the beautiful and the ugly, there still exists a province of irreducible, always present experience of beauty. But how can you maintain this view after 15 years of architectural Post-Modernism, neo-Classicism and the semiotics of architecture? Besides the technologisation of architecture, we've also had its semiologisation. What leads you to think that there's still something behind it, now that the relationship between substance and sign has been broken so ceremoniously?

! Take a look at Marion Segaud's essay Pour une Sociologie du Goût en Architecture (Paris 1989). This dissertation, and the research accompanying it, makes it clear that the concepts of 'Beautiful' and 'Ugly' still continue to function, albeit 'in the background' (which does not mean that they are eternal). As far as 'Beautiful' and 'Ugly' go as essences, this is something that metaphysicians, philosophers, sociologists and psychologists have attempted, more or less in vain, to shed light upon; next in line are the neurologists. But we won't have to wait very long for that, if we read J.C. Changeux's very intelligent essay introducing the catalogue for the Meaux exhibition. Let me repeat: the permanence of 'Beautiful' and 'Ugly' is beyond doubt; where they come from is another question…

? The specificity of architecture you are advocating with respect to its Rule can perhaps contribute to an improvement in the quality of our built environment. But at the same time architecture is then able to protect itself improperly from the process of modernity that has inflated that rule. You cannot dispose of the deconditioning strategies of Modernism as an aberration. There was also an historical fatefulness connected with it. How can you reintroduce the rule, without the risk of historical regression?

! As you know, the Modern is a relative quality: for the Baroque period 'modern' meant respect for the Rule; for Apollinaire, Christ was 'more modern than the Eiffel Tower'. In short, whoever cuts himself off from Modernity lays the basis for a new modernity. Whichever way you look at it. For Jacques Lucan for example, 'modern' is simply what's printed in the newspapers. It's not something we have to worry about very much.

? It is striking that both you and Venturi, on the basis of a completely different understanding of quality and the essence of architecture, think you know 'what the public wants', or, as the case may be, suffers. You surely have your sources for your list of the public's wants. Why do these not correspond to Venturi's?

! Venturi has made himself useful by leaving simplists like Mies and Corbu to their cubes, their four functions, their 'less is more'. As to what the public wants, we just have to ask them. This is what Marion Segaud analyses in her thesis, which is precisely about the 'public'. For that matter, all historical research into architecture should likewise consider the public. Why do you think that architecture was dominated by such a consensus in the Baroque period? There is a similar consensus today; it's just that modern architects are unable to articulate it. To use a big word, I think Venturi's Baroque is a diversion from contemporary Modernity, just as the Baroque of the Jesuits of Perugia is a diversion from the Gésu church in Rome. And that's no small a compliment.

The Rule is anchored in History; since the Renaissance it has been passed on orally in the fraternity of construction workshops. I think it is appropriate to distinguish between Rule and Doctrine: the Doctrine is the face, the proclamation of the Rule. The Rule is mainly laid down in negative examples ('do not do this') of the sort that we find with Philibert Delorme and which do not lend themselves to systematic prescriptions. Of course architectural doctrine encompasses the Rule, but in so doing it masks it so that it becomes difficult to analyse it in *opus operatum* and *modus operandi:* in an understandable pursuit of essentiality it often refers to a transcendence (particularly in the case of Philarete) or to a human measure (as with Alberti), while on the other hand Philibert Delorme's *The Art of Building* is more a collection of practical advice.

What we are left with, then, is that the considerations of architects bear as little witness these days to the existence of rules as do the views of architectural critics. Such rules nevertheless lie at the bottom of an architecture that would like to be subordinate to public judgement, instead of being satisfied with the nihil obstat of technocrats and contractors. Well then, the principles enabling judgements to be made do still exist in this public that is so disparaged:

- Symmetry as the organising principle of a building, which means not a total, but precisely a moderate symmetry, in other words one that rhymes with its surroundings.
- A building must have a beginning and an end, particularly when it is part of an urban complex.
- Without a well-defined accord between street and the pattern of moulding one lapses into a sort of 'natural architecture', in other words into nothingness. What this means is if there is no rule making the building height subservient to the possibilities of recognising architectural meanings, one ends up in imperceptibility, that is to say, in nothingness. Then the door to Venturi lies open: let's give skyscrapers skirts.
- Finally, and this is most important for the public, architecture is also the art of making the whole and the parts of a building mean something. Modern architecture has become incapable of looking for this and of grasping and communicating the sense of a building. ?

What we are left with, is that the considerations of architects bear as little witness these days to the existence of rules as do the views of architectural critics. Such rules neverthe-less lie at the bottom of an architecture that would like to be subordinate to public judgement, instead of being satisfied with the nihil obstat of technocrats and contractors.

? What do you think of the idea that the reduction of aesthetic satisfaction to the level of a picture postcard collection is a clear signal of the way involvement in the environment has been reduced to the tourist gaze, which concentrates on those very monumental 'punchy operations' that Bernard Huet talks about, and forgets what the relationship had once been between the two mastodons of urbanity and the landscape. Or should we regard the one just as much as the other as surrogates, which would then prove your assumptions of an immanent norm?

! This idea of yours is certainly a result of the hyper-elliptical nature and obscurity of Prof. Raymond. Of course you cannot equate the effect of categories of beauty with choosing postcards. Just look at home furnishings stores: there you see that people constantly follow these categories when it comes to their own home. You don't think, do you, that people buy curtains without thinking of Beauty?

Basically, the idea we stand for is as follows: unlike the plastic arts, modern architecture does not have the possibility of betting on the disappearance of aesthetic judgement; this is always present with the public and it is from this minimum that the guarantees have to come against the disasters described by Manfredo Tafuri and Bernard Huet.

Cynicism in Architecture and what comes Afterwards

Architecture in France has fallen into the hands of bureaucrats. Their simple and poorly informed idea is that this confiscation has happened for the benefit of a public that is still dumb and that will gradually gain access to happiness through information provided by the media. But we have strong doubts about whether architecture contributes to happiness – it is not its task and it is completely incapable of developing plans for this. Architectural cynicism is collapsing by itself in Vaux en Velin, just as it has collapsed in Briey or in La Courneuve. Architecture as social planning has as little sense today as 'scientific socialism'. It is a pity, but that's simply how it is. As regards the practice of aesthetic judgement we have to acknowledge that this takes place nowadays on a pile of rubble even worse than the most brutal eclecticism. One could begin to despair, but the sale of millions of picture postcards makes us confident that, far beyond this chaos, a latent order lies in wait. It needs time, a lot of time. ?

Architecture is too Important
to Leave to the Architects

A Conversation with Giancarlo De Carlo

Giancarlo de Carlo has a long career as an architect and writer behind him. As an architect he is self-taught, having mastered the profession during the war while at the same time being involved in the resistance. In those days he was an enthusiastic admirer of the masters of the Modern Movement. Later on, however, in the fifties, together with contemporaries such as Aldo van Eyck, Jacob Bakema and Ralph Erskine, he founded Team 10, a group that was fiercely critical of the rigid functionalism of the CIAM. Since that time De Carlo has not ceased to analyse and criticise new developments and trends in architecture. In his public appearances and in his writings De Carlo denounced the anonymity of bureaucratic clients, the frivolous concern with symbolism in architecture that ducked any attempt to discuss its content and the prevalence of special interest groups in the field of architecture. A constantly recurring theme was accountability in architecture.

In the eighties architecture went through a phase of being depoliticised; now in our own age his approach has again become amazingly topical. One article of his that is particularly striking is entitled 'Legitimising Architecture' (*Forum* Vol. XXIII, 1972, no. 1, pp. 8-20). In it he accused the profession of surrendering to the interests of people without any principles ('the expert exploiter of building areas, the manipulator of building codes, the cultural legitimator for the sacking of the city organised by financiers, politicians and bureaucrats'). This article deserves to be quoted in detail.

'Any discussion of the purposefulness, or historical legitimacy, of architecture in the contemporary world must necessarily begin with the acknowledgement of its present futility, assuming it as the origin of any investigation of architecture's future or past. (...) Thus with the rise of middle-class professionalism, architecture was driven into the realm of specialisation, where only the problems of "how" were relevant, as the problems of "why" were assumed to have been resolved once and for all. (...) Working on "how" without a rigorous control of "why" inevitably produces the exclusion of concreteness from the process of planning. Proposals for solving problems necessarily stand midway between the definition of goals and evaluation of effects. The refusal to correlate one's own contribution with the two poles of motivation and control is a typical manifestation of the idiocy of forced specialisation. A manifestation which also influences the quality of the proposals and their capacity for resisting attempts to alter them.'

De Carlo goes on to argue for a renewed dialogue with the user in specific situations and concrete places. This attitude is reflected in the very modest place in his own practice that he gives to design. First and foremost for him is the social context in which the artefacts are situated. He states his viewpoint as follows:

'A building is not a building. A building, in the sense of walls, floors, empty spaces, rooms, materials, etcetera, is only the outline of a potential: it is only made relevant by the group of people it is intended for'. Giving form to a building implies an organisation and every organisation includes a problem of form. In this sense De Carlo's ideas about the organisation of society and his view of design are inseparable. His demand for legitimacy is given real weight by his genuinely committed attitude.

Even though his unquestioning belief in the 'real discussion with the occupants' has proved in practice to be not always justified, De Carlo's analysis of the marginalisation of architecture has lost none of its force. Now that the question of the cultural legitimacy of architecture is being raised on all sides, his criticism has begun to attract attention once again. The question here is how this criticism can be restated at a time when architecture has become more popular than ever.

The semiotic concern with meaning in architecture has undergone an explosive development since the late seventies. Can you explain where this concern comes from?

I can give two reasons for this extraordinary concern, one direct and the other indirect. I can state the direct reason in a sentence: the mass media show up everywhere sooner or later. Now they have discovered architecture as a relatively unknown territory and they can make use of it for a while. The indirect reason why people are at present so interested in finding meaning in architecture is the increasing complexity of the Western world; people's powers of observation are continually improving; they are also continually being subjected to new stimuli. There is an enormous amount of information that is apparently permanently available. There are more and more possibilities of studying something in depth, but the fact that the flow

Giancarlo de Carlo

Mazzorbo Housing, Venice, 1983

of information is so continuous also means that there is no context for this in-depth study. If this goes on too long it is only natural that you end up feeling a need quite literally to decide where you are. You start wondering about the character of the place you live in, and about how this place is made. As one of the most important parts of the environment, architecture can gain from this increased interest. Those architects who are conscious of this will emphasise the symbolic meaning of architecture. A building will then not just be a point to refer to, but also a pretext for conjuring up memories, an occasion for creating a scenario that enables individuals to feel a bond with past, present and future. ***We can trace a relation between the increased concern with architecture and the weakening of social conventions or even with a despair about the absence of rules.*** It is a case of an attempt to restore the rules somehow or other. Even so, if I say that despair also plays a role here, this does not mean that I am completely pessimistic. What is at stake in fact is powerful feelings and passions. Restoration too is a question of passion and I cannot and will not be negative about that.

Can you place this development in a cultural perspective? Is it a part of the contemporary situation and if so what is your attitude towards it?

Christian de Portzamparc, Cité de la Musique, Paris, 1992

Post-Modernism is a historic fact; Lyotard was right about that. It is not something that you can be for or against. We are already Post-Modern if only because we don't live in the Modernist era any longer. I don't only mean Modernism in architecture but in the culture as a whole. We no longer have a mechanistic faith in Progress. New discoveries are no longer good by definition; on the contrary, they are more likely to prove a disaster. We are becoming more cautious and critical. We can call this new period Post-Modern, post-industrial and post-Marxist. But we have known for a long time already that this has nothing to do with Post-Modernism in architecture. In this field – even though it is on the wane now – it has acquired the character of a party complete with dogma. It has sometimes actually taken on the form of a Mafia, with mutual favours, interests in the media and a control over prize competitions. This is another story entirely. Team 10 was in a sense already Post-Modern because it was concerned with a fundamental redefinition of the CIAM. But Post-Modernism is a self-selected name for a self-appointed sub-group and something like that is a stunt, not a historical term.

All the same, my attitude is not entirely negative. It is abundantly clear that some of these Post-Modernists are extremely talented. The fact moreover that their designs are based on a general notion of a pluralistic society is something that I agree with completely. It is generally understood that everything is undergoing a process of considerable change and that an univalent language is no longer adequate. What the rationalists do with their unambiguous design vocabulary is no longer relevant. The Post-Modernists with their hybrid style have understood this very well and have opted for eclecticism, for a multiplicity of forms. Despite their decline in popularity, eclecticism still remains intact even if in a less fanatical form. Eclecticism is a super-style. The sense of unease with a language that has only one level of meaning is fundamental to eclecticism and it is something that I feel too. Only what I am looking for is a completely different solution to the problem. I am looking for a style that is pluralistic and a-stylistic. What I am arguing for is a language and working method that has already been stated in much greater detail in other areas of the culture, for instance, in music. Someone like Frank Zappa or Prince, for instance, who does not think twice about working with a jazz saxophonist, succeeds in making a polysemic language. As architects we should take a much closer look at this kind of collaboration because it is a rich source of inspiration. In any case I think it is much more interesting than institutional music. Stockhausen, Berlioz and Cage are very fascinating, but for very few people. On the other hand there is music that is rich and multi-faceted and that has a huge audience everywhere. These people are interested in polysemic forms of music. The same is true not just of music but also of video and television as well sometimes; new forms are being generated. This is something that we can't ignore; present-day society functions on so many different levels that no form of art, including architecture, can remain unambiguous. To talk about the eclectic style of Post-Modernism is therefore a contradiction in terms. A style by definition cannot be eclectic. A style is monological. Everybody should be able to find a meaning in architecture that is able to correspond with his or her cultural level, history or background. It is this sort of multi-faceted meaning that I am looking for in my own work. This is not easy. I would recommend that you read Italo Calvino's book, *Le città invisibili* (Turin, 1972). Calvino's intuition was very strong just because his descriptions of cities aim to create multiple layers of meaning.

As you are stating it now the question of Post-Modernism in architecture gets bogged down in an abstract concern with meaning. Sometimes it seems that the discussion about meaning ends up with meaning becoming a value in itself. What is your view of the relation between being open to meaning as a point of departure for a social critique of architecture, and the dogmatic exclusion of meaning at the end of the seventies and in the eighties?

It's quite true that symbolism and meanings become more and more things in themselves. Instead of being results that one arrives at they become goals that are assumed before one starts. Peter Eisenman is a good case in point. In his programme he searches for meanings, or to be more precise, meta-meanings. He searches for a grammar, for deconstruction, for catharsis and all that sort of thing. This is however a completely unjustified abstract manipulation of the design process. It is sheer folly for an architect to be so arrogant as to say: here you are, here are your meanings from one to a hundred. If value in architecture is dependent on the say-so of a single person, even if that person is someone like Eisenman who constantly negates himself, then architecture as a whole becomes a complete failure. Fortunately, meaning in architecture is something that is much more concealed. Meaning will only appear after you have made a painstaking analysis of the assignment, taking into account the context in which it occurs, your own personal background, your view of society, your hopes and disappointments. It is a question also of how the people you are working for alter the process in order to give it life as they see it. Only after this process is complete will you perhaps achieve meaning, with the emphasis on the word perhaps. You cannot programme meaning in advance. One diagonal and then another diagonal and, hey presto, there's another pretty geometrical construction for you. You never get architecture like that. I recall a very odd lecture at

Yale University where Palladio was reduced to a list of modules, so that his work ended up sounding like a petty cash book, a sum of credits and debits, pros and cons. No longer was any historical reference made to Venetian society in the sixteenth century; not a scrap of attention was paid to the needs behind his work. Palladio wanted to persuade people to organise space in a different way; he was a pioneer in the change that has taken place in our notions of space. Things like this also have a bearing on architecture. It isn't just a geometrical game. The science of architecture aims to develop an understanding of all the forces that may have an influence on the creation of space and spatial organisation. Understanding architectural space involves understanding the whole history of the particular place, city, land and culture that is involved. Also in designing possible future buildings – if that is still a possibility – you can state a view of the world and create a space in which balance or conflict become explicit. In the long run an approach like this gives you a broad perspective for dealing with details so that you are not confined to your own specialised field. In this way you make space for criticism.

Do you regard this as being so important that you conclude your argument with it?

Criticism is the beginning of change and anyone who doesn't keep his eyes closed can only approve of any changes in the status quo. The purpose of art always was to sharpen one's thought processes and to be open to criticism, not to gloss things over. The thing about the formalists in architecture that makes me so

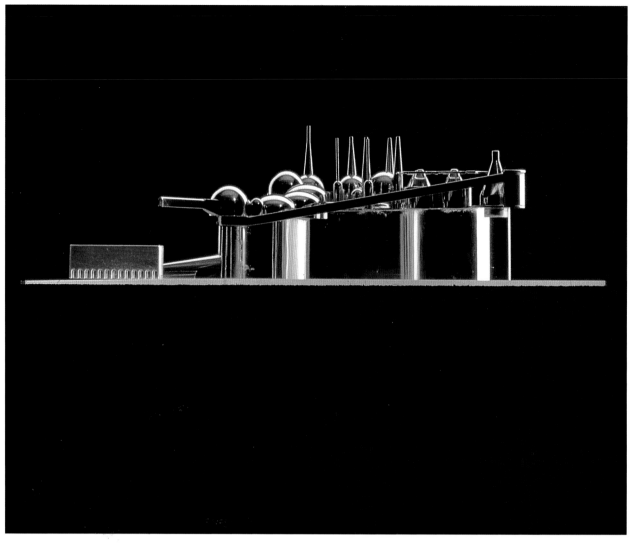

Salzburg Guggenheim Museum, competition entry, 1989

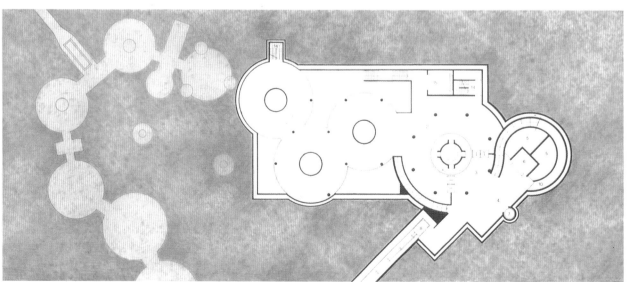

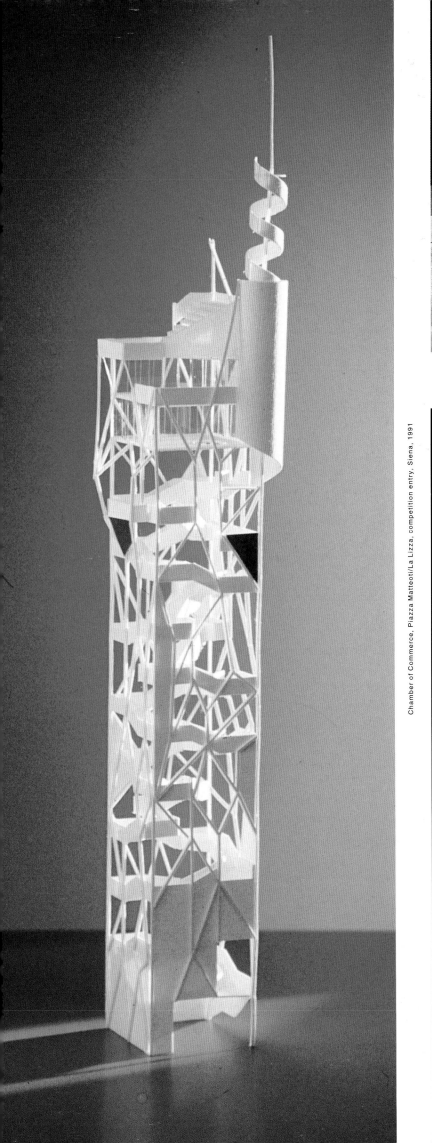

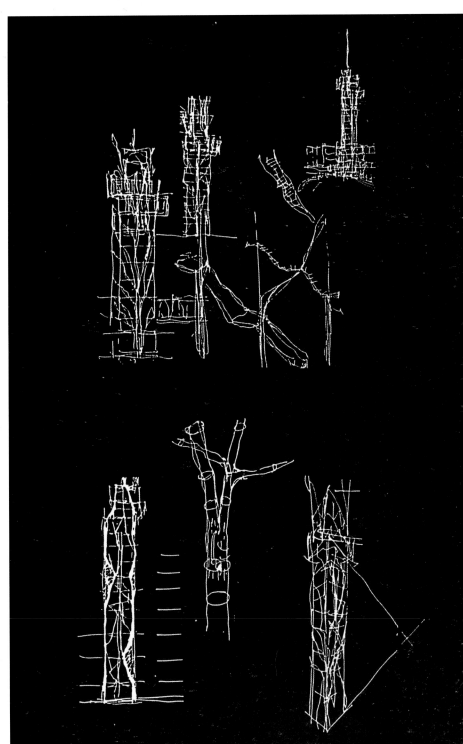

Chamber of Commerce, Piazza Matteoti/La Lizza, competition entry, Siena, 1991

angry is that they prettify conflicts with a lot of pretentious rubbish. There are conflicts all around us and they are ingredients of our imagination.

How can one arrive at a critical stance and the resulting attitude of commitment in a pluriverse like ours?
How can one feel sure enough of what one is doing and of the criteria for one's criticism while at the same
time accepting the present cultural situation?

The more this 'pluriverse' develops the more necessary a new sort of criticism will become. A criticism that no longer regards the variety of forms and the multiple layers of meaning that belong to an architectural event as being sufficient, but which also contains a value judgement, a judgement that will of course be much more complicated than is usually the case at present. It is a case of a preparedness to make a judgement without the finalistic pretensions that usually go with such an attitude. Manfredo Tafuri is well known for his finalistic aspirations and that is a bad thing for the living architecture that I believe in.

Even though they have plenty of power, the critics are having a hard time at present. They get their power from the fact that architects are so afraid of criticism that they stuff their work as full as possible with the pet notions of the critics. Critics often sit on competition juries; this means that they exercise an influence on architectural production that is by no means open. Despite their power the critics are afraid of missing the bus. Not in the sense of not spotting a new trend, because they are the ones who launch them, but rather of being too late for history in general. They don't want to repeat the mistake of once again overlooking a *Salon des Indépendents* or a Van Gogh. That means that they get on every bus that turns up and it's often the wrong one. They know that themselves and that's why they get off again at the next stop. The result is a chaos of publications.

Do you think that something like that can still be called criticism? Being critical presupposes a certain belief
in yourself. The critics you mention apparently don't believe in themselves, in fact quite the reverse. Is that
the end of criticism or can we just see it as a failure of certain individuals who, because of their profession-
al position, are called critics?

There is no end of criticism, but there will be a change. The way in which criticism is practised nowadays hardly works any more. There will be critics who will write criticism that is parallel to a new architecture. The two do of course go together. Criticism won't disappear because its mediating role as well as its function of proclaiming and identifying new developments will always remain intact. A study like that of John Ackermann on Palladio that situates architecture so clearly in its cultural context could never have been produced by writers who did not have the historical or critical equipment. Criticism must be endless, especially in a time when increasing numbers of people are coming into contact with art. It will not be sufficient just to explain; hypotheses will need to be put forward as to how something is to be understood.

And what about the situation of the architect himself? If you acknowledge the political and cultural value of
architecture, how can a specialist in this form find his or her way back to politics and culture?

Architecture is such a vague discipline that it can never become a fully specialist one. People often complain that architecture is really difficult, because it doesn't have any parameters; it isn't a form of arithmetic, nor is it just a branch of design. This is in fact a very good thing, because it means that the profession can never degenerate into being a purely specialist field. Architecture is always enlarging its scope; you can't impose boundaries on it. This means that I am not a specialist but someone with certain capacities. In other words, I do not just know how certain specific things have to be dealt with, but increasingly I attempt to understand why I deal with them in a certain way. This is also why I try to find a balance between the way that I work and the reason why I work.

It is a question of finding a unity between skill and motivation. This brings you to politics, because once you know what motivates you, you are also in a position to understand the role that is allotted to you in society. The idea that architecture is able to change society is out of date; but I continue to believe that architecture can produce concrete material stimuli that can lead to a change of this sort. It can provoke situations; it can create an atmosphere that is balanced or even unbalanced. You can use it to produce an expression of society or of that part of society that you work for or want to work for; you can also organise space in such a way that balance and conflict are both made explicit. This is the intellectual challenge of our profession. Of course you can never do it in a directly explicit way as one can with the written word. It is always indirect. Forms generate repose or a lack of repose and this is what opens one up to criticism.

Once again, change begins with criticism. In my view the function of art and architecture continues to be to encourage the viewer to think critically and so to be open to change. In itself architecture cannot change anything; what it does do is to prepare the way for change. We must do everything in our power to avoid using form to disguise reality. This is something that happens all the time and it makes me furious. In this respect my profession, despite all its theoretical power, doesn't relate at all to the situation as it is. That is a crying shame. If there are conflicts, it is our task to expose them.

Since you lay such emphasis on the social aspect we would like to ask you a typical Beaux-Arts *question. In the approach you are suggesting is there any idea of architecture as an art form? Do you believe, to use Nikolaus Pevsner's classical terminology, in a difference between architecture and building?*

That's something that I don't believe in. At most there are different talents with the usual differences in quality. I believe in a difference between relevant and irrelevant architecture, and in everything in between. Even the cheapest or most shabby building is architecture, because in my view architecture is an organisational activity; it has to do with the ordering of space. Every building transforms a space into a site, and so it becomes architecture, for better or for worse. This means that I do not believe in architecture with a capital A as the most perfect sort of building, because that way of classifying things leads to a completely false hierarchy. Classifications like this are arrogant and have no *a priori* justification; they have little to do with real problems. They make things easier for the critics maybe because they like to have a well-defined profession, but it is nonsense from the point of view of the actual occupants of the buildings. Just think for a moment of all the places that people occupy where you haven't a clue if they are worth anything as architecture; I am still obliged to take these places seriously. In cases like this the use justifies the form, and it is my job then to find out how something like that works: I have to learn from life; life doesn't have to learn from me.

But the advantage of an approach like Pevsner's is that it gives us certain conventions for what attractive architecture is.

Yes, that's true, but conventions wear out. Pevsner forgot a great number of buildings that I personally think are very attractive.

Let's put it a bit more generally then: when you look back on the whole tradition of architecture, your memory will still tend to select very 'architectural' architecture. Professionalism and artistic appeal are still apparently the criteria for the choices one makes.

In no sense do these criteria have any general validity; it depends on the taste of a person or group and is also very much dependent on the period. Many of Pevsner's choices are no longer so self-evident. Many buildings that he left out might now be included in a book like this. Even in my own career there are buildings that have sometimes been very important for me and at other times not. I would, however, like to make a qualitative distinction. The fact that in certain circumstance certain buildings can become exceptional long after they have been built, does not mean that all buildings are potentially good. (This is similar to the question of the critics all jumping on the bus: we would no longer be able to pass judgement on buildings because time is always capable of proving us wrong.) Some buildings are irrelevant; they have no special qualities. There are also buildings that do undoubtedly possess special qualities. In other words they have an additional excellence that enables them to transcend the ancient Vitruvian principles of *firmitas, commoditas* and *venustas*. You have to judge every building according to these criteria. Some examples of architecture will stand the test better, some worse: this is how you calculate the value of a building. But on top of this you sometimes achieve a super-quality: *concinnitas*. It is a question of something that Cicero saw in the rhetoric of someone who was capable of moving his public.

It is no longer a question of clarity or of being interesting, but also of an atmosphere whose fascination is universal. According to Alberti – and I agree with him totally – architecture is capable of attaining this level. It is at precisely this point that there are no longer any conventions or rules such as were still applicable to the other Vitruvian categories. I believe that this quality of perfect elegance has the power to enthral everybody.

For instance?

In my lifetime I have seen only a few buildings that can lay claim to this quality. The Hagia Sophia in Istanbul, Hadrian's Villa outside Rome and perhaps Le Corbusier's Unité d'Habitation in Marseilles. I have felt it in the Palazzo Ducale in Urbino. Everyone, no matter from what culture, gets a shock on seeing that palace. That is when architecture becomes a miracle. *Concinnitas* is a category of super-quality, a *qualité suprème*. Anyone who experiences something of this order will never be the same person again.

Dormitories for students, Urbino, 1962

Hagia Sophia, Istanbul, 537

A Conversation with Giancarlo De Carlo

The Invisible in Architecture could be conceived as identity. Whether we take this term in its philosophical or its psychological sense, it is the character that people and things give one another, and derive from one another. Since identity takes shape through social intercourse, there are always agreements involved too – invisible agreements.

As an attribute of the individual, identity decomposes into at least two parts: personal identity and ego-identity. Personal identity is based on the perception that someone remains the same as time passes by. It is the idea of identity that we use in everyday life. The ego-identity is more complex, and breaks down into three levels. There is a somatic level, at which a person maintains his equilibrium by adapting to and separating himself from the environment. Then there is a personal level, at which, in the long term, the person integrates his inner world with his experience. Finally, there is a social level, at which the identity is upheld by means of interactions among a group of people with a common geographical and historical background.

The development of identity gains momentum in adolescence, a phase in which the young person has to integrate the *ego-ideal* of his childhood into a coherent picture of the future. The adolescent has to amalgamate the succession of widening perspectives and more intensive experiences into a single whole, at a personal level. At least as important as this is that, at the same time, the collective must furnish the adolescent with an identity at a social level, from which he can draw support and which offers him the possibility of recognition, association and solidarity. Owing to the ever greater prolongation of adolescence, coupled with the breakdown of those authorities that were once the source of permanent values, the formation of identity has become a permanent problem in Western society.

Substantial libraries could be filled with the countless publications that have already appeared on the subject of the identification process at the personal level. The role of the collective identity and the social level has been much less closely studied.

The modern process of individualisation seems to be accompanied by the disruption of many traditional codes, values and structures. But at the same time masses of codes, values and structures – in short, a collective identity – is installed in accordance with the laws of the market. A reterritorialisation takes place within a system of state, law, commonality, multinational economy, consumerism and other normalising conditions. These all-pervading identity mechanisms are ignored in the great majority of democratic news and communications media. Still, the actions people undertake stand in an undeniable relation to the dominant collective identity. And when we probe for this relation in an architectural oeuvre, hidden authorisations emerge.

The group-forming, identity-determining forces are perhaps not as obvious as they used to be. The socialising counterpart of individualisation has to make do without all too specific a name. But nameless does not mean irrelevant. The 'identity' vector attempts to address this insight.

Since the Renaissance, and above all since the mid-eighteenth century, there has been a growing tendency to objectivise the purely subjective. As natural science, visual art, architecture and even politics drew the universal, 'divine' rules, so enthusiastically recorded by the humanists, into doubt, and it gradually became acceptable to postulate the relativity of the 'here and now', the great adventure of self-research began. For romantics, the inner world was no longer an uncontrolled morass of vice, but an intriguing and favoured theme. This led, in the late eighteenth century, to the establishment of an introspective tradition that continues to this day. The most intimate private circumstances and feelings are now brought out into the open and exploited. In brief, abstract terms, we can summarise this development as a progression from the 'What do I know?' of Montaigne, to the 'Who am I?' of Stendhal, to the *Ecce Homo* of Nietzsche and the 'Where am I as an author?' of Roland Barthes, to the 'Here I am!' of Oprah Winfrey.

Black skin, white mask Honduras

In the footsteps of this tradition, the term identity seems to have gradually become a catchword in various forms of cultural criticism. People refer to ethnic identity, sexual identity, the 'own' identity or the identity crisis of anything under the sun; and this is generally accompanied by the unspoken assumption that identity is a right. In these cases people talk of identity when they have an idea that they are not getting the respect due to them. Whenever the term 'identity' is mentioned, it tends to be associated automatically with an emancipatory cultural politics. Naturally, the dominant culture has its own character too, the peer group also has its own identity, but this is widely accepted as a self-evident matter. People generally place special emphasis on the inalienable identity of the minority, the 'difference', the 'other', and leave the identity of the collective consensus out of consideration.

But, whereas a politicised use of the term identity is frequent, doubts have been cast on the tenability of this concept on a number of fronts. Identity has become a popular theme in psychology, philosophy, art and even science fiction. The issue is invariably whether thinking in terms of identities can still be valid in a post-modern condition, i.e. in an age that places little value on consistency, integrity and responsibility, the keywords of rationalist identity philosophy since Descartes and Spinoza. There is also a rising tension between the former certainty of the need to form a personal identity, and new developments in areas such as pedagogy, communications technology and semiotics which increasingly make the ultimate personal responsibility for behaviour into an either necessary or unnecessary illusion. Pessimistic philosophers of culture warn repeatedly against this erosion, against the decay of the responsible, always-recognisable individual, against chameleonism. However, there are also many theoreticians who see these new facts in a positive light and perceive in them a modernised conception of freedom.

It is in this field of force between self-definition and transgression, between optimism and pessimism, between identity and 'the other', that various forms of angst can emerge. Firstly, there is the panic that arises in the face of new facts, such as discoveries and inventions that radically widen and change our whole world view. Then there is a vaguer sinking feeling aroused by the symbolic dangers that people experience through the decline of existing ideologies. And finally, in the wake of disintegrating belief, there is the fear of an existential hell without any spiritual meaning.

It is in this ethical vacuum that today's debates on cultural, national, ethnic and other identities take place. Nobody wishes to succumb in this vacuum. But neither does anyone seem capable of escaping it by formulating durable criteria.

Identity in architecture, a result of the interaction of space, image and programme, is directly linked to the problems highlighted above. The identities of the designer, the client and the distribution and production process, have their resonance in the project's purpose, location, materials, tectonics, spatial form, cladding etc. The user's identification with this ensemble takes place by recognition and in usage.

Following the rising awareness that architecture is not only a functional and aesthetic phenomenon but also a means of communicating an identity, a lively discussion has ensued on the relation between the meaning of the architecture and its meaning as understood by the public. Since the sixties and the pioneering work of such social psychologists as Alexander Mitscherlich, Kevin Lynch and Klaus Horn, and since the architectural criticism of Colin Rowe, Christopher Alexander and Jane Jacobs, we can no longer believe in the one-dimensional vocabulary of Modernism. Its sterility and lack of identification points were recognised as a psychological deficiency. We might even suggest that architecture's modern project has failed precisely because of this 'less is more' approach. Since identity went hand in hand with a certain level of humanity, and hence a lack of identity with a certain shortage of humanity, it was inevitable that the Miesian idiom eventually came to be the butt of intense criticism.

The failure of Modernism in architecture did not, by the way, come about through logical reasoning. Although the above mentioned theoreticians introduced an accompanying analytical vocabulary, the bankruptcy of Modernism could be linked to a reason more inherent to culture. It became apparent that man was incapable of the voluntary behaviour for which Modernism was the neutral platform – certainly not while that platform was becoming ever more expressionless, for reasons of financial efficiency. Recognisable, representative identities were supposed to compensate for this 'expressionless' character. But such *Ersatz* qualities can only be of restricted value. Passionately wanting an identity raises the gravest suspicions about actually having an identity. In architecture, representation has gained immensely in importance, but the value of architecture for the process of identity formation has clearly not always kept pace. Our individual capacity to form judgements about social and institutional identities is sometimes seriously impaired by the aesthetisation of the architectural object.

Three strategies and three architects The work of the architect always has an identity. Users and passers-by derive an identity from buildings; they let their own identities be partly determined by the built structures around them. Since there is an awareness of this dimension in architecture, it is consciously taken up in designs and in criticism. In this respect, we may distinguish three approaches.

Archaism
Archaism interprets identity as being dependant on locus and on social organism. Using its inherent capacity for differentiation, archaism hopes to do justice to differences while at the same time being able to universalise its claims to validity. Identity constitutes an irreducible entity, but survives by means of differentiation. The attention of the archaist is thus drawn to the unique contacts between one person and another, in relation to unique places. **Lucien Kroll's** attention is drawn to everyday life, with its anthropological character of interaction between individual and group. For him, this is a way of staving off the colonialisation of the life-world by technology, specialisation and the commodity culture. Kroll supports a participation in which the future inhabitant discovers (or rediscovers) the architect, the *homo faber*, in himself. He designs complex villages where every building and every residential unit has a face of its own, and where time 'contributes' to the design. Here, anarchy and identity go hand in hand.

Façadism
For façadism, the positive expression of identity is an extremely important matter. Particularly when this tendency works from a radical criticism of the modernist poverty of meaning, it sees the façade as the iconographic means by which architecture can generate identity once more, both for itself and for the public. With this in mind, the façadist incorporates countless cultural references, signs that represent an 'identity'. **Ricardo Bofill** is largely specialised in giving monumental shapes to squares and boulevards. In his way of doing this, it is not the individual who stands out, but rather a collective self that seeks its expression in dream palaces. The lack of 'artistic' identity of the moderns is compensated by a majestic packaging that is meant to offer a psychological foothold. High-quality prefab components make the grandiloquent gesture possible, and bring the historically established emblems of self-confidence within everyone's reach.

Fascinism
For fascinism, the coherent identity is dead. The one true identity, the thing identified by a name, is an attribute of a lost 'classical' world. Fascinistic architecture confirms the impossibility of such an identity in a post-modern condition. It prefers to offer either a complex, confusing and fragmented atmosphere which is a reflection of our world as it is, or it restricts itself as clinically as possible to the milieu around this confusion. The architecture of the latter kind is hence also a metaphor for the end of metaphor. **Norman Foster**, in his fascination for the dynamics of the age of communication, is beyond a politics of identity. He creates a cordon sanitaire, a flexible platform, a stately structure built with state of the art technology. It is a transparent architecture that barely gives an identity a chance to consolidate itself – apart from the 'minimal' identity that is stimulated in and by the machinery. Foster's architecture is like the sterile sheet with an aperture that is placed over the patient during an operation, so that the surgeon is not obliged to identify with the object of his technical performance.

For us every building has something unique, something natural that arises from working with its users. The interplay of form, colour and materials forms a harmonious whole in which people occupy a central place. **Ton Alberts & Max van Huut**

Within a site, architecture tries to dominate emptiness, but at the same time emptiness dominates the architecture. If a building is to be autonomous and have its own character, not only the building but emptiness itself must have its own logic. **Tadao Ando**

The history of forms, the history of architecture of which Modernism and the International Style are part, is the basis on which our architecture erects itself. There it will reintegrate the values of this history. So that the glance comes to rest on it, recognises it, and wonders at the intangible future. **Ricardo Bofill**

Transparency today is intrinsic to our perception, buildings need not be built transparent. They must now simplify and solidify. Julia Bolles & Peter Wilson

Picasso said that the best place to learn painting was in the museums, observing and studying what other people had painted. I think that what originality there is in my work lies in my extrapolation of certain aspects contained in the work of others. **Santiago Calatrava**

What planning as a principle ignores is the synthesising instinct of experience – that the proximity of dissimilar images and events can release architecture from its object status. This may be why most of us feel livelier in cities complicated by the imprint of one reality upon one another. Nigel Coates & Doug Branson

If by identity, in a transgression with respect to its literal meaning, we mean the capacity to be recognisable for the quality and specificity of the message within a complex accumulation of communications, then we are talking about the evidence of a difference. **Pietro Derossi**

The body is a plastic form, moulded to con-form to the idealised normative body. Prosthesis, here, is de-mechanised, sometimes camouflaged and in fluid exchange with steroids, silicone, spandex and skin. Its programme of completion is replaced by one of mutation. Elisabeth Diller & Ricardo Scofidio

The appearance of the Hong Kong Bank both inside and out, its internal organisation and the spatial experience that it offered were all defined, ordered and modulated by the structure which supported it and the walls which enclosed it. The design of Stansted Airport gives a compact building which reduces walking distances for passengers and enables them to move through the building on simple linear routes. **Norman Foster**

Oriented to the North, the façade of the Joan Miró Library takes on the significance of an architecture meant as container of books. **Beth Galí**

What I like doing best is breaking down the project into as many separate parts as possible. So instead of a house being one thing, it's ten things. It allows the client more involvement, because you can say, 'well, I've got ten images now, that are going to compose your house. Those images can relate to all kinds of symbolic things, ideas if you've liked, bits and pieces of your life that you would like to recall...' Frank Gehry

I suspect that over the last ten years, I've been simply trying to say two things. First, that my work is abstract by nature because of the geometric compositions that I use, and that it can therefore risk being very obscure in terms of the layman. But at the same time, it has to be figurative enough to allow the layman to participate in it. **Michael Graves**

Having completed the Shonandai Cultural Centre I realise quite clearly now that I want to create an inclusive architecture that accepts a multiplicity of things rather than an architecture arrived at through reflection and elimination. The idea is to make architecture more realistic through what might be called a 'pop' reasoning that allows for diversity as opposed to a logical system of reasoning that demands extreme concentration. Such an approach represents a shift to a feminist paradigm, in the sense that an attempt is made to raise the consciousness of as many people as possible. Itsuko Hasegawa

What is really in our way, is not the fact that we have to open and close doors, but a specific difficulty that is part of our time. There is this lack of identity...

Jacques Herzog & Pierre de Meuron

The essence of a work of architecture is an organic link between concept and form. Pieces cannot be subtracted or added without upsetting fundamental properties. A concept, whether a rationally explicit statement or a subjective demonstration, establishes an order, a field of inquiry, a limited principle. **Steven Holl**

The shape of a building does not develop out of the material condition of its purpose. A building shall not show its use. It is not an expression of structure and construction, it is not enclosure or refuge.
A building is itself. **Hans Hollein**

The traditional and modernity are not contradictory notions. One can be a modern man of tradition. There is no contradiction. **Leon Krier**

Isn't it criminal to design places deliberately as mass-produced, cloned, impersonal structures, when the aim is to implement a sensitive, non-regimented upbringing? Do we not have the right to measure the value of the building against its end product, i.e. the behaviour of the users? In other words, what becomes of the children who are taught in one specific environment or another? It seems, in this era that terms itself rational (is it that, or is it simply regimented?) that these questions are never considered. Would that be such a sacrilege?
Lucien Kroll

The street is an intermediary zone where the private interior space of the individual dwelling meets the public exterior space of the road. These two natures interpenetrate, exist in symbiosis, and stimulate each other, creating a zone that can be described as extremely warm and suggestive. This symbiosis of interior and exterior represents a typically Asian attitude. **Kisho Kurokawa**

Buildings have to fit in, have to conform to existing buildings. Nowadays autonomy is seen as a quality, but I think that is because architects are too eager to leave their mark on the situation where they are building. Often it is the case that the more autonomous the building, the worse the situation is. **Lucien Lafour & Rikkert Wijk**

How does one change such a process? How does one bring back the urgency, the immediacy which must have existed at some point sometime, that violence which has to do with breathlessness'? Where is the breathlessness in architecture! Why is everybody so full of confidence? Why are people not breathless? Or why are they so out-of-breath for the wrong reason, running from one office to another co-ordinating imbecile data. It is mysterious that architecture's respiration suffers from its in-spiration. **Daniel Libeskind**

Architecture implies the distance between our work and ourselves, so that in the end the work remains alone, self-supported, once it has acquired its physical consistency. Our pleasure lies in the experience of this distance, when we see our thought supported by a reality that no longer belongs to us. What is more, a work of architecture, if successful, may efface the architect. **Rafael Moneo**

My pleasure has never surfaced in looking at buildings, at the 'great works' of history or present of architecture, but rather in dismantling them.
Bernard Tschumi

In all our projects but particularly in our major museums, we have tried to derive an identity for the building by 'learning from' the site, the city, the campus, and the goals, values and need of our client. This identity turns out to be as complex and contradictory as we are. A multivalent identity that confronts both the collective and the individual, public and private, the present and the future, the rootedness of the institution and the flux of the civilisation, to say nothing of conflicting values and roles within the individual, probably needs a modicum of irony in its make-up to smooth the ride. For us, allusion to many other sources and ways of thought is a means of establishing such an identity, but the allusions are fleeting and themselves multi-layered and they give rise to further questions about meaning.
As for the architect's own identity, the ideal is that the architect too be glimpsed only fleetingly, moving between columns, not like Frank Lloyd Wright in a flowing robe, but in an undistinguished suit high-tailing it from the controversy.
Robert Venturi & Denise Scott Brown

Lucien Kroll
The Voice of Libertarian Socialism

Editors' note: Lucien Kroll is a man who never smothers social empiricism with an imposed discourse. Situationism, casuistry, situational ethics and ethnology are the keywords of an approach to architecture in which it is not the architect, the artist or the client who determines who and what people are, but the people themselves. A good proof of the success of this non-prescriptive architecture is a telephone call Kroll received from the photographer of a Japanese architectural magazine. Phoning from a call box in the middle of one of Kroll's urban projects, the photographer asked 'Where can I find your architecture?' Kroll's architecture does not stand somewhere, it happens somewhere. Owing to his near-obsession with the value of grass-roots democracy, every coercive, authoritarian or technicist intervention is foreign to him. Kroll is at most a primus inter pares, and then only during the design phase. After that, time will have its say. The identity of the profession is overshadowed by countless sub-identities from homo faber to homo ludens. In Kroll's view, the environment is a function of human behaviour. Making behaviour a function of the environment is terror. That much is about to be rammed home... We head Lucien Kroll's letter as follows:

Dear Editors,

We are not simply manufacturers of objects with a mechanical function. We use our powers of empathy to render the constraints, the capacities and the conflicts of a neighbourhood and a place as architecture; and we do the same for the users' desire to congregate, in as far as we can predict it. So the main task is to create a kind of landscape. Architecture then becomes an instrument of human behaviour, and this is a sufficient justification for its existence. I received your questionnaire on the eight themes you considered important to give your book a scholarly structure. Your questions★ are only partly relevant to a method such as ours. Moreover, their intellectualist tone gets in the way of architecture. They fail to get down to the meat of the matter. Shall I try to do that for you?

★ See the introductions to the eight vectors: durée, context, border, topos, programme, space, identity, representation.

Durée

It is true that the concept of durability seems to stand for the permanence and continuity of culture. And Modernism (or, if you like, modernity) is apparently in the throes of an accelerating process of change. Is it possible to assert that we must keep becoming more modern (although in what respect?), must keep moving faster (but where to?), must persevere with limitless economic growth (thereby frittering away our resources) and must internationalise all cultural action (as in a melting pot – or perhaps towards universal justice)? Such a row of contradictions may seem rather artificial – exaggerated, Manichean etcetera. Or perhaps they are 'pre-war Modern', i.e. belonging to that awful period (I do not say awful people) of illusions in the areas of technology, psychology, society, humanitarianism and war.

396

Preliminary School, Woluwé-Saint-Lambert, Brussels, 1971

Groothandelsmarktterrein, urban planning, The Hague, competition entry, 1988

Zero growth, respect for *existing* (i.e. contemporary but not necessarily modern) cultures, respect for the animal and vegetable species and for the landscapes which seem to be destroyed cursorily by our progress, the right to intervene in other countries' internal affairs – are these a form of repression or are they *also* part of that progress?

I have no intention of spouting sociology and I have no economic pretensions. But I would be only too happy if I could get to grips with the concealed or indirect motives that dominate architecture far more strongly than the pencils of the architects. Is that a foolish concern? You might well think so if you read the professional magazines, with their autistic exegeses and their dismissive commentaries on anything that has to do with context, with spontaneous expressions of culture or with the spirit of the times etcetera. They present the architectural object 'as such', as a work without temporality, without antecedents, without past and without future.

For example, there has been a recent recrudescence of articles on the architecture of the twenties. These include photographs taken in that period, and these sometimes have a sinister look: they are in monochrome, and were often taken immediately on completion, the building still surrounded by mud, without greenery, without neighbours and above all without traffic. Instead of this practice, one could make an attempt to show the evolution (good or bad?) of the same buildings – their history, the roots they have put down, the way they become estranged from their original form, evolve and age. Architecture should never be reviewed until it has existed for at least twenty years. The only positive instance I can think of is Philippe Boudon, who studied Pessac as experienced by its inhabitants at a time when Le Corbusier had become no more than a distant name for them. If architects were conscious of the time dimension when designing a building, they would be able to anticipate how the landscape would take the abstract and alien object and consume it, assimilate it and make it one with the environment – however indigestible it might have been to start with!

But is this modern? Respect for time and duration is not just nostalgia. It means making allowance for things as they are and refraining from imposing tyrannical utopias. On the other hand, it is absolutely clear that we can not extrapolate an existing context into the future (that is romanticism!). Our contemporary context is mobile, multi-racial, ever more diverse (what a wealth!). Thus the present situation calls for architects who are capable of working very personally but also with great complexity.

Thought about time and duration gives architecture an invisible quality, as one can see if that thinking continues far beyond the design phase. The more functional the thinking is, the shorter the building functions. The thinking should be of a cultural (multi-cultural) character because the aim is to produce a building (not a mere construction) which should be at the service of everyone who appears on the scene – announced or unannounced.

I am not referring here to the projects of ineffectual intellectuals who prefer the conceivable to the actual and who lead their readers up idiosyncratic dream paths, far from the heat and the sweat of the day. Nor am I referring to the surrealist projections of schizophrenic geometrical figures (whose only market value is their surprise effect).

Context

One can not reduce context to tradition. That would be ignoring the fact that social relationships (visible or otherwise) continually reconfigure themselves, every day, according to the new circumstances. As a result, the various kinds of nostalgia for older, stable forms of society retreat in favour of active social construction in the present. This activity is synthetic, not analytic (I am no Cartesian!). It permeates the entire context and knows no bounds. It involves every aspect of human existence.

Taking the context into account simply means feeling part of the geographical, human, cultural, economic world you have chosen to operate in, not shutting yourself up in abstract and destructive forms of logic. Modernism, from which we are freeing ourselves at such great effort, suffered from monomaniac anxiety. Consequently it refused to admit to emotion, and remained fixated purely on the architectural object, the urban grid, the residential boxes – all that obsessive self-repetition that they termed industrial

Medical Faculty, University of Leuven, Woluwé-Saint-Lambert, Brussels, 1971

but was really just regimentation and abstraction. Perhaps that neurosis was originally necessary to drive out other, now forgotten, forms of commercial sentimentalism. But nowadays...

Border

Despite the invention of bureaucracy and of its mechanical organisation at the beginning of the twentieth century, architecture knows no bounds: its apparent limitations are rapidly dissolving. Only modern architects imprison themselves in their own pigeon holes – for example, have you noticed their unanimous aversion to buildings that project above the roads? Antoni Gaudí was the only one to lean his buildings on the footpath. Siza tried to do the same in Berlin but his column failed to make contact with the pavement! Thus there is no longer any *homogeneity*. There is merely a certain permeability in the partitions, a potential for dialogue, which the future will exploit. The result will be a blurring of borders of a geographical or psychological nature etcetera and hence a fusion into a continuum.

Chaos is a creative virtue of cities. 'Liveable town planning is a result of bad architecture', said certain Moderns disconsolately. Let us therefore build that 'bad' architecture, but let's do it well! Simple enough, but is it 'art', and who decides?

Topos

Why should we fill in the surroundings only as an abstract pattern of dots? When we are talking about densely populated areas, isn't that a racist way of thinking – this is white, that is black? We must not confuse Topos with Condominium.

The condominium is the obnoxious American bastard child of the European housing association. Just as the housing association, invented in Europe's nineteenth century cities, was the result of open and co-operative urban behaviour, so is its degenerate American form the result of urban enclosure (shutting the others out), of the city-dweller's insecurity that creates and seals ghettos of every shape and size. Housing associations originally grouped people of all different kinds. The condominium

enforces a uniformity of race, of material wealth, of culture, of spending power etcetera.

The condominium is most clearly represented by the New York skyscraper with a porch leading from the sidewalk to the lobby, where a security guard, revolver on belt, waits to welcome you. He asks who you wish to visit and checks on his intercom.

No, that is not what a city ought to be like.

The USA also has some very nice condominiums with ten or twenty thousand inhabitants, who lead a pleasant life behind a wall topped with barbed wire, permanently guarded by armed men driving around in jeeps. One of the many residence rules: nobody less than 55 years old. Sinister, but expedient.

We should never start *inventing*! When rationalists invented houses arranged in lines along a street plan, they robbed the inhabitants of all the reptilian habits that prevailed in the old urban spaces and in their articulations. When they thought up the tree model for functionally stacked dwellings, they robbed the inhabitants of their equally reptilian patrimony of old-style house plans that paraphrased the human body.

Let's get subjective, right now!

Programme

The architect's sense of honour is generally so highly developed as to respect the brief and the client's wishes (however absurd) right down to the threshold of pain. They thus make themselves willing victims of the worst kind of Taylorism (one person commands, the rest blindly follow...). Of course a solid programme is necessary to build something that will stand up to the test of utility. The question is, though, how is this programme implemented in practice? Is it the architect's fate to always follow the schizophrenic wishes of the specifier of the brief? Or is it the brief-writer who must expect the architects to come up with ideas that will give their precise, regimented schemes life and blood, body and clothing?

Sometimes I think I am the only architect who has ever experienced a normal briefing procedure. During the construction of the Medical Faculty at the University of Brussels-Woluwé, I proposed incorporating a small primary school into one of the buildings specified in the brief. Astounded at this suggestion, the University put off taking a decision until circumstances made it imperative to do so. Note that if I had not designed the primary school in, they would have had to build it on a separate plot of land.

Nowadays, at least in France, the architect is invited to attend the discussions right from the start, before the brief-writer has a chance to mummify amid the sheets of surfaces, connections and partitions. The sensitive architect is able to interpret the elusive values of society, geography, cultural landscape etcetera, and can also anticipate requirements of future users.

Emerainville, housing, Marne-la-Vallée, 1980

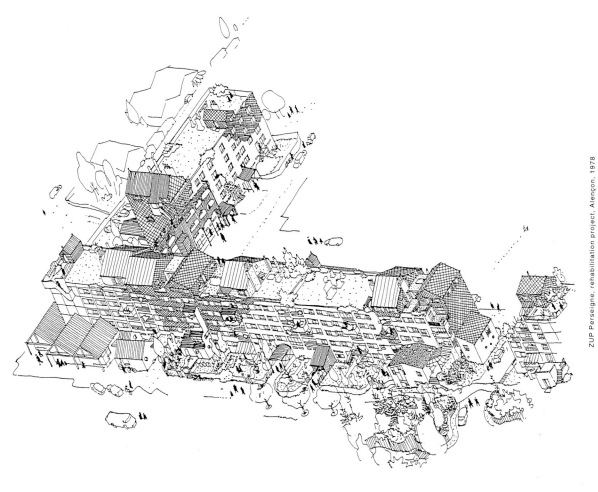

ZUP Perseigne, rehabilitation project, Alençon, 1978

David Hammons, House for the future, 1991

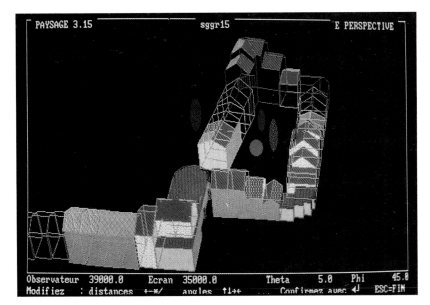

Wire frame, from 'Paysage', computer-aided-design
programme developed by studio Lucien Kroll, 1981-1987

Space

It is a mistake to identify *space* with appearance: can we not imagine an architecture for the blind, for instance? Equally erroneous is to equate quantitative space with qualitative space. This is seldom realised. It is much like confusing *scale* with *proportion*. In fact, many architects work only two-dimensionally. The third is more complicated! Ideologies are often accused of manipulating quantities of space, but they have a much more powerful influence on the qualities, the joints, the complexity. That Haussmann's city plans were dictated by the need to deploy artillery against slum uprisings is probably a myth; but he was definitely an adherent of a particular ideology, namely that of the regimented image! Everything in its proper place – that is a fundamental tenet of the bourgeoisie, and it generates a very particular form of city. Later that form was termed 'hygienic' and was used to design working-class districts and then entire social complexes. Some people have ascribed the 'hygienic' regimentation to the use of prefab architecture. But prefab is in fact merely a convenient extension of the same formal principles. We, on the other hand, seek to foster the development of self-organising social autonomies out of disorder. Is that an ideology too? The times have changed, at least. A feeling for space (full or empty) and for the concerted action of materials that go together to build a space brings a great deal more clarity than does a feeling for semiology.

Identity

Is it really still possible to design a school, for instance, as a series of identical rectangular rooms in a row? Is education a process that takes place in clear-cut and objectively definable spaces? Shouldn't we rather differentiate the space and architectural attributes, at all costs, to prevent the children confusing people with objects? Isn't it criminal to design places deliberately as mass-produced, cloned, impersonal structures, when the aim is to implement a sensitive, non-regimented upbringing? Do we not have the right to measure the value of the building against its end product, i.e. the behaviour of the users? In other words, what becomes of the children who are taught in one specific environment or another? It seems, in this era that terms itself rational (is it that, or is it simply regimented?) that these questions are never considered. Would that be such a sacrilege? Let us escape from this architectural torpidity! Shouldn't we actually search for the maximum variety in identities, for composite building projects; and thus avoid that repulsive fad for identifying everything by numbers (streets, buildings, doors etcetera), sometimes with extra large numerals like those on warships?

The inhabitants will eventually come to identify with their neighbourhood, their street or their home – or so we hope. But shouldn't this be possible straight away, instead of after years? Surely it cannot be achieved by keeping architects anonymous – even giving the narcissistic types their head would be better than that. Or would it...?

Representation

The image: even the blind form one! In our urban district renovation projects, I deliberately chose to represent a kind of pedestrian civilisation – one which might have prevailed in a peaceful way, without (or in opposition to) the whole superimposed mass of technology, regimenters, subjugators, authorities etcetera. Naturally, this is just a metaphor, but I make no secret of my feelings about it towards clients and authorities. They understand that it is often a matter of their own survival: these forms reflect a cooperation between those who command and those who obey. Is that a model of democracy? Sometimes it is the everyday, popular (folksy) attributes that make a neighbourhood more liveable than an architect can ever achieve deliberately;★ for once the inhabitants install themselves, they soon find their way around and start organising things spontaneously to please themselves. ★ I have never found this a problem. The architect's work is located at a different level, that of collecting and articulating spaces to produce a non-regimented, i.e. civilised, architecture.

★ In Cergy-Pontoise, we waited to see how the inhabitants themselves would design their houses. We were able to organise a considerable level of disorder (complexity). At this level, our work does not depend on a homogeneous and maniacal definition of all the elements involved.

★ In Haarlem, we housed Dutch families opposite a garden along the bank of a canal. Within a few months, they had completely transformed the garden and its relation to the water.

And... Institution

The dimension of 'institutional analysis' seems to be entirely ignored in your questionnaire! I know why this is. How is it possible for architectural colleges to design foundation courses without giving any practice in institutional analysis? They park the kids on stools, give them pencils and say, 'Just draw away, don't be afraid, be nice to Mummy and all will be well'!

If we taught institutional analysis we should be able to forestall a whole generation of Left-wing architects who practise Right-wing architecture. Here are two examples. Firstly, under the pretext of democracy, they prefabricated the same for everybody and so ushered in the calamity of suburbia. Secondly, when people wanted meeting places the architects provided them with shopping malls and luxury stores; then within a single generation the whole model collapsed. Now there is fire in the suburbs. Something positive at last!

In spite of the generous subsidies, social sector housing has caused the greatest uprooting of all projects in large towns. You have to realise this in order to correct your course and develop a concept of spatial organisation and architecture which accords with a changed attitude.

The use of 'modern' building materials goes hand in hand with the 'importation' of millions of foreign labourers into European countries. At the same time, it brings in its wake the destruction of the craft knowledge of many building tradesmen. As an architect, you ought to be able to take this kind of thing into account when making decisions, without being romantic about it. The formal world of architecture and urban design embodies a clear ideology, which the 'creators' apparently do not wish to know about. But the damage done by that ideology will only become clear in the next generation, during the de-Stalinisation of architecture!

Etcetera.

Yours sincerely,

Lucien Kroll

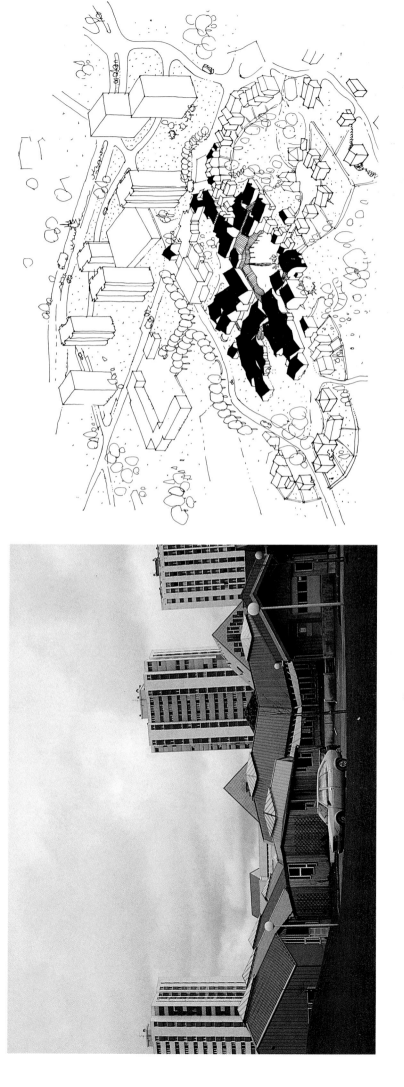

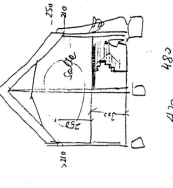

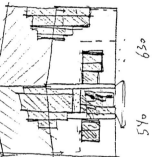

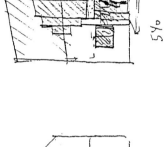

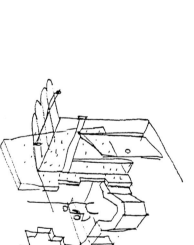

Our secondary school for technical education in Bavilliers, 12,000 square metres in size, is nestled into the frayed edge of Belfort, next to a post-war city extension quarter. We wanted to approach the school as a means to influence behaviour, as a complex landscape and not as an egocentric 'functional' object. The exterior and the inside of the school are determined by only one motive: the open network. The highschool will immediately come in contact with the neighbouring low-grade habitats. It will climb up their façades and reorganise the intermediate area when the houses are redone. We placed 'the outside in the middle' to be assured of a permeable environment: we kept off enclosures and divided the area by means of streets and squares that were placed under public rule to ensure free entrance. Narrowing down and widening, they become a natural extension of the adjacent area. The network of streets divides (or unites?) the territory into half a dozen distinctive units. They encircle two important public spaces: the 'entry' towards the social habitats and the large plaza in the centre of the high school. This plaza has been covered with glass for playground as the programme demanded. The central plaza gathers the largest variety of buildings: the diverse studios, the foyer-bar, the classrooms for general education, the restaurant, the staff rooms, the administration in the back of the square and at the side the caretakers' house, waiting for neighbours. Thus there are some fifteen 'houses' grouped according to their own logic. They personalise themselves, as much as we could allow them to, by their activities on the spot, the locations, the volumes, the forms, the slope of the roofs, the construction techniques, the colours, etcetera. Every house will get its name spontaneously, as in the old regions. The landscape will become so complicated that even we will no longer be able to control all its forms and assemblies. It lives its own life and manages to surprise us during its construction. Thanks to the division into a federation of units, we were able to spread the assignment over several bricklayers and carpenters; thus we were able to work with a limited budget, avoiding expensive contractors. Already in every one of our projects we tried to deconstruct not the architecture – that is just a passing trend – but the homogeneity of the object, its cohesion, its autism, to make it more open towards its neighbourhood and to its urban and spiritual responsibilities. For that reason it becomes a landscape itself.

Lucien Kroll

Location Rue de Zaporodje, Belfort, France **Assistant** X. Nuttin **Client** Société d'Equipement du Territoire de Belfort (SODEB) **Design** 1983 **Completion** 1989

Atelier d'Urbanisme, d'Architecture et d'Informatique Lucien Kroll *Technical College Denis Diderot*

JANUARI   FEBRUARI

Z   M   D   W   D   V   Z

30   31   1   2   3   4   5

On the Work of Ricardo Bofill
The Man who Mistook Style for a Living

Ricardo Bofill is perhaps better known to the general public than any other living architect. It is hard to imagine a more photogenic style of architecture than his. Countless viewers must have seen, at some time or another, a television fashion show, an erotic film or an Open University programme with one of his buildings in the background. Yet his work is at the same time extremely controversial, probably precisely because of his mass popularity. Commentary on Bofill's palaces has often been devastating. Here are a few phrases, just to remind you: mastodons in the urban tissue; disregard for the public sphere; you cannot make a gentleman out of a prole; soulless prefab Classicism; with Bofill, if you want to be beautiful you have to suffer in a cramped little box; the iron will of a flamboyant superstar... These are just a few snatches from a discourse that needs no repetition here. These critiques have always given the impression that no one could really wish to live in such lordly mansions. But in the meantime it is surely clear that quite the contrary is true.

Many of Bofill's projects betray a passion for the crescent. Bofill succeeds in using this type to give his housing developments a grandeur recalling the stately architecture of the aristocracy of former centuries. Now, however, this grandeur is available to one and all. The renowned crescents of Bath stand as examples. Co-architect Peter Hodgkinson put it as follows:

'Within the Taller Bofill, we look to Bath as a dream model – by no means utopian, but totally realistic. Bath was built all in one go by a small group of financiers and developers and architects who could *impose* – and that is the important word – impose their will on the general public.'★ This approach has gained a fitting epithet in history: enlightened despotism. Everything for the populace, but nothing by the populace.

The populace may now live in Walden, Les Arcades du Lac, Les Echelles du Baroque, Les Espaces d'Abraxas, Le Théatre, l'Antigone. When you take up domicile in one of Ricardo Bofill's residential projects, you don't live just *anywhere*. The inhabitants often have visiting cards proudly printed with logos of their imposing dwellings. The power of style seems to have turned into the style of power. As long as one can identify with the greatness of the past, that is to say the past of the big male overlords (slight exception for Antigone), it doesn't matter too much if there is something missing from these *grands ensembles* of reincarnated self-respect. As long as the inhabitants can flatter themselves with the idea that their home is literally their castle, they are hardly likely to be put off by the thought that the justification for these castles is no longer their social legitimacy but the added value of an architecture with an arrestingly dramatic iconography. As long as one's own lifestyle is fully furnished with the right status symbols, the empty centre is not a problem. So Bofill has no reason whatsoever to be concerned about the dubiousness of the content. His concentric courtyard is empty and partly forbidden territory, a

★ Peter Hodgkinson, quoted in Games, Stephen, *Behind the Façade*, London 1985, p. 22.

Port Juvenal, Antigone, housing, Montpellier, 1989

domain for the all-seeing eye of the unsurpassed French concierge whose presence you suspect somewhere behind the mirror glass of the fake colonnades. It is not a (chaotic) public sphere that prevails here, but the self-centred morality of imposed beauty. A certain message seems to keep springing to mind: *il est interdit de...*

From *Noblesse Oblige* to *Sine Nobilitate*

The urban complex in Cergy Saint-Christophe forms a notable exception to the above point of view. The artist Dani Karavan has been permitted to add a central sculptural accent. At first he wished to mark this location with a gigantic obelisk. When he started working together with Bofill, he realised that the order an obelisk imposes on its environment would be too much of a good thing. So Karavan opted for a slightly twisted and leaning column which seems to compromise the morality of the strictly geometrical order. The rest of Karavan's contribution, on the other hand, supports Bofill's status strategy with all its might. It extends the chief axis of the residential complex for several kilometres intersecting, among other things, a majestic *belvedere*. No doubt the inhabitants will take their friends on evening walks to this viewpoint and boast 'Over there, in La Défense, in those tall towers, third from left, 38th floor, that's where I work'. (As Gertrude Stein said, 'There's no there there, when I get there.')

But that twisted column in the empty centre, that ironic commentary on the all-dominating focality, calls for a visit. When we were viewing this location and arrived at the heart of the complex, we noticed a door in Karavan's column. You could go up it. It was possible to stand at the centre, like a warder in your own panopticon, and imagine yourself the absolute monarch *par la Grâce de Dieu*. Up there, you could muse that you were the one and only master of this boundless empire. At your feet would lie the palace, with its many wings and gardens. On the skyline, you would be able to make out Paris, your capital, your subjects.

Alas, this pleasurable fantasy was denied us. The door was locked. A small board sul lenly informed us that we would have to visit the concierge if we wanted the key. The concierge, apparently, was the absolute master here over the dreams of the populace. Guardianship of the key allowed him or her to keep a close eye on whatever members of this already select community might harbour such high-falutin ideas. *Il est interdit de rêver*, or at least, you would first have to pass this concierge who – how could it be otherwise – might only be disturbed by key-requesters during closely specified hours. So save up your visions. For us, the only possibility was a purely imaginary levitation above this architecture. In the circumstances, a remark by neurologist Oliver Sacks sprang to mind:

'We have, each of us, a life-story, an inner narrative – whose continuity, whose sense, *is* our lives. (...) We must "recollect" ourselves, recollect the inner drama, the narrative, of ourselves. A man *needs* such a narrative, a continuous inner narrative, to maintain his identity, his self.'★

Bofill's architecture can be viewed as a display case of ingredients for this drama. By his acute emphasis on the stupendous façade, he offers people a dramatic sense of aliveness from ★ Sacks, Oliver *The Man who Mistook his Wife for a Hat*, London 1985, pp. 105-106. which, for want of anything better, they can draw their own identity. Bofill's work shows how people are prepared to offer up some of their privacy, comfort and social contact in exchange for this meretricious identity. Into the bargain, they accept the cramped, functionalist floor plan of their apartment, the dark, desperate corner for a dustbin, and the labyrinth of echoing, sombre, claustrophobic corridors. But what they get in every case is drama.

Mediterranean Cultural Centre for Barcelona, project, 1992

Since drama comes first, there are two prominent attributes that appear repeatedly in Bofill's work. Firstly the project must be as big as possible; for outside, in the drab urban periphery where it is normally situated, the drama sits oddly with reality. If the project were to stop suddenly around the corner, it would deny its own intentions. Secondly, the work must be as dramatic as possible in scaling and articulation. Everything must be subjugated to a coherent, overpowering narrative.

But the problem – and the crux of this argument – is that this coherence and overpoweringness is based on kitsch, on histrionics. Standing between the dream and the reality, there are regulations and practical impediments. So the drama is expressed solely in form. And it is prefab form, which you can order from the builders' wholesalers.

Kitsch Makes The World Go Round

The history of kitsch is also the history of the insurance trade, which arose when it became possible to spread and reduce the risks. Legislators and underwriters effected the spreading of risks by means of statistics and social laws. But reducing the risk was something you always had to do largely for yourself. The formula for achieving that was … good behaviour.

This formula found wide acceptance. Most people are keen to earn a substantial no-claims bonus. By leaving everything as it was, by daring nothing, they ward off nasty surprises. Besides getting a discount on their premium, they also enjoy a feeling of safety and pride in their own good sense. And meanwhile, the certainty, the guarantees and the reliability stretch much further than conditions on a policy. The spirit of insurance proliferates like a benign growth into the remotest corners of the life cycle. Life and burial were already insurable; soon, with the aid of prenatal gene therapy, birth will follow. And if that is not enough, Bofill's work will even insure you against the dark depression that strikes whenever you momentarily recall how your life course differs from what you pictured for yourself in May 1968.

That is kitsch, the dramatic form of a world where certainty, predictability, caution, problem avoidance and averageness are the senile senators; the world of code, consensus and convention. Kitsch is the dramatic mask of a calculating mind in a glass head. One can not be certain, of course, but there is a strong suspicion that the thousands of inhabitants of Bofill's palaces do not get all that agitated about what one might call the drama of life. On the contrary, their preoccupations are more likely to be as follows:

• Credit buying. We will worry about paying later, they say. But that worry is fragmented into *x* instalments, so the stress of repayment is continuous instead of deferred.

• Pension continuity. The threat of a pension gap does wonders to foster massive immobility, despite automobility. Commute, don't relocate.

• Insurance policies. Insurers increasingly insure only what is predictable. New risk categories are defined and carted off to the ghetto of uninsurability. (We'll bet you this ghetto will never be called *Les Echelles du Baroque!*)

• Daily amusement, i.e. the suffering of the world as a stream of infotainment, legitimised by the freedom of opinion and the press.

The Classical laws of proportion and harmony have subsequently guided Taller's design of everything from streets and squares to perfume bottles.
Bartomeu Cruells

The Taller has, in effect, put forward the model of the Mediterranean city, with its well-defined thoroughfares and public spaces and its absence of zones exclusively devoted to different functions, as the model to be followed in new town planning schemes. The accusations of gratuitous historicism and imitativeness have been numer-

defunctionalisation of their constituent neighbourhoods and a return to the allocation of mixed uses to their buildings.
Bartomeu Cruells

The orderly design of the Taller's parks or gardens, criticised on numerous occasions as being excessively strict, is something that Bofill has consciously pursued as a differentiating element in what would, otherwise, be nothing more than a natural space. The Taller's architecture does not work against nature but it does impose itself as an ordering element.

A profound conviction of the need for dialogue between people as the mainspring of culture and tolerance informs the design of all of the Taller de Arquitectura's projects for public buildings. This is the source of the spacious vestibules, the cloisters, the hypostile halls which seem not to derive from the specific programme for each construction. Nevertheless, any space that facilitates meeting and encounter contributes to the use for which a public building was designed and built.
Bartomeu Cruells

From the first studies for the city in space, by way of competitions, projects and proposals for various developers, the Taller has been involved in detailed study of skyscraper typology on countless occasions. Amongst the unbuilt schemes which now form part of the Taller's historical archive there are projects for skyscrapers ranging from basic premises in line with those of Kahn and Archigram through to Classical and High-tech schemes. The first of their tower blocks, constructed, naturally, in the United States, demonstrate the Taller's new dynamic and the versatility and experience in a variety of fields possessed by the team as a whole

La Place du Nombre d'Or, apartments and shops, Montpellier, 1995

Le Palacio, apartments, Marne-la-Vallée, Paris, 1982

Kitsch sells well and insures the buyer against excessive stress. Kitsch makes the world go round. It offers a place for everybody. Common place requires commonplace.

Reflections on Bofill's Counter Revolution in France★

We live in a staccato culture, a *Life* magazine of *faits divers*. Therefore the following:

 406

- A garden gnome, a weeping Madonna in a television set converted into a showcase; an electric coal fire; plastic roses; a fake palace with drive, formal French garden, Classical orders and all the other accoutrements of a palace.

★ With acknowledgements to Roland Barthes, Walter Benjamin, Hermann Broch, Edmund Burke, Gillo Dorfles, Umberto Eco, Gustave Flaubert, Ludwig Giesz, Klaus Kocks, Klaus Lange, Abraham Moles, Maarten van Nierop, Nathalie Sarraute and the rest of the world.

- This architecture is 'false'.
- Kitsch architecture is architecture of the stereotype.
- Kitsch is cliché, commonplace and – in the best cases – myth.
- Clichés: invisible quotation marks around a realistic effect.
- Commonplace: reference to bon ton and what the appropriate attitude should be.
- Myth: Ricardo Bofill, *cavalier seul,* foe of the tastelessness of existence. His weapon: lack of taste.
- Architecture for the kitsch personality: it holds nothing back, its signs have no depth, it does not conduct a 'subconversation'.
- The kitsch personality is one big façade, one big false claim to status. Dominates every conversation in which he or she participates. Complete identification with the discourse of a specific class. Subordinates his/her voice to the collective voice. No source, but authoritative. Appeals to timeless values – Family, Fatherland, Justice, Decency, La Révolution Française e *tutti quanti.*

- The kitsch of this architecture is a censure with a velvet glove which imposes values we can not evade.
- Architecture of the *Doxa,* the mind of the majority, the consensus of the petit bourgeois, violence of prejudice. 'Doxa, that is public opinion, the truth which is repeated as though there were nothing wrong with it. It is Medusa; it petrifies those who gaze at it.' In this architecture, the bottom point has been reached: the petrification of the soul's petrification.
- 'Kitsch is work that is eager for effect, that hopes to justify its function by flaunting beauty that was created elsewhere and that tries to sell itself as unalloyed art.'
- 'What is involved here is the concocting of a compensatory purpose as a reaction to experiencing a lack of purpose in reality.'
- '... a simulated space for action in compensation for an oppressively imposed everyday passivity or contemplativity.'
- In other words, the world is exorcised of its demons. The sharp edges of human existence are replaced by romantic idylls. A retarded attack on existentialism – and that in Paris, too!
- (By the way, did you know that the word 'kitsch' came from mud that is smoothed over with a Kitsche, for example in mud and wattle building? Appropriate, don't you think?)

To sum up, there are three classes of argument against kitsch:

- Subject qualification: shameless, pretentious, coquettish, unconvincing, snobbish. Kitsch is a comfortable lie that forces itself on you.
- Object qualification: stylistic imitations, glossy mediocrity. It discloses a discrepancy between the nature of the material and what that material is used to express, between

Subsequent to the construction of a pharmaceutical laboratory and the Taller de Arquitectura's own offices, the design of buildings as places of work constitutes the expression of a point of inflection in the Taller's style in the late eighties. While maintaining the validity of Classical proportions and laws of harmony, there was a progressive introduction of elements that had formerly been exclusively associated with the vocabulary of High-tech: steel and glass. The Taller de Arquitectura, with worldwide expertise in the most advanced techniques in the use of architectural concrete, shuttering systems

Marne-la-Vallée and Montparnasse, in order to obtain more architectonically suggestive façades.
Bartomeu Cruells

The designing and building of the *villes nouvelles* allowed the Taller to acquire and then transform the technological base which converted the dream of utopia into reality: the construction of high-quality, aesthetically attractive and harmonious subsidised housing at competitive prices. The considerable experience they gained in this field allowed the Taller to go on to design housing of all

In elevating housing design to paradigmatic urban dimensions and linking it to a broader set of social intentions, Bofill places this work within a rich French tradition of 'ideal city' proposals. It is a comparison he invites through written and visual references to Ledoux, Fourier, and Le Corbusier, among others. With these forebears Bofill shares a philosophical intent to link built form with an ameliorative vision of human society. In pursuing this goal through a limited public housing program, which includes no shops, workplaces, or social institutions, Bofill imputes to formal imagery alone the power to trans-

'Post-Modern' label, who also employ historical motifs to give new allure to conventional building programs. At the same time, however, there is a serious question as to whether Bofill's formal approach is adequate to his social purpose: can daily life be exalted by a dazzling set of historical images when the fundamental structure of that life remains unchanged and unheralded?
Tony Schuman

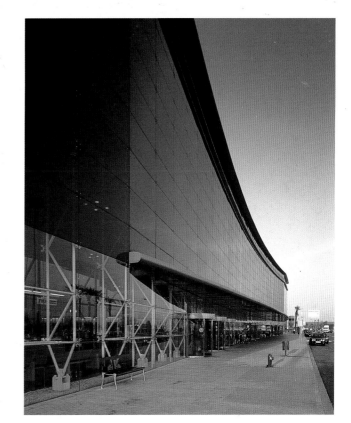

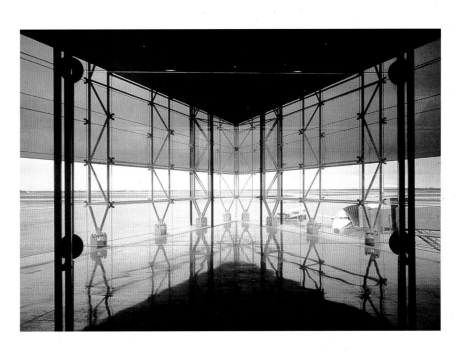

the new use and the original source of the form, and with the environment.

• Social contextual qualification: mass production, mechanical reproduction, commercialisation.

After his victory over the Austrians, the enlightened despot Frederick the Great had a huge new palace built near his beloved Sans Souci. He was heavily criticised for this gesture in the later DDR. Visitors to the Sans Souci palace prior to the *Umwertung aller Werte* of 1989 were given to hear that this residence was worthy only of scorn, built as it was by a ruler who had led his people to the slaughterhouse and had bankrupted his country. These crocodile tears from the moribund regime were kitsch, not criticism.

When Bofill's buildings are criticised with the remark that they are nauseating if one considers how much social and cultural harm was involved in their erection, that is the kitsch of criticism. Palaces do not come into existence without harm, not even those built for the man in the street. Does that mean we have to do away with all palaces? According to Bofill, it is a mistake to take it all as seriously as it looks. (After all, kitsch is related to the unbearable *lightness* of being.) 'I would like to point out that all the terminology we use, all the communication systems at our disposal, remain strictly in the domain of suggestion. None of it should be taken too literally. It's a mistake to think that way.'★ This same paragon of modesty also stated: 'They took me along to see the Les Halles site. (...) In an almost unconscious manner, I accepted the invitation to take part in the competition. But with one condition: total freedom, without having to justify myself towards any restriction or programmatic demand whatsoever...'

This reminds us of the tale recorded by the Brothers Grimm called 'The Fisherman and his Wife'. The fisherman of the title catches a fish which grants him and his wife a wish. So she wishes for an endless number of wishes. The moral of the story is known to us all – 'Pride comes before a fall'.

★ Ricardo Bofill, *Architecture d'un Homme, Entretiens avec François Hébert-Stevens*, Paris 1975, p. 216.

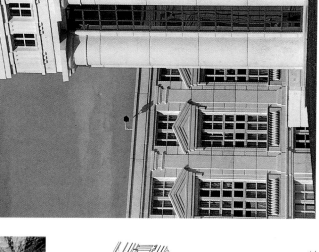

Les Colonnes is a polymorphous complex of 380 apartments, shops and public garden areas, occupying the highest point of the valley of the river Oise. The project contains three buildings that enclose a circular central plaza. Lawns run from the plaza toward the six-storeyed crescent at the south side of the project. This building is oriented towards the valley, overlooking downward sloping lawns and the public gardens to the south-east. The apartments are at this side vertically separated by protruding blocks which contain the staircases. At the inner side of the crescent, the façade is dominated by columns. At the north side, the central space connects with a cross-shaped passage that is formed by four volumes protruding from two square buildings, each containing four storeys. The grand lawns surrounding the crescent are repeated on a more intimate scale within the two squares. From the central space, one can enter these courtyards by means of a narrow passage; a similar passage runs through the crescent to the south-east into the gardens. While the façades have a residential character, the buildings comprise in fact small family apartments. The French windows, deriving their scale from palatial prototypes, conceal the fact that they run over two storeys of apartments. The details remind one of the classical tradition. Overblown, flattened out or in other ways adapted, they are not simply citations of this style. In the centre of the circular plaza stands a tower-like sculpture. In contrast with the orthogonal geometry of the architecture, the four-sided white tower is slightly tilted and twisted. The sculpture and the plaza are part of a landscape design by Dani Karavan, which also includes a monumental axis over three kilometres in length. In fact, the commission of Karavan preceded the choice of Bofill as architect. Originally, Karavan intended to put an obelisk in the centre of the plaza. In interaction with the design of Bofill, this might have given an absolutist air to the axis. The present tower, reminiscent of the family towers in medieval Italy, refers instead to specificity as opposed to the centrality of the general layout. In the same line of thought, the axis cannot be said to have a starting or ending point in the tower. The passage through the crescent is part of it, and prolongs itself into the gardens from where La Défense shimmers in the distance. *Based on: Daniel Abadie, et al. (eds.), l'Art et la Ville. Town-planning and contemporary art, Geneva 1990; and: Tzonis, Alexander, Liane Lefaivre, 'Memory and Invention', in Architecture in Europe since 1968, London 1992.*

▼

Location Cergy-Pontoise, Paris, France **Assistants** P. Genard, P. Hodgkinson, R. Collado and others **Client** Foyer du Fonctionnaire et de la Famille **Design** 1981 **Completion** 1986

Ricardo Bofill Taller de Arquitectura *Les Colonnes de Saint-Christophe Housing*

Albert Hien, Untitled, 1982-83

On the Work of Norman Foster

Teflon Tech:

Quarantine in the Big Shed

Since the Prince of Wales first entered the arena of architecture in 1984, the United Kingdom has placed at least 500,000 buildings on the list of historic buildings and ancient monuments. Half a million buildings are now legally protected from demolition or significant alterations, an unprecedented total. No country has ever taken such wide-scale and radical action to preserve its heritage as has Britain during the eighties. It is an attempt to employ official measures by government authorities to curb the destructive maelstrom of Modernism which until recently was welcomed by those same authorities with open arms. If the 'heritage industry' has anything to do with it, then from now on Britain will be preserved in aspic to become an eternal memento of bygone glory. The end of history is likely to meet little resistance here.

While Britain goes further than any other country in its advanced degree of historic somnambulism, it is simultaneously home to the most avid cult of technology in architecture. England clearly still identifies itself as the founder of the machine age. The country that once unleashed the Industrial Revolution and gave it its ideological ground rules ('Knowledge is power, time is money') can still pride itself on what Charles Jencks once called 'High Church Tech'. The buildings of such architects as Richard Rogers, Michael Hopkins, Nicholas Grimshaw and Norman Foster are recognised throughout the world as the thoroughbreds of 'High-tech' architecture. These architects prepare us for an Odyssey to the New Atlantis about which Francis Bacon once speculated. Of this illustrious company, Norman Foster is the one who has taken the technological aesthetics the furthest. Technology forms an ever recurring theme in his work and is exposed in all its beauty. He has little need of intellectual justifications. A multimillionaire, manager and aesthete is at work here. Thus Foster is our best choice when it comes to assessing the cultural impact of this 'technicist' approach.

'Supernorm'

Some say the contemporary architect has no contribution to make to society. The architect may well get the assignment, but the investment decision, the programme of requirements, the site and ultimately a whole mass of details from climate control to potted plants, is defined by someone else. So what is left for the architect to do, permitted as he is to do his little turn somewhere halfway between the commission and the completion? The following: form. Form is his speciality, the domain of the profession. But even if form is the architect's only preserve and he has to leave the greater part of the project to the ministrations of the developer and the contractor, there are always margins within which the architect can find the elbow room to say something individual. If he does have something to say, then he can say it in those little bits of no man's land: domains like the manipulation of scaling, the areas between the served spaces, the vertical infrastructure, the corners, the boundary markings, the structural joints. The points where you think it really doesn't make any functional difference are exactly

Hong Kong Shanghai Bank, 1986

those where there is most that the architect can do. For that is where things are not rigidly defined by standards, conventions and the demands of the programme. The fact that the space has already been allotted to its various functions does not necessarily mean the final word has been said on the materials to be used, the positioning of the various spaces within the total building volume and the location of access routes. The architect who sets his sights further than the standard catalogue of solutions offered by the major industrial builders and the tried and tested typologies of form and system, can transmute the restrictions placed on his craft into an astonishing elegance and originality. There, in the margin between form and function, lies the promise of architecture as an art form. Once that point has been reached, the world opens and the whole litany of architecture's loss of meaning becomes a nonsense. And if an architect proves capable of continually ringing the changes within the specified constraints, of developing a unique style that may well mask the limitations of the institution but nonetheless overwhelms the public with an ostensibly functional display of meticulous precision, then he stands a good chance of achieving worldwide fame.

Sir Norman Foster is one who has achieved that lofty status. His success with the Hong Kong Shanghai Bank (1986), a megaproject without equal, rumoured to be the dearest building in the world, and documented in no less than twelve leading journals, has delivered him an aura of unassailable glory. His widening of the professional margin of action, his perfectly designed details, his hypertechnological innovations that trickle natural light down into the building's darkest nooks and crannies, and make it possible to adapt the structure to a new function 'in a single weekend'. These, together with his 'High-tech' image and his bulging portfolio, all go to make it possible for him to get done things that have long been classed as outside the competence of his less famous confreres. As soon as Foster's name is mentioned, financiers throw open their coffers, licenses are granted undemurringly, zoning plans are modified and the whole technical

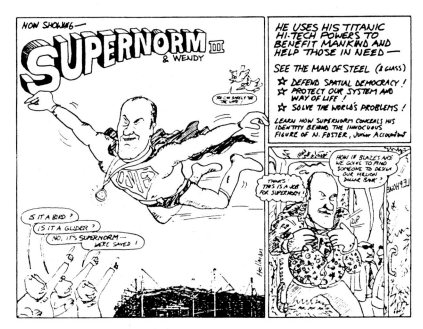

team is made subject to the word of the maestro, who, in passing, pushes certain products and methodologies. Ergo: the more flexibility you demand of him, the more the result will be a real 'Foster'. And that is his secret. He designed the Century Tower in Tokyo in 1991 and is now working on a Millennium Tower, 800 metres tall. Not even the sky is the limit. It seems that someone with Foster's ability is able to give architecture its old authority back. For a proven talent like his, the institution of architecture appears to be capable of more than most people think.

The Quintessential Foster

Foster's Stansted International Airport, completed in 1991, pairs exemplary simplicity with exceptional refinement in design. In functional respects the project is little more than a gigantic hangar or shed of steel and glass which rises out of the landscape. All the public facilities are placed on a single floor level. All the technical spaces are hidden below ground. In as far as technical elements such as heating, ventilation, air conditioning and lighting have to appear above ground, they are generally concealed in a graceful supporting structure. Light, both natural and artificial, plays subtly among the roof trusses.

The interior displays a virtually limitless isotropy. Everything is smooth, flat and uninterrupted. The whole building is the very enemy of delay. It has practically become an aircraft itself: a medium for ultrarapid transit to nowhere, to the next halt. It is an architecture that demands a perspective as open as the sky itself. We can detect an ambiguous attitude to the image in Norman Foster's oeuvre. On the one hand, the work is marked by a considerable transparency. The buildings have been 'purged' of iconographic extras and radiate a narrative modesty. Imposed meanings are not allowed to obscure the function. The architecture is a neutral platform, a tool.

On the other hand, whether you take the neutral transit hall of Stansted, the cathedral of big business in the Hong Kong Shanghai Bank, the speculative floor space of the Century Tower or the prestigious heights of the Millennium Tower, his work is invariably designed. For him, no monstrous tangles of piping, no brutal lines of rivets or locknuts; just suavely recessed Allen screws. His buildings often have an 'aerodynamic' skin of smooth steel or glass panels, as though they were about to shoot off at any moment. As a concession to the Miesian need for reserve and classic integrity, colour is used only sparingly. The structure stands aloof with a air of monochrome autonomy. Within an image which is polished in the extreme, Foster favours escalators and lifts as his most expressive element. Every building is self-evidently one-off, despite its overtly industrialised forms. Here the genius of the architect prevails over the pragmatism of the engineer.

The building materials are smooth, hard and 'industrial' – steel, glass and plastics. Even the stone paving at Stansted has a polished perfection that takes away its natural character.

The construction is unambiguously technical both in fact and in appearance. The umbrella structures of the Renault Distribution Centre (1983) and the suspended floors in the skeleton frame of the Century Tower result in a scaling up of the engineering metaphor. The oversized quality and expressive dynamism of the structure bring the architecture onto a practically metaphysical/ideological plane of meaning with strongly utopian connotations. With this, we move on from empirical observation to the realm of cultural interpretation.

A Shed as a Servant Space

The act of construction itself is not made manifest in Foster's work. Technology, in his view, is only interesting when associated with a skilled hand, with 'love and care'. He hereby explicitly introduces the notions of individual craftsmanship and artistry into a work that at first sight has such a impersonal aspect. In nineteenth century terms, what would previously have been treated as 'core form' is now articulated by Foster as 'art form'. What began as mechanical aesthetics here becomes the aesthetics of form. The engineer turns out to be a masterly visual designer. This is almost certainly exactly where the secret of Foster's global prestige and portfolio lies. Not only do his 'High-tech' designs appeal to countless industrialists and politicians who are keen to underline their ambitions with a 'scientific' allure, but he offers the ingredients of an optimistic world-view. Since he does not supply these services in the guise of an anonymous manipulator of prefab elements but as a unique artist with a unique style, he also appeals to those who seek the salvation of architecture in the consolidation of its 'artistic' qualities. Foster thus kills two birds with one stone: he advances the march of progress by a technological revitalisation of architecture; and, at the same time, he bolsters the image of the architect as artist, locked in a one-man battle against the uncaring world.

Since there is nothing else that 'defines' the space, it is dominated by the expressive properties of the structure. Foster's unique achievement is to bridge the seemingly

413

Architecture is a bridge over time, spanning between those cultures of the past and the future. Buildings created today are sited in places which have evolved over the history of past cultures. Each of our projects attempts to be a special response to its own place, influenced by and sensitive to the past also shaped by an anticipation of the future.

One may claim that, unlike either science or art, architectural practice favours stasis rather than process and that it tends, however weakly, to resist the fungibility of the industrialised world. In this regard, latter-day appeals to science and art may be seen as subtle efforts to accommodate architecture to the dominant categories of a totally priva-

Today, technology is no longer distinct from science; there is instead, 'techno-science' (Lyotard), the instrumental integration of research and development, knowledge, and power. This system erodes definitions on all sides: the difference between body and not-body, the difference between life and death, the difference between nature and not-nature. This

Without a clear definition of needs, there is no basis on which to design. But often an honest 'don't know' is a far more precise acknowledgement of the reality of a situation than some spurious attempt to quantify an unknown future. Unlike the design of artefacts, buildings are conceived in the present for a volatile future, but, culturally, they can-

unbridgeable gulf between technology and architecture, which has held the discipline in its grasp for some two hundred years; and he does this not so much by striving for technical efficiency as an end in itself but by glorifying technology as a potential source of architectural form. The Kahnian 'servant space' has here become the entire building. All space has become subservient to the machine. In other words, Foster's architecture involves obeisance to technology without a proper consideration of its social consequences, namely the dissolution of authorship in an anonymous productivism. He manages to escape the reality of his object of adulation, namely technotopia achieved. His work remains a stereotype representation of the possible, of the future as a 'High-tech' Utopia. It is precisely the all too familiar image of the good old march of progress that conveys a sense of nostalgia.

This is palpable in the case of Stansted, where the building deliberately refers to 'the pioneering days of civil aviation'. Foster wishes to celebrate mobility in its finest hour, without a thought to the price we have since had to pay for it: the constipation of every infrastructure by an excess of motion, the destruction of place, the isolation of the individual, the economisation of society and, finally, the virtualisation of life itself.

Belief in Technology is a Matter of Technique

Foster derives his 'High-tech' idiom from the methods of engineering construction, especially of bridges, ships and aircraft. This architecture also has an air of 'manufacturing industry' about it, with a suggestion of production facilities, assembly halls, distribution centres and warehouses. This represents a curious narrowing of the whole idea of technology. Today the cultural significance of technology lies in the problems of identity associated with cybernetics, mediatisation and biotechnology. Manufacturing industry is becoming less and less fundamental to our society. The keyword of the post-industrial age is 'communication', and that is largely an electronic affair. Thus Foster's work is a representation of an outmoded idea of technology. It is a perfect futurist metaphor for the past – no less so because this architecture corresponds to an obsolete collectivist conviction, namely that 'we are all working together to achieve something great'.

Foster's position inevitably leads to a number of internal contradictions. Firstly, the plea for 'appropriate technology' is linked to consistent Fosterism. Foster aims to find an 'appropriate technology' for every project. He hopes to find the architectural means that fit the assignment as exactly as possible. This is the reason for his resistance to repeated attempts to elevate him to a sort of pope of high technology. Still, his work has remained unmistakably Fosterian over the years.

Secondly, the suggestion of standardisation ends up as technological symbolism. Robert Adam noted how much the 'High tech' rests on false premises. Although the 'High-tech' imagery suggests otherwise, the production of a building bears no resemblance to industrial manufacturing.

> 'On a site the operative must move to his task whereas the essential quality of factory flow production is that the task must move to the operative. In fact, the Modernist ideal of factory-inspired production is largely symbolical.'

Concept models, BBC Radio Headquarters, London

Thus, in Adam's opinion, the superplastic aluminium used in the Sainsbury Centre (1978) in no way introduces a new, universal factory standard; and thank goodness for that, for if building were really to take place strictly according to mass-production principles, it would make a horrible world. If 'High-tech' remains purely symbolic we should certainly not regret the fact. ★

Thirdly, technological anonymity is coupled to world renown for the 'unique' talent. Something that Adam misses is how Foster's work helps clarify our thinking in this area. You would expect an advanced, 'High-tech' architecture like that of Foster to diminish the architect's role even further than before. But, on the contrary, Foster's ability to interpret technology as a design element seems to enlarge that role (at least in his own case, considering his promotion to knight and media personality).

★ Adam, Robert, 'Tin Gods', *Architectural Design* 61 (1990), pp. VIII-XVI.

Fourthly, the pretence of offering a forum for human emancipation is undermined by measuring the human image in terms of technological rationality. We shall examine these four points one by one. Foster's style relates to a widespread psychological belief. The work is grounded in the Modernist idea that in this world people have to sort things out for themselves, individually and together. This thinking leaves no room for architecture to be anything other than a functional precondition. To paraphrase Karl Kraus, if it's a friendly atmosphere we want, we shall just have to create it with our friends. Foster's work is totally unrelated to Team 10's concept of an informal shelter intended for a non-authoritarian society. His buildings are not social condensers. On the contrary, their teflon technicism projects pure formality. Their neutrality does not come from a reduction to basic necessities to provide a backdrop for life at its most intense; it is an explicit and whole-hearted statement.

An Abstract Space for the Abstracted

This last observation brings us to the fundamental paradox of Modern architecture and its preoccupation with space. At the very point in history that architecture gave people all the space they needed, they suddenly became uncertain about what to do with it. This architectural tradition of creating space reveals a thirst for liberation. However,

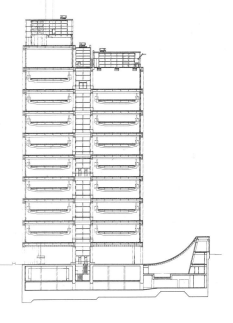

Century Tower, commercial building, Tokyo, 1991

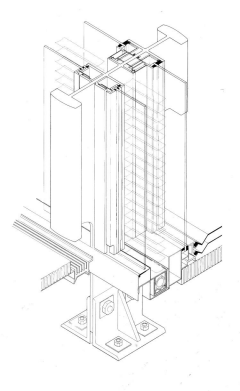

there was no new purpose of life available, to which the new-found liberty could be applied. In this sense, we can construe Foster's ultra-Modernist design as an expression the bankruptcy of Modernism's pretensions to emancipation. Foster does not pause to reflect on this bankruptcy. Now that architecture no longer appears to serve as a social platform, Foster has decided to dress the platform up a bit. But however pretty it is, it remains a platform without a purpose.

It's really tragic. First people failed to get a grasp of Modern abstract space, owing to their incapacity to find a replacement sense of purpose after the disenchantment of the world. Then Modernism thinks of nothing better to use than 'design' to make this abstract space bearable. We can only console the new-born with the formal perfection of the forceps.

416 From an Architecture of Opportunity to an Architecture of the Golden Opportunity

Technology is a threat to the social status quo, but of all imaginable threats it is probably the one which is most widely tolerated. Technology is the one area where the world may freely be turned on its head. After all, it satisfies human curiosity about the future and promises a fix for every problem (except ethical ones, of course). So everyone wants it. How remarkable it is, therefore, that behind the 'High-tech' façade there lurk such unrevolutionary institutions as banks, offices, air terminals and military functions. The design invariably makes a suggestion that is never redeemed. Foster's work is an out-and-out celebration of the possible, and that would be heartwarming if it were not that his rendering of the possible has an alienating effect on people. Owing to the character of the institutions that occupy Foster's buildings, we are left with an impression that the visionary updraught of the possible is under the control of people who are only aware of it when they perceive a golden opportunity to gain riches and power. And how could it be otherwise when the 'appropriate technology' carries such a hefty price tag?

Technology has lost its Promethean heroics. The audacity of the inventor has long been a thing of the past; all that matters is calculation, profit, business. Some people find Foster's spaces fascinating, others find them tedious. In neither case do they

encourage the frame of mind and energy that traditionally went with Modernist space: wide awake and striving for a goal. In Le Corbusier's words, *'l'Homme marche droit parce qu'il a un but'*. In Foster's work it is mainly the labour and production processes that march onward. Thus this work pre-eminently expresses the monotony of a society that continues to applaud a rudimentarily utopian view to life. Utopianism is an endless postponement of enjoyment and fulfilment to the future. All we have for the present is the dull routine of labour – and that must not be interrupted, so everything must be smooth and undistracting. Dormant dissatisfaction must be not stimulated but sedated. For example, Foster's office building in Ipswich for Willis, Faber and Dumas (1976) presents an egalitarian, isotropic, homogeneous space which accords with a non-hierarchic concept of the office. It is a conflict-free soma vision, complete with swimming pool and roof garden. It is not designed for an awakening individual but for the Gammas of Aldous Huxley's *Brave New World*. Foster's forte is *machines à gagner*, machines to make money in.

All Power to Architecture... but Please Disinfect it First

We do not live in a technological era because we live in machines; on the contrary, we are machines because this is a technological era. The era has its own dynamic quality and its own laws, which affect us whether we like it or not. Foster's 'appropriate technology' is not so much a satisfactory solution to this problem, as a piece of technicist appropriation designed to impress.

True, we are very impressed. Foster actualises an exceptionally beautiful dream and displays consummate craftsmanship. The technology is so overwhelming that we keel over at the sight – despite the falsehood of the arguments repeatedly used to justify it.

But back home at the writing desk, another thought strikes. It is impossible to justify treating a single, isolated product of Enlightenment ideology – albeit a very important one, namely purposive-instrumental technology – as a solution to the problems that come from the dialectics of that same Enlightenment. At its best, the machine aesthetic has always been coupled to a consideration of these dialectics, and the same ought to apply to new versions of that aesthetic.

The transparent aesthetics of Foster's buildings tell us something about the workings of society; but what pleases his clients, it must be said, is being able to observe the behaviour of their staff and customers. While Foster has carved himself out an elbow room of mythic proportions in order to give architecture back its social value as a meeting place of aesthetics, technology and organisation, the architecture that emerges looks like a perfect machinery for the perpetuation of our present social condition. The omnipresent Teflon skin of this architecture gives the world a spotless, uncontaminated look. The architecture is immune to the dirt of real life. Never was architecture as antiseptic as it is here – and that just when the immunity of organic life itself is showing the strain...

When civilisation goes past a certain point it seems to become pathogenic. The mastery over nature which was the original goal of technology proves to have the destruction of nature as an undesired side effect.

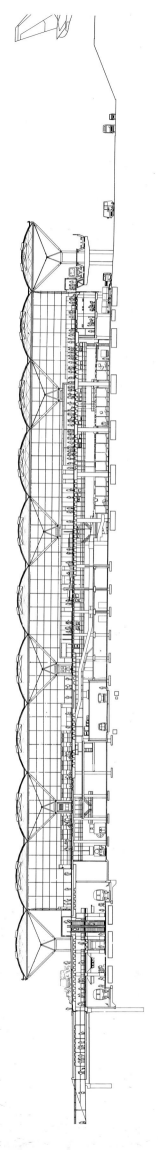

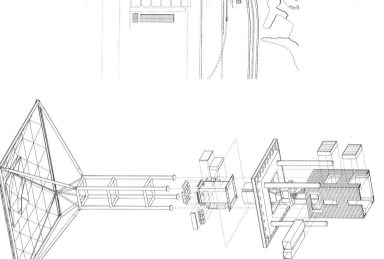

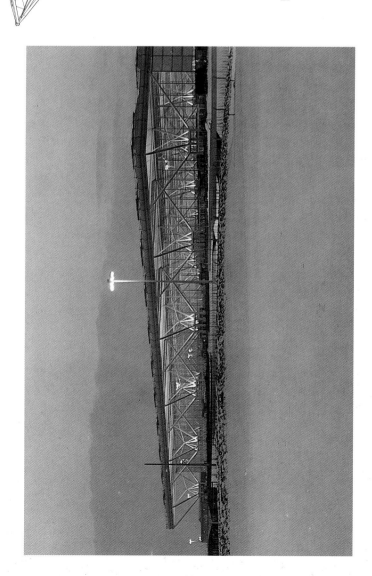

The terminal design seeks the simplicity and convenience of the earliest flying era. All public facilities are provided on a single concourse floor. The design gives a compact building which reduces walking distances for passengers and enables them to move through the building on simple linear routes. The terminal is very closely integrated with all transport links to Stansted. The landside vehicle forecourt and passenger set-down are constructed at the same level as the main concourse. The short term car park and coach station are situated to the south of the forecourt set at a lower level to minimise visual impact and give easy access into the terminal. The British Rail station is located below the landside forecourt as an extension of an undercroft. Lifts, escalators and ramps bring passengers from the railway station, coach station and car park, directly up to the concourse level. Passengers then proceed through the check-in area, security and immigration controls and departure lounge to a tracked transit station. From here automatic tracked transit vehicles transport passengers to satellite buildings from which they board their aircraft. In addition to containing the proposed British Rail station, the undercroft serves the main concourse level above with baggage handling systems, the environmental engineering plant for the building, a service road with associated service areas and related commercial storage. The structural

columns at concourse level are set on a 36 metres square grid, generated by the functional requirements of the terminal – in particular the check-in – and the need to provide maximum layout flexibility. The supports for the roof form tree-like structures comprising clusters of four tubular steel columns. All equipment for heating, ventilation, air conditioning and lighting serving the concourse is contained within these 'trees'. There are no engineering services at roof level in the terminal. To allow the airport a high degree of flexibility for growth and modifications, all passenger facilities at concourse level which require enclosure have been designed as free-standing enclosures or cabins, which can easily be dismantled. Internally there is natural light throughout the concourse, provided by both the fully glazed cladding and the roof lights in the lattice domes. This emphasises the feeling of calmness and airiness. After dark, the concourse is lit indirectly by light reflected from the roof; from the outside no harsh light sources are seen. The building gently glows. The form and external appearance of the terminal are designed to have an assertive but low profile. The main floor level is set at existing ground level. The overall height of the building is similar to that of trees in the surrounding landscape. *Norman Foster*

Location Stansted, Essex, Great Britain **Assistants** S. de Grey, C. Chabra, J. Silver and others **Client** British Airport Authority/Stansted Airport Ltd **Design** 1981-85 **Completion** 1991

Sir Norman Foster and Partners *Stansted Airport Terminal*

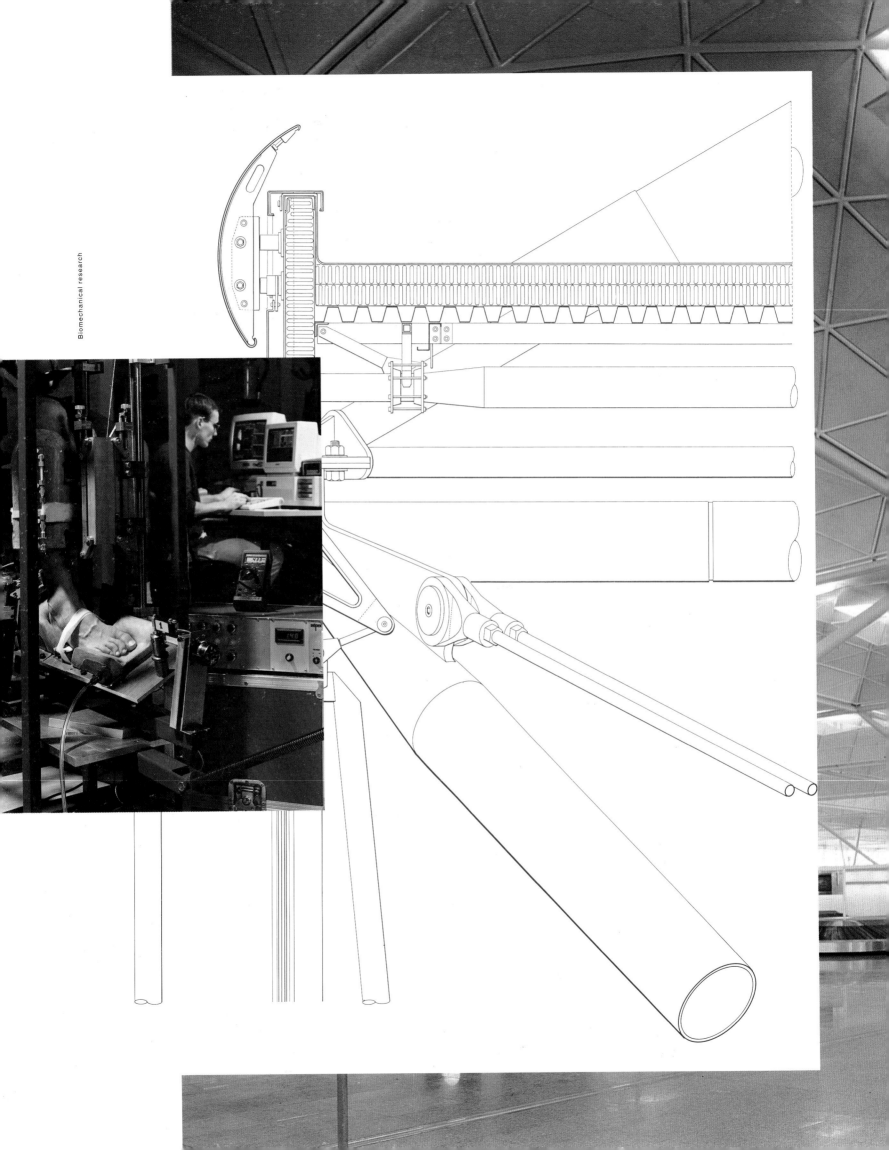

Biomechanical research

Rendezvous with the future

The Invisible Political Economy of
Architectural Production

David Harvey

Look at Canary Wharf in London's Docklands and what does one see? A collection of buildings by some of the world's better known architectural firms – one building by I.M. Pei, two by Skidmore Owings and Merrill, one by Kohn Pederson and Fox and the 800 foot tower designed by Cesar Pelli – lavishly appointed and equipped to be Europe's most prestigious, most elegant, most beautifully manicured and above all most internally efficient office complex. Each of the buildings is, within the limits of its own style and space, competently executed and in some cases designed with some flair. The finishing and detail is exquisite and attention has also been paid (unlike most of the haphazard development of London's Docklands) to how each building might offset the other as part of a complex whole in which visual interaction, both from afar and from close at hand, might prove imposing and even, perhaps, intriguing.

But if Mies van der Rohe was right and architecture is indeed 'the spirit of the age conceived in spatial terms', then presumably we should also take account of the 'spirit' of that age which led Canary Wharf's developers, Olympia and York, to go bankrupt in the biggest property company crash the world has ever known (owing some $20 billion to banks and other creditors). For many, the whole complex has, as a result, come to be read as the last instance of the insane, credit-fuelled real estate boom of the late eighties.

Not, of course, that the physical design of the complex is above criticism. There are, to begin with, questions of scale ('But why does it have to be so tall, Mr. Pelli?' asked Prince Charles of the tower's architect). It has all the air of a moribund office space that will wake up only when the rhythms and flows of office work dictate. There is no truly liveable space in sight. The only attempt to instill any sense of life, diversity and difference relies on playing the game of upscale ethnic commodity markets (Peruvian rugs and Brazilian beauty products) on the ground floor shopping spaces and creating neatly manicured flower-pot spaces elsewhere so that at least something other than money might be seen to grow in the place. It announces the death of public space and the street as a site of heterogeneity and difference, and commemorates the universal and homogenising uniformity of money power without even a trace of guilt. It will take tremendous dedication and effort on the part of London's more ambitious street-dwellers, skateboarders, performers and urban ravers to create anything at all out of this hostile, alien and isolated terrain. Even the Situationists at their best, would have had a hard time to liberate this space, even for a day, from its pervasive and oppressive business-class, space-age mix of surface glitter and inner gloom.

Hardly surprisingly, there has been a certain reluctance of office workers to get trapped in such a sepulchral place – presuming they can get there, given the lack of any decent transportation infrastructure to access the site. The employees of the conservative *Daily Telegraph* newspaper, whose proprietors were apparently determined to be one of the first on board Margaret Thatcher's flagship Docklands Development project (she began her 1987 electoral campaign with a political stunt in the Docklands to make the point that her brand of capitalism could fix up anything), are reputed to hate the place. The civil servants whom the government are now considering as filler for the empty unlet spaces (with an extra hour's commuting time) and hence as a hidden bail-out for the project are hardly enthusiastic. They are probably viewing with alarm the latest reports which say that the Department of the Environment is actually going to buy one of the buildings to house their own offices as part of a deal to galvanise investors to continue funding for the project while simultaneously helping reluctant corporate tenants and their office workers shed the feeling that they are about to be stranded on the far edge of some space-age financial monitoring station.

But then what more could we expect, given the spirit of the age which produced such a use of urban space? For Canary Wharf is the product of massive investment by financial institutions in an office complex designed to house other financial institutions which themselves make money out of, among other things, real estate ventures like Canary Wharf. When that spiral becomes a circle then small wonder that it snaps, as it has for so many property developers in the Docklands and elsewhere as well as for

Klaus Staeck, 1974

David Harvey

the bankers who finance them. What is not immediately visible about Canary Wharf is exactly its relation to this process of money-making and money circulation. Yet here, too, it does not take much imagination to visualise the space as a pure product of the money which circulates through it. Think of Simmel's observation: 'To the extent that money, with its colourlessness and its indifferent quality can become a denominator of all values, it becomes the frightful leveller – it hollows out the core of things, their specific values and their uniqueness and incomparability in a way which is beyond repair. They all float with the same specific gravity in the constantly moving stream of money'.★

★ Simmel, G., 'The Metropolis and Mental Life', in D. Levine (ed.), *On Individuality and Social Forms*, Chicago 1971, p. 330.

Then think of Canary Wharf, floating like a lost ark downstream from the City on the tide of the Thames, and floating even more emphatically in that moving stream of money which hollows out the

421

Hilton Hotel Pool, Sidney, 1984

core of things and destroys all alternative senses of value. Even the most habituated and thoroughly socialised office-worker must feel some sense of loss when they find themselves consigned to the hollowed out core of nothingness which lies at the heart of financial capital. When money destroys the community it becomes the community, said Marx, yet most of us resist, in some way or other, that simple equation. Even the capitalists demur, but the only way left for them to compensate for money's hollowing out and levelling powers is to accumulate more and more of it. So when they build, they build up and up to clutch at the only distinction that monuments to capital have left: to scream at the skyline of every capitalist city that 'I am bigger, larger, richer and more important than you!'

But it does not take much to see through that bravado. The moving stream of money, having passed like the hand of mammon across the land, flows on and on leaving all kinds of places that once were awash with the stuff drained quite high and dry. Just before the bankruptcy of Olympia and York, it was reported that the interest bill alone was draining cash at the rate of £40,000 an hour. While that may be quite invisible to the seeing eye, it poses a potentially deadly physical threat to large swathes of London's built environment. If nothing flows in, then only reserves can flow out and when reserves run dry only bankruptcy remains and that implies the devaluation or even physical run-down and destruction of some portion of the built environment. Not that Canary Wharf will necessarily fall down. It is often the case, Marx commented, that those first in the field in projects of this kind fail, but those who take over from them reap the surplus. Canary Wharf will almost certainly be snapped up at a fire-sale price by some investor or other, in exactly the same way that Olympia and York became so big and powerful in the early eighties by snapping up properties cheap in New York City at the bottom of the real estate cycle and making huge profits on them on the up-turn – why Olympia and York entered the London market at the peak of the boom is still a mystery unless it is to be explained simply in terms of hubris. The problem in London will lie with all of that secondary surplus office space which now lies half empty and which, lacking the accoutrements and attractions of Canary Wharf, may indeed bite the dust physically as well as financially. But no matter, the beacon of financial power at Canary Wharf ought still to be visualised as an obelisk commemorating those who lived and died by speculative greed. But, sadly, it was not only the speculators and their financiers who got hurt. The obelisk of Canary

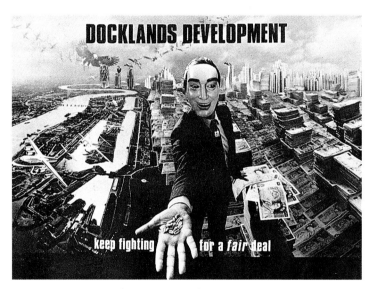

Docklands Community Poster Project, The Changing Picture of Docklands, photomural in Wapping

Wharf also commemorates the victims of an eighties politics of urban apartheid. 'The fortified wall which had once circled the docks,' David Widgery suggested, 'was not so much torn down as rearranged as a series of fences, barriers, security gates and keep-out signs which seek to keep the working class away from the new proletarian-free yuppie zones.'★ Canary Wharf cuts itself off from any relation to its potential neighbours. Olympia and York made some attempts to mollify restive local populations and reconcile them to their inevitable fate, though the employment compact which was supposed to link indigenous workforces

★ Widgery, D., *Some Lives!* A GP's East End, London 1991, p. 219.

to construction and other jobs never worked and irate local residents are sueing them for compensation for the deleterious health and other effects of ten years of blight, disruption, dirt and construction noise. But the overall project has to be seen in the context of the despoliation of a whole zone of London of its human resources. Said Widgery, a local doctor long resident in London's East End: 'Mrs. Thatcher's chosen monument may be the commercial majesty of Canary Wharf topped out only two weeks before her resignation in November 1990, but I see the social cost which has been paid for it in the streets of the East End: the schizophrenic dementing in public, the young mother bathing the new-born in the sink of a B-and-B, the pensioner dying pinched and cold in a decrepit council flat, the bright young kids who can get dope much easier than education, wasted on smack. I also see the pain of those trying to cope in the social services whose collective provision the Thatcher era systematically derided, underfinanced and then "reformed".'

Cesar Pelli, Canary Wharf Tower, London, 1989

? How come the American Grand Old Party and the English Tories got re-elected time and again, often by a landslide? What is their edge over their hardly less conservative rivals? Do we have to take your words as criticism of the concept of democracy?

! I have never regarded the electoral victories of Thatcher/Reagan (and later, Bush and Major) as massive landslide victories. The rate of abstention in elections in the USA has been so high in most presidential elections that Reagan was in fact getting elected with only 26 percent of the eligible vote (which itself was much less than the potential voting population). In Britain, the highest score the Conservatives have ever achieved is 43 percent. What we have had in these countries these last few years is an electoral dictatorship of minority right-wing governments. This in part could continue because of the failure of the left to define a significant alternative. As soon as someone like Clinton offers even a glimmer of hope (even though I do not consider it a real alternative) he gets elected.

It was very much the spirit of that age which we call the eighties, particularly in Thatcher's Britain and Reagan's United States, to deliberately marginalise and beat down whole swathes of the working class population who, from the standpoint of the ruling interests of the time were thought to have acquired far too much influence over capitalist affairs. The eighties was not, it must be said, an easy time for world capitalism in general – with low growth and heightened international competition –, but politics also played its role. A starkly honest version of Thatcher's politics in Britain, for example, has been given by Alan Budd, an economic advisor to government. The eighties policies of tackling inflation by squeezing the economy and public spending were, he suggests, 'a cover to bash the workers'. 'Raising unemployment was a very desirable way of reducing the strength of the working classes. What was engineered, in Marxist terms – was a crisis in capitalism which re-created a reserve army of labour, and has allowed the capitalists to make high profits ever since.'★ Interestingly, Stockman (Reagan's hatchet man at the Office of Management and Budgeting the early eighties) tells a similar story in his book of reminiscences: the budget deficit of the United States was deliberately ★ *The Observer* (21 June 1992). created and allowed to become astronomical in the early eighties in order to force reductions in welfare expenditures and social programmes on a recalcitrant Congress and a resistant U.S. public.**?** It may seem wrong to invoke all this in connection with Canary Wharf, yet it is important to visualise the connection which otherwise eludes the seeing eye. For Canary Wharf is a piece of architectural production which relates to its period and place and which in all sorts of ways reflects the political economy of its times. It is, as Widgery put it, 'the most ostentatious example of a process by which multinational commercial developers, largely financed and controlled from outside Britain, have been allowed to create a new "free market" metropolis.' Within a metropolis. It has also been central to the re-shaping of London's urban space in ways reflective of an increasing segregation between the rich and powerful and their favoured financial institutions on the one hand and an increasingly marginalised and impoverished population on the other. The eighties was a decade in which the rich got very much richer and the poor became significantly poorer and that has been inscribed into urban space either by increasing territorial

Capitalism is always about individuals making money by whatever means and that has nothing whatsoever to do necessarily with making long-run rational allocations of financial resources.

segregation of populations or by exercising ever tighter social (even military) control over the uses of urban space. 'A typical action', reported Widgery 'is that of a group of high-income Dockneys (the yuppy Isle of Dogs residents' self-designation) who sued their private landowners because they failed to curb the "nuisance" of indigenous neighbours who had the propensity for shouting and hanging out washing'. 'As the walls have come down in Eastern Europe', Davis remarks in the quite different context of Los Angeles but in terms which are remarkably appropriate for Canary Wharf, 'they are being erected all over (our own cities)'.

But how and why could all of this happen in the way it did? A useful way to reflect on that question is to situate Canary Wharf against the background of the temporal and spatial changes occurring within global capitalism in the eighties. The recession of 1979-81, although it was, as we have seen, politically exaggerated by both Reagan and Thatcher, was real enough. It implied no easy end in sight for the difficulties into which global capitalism had lapsed after the long post-war boom came to a shuddering halt in the deep recession of 1973-5. Fundamental to this recessionary process was yet another bout of what we political economists call 'overaccumulation' – a periodic condition of capitalism in which idle capital (manufacturing capacity, goods, facilities, or money) lies side by side with surpluses of labour power (the unemployed or underemployed) and there seems no way to bring the two elements of production together because the prospects for profit are so poor. In the manufacturing sector, overaccumulation is typically manifest as 'deindustrialisation' and 'rationalisation' of existing job structures. The effect is to put workers employed in manufacturing and ancillary activities under the strong disciplinary threat of unemployment and in the process leave working class communities as derelict and despoiled zones of human despair, left high and dry by that flowing stream of money that has sucked the living labour out of them for so many years in ways that the developers of Canary Wharf, itself left stranded, will never have the misfortune to know. Symptomatic here was the fall in registered employment in the London docks from nearly 25,000 in the late sixties to barely 4,000 in 1981 and its ultimate total demise, leaving something like a 32 per cent male unemployment rate in the area by the mid eighties and a terribly depressed set of communities in London's East End. **?**

The political choice of the Thatcher and Reagan governments, however, was to blame capitalism's evident failures in the recession of 1979-82 (which they themselves partially engineered) on the excessive power of organised labour and on the burdens placed on entrepreneurial endeavour by excessive state regulation. Deregulation and privatisation, coupled with attacks upon trade unions and the welfare state, became crucial aspects of a government policy which bore all the hallmarks of naked class aggression. The deregulation of financial services was regarded in this light as one of the keys to economic success. Free up financial capital flows and financial services, the argument went, and the natural proclivity for money to seek out the best rate of return would lead to the reallocation of economic resources in such a way as to provide the grounds for renewed economic growth. The further implication was that national boundaries should also become much more permeable to capital flow and that financial capital should be able to operate more freely at the global scale. Territorial barriers to capital flows were reduced as were state powers to regulate the inflows and outflows of capital. But, at the same time, concentrations of financial power never seen before emerged in the world's financial mar-

Blade Runner, movie by Ridley Scott, 1982

Hong Kong

424

? *It is not very long ago that full-scale protests were launched by the victims of the governmental and capitalist politics you describe in no uncertain words. The demonstrations however were targeted against substantially less flagrant developments. At the time unions displayed strength. So-called left-wing political parties – Labour in England and on the continent, and to a lesser degree Liberals in the U.S. – succeeded in implementing measures such as capital gains sharing, participation councils, and social housing programmes. You sketch a monstruous condition of our time, you volunteer arguments which resemble all properties of an apocaplypse. How can a critical movement fall silent the moment interests of large sections of the population are more tampered with than ever before?*

! The critical movement has in part fallen silent because of institutional repressions (organised by minority electoral dictatorships as well as through capitalist control of the media) and the massive effects of deindustrialisation and unemployment. It has also failed to mobilise anything more than an often fragmented political response out of its own soul-searching and disarray. But the potential for massive response is always there, as we have seen in Britain in the public response to the Tory government's proposals to destroy coal mining production and, with it, one of the strongest bastions of working class politics.

kets, based primarily in New York, Tokyo and London. Led by New York, London was one of the first financial centers to follow the deregulation game in what came to be called the 'Big Bang' of 1986. This was touted as the way to make London economically secure by positioning itself as switching point within the never-ending flow of money and as host to the seemingly unlimited variety of financial services that would accompany that. Overaccumulation in the economy in general could be absorbed within the world's financial system at the same time as all that unemployment in the London Docks could be offset by the booming employment in financial services. And that booming employment would mean burgeoning demand for custom-equipped high-tech office space.

The project had all manner of defects. Deregulation did not necessarily lead to better allocations of economic resources. Instead, it provided abundant opportunities for corruption (Ivan Boesky, Milken, Guinness, the BCCI banking fiasco) or speculative recklessness (the Savings and Loan scandals in the United States lost some $300 billion in a decade, much of it on reckless real estate ventures). Capitalism is always about individuals making money by whatever means and that has nothing whatsoever to do necessarily with making long-run rational allocations of financial resources. Deregulation and privatisation merely provided multiple opportunities for financial wizards to get rich quick simply by punching the right numbers into their computer screens. Dockers, furthermore, do not easily convert into

David Harvey

? *Viewed from your ethical points of departure, this is no less than hell. Your theoretical inclination towards diagnosing the crime contradictions of capitalism, might signal an oncoming revolution. No such thing however is about to happen. How much more time do you grant capitalism?*

! Capitalism, as a political-economic and social system, is in a very sick state. I do not say that we are into the 'ultimate' crisis, but plainly the supposed victory over communism has been a hollow one (witness Germany) and the power centres of capitalist development over the last decade or so – Japan and Germany – are experiencing all sorts of difficulties. What I fear most of all is collapse of capitalism into warring trade blocks (of the sort that arose in the thirties) as a prelude to nationalist/fascist takeovers in significant parts of the world. The left has to get together in the face of threats of that sort.

stockbrokers, and long-term structural unemployment became more and more of a chronic problem in the midst of get-rich-quick financial capitalism. And then came 'Black Monday' of October 1987, which saw the crash of the stockmarket which forced financial institutions to cut back their employment. The vast debt-bottling plants and swathes of office space under construction across London suddenly lacked tenants as profit margins shrank in the financial sector and as brokerage fees and all manner of other business dried up. **?**

The search for financial solutions to problems of capital overaccumulation in the eighties had by then also spun off into the real estate sector in a very big way. Real estate borrowing in Britain shot up from less than £10 billion in 1987 to close to £40 billion in early 1992, while in the United States, even after a year of solid shake-out which followed upon a decade of extraordinary growth, the debt mountain on real estate borrowing topped $160 billion. Here, too, the climate of deregulation of financial flows, laxer planning restrictions all coupled with grumbling problems of overaccumulation in general, led to a sudden flood of surplus capital into the construction of the built environment (office space, shopping malls, etcetera) without a thought that this could or even certainly would (as many past speculative episodes had showed) create a situation in which overaccumulation of assets in the built environment

Anthony Hernandez, Landscapes for the homeless, 1989

was likely to become a serious problem. Nowhere did this become more spectacular than in overproduction of commercial office space which, by 1990, already exhibited an appallingly low and quite unremunerative occupancy rate in most of the world's major cities, including London. The crisis of overproduction of office space which has broken out over the last few years, with all sorts of ramifications for the viability of financial institutions (to say nothing of the developers) is, then, a thoroughly predictable aspect of capitalism's general penchant for overaccumulation. Furthermore, the slackening demand for office space pointed down a very slippery slope. As the developers of office space went into bankruptcy they left even more massive problems for the financial sector which meant even less demand for office space. Spirals built on feedback effects of this sort can just as easily point down as up. And it is exactly in such a context that both the production of Canary Wharf in the midst of that flood of surplus capital into the built environment during the late eighties and the financial collapse of its developer, Olympia and York, at the moment of withdrawal after 1990, has to be placed.

But to look at the question solely in temporal terms is also to miss something vital to the story. Of all the material forms that capital can assume, the financial form is by far the most geographically mobile and hence most global in its field of action. It is not always easy to lure it to earth from out of the telecommunications ether in which it is typically wont to float. And if it is to become transformed into a fixed and long-lived physical element in the built environment, financial capital increasingly demands all manner of strong inducements and guarantees. State powers (national or local) become crucial to offering such inducements and financial capital increasingly looks to come down to earth only in those places where its returns are guaranteed or subsidised and its risks minimised. Competition between places to attract inward investment of any type has, as a consequence, become much sharper as community after community falls over itself to offer more and more inducements to capital to come to town. London, for example, was in clear competition with other financial centres for business (not so much with New York and Tokyo with which it tended to share the spoils, but with Frankfurt, Basle, and other European rivals). Canary Wharf was meant to make London Europe's most attractive financial centre precisely by virtue of its qualities and to make sure that as little of that supposedly lucrative financial business as possible went abroad. But if Canary Wharf was to perform that function, then it first had to be built.

Inter-urban competition on the European scale for financial services has become acute in recent years. National governments and municipalities behave like the Cargo Cultists of Papua New Guinea, who seek to lure passing aircraft to earth by building imitation landing strips in the vague hope that some might land. This comparison is not so far-fetched as it might seem. In the Canary Wharf case a suitable landing strip was prepared to lure in totally unregulated foreign finance capital to build the office space that would lure major financial institutions to set up in London. The London Docklands Development Corporation, set up by the conservative government in 1981, had all sorts of powers devolved to it (it was also enabled to circumvent the wishes of democratically elected local authorities at will) with the express purpose of luring in capital of the sort needed to support the Canary Wharf Project. The Docklands Consultative Committee estimates that the LDDC expended something of the order of £1.3 billion of public moneys to prepare the ground for a project that was supposed to be a monument to the spirit of free enterprise capitalism and private entrepreneurial endeavour. Ironically, when the govern-

426 *The rebuilding of urban space becomes, as it were, a 'spatial fix' for capitalism's overaccumulated capital. The game of completely re-shaping the interior spaces of cities, shifting its populations around at will, disrupting older and received ways of living and where necessary clearing out whole populations from off their preferred terrain, is background accompaniment to the 'hymn to greed'.*

ment was faced with panic demands that it bail out Canary Wharf not only to save London's competitive position in the struggle to bring in financial services but also to prevent some threatened *meltdown* in the world's financial markets, it at first demurred on the grounds that it had already put in enough! Later, as we have seen, it has opened the way for a covert subsidy to the project by proposing to move one of its largest departments into the complex either as tenant or buyer. But the plain fact is that Canary Wharf, for all the governmental proclamations to the contrary, is a state subsidised project which has been nevertheless used to proclaim the virtues of private enterprise.

But here another even more localised element of spatial competition enters into the picture. For though the famous Square Mile that is the City of London appeared to be running out of space and although the buildings there were difficult to adapt to the high-tech needs of modern financial services (compared to the ability to custom build in Canary Wharf), it turned out that relaxation of planning restrictions and the coming on the market of some new development opportunities around railway stations like Liverpool and Broad Streets allowed the City to try and out-compete Docklands in a free-for all of spatial competition. The consequent competitive overproduction of office space became all-too-apparent after the stockmarket crash on 'Black Monday' of October 1987 had led to all manner of cut-backs in financial services. Potential rents on Canary Wharf fell as a consequence of intense competition from the much better positioned Square Mile. Rents which ran as high as £35 per square foot in 1987 in Docklands fell to as low as £6 per square foot with some potential tenants being allowed in for nothing (and their old leases being bought out in complicated deals by Olympia and York so that net rental may in fact have been negative). Heightened intra-capitalist competition (and in this case inter-territorial competition) in times of slump can produce quite ruinous results. And so it was for Olympia and York. But creating landing strips for highly mobile financial capital presumes a clearing of the land of all previous tenants as a prelude to redevelopment. Such clearance can in part be accomplished as the seeming-

? *The political-economic background of the contemporary architecture you describe should be studied by architects. But, if they actually realised the scope of Canary Wharf for instance, they could not any longer take their profession seriously as a critical instrument. Could you please specify your recommendation to architects, and do you happen to know instances in which architecture was able to operate along the lines of this kind of insights?*

! Architects, precisely because they do not build buildings with their own money, cannot be in the revolutionary vanguard except in the narrow sense of exploring the possibilities inherent in new materials, design systems, production systems and philosophies in the social construction of space. Precisely because of their expertise in these areas, they can sometimes be subversive of their client's intent (e.g. producing office spaces that will be friendly for the homeless needing warmth and shelter) and sometimes make direct proposals for designs that cannot be built under existing social relations. Within the latter, however, they can also produce community forms of architecture, disorganised spaces and micromonumental forms which serve more popular ends than simply working for Olympia and York.

? *How could you help making people critical, in a world in which the problems of this world are no longer reflected in the lives of the people who could do something about it?*

! I simply disagree that the problems of this world are not reflected in my own life. I encounter more and more homeless people on the streets of Oxford every day, more and more burglar alarms are visible (including fake ones) and the safety with which I and my friends can use the spaces of the city is diminishing. I do not want to live in a fortress society or an unjust society and a lot of people now feel that (including a very Conservative architecture critic for a major right-wing newspaper whom I met the other day). The battle is not so much to make people aware of these problems, as to come up with an articulate programme as to what to do about it all.

ly 'natural' corollary to capitalism's in-built penchant for what the economist Schumpeter liked to call the 'creative destruction' of capitalism's dynamic. If 'progress' is inevitable, then the wholesale decline of London's once thriving Docklands with its tightknit working class communities, can be viewed as an inevitable byproduct of that progress which brought us far more efficient means of overcoming spatial barriers through containerisation, computerisation, roll-on-roll-off ferries, and jet cargo transport. But this is not all that is involved, for even when the jobs are gone, the communities, however impoverished, often struggle on, refusing to leave the spaces they occupy. It frequently takes a quite savage attack upon them to clear the land so that redevelopment of the Docklands sort can be achieved. Clearance becomes even more imperative when overaccumulated capital with, seemingly, nowhere else to go, is poised to flood indiscriminately into real estate development. The hunger for more and more development sites places a great premium upon taking no prisoners as the land is ruthlessly cleared of its indigenous population. The rebuilding of urban space then becomes, as it were, a 'spatial fix' for capitalism's overaccumulated capital. The game of completely re-shaping the interior spaces of cities, shifting its populations around at will, disrupting older and received ways of living and where necessary clearing out whole populations from their preferred terrain, is background accompaniment to that 'hymn to greed' (to use Richard Rogers' phrase) that always emanates from redevelopment projects of the Canary Wharf sort.

Wim Quist, Morgan Bank, Amsterdam,

427

So what then should we visualise when we look at Canary Wharf? Architecture, it has been remarked, 'is the one art form that deals with space directly'. 'Painting can depict space, poetry can form an image of it, music can offer an analogy, but only architecture can actually create it.'★ But what sort of space is it that architecture works with and what does the architect-developer do to that space when he or she works to create it? The traditional view, Kern argues, was 'that space was an inert void in which objects existed' but at the turn of the century this began to give way to a view of space as 'active and full'. This meant in turn that architecture began to be viewed as constitutive, not only of spatial organisation but of social life itself. The foreground (positive space) had now to be seen in relation to the background (negative space) and this led, Kern suggests, to a vision of 'positive negative space' in which the 'background itself is a positive element, of equal importance with all the others'.

★ Kern, S., *The Culture of Time and Space 1880-1918*, London 1983, p.158.

So what background constitutes this positive element of equal importance to the foreground of Canary Wharf? For the most part, architects would probably interpret that question solely in terms of the kinds of proportionalities required of aesthetic forms as they lie physically in space. But buildings also exist against a background of that moving stream of money, of capital accumulation and overaccumulation, of imperatives to reconstitute urban space to absorb surplus capital, all in ways that bear little or no relation to human need but which submit entirely to the dictates of human greed. Learning to visualise the background space in these terms giving it equal importance (as positive negative space) to the foreground appears to me to be the first step towards a critical architecture, an architectural discourse which opens up the invisible for inspection. **??**

In the Place of the Public;
Observations of a Traveller

Martha Rosler

'You've the effrontery to tell me I must go to Kansas City to get to New Orleans. You people are rewriting geography! You're mad with power.' (An irate traveller in Arthur Hailey's novel *Airport*, New York 1968)

'Capitalism and neo-capitalism have produced an abstract space that is a reflection of the world of business on both a national and international level, as well as the power of money and the "politique" of the state. This abstract space depends on vast networks of banks, businesses, and great centres of production. There also is the spatial intervention of highways, airports, and information networks. In this space, the cradle of accumulation, the place of richness, the subject of history, the centre of historical space, in other words, the city, has exploded.' (Henri Lefebvre)

Martha Rosler, Untitled (Minneapolis), 1992

As a teenager in the fifties I sailed the Atlantic and Mediterranean a couple of times. In the sixties and seventies I drove back and forth across America. Also in the seventies, I traversed the country in long-distance buses, experiencing the bald regimentation of passengers that is suggestive of custody for minor crimes. I photographed these trips in black and white. By the end of the seventies, with my tickets paid by various employers and inviters, I had all but abandoned the buses for aeroplanes. I offer this history as typical of the possibilities awaiting the upwardly mobile middle-class city dweller in the postwar United States.

In the past fifteen years, living an artist's life, I have found myself flying many times a year. I found myself in the company of the besuited and the befurred, of those in trenchcoats carrying attaché cases and garment bags or those in leisurewear toting skis or pedigreed dogs. I discovered that at many small airports the flyers included the same people who might have been riding the bus. I changed my black-and-white film for colour, and my serious 35-millimetre camera for a less weighty pocket version. I became interested in the ephemera and experience of this form of travel, so different in time, space, and (self-) organisation from train and particularly long-distance bus travel. In a time in which production in advanced industrial countries is increasingly characterised by metaphors of transmission and flow, I am interested in the movement of bodies through darkened corridors and across great distances but also in the effacement of the experience of such travel by constructs designed to empty the actual experience of its content and make it the carrier of another sort of experience entirely. This totalised representation of air travel and its associated spaces as 'a world apart' is different from that of any other form of mass transport.

Walter Benjamin, unexpectedly, ends *The Work of Art in the Age of Mechanical Reproduction* with a pocket analysis of architecture: 'Architecture has never been idle. Its history is more ancient than that of any other art, and its claim to being a living force has significance in every attempt to comprehend the relationship of the masses to art'. 'Architecture', Benjamin continues, 'is "appropriated" not only through sight but through touch; it is experienced by the body as presence, through "distraction", or habitual use, not through optical contemplation'. He likens the new art of cinema to architecture, holding out the hope of the education of the senses and therefore a means to combat the fascist aestheticisation of politics through spectacle. Despite the focus of his essay on the social effects of photography and film, Benjamin could hardly have anticipated the invention of virtual reality, a computer simulated 'environment' or 'architecture' that envelops the spectator in a sensory phantasmagoria offering apparently spatial, auditory, and tactile cues★ – in other words, 'experience'. Virtual reality, and 'cyberspace', a broader conception of a computational environment, exists more in the promise than in the fulfillment; but it is not news that in the organisation of physical space and the design of buildings in advanced industrial society there are elements that relinquish presence or presentness in favour of signification: *the Empire of Signs*. Those seeking cyberspace dream the future by literally moving space to the plane of the imaginary.

How far can one advance a discussion of air travel and its associated spaces, structures, and experiences by broaching the subject of virtual reality? Not far, perhaps. Nevertheless, as the opening quotation

★ The term 'virtual reality' was coined by one of its inventors and promoters, Jaron Lanier. The creation of this simulated body of experiences, which is being developed in conjunction with the military-industrial complex, generally involves the donning of goggles or a helmet with tiny video monitors and a glove containing elements that allow the wearer to see and apparently to touch and manipulate objects not present in the same space or not existing in the real world. (Various developers are hoping to get rid of the wires.) The synchronicity and multiplicity of these cues serves to 'inform' the experiencing subject that s/he is 'in'; the other space. The term 'cyberspace' was coined by the science-fiction writer William Gibson in the mid-1980s in his Neuromancer future-dystopia novels and refers to a vision of an entire world based on computer simulations. There is a certain irony to the fact that these nightmarish and paranoic visions of a future far more bleak and disorienting than Orwell's *1984* are likely to be realised through the intervention of the military. See, among other sources, Michael Benedikt, ed., *Cyberspace: First Steps*, Cambridge, 1991.

★ Debord, Guy, *The Society of the Spectacle*, Detroit 1970.

suggests, Henri Lefebvre – followed by a host of commentators – has shown how space is produced by the relations of production, mapping political economy onto the physical world. Cyberspace too, although only a simulation, is thrown up by the collective imaginary of late capitalism, a translation of Lefebvre's 'abstract space' to an intangible realm. In describing the role of processes of image reproduction in contemporary society, the situationist Guy Debord★ has pointed out that 'the spectacle', is created by the mode of production and is not a technological accident, not a freely created spectral other world standing against 'the real': 'The spectacle is not a collection of images, but a social relation among people, mediated by images. (...) The spectacle cannot be understood as an abuse of the world of vision, as a product of the techniques of mass dissemination of images. It is, rather, a Weltanschauung which has become actual, materially translated (…). The spectacle, grasped in its totality, is both a result and the project of the existing mode of production'. Ultimately Debord and Benjamin are on the opposite sides of the question of technological optimism, but in terms of diagnostics, Debord's proposition that 'this society which eliminated geographical distance reproduces distance internally as spectacular separation' seems equivalent to Benjamin's concept of fascist aestheticisation.

The history of flight is not separate from the history of information management – nor from that of image production and, ultimately, of 'simulation'. An embryonic start toward virtual reality was the flight simulator. As soon as it became practicable, video became part of flight-simulator training, and video and flight simulation have developed in tandem. Air-traffic controllers spend their free time playing video games and are able to handle their jobs only through derealisation: If they thought of the radar blips as *planes* with *people* in them, they say, they would not be able to last a single day. The recasting of movement as information flow is a consequence of excess complexity.

In the brief compass of the present essay, I want to invoke some features of air travel and airports that, among other things, touch on matters of simulation and representation. I frame my discussion not from the point of view of an expert, an outside observer, or even a student, but from that of a traveller. That is, a traveller and an artist.

Those seeking cyberspace dream the future by literally moving space to the plane of the imaginary.

★ Emerson's journal entries are cited and discussed in Kasson, John, *Civilizing the Machine: Technology and Republican Values in America, 1776-1900*, New York, 1976, pp. 114-116.

In 1834 the American Transcendentalist poet and philosopher Ralph Waldo Emerson described railroad travel as a salutary drug of sorts, disconnecting the traveller from place and loosening the perception of stability – or the stability of perception: 'One has dim foresight of hitherto uncomputed mechanical advantages who rides on the rail-road and moreover a practical confirmation of the ideal philosophy that Matter is phenomenal whilst men & trees & barns whiz by you as fast as the leaves of a dictionary. As our teakettle hissed along through a field of mayflowers, we could judge of the sensations of a swallow who skims by trees & bushes with about the same speed. The very permanence of matter seems compromised & oaks, fields, hills, hitherto esteemed symbols of stability do absolutely dance by you.'★

Back home in the States, railroads were soon extended across the 'empty' continent, linking communities and regions together. Emerson wrote, in 1840, six years after his initial euphoria: 'The railroad makes a man a chattel, transports him by the box and the ton, he waits on it. He feels that he pays a high price for his speed in this compromise of all his will. I think the man who walks looks down on us who ride.' Even in his initial account of the train's perceptual effects, Emerson had noted the habituation to this technological marvel that the English – both travellers and roadside observers – had achieved. A century later Charles Lindbergh lamented his own loss of poetic perception resulting from habituation to flight.

All histories of art's responses to technology invoke the early twentieth-century effusions on modernity offered by the Italian Futurists that ended up affirming the technology of death. War – and its pornographic appreciations – helped dampen technological optimism, even among artists, until it was giddily reawakened by the 'global village' of postwar communications technology and, more recently, by cyberspace. These fictive 'spaces' created by instantaneous transmissions are compensatory for the destabilisations and fragmentations – the clichés of urban life – produced by the 'globalisation' of production and of markets. Despite industrial interest in a yet-to-be-realised technology of environmental simulation, at present the play environments of cyberspace are created by and for restive young men

Martha Rosler

who find few places for mastery among actually existing social relations. ★ But even at present the computer and telecommunications networks that join discontinuous actual places into working units create a functional cyberspace, however primitive and lacking in simulation cues. 'The technological universe is impervious to the *here* and the *there*. Rather, the natural place for its operations is the entire human environment – a pure topological field, as Cubism, Futurism, and Elementarism well understood.' ★ The movements of industry and information that link discrete areas of the world and simultaneously create localised discontinuities in ways of life and daily experience are not most notable for their transitory perceptual effects, and they have their greatest effects on those not aboard the train. The scale of social and psychic fragmentations occasioned by the globalisation of advanced industrial production and distribution is incomparably vaster than those produced by train, plane, or space travel; yet these movements of individuals are symptomatic.

After a century of fascination with the ever-increasing speeds of transportation and information, we find speed alone not particularly discomfiting but possibly reassuring. Motion parallax, no longer confusing, is simply another special effect of travel. Unlike one's pet cat, we have learned to cope with rapid passage across the ground and the water, in conveyances powered by complex hidden mechanisms. Jet travel, in contrast, introduces a dislocation or destabilisation so complete that it is as well to suppress the realisation of where one really is in favour of illusion. The development of technological illusionisms has adequately kept pace with the technological development of motion, and it appears that those who have a taste for imagining the future prefer to do so through simulations rather than through anything as normalised and apparently orderly as jet travel.

The possible euphoria of actually flying, of being in flight, is not capitalised on by those whose business it is to keep us from excessive curiosity or from panic while acting as passengers in commercial aircraft. The determinism of speed has no meaning in the sky, and the detachment occasioned by the dream of flying helps organise each person into private space, making us the perfect audience for an in-flight movie, perfect suckers for the unyielding babying inflicted on us by cabin attendants. The illusions that are provided in mid-air replicate the banalities of everyday life, or worse, the experience of institutionalised infancy in an imperfect womb. The dignity of both passenger and attendant is left at the gate.

Look out of the window of the plane during flight. Below is a vague array of generic sights: rivers, mountains, agricultural parcels; towns and cities; or cloud cover and horizon. Rising sun, setting sun, a plane or two flying above or below. Except for the occasional wonder of the world, the scene lacks impact, dreamlike but without compelling narrative. You object that a trip across the ocean in a commercial liner is not different, only emptier and longer. But on the ocean one sees the water and the waves, one remembers maps and globes, one recognises one's place in a microcosm with a daily round of events, on a voyage that makes no pretence of instantaneity. Flying says there is no journey, only trajectory. Look at the maps at the back of the airline guide: the arrows dominate the featureless shapes on the map. Less to identify with here than with the image of the globe from outer space.

Denial is a powerful psychological mechanism in air travel as in much of the rest of everyday life. Deny speed and elevation. Deny the thinness of the aeroplane's aluminium skin providing warmth, oxygen, protection. Deny the totality of air crashes, the dangers inherent in ageing air fleets, the possibility of incompetent or inadequate maintenance. Deny the terror of completely relinquishing control to the hidden men/machines up front. Deny the small chance of hijacking or the larger one of 'pilot error'. Deny the absurdity of the space into which you are shoe-horned. But think about this particular physical space. The bit of social space hurtling through the air that is the aeroplane is regarded by its masters as very expensive real estate, and the smallest margin of comfort above the outrages of cabin class is expensively obtained. (There is a certain historical irony here, since Le Corbusier referred to aeroplanes as little flying houses [!] and attempted to adapt some principles of house design and production from aircraft production.) Even under the best of circumstances, the commercial airliner is much like the least wonderful specimen of long-distance autobus, and certainly is nothing like the ocean liner or even the railroad train, which gather their inhabitants in communal spaces for dining or recreation and do not insist on strapping them to their beds.

One of the great blessings of railroad and then plane travel was the inaccessibility it afforded the traveller: no phones. Now the perpetually plugged-in lower-level executive cannot abandon the telephone,

★ One wonders what the implications are of the fact that when the industry in question is information transmission, technological development may arise from an initial beginning in fantasy projection, in the space of desire, rather than in 'reality'-oriented problem solving. Magic versus science, the predictable antipodean choices. For a consideration of the encoding of computational space as private (real) property, see the discussion of 'hacking' as trespassing versus the computer invader as 'a polite country rambler' traversing 'picturesque fields', in Ross, Andrew, *Strange Weather Culture, Science and Technology in the Age of Limits*, London 1991, p. 82.

★ Tafuri, Manfredo, 'The Crisis of Utopia: Le Corbusier at Algiers', in *Architecture and Utopia: Design and Capitalist Development*, Cambridge Mass. 1976, p. 129.

which accompanies him in cars and restaurants and, along with computers and fax machines, into the air. Phones are implanted in seat backs on some aircraft. Fax modems will soon be able to link computers, phones, and land terminals with their flying users; the functions, moreover, will likely be combined into a single pocket-size instrument. This telephone slavery completes the circuit of physical passage from point A to point B. As the plugged-in body moves through real space, the plugged-in mind, in the loop of information in transmission, has no respite. How different is this condition from that of the social offender who under house arrest must wear an electronic bracelet? Alternatively, a passenger dons the earphones provided by the cabin attendants or those of a personal Walkman. The interval that might be used for private purposes or socialising, for anything at all, is recast as a duality: produce or consume, work or be distracted. This never-terminated hook-up – an ad hoc version of cyberspace, after all – reflects the auditory horror vacui of all formerly silent public spaces, such as elevators, restaurants, and dentist's offices, not to mention nature shows on television, venues that used to be without piped-in sound, a condition of auditory freedom now apparently forbidden – except in terminals, which unlike the aeroplane and the telephone 'hold' mechanism, is not yet deemed conveniently colonisable by 'easy listening'.

Eventually, the plane lands, the traveller arrives. As an invitation to theorising, the airport suggests the meeting point of theories of time and of space, of schedules and of layouts. The airport is a multi-dimensional, multi-function system whose overriding concerns are operational. To state the obvious, airport design requires a consideration of a set of flow trajectories in vertical space, a dimension normally regarded as more or less stable. The most intensive period of airport construction coincided with stripped-down functionalist Modernism. It would be interesting to compare airports built in the early postwar period and more recently, when the dominant metaphors of flow dynamics shifted from water to information. Airports, unlike railroad terminals, are not in the heart of an urban milieu but situated out of town and so not subject to the same kinds of siting and façade considerations as other major structures. Furthermore, they are often under the control of different agencies from those responsible for town or city planning. Falling under the reign of the technocrat, they do not encode capital the way large urban structures do. Since the airport is conceived of as a web of functionalities, the idea of an architecturally imposing gateway structure, while certainly present, is secondary. The conception of the façade is also altered by the fact that in the best circumstances airports are approached by ground travellers not from roads but from trains – preferably underground, though this is rarely so in the United States. Increasingly, they are approached by people getting off one plane only to get on another. That technical efficiency, not the state of the public, is venerated by the airport and has resulted in structures whose experiencing subjects are atomised. Inside the terminal buildings, each atomised subject is the same consumer created by other commercial transactions: an irrationalist, operating in the realm of desire.

Except for a few high-profile terminals, the airport may not be usefully described in terms of 'architecture'. Airports reflect the thinking of engineers, underlining the historic split that turned architects into a profession of more or less willing mandarins. While the airport does not escape its conception as a system composed of a linked series of operational 'modules' – a term interestingly incorporated not only into the lexicon of space travel but also of the 'architecture' of the computer 'environment' – it is useful to elide the distinction between architected and engineered space.

Architecturally, the terminal is conceived as a hangar or shed. Many terminals celebrate the functionality of glass and steel, elements not only held to be essential to the construction of the terminal structure but signalling the fabric of the plane and the act of navigation. Facade elements are de-emphasised in favour of an interior often defined by glass but generally lacking Crystal Palace triumphalism. Central areas or concourses range from the humdrum to the grandiose, with little in-between. Huge aimless spaces are marked off by rope-and-stanchion arrays to keep order among those lined up at ticket counters. Away from the central hall, acoustic tile in grim tracks, self-effaced flooring, fluorescent-lit low-ceilinged corridors, reductive directional signs no more inflected than road signs – although the latter are meant to be grasped at a high rate of speed – are ubiquitous. The accountant and the crowd-control manager are the gods supplicated within.

At Kennedy Airport, Eero Saarinen's biomorphic 1962 TWA terminal, while attempting an inspiring

Martha Rosler, Untitled (Philadelphia), 1992

Martha Rosler, Untitled (LAX), 1990

Martha Rosler, Untitled (O'Hare), 1986

Martha Rosler, Untitled (Schiphol), 1992

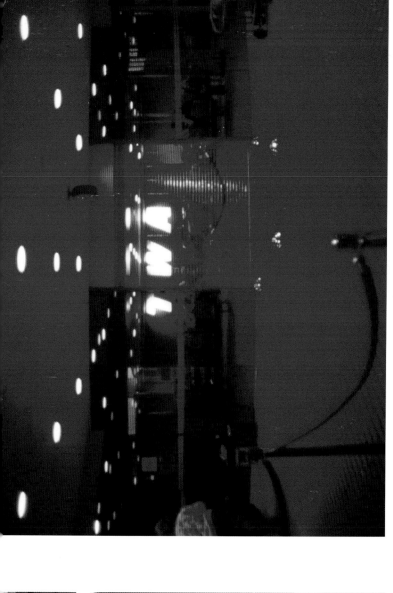

Martha Rosler, Untitled (TWA, JFK), 1990

Martha Rosler, Untitled (London), 1984

Martha Rosler, Untitled (TWA, JFK), 1992

Martha Rosler, Untitled (United, O'Hare), 1990

interior, is probably more comprehensible from the air than from below. Helmut Jahn's celebrated late-eighties United Airlines terminal at Chicago O'Hare Airport, America's busiest, organises our perceptions in a straight ahead interior runway with a big sky. If the great railway terminals created a pseudo-sacral public space with soaringly meaningful overheads, the Jahn terminal is mausoleum-like, a reminder of individual insignificance. And that authoritarian black-and-white chequerboard floor! But Jahn, although predictably megalomaniacal, can be held accountable only for his design, not for its emptiness, which surely is a cultural product rather than simply a personal shortcoming. Underground at O'Hare are very dim tunnels linking the terminals, tunnels through which homeless people guide their shopping carts.

The airport is not organised as a signifying space that creates a public any more than the aeroplane itself is – unless we accept the message of the plane and the terminal equally to be human docility, homogeneity, replaceability, transitoriness. If money and crowd control are the prime movers, surveillance is the constant practice. Surveillance may or may not be accomplished with the aid of hidden cameras. There is always in place some dangerous and invasive Other to be invoked, and every airport now appears organised around the spectre of the international terrorist, a sufficient excuse for the remilitarisation of flight.★ Especially in certain European capitals, terrorist explosives must be guarded against. Yet ordinary armoured-car robbers of airport payrolls and payments,★ not to mention baggage thieves and pickpockets, are more likely to be the interlopers at American airports – thieves and those with no homes. One effort of policing terminals is to prevent homeless people from seeking shelter at the airport. In this task the airport managers are fortunate, because airports, unlike ground-transportation terminals, are located well away from urban centres. O'Hare is one of the few U.S. airports that can be easily reached by rail from the city. The airport, like the modern corporate space, cleanly embodies Foucault's observations on the ways that information is used to organise and control people.

Information, a necessity for every traveller, is not easily obtained. With any change in schedule or plans, whether caused by accident, mechanical failure, bomb threat, or weather, the system breaks

★ Realism breaks through the implacable denial of the fragilities of flight when the anti-terrorism 'expert', paid to create a *frisson* in his employers and other listeners, refers to a 747 as 'a tin can full of several hundred hostages at forty thousand feet'.

★ Surveillance, of course, misses the big crimes that are the ordinary accompaniments of big business, ranging from extortion of protection money from freight carriers to the far more significant and successful profiteering at public expense occasioned by the constant building and rebuilding at airports.

434

The space created by capital perpetually re-creates its own underworld, its own space of 'underdevelopment' and immobility, its own wasteland.

down, and the flow of passengers stops. The oldest model of bureaucracy – information constriction, information sadism – takes over. People stand in long lines or in clumps trying to find out what is occurring, with almost no effort at co-operation from the airline employees, who stand behind counters, manipulating computer terminals, and decline to make eye contact. Hours pass. Food and drink are rarely offered. Sometimes hotel accommodation is offered, but regardless of the nature of the emergency, information is as far as possible withheld.

On the other hand, the search for *impersonal* information on the part of the authorities extends to a microscopic level. High-technology bomb detectors, 'thermal neutron analysers', have been announced as being readied to search luggage at international gateways in the hunt for plastic explosives. More routinely, all hand luggage (and much checked baggage) is scrutinised by means of x-ray machines and hand searches, and people must pass through magnetic metal detectors or are physically searched. More personally, customs and immigration officers, inspecting people and documents, apprehend illegal entrants and turn them back.

As a teenager I would drive out with friends to Kennedy Airport (then Idlewild) to watch the planes take off and land, but now people who watch planes prefer to do so casually, in the airport bar. Even so the bar is more likely to have no windows facing out. In the airport terminal, pseudo-sidewalk cafes and theme restaurants are common. In the United States, the airport is so far removed from the model of the public plaza or terminal that the fundamental right to solicit money or to hand out political and religious leaflets was uniformly denied until reinstated by the Supreme Court. In this effort at a tidy order free of political or religious displays, airport authorities revealed their conception of the facility as a private space much like a store or a home. 'Public spaces' are rethought as 'non-private' spaces, spaces of consumption and control or spaces of disorder, characterised by homeless people, by crime, vehicular traffic.

In countries less dominated by the reign of commodities, in the peripheral reaches of the Empire of Signs, the totalisation of the airport as singular unified space is less advanced. In Johannesburg, commercial signage is minimal, the modest bit of art is commemorative bronze statuary, and passengers ascend and descend the planes via staircases moved onto the runway. This is a society in which consumers know themselves, and the State has other preoccupations than facilitating consumption. In the United States, the air-travel market was given free reign by the deregulation process begun in the late seventies. The onset of Reaganism forestalled the minimal protections proposed for small airlines and unprofitable routes. Competitive practices were touted as allowing customers to achieve lower fares on small airlines; instead, increasingly monopolistic control over pricing, scheduling, and routing led to higher fares, far fewer airlines and a reduced schedule. The U.S. market, dominated by a few carriers, is an unstable oligopoly.

At U.S. Air's hub in Pittsburgh, a new terminal includes a shopping mall (with regular mall prices, not the usual extortionate air-terminal prices), apparently still the only model to which an air terminal can aspire. The huge terminal also contains a 'meditation room' designed by a New York artist and works by other internationally known artists, among them Robert Morris. Many U.S. airports incorporate art, much of it mandated under municipal 'percent for art' programmes. A *New York Times* article called attention to the differential between the potential audiences at airports and at museums.★ Unconcerned with the private property argument about airports, the *Times* treats these works as examples of public art. The article compares Chicago O'Hare airport's sixty million passengers and uncounted other visitors in 1990 to the four and a half million who visited New York's Metropolitan Museum of Art. The elision of the difference between travellers passing art works and paid visitors to a traditional museum tells. What also tells is the article's description of a planned Baudrillardian simulation in the Denver hub in the Rockies: 'the facility will use its multimillion-dollar art budget to bring the essence of Colorado to the many transfer passengers who never venture outside the airport. Among innovations planned are a light sculpture that will cast changing Colorado cloud formations onto an atrium roof, and a 60-foot-long water sculpture reproducing nearby mountain landscapes.

The terminal earnestly approaches the status of the enormous room, the prison-house of culture, described by people as disparate as the poet Cummings and the philosopher Adorno.

This conception of the airport as museum is municipally imposed and does not follow the logic of the resident airlines, which naturally want to colonise your mind with notions of big and little trips. The works of art – often screwed to the wall like fire hoses in thick Plexiglas cases – generally seem negligible, out of place, absorbed into the 'architecture' like inexplicable 'beauty marks' or eruptions on its office-interior skin. Airlines, as I have suggested, want terminals to be more like virtual than actual spaces. Airport corridors are generally no better lit than the average department store, with similar intentions – to cast you inward to the psychological space of desire. In the airport, desire is always infinitely deferred, and meaning is elsewhere and otherwise. Back-lit photos lure us to Tahiti or Cincinnati (unless we are in Tahiti or Cincinnati), to Disneyland or the Eiffel Tower, to Marlboro Country or to the land of financial accumulation, telephones, and computers or of remote outmoded forms of transportation, such as a canoe trip in rural Africa – sometimes both simultaneously.

'The economic organisation of visits to different places is already in itself the guarantee of their equivalence. The same modernisation that removed time from the voyage also removed from it the reality of space.'★ Photography and the creation of (commodified) space, which share a common origin, continue to develop together; preservation efforts, always a project of elites, are being carried forward via electronic digitisation of images, the latest linkage of photography and computerisation. *Projet Patrimoine 2001* will photograph 200 'cultural and natural wonders' and make the images 'instantly available worldwide through digital transmission'. What makes this preservation through image appropriation notable is that it is a project of UNESCO, the United Nations Educational, Scientific and Cultural Organisation, under the impetus of its new Spanish director, Federico Mayor. The project will be substantially underwritten by grants from the immensely rich La Caixa Foundation, based in Barcelona and supported by its municipal pension funds. Technical services will be donated by Kodak, France Telecom, and the Gamma photo agency. The idea is to make images of endangered treasures before, according to the *New York Times*, 'they are further damaged by war or the environment'. It is important that it is UNESCO initiating this project, which can be of interest only to the advanced industrial countries, because under its previous, African director, UNESCO was boycotted by them because of its challenge to their control of information. (The U.S. withdrew from UNESCO in 1984.)

★ Carmichael, Suzanne, *Stuck at the Airport? Then Look at the Art*, in New York Times, 15 December 1991.

★ Debord, Guy, *The Society of the Spectacle*, Detroit 1970, prop 168, n.p. The frustrating sameness of tourist destinations has been described by Jean Baudrillard and such other commentators as Donald Horne. All these accounts, overstated as they surely are for theoretical effect, point out the homogenisation of culture: the beaten path beats down that which it managed to reach with such difficulty. Erasure of difference always leads to efforts by the coloniser to 'preserve' it, but as a depoliticised, aestheticised set of cultural practices – as a 'destination'.

Martha Rosler

435

Under Mayor, UNESCO claims to have turned toward 'universality'. Experience tells us that claims for universality translate into alibis for domination.

Allowed past security checks, ticket holders hurry to the gates. Aeroplanes do not rest like ocean liners in a great public arena, and airport bays and piers do not replicate the docks of ships. Instead, they run up and down terminal buildings placed alongside the runways rather than along the 'natural' juncture of ocean and land. Thus for passengers there is no immediately intuitive logic to the terminal layout, which is often described in terms of 'fingers'. Such biomorphic analogies notwithstanding, the fingers may be on far too many 'hands' to make obvious sense. Mystification of place and space appears to conflict with the operational aim of routing people efficiently. The passenger must be directed by signage as well as by moving walkways, passageways, and tunnels designated more like the rows in parking garages than like public streets. In the airport as in the giant shopping mall or immense natural history museum, an aerial schematic map tells you 'You are here'.

As the space of the terminal does not explain itself, so the plane does not beckon. The aeroplane does not match the majestic image of either the big ship or the long-distance train. It is just another information/transportation module. At best, to stick with metaphor, the plane is likely to call to mind a tiny vessel lost in vastness, a storm tossed boat rather than the iceberg monolith of a big ship with its deep airhorns, rather than the long stretch of a passing train Doppler shifting through space and time. Inside the craft the meanness of space allotted each person, the relentless miniaturisation with no opening into a larger space, helps create this image of puniness and fragility. But the interior and the exterior of the plane itself do not coincide. Rather than participating in a grand display of arrivals and departures, air passengers are politely hustled onto and off the planes preferably through 'jetways' channelling them from terminal to plane and vice versa. These elevated walkways share something with the elevated shopping arcades, or skywalks, in malled-in America, although they are narrower – featureless passages perhaps more reminiscent of a birth canal leading from the plane's shrouded entrance. Indeed, the airport itself can be seen as the subterranean erupted upward, a series of blind passages and darkened tubules with walkways moving passengers in an approximation of peristalsis. Out on the field, the aeroplane, with its female name, lies quiescent, serviced by shuttling fuel tankers and 'honey wagons', food trucks and cargo carriers. These evocations of the body are the closest approach to the possibly female in the phallocratic regime of flight.★ That it calls to mind structures of domination replicates the relationship of air travel to the land, to the sky, and to the earth itself.

What of the airport as a gross physical, a geographic, entity? Airports are tremendous colonisers, rendering the land they occupy and the surrounding areas into wasteland. Like the ground under a city, the airport bulldozes and flattens out the spaces of nature. It brings the land as close as possible to the condition of perfection, in which geometry has conquered diversity or incident. Air travel wrecks more than the land on which the airport sits; aside from the chemical pollutants inevitably introduced into the surrounding landscape, human and animal life in a wide area around the airport is disturbed by airport noise. But money talks, and pilots are often required to loop about in the air, giving up a direct route in or out of the airport in order to preserve the quiet of wealthy homeowners below. Land values around airports and in the flight path are depressed, and working-class dwellers are annoyed and sometimes killed by overflights.

When catastrophe befalls a plane carrying large number of Americans, when such a plane crashes or blows up, routine is left behind. Along with emergency services, news and information are marshalled for various purposes. The machinery of containment is deployed by the airline and the State, human-interest stories are written and grief is exploited by news agencies, blame is sought as a cathartic act. With crashes of international flights, the rationalist efforts of state agencies are offset by sudden suspicions of conspiracy and secret terror. Pilot error, the preferred explanation, is not particularly reassuring to travellers, traffic-controller mistakes or mechanical failure even less so. Foreign acts of aggression may suit state purposes. Worst are the suspicions or confirmation of sabotage. Sabotage, formerly perpetrated by persons seeking life-insurance gains, is now inescapably the purview of international terrorists, almost all Islamic. Mass paranoia, generally repressed, surges around such incidents, fuelled by the families of victims, who brush aside explanations offered by the State. As time passes, the families'

★ The interior of the plane, however, does little to evoke the female, drawing upon the masculinist realms of the factory and the office.

★ Lefebvre, Henri, 'Space: Social Product and Use Value', in Freiberg, J. W. (ed.) *Critical Sociology*, New York 1979, p. 287.

436

Jan Benthem, Mels Crouwel and Khio Liang le Associates, extension to Amsterdam Airport (Schiphol), 1993

dragnet is cast wider and wider, invoking secret plots and counterplots by intelligence and other, unnamed clandestine forces, involving explosives and drug smuggling, agents and double agents. This was as true of the Soviet downing of KAL flight 007 over Sakhalin in 1983 as of the still-unresolved bombing of Pan Am Flight 103 over Lockerbie in 1988 and the crash of the military charter flight over Gander in 1985.

Airports, like all modernising modalities, serve the needs of capital above all and leach away resources from those who are not integrated at a sufficiently high level into the political economy. Just as in suburbia or in inner cities, and on the streets below the skywalks and the outer perimeters of the indoor malls, service workers can be seen waiting for hours at bus stops or riding for hours to and from work, because car ownership is presumed to be 'universal', the ubiquity of air travel underdevelops more modest forms of transportation, such as the railroad and the long-distance bus. Some cities, like St. Louis, sink millions into light-rail lines to the airport while neglecting internal transport in the highly segregated city. Lefebvre again: 'Abstract space reveals its oppressive and repressive capacities in relation to time. It rejects time as an abstraction – except when it concerns work, the producer of things and of surplus value. Time is reduced to constraints of space: schedules, runs, crossings, loads. Time has disappeared in the social space of modernity... Economic space subordinates time, whereas political space eradicates it because it is threatening to existing power relations. The primacy of the economic, and still more, of the political, leads to the supremacy of space over time'.★ The reigning paradigm always casts its meanings back through time; wherever possible those meanings are newly embodied in social practices, in landscape, in the built environment. On the way to the commuter railroad that takes me to work from the 'new' Pennsylvania Station in New York City, an enormous, hideous pit with low-ceilinged, dreary areas, uncomfortable in every detail, I pass a series of photographs of the old Beaux Arts-neoclassical Pennsylvania Station (McKim, Mead & White, 1906-10) razed by the Pennsylvania Railroad in 1963. The face presented to the street – the architect's face – of this terminal, meant to replicate the Roman Baths of Caracalla, was that of monumental Classicism and stability. Inside, the 'face' the traveller saw was a soaring hymn to engineering. Without romanticising the 'lost' edifice, one may still invoke this grand advertisement for capital as the epitome of the public space, the physically embodied metaphor of an imperial people – as is the still-standing Grand Central Terminal on the other side of town. In these terminals one realises oneself, for good or ill, as part of a totality. In contrast, in the airport, the space on which the new Penn Station clearly is modelled, everything and everyone is weightless, anomic, and the appeal is to consumerism, not to sociality. There is no middle ground between imperial citizenship and the vacuum. Both terminals, the carceral and the grand, house populations of people who would otherwise have to sleep in the street. Their passage across the landscape is in inverse proportion to the speed of those above them. The space created by capital perpetually re-creates its own underworld, its own space of 'underdevelopment' and immobility, its own wasteland.

'...the twentieth century is a century which sees the earth as no one has ever seen it, the earth has a splendour that it never has had, and as everything destroys itself in the twentieth century and nothing continues, so then the twentieth century has a splendour which is its own and Picasso is of this century, he has that strange quality of an earth that one has never seen and of things destroyed as they have never been destroyed. (Gertrude Stein)

How is it that we are confronted with a choice between the intrusive reminders of capital's aspirations toward domination and the blank-eyed emptiness of nowhere and no-body?

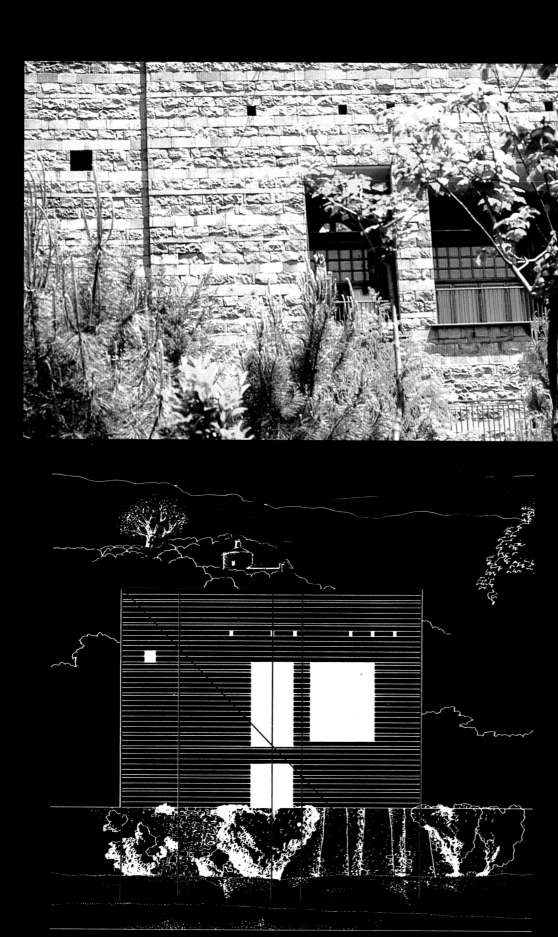

'No explanation is necessary' (Francesco Venezia)

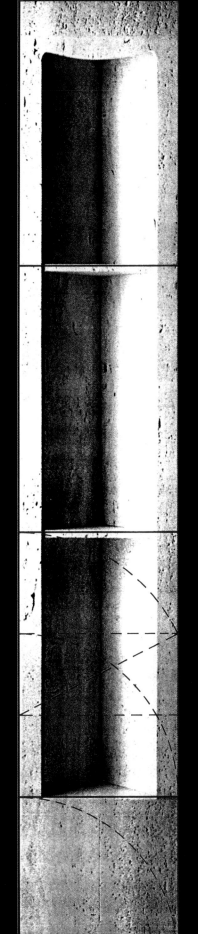

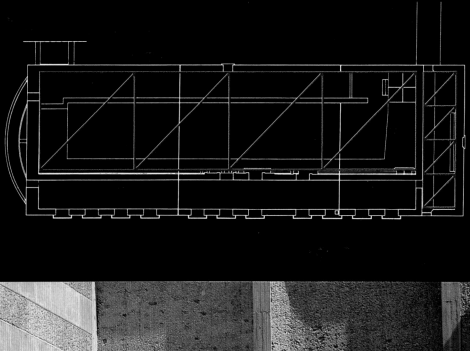

One of the aspects of *our work as architects is to offer a certain resistance to the rapid exhaustion of the practical reasons behind the structure of a building; to evoke a concealed time that resists the apparent time of its usefulness.* ■ Everybody is familiar with the inexhaustible character of some buildings: their ability to capture our imagination and inspire us, to extend the material life of the space beyond all reasonable expectations, staying the course while still remaining true to their functional goals. ■ Many people will also be familiar with how an experience of this sort – whose duration is so exceptional – is renewed and enhanced whenever we chance to revisit the building in question; it will seem the same and yet not the same compared with our previous experience of it. ■ In architecture itself the mystery of this concealed time – which is a nexus of relations, only partially apparent, which are capable of suggesting this idea of inexhaustibility – is the result of the rigorous and patient activity of the designer. ■ An activity that is based on ideas and techniques. ■ The basic idea is that various elements combine to create the outward form of the building and that these are only partially visible in the immediate picture one gets of it. The remaining elements withdraw, so to speak, behind the surface; only at certain points do they reveal their hidden texture. ■ The basic layout, the modulations in the design, the shape of both structural and plastic elements, the shape of the component constructional materials operate on various levels. ■ The respective geometries that unite them to form precise mutual relations coincide only in part. They often deviate from each other. ■ It is in this action of geometrical systems, operating on different levels and with a degree of mutual divergence, that this extremely long duration, that is the concealed and inexhaustible part of the building, comes into being. ■ I said building, but I should have said half of the building: the other half, the shadowy half, takes shape and transforms slowly – it appears, disappears and reappears. ■ In retrieving these elements of rhythms and textures from the darkness that silences them and renders them featureless, in combining them like the instruments of an orchestra, the light discloses an ensemble of mutual responses: their shadowy half. ■ Variegated and ineluctable, defined and ordered, related in their predictable realisation to the unpredictable evolution of the changeable harmonies of the tune, every element, while being ordered in sequence with other elements, registering in them the *raison d'être* for its own position, generates in turn the sequence of its own shadows. ■ The interplay between duration and the fleeting moment, between the event and its development, becomes more complex. ■ The rhythm that organises the duration of the event captures it with a time that is enhanced and accumulates. ■ This movement that takes as its point of departure the abstraction of systems of measurement and scale, this meticulous construction of a nexus of relations that do not correspond and round which the material elements of the structure are built – to arrive at the inexhaustible flux of sensations that are only predicted in this nexus of relationships – all this comprises the adventure of the work of construction: the project as a design consisting of predictions and of the fragmentary and chaotic universe of materials awaiting construction. ■ The tension between the design that aspires to order things and the material that offers resistance. ■ The critical point of impoverishment in a great deal of present-day architecture is the deliberate – at times paradigmatic – elimination of every element of divergence and the assumption that the geometry of the design and the geometry of the component materials will at all points coincide. ■ The process of composition that is based on the form of the square – the square as a concealed figure that gives rise to a flowering of relationships – is replaced by the stupidity of a process of a division into squares that governs all the component elements of the building in a way that can only be called superficial. ■ Pride of place is given to a banal choice that does nothing but give a rhetorical explanation of the rationality and logic inherent in any process of construction. ■ Everything is resolved and exhausted in a swift glance of comprehension – in a

Francesco Venezia

Uno degli scopi del **nostro lavoro di architetti è opporre una certa resistenza al rapido esaurirsi della ragione pratica che determina la costruzione di un edificio: suscitare un tempo nascosto che resista al tempo apparente del suo uso.** ■ *A ciascuno è nota l'inesauribilità di alcuni edifici: la loro capacità di eccitare e catturare la nostra sensibilità, di dilatare oltre ogni ragionevole misura il tempo necessario ad esaurire il percorso materiale dello spazio, coprendone le distanze e raggiungendo le mete utili.* ■ *E a molti è noto come tale esperienza – peculiarmente lunghissima – si rinnovi e si dilati quando ci accade di rivisitare quell'edificio, che ci appare lo stesso e non più lo stesso rispetto alle precedenti esperienze.* ■ *Il mistero di questo tempo nascosto, una rete solo in parte manifesta di relazioni in grado di suscitare quell'idea di inesauribilità, è in architettura il frutto di un paziente e rigoroso lavoro di progettazione.* ■ *Un lavoro che si basa su idee e tecniche.* ■ *Idea primaria è che alla forma dell'immagine immediata. I rimanenti sono per così dire arretrati rispetto al piano più esterno e solo per punti svelano la loro trama nascosta.* ■ *Tracciato regolatore, modulazione, forma degli elementi strutturali e degli elementi plastici, forma dei componenti materiali della costruzione si muovono in piani diversi.* ■ *Le rispettive geometrie, che li collegano nella precisione delle mutue relazioni, solo in parte coincidono. Sovente sono tra loro slittate.* ■ *In questo agire su piani deversi e con un mutuo slittamento dei sistemi geometrici si forma quel tempo lunghissimo che è la parte nascosta e inesauribile dell'edificio.* ■ *Ho detto dell'edificio e avrei dovuto dire di una metà dell'edificio:* ■ *l'altra, la metà d'ombre, si forma e si traforma lentamente – appare scompare riappare.* ■ *Nel trarli dal buio che appiattisce e tacita, nel chiamarli a raccolta come strumenti di un'orchestra, la luce svela agli elementi dei ritmi e delle tessiture un insieme di risposte a se stessi: la loro metà d'ombre.* ■ *Molteplici quanto ineluttabili, definite e ordinate, legate nel loro attuarsi prevedibile all'imprevedibile evolversi dei mutevole equilibri dell'aria, ogni elemento, mentre è ordinato in sequenze geometriche con altri elementi, registrando in esse la ragione della propria posizione, diventa generatore della sequenza delle proprie ombre.* ■ *Il gioco tra istante e durata, tra evento e suo sviluppo, diventa complesso.* ■ *Il ritmo, che organizza la durata dell'evento, cattura per un tempo che si dilata e si accumula.* ■ *Questo muovere dall'astrazione di sistemi metrici e proporzionali, questa meticolosa costruzione di reti rapporti non coincidenti entro cui sono imbrigliati gli elementi materiali della costruzione – per approdare al flusso inesauribile delle sensazione da quelle reti di rapporti solamente previste – rappresenta l'avventura della costruzione: il progetto come piano di previsioni e l'universo frammentario e caotico di materiali da costruzione in attesa.* ■ *Tensione tra il progetto che aspira a dare ordine e la materia che vi resiste.* ■ *Il punto cruciale dell'impoverimento di molta architettura oggi è la voluta – talora paradigmatica – eliminazione di ogni slittamento, la collimazione tra geometria del disegno e geometria dei componenti materiali.* ■ *Ad un procedimento compositivo 'ad quadratum' – il quadrato quale figura dissimulata che genera una fioritura di rapporti – si sostituisce la stupidità della quadrettatura che regole epidermicamente tutti i componenti l'edificio.* ■ *Si privilegia una scelta banale capace solo di esplicare retoricamente la razionalità e la logica insite in un processo costruttivo.* ■ *Tutto si risolve e si esaurisce in una velocissima comprensione – in una repentina indifferenza.*

441

Architecture at Remdom;
The Blinkers that Make the Visionary

A Conversation with Rem Koolhaas

Rem Koolhaas, or rather, the continuously jetlagged avant-gardist. His image has always been that of an architect who is not entrenched in his own discipline but who uses architecture as a base to carry out raids on the whole culture. His work is a non-stop running commentary on *la condition contemporaine* and its impact both on architecture and on our ideas. His work is distinctly conceptual, and contains hidden intellectual depths. He is not afraid of reformulating a given project in terms of a strategy that undermines outworn conventions. His work is a stumbling block, literally and metaphorically. OMA is not a company that deals in amenities, but a place where the future of our culture is discussed. It seems almost incidental that architecture and city-planning are the media employed. With his inimitable mix of paradoxical statements and spectacular objects and images, Koolhaas is an architect who has transgressed the limits of his specialism and has made inroads into the realms of economy, philosophy and art. In 1990, for instance, he participated in the huge exhibition, *Energies*, in the Stedelijk Museum in Amsterdam. His competition entry for the Très Grande Bibliothèque in Paris was shown there alongside the work of artists such as Bruce Nauman and Anselm Kiefer.

Koolhaas is an architect who has often expressed his disgust at the self-imposed limitations of his colleagues. This attitude has made him a fruitful subject for social analysis. A group of intellectuals and other trendsetters feels increasingly at home in Koolhaas' work. We however can't resist asking whether there isn't a certain contradiction inherent in his work: everything about it suggests that it does not so much point to a new direction as to lead us to the pseudo-organised no man's land of the present-day megalopolis. Once Fredric Jameson described Koolhaas as suffering from the 'bladerunner syndrome' which he describes as:

'...the interfusion of crowds of people among a high technological bazaar with its multitudinal nodal points, all of this scaled into an inside without an outside, which thereby intensifies the formerly urban to the point of becoming the unmappable system of late capitalism itself: the abstract system and its interrelations are now the outside, the former dome, the former city, beyond which no subject position is available, so that it cannot be inspected as a thing in its own right, although it is a totality.'

It is clear that this architecture has a distinct psychopathological dimension. The city of the Fascinists has ceased to be a forum where public affairs can be debated; what it offers is the kick of a psychic dance on the edge of the abyss. Koolhaas' only objective to date, according to Jameson, has been 'to model what is no longer a public sphere or realm but rather a no man's land'.

Our heads must have been turned in another direction, because the very thing we wanted to talk to Koolhaas about was the importance of his approach for the public domain. We were interested to know what his almost cinematic atmospheres might mean to concrete human beings on the level of their concrete experience and above all what plans, hopes, ideas and critical potential an encounter with his work might generate. How do you escape the purely practical application of theoretical concepts? How do you prevent this adventure from only being interesting to the 'happy few' who possess both the critical distance and the liquid assets to get the chance to actually enjoy Koolhaas' hyperreality?

We tried to get Koolhaas to talk about these and other matters. It wasn't exactly a success. The author of *Delirious New York* and other manifestos is no longer with us. Language is not meant to clarify things but to make them more complicated. Koolhaas does not suffer from any shortage of words; they have, however, lost their innocence.

We'd like to begin with a couple of quotes from you. 'The world is nostalgic for the architect as philosopher'. And: 'The world is ripe for the architect as visionary (...) What we require is a programme of reconstruction for the mythology of the architect'. Architecture for you is above all 'petrified thought'. That is presumably the reason why you have no qualms about pouring ridicule on your colleagues' lack of vision and lazy-mindedness, and the fact that they so often judge your work on the basis of purely technical criteria. Does this make sense?

Ridicule? I never meant to sound so didactic. I think that part of our activity has to do with creating a sort of *Lebensraum*, a context in which we can do what we want or rather, to put it more modestly, what we are

capable of. As far as I am concerned, then, it has very little to do with some didactic need to give people a good ticking off. What does astonish me is that the things that are self-evident to us are not so for them.

All the same, after so many years of being astonished you should now be able to spot a number of examples of the Koolhaas recipe? I would have thought that you would gradually be beginning to see certain constants in the way that you and your approach are received.

It is very difficult for me to see any constants because we have changed so much ourselves. In recent years in particular we have actually landed up in a completely different world with the result that I lead a sort of double existence. I have one life in Holland and another abroad. Life in Holland is hard and abroad it is... certainly not easy but at least it is a completely different life. We also make different things abroad from what we make here. That means that people's responses are also different. The financial conditions under which one has to make architecture in Holland simply don't exist abroad in our experience; that also means that a number of criticisms that may be quite legitimate here, do not apply elsewhere. As far as use of materials and detailing are concerned, our block of flats in Fukuoka in Japan, for instance, is stunning in its perfection and everyone who has seen it so far as told us so. It even won the prize for the best building in Japan in 1992! I felt that the building should have something Japanese about it but that it also shouldn't be too beautiful. For that reason we opted for a very banal polyester/polystyrene matrix that was cast in black concrete; I calculated that they would come up with such perfection that that would be enough to give it some dignity. Conditions and possibilities of this order don't occur in Holland.

Nexus World, residential complex. Fukuoka, 1991.

To give you another example: I recently tried an experiment with the Byzantium building that we designed at the entrance of the Vondel Park in Amsterdam. I invited two foreign architecture critics, Klotz and Von Moos, who did not know who it was by. I asked them what they thought of it. They both thought it was an extremely interesting building. I've never managed to get a Dutch person to react that way, so you will have to put your question a little bit more precisely before I can really give you a proper answer.

Maybe there is a difference between the responses you get in Holland and elsewhere; what we are interested in, however, is the fact that you often criticise people for playing dumb about questions of historical conditions. You want to use architecture to renew a certain historical consciousness or, at any rate, to bring architecture up to date, to make it contemporary once more. This is, of course, an intellectual project that is way above the standard discussion in the trade in Holland at the moment; it revolves around a situation in which the whole Western world is involved. This constant 'updating' of architecture is in this sense also a sort of struggle against the refusal to know; it is a critique of the deliberate attempt to ignore the present historical situation.

I don't see it as a struggle against this negative attitude but as a professional operation that creates something like the wake of a ship but in reverse, something, that is, that opens up in front of you. Something that you yourself can use to operate practically in the theoretical space that is created. It is then a sort of communication about the status of our profession and about what themes are important, sometimes as an intuitive registering of things that will become important, that you can feel coming before you have encountered them in reality. This can be explained quite simply and banally by saying that you are someone who is on the lookout for these things and that that gives you the right to be active in the front line of architecture.

Do you imply by this that you are taking up an avant-garde position?

My approach has never been that of a guerrilla or a member of the avant-garde, if anything the opposite. *Delirious New York* (Oxford, 1978) is a 'retroactive' manifesto about what has happened and not about what has got to happen. What it actually dealt with was the possibilities, the relations between architects and power, without making any claim to be subversive. The front line is not exclusively the terrain of the avant-garde. It is not only the reformers who are active there but also the researchers. In *Delirious New York*, Manhattan was the Rosetta Stone and I was Champollion.

Is it really just an individual need to establish a position for yourself in the world of architecture, or is there more at stake? Are you in fact operating in a context where you are concerned not just with gaining a position as an individual, but where you also have to bring about a change that will be of benefit to architecture or have even wider implications? If that is the case, then you could well describe the critical activity involved as 'exposing to ridicule'.

I have a horror of the expression, that's all. But this feeling of horror is probably just a form of hypocrisy, because I can't bear to see myself as a sort of schoolmaster. It is true of course that it does have two aspects: on the one hand I am concerned with publicising our own work as individuals and as a firm of

444

architects and on the other hand with my capacity or need to make statements about what has taken place in architecture and about what will or could happen in this field in the future.

But do you mean in architecture itself, or do you think you need to be active outside architecture as well? Your work still seems to take what is utilitarian very much as its point of departure; it is very project-dependent and it tries to express an idea or an atmosphere that is inherent in the project. This means that you touch on matters that in themselves don't have any direct relation with architecture, that refer rather to other aspects of our culture.

We are totally dependent on the culture; that's exactly why it's so important that we make some kind of statement about it from an architectural point of view. I am writing a book about Tokyo, Paris and Atlanta at the moment. The book deals with the thesis that the only relation an architect can have with chaos is to take his rightful place in the army of those who struggle against it. It is through our *a priori* failure in that struggle, moreover, that chaos comes into being. This isn't something that you can deal with as though it were a matter of style or aesthetics. The book argues for a total review of the situation; I relate architecture to all kinds of developments: in politics, in culture and in economics. In any case I want to carry out an analysis of the sphere of influence in which architecture operates. Although it looks at present as though the context is the most important factor, it is the architecture in fact that remains the most important thing for me. I want to work out in detail the way that we can most effectively relate and respond to what is going on at the present moment.

But is your architecture only a neutral mirroring of the age or does that mirroring also imply criticism?

In everything that we do there is a critical layer. An operation such as we are carrying out in Lille (the Urban Plan for International Business Centre) is a thousand times more than just a neutral reflection. We are involved either in sending a large part of Europe to hell or else we are giving it a completely different character. The question then of whether or not what I do is to reflect what is going on becomes a bit academic. I myself have the feeling that it no longer has anything to do with reflecting what is going on. Existing possibilities and conditions have been assessed and interpreted so many times and have been subjected to so many different trends, some critical and others ecstatic, that you can't speak of being a mirror any more.

Is there a moment when this processing of existing conditions becomes 'fashion', or aren't you interested in that particular connection?

It is interesting to me only for my own count; the others can do what they like. For myself I always try to retain an element that is hard to assimilate. I can think of nothing worse than becoming really popular, being all the rage: we should always retain something that is difficult. On the other hand there is some very fashionable architecture that I find really attractive. I experience it as very difficult to pass any moral judgement. All I know is that I myself don't want to circulate effortlessly in those smooth circles; I need the sound of grinding cogwheels too.

You once described a very particular moment: the moment when you are allowed to do whatever you want coinciding with the moment that you can no longer think up anything. Does the fact that you are at present so preoccupied with that moment mean that it is rapidly approaching, or was it always a danger right from the beginning of your career?

I think that it is by definition a constant danger; one of the ways of exorcising that fear or danger is by carefully studying the career of other architects. How did your colleagues deal with it? Self-criticism and just keeping on one's toes also remain essential. Up till now I don't get the feeling that we've run out of ideas or that we have succumbed to the temptation of repeating ourselves. In one thing at least we have been successful: there is no predictable trend in our work.

Your social and cultural diagnosis makes your architecture a cultural medium of some significance; in the long term this is perhaps more important for the world than any purely architectural intuitions that in a specific place or at a specific time lead to certain design choices. The narrative element in your work is the diagnosis. Isn't that also the most essential element of your criticism in the long run?

As an architect I want to make one thing quite clear: it is very important not just to be an artist with language or a talented diagnostician. As far as that is concerned the block of flats in Japan, the Villa dall'Ava in Paris and the Media Centre in Karlsruhe are, in our view, unusually aggressive ventures that also give one an extremely good idea of the spectacular and spatial aspect of our work. I wouldn't like to say which of the two buildings I prefer. One of the great problems with what usually passes for criticism is that it is too one-sided. We are so ambitious that we want to do everything at once. And that immediately turns out to mean we can't do everything at once. No critic has succeeded in understanding this dialectic. Take for instance the problem of detailing; this is something that we are beginning to be reasonably good at. In fact we got a prize for the best building of 1992 with the Villa dall'Ava. It is also strategically important at a given moment to avoid being constantly carped at for reasons like that. But I would never criticise it in isolation as critics of architecture usually do.

You talk about the question of detailing as though it was the opposite pole to the general cultural signifi-cance of your diagnosis, but couldn't you imagine a brilliant theory of culture about an architecture that is not itself refined or polished and which rejects detailing as a sort of cultural prise de position?

Something resembling this theory does in fact exist, but it doesn't explain everything. In the Media Centre in Karlsruhe there are things that are pretty rough, but anyone can see that they are deliberately rough; they aren't just accidents. What we are doing is using a kind of failure in detailing as a sophisticated form of detailing. In the Danstheater in The Hague there are some details that come into that category, but others that don't. However that may be, I refuse to be identified with what is no more than one aspect of our work.

That's fair enough, but the diagnosis you are offering is of course the diagnosis of a situation where you can no longer identify with just one aspect of your work, if only to be able to continue to take yourself seri-ously.

That's quite true. What is involved is a permanent process of adaptation. It is a case of cultivating new forms of recalcitrance or difficulty.

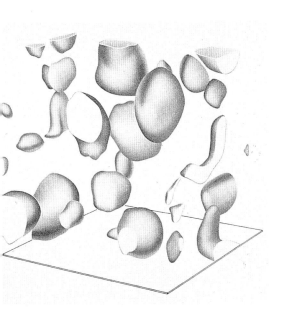

Superclusters and voids

Très Grande Bibliothèque, competition entry. Paris, 1989

But supposing we take spatiality and, by implication, the profession itself as our point of departure. You constantly stress that emptiness is more important than space, because as you once said: 'Where nothing exists everything is still possible, and where architecture exists almost nothing is possible any more'. For the outsider who is intrigued by your architecture but doesn't necessarily want to know about any problems you may have had of a technical-professional nature, the interesting thing is just that historical transforma-tion from space to emptiness that you have apparently made into your theme.

If you want to refer to the profession in general, I would rather talk in terms of going from volume to empti-ness. Some of the empty areas we have devised are exceptionally spatial, so I don't understand what you mean by 'transformation'. But go on please.

You seem in your work to address yourself more to a notion of an atopia than to the positive idea of space that the Modern architects wanted to break open to liberate a utopian energy where everyone could have their say in society. Emptiness as an architectural principle is of great cultural importance because it is a commentary on the positively interpreted space of the Moderns.

I think I've entered a new phase. I think that what you say is a good interpretation of our work but I see absolutely no reason for further comment on it. In any case I never conceived of it so precisely. It wasn't my intention to deliver a deliberately cynical attack on the idealism of the Modernist architects, by opposing their space with a notion of emptiness. In some respects what I was doing was much more banal and

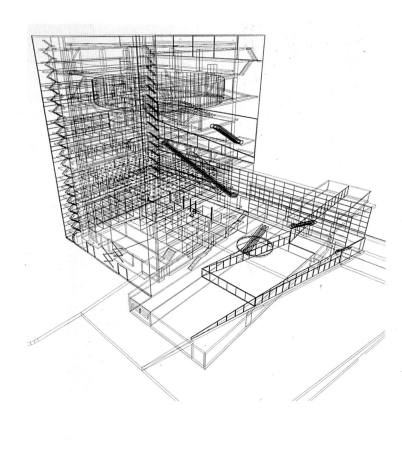

ZKM, Centre for Art and Media Technology, competition entry, Karlsruhe, 1989

Nexus World, residential complex, Fukuoka, 1991

Secciones transversales / Cross sections

literal. Everything that has been built has become increasingly unmanageable: for that reason if for none other the things that have not been built are of great importance.

Our interpretation is also based on your speech in the symposium on 'How modern is Dutch architecture?' ★ You gave a brilliant speech about Nietzsche and the Modern Movement, that had at least a latent intention of encouraging your audience to draw conclusions about the architectural element in it.

★ Published in Bernard Leupen et al., *Hoe modern is de Nederlandse architectuur?* Rotterdam, 1990, pp. 11-20.

I certainly don't want to give you the idea that I am an uncomplicated person; on the contrary, I am really interested in the moments when my articles cause a furore. But it is also exactly these moments when I'd rather have kept my mouth shut. There's nothing unusual about that, surely?

It's still a problem for us. As authors of this book the temptation to go deeper into that is irresistible. That's why we'd like to ask you what you think of the notion of the German historian of architecture, Michael Müller, who made a comparison between your architecture and the 'destructive character' of the modern to use Walter Benjamin's expression ★ Benjamin talks about the execrable Étui-Mensch; *with you it is more a case of holding people up to ridicule, or providing diagnoses or wanting to explode the present situation to which people continually respond by deliberately thinking up yet another reassuring answer.*

★ Michael Müller, 'Destruction and Deconstruction. Traditional Pathways in the Avant-garde'. In *The Production Book*; The Delft International Working Seminar on Critical Regionalism, Delft 1990.

Of course that's something I'm interested in. But some of my articles, such as the one in which I present the architect as philosopher and visionary are exaggeratedly rhetorical. That aspect of my work is based on a momentum in myself that I can hardly stop, an attitude that has something to do with my sort of intelligence. So it's definitely not something I think of as a personal message, but rather as a commentary on an incurable condition. I'm always looking for that sort of thing; I have a feeling for that sort of contradiction, that sort of sentimentality.

That's okay, but if someone in your audience takes you seriously and openly takes issue with you about it, you have to take some responsibility for that, surely. Do you really think that once you've done your performance, people can make of it what they like?

Maybe I feel dreadfully responsible; that's my business. But I don't feel that obliges me to orchestrate the verbal aftermath. It's been enough for me to have had a bit of fun saying things that have apparently stirred something up. One of the things that I regard as extremely questionable in the present-day architectural world is the notion of important people. You may be an important architect but that doesn't mean that you are an important person whose seal of approval is required for all kinds of things or whose opinions have some kind of hierarchical status.

We talked about bringing architecture up to date. Or rather about seeing that contemporary trends are actually incorporated into architecture as it is practised. One of the most typical features in that project is the confrontation you get with the people who want it to be 'easy' and don't look at contemporary developments that are anything but easy. You could say that architecture is an ideal medium for clearing the intellectual backlog; but you might also say that, from the point of view of its limits as a discipline, architecture is neither the only nor necessarily the best means for doing this.

I am once more, quote-unquote, seriously involved in writing. That is of course another means of expression. In the Centre Pompidou, where they now give the new media the same status as painting, there is a virtual reality project in progress. I'm taking part in it. Public appearances and teaching is in a sense a sort of sideshow. For the moment I don't get the feeling that I've hit my limits. On the contrary, I feel more and more enthusiasm for defining the territory myself. By the same token I could have been a writer and I think that that wouldn't have changed very much. For humanity, maybe, but not for myself.

But isn't the far-reaching specialisation that is typical of our society also a limitation? Or, rather, doesn't it lead to an illusion of freedom that this society creates and which makes it impossible to bring about any real changes any more?

Do you really think there is so much specialisation? All the people who try to get me to do something else, films for instance, I really have to brush them off like flies. For the time being at least it's my own limitations, my own caution that is the problem.

We meant something else by that. Have you never had the feeling with a commission, that another problematic ought to be playing more of a role than the one dictated by the project? Haven't you ever felt boxed in because you were called in as a specialist in design and your client never asked you to make any kind of statement about the social character of the project?

There is a correlation between the sort of commission you get and the kind of architect you are. I've noticed that particularly recently. Take for example the (cancelled) Media Museum in Karlsruhe where the definition of the commission was one of the most essential parts of the design. The same goes for domestic architecture. With the housing project in Fukuoka that I just mentioned I was almost given *carte-blanche* to do what I liked. For the time being then I really can't say that I am limited in what I am allowed to do; and I won't use other people's limitations as an alibi for any limits in my own content.

So, it's not architecture that's the problem, but your own limitations. If the occasion arose, could those people whom you once talked about hypothetically as being potential visionaries, also succeed in being so in the realm of architecture? Does architecture really allow one the space to be visionary?

I certainly think so. **At the present time architecture has an enormous potential for influencing the course of culture.** But perhaps that opportunity will only be there for a moment. Perhaps it's just a small opening that will last about four years. I'm not going to make any predictions about that.

Can you give an example of a work of architecture having had a decisive impact?

It depends what you mean by decisive. I can imagine that a building like the Media Museum in Karlsruhe might have had that sort of impact on the classical idea of the museum; that the new media may be able to bring about a sort of redefinition of what architecture actually is. One of the temptations with that project was to make as great a use of the media as possible, but in the end that was of course somewhat naive because the media themselves are exposed to a sort of ongoing process of change; and for precisely that reason they need a sort of crude skeleton for them to remain viable themselves. I also have the illusion that something like that can happen in Lille. Perhaps it doesn't amount to a revolution in European culture, but it is certainly a decisive intervention in Northern Europe.

The question of course is which came first. Isn't it rather a case of architecture being called in to give a helping hand during a certain period of historical transition?

Yes, of course! But then I never claimed to be the first in the field. On the contrary. In the seventies and eighties the situation was so arid that we all went round with a host of ideas that nobody wanted; we were like lovers who had been rejected. The situation is more exciting now and possibly more dangerous. In contrast with the previous decade, I get the feeling that we are now actually being called on to give some kind of coherence to a number of operations that are under way. These operations are by no means unambiguous, but at the same time it is clear as daylight that a movement is going on that is wider than architecture alone.

But even if you come second, you claim that your influence is decisive. But what proof is there for that? Is it an influence on space or the debate about space or on the iconography of buildings...?

On everything in a way. If Lille turns out to be a success, then it will above all be as an irrefutable proof of Virilio's propositions, that distance doesn't exist any longer and that everything has turned into time and speed. This means that a number of things are eliminated and that a number of other things become prominent. I believe that this is the direction we are heading in. The spatial dimension will in this case therefore have to be interpreted as making a sort of commentary on our time and I also hope that a sort of equivalent iconographical expression will emerge.

A number of your colleagues have appropriated that iconography in advance without taking any account of what you call the impact on our time. The reputation of your oeuvre is based on its design vocabulary. Even though one would think this iconography was a good expression of a certain attitude towards all these rapid changes, there seems to be a rather 'Beaux-Arts' response to this iconography. What do you think of that? That hardly suggests that it is having a decisive influence on what's going on?

We are not interested in being original and I am trying to get the firm to give up its habit of looking at things that way. We know that in a lot of ways we are not particularly original. Luckily that realisation has so far always helped me to avoid making the mistakes of others.

For the rest, I agree completely with your comment. As far as that is concerned, France is at present a very good example because their whole idea of what is modern is completely conservative and reactionary. Instead of symmetry they now give us asymmetry; instead of the classical materials everything is now transparent and made of steel and glass. It is actually extremely vulgar. In fact I think that you can also say that about the Institut du Monde Arabe, even though it is an absolutely fascinating building, even including the fact that it is so absurd. That wall with the diaphragms is really crazy and that makes it a sublime success, but if one thinks about it, its impact on the city is rubbishy. I really admire that building, yet there is nothing dynamic or modern about it, even though that's exactly the feeling it was supposed to convey.

It is important to realise that inherent in every project is an upper level of what you can achieve with it. With the Media Museum in Karlsruhe, for instance, where that level is very high, we were for the first time able

449

Villa dall'Ava, Saint Cloud, Paris, 1991

Kunsthal, centre of temporary exhibitions, Rotterdam, 1992

Urban plan for Business International Centre, Lille, 1994

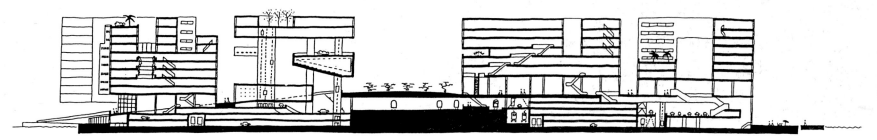

OMA, Van Berkel & Bos, Christiaanse, Neutelings, West 8 and Light, Masterplan Amsterdam Waterfront, 1992

Convention and exhibition centre, Lille 1994

to identify 100% with the aims of the commission. That is also a sign that the culture is pressurising architecture to come up with things that are new. In *Delirious New York* the question was still how conscious or unconscious an architect had to be to ride the waves of modernity like a surfer. The thing that was really brilliant about the first generation of New York architects is that they were extremely intelligent while still managing to avoid being so self-aware that they had to automatically distance themselves from their own self-awareness. They preserved an artificially maintained innocence.

Most masterworks have been a result of this combination of intelligence and innocence. They embodied a collective ideal while at the same time managing to provide a distanced commentary on it; they enabled the aspirations of the collective to coincide effortlessly with those of their client. I had the idea that this was something we would never see again. That we were condemned to consciousness. The remarkable thing is that in our recent projects we have the idea that this innocence can return again. That this total identification has again become possible. Only in this way can architecture also be more than an illustration and succeed in inspiring a cultural movement instead of merely commenting on one.

When is someone too conscious to be capable of doing anything?

You can always do *something*, of course. Even someone as hyperconscious as Eisenman still does something. But in some cases we notice that we are much less committed and this means that a more cynical building is erected than in cases where our commitment was more genuine. In the first half of the eighties we were tending much more in that direction; that's why it's such a good thing that we have regained a certain innocence. Recently **interviews have also become a problem for me because they force you to speak in terms of complex motivations that are in some respects of minimal importance to me right now.** I'm not so naive that I think that if you know what motivates you immediately lose it. That was the classical reason why people refused to see a psychiatrist: that you would no longer be creative if you did so. At the present time however it is very important for all of us to insist on the rights of our unconscious. Part of these rights involve a reserve about explaining all our motivations.

That could make it difficult for us to continue this interview.

Just carry on. Look, I think it is certainly interesting for you to ask me what my motives are but I don't think it is interesting for me to answer you. Tomorrow if I feel like it, I defend my right to be interested in space and space alone and to build an extremely reactionary building. That could even be an incredible challenge.

Are you waiting till the programme fits in with that, or should every programme fit?

Perhaps the end result will sometime even have to go completely against the project. I don't want to discount any possibility. Currently there is in any case a tendency towards behaving recalcitrantly or at least people have a sense of the importance of being difficult, something that expresses itself in an inexplicable discrepancy in statements. It can of course be a very good thing if at a certain moment we say that speed is totally unimportant or if we punctuate that speed with something that doesn't go past in a flash.

In other words your themes may change but your recalcitrance marches on? My question then is: why?

To stay innocent?

No, definitely not. One of the things that interests me in a way that is almost literary is how the career of the average architect looks. I am extremely fascinated and spend a lot of time trying to understand how someone like Meier or Isozaki function, and how it is that some people have nothing more to say while others are doing new things all the time. For that matter it's no more than a kind of curiosity that has everything to do with my own self-interest.

Isn't it almost a fear of becoming old-fashioned?

No, not at all. There is a well-known drawing that shows the correlation between one's creativity and one's portfolio of commissions.

An awful lot of people operate in the execrable right-hand area. Maybe it is a great pleasure to operate there but in any case it is not particularly respectable. This recalcitrance and unwillingness to be pinned down have a lot to do with this. Tactical considerations are very important for me. There are a lot of things about running a firm with forty people that are of course anything but pleasant. That means that in one way or another I have to get some kind of pleasure out of life.

Learning lessons from the careers of others, however, is a bit of a long way round; you can hardly call it an inner necessity. You are not only conscious of your own position, but also of the way others have managed to escape falling into traps. Isn't the appeal to allow room for the unconscious and to put innocence back on the stage, particularly strong in your case just because you are already all too aware of a similar switch in your own career?

Correlation between one's creativity and one's portfolio of commissions.

Creativity / Commissions / Repetition / Difference / Time →

I don't believe its possible to be 'all too aware'. In my opinion you can never be conscious enough, but let's say for the sake of argument that there needs to be another source of inspiration parallel to the conscious one. Perhaps it is a naive illusion that these are a sort of communicating vessels; that the more that consciousness increases, the less there remains for the unconscious. It could be the case that when the one increases, the other does so too. It is at any rate very important for you to keep on working and not to get bogged down in endless ruminations. That almost always ends up in gloomy generalisations. I have an enormous dislike of all the prophesies of the merchants of doom; I refuse to join in the forecasts of disaster that have for so long now been a sort of signature tune for intellectuals analysing society. I get the feeling that it leads to an enormous blindness. The simple fact that the apocalypse continually fails to show up becomes problematic for thinkers like Virilio. At a certain point anxiety becomes an end in itself. I think it is just as rewarding if one postpones one's apocalyptic view of life – a tendency I also have latently – for as long as possible.

And what do you think of the reaction of people like Siza, Ando and Frampton in his critical writings who fall back on the notion of the 'tactile'. What do you think of Siza when he says: 'If the world is speeding up I respond by deliberately making peaceful-looking buildings and I put the materials first'?

The Villa dall'Ava in Paris is also tactile and very physical just because it is a house. What I mean is that with regards to the body the relation is so undeniable and self-evident that tactility is almost inevitable. I also feel a great deal of sympathy with that attitude. But if you look carefully at these people you will notice a sort of speeding-up right now; Ando and Hertzberger, for instance, are adapting their own sobriety to a sort of mobility. The curious thing about Ando is that the less you see of Ando, the more impressive he is, and the more you see of him, the more it strikes you that he employs the same aesthetic regardless of the project involved – a boutique, a sort of Zen Buddhist monastery, a Protestant church or a dwelling. I hardly need to say that at a certain point it becomes hard to take him seriously.

But don't you think that a certain commitment is beginning to develop that this architecture is also a part of? Or do you think that is also just a passing fashion?

The tactility of his work is undeniable and it is everywhere, even in his most streamlined and so least tangible design. That's the first point. I also think that in a number of his projects it has a lot to do with his frustration about scale. There are any number of good architects who work on a scale that is too small, especially in America. That leads to an obsession with tactility or with the craft. The tactile is given a preference and attention that is completely one-sided. Someone like Holl, as soon as he gets to make a public building or something large-scale, I think he'll turn out to be completely different. It is a phenomenon that is easily explained; it's almost sociological. Or take Morphosis, those people are involved with an obsession that is quite ridiculous, but that has to do quite simply with the scale of their megalomania; I mean they are megalomaniacs, but are condemned to realise their megalomania in minimal projects.

What about your own sense of commitment?

I thought the library in Paris was an interesting project in that it showed that there is something really quite important that still remains: that is, a large collective space where (as far as that goes 'shelter' isn't the right word) fragmented humanity at any rate now and then for specific reasons can reconstitute itself; that a process of reuniting of a collective population, a regrouping can take place.

But is that still collective? Is that space not just a symbol of the impossibility of forming a new collective? Is the fact that a project of this sort is included in an exhibition with a neutral name such as Energies (Amsterdam Stedelijk Museum, 1990) not in itself, to say the least, indicative of this anonymysing and decollectivising tendency? A certain abstraction is introduced that is subversive of collectivity in all its aspects.

It is more an answer to the question of what collectivity means now. Or of how you might be able once again to give form to the collective. I think that the word collective is very applicable to it. I think that at the moment one question is particularly relevant: in the light of the dissolution of matter, the disappearance of the need for centralisation, what roles of architecture are in any case made redundant? Apparently some of the roles remain relevant, if only through the fact that we ourselves continue to exist. That is another meaning for the collective value of our architecture: to investigate and determine the implications of our profession for the present moment in our culture.

We are beginning to run out of steam...

I know what you mean. Have some more coffee.

The Invisible in Architecture could be conceived as representation. Perhaps this seems self-contradictory: representation is the externalisation of an 'underlying' meaning and as such is eminently visible. But representation is also the process by which meaning comes about. The causes and mechanisms of this process are nowhere near as visible.

The lesser visibility is in no small part due to today's plethora of representation. We live in a time in which representation predominates over presence. People and things seem to be changing more and more into clones from the production lines of the representation industry. Our actions, too, the meeting of persons and things, make way for a surrogate encounter in the domain of representation. True, the technology of representation gives us access to the whole world, but it never lets us intervene. We can say what we like, but nobody hears us. It is as though the world were becoming ever more visible, while our potential for intervention in social and historical conditions is vanishing over the horizon.

In this situation, the sign no longer represents reality. Representation slides into simulation. It becomes a self-referring sign system, as though it were reality itself. It is true that this receives some discussion in the media, but the commodity structure of reality is generally unimpaired. The media do not so much unmask this kind of structure as put it into practice. There are a few people who react against this situation and turn away from the domination of representation, seeking a wealth of experience that escapes the hegemony of the image. They appeal to the three-dimensional experience of space and substance, often suggesting that representation is the very opposite of a physical experience. But image and reality are hard to sunder, for 'reality' is inevitably an image too.

As soon as we speak of representation, we speak of politics in the same breath. Systems of representation are a territory in which countless social interests compete. To a certain extent, it is these systems that generate reality. For that reason alone, it

454 Representation

is vital to investigate both the interface between the political and the personal in daily life, and the place occupied in this interface by the image. Only when this is clarified will it become possible to devise strategies by which people can relate to these systems – or, if they wish, try to escape them by means of artistic manoeuvres.

Representation is not neutral, nor has it ever been. The problem is that we are now more aware of this than ever before. The link between the word and the thing, between the sign and its reference, which was once regarded as a natural phenomenon, now exists only as an arbitrary consensus. Once there was a strong association among the sign system, the meaning and the action, but the connection has now become utterly tenuous. The system of signs has become self-referent, and those who attempt to trace meanings by philosophical, psychoanalytical or semiotic means invariably find themselves faced with yet another set of signs. In this process of endless semiosis, motives for action eventually disappear altogether. (We may note here that the Left, the traditional holder of the patent on historic breakthroughs, has, in focusing its attention on the sign system, shed its time-honoured catalytic role.)

The disengagement of *signifiant* and *signifié* is the final stage of the triumphant march of nominalism. While for the one this decoupling may be a licence for untrammelled pragmatism, for another it means a ceaseless grappling with a loss of purpose. Representation is recognised as the problem at the heart of the matter, and this has inevitably spurred people to theorise about its rise and fall – from divine presence, to presentation, to representation, to simulation, to virtual reality, to morrow.

Our shift of attention from the action to the sign erodes the debate on the ideological and disciplinary mechanisms that drive us. We thus find ourselves in a paradoxical situation in which the media flood us with information, while the public domain in

which we can act on this information has practically vanished. To put it another way, the moment the system of representation seems to be working at its best (to judge by its profuseness) its social effect diminishes to zero. Representation, in as far as this word fairly expresses the process of obfuscation, has turned against itself. The emancipatory effect of freedom of opinion has degenerated into a cacophony in which everyone is occupied with his own problems instead of with a public concern. In short, the free availability of information has overshot its mark as a social precondition and can scarcely still claim credit for actions that genuinely lead to the improvement of society. To the extent that changes are achieved, they look much more like the outcome of non-public mechanisms, of decisions on private matters in which only a few people are involved. Moreover, those few are often so tied by the system, that the changes they decide upon are more affirmative than subversive. A public arena of this calibre can scarcely be a source of momentum. The ideal of representative transparency has veered around to become a dead public space.

When criticism of the Modern Movement began making itself heard in architecture, interest grew in the problem of representation. Representation even emerged as a key concept of this criticism. In the eyes of many, modern architecture had fallen short in meeting mankind's need for a visible meaning. Its bareness, its blankness and transparency represented only such abstractions as a Better World, Hygiene, Rationality and the like. Hence this architecture failed to mirror a far more complex lifeworld. In as far as Post-Modernism aimed to introduce change into this situation, solutions were sought principally in the area of representation.

Simultaneously, however, this Post-Modernism also broke through in philosophy. Post-Structuralism established the precise impossibility of such compensatory programmes to establish purpose. Some saw it as impossible simply to disregard, in the visual sphere, this crisis of meaning in the philosophical sphere. Thus, within architecture, there arose a tendency that aimed to represent the problem of meaning itself: for even a problem can be a source of inspiration.

Be that as it may, with respect to the two major tendencies of Post-Modernism in architecture, namely historicism and deconstructivism, it is the representation not *in* but of architecture that has burgeoned so enormously. The architectural press has won a completely independent status and makes buildings not only into commodities but into reproducible concepts that receive world-wide discussion. Architects, in principle the makers of buildings, have consequently acquired the status of talk-show celebrities. They live increasingly as ambassadors of the representation industry, leaving less and less time for the actual making. The actual makers stay behind at the office: they are the 'assistants'.

It was a matter of course that there would be a reaction to this dematerialisation of the architectural object. Accordingly, regular pleas are to be heard for an architecture that seeks a way out of this scenography, one that concentrates solely on its own *presence*. We are referring to a movement that aims to react against the prevalent simulation of a reality which, if we do ever experience it as it really is, turns out to be a falsehood. Hence the revival of interest in the building *an sich*, its reality, construction and sacrifices to gravity. It was inevitable: some people have become allergic to signs.

What links the above three approaches is the marginalisation of architecture to a speciality of form. Concern for representation did not grow only out of a critical standpoint towards the modern, but also out of restriction of the craft to purely outward matters. The architect has been driven further and further from the rooms where the programme, the action, is decided. Thus he is increasingly forced to restrict himself to the packaging. The stress on representation is thus also an inevitable consequence of a loss. The architect who hopes to stimulate speculation on the content finds his room for manoeuvre limited to just a few aspects of a building, of which the main ones are the circulation routes and, above all, the façade. This restriction has resulted in a superfluity of expressiveness within a paltry domain. And, what is more, that little domain has been absorbed into the society of the spectacle. Doubtless this is why the sublime, that elevated, unrepresentable aesthetic moment that only a Great Artist could achieve, is staged so often.

Three strategies and three architects Representation is an unavoidable subject for contemporary architecture. Meaning has proved to be a process, and if you do something then you influence only the operation of this process, not the cause. In this connection, we once again distinguish three strategies.

Archaism
Archaism aims to resist the media-cultivated perversion of the 'unrepresentable'. It strategy is a pursuit of authenticity. It tries to distance itself from a modernisation process that has come to show features of pure simulation and that has long lost its élan of progress. Thus this tendency seeks its salvation especially in the landscape elements that are not yet contaminated by the virus of civilisation, and also in the 'eternal laws' of construction, foundation, gravity and materiality. The eye is not consoled with beautiful images, but is itself obliged to become sensitive. The image that this generates (some kind of image is unavoidable, alas) is generally bare and sober. Naturally, there really is a representational strategy at work here: the image can only express the wish not to be an image by virtue of being an image. There is no way to avoid getting your hands dirty with the mud of representation. **Jacques Herzog and Pierre de Meuron** balance delicately on the horns of this dilemma. Their buildings, to put it paradoxically, glow with tactile sobriety. It cannot be denied that, as well as images, they are things. But they are remarkably articulate things: they announce their speechlessness with much emphasis. They simulate immediacy and illustrate the iconophobia of the image addict. The architects are exhilarated by impossibilities such as these.

Façadism
The architecture of façadism behaves as though it reflects no values other than those it *aims* to reflect. It is intent on a limpid, honest and democratic communication, which is accessible to everybody. The unrepresentable is not seen as a possible subject, for signs make the world go round. This approach comes out principally in the treatment of the exterior of the building, but as an attitude it can also be detected in the programming and even in the way the psychological experiencing of the programme is staged. This always involves the consumption of conventional meanings, without problems and without questions. For **Michael Graves,** this approach comes mainly down to a literal surface treatment, directed at the application of striking iconography and ornament. In Graves, architecture has become monumental entertainment, comprehensible to one and all. If 'comprehensibility' has become the main positive criterion in a complex world, then Graves is one big success.

Fascinism
Fascinism is in its element with the semiotic alienation of sign and content. Within this tendency, meanings are never adopted as a way of conveying knowledge but are stripped of their referent and are staged again as signs. The world is a grotesque meaning process in which you let yourself be dragged along in total fascination. The system of representation is an accepted fatality. The individual is no longer in a position to change anything, for we find ourselves after all in an endless chain of representations of representations of... Ultimately, no meaning is definite, and there is no criterion on which a criticism could be based. **Itsuko Hasegawa** shows how far the category that, seen historically, preceded the present condition – the state of nature – has been assimilated into this process. This is not an ecological criticism that attempts defensively to rescue whatever is left of the wreckage, but an explicit display of the representation of nature as a fully-fledged substitute for nature. Nature as sample.

The ING Bank presents itself as a diverse, innovative and quality-oriented financial institution. This is also reflected in our design of the head office.
Ton Alberts & Max van Huut

A wall that has been drawn on becomes a signboard and is robbed of its material significance. In becoming a sign, it loses its presence. **Tadao Ando**

In order to conceive an architecture, we talk about temples, columns, triumphal arches, archetypes and also rocks and icebergs.
What we represent is what you represent yourselves. **Ricardo Bofill**

In launching the shipshape we were also experimenting with the hyperactivity of architectural media in disseminating the latest form. It was a catchy name and a catchy shape, and we wanted to see how quickly it would be taken up by the architectural world. In this sense I view the experiment as an unprecedented success. More than ever I believe that Function follows Form.
Julia Bolles & Peter Wilson

Drawing and architecture are two different things. Architecture is a phenomenon in itself. It comes more from the world of ideas directly applied to the materials used in building. Graphics intervene: they have now become almost a hindrance.
Santiago Calatrava

Television is the new measure of our perceptions.
Nigel Coates & Doug Branson

Representation is a 'fragment of being' which speaks of ancient, secret rapports with the world, but which wants to reconcile itself with the world, wants to be understood by the world. Representation does not refer to another meaning, but is itself the meaning of this expectation. **Pietro Derossi**

It is common practice to try to retrieve experience in drawing, to return a semblance of the third dimension, to embody the quality of light and the anticipation of the material, to suggest the presence of time and movement. We are attempting the reverse; to absorb notational principles directly into the architectural project... **Elisabeth Diller & Ricardo Scofidio**

The very core of the set problems and the way they are resolved will largely generate style. **Norman Foster**

The blind walls of the Joan Miró Library give the character and imagery of library, while at the same time supporting the stacks where the books are kept. On the outside, rows of cypress trees form green walls which border the lake and thicken between the waterfalls. These cypresses can be seen as a replica and natural extension, in vegetation, of the stone wall system. **Beth Galí**

Gehry talking to his neighbours: What about your boat in the backyard? What about your camper truck? It is the same material. It is the same aesthetic They say, 'Oh, no, no, that's normal'. I am always surprised that other people don't see it.
Frank Gehry

The idea of decoration on a wall – it's pure invention; we don't have to have it in a pragmatic sense. But it might be said that our lives would not be terribly rich without it in a symbolic sense. *Michael Graves*

The highly confident and flourishing arguments from the point of view of production for production's sake have called into being the aspects of over-consumption and homogeneity. In order for modern architecture to break through and run past these undesirable aspects to face the next stage, it is thought we must depend even more on information technology to enlarge our imaginations by planning on some kind of 'science fiction' connection of the classical human brain to the peripherals of the 'digital-thinking circuits' called the computer. It is important to bring a fresh impetus to this kind of media environment by continuing to paint universal dreams through architecture.
Itsuko Hasegawa

What else can we do but carry within us all these images of the city, of pre-existing architecture and building forms and building materials, the smell of asphalt and car exhaust and rain and to use our pre-existing reality as a starting point and to build our architecture in pictorial analogies? The utilisation of these, their dissection and recomposition into an architectural reality, is a central theme in our work. **Jacques Herzog & Pierre de Meuron**

Writing's relation to architecture affords only an uncertain mirror to be held up to evidence; it is rather in a wordless silence that we have the best chance to stumble into that zone comprised of space, light, and matter that is architecture. Although they fall short of architectural evidence, words present a premise. The work is forced to carry over when words themselves cannot. Words are arrows pointing in the right directions; taken together they form a map of architectural intentions. **Steven Holl**

Architecture is a medium for communication.
Hans Hollein

Classicism really transcends the limits of any political period or tenancy. And that is why you can revive it – because it is completely independent of political expression.
Leon Krier

In our urban district renovation projects, I deliberately chose to represent a kind of pedestrian civilisation – one which might have prevailed in a peaceful way, without (or in opposition to) the whole superimposed mass of technology, regimenters, subjugators, authorities etc. Naturally, this is just a metaphor, but I make no secret of my feelings about it towards clients and authorities. **Lucien Kroll**

Architecture and urban planning must serve to facilitate not only function, but meaning too. Clusters of signifiers divorced from meaning now produce 'simulacres' of meaning or pseudo-meanings, which colour and humanise spaces with humour, wit, speculation, and conviviality. The metamorphosis of free-floating signifiers and 'simulacres' creates realms of 'atmosphere' or 'mood'. These poetic spaces open up not through the recombination of signs, but in stretching ambiguities to the very periphery of sign systems, to the ambivalent interplay of diverse 'simulacres'. **Kisho Kurokawa**

Here in the West you see that a lot of people have nothing to go by and seek salvation in formalist solutions. This is reinforced by the architectural journals. You don't need architectural journals at all. They can help a little, but they also distract you from your own route. First you have to look inside and develop what you have in your body and soul.
Lucien Lafour & Rikkert Wijk

True architectural drawings, and those may be rather incomprehensible or more difficult to read, don't have the codes of convention built into them. Let's say, the drawings that are not part of the presentation process are the most interesting because they are not 'present'. **Daniel Libeskind**

The work alludes to Roman architecture, but naturally it isn't Roman. However, the authenticity of the image is kept by the reality of the construction. This building is probably not far from what Roman architects would have done... I tried to go about making a Roman architecture in a direct and real way, not by means of representation but by means of strict reality. And for me the problem of realism is connected to construction, to the logic of building itself. It is one of the issues in which I am most interested.
Rafael Moneo

Any analysis ('deconstruction') of the material of architecture may be performed through its documentation rather than through the material itself. As opposed to plans, maps or axonometrics, the perspectival description of existing buildings is concomitant with their photographic record; the photograph can then act as the origin of the architectural image. The perspectival image is no longer a mode of three-dimensional drawing, but the direct extension of modern photographic perception. **Bernard Tschumi**

We have said many times that allusion in our work is achieved not through reproduction but through representation. The fake should be easily visible, no more than half an inch deep, and you should sense the shed behind the decoration.
The façade is, where outside and inside meet and where, metaphorically, public and private collide and the community and the individual negotiate. This 'in between realm' of Aldo Van Eyck is the locus for decoration and representation and carries the larger freight of symbolism, being between and part of two aspects of the building. In our work, we both set up this façade and erode it, taking the outside through it, the street through the building. Metaphorically, the highway has gone through our lives and therefore through our architecture. We will never be the same again. The façade is broken; what remains is representation and a thin glass skin to help condition the inner air.
Robert Venturi & Denise Scott Brown

Reculer pour Mieux Sauter?

The buildings of Jacques Herzog and Pierre de Meuron do not have the kind of looks you immediately fall in love with. They are too stodgy, impersonal, too Kafkaesque for that. Especially in their residential designs, these architects have devoted themselves to a formal typology that is more reminiscent of utility architecture, barracks perhaps, than of the fresh-faced stock-in-trade of today's prefab merchants. The overall image, at least as it reaches the world in printed reproduction, is monochromatic and repetitious. Still, if we persist in looking a little beyond the first impression, an expressive texture begins to emerge. These designers know perfectly well what the real meaning of form and material can be. The emphatically tactile quality of their architecture makes it immediately clear that the attribution of meaning is no mere accident. On the contrary, tactility, which is usually meant to reach the observer's brain stem directly through the sense of touch, here makes a detour via the most sophisticated regions of the intelligence. The tactilism has become an artistic form of *representation*.

Architecture Between Jean-Paul Marat and JFK

According to the makers of this sober, alienating architecture, their childhood memories from the fifties play an important role. But, they claim, their work also has within it a concealed 'potential for enlightenment' (*Aufklärerisches Moment*). This assertion contrasts oddly with the fifties air of despondency that the buildings do in fact have at first sight.

Sometimes it looks as though what the eighteenth century was to world history as a whole, the fifties are to this century: a period in which a historical and moral breakthrough was coupled to an abysmal deception about what mankind was capable of. The Enlightenment brought forth the emancipation of the bourgeoisie, of the individual and of reason. Common law made way for a mature statutory system, and knowledge gained precedence over faith and superstition. The guilds system and slavery were

abolished and the free market won a definitive place as the guiding principle of economy. At the same time, however, the foundations were laid for an antithesis. Without people fully realising it at the time, the invention of anthropology, of the concept of History, of the Self and its shadow, of utilitarianism, of style and of sexuality as a human 'attribute', later provoked the greatest doubts about the Enlightenment project. In the latter days of the French Revolution, with the death of Marat and the ascendancy of *la Terreur* as a political tool, disillusion was already widespread.

The nineteen-fifties show much the same dialectical pattern. Most of those who lived through the liberation of Europe thought that the war had ended not only militarily but also morally in 1945: that it was time for reconstruction and for a major breakthrough in a culture that was still rooted in the pre-war political caste system. But the war was not over. There was a feverish spate of building, and the world began to regain its old reassuring solidity, but it became apparent that a certain point had been passed during the war, after which courage, optimism and the will to start afresh no longer had any meaning. The baby boom cut its teeth to the accompaniment of clattering pile drivers and moral disillusion – a situation that culminated in 22 November 1963. The assassination of Kennedy, the Marat of the twentieth century, shocked the progressive tendencies of the West. The obfuscation and sense of cover-up around Lee Harvey Oswald were symptomatic of the prevailing condition – the institutionalisation of false optimism. We are not naive out of free will, but we are kept naive. Keep smiling, life goes on even if it has no obvious purpose. *Huis Clos*. Neither Mankind nor Future nor History nor the *Prinzip Hoffnung* retains any vitality. Instead, we are confronted with the theatre of Samuel Beckett, Albert Camus, Harold Pinter, John Osborne. And, of course, Jean Paul Sartre.

Jacques Herzog and Pierre de Meuron, two boys who were mangled by the dialectics of their own fifties Enlightenment, who even in neutral, perfidious Switzerland must

Thomas Ruff, House no. 12, 1989

House for an art collector, Therwil, 1986

What is the architecture that we seek, that we rush to meet? The architecture that urges and motivates us, that wants to be discovered, taken out of its hiding-place in our architectural consciousness, or rather our unconscious? What architecture, compelled like an insect to light, fulfils its inevitable fate? Why this architecture and not another although an endless number of other possibilities exists? The architecture for which we battle, which we attempt to define as a stance, which we let be defined by friendly, hired or volunteer critics so that this architecture, now a stance, can be defended against other stances, built up from the inexhaustible multitude of other forms, other masses, other surfaces, other static systems and other transparencies.

Jacques Herzog & Pierre De Meuron

Like all people alive today, we experience of course the ruptures in our cultures, i.e. the impossibility to define things clearly. We too face this non-monolithicness which surrounds all subjects; it becomes the central motive of our work. We can't rely on anything: neither on an existing mode of building, nor on any tradition, since these things actually rendered useless. Concerning architecture, even the architecture of the fifties and sixties already turned historical. We can't stake them as images. Technology at large has developed far beyond that point, so that a direct application leads to unsatisfying results.

Jacques Herzog

Herzog & de Meuron are not keen on telling their own story, neither do they want to tell stories at large. What they are trying to do is find images that appear just as they do when we zap between television programmes, to apply them to buildings that tell their own stories and act as suggestive supports and catalysers for so many other personal stories.

Marianne Brausch

The fundamental event of the modern age is the conquest of the world as a picture (*Weltbild*). The word picture (*Bild*) now means the structured image (*Gebild*) that is the creature of man's producing which represents and sets before. In such producing, man contends for the position in which he can be that particular being who gives measure and draws up the guidelines for everything that is.

Martin Heidegger

Cultural Centre, Blois, competition entry, 1991

have gaped at a world full of people with rolled-up sleeves but without the appurtenant resolute eye fixed on the horizon, are now themselves builders. And part of that personal past now returns in a heightened form. For Herzog and De Meuron, tradition has lost its relevance and no single architectural form has an eternal validity. Memory goes back only as far as your own life-span, they argue, and everything before that is hearsay. And even your own early memories must be treated with an appropriate distance. Accordingly, these architects make conscious use of their personal history and remain ostensibly unfeeling towards any inclusive, optimistic view of life.

Yet in their negative, almost dehumanised formal vocabulary, there remains something irreducibly utopian. Theodor Adorno (with Max Horkheimer), although acutely aware of the contradictions of the Enlightenment, was not immediately prepared to abandon a critical theory with emancipatory intentions. Similarly Herzog and de Meuron, despite their 'negative' architecture, appeal to our powers of imagination to envisage something other than the mediocrity that leers at us in its barely distinguishable gradations all around the world. But what is that Other, and how do they make that appeal?

Negative Dialectics

One thing becomes clear in a confrontation with this subdued architecture, which seems so familiar yet at the same time so alien and remote. The Other, the suggestion that this work puts out, remains nameless and is never expressed as an image. If you look carefully at the contrived poverty of certain details while bearing in mind the craftsmanship betrayed by certain others, you may conclude that a deliberate strategy of anti-mimesis is in action, one that is fed by a heavily repressed iconophobia. The interior barely seems to have any importance attached to it and bears the stamp of the current standardised productivism that is so successful in that area. But neither does the exterior compensate for this restraint. The images generated by this architecture are of an unprecedented sobriety, yet at the same time they practically succumb under the weight of their doom-laden message. In the bunker-like – or should we say prison-

camp-like – façades of their 'garden suburb' in Vienna-Aspern, they mask their deeply-felt sense of a stylistic and historical endgame with an architectural poker face. This architecture, with its high windows, its blind walls, its turret-like cantilevers, its bare simplicity and its sinister loneliness suggests a moral, a purpose. But this purpose is never expressed directly in the form of imagery. Only 'negative dialectics' (to use Adorno's term) are allowed to operate. A better world can, it seems, only be achieved by forming a conception of what it should NOT be like. The *promesse de bonheur* is to be found only in its opposite, absolute desolation. ★ Adorno, Theodor, *Aesthetic Theory*, London 1986, p. 161.

As Adorno wrote, 'Dissonance is the truth about harmony.'★ Or, to put it more strongly, this is the architecture of the Second Commandment. It is permissible to evoke the hallowed Other only by negation. 'The utopian is not even conceivable in positive form, for no image is powerful enough to illustrate it without ridicule (...) The objective of modern art is to make people aware of the terrifying aspects of everyday life. Given the *circumstances* (italics Ole Bouman/ Roemer van Toorn), negativity is the only possible way to keep the ideal of the utopian vivid.' ★ But these subtleties are reserved exclusively for the circle around these architects. At the same time, the unfortunate inhabitants have been landed with a myth that bears a passing resemblance to *Arbeit macht frei*. Fortunately, flourishing greenery is now alleviating the worst of the smart.

★ Heynen, Hilde, 'Architecture Between Modernity and Dwelling: Reflections on Adorno's *Aesthetic Theory*', *Assemblage* 17, (1992), p. 83.

In Vienna-Aspern, the architects employed the 'negative' shock tactics of quoting a suffocating fifties mass-construction architecture as a way of simultaneously offering relief from it. Their Schwitterblock in Basel similarly offers such a passionate show of mediocrity that the perspicacious observer (but how many of you are there out there?) can momentarily escape from the predominant kitsch simulacrum, and make brief contact with the latent power of architecture itself. Herzog and de Meuron offer no alternative, no consolation or new Utopia, but an instant at which mediocrity and tunnel vision come face to face with themselves. This is, of course, a hyper-intellectual game of

461

We are not interested in any material as material, in any architectural tool as such (like letters, styles, images) but we use them all just in order to be flexible, to move our heads like a camera in and around this world. We use our architectures to take and to make pictures of this world.

Jacques Herzog & Pierre de Meuron

We are not interested in a 'personal style' but very much in a specific *attitude* aiming towards one direction of architecture which is both intelligible and politically enlighten-

Enlightenment today depends on two crucial efforts. First, substantive reason must be reconstructed as a modality of sensory, imaginative experience; and second, a 'public sphere' which could serve as a forum for individual imagination and unconstrained public debate must be created to respond to the contemporary threats of media concentration and the industrialisation of consciousness.

Fredric Jameson

Never in the history of architecture has there

There are things known and there are things unknown; in between there are doors.

William Blake

What really bothers us, is not that we have to make doors open and shut, but those signs of our time problems.

Herzog & de Meuron

Collective as well as individual identity is defined by a strategy of cultural appropriation and both symbolised and realised by visual consumption.

The fifties are much closer to us, therefore, from the images we can understand the era correctly. These buildings possess an inherent faith in progress, almost in the naive sense.

Herzog & de Meuron

Buildings of the past can only be relevant to us today if they never had presentness at all but rather a spirit of all time because it is this which gives it relevance over a long period of time.

Peter Eisenman

Ricola factory addition and glazed canopy, Laufen, 1991

theirs that calls for a sensitivity of spirit to equal their own. In as far as architecture is both a participant in the public discourse and serves as a forum for that discourse, their method is exasperatingly recondite. But for those who have lost all confidence in this discourse and can only hang on until retiring age in a kind of Sartrian nausea, the instant of confrontation can offer a moment of great relief. The architects' intention of proffering a 'potential for enlightenment' must thus be sought principally in this 'reality therapy'. Now that the surgical approach to curing the social condition has lost its credibility for the tired intellectual, he can still clutch at this one final straw of homeopathy – a dose of negative dialectics, an image at infinite dilution but maximum potency.

So perhaps homeopathy is the real social role of this oeuvre: a mirror in which mediocrity is shocked to recognise itself, a trampoline that bounces the symbolic order of architectural totalitarianism (*Heimatstil*, garden cities and *Neue Sachlichkeit*) back onto itself.

The Tactile as a Mental Tactic

Besides a spine-chilling iconography and an ultra-dilute, almost transparent image, there is another respect in which Jacques Herzog's and Pierre de Meuron's subversive strategy thwarts the pure, tactile experience. Their architecture is visibly steeped in the Husserlian precept of 'back to the things themselves'. Their buildings do not so much attempt to speak out, as to be themselves in a cryptical, reserved way. It is this 'self' of a building, its actual identity, with which they wish to confront the spectator in a phenomenological perceptual relationship. Through the continual references to the importance of perception and the repeated emphasis on tactility, we can guess an influence from the existential phenomenology of Merleau-Ponty. This philosopher wished to restore the lost primacy of existence by positing a preconscious implication of bodily existence in perception.

The work of Herzog and de Meuron derives much of its strength from its ambiguity at a similarly preconscious level. However, this ambiguity is not only deployed for the sake of the existential experience itself, but as a tactical device: the work seizes us by some ill-defined part of the body only to let us drop in confrontation with the results of their montage.

In the Ricola warehouse (Laufen, 1988), the underlying construction is almost obscenely displayed. Everything, the stacking of the material, the material itself, the structural joints, the slight elevation above ground level, the incidence of light, the horizontal articulation of the cladding, makes it obvious that the architects are playing a strategic game of tactility here. In their own words, they generate a 'corpus experience' which initially forces the public (in as far as there is one) back to a phenomenological level of experience in which the entire body plays a role. In the first instance it looks as though these architects must feel perfectly at home in the school of sensory realism which includes Alvaro Siza, Luigi Snozzi, Peter Zumthor and Tadao Ando. The Ricola warehouse design is unarguably rooted in the architects' keen interest in the haptonomy of architecture. On further consideration, however, this is clearly yet another example of the heightening of experience as a tactic within a highly cerebral strategy. Just as you start thinking that here, for once, the authentic experience has managed to stay one step ahead of representation, you realise that this tactility has degenerated into a code. However physically immediate the building may seem at first, it remains utterly remote in conception. Again, the game is played using the opponent's weapons and on the opponent's territory. Herzog and de Meuron are not interested in the tactile as an

462

The reality of architecture is not built architecture. An architecture creates its own reality outside of the state of built or unbuilt and is comparable to the autonomous reality of a painting or a sculpture. The reality of which I speak is also not the real building, the tactile, the material. Certainly we love this tangibility, but only in a relationship within the whole of the (architectural) work. We love its spiritual quality, its immaterial value.

Jacques Herzog

Making architecture superfluous, letting it disappear from our consciousness, directing attention to something else: then the city becomes like nature. It needs no more inventions. It cannot be expanded upon. It is omnipresent. It cannot be copied again since it has already copied itself infinitely. The entropy of architecture.

Herzog & de Meuron

We used to think of culture as the thing that would protect us from nature – from the earthquake and the famine and the cold. Now we look helplessly to nature for some cure for culture. And nature might not be there to offer a cure, having reciprocally been absorbed into culture at the same time that culture was being revealed as sunken into the chaos and randomness of nature.

Thomas McEvilley

It is the physical-sensual presence of the film in the movie theatre and of the sound in the loudspeaker (and not any biographical or entertaining component) that fascinates us, that moves us, that enables us to meet with our own physical presence. Thus the architecture, created by us, embedded in our biography, would be a corporeal part of ourselves? A projecting being constantly projected by us who soon turn from this to new projects, untrue, merciless, abjuring, moving away from it, pushing it off like the burnt-out projectile of a rocket.

Storage building for Ricola, Laufen, 1987

end in itself. They show, by means of exaggeration, monumentality and a patent irony in their manner of presentation, that even the body is a concept, a mere projection of (artificial) intelligence. Only the naive observer would believe that this material embodies true authenticity. It all looks so honest and truthful, but in fact the warehouse is a specimen of pure Baroque, more a suggestion than a reality.

Once more we note the iconophobia. No positive declaration of architectural postulates is issued; no model is presented, no act of obstetrics committed. The only means deployed are the means of those who are forever trying to give architecture an ontological basis, the lovers of ground and foundations. The net result is that the intentions behind these means are ridiculed. The two architects thus situate themselves half-heartedly somewhere between fascinated awe for the authority of the *fête accomplie* of a carnival world, and those efforts to resist it that are still undertaken. *Das Ding...*, sure, but no longer *an sich*. Their architectural image has an 'open' character; every individual observer can experience a sensory stimulus. Meanwhile, the institutional programme is explicitly upheld.

So this is as far as their 'potential for enlightenment' goes. The two architects search continually, seriously and assiduously for an architecture that is capable of communicating 'directly from body to body' with the observer, for an artistically manipulated architectonic surface that by direct confrontation sets the observer thinking about the identity of the things he perceives. But – and this is something that distinguishes them from many of their professional colleagues – this thinking has in no way to be guided to a conclusion. It is good enough that thinking takes place – let everything well up in a transgressive fever that opens up the darkest crypts of feeling. Homeopathy is one thing, but at a certain point it becomes catharsis. If architecture really can contribute to a better time and a different world, then it will have to rise up from the mud and excrement of an absurd present. *Reculer, pour mieux sauter*. Hands will have to be dirtied.

Rebels Without a Cause

Herzog and de Meuron commit the architectural tradition resolutely to the scrapheap of history. For them, a building must never be a representation of realities that have long been dispensed with. The architecture of the past can, in their opinion, still serve only as part of the arsenal of images on which the architect draws when assembling an architectural image. The contract between image and meaning has been broken, and betting on God, as George Steiner suggested, is no solution either. Herzog and de Meuron describe the act of montage, which plays a significant role in their strongly image-oriented design process, in physical terms as a 'bodily filtration' or a 'Turkish bath'. The process is supposed to result in an image that coincides perfectly with 'architectural reality'. In the long run the building must speak 'a language of its own'. They want their buildings to be without 'bad faith' (to use Sartre's term). They must be buildings whereby architectural autonomy may be claimed with conviction. They are pure surface, without centre, without a subject in the literal sense of the word.

Herzog and de Meuron cleverly run with the hare and hunt with the hounds. We can detect the serenity of the phenomenological but it seems to penetrate no deeper than the retina. It looks somewhat as though Herzog and de Meuron are not quite sure which 'reality' they prefer. This disturbing impression is underlined by the observation that the provocation in the final montage is hyper-aesthetically crafted; it is so well-finished that there is a slight effect of a mildly ironic embracing, a sanctioning of the 'represented' reality. The provocation is disarmed, and this architecture thereby loses its character of a statement. Herzog and de Meuron say themselves that it is the observer who decides on the nature of what he encounters, and hence 'makes' the architecture. But the buildings themselves project no identity against which the viewer can test his conclusion, so it really is an anonymous power that continues to rule the world after all. Indeed, the potential for enlightenment is... no more than that.

Schwitter apartment and office building, Basle, 1988

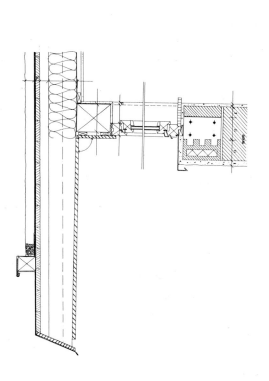

The development on a level tract of land in the east of Vienna consists of some two hundred single-family row houses. The town planning concept was realised in collaboration with Adolf Krischanitz and Steidle + Partner. Each group of architects who participated designed about a third of the low-rise dwellings. The artist Helmut Federle collaborated in the Herzog & de Meuron design for colour and surface treatment. The goal was a maximum simplicity of design in order to underline the flatness of the terrain. The curved rows of houses emphasise a certain movement toward a centre without giving this centre undue weight in relation to the lateral spaces. The curving external spaces help to give specificity to the houses while at the same time emphasising the unity of the urban scheme. Herzog & de Meuron pursued essentially three house types. Type A is an L-shaped unit that encloses a more intimate, private garden by the 1.5 storey studio wing. The lower ground floor, designated as a workshop, could be used as an additional living room. Type C is a rectangular unit that has all the

services contained in a slot placed to one side together with a winding staircase, whereas type D is organised around a single-flight stair that, with the guest WC and a store, forms a core at the upper ground floor. The exterior finishes were originally to have been alternating vertical stripes of smooth and rough self-coloured plaster render. Later on, this idea was dropped for reason of production technology in favour of a concept that was to have left the surfaces and materials in their own colour (unfinished external render), and Federle only permitted the coat of paint as 'protection' to balustrades and window frames. In the end all façade surfaces were painted in the colour of the bearing material, contrary to the intention of Herzog & de Meuron and the artist Federle.

Based on: Theodora Vischer, et al., *Architektur von Herzog & de Meuron*, V° Venice Biennale Swiss Pavilion exhibition catalogue, 1991; *and:* Wilfried Wang, *Herzog & de Meuron*, Zürich 1992; *and:* Dietmar Steiner, et al., *Siedlung Pilotengasse Wien*, Zürich 1992.

Location Pilotengasse, Vienna-Aspern, Austria **Assistant** G. Wiederin **Client** Österreichisches Siedlungswerk **Design** 1987–88 **Completion** 1989–92

Herzog & de Meuron Architekten **Pilotengasse *Garden District Masterplan and Housing***

▶

Allan McCollum, Plaster Surrogates, 1982-1984

Thomas Ruff, House no. 7 I, 1988

On the Work of Michael Graves
The Eye Takes Command

If there is one architect who has contributed more than anyone else to the general reevaluation of the architectural image since the late seventies, surely it must be Michael Graves. With the intellectual backing of star author Charles Jencks, whose *Language of Postmodern Architecture* (1977) announced the death of Modernism, Graves has made a sterling contribution to undermining the Modern iconoclasm that has dominated the built environment for so long. Modernism's hate of ornamentation was originally meant as a way of spreading Kant's 'condition of the possible'. After the war it became clear that this condition was also a money saver. So, largely for economic reasons, the visual value of architecture was given bottom priority. Iin the seventies, however, architecture woke up to the cry of 'power to the imagination' that was already resounding in other quarters. It shook off its sombre cloak of visual abstinence and went in search of a richer vocabulary. Michael Graves was the first to do justice to this aspiration with his now famous Portland Building (1980). This work brought him international renown and a flood of commissions. During the eighties many people came to regard his hybrid, collage-like wealth of forms as a *pars pro toto* for Post-Modernism. Once the strict barrier between high and low culture had been levelled, architecture could devote itself to its task of communicating with the masses. Here it was not the esoteric references of Modernism that were now appropriate, but the kitsch and clichés of mass culture – the ingredients which according to Milan Kundera keep the world turning. Michael Graves and his recognisable architecture brought back aesthetic and psychological certainties to a humanity which had suffered so long under the stern neutrality of an ornament-free world. The captive audience felt reassured and everyone was happy.

468　　From White to Grey to… Kodak Gold

For an inquisitor of Modernism, Graves' own record is far from clean. Prior to the Portland Building, he boasted a lengthy career as a henchman of Modernism. As one of the local architectural avant-garde, the *New York Five*, Graves had been interested in the Modern Movement's exploration of geometrical themes – abstract form, space, intersections, the grid, the corner, the plane, the line, the point – since way back in the sixties. Not that this was a token of respect for Mies van der Rohe's 'less is more' dictum, but a way of livening up Modernist abstraction with post-war complexities derived from philosophy and linguistics. In a certain sense this approach could still be termed 'Modernist' because of its emphasis on the autonomy of architecture and, in particular, on its *syntax*. The work invited the user – or rather the connoisseur of architectonic vocabulary – to trace the coded references and symbolic relationships. Graves combined the ground plans of Le Corbusier with variants on Giuseppe Terragni's and Cesare Cattaneo's apportionment of elevations and of space, thereby dramatising the tensions between surfaces, grid structures and volumes (e.g. the Snyderman House, 1972). The important thing was to reduce architecture to its fundamentals and so give insight into the mutual relations of isolated design elements. The cleaving of mass and

the dynamic interplay of columns, openings and surfaces, resulted in a mysterious spatial transparency. The metaphoric strength of these works was supposed to make the intellectual user aware of himself as being embedded in a linguistic structure. All this, however, took place within the familiar idiom of Modernism.

During the seventies, Graves took his leave of academic research and the cubist repertoire (e.g. the Schulman House, 1976). Owing to the esoteric nature of his methods, only a small group of initiates were still able to follow his development. He tended more and more to a populist approach. In this respect, the Post-Modern revaluation of history proved particularly opportune. The result was a rapid rise in the recognisability of his work – and an increasingly well-filled portfolio of commissions. Henceforth the ground plan had to embody a volumetric concept and enter into a mutual relationship with the demarcations formed by walls, floors, ceilings, columns, colonnades, doors and windows. An arsenal of classical forms – headstones, round arches, pyramids, porticos, posts, columns, colonnades, pylons, steps, stairs etcetera – replaced the whole biscuit tin of cubist quotes. The cube itself was reinstated, placed on the axis of symmetry and apportioned in the classical rhythm of basement, middle and top. The cube no longer had to be hollowed out, but was given a surface treatment. *Exeunt* tectonic and technical elements. The wall regained its traditional iconographic role. For Post-Modernist Graves, items like the floor and ceiling might well be horizontal surfaces in the formal sense but the dramatic difference in their signification – the ground and sky respectively – called for a distinction in material, texture and colour. He no longer used the primary colours of Mondrian but colours evocative of the natural world: brown and yellow (earth), various greens (vegetation), and blue (the sky). The underlying thought was that these ingredients were needed to recount *our own* myths and rituals in our buildings. But running like a thread through all Graves' work there is a continuing love of aesthetic play. Another obvious constant is his use of collage techniques, a game of fragmentary quotations devoid of any deeper meaning. The gulf between architecture and the public at large has undeniably been bridged but the autonomy of the visual language still predominates. Behind the decorative Post-Modern façade, modernity hurtles on.

Cut and Paste

In Graves' architecture, various functional activities are concealed beneath the surface of the standard box, i.e. inside the building. We use the word 'concealed' because the programme as such hardly matters. On his way to a design, Graves rambles through the archaeology of form, easing all kinds of historical references free of their original context, scale and material. He combines the fragments and moulds them into a new, collage-like totality. Memory and association are inextricably interwoven. An a-historical symbolism surfaces on the building's outer skin – a-historical, because the relatively arbitrary pasting method blocks any real historicising action. But the abstractions remain identifiable and offer a form of urban collective memory. For instance, the little huts on the roof of the Portland Building are meant as a reference to the houses on the surrounding hills. Graves hopes to contribute a meaningful building to the environment by these two-dimensional façadist methods. But since Graves decouples Substance from Phenomenon, and concentrates on the surface, meanings become assigned in a (literally) superficial way; the result is reminiscent of the gigantism strategy of the closed but dressed-up box, familiar from contemporary shopping malls. The internal organisation remains a prey to Modernism.

This radical distinction restricts the architecture to a two-dimensional, or, in a philosophical sense, a one-dimensional reality. While we find ourselves confronted with an endless series of updated neo-historicist references (with corresponding cultural suggestions), the architecture forms the perfect counterpart to the state of the art, the requirements of the users and the demands of the project developers. From that point of view, Graves' recent buildings are catalysts for the amusement-cravings of today's money market.

Medium = Message

If we are to fathom Graves' metamorphosis from geometrical abstraction to figurative tinsel, we must pause briefly to consider the growing absolutism of the 'architectural language' concept. Graves' main reason for stressing language is his wish to communicate with as many people as possible.★ By his exceedingly free interpretation of the Classical canon, he hopes to call a halt to the Modernists' visual (or visual-linguistic) impoverishment, which was once meant to help maximise individual self-realisation. Now that the Modern project has collapsed and its visual diet of starvation has lost its *raison d'être*, architecture would be better off going back to speaking a language everyone can understand. On the basis of that agenda, the his-

★ See Graves, Michael, 'A Case for Figurative Architecture', in *Michael Graves; Buildings and Projects 1966-1981*, New York 1982.

Hanselmann House, Fort Wayne, Indiana, 1967

toricising and popularist architecture of Michael Graves ought to be one hundred per cent democratic. But the question is, what is this architecture actually trying to communicate? On the one hand, the colourful metaphors, the apt historical references and similar representational devices, the importance accorded to a richly landscaped look and the revaluation of architectural history, combine to help us identify with our surroundings and thus foster urban (or even social) cohesion; for surely the ability to recognise figurative references must give us a feeling of closer involvement with our immediate social milieu. But, on the other hand, the ground plan and the idea underlying the design lose their critical value. That becomes especially clear in connection with the position of the body and the intellect. Physical movement has become irrelevant, the eye takes command. We are not referring here to the free eye of the free citizen, but to the eye that already 'knows' how it is supposed to see things, the programmed sense. Graves panders to the eye that craves the recognisable, the look of something familiar.

Graves' present work seems at first to refer to matters outside itself, to the world of ordinary people. But it soon becomes clear that the stress on the figurative places the architectural language in a new isolation – this time not within the discipline itself, but within the linguistic conventions. To stay with the jargon: specialised research into architectural syntax makes way for equally specialised research into architectural semantics. Admittedly, the public recognises much more of itself in the new semantics, but these fail to rise above the level of cliché. The 'research' on which the semantics are based remains as esoteric as ever. No sooner does it open up than the semantic universe implodes. Architecture no longer leans on language as an analogy but sees itself as being at one with language. The medium is the message. The Moderns wanted

469

Human life takes place between earth and sky, and architecture as an art is the means to render this condition visible. An architectural figure is a nameable thing which gathers earth, sky and between of human life in a certain way. It reveals how life takes place and helps man to understand and master his condition. The basic figures are archetypes, which have to be interpreted over and over again in ever new ways.

Christian Norberg-Schulz

We as architects must be aware of the difficulties and the strengths of thematic and figural aspects of the work.
If the external aspects of the composition, that part of our language which extends beyond internal technical requirements, can be thought of as the resonance of man and nature, we quickly sense a historical pattern of external language. All architecture before the Modern Movement sought to elaborate the themes of man and landscape. Understanding the building involves both association with natural phenomena (for

example, the ground is like the floor), and anthropomorphic allusions (for example, a column is like a man). These two attitudes within the symbolic nature of building were probably originally in part ways of justifying the elements of architecture in a pre-scientific society. However, even today, the same metaphors are required for access to our own myths and rituals within the building narrative.

Michael Graves

The codes are too esoteric, the meanings too private to Graves and architectural scholars, to communicate the depth of reference intended. For those willing to go through the above analysis the bridge is, no doubt, a multivalent work sending out a criss-cross of elaborated meanings quite marvellously complicated in their inter-relations. But for the uniformed beholder there are not enough explicit cues for this rich interpretative process to take place; in this way the scheme is characteristic of the private language games of Late-Modernism.

Charles Jencks

their abstract syntax to steer the actions of the individual in the direction of a better future. Ironically, the decoding (and then decoration) of this system by Graves seems only to prolong the iron rule: now the image is prescribed, too. Thus language becomes the new straitjacket and criticism is forced to start again from scratch.

Disney, the Unbearable Lightness of Being

According to Graves, Modernism's unceasing production of non-figurative architecture has led to the dilapidation of the cultural language of the past. The machine aesthetic is the major culprit here, for it proffered a metaphor that referred not to the bounty of culture but to the sterility of technology as an end in itself. No real poetry lay at its root, no ritual gesture, no symbolic riches, no literary moment, no mythical aspiration. Apart from the design of several unique spatial configurations, the outcome had by and large been a dismal decay of the architectural tradition's historic capital; in the end architecture lost its anthropomorphic character, its human face. In contrast with these darker

ture as a distinctive social institution. Architecture only manages to keep going by distending its power of *design*. Once that inflation has taken place, leaving architecture itself correspondingly deflated, the architect can expect a warm welcome at the bureaux where commissions are handed out.

With a client like Disney, there is no need for complex appraisal – the kitsch of criticism should be good enough for the criticism of kitsch. Critical analysis of the Disnification of society is a long-familiar theme, but it is still relevant. Disneyland, Disney World and Disney Universe unite everything the independent spirit despises:

'This is a landscape for the eye of the child in the mind of an adult. (...) a Disney landscape replaces the narrative of a socially constructed place with a fictive nexus derived from the market products of the Disney Studio, the whole representing the jealous cultivation of the common mean.' ★

★ Zukin, Sharon, 'Postmodern Urban Landscapes', in Lash, S. and J. Friedman (eds.), *Modernity & Identity*, Oxford 1992, p. 233.

This kind of criticism is practically a foregone conclusion, if we are to judge by the

Costumes for the ballet 'Fire', choreographed by Laura Dean, 1982

Disney Office Building, Burbank, California, 1990

Humana Building, offices, Louisville, Kentucky, 1982

aspects of the Modern Movement, Graves' contribution must seem overwhelming. It has been elevated to become practically an exemplar of the new mentality. Graves is not the only one to have charged architecture with this culture-critical task, but few have gone as far as Graves in pursuing this criticism to its logical conclusion in form: the design of buildings for the Walt Disney Company. The need for metaphors richer than that of the machine culminates in the new (stage-managed) naivety of the amusement park, where there are clichés to answer your every need. Unlike the cliché of the Modern, the Post-Modern cliché of Graves' work makes it quite clear that 'top-ranking' architecture needs cliché to hold its position at the summit. The kitsch, the reduction of architecture to a recognisable and seductive show, is essential for rescuing architec-

words of those who initiate these megaprojects. 'What we create,' one of the project developers frankly revealed, 'is a "Disney realism", sort of Utopian in nature, where we carefully programme out all the negative, unwanted elements and programme in the positive elements'. 'Obviously there's no homelessness in Disneyland,' concurred Michael Eisner, chairman of the Walt Disney Company. 'We don't deal with the social problems. Maybe Disneyland is an idealised version of the city.' Stop whining, in other words, 'Disney is Fun' (Robert Stern) and hence not open to any serious criticism at all. The synthetic feeling of homecoming, the total control and predictability of the amusement, the exclusion of everything alien to white middle-class culture, the ultra-conservative values preached, the absurdly feverish pace with which the maximum number of

---

Individual voices speaking a commonly understood language.
Robert Stern

Here is the theory: anywhere in the world around us there is a lot of truths for humans to go by, and all of them are beautiful - the truth of passion and love, the truth of honesty and soberness, the truth of patriotism, the merit of individual self-reliance, etcetera. However, if people try for self realisation, they go by their own principal truth, excluding others. And when this happens, the moment somebody does that - clinging on to one truth with desperate tenacity - this clenched truth becomes a lie and turns this individual into a grotesque character.
E. L. Doctorow

The striving for individuality tends to express itself in adornment, for by adorning anything, be it alive or inanimate, I bestow upon it the right of individual life.
Gottfried Semper

You are really decorating, which is the adjectival condition of the theming of a building. (...) In Modernism, the theme was technology or function, which was more mute. When you start putting flowers on the wall how can that differ from all that Modernism fought against? Modernism was singular in its pursuit of the machine metaphor. Traditional architecture acts more like literature; a lot is said simultaneously, and unpredictable combinations are made.
Michael Graves

Having established a system of limitations and of exclusions, Graves can manipulate his materials in a limited series of operations; but at the same time, this system permits him to demonstrate how a clarification or explication of his own linguistic procedures exerts an indirect control of the plan, always *from within the system of predetermined exclusions.*
Manfredo Tafuri

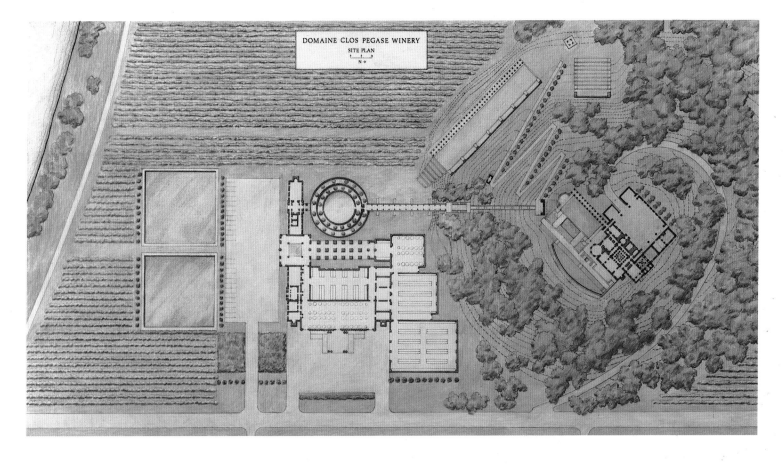

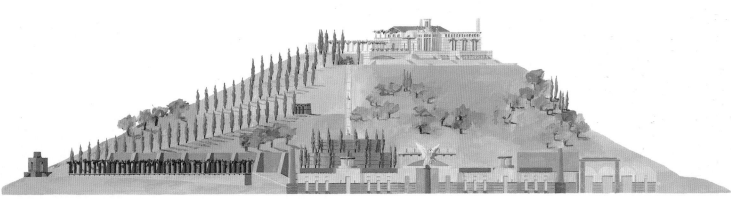

Clos Pegase Winery, Napa Valley, California, 1984

attractions must be consumed in the minimum possible time (what a relaxation!) and, finally, the impertinent paradox of the ultimate in public-friendliness combined with an unmitigated regulation by a central apparatus: but this catalogue of affronts to sensibility hardly exceeds what critics have already muttered on the sidelines. It won't harm Disney anyway, nor Michael Graves, although he did find it necessary to explain why he accepted the commissions: working for Disney has earned him

'as much criticism from my architectural colleagues as almost any building I have done. (...) All of us worry a little bit. It's very hard for most architects to overcome the kind of Gropius morality. But could you imagine Lutyens saying no? Bernini saying no? Or Michelangelo? Not on your life!' ★

For Graves, the Michael-angelo of our time, the Disney cycle was a wonderful opportunity to put his insights of the preceding years into practice. Having wrestled free of the ethics of the Modern, he found the time had now dawned to maximally explore the amorality of language for its purely expressive, ornamental value. There were so many combinations still to be tried, and life is so short... 'My life isn't empty, it's quite full. I can't wait to get up tomorrow morning.' ★

★ Michael Graves quoted in Abrams, Janet, 'The World According to Mickey', in *Blueprint* 2 (1991), p. 34.
★ Games, Stephen, 'Digging Graves', Interview with Michael Graves, in Games, Stephen, *Behind the Façade*, London 1985, p.44.

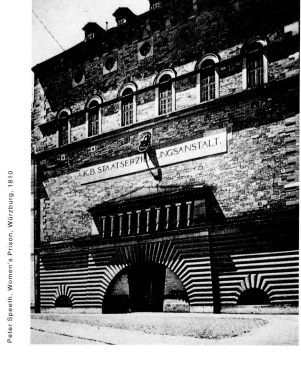

Peter Speeth, Women's Prison, Würzburg, 1810

Façadist Weight-watching: Architecture Without Gravity

The façades of Michael Graves are worth their weight in gilt when it comes to research into the values they represent. The image has an incontestable sensory potency and possesses a strong coherence which enables it to embody apparently conflicting meanings side-by-side. Historical shapes of every variety, Modern plans and Post-Modern elevations: they all cohabit affably in this architecture. The work is moreover unambiguous in its representation of the architect's ideological choice. Without intellectual legitimisations, it offers an excellent metaphor for the turn late capitalism has taken. It unashamedly displays the social conditions of the present day – as a realised but selective Utopia. Graves is candid about a stage-set democracy, a politics of tourism, which colonises life itself with its new dictatorship. From that point of view, his work is uncommonly transparent; the hidden agenda behind the formal profusion remains instantly legible, in spite of his highly individual expressiveness, because Graves' language refers to that redundant banality to which intellectuals are always so averse – namely, kitsch. In that sense Graves is unusually honest. Through his literally paper-thin decoration, Graves demonstrates (via the roundabout route of criticism) how modernity scurries on with unabated energy in spite of – no, thanks to – its snappy new suit. The tourist model of Graves' work fits in perfectly with this process. He offers an adequate *Ersatz* to every passive spectator: as a tourist, the idea is to remain uninvolved without actually feeling like an outsider. On the contrary, the irresistible visual quality of the imagery, the simple coding and the unceasing explanations of an army of commentators give us a sense of standing close up to it. Yet at the same time, we are so near to it that the distance needed for critical reflection has disappeared. You let yourself be taken in and at the same time you don't. What you gain on the swings ...

In recent work, Graves seems to have chosen definitively in favour of the tourist experience. In a sense it is a new religion, where the objects of devotion can be seen as self-depicting idols. What actually takes place is that a highly effective interface, which most users do not experience as an interface at all, is used to manipulate technological and other (future) developments in such a way that we can or may undergo some of them but not others. In the use of traditional forms, a very specific strategy is being defined for the future and for the present. It is an interface like a mask, which the client and the architect use to fine-tune the message and/or the experience.

Disney as *Genius Mundi*

The general acclaim for the beautiful image, which was originally meant to welcome the reincarnation of architectural communication, turns out to act as an inducement to mere sightseeing as well. The historical development from the discovery of architecture-as-language to the application of linguistics in architecture, can be boiled down to a simple category error. Even if architecture is language, language isn't necessarily architecture. We can see a somewhat similar process at work in research into what language 'people' actually prefer: the sociologists concluded that a particular taste-culture belongs with a particular social group, and this was transformed by the marketing boffins into a plan for the future. What sociology proved *a posteriori*, must apply tomorrow *a priori*, or so the market researchers dictated. In Graves' architecture, too, we can recognise a similar inversion of description and prescription. We owe our gratitude to this marketing trick for what is perhaps the most charming paradox of the late twentieth century. The arrogance of those who would programme the language of the future with compulsory meanings ultimately leads to a sublime honesty in that it divulges the cultural logic of the American Dream democracy: what the people want is what the people are persuaded to want.

The poetic form of architecture is responsive to issues external to the building, and incorporates the three-dimensional expression of the myths and rituals of society. Poetic forms in architecture are sensitive to the figurative, associative, and anthropomorphic attitudes of a culture.

Michael Graves

The Modern Movement based itself largely on technical expression - and the metaphor of the machine dominated its building form. In its rejection of the human or anthropomorphic representation of previous architecture, the Modern Movement undermined the poetic form in favour of nonfigural, abstract geometries. (...) While any architectural language, to be built, will always exist within the technical realm, it is important to keep the technical expression parallel to an equal and complementary expression of ritual and symbol. (...) This language, which engages

inventions of culture at large, is rooted in a figurative, associational and anthropomorphic attitude. If (...) that part of our language which extends beyond internal technical requirements, can be thought of as the resonance of man and nature, we quickly sense a historical pattern of external language. All architecture before the Modern Movement sought to elaborate the themes of man and landscape. Understanding the building involves both association with natural phenomena (for example, the floor is like the ground), and anthropomorphic allusions (for

example, a column is like a man). (...) The cumulative effect of non-figurative architecture is the dismemberment of our former cultural language of architecture. (...) It is crucial that we re-establish the thematic associations invented by our culture in order fully to allow the culture of architecture to *represent* the mythic and ritual aspirations of society.

Michael Graves

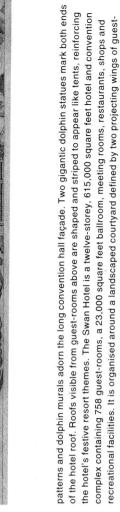

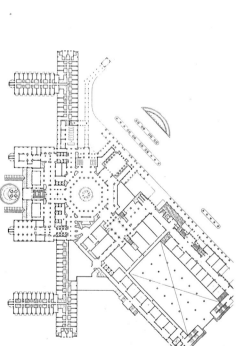

patterns and dolphin murals adorn the long convention hall façade. Two gigantic dolphin statues mark both ends of the hotel roof. Roofs visible from guest-rooms above are shaped and striped to appear like tents, reinforcing the hotel's festive resort themes. The Swan Hotel is a twelve-storey, 615,000 square feet hotel and convention complex containing 758 guest-rooms, a 23,000 square feet ballroom, meeting rooms, restaurants, shops and recreational facilities. It is organised around a landscaped courtyard defined by two projecting wings of guest-rooms. An octagonal lobby in the centre of this courtyard connects the hotel, restaurants, and other facilities with the causeway that crosses the lake to the Dolphin. Two swans, each 47 feet high, rise above the roof of the hotel. The façades are painted with large wave patterns, and clamshell fountains mark the ends of the two guest-room wings. The colours and decoration of the hotels and their surroundings suggest the character of Florida resorts and provide a thematic context consistent with Disney's programme for 'entertainment architecture'. *Michael Graves*

▶

The Walt Disney World Swan Hotel and Dolphin Hotel are organised around a common crescent-shaped lake. Though their size, services, programme, and operators are different, the two hotels were designed as an ensemble with consistent character and similar themes. A covered causeway for pedestrians and trams traverses the lake and connects the two hotel lobbies. The Dolphin Hotel is a 1.4 million square feet convention centre with circa 1,510 rooms, a ballroom of 57,000 square feet, and an exhibit hall of 50,000 square feet as well as meeting rooms, restaurants, shops and recreational facilities. It is organised to take advantage of the waterside views. Four nine-storey wings containing guest-rooms project into the lake, surrounding a restaurant court with a waterfall fountain supported by dolphin statues. The large vaulted entrance foyer leads to a tented octagonal lobby with a central fountain. From this lobby, visitors gain access to the rest of the complex. The lakeside façade of the Dolphin Hotel is decorated with murals depicting large banana leaves resting on a trellis base. Wave

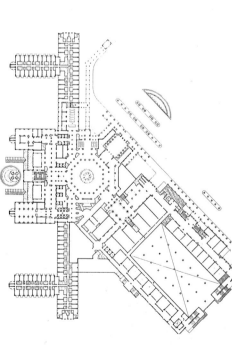

Location Lake Buena Vista, Florida, United States of America **Assistants** Mr. Macary, X. Menu **Client** Walt Disney World **Design** 1986-87 **Completion** 1990

Michael Graves Architect *Walt Disney World Resort Hotels and Masterplan*

Swan Hotel Fountain Lobby

Swan Hotel 'Palio' Restaurant

Dolphin Hotel

Swan Hotel

Swan Hotel Lobby Foyer

Swan Hotel Prefunction Corridor

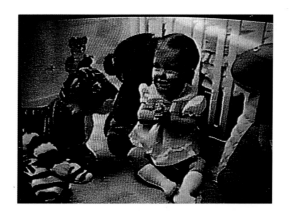

Let's play "Peekaboo."
Peekaboo! Peekaboo!

Wave to grandma!

Smile for mommy!

Play us a song.

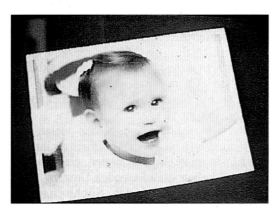

Have the fun but not the trouble. 'Video Baby', 8 minutes interactive videotape with manual, birth and health certificates

On the Work of Itsuko Hasegawa

Man Without Qualities...

is a Woman!

The aftermath of the Third World War is a theme familiar to science fiction readers. The spiralling tension between Nato and the Warsaw Pact that reached its chilling height in the 1962 Cuba crisis inspired many a literary doom-monger to fantasies of the final Armageddon (and the morning after). At the time everybody must have been wondering what it would be like to glory in that radioactive dawn, to be one of the few survivors chosen by Dr. Strangelove to perpetuate the human race. The grim prospect of a nuclear winter, which in retrospect seems to have helped tip the moribund Soviet monolith off its pedestal, seems also to have left its tracks in the Western spirit. The greatest post-war mass demonstrations were the peace rallies. Politics was overshadowed by Pershings, Cruise missiles and SS-20s. But what touched people at a deeper, moral level was the fact that if the statistics of the ballistics were anything to go by we could soon all be killed 40,000 times over.

Should we, in this cultural condition of as yet unconsummated annihilation, now think about Japan? It too felt the strains of the Cold War, at least in a military-strategic sense. But the widespread anxiety from which the *no nukes* movement flowered passed it by; for Japan had already had the Bomb, and without the privilege of agonising in advance. So there the future had already arrived. Only Japan had already had a foretaste of the Third World War as we feared it. Now that the tension has drained out of the superpower stand-off and military politics is losing ground to economic strategies, Japan finds itself on the far side of our era. Can there still be poetry after Hiroshima and Nagasaki?

Apparently yes, as long as poetry is not seen as the art of the true, the beautiful and the good, but as the art of the contingent. Itsuko Hasegawa displays all the features of the present Japanese building frenzy, which from outside looks like advanced lunacy but sometimes, in isolated projects, achieves a state of undeniable poetry. In a culture where mass destruction passes for a collective experience and in which architects prefer to shut themselves off from metropolitan chaos by striving for the autonomy of their objects, there is sometimes one who manages to emerge as an interpreter of a hopeful common voice. Itsuko Hasegawa, poet, architect and woman, is such a person. And that is something very exceptional amid the ubiquitous and deeply traditional male chauvinism of Japan. For however grotesque the impact of Western modernity may have been in and after August 1945, some things never change.

Post-nuclear *Feng-Shui*

At first sight Hasegawa seems fairly immune to the new condition. She describes her work as an attempt to do justice to the Asiatic philosophy of *feng-shui*, which holds that architecture should represent nature by referring to natural elements such as air, earth, water and fire. According to this concept, architecture is meant to contribute to a kind of natural state of the spirit, in which consciousness can flow freely inspired by the

Advertisement for International House Design Competition 1993, chairman of the jury Itsuko Hasegawa

place and its spatial qualities. In Itsuko Hasegawa's view, this cherished philosophy has come off worse in a collision with Western modernising tendencies. Architecture is the field where the damage is most visible. It is increasingly anti-aesthetic in respect of its relation to nature. It suffers from fragmentation, a disruption of the cosmic harmony, and has sacrificed its bond with nature to formal homogenisation.

Hasegawa's ambition is to put a stop to this process. She wishes her architecture to instigate a revival of the nature experience, as she puts it, in the urban scene. In contrast to those she calls the 'Modernists', she wishes to give architecture back to the 'ordinary citizen' who, without exception, longs for 'an environment in which he or she can be aware of the changes of the season'.★ But that is not all she wants. Architecture must also express the world of today in a way that offers greater freedom. She means here the *suggestion* of freedom. Architectural and technical details must 'evoke' nature. Natural and cosmic details must do the same for the architecture. While the architect puts nature on show and attempts to rescue it by design, nature is taken up into the realm of the artificial. The result may not always please the critical mind, but the architect has found her calling: architecture is supplying suggestion. That is why Hasegawa's work fits so perfectly into the virtual universe that has become such an integral part of Japanese culture. Imagination shows its power in compensating the physical constraints of an over-successful island surrounded by ocean.

★ Hasegawa, Itsuko, 'Projects', *The Japan Architect* 11/12 (1986), p. 54.

Natural Glue for the Boulevard of Broken Dreams: Shonandai

If there is any one architectural project in Japan that is an example of this suggestive role, then it must be Hasegawa's Shonandai Cultural Centre in Fujisawa. Although theoretically we no longer need physical propinquity in this our telematic universe we seem to have an unassuageable need for *direct* personal contact as in some archaic ritual. Centres like Shonandai, with a promenade, offices and cultural facilities, offer us an opportunity to meet and chat now and then on neutral territory. ★ Owing to the speedy growth of the communication culture, these projects are shooting up like *shiitake* all around Japan. Hasegawa's cultural centre is both a manifestation of this development and a commentary on it. She does nothing to gloss over the schizophrenic contrivance of a meeting between people who are completely alien to one another. On the contrary, she succeeds in using her architectural means to reinforce that schizophrenia. On second thoughts, the 'neutral territory' mentioned above is not at all neutral, but bears witness to a post-humanistic condition in which the concept of nature has completely overshadowed the physical reality of nature. The aim seems not so much to offer a material basis for the encounter as to build a suitable *atmosphere*.

★ See Vitta, Maurizio, 'Shonandai Cultural Center', *l'Arca* 42 (1990), p. 26.

Many of the characteristic features of Hasegawa's architecture can be identified in Shonandai. The elongated plan lacks any central perspective or ordering grid, but is more like a kaleidoscopic mass of fragments, each offering an explicit experience in its own right. Curves and spherical volumes, always in cheerful colours, dominate. The overall image is marked by a multitude of figurative references, most of which are easily recognisable. Natural phenomena such as rivers, mountains and clouds abound in this architecture in metonymic form. (Is metonymy perhaps the only way nature is still available to us?) A notable feature is the repeated use of perforated sheet metal as interface, so softening the boundaries and the contours of the volumes. 'These translucent membranes on the boundaries of buildings are thin and lightweight', says Hasegawa. 'They make us aware of the new aspects of nature; bathed in sunlight, they change constantly in appearance from hour to hour and from season to season; they may shower the interior with strong light or produce a hollow, metallic sound with the passing breeze. It is hoped that the façades of these buildings will become parts of their respective neighbourhoods and create bright, invigorating areas.' ★

The boundary of the building is thus not only used iconographically but generates events in its own right through the continual interaction with the natural elements. Thus nature is brought on the scene once again, on this occasion by appropriating the last remaining natural elements that are present in the city: light, air and sound.

★ Hasegawa, Itsuko, op. cit. p. 54.

Covering Up the Modern

Although hidden to the eye, the placing of offices and other 'modern' functions underground is very significant in the cultural analysis of this project.

'My intention', says Hasegawa, 'was to bury "Modern" architecture underground and to create above it "topographical" spaces continuous with the site'. Shonondai looks likely to be the next milestone in contemporary architecture after the *Language of Postmodern Architecture*, in which the exterior was detached from the Modernist interior and acted out a range of symbolic meanings. Now the iconographic function devolves on the whole aboveground structure. That creates space for a theme park world, a pacifying universe of edutainment. The modernisation process no longer hides behind the façade but has descended into the bowels of the earth. While subterranean time runs faster than ever, we crust-dwellers can carry on functioning within the same old anthropological and historical schemes. Now modernity has devoured nature we build a museum above the ground to *resemble* nature. Architecture no longer packages its Modernist content but effectively covers it off. That way it at least manages to recover its three dimensional significance, albeit without much conviction. Conversely we could say that Modernism has become so ashamed of its own ugliness that mere façades are no longer enough to mask it. Now a whole world has to be created, with life and all, in order to conceal the forces of Modernism. Façades alone have become too flimsy. In comparison, life may be a little sturdier. Unfortunately life is getting lighter all the time too...

477

'Architecture as Another Nature' or Nature as Another Culture?

Hasegawa sees the chief aim of her architecture and her profession as being to create 'another nature' out of respect for the *feng-shui* tradition. The critic Botond Bognar draws the distinction here between two levels in Hasegawa's adoption of nature. Firstly, she uses 'natural elements' like water, wind and light to evoke and provoke the

NC House, Tokyo, 1983

make them manifest architecturally. I call this approach 'architecture as latent nature'. In other words, to create architecture is to use a completely different vocabulary in expressing what one has experienced in life as a human being.

Itsuko Hasegawa

Tokyo is a city which expanded by embodying versatile factors and accumulating invisible systems without applying urban development planning. It continues to transfigure with no composition or coherence. It has no place to go but becomes saturated, and therefore, a site of extraordinary dynamism. The architecture which I design undergoes the process of developing new concepts through

my own spiritual filter, as I live in a town like Tokyo. This gave me the opportunity to speak here today on the theme of 'searching for a new direction of city and architecture as viewed from the scenes of Tokyo'. While it retains Asiatic village style in its total space or people or objects, huge economic structures and high technology are impregnated throughout its body, making it a swollen, chaotic city.

Itsuko Hasegawa

Japan continues its trend as a place of great consumption, and both the city and nature not only continue their decline, but also through some kind of 'simulated miracle', the highly developed mass media have kept up a constant battle cry arguing for the benefits of 'artificial information cities' in an effort to compensate for those visible aspects of decline. The simulated cities that are a result of this are impoverishing our society and finally many people are beginning to take notice.

Itsuko Hasegawa

The bird's eye view of Tokyo is a forest of large and small buildings. Close-up, each building is full of ultra-modern and unique expression and detail. Architecture is partly a direct expression of commercial greed. Tokyo is a theatre where symbols of the consumer society flit, or an electronic information society where invisible signals flow. Architecture is a component of an intelligent and emotional city, where nature and technology coexist naturally.

Itsuko Hasegawa

power of nature. Secondly, she uses an analogous nature, in the form of a highly suggestive imitation. ★

As to the former use, the elements, is that all nature is? If so, then Charles Moore's Piazza Italia is true Italian soil. And as to the second, the analogy, it is exactly the fate we all feared. Not only is nature imitated but it is cut up into categories and redistributed in decorative

★ Bognar, Botond 'Architecture, Nature & a New Technological Landscape', *Architectural Design Profile* 90 (1991), p. 33.

blobs. It is not 'architecture as another nature' but architecture *after* nature in both senses of the word. Hasegawa imitates nature, in form and in effect, in purely Aristotelian terms. But she is also post-natural. Mother nature is dead, long live Mother Nature.

Although Itsuko Hasegawa claims that she wishes to 'reinstate' nature, her work possesses all the trappings of a stylish funeral. She would seem to align with the decadent tradition of *fin de siècle* poets who believe, along with Joris-Karl Huysmans (in *Against Nature*), that 'the admiration of all true artists for that eternal old nag (nature) is a thing of the past and the time has come for the natural to be replaced wherever possible by the artificial.'

This seems to be precisely what Hasegawa is aiming at, for although her intention seems to relate to the *experience* of seasons and natural phenomena, her buildings are so totally embedded in the post-natural order of the metropolis, where virtual odours, virtual sounds and virtual images compete for every moment of attention, that her 'architecture as another nature' can only be interpreted as 'another virtual reality' and hence as a techno-topic manifesto *against* nature. Hasegawa's architecture is totally staged, artificial conditioning: air conditioning, water conditioning, earth conditioning and ultimately life and death conditioning. The final step to the conditioning of God, reality and metaphysics has almost been taken. So who is still talking about Experience?

478

At one time an aversion to the natural idyll was a sign of a Modernist resistance to bourgeois culture. Now Modernism seems to have won the match and nature can no longer be the putative opponent, it is better to affirm and represent this condition than to keep acting as though nature still existed. Hasegawa imagines she can restore nature but in fact her camp architecture deals it the death blow. Nature used to be bourgeois (as Oscar Wilde put it) but now it is our final avant-garde. Only nature can still be grotesque; Hasegawa's grotesqueness has long been mainstream.

Nomadic Feminism?

Hasegawa finds herself in invigorating company with her critique of rationalism, which is based on 'fuzzy logic' and 'soft technology'. She can reckon on the intellectual support of several feminist philosophers. Her iconography, with its undulating lines connoting the natural forms of the sea, a line of hills or a female body, its teardrop-shaped windows, its cut-out trees and clouds of metal, the softened contours of the volumes, the diaphanous membranes, the fragmentation of structure, the burying of Modernism's logo-centric, phallo-centric order beneath the surface of Mother Earth, all go to make Hasegawa's work fascinating material for a study of feminist philosophy.

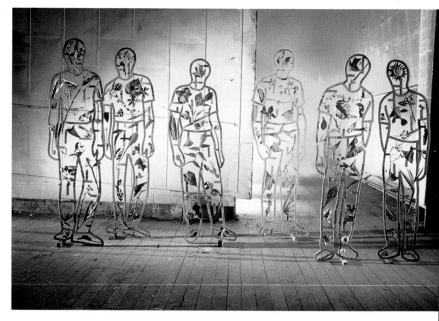

Rhonda Roland Shearer, Anthropocentrism Series: Studies §1 through §6, 1990

According to the Italian philosopher Rosi Braidotti, philosophy shares 'the unhappy and contradictory fate of the oppressed for the first time in its history, owing to the logic of a well-defined historical situation'.

One of the positive effects of this repressed position was that the philosophical discourse became conscious of all that had previously been seen as 'different' from the all-inclusive rational subject, i.e. 'the uprising of suppressed forms of knowledge'. ★ By 'the oppressed' Braidotti meant principally women, whose voice had hardly been heard in philosophy until the present day. There has been an increasing amount of attention for 'the Other' in

★ Braidotti, Rosi, 'Beelden van de Leegte', *Tijdschrift voor Vrouwenstudies* 41 (1990), pp. 5-17.

the Western philosophical discourse, and in the first instance this 'Other' is womankind. Moreover, since women have perhaps been the most successful of all 'minorities' to strive for emancipation in the present century, the philosophers of difference have, in their concern for this 'Other', concentrated more than anything on the female. The woman can personify the notion of the Other on the grounds of her historical subordination. Therefore the protagonist of Robert Musil's *The Man without Qualities*, whose search for his own identity ultimately brought him to the conviction that he had none, could be described as a woman in a philosophical sense. Woman (the Other) appears where the *principium identitatis* disappears. The man without qualities appears to be a woman – perhaps one imbued with impressive qualities, for that is always possible.

Itsuko Hasegawa's statements lead us to surmise that she not only wishes to see her work as the solution to a local problem, but as a manifesto of our times.

'The idea is to make architecture more realistic through what might be called a "pop" reasoning that allows for diversity as opposed to a logical system of reasoning that demands extreme concentration. Such an approach represents a shift to a feminist

The highly confident and flourishing arguments from the point of view of production for production's sake have called into being the aspects of over-consumption and homogeneity. In order for modern architecture to break through and run past these undesirable aspects to face the next stage, it is thought we must depend even more on information technology to enlarge our imaginations by planning on some kind of 'science fiction' connection of the classical human brain to the peripherals of the 'digital thinking circuits' called computers.
Itsuko Hasegawa

To effectively use the computer requires us, at certain times, to objectify and rearrange our ideas and what we want to express on a molecular level and with numerical expressions. At this point we think on the same level as a cosmic phenomenon and even feel mysterious as if we are reconstructing something. To pour all our imaginative powers which have been placed into this kind of space into architecture means, once again, we are asked how we really should live and how we can really take hold of the quality of our lives and the quality of our lifestyles.
Itsuko Hasegawa

It is important to bring a fresh impetus to this kind of media environment by continuing to paint universal dreams through architecture. However, for that to happen, it will be necessary to bring together and stratify all that surrounds the daily lives of people, both the questionable and physical things, especially among the Asians including the Japanese.
Itsuko Hasegawa

Being an informed society attracting all the people and commodities, unipolar concentration is accelerating in Tokyo. Sprung by technology, greed and dreams amplify causing a dynamic reality which even absorbs art into public manners and customs. Science and technology have entered the human elec-

tronics age combining living creatures and machines on common grounds, replacing the old-fashioned mode of the twentieth century where nature and men conflict.
Itsuko Hasegawa

Molecular biology discovered that every living creature has DNA genes. Subsequently, life has been comprehended as a complete and informed micro-system, which opened its utilities on energy-saving type technology. Thus, men and nature and science and technology can stand on common grounds with each maintaining their own features as men and nature (bees, for example).
Itsuko Hasegawa

House at Higashitamagawa, Tokyo, 1987

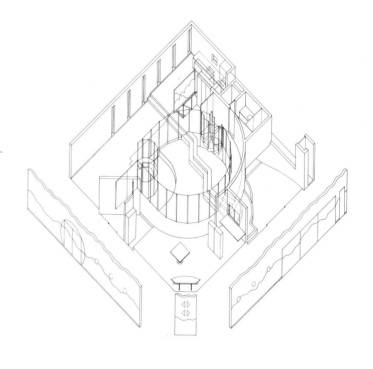

STM House, Tokyo, 1991

paradigm, in the sense that an attempt is made to raise the consciousness of as many people as possible.'

To Hasegawa, the 'system of reasoning that demands extreme concentration' is clearly not realistic, while 'pop reasoning' is. Hence she is not merely making an observation but is taking a definite stand on our post-humanist paradigm. Masculine world domination has run its course, she believes, the centre is unoccupied and the world is all the better for that. Thus woman, as a manifestation of the eccentric Other, gets her chance at last. Now is the time to accelerate a return to nomadic thinking.

480

Provisional Strategy

This fine aspiration is open to two objections. Firstly it is becoming increasingly clear that late capitalism needs a different discourse to the modern, goal-oriented rationalism. The philosophy of difference can be interpreted as the pattern of thought needed for a flexible, global economy. It is just possible that all the interest being taken in women's issues is something that really serves 'masculine' interests. Secondly, this widening of the field of knowledge, the attention being paid to what was previously suppressed, may have fostered emancipation but failed to stimulate any development in the value system towards which emancipation could be directed. The liberation of the Other is thus *mutatis mutandis* a purely negative freedom. In *Les Mots et les Choses*, Michel Foucault proposed that 'in our times one can only think in the emptiness of vanished

★ Foucault, Michel, *Les Mots et les Choses. Une Archéologie des Sciences Humaines*, Paris 1966, p. 353.

man. This emptiness does not excavate a shortage, nor does it prescribe us to fill a hole. It is nothing more or less than the opening of a space in which it is finally possible to think again.' ★

Well, the opening is there – now for the thought. About that, however, this philosophy

has nothing more to say. It can contribute no more. After all, it would otherwise regress into centrist thinking. In this respect, the philosophy of difference is paradoxical. It is emancipatory in as far as it exposes the oppressive presuppositions of our culture. However, it is passive in that it shrinks from revealing the ethical motives behind that act of exposure. Thus it is yet another provisional strategy, and that is typical of the bourgeois policy of status quo, a device for ever postponing the making of choices. From that viewpoint, Hasegawa's appeal to a feminist paradigm and her architectural articulation, offered to the post-nuclear urban nomads who must find their culture in a 'cultural centre', is problematical.

Sleeping With the Enemy: Fuzzy Logic

According to Luce Irigaray, 'those who have distanced themselves so far from their body that they have forgotten it (...) need the truth. But their "truth" makes us as immobile as statues, unless we shake off its power by attempting, here, there, immediately, to voice how moved we are.'

Does Hasegawa do that? No, she does not. On the basis of the modality of difference thinking, in the present case a linguistic, relative consciousness, the true world is reduced to a fable of blobs of body, blobs of nature. That fits the masculine world view in its late capitalist form perfectly. If this is feminism, then feminism has let itself be tricked into doing its opponent's dirty work.

The castration of Western metaphysics is, in this view, perhaps better explained by the impotence of man than by the potency of woman. 'Who' asks Braidotti, 'says that the Man, in his historic exhaustion, does not offer his companion, who is now emancipating herself, the poisoned apple of knowledge?' Woman may perhaps flatter herself with the idea that the crisis of the rational subject is her handiwork. But there is far more evidence to support the position that this crisis is a cultural function of the reorientation of capital. So a fat lot of good your *fuzzy logic* does you.

Commemorating Destroyed Nature

Hasegawa is known as a 'working' rather than a 'chattering' architect. But her projects 'as another nature' are invariably monuments of the time-honoured urban tendency to couch everything in abstractions and then to subordinate, manipulate and finally dispose of the original. Perhaps she is not all that verbose and her design strategies could often be described as phenomenological. All the same, her ideas are based entirely on linguistic concepts. Nature as landscape, in its *feng-shui* version or otherwise, has long ceased to exist. It was discovered by painting and sent packing by photography. We all know the look of nature ravished. We all know, too, the ostensibly unspoilt scenes that seem reserved for the museum and the chocolate box. Nature no longer exists except as abstraction or as a threatened environment. 'I want to help to create a new nature in the place of the one that used to be here,' says Hasegawa. 'I feel any new building ought to commemorate the nature that had to be destroyed because of it and serve as a means of communication with nature.' She is the architect who sublimely manifests this tragic predicament.

People are beginning to notice the appearance of the 'Second Nature', as the construction of a new environment by Tokyo's technology makes progress. I have persisted in an ad hoc style of development, rather than an attitude of exclusive development which does not mind rejecting whatever is objectionable. This means an inclusive type of architecture which accepts various factors in a comprehensive plan.

Itsuko Hasegawa

I believe architecture can stand on a popular rationale embracing a multipolar value system, rather than logical rationality based on unipolar value. Such posture will give rise to people's subconsciousness into a consensus, and trigger a feminist paradigm. Nature is an intelligent creature, and I intend to remain in Tokyo to continue my theme of 'Architecture as a Second Nature'.

Itsuko Hasegawa

Traditional Japanese architecture looks dignified, but, in fact, is a living space and conception based on free and vague rules of Nature, without being tied to architectural precision and strict space concept, as houses described in Kamo no Choumei's 'Houjouki',

and Kenko Hoshi (the monk's) 'Tsurezuregusa'. Another way to look at it is to recover the emotional side of culture, which has been cut off from the rich yet materialistic world in the name of rationality of the modern society, allowing no room for human mutual sympathy, or to open our ears to listen to the mysterious music of the universe. This means to aim and build a new type of architecture under the leadership of the citizen's society on the basis of modern science and technology, where rationality and irrationality, internationality and locality can live together in Nature.

Itsuko Hasegawa

The future success of Hasegawa's 'architecture as a second nature' presented by way of her new interpretation of technology, will ultimately depend upon whether she is able to avoid succumbing to, while flirting with or utilising, the tempting world of simulations in order to shift the course of recent, consumerist urban development towards new realities.

Botond Bognar

Chassez le naturel, il revient au galop.

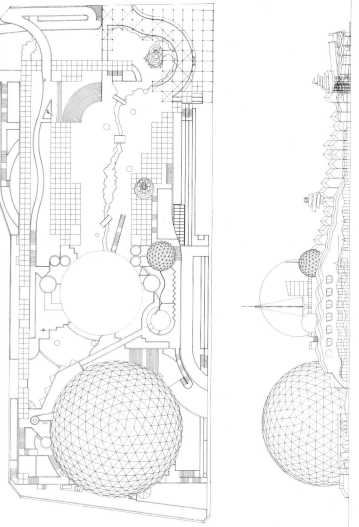

forest or a field. This image was chosen in part to symbolise the hope that here everyone will live in harmony and also to remind visitors of the natural environment that we are in danger of forgetting. In experiencing the huge globes and the spaces suggestive of the forest and the sea, visitors will no doubt begin to see this technological installation as itself a limitless natural landscape.

I felt nothing would come of building cubical structures in the style of modern architecture and fretting over their design or size. My intention was to bury 'modern' architecture underground and to create above it 'topographical' spaces continuous with the site. In the underground portion, the peripheral walls serve as anti-seismic features and lessen the horizontal forces within, making it possible to use a structure without beams. The aboveground portion is completely divorced from the basement, allowing the use of a very free structure of lightweight, randomly arranged steel frames. Light and air introduced below ground through toplights and dry areas will produce a mysterious effect. Visitors to the centre will not want everything to be prearranged. The interior design must not restrict the way the facilities are used but allow visitors to use their own imagination. *Itsuko Hasegawa*

▶

My theme of 'architecture as topography' has developed in response to the general social and intellectual climate and my goal is to create a new natural environment. Modern architecture was designed to be purposeful and people without a definite goal were not welcomed within. However, with a building like a cultural centre (in this case comprising a children's pavilion, a community centre and a public theatre) people ought to be able to just drop in. A public building must have a very definite character, one responsive to the needs of many different classes of users: children and the aged, women and men, and the handicapped and the healthy. A building ought to be seen as a space in which users will take part in an ongoing performance. Taking such an approach, one begins to design buildings, not singly but as an ensemble having a specific character. Places with definite character can be flexible and diverse and be made to accommodate multiple happenings simultaneously.

Ultimately my goal is to create a place that houses the world, to enclose the universe within an apparently delimited space. Trying to incorporate in the Shonandai project all that had been excluded by modern planning, I discovered I was designing not so much a work of architecture as a topography. Overall, the project suggests a

Location 1-8 Shonandai, Fujisawa, Japan **Assistants** M. Shitaka, M. Sasaki, N. Saito and others **Client** City of Fujisawa **Design** 1986-88 **Completion** 1987-90

Itsuko Hasegawa Atelier *Shonandai Cultural Centre*

On Kawara/Alberto Giacometti, Conscience (installation), Le Consortium, Dijon, 1990

こども館
展示ホール2〈円環ギャラリー〉

Children's Museum
Exhibition Hall #2(Loop Gallery)

日常から天文・宇宙までの広域な世界を理解するためのギャラリーである。いろいろな種類の映像を自分で選択できる〈ビデオギャラリー〉、気象衛星の画像を直接受信し、雲や台風の動きを知らせる〈ひまわり〉、自分で操作して楽しめる〈私達の情報コンピュータ〉など、最新の地理・物理などをわかりやすく解説する。

❶展示ホール1・全景 ❷森 ❸からだ ❹民族楽器 ❺民族衣裳

❻展示ホール2・全景 ❼フラーコーナー ❽ビデオギャラリー

Architecture or Status Quo

If we challenge the future, we have to learn that 'styles' are abundantly amongst us, that the style belonging to our own period is an all-embracing style. Revolution has become impossible.

Our minds have consciously or unconsciously apprehended this condition and new needs have been numbed. The machinery of society, too much in gear, oscillates between ages of boredom, and a catastrophe.

It is a question of building which is at the root of the mental pacification of today; architecture or status quo.

'Styles' no longer innovate, they are too much in our ken; if they still satisfy us, it is as teddy bears. If we set ourselves against the future, we are forced to the conclusion that the ever-occuring boring little shock of the new is no longer of any interest; it no longer concerns us: all the values have been neutralised; there has been a total ossification in the conception of what Architecture is.

There reigns a great agreement between the Post-Modern state of mind, which is a drug for us, and the stifling accumulation of hot news.
The problem is one of awakening, in which the irrealities of our life are in question.
Society is filled with a omnipresent somnambulism, caused by oversaturation. Everything lies in that: everything depends on the effort made and the attention paid to these symptoms of mass hypnosis.

Architecture or Status Quo.
Status Quo can be broken.

---

codes have been overturned. If we challenge the past, we shall learn that "styles" no longer exist for us, that a style belonging to our own period has come about; and there has been a revolution.

Our minds have consciously or unconsciously apprehended these events and new needs have arisen, consciously or unconsciously. The machinery of Society, profoundly out of gear, oscillates between an amelioration, of historical importance, and a catastrophe.

It is a question of building which is at the root of the social unrest of to-day; architecture or revolution.

the " styles " no longer exist, they are outside our ken; if they still trouble us, it is as parasites. If we set ourselves against the past, we are forced to the conclusion that the

old architectural code, with its mass of rules and regulations evolved during four thousand years, is no longer of any interest; it no longer concerns us: all the values have been revised; there has been revolution in the conception of what Architecture is.

There reigns a great disagreement between the modern state of mind, which is an admonition to us, and the stifling accumulation of age-long detritus.

The problem is one of adaptation, in which the realities of our life are in question.

Society is filled with a violent desire for something which it may obtain or may not. Everything lies in that: everything

depends on the effort made and the attention paid to these alarming symptoms.

Architecture or Revolution.

Revolution can be avoided.

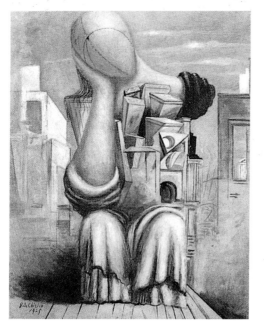

De Chirico, Il filosofo, 1925

Extension to the State Gallery, Stuttgart, 1977-1984. James Stirling and Michael Wjlford

Ole Bouman Roemer van Toorn

A Never-Ending Metaphor

Anyone seeking insight into a cultural or historical situation will find rich spoils in the accompanying architecture. Architecture gives expression to mentalities, visions, cultural and local identities, economic circumstances, political choices and much else. In the consciousness of many people, architecture is a metaphor for reality: architecture gives concrete form to reflections of the world, contemplations about the world, postulations of an imaginary world and speculations on a world of tomorrow. Moreover, its materiality, durability and functionality invariably return to take the gloss off all those bright imaginings. The scope of architectural metaphor is practically universal. Owing to its anthropological and biological basis, it reappears in every time and every place. All participants in a cultural dialogue avail themselves of its stone, its volumes and its space. Everyone has an opinion about architecture; everyone uses it, and hence it is the most public of all art forms. Presumably it will also continue to be so for a long time yet. While several forms of art have been declared dead at least once in their existence, it is sheer effrontery to do the same to architecture. While there is life, while the brain still needs a body and is not yet entirely transformed into artificial intelligence, an 'end' of architecture would be unthinkable. Architecture is the only art form which cannot, by definition, be pure art.

But this material bottom-line does not diminish the fact that architecture *is* an art form, a vehicle of cultural speculation. As such, the profession can not simply turn a deaf ear to the intermittent pronouncements of the 'death' of architecture. It is precisely its dual character, its constancy as a human need on the one hand and its inconstancy as a cultural medium on the other, that makes it such an excellent host to cultural debate. No wonder philosophers have been so fond of using it as a metaphor to exemplify their arguments. And no wonder it has been one of the most prominent subjects of the discourse on the Post-Modern which has been going on since the seventies. The various crises around which this discussion has centred have all found a ready and cogent illustration in architecture; yet at the same time, they have met an obstinate resistance in it. Architecture is the last guardian of the archaic world of foundations, gravity and eternal values. It is also the last guardian of the Modernist ideal of building for tomorrow; and perhaps the last guardian of free will, which it arouses by offering space for human action. In this respect, architecture can never be totally outmoded. Will bodies become irrelevant? Will places be homogenised out of existence? Will identities vanish? Perhaps – 'all that is solid melts into air', according to Karl Marx. But one thing remains, and that is architecture. And even while knowledge continues to splinter into ever yet finer specialisms, the architect remains, willy-nilly, a *homo universalis*. Architecture, seen as the integral process of commission, plan and execution, is the final generalism; and this could well prove to be its strength in the near future.

Apart from some isolated and often peripheral intellectual circles, the practice of describing the contemporary social and cultural situation in wide-sweeping terms of 'colonialism', 'imperialism' or similar jargon sprung from the vision of a utopian world, has all but vanished. Like practically any future vision couched in positive terms, such utopian worlds are suspect because they lay down the law for the perfect life. A Post-Modern society – fragmented, individualistic, multicultural, pluriform and anonymous, yet prepared to write off masses of humanity – no longer has any use for a metaphysics of universality. All that is now acceptable, it seems, is an appeal to the *relative* validity of an idea or a value. This condition of undecidability in an all-embracing atopia of the Now, lacks an escape route to any *terra incognita* whatsoever. It supports only individual worlds of meanings. Nearly all the philosophical capacity of the Western world is being deployed to map out this fragmentation. *En passant*, we forget that our pluriform culture is a mechanism that reproduces and distributes a uniform civilisation.

From the inside, this situation gives the appearance of a huge emancipation. The experience of individual self-determination has become a real possibility at last, at least for those of us who can afford it. Each of us can compile his own world-image and experience his own micro-history. Briefly, around 1990, in a crescendo of ill-informed triumphalism, this liberal view passed for the essence of paradise on earth – a New World Order, some said, whose further actualisation was merely a matter of time.

Now we are sadder and wiser. The New World Order extends no further than the dollar bill on which the motto *novus ordo seclorum* is printed. Deprived of the reassuring clarity of a colonial, Eurocentric world-view or a Cold War, the world finds itself in a situation where populations go adrift, nationalistic fanaticism and economic buccaneering flourish, religious fundamentalism shows its muscle and frontiers are inexorably closed to the despairing hordes of asylum seekers. Even tormented nature bites back at us without mercy.

But what can we do about it? The world is becoming more and more uniform, yet the resulting 'normality' seems to lack any real ethical depth. We stick decorously to the rules, while those vague, indefinable feelings of dissatisfaction seem to have gone into internal exile. Because the rules are accepted as a matter of course, the only thing people can still believe in is a limited individual self-fulfilment. The resulting Me-culture is the primary means by which the social mechanisms of cultural production are

perpetuated. To win any kind of social standing, the individual is forced to develop a 'unique' profile for himself and thereby claim a niche within the existing structure. The overwhelming **pluralism** of society **is a** consequence of this. We live in an up-to-date version of the **panopticon,** which now provides a multitude of fragmentary glimpses instead of a 360-degree perspective. The festival of forms legitimates and controls the status quo. Pluralism is part and parcel of an inescapable social homogeneity.

At the same time, this situation is marked by a kind of schizophrenia which combines the ultimate in well-informedness with the pinnacle of paralysis. Never before have we been so well aware of what things should *not* be like, but so little able to take the consequences. Never before have we known so much about so much, but been able to change so little of so little. Never before were we so good at communicating, but struck so profoundly speechless. The above-mentioned emancipation is totally inapplicable to the great majority of the world population, which, according to Eduardo Galeano, tends to be selectively forgotten. 'The problem of this world is that the problems of this world are no longer reflected in the lives of those who are in a position to do anything about them', said the German politician Gregor Gysi. We would go a step further: the media give the illusion of reflection, but, for the spectator, annihilate the relationship between experiencing and reacting to the represented reality.

Instead of that relationship, we see private interests invading a public space in which there is barely any communication between those present. The individual shields himself from reality because the obligatory interior monologue encapsulates or excludes other perceptions than his own. And should someone nonetheless feel an urge for change, he is confronted by the façade of legitimacy on which the (pseudo) public sphere is based. Behind this façade, however, there no longer appears to be any supporting structure. There is certainly no obvious forum where the public interest can be debated. There are no people to address any more. 'Instead of private faces in public places, there are only public faces in private places' (W.H. Auden). Naturally this situation has a certain transparency, but one that was never intended. We live in a time in which the engineering of consent plays first fiddle. Dissent exists only as a game of the 'alternative' – the alternative as a life-style, as an indulgence. The Other becomes a partial excuse for the monoculture industry. Critical awareness has become a placebo, instead of a disruptive attribute, an *Anleitung zum Handeln* (El Lissitzky).

From Nie Wieder Krieg to Anything Goes

Ole Bouman Roemer van Toorn

We would like to propose an Oedipal thought: the proclaimed end of the great ideologies about the true and the false or the beautiful and the ugly, is a conjecture strongly tied to demography. We are referring to the post-war boom babies who, in all parts of Western society, have now made their way up to the social cadre. This generation has now reached the age at which it no longer needs an ideology (as it did around May '68) in order to form an image of the world; it prefers to confine itself to its own life experience. After all, he who is not an idealist when he is twenty, has no heart; he who is still an idealist at forty, is a fool. The first post-war generation is acquainted with human folly at first hand, and this has scooped the utopian momentum out of its thinking; and seeing that the current discourse is largely determined by this post-ideological demographic cohort, the death of ideology tends to be proclaimed as though it were a plain fact. Meanwhile, the baby-boom generation now has more life behind it than in front of it. This must inevitably shape their view of the world.

Another reason for this transformation in the structure of idealism is the nature of the wars that preceded their birth. After Total Wars, a chorus of *nie wieder Krieg* came as no surprise. This cry, and the ineradicable memories of the holocaust and of Hiroshima, have made their mark on all contemporary thought. No longer can an ideal be elevated to absolute status: any ambition of universal validity for a theory, a viewpoint or a vision is suspect as the germ of a new Auschwitz. This state of mind, whether conscious or unconscious, has resulted in a philosophical concern for what was formerly excluded, what was in danger of being overlooked. Instead of stamping things as right or wrong, people prefer to leave the options open. To each his own, they say. Repression and exclusion exceeded a critical point in the past, at the zero point of history, and since then these mechanisms have been permanently tainted – even when their intention is to replace today by a better today. Judgements seem to have become impossibly difficult. People find it more important to restrain the undesirable than to strive for the optimum. They would rather be politically correct than politically active. So anything keeps going.

It all looks very liberal and democratic, but the avoidance of ethical errors can be an alibi for social passivity. And those who live on the wrong side of the affluent society have to bear the consequences. Inclusivism seems to imply pacification, but in fact it is violence. And we do well out of it. Our fear of taking a stand has repercussions that affect the lives of so many people that we have to shut them out of our minds for our own psychological protection.

Promotion leaflet Rokko Oriental Hotel 1992: 'Summer or white wedding pack'. Chapel on Mount Rokko Kobe, Hyogo 1985-86 by Tadao Ando

Billboard Barcelona airport: 'The art of being local'

Fear of taking a stand? But aren't we going through a period of revival in social involvement, right now in the nineties? Hadn't we all tired of the free-booting eighties, the decade of the bubble economy and the Post-Modern lightness of being? Under either practical or moral pressure, many people take up issues again, such as those surrounding racism, sexism, environmental destruction and AIDS. But these are inevitably reactions to acute threats, rather than visions of a better future. In effect, the pursuit of a moral condition takes second place to the preservation of preconditions. Not life, but survival, has priority. A similar retreat can be seen in politics, where those involved struggle against the effects but stay silent about the causes. It's a bit reminiscent of the kind of philanthropy in which the factory-owner's wife visited the slums bringing charitable aid to her husband's poverty-stricken employees. But we seldom hear a coherent argument – let alone see practical action being taken – about the relationship between all those micro-problems which can loom so gigantically in the mind and the macro-problems that refuse to take root there. Today's intellect seems to be incapable of anything more than a cocooned critical awareness.

For anyone in danger of succumbing to an excess of awareness, there is a way out: the sublime aesthetics of unrepresented authenticity, an experience of reality amid an ocean of simulacra. The sublimity of art is the ideal compensation for a false life. But it says a great deal that the sublime has become an endorsement instead of an observable fact. Once the experience has been named, it loses its innocence and can be

manipulated and faked. The result is that collective hope is replaced by the fetish of individual artistic talent. The work of art – and of architecture as art – becomes a bulwark of elevated feelings in a ruined world, the text an isolated moment of pleasure in an ocean of frustration. Artistic and architectural production safeguards its own existence by shutting itself up in aesthetics. Most practitioners think they can keep their hands clean of real-world necessity by pretending the innocence of an amoral aesthetic urge. People are afraid of art and architecture that takes a social stand. The work may freely contain all kinds of social and political hints, but never become an implementation of them. Art has been neutralised by absorption into freedom of opinion. It now has barely any impact on society, and a critical evaluation of this position is no longer considered relevant.

Art has let itself be caught in the net of dialectics by setting itself up in opposition to reality instead of residing in reality. Aesthetics becomes a component, a legitimation, of power. All that remains is artistic narcissism, in which monographs, one-man shows, artistic recognition are everything. Critical judgement has no place in all this. People rather let themselves be enticed by the most concrete form of involvement there is: *Einfühlung*, empathy.

One vein of contemporary art and architecture reflects a longing for the haptonomy of the object, for the touch of material and for the optical caress, for a rebirth of authenticity. This kind of work aims to offer a touchstone for experience, something to hold onto in a volatile world of simulation and experiential poverty, a pause in the endless flight forwards, a point of rest in the unstoppable mobilisation of the world and of our minds. Another current in art and architecture offers a state of excitement for those less in need of psychological reassurance – an aesthetics fascinated by speed, technology and virtualisation. Here, the spectator's empathy is not held by a thing but by a suggestive, evanescent, even hypnotic atmosphere. Fascinism is a high-energy art that has no time for the makeability of society.

This is the new involvement that can make do without ideology. The craving for a physically experienced meaning in the *fin-de-siècle*, and the mature awareness of human fallibility in a post-ideological world both lead to a belief in *Einfühlung*. Everyone can agree with a purely reptilian social critique based on a phenomenological apprehension of the world. This social critique makes a direct connection with the mid-brain, with the undercurrent of our humanity, which eludes every cerebral counter-argument. As critical spirits, what else can we do but heartily wish everyone the pleasure of this most individual of all experiences? And it is just as hard to argue against the fascination of social acceleration. Fascination invariably knocks criticism into a cocked hat.

Façadism *tries to attract. This strategy aims to show life as it is by means of the autonomous image.*

489

Fascinism *tries to draw us on. This strategy aims to give us a foretaste of the near future (at least according to current projections) by means of an autonomous atmosphere.*

Archaism *tries to retreat. This strategy aspires to modesty and pays its respects to the timelessness of eternal values by means of the autonomous thing.*

We can conceive of various levels at which architects decide their attitude to and, especially, their position *in* society. Firstly there is the narrative level of the form, the outward appearance, the façade. This is the former *venustas*, one of the few traditional aspects of building still left exclusively to the architect following the industrial division of labour. Secondly, there is the constructive-material level of the skeleton (*firmitas*) and other 'hardware'. This is generally already the work of the civil engineer, who specialises in 'working out' what is required. Finally, there is the programmatic-functional level of the 'life' that is accommodated by the architecture (*utilitas*). This is generally organised spatially by the architect, but falls largely under the responsibility of the investor, the client, the bureaucrat and the user.

It is not easy for an architect to pay due respect to all the dimensions that play a role in his work. The production, the distribution, the networks and many other mechanisms of architectural practice have forced the architect into ever greater specialisation. As a result, it is exceedingly difficult to operate beyond the bounds of one's own vocabulary. The architects is free to manipulate only those variables for which she or he is authorised. All the rest falls outside her or his expert scope, and in any case would exceed the budget. No wonder even the internationally renowned architects in this book are tightly restricted in what they can do, despite their efforts to expand the range of their specialism. If you want to survive, there is not much alternative to doing what the practical world demands of you. And the practical world demands of the architect that he behaves as a manager of the programme and a creative designer of the space. The architect's role thereby becomes marginal: the measure of freedom within one's own domain is coupled to total obedience as regards practically everything that precedes or falls outside it. In concrete terms, this generally means that the architect can seek at most a formal relationship between form and content, but can never act in structural conflict with the political and social tenor of the commission. In relation to culture at large, he can occupy an innovative and critical position only as far as the form is concerned.

Once it is narrowed down to merely the aesthetic aspect of what used to be its total programme, architecture becomes simulation – a far cry from a public forum in which the acts of power can be subjected to debate. The programme is lost from view. If architecture is able to accord a shape to the function, then it is only in the classic functionalist (i.e. technocratic) mode; thus the political implications of the function no longer have any visual or material point of reference.

Of course, this state of affairs reflects a development that is taking place quite independently of architecture. The more the human body and its acts are robotised and digitalised, the less visible the political identity of an act becomes. It is not the act itself, but how it is done, that matters. For architecture, this implies a strong emphasis on the solution to the exclusion of cultural speculation, i.e. the articulation of a social problem within the solution. Architecture is expected to be purely part of the solution. That much of the notion of the house as a machine to live in has become a reality, after all.

Architecture, as an art form, adopts the time-honoured survival strategy of an artistic discipline: it abandons whatever it shares with other disciplines and concentrates on that which makes it unique. The result is, indeed, a kind of survival. ***Thank God, we know the difference between Lincoln Cathedral and a bicycle shed.*** Architecture has definitively emancipated itself as Art. But at the same time it has sacrificed its programmatic capacities. Its newly won sublimity is thus at the cost of a significant reduction in its relevance.

Wim Wenders, Lid sinds 1988.

Daar kunt u gerust mee van hu

Bel voor informatie 020 - 5 to 13

Ole Bouman Roemer van Toorn

True, architecture has survived as art. As art, it is free and autonomous. This autonomy has a number of characteristics. Firstly, the freedom only applies within the strict bounds of the discipline. Secondly, the aesthetic aspect is presented as a way out of the violence of the 'everyday world'. This aspect is not so much a rational thing as an attribute of an elevated, poetic domain. Thirdly, the autonomy is characterised by mutual competitiveness which largely centres around being up-to-date and different. Everyone who wishes to take part is obliged to take a distinct stance towards his contemporary surroundings and the status quo. Originality and a unique style are the primary requirements, and these have to be accompanied by intellectual arguments of high quality. Still, this architecture rarely has anything to do with criticisms of current social developments.

Architecture produces objects that no longer actively relate to social reality. It objectivises its own morality in a purely analogous, illustrative way, by 'sticking' discursive ideas onto the architectural object. The result is a huge discrepancy between the complex reality, defined as the 'outside world', and the architectural reality 'inside'. This architecture gives free scope to the most varied functions and interpretations, and is hence able to perpetuate its own impeccable autonomy. It withdraws into a shell of meaning which is conveyed by the material. This meaning is determined not so much by the mutual relationship of the programmatic content to the material, as by the relationship between the different material carriers. The material carrier can, admittedly, have a radical influence on the space, but that influence is not conceived from the standpoint of the spatial organisation itself independently of the material.

The critical architect, having realised that the innovation of a sign *within* the signing system is no longer an acceptable substitute for significant change, would no longer restrict his alternative ideas to the form alone.

It is very important to show explicitly how the form operates separately from the content and thereby keeps the dominant mechanisms of late capitalism in the saddle. This would in turn demonstrate the untenable position of the kind of artist who believes s/he can be socially involved through form alone. Furthermore, it is important to bring form and content into a deliberate relation once more. In this way, we believe, it will be possible to find an alternative that does not distance itself from the constant developments of technology or take refuge in the tactility of the tectonics. This is an approach which could open a new perspective, in which the invisible and visible processes would become transparent without losing their emancipatory momentum in an apolitical, neutral rendition. In practice, this would mean architecture making it its business once more to create a genuine public domain. It would amount to the development of an architecture in which the satisfaction of basic human needs would go along with a critique of the cultural stasis in which we find ourselves. Both the professional community and the user would then be able to evaluate the merits of this alternative approach in built reality. The precondition of this alternative is not so much the discipline's autonomy or a recognisable artistic signature, as the architect's willingness to bring his own professional competence to bear on not only the functional programme, but also the programme of the context and of the location.

491

Still from *Tout va bien* by Jean Luc Godard, 1972

Architecture Pro Gramme of Life

Before s/he makes a single mark on paper, every architect has to deal with a programme formulated by the client. In many cases the client knows next to nothing about architecture. He would like to accommodate all kinds of activities, but is incapable of imagining how it might look. It is the architect's job to dispose of any inappropriate preconceptions the client may have and thus provide insight into the actual implications of the client's idea in terms of square metres and mutual relationships between the various functions. This puzzle is almost invariably solved in a way that functionally accommodates the programme of requirements, while the architect retains a little elbow-room in which he can exert his own interpretation. Obviously, this does not mean that the functional programme and the programme of the architect are mutually independent. However, the programme of requirements is seldom interpreted in such a way that, before being converted into materials and space, a critique of or alternative to the status quo is expressed. The architect rarely penetrates to the functional issues themselves, but usually operates only at the level of clothing the programme in a material shell.

Our view is that the programme of requirements must be scrutinised as a social institution, against the background of the mechanisms on which that institution relies. This is precisely the activity in which the specialism of architecture should be prepared to go beyond its presently prescribed bounds – naturally, in connection with a spatial form. This could hardly be achieved without drawing on other domains of knowledge. All in all, our plea is as follows: firstly, the architect should aim to throw the constraints that affect him open to discussion and insist on the right to exert an influence on the programme; secondly, the architect should seek opportunities to achieve the closest possible relationship between form and programme, taking into account the situation and the scale of the assignment but without deference to the prevailing institutional constraints. And these desiderata should be seen as steps on the way to an alternative that bears a true relation to the public sphere.

Ole Bouman Roemer van Toorn

This book is an open work that raises more questions than it can answer. An architectural project can be an open work too. A project does not have to be an attempt to solve everything in one go or to have some unequivocal 'meaning'. Rather, it should offer a critical insight into both the use and the thinking behind that use. In this sense architecture could share Hegel's characterisation of philosophy - *'Die Philosophie ist Ihre Zeit in Gedanken erfasst'* (which with a slight but essential modification gives us Mies van der Rohe's dictum 'Architecture is the will of an epoch translated into space'). The difference between architecture and philosophy is that the latter analyses or characterises reality without having to accommodate itself to it. But architecture does not have the option of such independence. With architecture, you inevitably get your hands dirty, and it would be wrong to pretend otherwise; on the contrary, this necessary fact should be recognised as a stimulus for the development of a practical alternative – in advance of theory, perhaps. Architecture's down-to-earth obligations mean that it can never be completely reduced to a (visual) language, which can at most represent reality. The widespread belief that architecture 'is' language is often pushed to the point of claiming that a new reality can be created only through language. Architecture cannot permit itself this luxury because its three-dimensional presence means that the image and reality can never shut one another out. In this sense, architecture is an 'in between'. Architecture houses a real-life programme that obliges it to act with a sense of reality. This involvement with life is the source of its strength, but it imposes constraints. Architecture remains closely tied to the institutional mechanisms with which it has to function, despite its inclination to see itself as an art form. Architecture is characterised by both a capacity to take distance and a need for nearness. This difficult combination of requirements should also be the determinant of its expressiveness.

It is our conviction that when architecture really aims to offer an alternative to the status quo, it has to cross the traditional boundaries of its field. In doing so, it automatically becomes a critique of the internal logic of Design, and will act in consciousness of its institutional role. An 'open' architecture challenges the public and stimulates critical involvement without ceasing to be architecture. Its author, moreover, will not be a passive producer of someone else's standpoint, but will be highly alert to the dialogue between daily life and the array of beliefs his work perpetuates, satisfies, probes or reinforces. Her or his work exposes the internal contradictions and does not shrink from confrontation. The absence of an original personal or homogeneous style is not an unintentional weakness associated with this position, but an essential principle. In this way, opposing discourses will be taken up into a process of mutual illumination and influence.

An architecture that is open has specific structural attributes that allow, and also channel, new interpretations and shifting perspectives. The relation between form and content is openly presented as a problem with roots in the nature of the programme, the scale and the context. Within this concept, the aesthetic component takes on meaning only when coupled to the practical requirements and the context. The image must add something to the given reality without flinching from baring that reality. **Open architecture** is critical in that it aims to be an ongoing stimulus to criticism. The spectator/user should not be simply orchestrated by the artist/architect, but should be able to contribute to the meaning. A crucial precondition for this is a fluidity of perspectives that offers resistance to an unequivocal reading of the form. The purpose of this systematic ambiguity should not be to lose the surprise which is inherent in every perception in an infinity of fascinating (false) trails. It should be, rather, to provoke a thought process by offering a series of alternatives, and hence to stimulate open use. We believe the real world always allows multiple interpretations that have not yet been swallowed up by the established perception. If we succeed in keeping these alternatives alive, then we can avoid clichés, open up new perspectives and perhaps enter the real world.

493

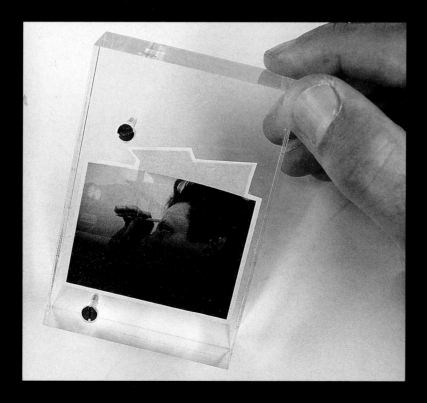

Anton C. Alberts & Max van Huut

An austerely planned bed of roses, now that's what I call chaotic

Anton C. Alberts, born in 1927 in Berghem near Antwerp, Belgium, started his education at the Higher Technical School of the Art of Building, Amsterdam, studied at the École des Beaux Arts, Paris, and finished his study at the Academy of Architecture in Amsterdam. For more than twenty years he was teacher at the Academy of Architecture in Amsterdam and Tilburg. He made a study of yoga in general and a specific study of the esoteric training of the Raja-yoga. Through many years of experience searching to express esoteric principles in buildings, he developed his 'organic architecture'. In 1963 he established his architecture office. **Max van Huut**, born in 1947 in Jakarta, Indonesia, has lived in the Netherlands since 1957. He studied at the Higher Technical School and the Academy of Architecture in Amsterdam. Since 1987 has worked at the office of Alberts which then changed its name to **architecture office Alberts & Van Huut**. During the development of the projects Alberts forms the conceptual framework, Van Huut completes it and makes a direct relation between the organic architecture and other arts, like music, dance and visual art. **Projects** House *De Waal*, Utrecht, (NL) 1979-1980; ING (formerly NMB) Bank head office, Amsterdam, (NL) 1982-1987; Gasunie head office, Groningen, (NL) 1989-1993; and more than 12,000 houses (social housing) over the years in various urban planning projects. **Publications** Alberts, T., *Een organisch bouwwerk. Architectuur en spiritualiteit*, Utrecht/Antwerp 1990; Alberts, T., *Obeying the organic*, Friends of Kebyar, vol. 9.2, no 50, 1991.

Tadao Ando

Architecture is half dependent on thought; the rest comes from existence and spirit, i.e., the invisible

At seventeen **Tadao Ando**, born in 1941 in Osaka, Japan, was a qualified professional boxer. He didn't follow any architectural training; instead, he instructed himself in architecture (1962-1969). In those years he also travelled in the United States, Europe and Africa. In 1969 the **Tadao Ando Architect & Associates office** was established. Since 1981 the office has been situated in the first completed work of Ando: the Tomishima House. He has lectured at many universities as visiting professor: in Norway (1984), in the USA, at for instance Princeton University (1985), Harvard University (1985 & 1990), Cooper Union (1985), Columbia University (1985 & 1988), London (1985), and Australia (1985). **Projects** Row House Sumiyoshi, Osaka, (J) 1976; Rokko House I, (J) 1983; Church on the Water, Hokkaido, (J) 1988; Church of Light, Osaka, (J) 1989; Museum of Literature and Children's Museum, Himeji, Hyogo, (J) 1991; Japan Pavilion EXPO'92, Sevilla, (E) 1992; A factory of different cultures and traditions for Benetton, Treviso, (I) 1992. **Publications** *Tadao Ando: The Yale Studio & current works*, Rizzoli, New York 1989; 'Tadao Ando', *El Croquis* 44, 1990; 'Tadao Ando', *GA Details*: A.D.A. Edota Tokyo, 1991.

Ricardo Bofill

Through my buildings I want to receive the kind of adulation usually reserved for pop stars

Ricardo Bofill, born in 1939 in Barcelona, Spain, studied at the Escuela Téchnica Superiór de Arquitectura, Barcelona (1955-1956) and the School of Architecture, Geneva, Switzerland (1957-1960). In 1963 he brought together a group of architects, engineers, sociologists, philosophers and artists, creating what is known today as the **Taller de Arquitectura** *(Architectural Workshop)*. Taller proceeds from a multi-disciplinary approach. In the sixties, a new housing typology was developed and realised with the construction of, for instance, *Barrio Gaudi*, Tarragona and *Walden 7*, Barcelona. In the recent projects it isn't the typology but the monumentality of the building that gets the attention. Over the years the Taller office established new project-teams in Paris, New York and Tokyo. Bofill lectured at the Columbia School of Architecture. **Projects** *Walden 7*, Barcelona, (E) 1970-1975; Le Jardin des Halles, Paris, (F) 1975; St. Quentin-en-Yvelines, Paris, (F) 1972-1975; Marne-la-Vallée, Paris, (F) 1978-1983; Montpellier, Paris, (F) 1983-1990; Olympic Village, Barcelona, (E) 1989-1992; Airport of Barcelona, (E) 1988-1992. **Publications** James, W. A., *Ricardo Bofill. Taller de Arquitectura. Buildings and projects 1960-1985*, New York 1988; 'Ricardo Bofill. Taller de Arquitectura', *GA Document* 4,1985; Futagawa, Y., 'Bofill's last Spanish projects', *GA,* March 1992.

Oriol Bohigas

The fact that I occupy this office in the municipal department of cultural affairs means that I am completely in agreement with the mayor

Oriol Bohigas was born in 1925 in Barcelona, Spain. After his graduation from the Escuela Tèchnica Superiór de Arquitectura, Barcelona (1943-1951) he went into partnership with Josep Martorell. In 1961 he got his technical diploma in town planning. One year later he went into partnership with David Mackay. Since the sixties he has spent his time building, teaching and writing. From the beginning Bohigas was involved with town planning. He was the co-founder of **Grupo R.** which was directed against the town-planning principles of the CIAM 1951. The existing traditional and local urban structure had to be the starting-point for new projects to be developed, in keeping with the basic tenet of Grupo R. that the architect's task is not to change but only to improve the urban environment. In 1980-1984 Bohigas was director of planning in the city council of Barcelona, and from 1984 personal advisor on urban affairs to the mayor of Barcelona. He became councillor of culture on the city council in 1991. **Projects** built by the Martorell, Bohigas, Mackay-office: House *La Maquinista*, Barceloneta, Barcelona, (E) 1979-1988; Housing Block, Mollet, Barcelona, (E) 1987; Olympic Village, Barcelona, (E) 1992. **Publications** Frampton, K., *Bohigas, Martorell, Mackay; 30 anni di architettura 1954-1984*, Milan 1984; 'Martorell/Bohigas/Mackay', *El Croquis* 34, May-June 1988; Gili, Gustavo, *Martorell, Bohigas, Mackay, Puigdomènech. La Vila Olímpica. Barcelona 92. Architecture, Parks, Leisure Port*, Barcelona 1991.

Santiago Calatrava

I don't care if they call me engineer or architect; architecture needs both of them

Santiago Calatrava, born in 1951 in Benimamet, Valencia, Spain, went to several academies: the Art School in Valencia (1968-1969), the Escuela Téchnica Superiór de Arquitectura de Valencia (1969-1973) and visited the Eidgenossische Technische Hochschule in Zürich, Switzerland, to study civil engineering (1975-1979). Finally he did his doctorate of technical science at the Architectural Department of the ETH, from 1979-1981. His thesis was titled 'Concerning the fold ability of Space frames'. This preoccupation with space frames is notably present in his Calatrava's work: in the various bridge-projects it is divided in two directions – the technical and the architectural. In 1981 Calatrava established his **Architecture and Civil Engineering office** in Zürich. His second office, based in Paris, opened in 1990. **Projects** Bac de Roda – Felip II bridge, Barcelona, (E) 1984-1987; Stadelhofen Railway Station, Zürich, (CH) 1983-1990; Telecommunication Tower for the Olympic Games, Barcelona, (E) 1989-1992. **Publications** *Santiago Calatrava. Engineering architecture*, Birkhäuser, Basel 1990; *Calatrava. Recent projects. Dynamic equilibrium*, Artemis & Winkler Verlag, Zürich and Munich 1991.

Giancarlo De Carlo

I always believed in dualistic reality, in oppositions and consensus, in that dialectical play which is the salt of life

Giancarlo De Carlo, born in 1919 in Genova, Italy, studied at the Technical University, Milan (1942) and the University of Venice (1945-1949). He lives in Milan and many of his building projects were realised in Italy. Besides his architectural projects he has also worked on many urban design projects and entered many international and national competitions. He was leader of the collection *Struttura e forma urbana,* published by Il Saggiatore, A. Mondadori, Milan. The introductions to these works were written by De Carlo. He has organised several exhibitions, including the VIIIe, IXe and Xe Triënnale, in Milan. Between 1952 and 1957 De Carlo was the editor of *Casabella,* and since 1977 he has been the head editor and publisher of *Space and Society.*

Projects Housing, Materna, (I) 1959; University building, Urbino, (I) 1966; Housing Matteotti, Terni, (I) 1974; Operazione Mercatale, Urbino, (I) 1980; Collegio Universitario del Tridente, Urbino, (I) 1980; Housing, Venice, (I) 1983; Housing Murano, Venice, (I) 1986-1987.

Publications De Carlo, Giancarlo, *Urbina, la storia di una citta e il piano della sua evoluzione urbanistica,* Padua 1966; De Carlo, Giancarlo, 'Legitimizing Architecture', *Forum* Vol. XXIII, the Netherlands, January 1972; De Carlo, Giancarlo, *Reflections on the present state of architecture,* London 1978; Zucchi, B., *Giancarlo De Carlo*, London 1992.

Nigel Coates

It'll happen anyhow. If architects don't do it, others will

Nigel Coates was born in 1949 in Great Britain. He studied at the Architectural Association School of Architecture, London (1974). After that he taught for many years at the A.A., first as assistant to Tschumi, who had been his tutor, and then as a unit master of Unit 10 (1977-1989). In 1978 he won the Year Prize Italian Government scholarship to visit Rome University.

In 1983 he and eight of his students from the unit of the A.A. formed the architects group NATO (Narrative Architecture Today) and started publishing the *NATO* magazine. In that same year he also established his own office: Nigel Coates Architecture. After two years he formed **Branson Coates Architecture** with **Doug Branson**. Besides buildings the office makes furniture, and video clips and collages about the contemporary city. In 1986 the office was licensed to produce

furniture in Japan, in 1988 for the United Kingdom and in 1990 for Italy.

Projects Metropole Restaurant, Tokyo, (J) 1989; K. Hamnett Shop, Sloane Street, London, (GB) 1989; Nishi Azabu Wall, commercial building, Tokyo, (J) 1990; Ecstacity, Installation, Architectural Association, London, (GB) 1992; Nautilus bar and seafood restaurant, Schiphol, (NL) 1993.

Publications *Arkalbion and six other projects*, London 1984; Poynor, R., *Nigel Coates: the city in motion*, 1989; Coates, N., *Ecstacity*, London 1992; film 'Signs of the city' for the BBC, 1992.

Pietro Derossi

It is the time of life which makes the measure, poses the issue of finiteness

Pietro Derossi, born in 1933 in Turin, Italy, studied at the Faculty of Architecture in Turin. He has been visiting professor at the Architectural Association in London, the Pratt Institute in New York, Columbia University in New York, Hochschule der Künste in Berlin and at the Lausanne Polytechnic. He has been professor of architectural design at the Faculty of Architecture in Turin. Since the end of the sixties Derossi has written many texts besides the building and furniture-projects that have been realised.

Projects Piper Pluri-club, Turin, (I) 1966; L'altro Mondo club, Rimini, (I) 1968; XIV Triënnale di Milano, Milan, (I) 1968; Social Leisure Environment, Museum of Modern Art, New York, (USA) 1972; Restoration of a nineteenth-century family house, Turin, (I) 1980 (Derossi and Ceretti); 'Aldo Moro' activity centre, Turin, (I) 1983 (Derossi, Di Suni and Caffaro Rore); Residential tower in Wilhelmstraße, Berlin, (D) 1985-1987 (Derossi, Caffaro Rore, Di Suni and Besso Marcheis); Biffi Scala Restaurant, Milan, (I) 1988 (Derossi, Besso, Caffaro Rore, Massa). Derossi's work has been exhibited on several occasions under which: MOMA New York 1972, Aedes gallery, Berlin 1986.

Publications Derossi, P., 'Intermediate city', *Chronicle in Urban Politics*, London 1974; Derossi, P., *La Città nella giostra del capitale*, Torino 1979; 'Ogetti semplici per funzioni complesse, e poi anche architettura', *Modo* 20, June 1979; Derossi, P., 'Modernita senza avanguardia, Modernism without avant-garde', 13 *Lotus Documents*, Milan 1990; Michelis, M. de, 'Pietro Derossi, Architecture and Figuration', *Ottogono* 94,

March 1990, pp. 68-88; Derossi, P., 'Radical Recall', *Ottogono* 99, June 1991, pp. 89-115.

Elisabeth Diller & Ricardo Scofidio

We are nervous presenting our work within the context of a comprehensive survey

Elisabeth Diller, born in Lodz, Poland, studied at the Cooper Union Schools of Art and Architecture, New York. From 1981-1990 she taught at the same institute. Since 1990 she has been assistant professor at the Princeton University School of Architecture.

Ricardo Scofidio, born in New York, USA, studied at the Cooper Union and at Columbia University. Since 1967 he has been full professor at the Cooper Union. In 1979 they started their cooperation as **Diller + Scofidio**. Their projects cover the fields of settings and body constructions, body building, hygiene, androgyne, uniforms, American industrial design, paranoias and pathologies of any kind, medical drawings and instruments, advertising, electronics etcetera. Their investigations go beyond the conventional expectations of (architectural) forms.

Projects Kinney House, (USA) 1983-1984; *The Bridge* in an arch below Brooklyn Bridge, New York, (USA) 1986; *A delay in glass* or *The Rotary Notary and His Hot Plate*, New York, (USA) 1987; *Withdrawing Room*: a probe into the conventions of private rite, San Francisco, (USA) 1988; *Parasite*-installation, MOMA, New York, (USA) 1989; *Slow House*, North Haven, Long Island, New York, (USA) 1989-1990;. *Tourism: suitcase Studies*, Walker Art Center, Minneapolis, (USA) 1990.

Publications 'Elisabeth Diller & Ricardo Scofidio, three projects' *AA Files* 14, London 1987, pp. 54-61; 'A Delay in Glass', *Daidalos* 26, 1987, pp. 84-101; 'Elisabeth Diller & Ricardo Scofidio, the withDrawing room', *AA Files* 17, London 1989, pp. 15-24; Teyssot, Georges, 'Erasure and Disembodiment – dialogues with Diller + Scofidio' and 'Diller + Scofidio. Pretext Machine', *Ottogono* 96, September 1990, pp. 56-105.

Peter Eisenman

I don't believe in happy people making art

Peter Eisenman was born in 1932 in Newark, USA. He studied Architecture at the University of Cornell (1955) and continued at the University of Columbia (1960) before gaining his MA degree and his PhD at the University of Cambridge, MA (1962 and 1963). He is professor of architecture at Ohio State University. In 1967 he founded the Institute of Architecture and Urban Studies of which he became director in 1982. The Institute is a gathering place for intellectuals as well as practising architects. He is also co-founder and editor of the magazine *Oppositions*. From the outset of his architectural career Eisenman has been preoccupied with the polemical, the practical and the theoretical side of architecture, activities visible in his projects, even in his first series of Houses (I-X, 1968-1977). In 1980, after years of teaching, writing and producing theoretical work, he established his professional architecture practice to focus on building.

Projects Fin d'Ou T Hou S, (USA) 1985; Moving Arrows, Eros and other Errors - An Architecture of Absence (Romeo and Juliet project) 1985; Choral Works, Parc de la Villette, Paris, (F) 1986-1990; Biocentre, University of Frankfurt am Main, (D) 1987; Wexner Center for the Visual Arts, Columbus, Ohio, (USA) 1985-1989; Koizumi Building, Tokyo, (J) 1989; Alteka Tower, Tokyo, (J) 1991; Greater Convention Center, Columbus, Ohio, (USA) 1993; College of Design, Architecture, Art and Planning, University of Cincinnati, Ohio, (USA) 1993.

Publications 'Eisenmanamnesia', *A + U*, August 1988; 'Dossier Peter Eisenman', *l'Architecture d'Aujourd'hui*, 279, February 1992, pp. 98-115; Graafland, A. (ed.), *Peter Eisenman*, Recente projecten/*Peter Eisenman, Recent projects*, Nijmegen 1989; 'Peter Eisenman', *El Croquis* 41, 1989; *Re:working Eisenman*, Academy Editions, London 1993

Hal Foster

In the face of a culture of reaction on all sides, a practice of resistance is needed

Hal Foster was born in 1955. He is a critic of art, architecture and culture. He was connected to the DIA Art Foundation in

New York and course leader at the Whitney Independent Study Program. He is associate professor of art history and comparative literature at Cornell University. He co-founded the journal *Zone* and has been senior editor at *Art in America*. He is editor of the journal *October*.

Publications Foster, H., *The anti-aesthetic: Essays on Post-Modern culture*, Washington 1983; Foster, H., *Recodings: Art, Spectacle, Cultural politics*, Seattle 1985; Foster, H. (ed.), *Vision and Visuality*, Seattle 1988; Foster, H., *Compulsive beauty*, Cambridge, Mass. 1993.

Norman Foster

In architecture we never talk about creativity, we just do the job

Norman Foster, born in 1935 in Manchester, Great Britain, studied both architecture and city planning at Manchester University (1961) where he was awarded a Henry Fellowship at Yale University, M. Arch. (1962). After travel and work in the USA, he returned to London to set up a private practice with R. Rogers, W. Cheesman and Sue Brumwell, (*Team 4*) in 1963. In 1967 he founded **Foster Associates** with his wife Wendy. From 1968 to 1983 he worked with Buckminster Fuller on various projects.

Projects Sainsbury Centre for Visual Arts, Norwich, (GB) 1974-1978; Stansted Airport, (GB) 1981-1991; Hong Kong Shanghai Bank, Hong Kong 1979-1986; Stanhope security office, Stockley Park, London, (GB) 1987-1989; new ITN Headquarters, London, (GB) 1988-1990; Century Tower, office building, Tokyo, (J) 1987-1991; Telecommunications Tower, Barcelona, (E) 1988-1991; Centre d'Art Contemporain et Mediathèque, Carré d'Art, Nîmes, (F) 1984-1992. On a smaller scale: the Nomos range of furniture and the first London shop for Esprit.

Publications 'Norman Foster', *A + U* Monograph, Japan 1987; *Norman Foster: Foster Associates Buildings and Projects Volume 1 1964-1973, Volume 2 1971-1978, Volume 3 1978-1985*, (ed. Ian Lambot), Watermark Publications 1990; Chaslin, F., *Foster Associates Buildings and Projects 1991*, Sainsbury Centre for Visual Arts 1991; *Foster Associates: Recent Works*, Academy Editions Monograph, London 1992

496

Kenneth Frampton

Sometimes I'm feeling like a dinosaur

Kenneth Frampton, born in 1930 in Woking, Surrey, Great Britain, studied at the Architectural Association School of Architecture, London and got his degree in 1956. Early in his building career Frampton started to theorise and publish about architecture. Today he is a well-known architecture historian and critic, and is invited to partake in a variety of activities by many international universities, institutes, juries etcetera. Since 1972 Frampton has been professor of architecture at the Graduate School of Architecture and Planning of Columbia University, New York, and besides this he has been fellow at the Institute for Architecture and Urban Studies (1972-1982), senior tutor at the Royal College of Art, London (1974-1977) and since 1990 a visiting tutor at the Berlage Institute, Amsterdam.
As mentioned before he has been publishing for many years in magazines, such as *Oppositions* (of which he was a co-founder), and *Lotus Architectural Design*. He has written introductions for monographs on architects and published numerous books.

Publications Frampton, K., 'Labour, work and architecture', in: *Meaning in Architecture*, ed. Ch. Jencks and G. Baird, New York 1970, pp. 151-157; Frampton, K., *New Wave of Japanese Architecture*, New York 1970; Frampton, K., *Le Corbusier 1933-1960*, Cambridge, 1980; Frampton, K., *Modern Architecture, A Critical History*, London 1980; Frampton, K., *Modern Architecture 1851-1945*, New York and Tokyo 1983; Frampton, K., 'Towards a Critical Regionalism: Six Points for an Architecture of Resistance', in: *The Anti-Aesthetic. Essays on Postmodern culture*, ed. Foster, H., Port Townsend 1983, pp. 16-30; Frampton, K., *Studies in Tectonics* (to be published).

Elisabeth Galí

What we understand as anonymous, disciplinary and conventional architecture, should be frequently

poked up, as one pokes up a fire, by avant-garde, revolutionary, and therefore 'artistical' architectural attitudes

Beth Galí was born in 1950 in Barcelona, Spain. Since 1966 she has been working as an industrial designer. Some of her designs, such as an amplifier, put together furniture and a streetlight have won awards. Since 1982 she has been connected as an architect to the 'Servicio de Elementos y Proyectos Urbanos' of the municipality of Barcelona, part of the now famous city council guided by Oriol Bohigas.

Projects *Dafnis i Cloë* design for the Parque de l' Escorxador, Barcelona, (E) 1980-1982 (together with A. Solanas, M. Quintana, A. Arriola); four holiday houses in Selva de Mar, Girona, (E) (together with A. Solanas); Jardín d'Emili Vendrell, Barcelona, (E) 1981; Parc Migdia, Fossar de la Pedrera, Barcelona, (E) 1986; Library Joan Miró, Barcelona, (E) 1985-1990; design for an information bureau of the municipality of Barcelona, (E) 1983 (together with P. Casajoana).

Publications Galí, Beth, 'Diez años de arquitectura española, 1966-1976', in Dorfles, G. (ed.), *Arquitectura Moderna*; Galí, B., 'Los muros verdes del Empordà', *Arquitecturas Bis* 27, March/April 1979; 'Barcelona: Public Spaces with Monument', *Lotus* 39, November 1983, pp. 20-24; 'Island Library', *Architectural Review*, July 1991, pp. 37-41.

Frank O. Gehry

Being accepted isn't everything

Frank Gehry, born in 1929 in Toronto, Canada, studied at the University of Southern California, Los Angeles (M. Fine Arts, 1949-1951 and B. of Architecture 1954) and at Harvard Graduate School of Design (city planning 1956-1957). Before he established his own office, **Frank O. Gehry and Associates, Inc.** in 1962, he worked with Victor Gruen Ass. as a designer and with Hideo Sasaki, Pereira (Los Angeles) and André Remondet (Paris). Gehry has been a visiting professor at various universities in the USA: Southern California (1972-1973), Los Angeles (1988-1989), Harvard (1983), Rice (1976), California (1977-1979) and Yale (1982, 1985 and 1987-1989). He has been design instructor at the University of South California and the South California Institute of Architecture. Over the years he has been on various juries. For his work Gehry has received more than eighty awards since

1967. Gehry has produced many public and private buildings in America, Japan, and more recently in Europe.

Projects Danziger Studio-residence, Hollywood, (USA) 1964; Gehry House, Santa Monica, California, (USA) 1977-1978; American Centre, Bercy Park, Paris, (F) 1989-1992; Schnabel house, Brentwood, California, (USA) 1986-1989; Winton residence guest house, Wayzata, Minnesota, (USA) 1987; Art museum and commercial centre, Santa Monica, California, (USA) 1988; Yale psychiatric institute, New Haven, (USA) 1989; Vitra museum, Weil am Rhein, (D) 1989; Euro Disney, Paris, (F) 1990; Walt Disney concert hall, Los Angeles, (USA) 1988-1990; American Center, Paris, (F) 1993.

Publications Arnell, P. et al (ed.), *Frank Gehry. Buildings and Projects*, New York 1985; *The Architecture of Frank Gehry*, New York 1986; 'Frank O. Gehry', *El Croquis* 45, 1990.

Michael Graves

My life isn't empty, it's quite full. I can't wait to get up tomorrow morning

Michael Graves, born in 1934 in Indianapolis, USA, received his architectural training at the University of Cincinnati (B. Arch. 1958) and Harvard University (M. Arch. 1959). In 1962 he became the Schirmer Professor of Architecture at Princeton University. Two years later, in 1964, Graves opened his professional practice in Princeton, New Jersey. After Graves' late seventies work, for instance the Portland Building, Portland, Oregon, (USA) 1979-1982, Charles Jencks proclaimed him as the figurehead of his own campaign for 'Post-Modernism'.

Projects Crown American Corporate office building, Johntown, Pennsylvania, (USA) 1985-1989; Walt Disney World Swan and Dolphin Hotel, Lake Buena Vista, Florida, (USA) 1987; Historical Center of Industry and Labour, Young town, Ohio, (USA) 1986-1989.

Publications Omer, A., and Weinel, E. (ed.), 'Representation', *Representation and Architecture*, Information Dynamics, Inc., 1982; Wheeler, K. et al (ed.), *Michael Graves, Buildings and Projects 1966-1981*, London 1983; Graves, M., 'A Case for Figurative Architecture', in *Modernity and Popular Culture*, Alvar Aalto Museum, Jyvaskula 1988; Vogel Nichols, K., et al (ed.), *Michael Graves, Buildings and Projects 1982-1989*, New York 1990.

David Harvey

I shop, therefore I am

David Harvey, born in 1935 in Great Britain, studied at St. John's College, Cambridge (1954-1957), where he also attained his PhD in Geography 1957-1960 with a thesis on 'Aspects of Agricultural and Rural Change in Kent, 1800-1900'. In 1989 he became adjunct professor, after having been associate professor and professor of geography between 1969-1988, at the Johns Hopkins University, Baltimore. In 1987 he was assigned Halford Mackinder Professor of Geography at the University of Oxford. He has been visiting professor at various universities in the USA, France, England and Spain.

He has published books on the themes of the city and the contemporary social and cultural structure: Harvey, D., *Explanation in Geography,* London/New York 1969; Harvey, D., *The City and the Space – Economy of Urbanism,* Washington D.C. 1972; Harvey, D., *Social Justice and the City,* London 1973; Harvey, D., *The Limits of Capital,* Oxford 1982; Harvey, D., *The Urban Experience,* Oxford 1989; Harvey, D., *The Condition of Postmodernity: An Enquiry into the Origins of Cultural Change,* Oxford 1989. In this book Harvey cuts beneath the theoretical debates about Post-Modernist culture to reveal the social and economic basis of this apparently free-floating phenomenon. The book Patterson, J., *David Harvey's geography* was published by Croom Helm in 1984. Harvey has published numerous articles in mainly geographical magazines.

Itsuko Hasegawa

I intend to stay in Tokyo to continue my theme of creating 'Architecture as a Second Nature'

Itsuko Hasegawa, born in 1941 in Shizuoka Prefecture, Japan, graduated from the Department of Architecture, Kanto Gakuin University, Japan in 1964. Between 1964-1969 Hasegawa worked at the office of Kiyonori Kikutake. After that she first worked as a research student at the Tokyo Institute of Technology (1969-1971) and later on as an assistant to the Kazuo Shinohara Atelier (1971-1978) at the same institute. In 1979 she established the **Itsuko Hasegawa Atelier** in Tokyo. In the late eighties she started lecturing at Waseda University (1988), the Tokyo Institute of Technology (1989) and Harvard University (1992). Since 1978 her work has often been exhibited in many capital cities such as Boston, New York, London, Paris, Copenhagen, Rotterdam and even Moscow.

Projects Kimura residence, Yaizu, (J) 1972; Tokumaru children's clinic 1979; Kuwahara residence (1980); AONO building (1981); Bizan Hall, Shizuoka (1982-1984) in Matsuyama, Japan; private house, Kumamoto, (J) 1985-1986; private house, Higashitamagawa, Tokyo, (J) 1987; Shonandai Culture Centre, Fujisawa, (J) 1990; S.T.M. house, (J) 1991.

Publications 'The Complete Works of Itsuko Hasegawa', *SD,* April 1985; 'The Age of Dwellers, a Dialogue with Takamisa Yoshizawa'; *Itsuko Hasegawa,* Academy Editions Monograph, London 1993. Hasegawa is also working on another title.

Manfred Hegger

When the social situation provokes it, out of many different kinds of opposition a huge river may develop, that seems to go to a new, better world. Nothing is more delightful than to swim in this river

Manfred Hegger was born in 1946 in Korschenbroich, Germany. He studied architecture at the University of Stuttgart and the Hochschule für Gestaltung in Ulm (1967-1973). He continued with studies in planning at the London School of Economics and Political Science (1975-1976).

He has lectured at the University of Stuttgart (1973-1990), Gesamthochschule in Kassel (1977-1979) and since 1984 has been connected with the Centre for Infrastructure Planning of the University of Stuttgart. In 1980 the **Partnership HHS Planer + Architekten** was established with D. Hegger-Luhnen und G. Schleif. In 1990-1991 he participated in the project-partnership GrünGürtel-Projectoffice in Frankfurt am Main with Professors P. Latz and P. Lieser. Hegger's main issue is today's ecological problems. In his writings he tries to come up with possible solutions to these problems through architecture.

Projects Ökologische Siedlung, Kassel, (D) 1984-1986.

Publications Hegger, M., Pohl, W., Reiss-Schmidt, S., *Vitale Architektur - Traditionen.* Braunschweig/Wiesbaden 1988; Hegger, M., Wolfgang, P., 'Bekenntnisökologie versus Ökotechnologie', in *Arch+* 94 (April 1988, pp. 44-48; Hegger, M., 'ÖkoBau. Ökologie ist unsichtbar', *Deutsche Bauzeitung* 7 1987, pp. 10-15.

Herman Hertzberger

People who want to think about architecture must be able to build

Herman Hertzberger, born in 1932 in Amsterdam, the Netherlands, got his engineering diploma in 1958 at the Technical University in Delft. In the same year he established his own architecture office. Besides his architectural work Hertzberger also expresses himself in other dimensions about architecture. Between 1959 and 1963 he was editor of the (Dutch) journal *FORUM,* together with Van Eyck, Bakema and others. He lectured at the Academy of Architecture in Amsterdam (1956-1970), has been professor at Delft's Technical University since 1970 and professor at the University of Geneva since 1986. In 1985 he was the initiator of Indesem (architectural workshops), and since then, a yearly week of exchange for architecture students and professors from several European Universities has taken place. Since 1989 he has been Dean of the Berlage Institute of Amsterdam. Hertzberger has been visiting professor at various institutions and universities.

Projects Centraal Beheer office building, Apeldoorn, (NL) 1972-1978; the Vredenburg Music Centre, Utrecht, (NL) 1973-1978; the Apollo Schools, Amsterdam, (NL) 1980-1983; Ministry of Social Welfare & Employment, The Hague, (NL) 1980-1991.

Publications 'H. Hertzberger 1959-1990', *A+U,* April 1991; 'Herman Hertzberger Recent Work', *Archis* 12, December 1986, pp. 7-43; Reinink, W., *Herman Hertzberger Architect,* Rotterdam 1991; Hertzberger, H., *Lessons for Students in Architecture,* Rotterdam 1991.

Jacques Herzog & Pierre de Meuron

Space never ends, especially not as a theme for architects. Think of the spatial effect your eau de toilette creates in your mind when you get up in the morning or think of the spaces between the words Herzog & de Meuron...

Both **Jacques Herzog** and **Pierre de Meuron** were born in 1950 in Basel, Switzerland and got their Architecture-diploma at the Eidgenossische Technische Hochschule in Zürich in 1975. In 1978 they established their own **Herzog & de Meuron office** in Basel. They have been visiting professors at Cornell University, Ithaca (1983), Harvard University, Cambridge (1989) and Tulane University, New Orleans (1991). From the start of their building career they have approached their projects in a conceptual manner: 'The conceptual level of each project acquires more and more importance in our work – it frees us from the obligation to have "a personal style" – which is actually impossible anyhow.'

Projects Blue House, Oberwil, (CH) 1979-1980; Photostudio Frei, Weil, (D) 1981-1982; Stone House, Tavole, (I) 1982-1988; Schwitter apartment and office building, Basel, (CH) 1985; Brunner residence, Bottmingen, (CH) 1985; Storage-building Ricola, Laufen, (CH) 1986-1987; Gallery for a private collection of contemporary art, Munich, (D) 1989-1992.

Publications Herzog & de Meuron: *Architektur Denkform,* Architekturmuseum Basel 1988; Herzog, J., 'La Parte y el Todo (The Piece and the Entirety)', *Quaderns* 175, October, November, December 1987, pp. 10-18; *Architektur von Herzog & De Meuron Fotographiert von Margarethe Krischanitz, Balthasar Burkhard, Hannah Villiger und Thomas Ruff mit einem Text von Theodora Vischer,* Bern 1991; Wang, W., *Herzog & De Meuron, Studio Monograph, Paperback,* Zürich 1992.

Steven Holl

Oops I changed a slide with my stomach

Steven Holl, born in 1947 in Bremerton in

Washington, USA, studied at the University of Washington (B. Arch. 1971), and at the Architectural Association, London (1976). He was instructor at the Parsons School of Design and the Pratt School of Design and since 1991 he has been a professor at Columbia University. At the beginning of Holl's architectural career the first projects were interiors of shops. In these shops Holl's preoccupation with creating flexible and specific spaces is already visible. In his later projects, mostly houses and housing-projects (1975-1988), he developed this theme further.

In 1978 he established his own office **Steven Holl Architects** in New York. In February 1989 he had a one-man exhibition at the Museum of Modern Art in New York.

Projects Metz House, Staten Island, New York, (USA) 1980; Autonomous Artisans' houses, Staten Island, New York, (USA) 1980-1984; Cohen Apartment, New York, (USA) 1983-1984; Bridges of Houses, New York, (USA) 1981; Hybrid Building, Sea-side, Florida, (USA) 1985-1988; American Memorial Library, Berlin, (D) 1988-1989, Stretto House, Dallas, Texas, (USA) 1988-1992; Void space/Hinged space, Fukuoka, (J) 1989-1991; Palazzo del Cinema, Venice, (I) 1990.

Publications Holl, Steven, *Anchoring: Selected Projects 1975-1991,* New York 1989; Holl, S., 'Within the City: Phenomena of Relations', *Design Quarterly* 139, Spring 1988; 'Meet the Architect (ten projects)', *G.A. Houses* 25, 1989.

Hans Hollein

All building is ritual

Hans Hollein, born in 1934 in Vienna, Austria, studied at the Academy of Fine Arts, Vienna, School of Architecture (Department of Civil Engineering, 1949-1956), Illinois Institute of Technology, Chicago (Graduated Studies, 1958-1959), University of California, Berkeley, College of Environmental Design (1959-1960), M.A.(1960). In 1964 Holl established a private practice in Vienna. He has been a visiting professor at Washington University (1963-1964, 1966). Since 1967 he has been professor at the Academy of Fine Arts, School of Architecture, Düsseldorf and since 1976 head of the school and the Institute of Design at the Academy of Applied Arts, Vienna. Hollein works on various types of projects, including houses, museums, furniture-

design, shops, exhibitions, papers, travel agencies, etcetera. In the field of product design he has dealt with all types of furniture, lighting fixtures and lamps, silver objects, door-handles, pianos, glassware and others.

Projects Schullin Jewelry, Vienna, (A) 1972-1974; exhibition MANtransFORM, New York, (USA) 1974-1976; Museum Abteiberg Mönchengladbach, (D) 1972-1982; Museum of Modern Art, Frankfurt am Main, (D) 1985-1990; Haas House, Vienna, (A) 1985-1990.

Publications 'Absolute Architektur', 1963; 'Hans Hollein', *A + U,* February 1985; Pettena, G., *Hans Hollein. Works 1960-1988,* Milan 1988; *Hans Hollein DESIGN MAN transFORMS, Concepts of an exhibition*, Wien 1989; 'Dossier Hans Hollein', *l'Architecture d'Aujourd'hui,* 279, February 1992 pp. 176-129.

Charles Jencks

You owe an obligation to the system of meaning quite apart from the position you cut within it. I owe something to my enemies because without them my position is nothing. If I were to win I would lose. The whole system of meaning depends on opposites

Charles Jencks, born in 1939 in Baltimore, USA, studied architecture and English literature at Harvard University (1957-1965). He was promoted as a Fulbright Scholar PhD at the University of London with Reyner Banham in London (1970). Over the years he has lectured at over forty universities in the USA, Europe and Japan. Since 1975 he has been visiting professor at the University of California in Los Angeles and in 1990 he was part-time teacher at the Architectural Association School, London. Not only by building but also by writing he contemplates architecture. His book *Meaning in Architecture* (with G. Baird), 1969, introduced one of the new directions in the interpretation of architecture and style. His other books follow the direction/tension of this book.

Projects *Garagia Rotunda*, Cape Cod, Massachusetts, (USA) 1975; *The Elemental House*, Los Angeles, California, (USA) 1977; *The Thematic House*, London, (GB) 1978.

Publications by Jencks, C.: *Le Corbusier and the Tragic View of Architecture,* London 1973; *Modern Movements in*

Architecture, London 1973; *The Language of Post Modern Architecture*, New York 1977;*What is Post-Modernism?*, New York 1986; *Post-Modernism, The New Classicism in Art and Architecture*, New York/London 1987; (ed.) *The Post-Modern Reader,* New York 1992; *Architecture Today*, London, 1993; *Heteropolis,* London, 1993

Rem Koolhaas

In one way or another I have to get some kind of pleasure out of life. I myself don't want to circulate effortlessly in those smooth circles; I need the sound of grinding cogwheels too

Rem Koolhaas, born in 1944 in Rotterdam, the Netherlands, decided to study architecture after a short career as a journalist for the Dutch magazine *Haagse Post* and as a screenwriter. Instead of joining the Dutch universities he went to London and was educated at the Architectural Association (1968-1972). After his graduation he went to the USA to work with O.M. Ungers, and with Colin Rowe at Cornell University (1972-1973). He was a visiting fellow at the Institute for Urban Studies in New York, directed by P. Eisenman (1973-1979). He taught both at Columbia University and at UCLA. In 1975 he founded with E. and Z. Zenghelis and M. Vriesedorp the **Office for Metropolitan Architecture** (OMA). In the beginning of the eighties Koolhaas came back to the Netherlands. In 1980 he opened the OMA-office in Rotterdam. Between 1988-1990 he was professor of architectonic design at the Technical University, Delft. During his stay in the USA, Koolhaas wrote the book *Delirious New York: A retroactive Manifesto for Manhattan,* 1978, coinciding with the exhibition 'The sparkling Metropolis' at the Guggenheim museum. Over the years Koolhaas has participated in a lot of competitions, so his project list contains built as well as unbuilt projects.

Projects extension of Dutch Parliament (first prize ex aequo) The Hague, (NL) 1978; National Dance Theatre, Projects 1 & 2 Scheveningen, Project 3 The Hague (NL) 1981-1987; IJ-Plein, Amsterdam, (NL) 1980-1983; Biocentre, laboratory for the University of Frankfurt, (D) 1988; National Library of France, Paris (F) 1989; Centre for Art and Media Techniques (winning project), Karlsruhe, (D) 1989.

Publications Lefaivre, L., 'Dirty Realism in European architecture', *Archithese*, January 1990; Lucan, J., *OMA- Rem Koolhaas Architecture 1970-1990*, New York 1991; 'Rem Koolhaas – OMA 1987-1992', *El Croquis* 53, February-March 1992; *S, M, L, XL, OMA projects*, OMA, New York, 1994.

Leon Krier

I do not build, because I am an Architect

Leon Krier, born in 1946 in Luxembourg, Krier studied architecture at Stuttgart University (1967-1968) but left his education unfinished. As a self-taught architect he collaborated with James Stirling in London. He has taught at Princeton University (1974-1977), the University of Virginia (1982) and at Yale University (1990-1991).

Krier has worked on many projects but most of them are not realised. They remain as masterplans on paper, for his vision on the built is a very specific one: '*I can only make Architecture, because I do not build.*' Most are planning projects with a focus on the politico-spatial problem.

Projects reconstruction of Luxembourg, (L) 1978; Point-Nord, new town near Munich, (D) 1983; new urban quarter on the Havel at Tegel, Berlin, (D) 1980; Façade of a Venetian house in the Corderia Venezia Arsenale, (I) 1980; Project for La Villette, Paris, (F) 1976; Atlantis project 1987; Main architect of 'Poundbury', Dorset, GB, 1989. Krier is personal advisor to the Prince of Wales for whom he drew up the masterplan for the redevelopment of British architecture.

Publications Krier, L., *Cities within the City*, Tokyo 1977; Krier, L., *Rational Architecture*, Brussels 1978; Krier, L., *Houses, Palaces, Cities*, London 1984; Krier, L., *Albert Speer, Architecture 1932-1942*, Brussels 1985; Krier, L., *Atlantis*, Brussels 1987; *Léon Krier. Buildings 1967-1992*, London 1992; Krier, L., *Architecture and Urban Design 1967-1992*, Academy Editions, London 1993. Krier writes for the magazine *AAM*, (Les Archives d'Architecture Moderne), in Belgium.

Lucien Kroll

Well, the fact is we simply aren't Calvinists...

Lucien Kroll, born in 1927 in Etterbeek, Belgium, studied architecture and town planning at the University of Brussels (1951). Kroll has his own office in Brussels.

Projects Medical Faculty buildings underneath student housing of the Université Catholique de Louvain, Woluwé-St.-Lambert, Brussels, (B) 1970-1982; Academy of Expression, Utrecht, (NL) 1979-1987; Subway station *Alma*, near Louvain University, (B) 1979-1982; Area *Vignes Blanches*, Cergy-Pontoise, (F) 1977-1979; General plan for city and commercial centre in Clichy-sous-Bois, Paris, (F) 1984- .

Publications Strauven, F., *De anarchitectuur van Lucien Kroll;* J. D. Besch, *Lucien Kroll, Componenten 1*, Delft 1987; Kroll, L., *An Architecture of Complexity*, (translated and foreword by P. Blundell Jones), Massachusetts 1987; *Lucien Kroll, Projets et Réalisations. Projekte und Bauten*, Wolfgang Pehnt (introduction), Teufen, Switzerland 1987; J. D. Besch, R. Hendriks, S. Ruiter, *Lucien Kroll, Componenten 2: Omtrent de Modernisering van de Architectuur*, Delft 1994.

Kisho Kurokawa

In my office I'm God; all ideas and theories come out of my head

Kisho Kurokawa, born in 1934 in Nagoya, Japan, received his architectural degree at Kyoto University, Japan. In 1962 he established **Bureau Kisho Kurokawa & Associates.** In that same year he was one of the youngest members of Team X (with J. Stirling, C. Alexander and H. Hollein). At Tokyo University, where he took his doctorate course in 1964 he and several others formed the 'Metabolist Group'. They perceived the city and architecture to be an organism capable of growth and change based on Buddhist philosophy. Architectural examples are the capsule pavilions at Expo 1970 and the Osaka and Nakagin Capsule Tower, Tokyo in 1972. From this concept Kurokawa developed his 'Philosophy of symbiosis', which probes the interrelationship between time and space, and man and technology, influenced by Buddhism and traditional concepts in Japanese culture.

Projects Roppongi Prince Hotel, Tokyo, (J) 1984; Melbourne Central, Melbourne, (AUS) 1986; Hiroshima City Museum of Contemporary Art, (J) 1987; Japanese-Chinese Youth Centre, Beijing, (PRC) 1990; New wing, Van Gogh Museum, Amsterdam, (NL) 1992-. Kurokawa has received twenty important design awards for his major works.

Publications by Kurokawa: *Urban Design*, 1965; *Thesis on Architecture I: Towards Japanese Space*, 1982; *Philosophy of Symbiosis*, 1987; *Rediscovering Japanese Space*, 1989; *Intercultural Architecture: The Philosophy of Symbiosis*, London 1991; *From Metabolism to Symbiosis*, Academy Editions, London 1992

Lucien Lafour & Rikkert Wijk

To design? It should be as if you are speaking to your mother

Lucien Lafour, born in 1942 in Amsterdam, the Netherlands, decided during his training as an interior decorator to study interior design at the Institute of Applied Arts, Amsterdam. Here Aldo van Eyck was one of his teachers. Van Eyck rekindled his interest in architecture. After finishing his study he went to work for Piet Blom, and later on at the Van Eyck & Bosch bureau.

Rikkert Wijk born in 1948 in Uithuizermeeden, the Netherlands, studied architecture at the University of Technology, Delft (1965-1975). He worked as an assistant of Tonny Zwollo (1975-1976) in Ecuador. During his stay in Surinam in 1977 he met Lafour, and they decided to work together: they established the office **Lafour & Wijk**. In 1981 they went back to the Netherlands. Most projects they built are housing-projects and public buildings, such as health centres.

Projects Ellen Health Centre, Marienburg, (SME) 1975-1981; 11 dwellings, Burmanstraat, Amsterdam, (NL) 1983-1985; 65 dwellings, Realeneiland, Amsterdam, (NL) 1985-1989; 313 dwellings, Abattoirterrein, Amsterdam, (NL) 1986-1989.

Publications Buch, J., 'For Free Sight and Open Space', in Brouwers, R. (ed), *Architecture in the Netherlands. Yearbook 1990-1991*, Rotterdam 1991, pp. 96-101; *Lafour & Wijk. Architects*, M. Kloos (ed.), Amsterdam 1991.

Daniel Libeskind

I've never seen a building. Architecture is dead, finished, vanished, terminated

Daniel Libeskind, born in 1946 in Lodz, Poland, got his primary education in Poland and Israel. He studied music in Israel and America. He became interested in architecture through his involvement in mathematics and painting. In 1959 he won a scholarship for the study of music. After moving to the USA, where he attended secondary school, Libeskind moved in the direction of architecture and went on to study at the Cooper Union, New York, (B. Arch. summa cum laude 1970). In 1971 he gained his Master of Arts Degree in the history and theory of architecture at the School of Comparative Studies, Essex University, England. He has been visiting professor at Harvard University, Ohio State University, University of Naples, University of Illinois, University of London, Danish Academy of Arts in Copenhagen, and was unit master at the AA, London (1975-1977).

Projects Micromegas 1980; Chamber Works, London, (GB) 1983; Three lessons in Architecture, Venice Biënnale, (I) 1985; City Edge Berlin, (D) 1987; Line of Five 1988; Nine books of Groningen, (NL) 1990; Competition entry for former concentration camp Sachsenhausen, (D) 1993.

Publications *Between Zero and Infinity*, New York 1981; *Chamberworks*, AA, London 1983; *Marking the City Boundaries*, Groningen 1990; *Architectural Monographs 16*, London 1991; *Monograph Daniel Libeskind, Countersign*, London & New York 1992; *Jewish Museum*, Berlin 1992.

Ernest Mandel

I don't have to convince anyone with arguments. Reality will do it better

Ernest Mandel, born in 1923 in Frankfurt am Main, Germany, studied economy at the Free University of Brussels and the Ecole Pratique des Hautes Etudes de Paris. Between 1954 and 1964 he was economic advisor of the 'Algemeen Belgisch Vakverbond' (General Belgian Union) and editor of the magazine *Le Peuple*. Since 1970 he has been professor of economy at the Free University of Brussels. He is a member of the RAL, the Belgian department of the Fourth International.

Publications Mandel, E., *Late Capitalism*, London 1975; Mandel, E., *Long Waves of Capitalist Development*, Cambridge 1978; Mandel, E., *The Formation of the Economic Thought of Karl Marx, 1843 to Capital*, New York 1983; Mandel, E., *Marx, The present Crisis and the Future of Labour*, Brussels 1984.

José Rafael Moneo

The turmoil we feel today has, in fact, always occurred

Rafael Moneo, born in 1937 in Tudela, Navarra, Spain, studied architecture at the School of Architecture, Madrid 1961 and became doctor of architecture in 1963. Between 1963-1965 he was a fellow of the Spanish Academy in Rome. Back in Spain Moneo established his professional practice in 1965, where it still resides. Moneo has been assistant professor at the Madrid School of Architecture 1965-1985, visiting professor at Cooper Union School of Architecture, (USA) 1976-1977, chairman of the department of architecture, Harvard Graduate School of Design (1985-1990). To date Moneo remains active as full professor at Harvard University. He has developed an extensive body of work as an architectural critic and theoretician, which has been published in magazines like *Oppositions*, *Lotus* and *Arquitectura Bis*, a journal co-founded by Moneo, of which he still acts as editorial consultant.

Projects Fabrica Diestre, Zaragoza, (E) 1965-1967; Urumea building, San Sebastián, (E) 1968-1971; Bankinter, Madrid, (E) 1972-1976; Town Hall, Logroño, (E) 1973-1981; Atocha Station, Madrid, (E) 1985-1992; National Museum of Roman Art, Mérida, (E) 1980-1984; Previsión Española Building, Sevilla, (E) 1982-1987.

Publications 'Rafael Moneo', *A + U* 227, August 1989; 'The Idea of Lasting: A conversation with R. Moneo', *Perspecta* 24, 1990; 'Rafael Moneo 1986-1992', *Monografías de Arquitectura y Vivienda* 36, 1992.

Jean Nouvel

I get in a state of panic at the thought that I am not making good use of the possibilities of my time

Jean Nouvel, born in 1945 in Fumel, France, studied architecture at the Ecole Nationale Supérieure des Beaux-Arts, Paris (1966-1972). In 1974 he was co-founder of the 'Mouvement d'Architectes Français' ('Mars'). In 1981 he was head of the second Biënnale d'Architecture de Paris with the theme 'Modernity and the Spirit of the Time'.
In 1970 Nouvel opened his first office and in October 1988 Nouvel associated himself with Emmanuel Cattani in *Jean Nouvel, Emmanuel Cattani et Associés*. Both have their specific departments, Nouvel deals with the concepts, the philosophy and the creation, Cattani with the organisation, administration and policy.
Projects Institut du Monde Arabe, Paris, (F) 1981-1987; Tokyo Opera House, (J) 1986 (with Philip Starck); Public Housing 'Nemausus 1', Nîmes, (F) 1985-1987; Restoration of Lyon Opera House, (F) 1986-1993; Tour Sans Fin, Paris, (F) 1989; Galeries Lafayette, Berlin, (D) 1991; Mediaparc Block 1, Cologne, (D) 1992.
Publications 'Jean Nouvel 77-1983', *l'Architecture d'Aujourd'hui* 231, February 1984; Goulet, P., *Jean Nouvel*, Paris, 1987; *A + U* 214, July 1988; 'Dix Projets et un Retour à Nemausus', *L'Architecture d'Aujourd'hui* 260, 1988; 'Jean Nouvel im Gespräch mit Patrice Goulet und Paul Virilio', *Arch+* 108, August 1991, pp. 32-43; Boissière O., Fessy G. *l'INIST dans l'œuvre de Jean Nouvel*, Paris 1992; Boissière O. *Jean Nouvel. Jean Nouvel, Emmanuel Cattani und Partner*, Zürich 1992; De Bure G., *Jean Nouvel Emmanuel Cattani und Partner. Vier Projekte in Deutschland*, Zürich 1992.

Amos Rapoport

I never show slides, but for this occasion I will submit to the wish of an audience of architects

Amos Rapoport, born in 1929 in Warsaw, Poland, studied at the University of Melbourne, Australia, (B.A 1954), Rice University, Texas. (M.A. 1956), and got his post-graduate diploma of town and regional planning in 1965 at the University of Melbourne. Since 1972 Rapoport has been a distinguished professor in the School of Architecture and Urban Planning at the University of Wisconsin-Milwaukee. He has also taught at the universities of Melbourne, Sydney, Berkeley and London. He has been a visiting teacher in Israel, Europe, Asia and South America, and is the author of four books and approximately 200 papers, chapters and articles. He is considered a pioneer in the new interdisciplinary field of 'Environment-Behaviour studies' and was editor in chief of *Urban Ecology* and associate editor of *Environment and Behaviour*.
Publications Rapoport, Amos, *House, form and culture*, New York 1969; Rapoport, Amos, *Human Aspects of Urban Form*, Oxford 1977; Rapoport, Amos, *The Meaning of Built Environment*, Beverley Hills 1982; Rapoport, Amos, *History and Precedent in Environmental Design*, New York 1990.

Henri Raymond

This idea of yours is certainly a result of the hyper-elliptical nature and obscurity of Prof. Raymond

Henri Raymond was born in 1921 near Paris, France. He is the former director of the European Centre for Research in Social Science (Vienna Centre), and 'Professeur Première Classe' at the University of Paris Nanterre. With Bernard Huet, Raymond was co-founder of the French school of architecture named UP8, now known as Paris Belleville.
Publications Raymond, H., *l'Habitat pavillonnaire*, 1964; Raymond, H., *Le Corbusier Mythe et Idéologie de L'espace* (with Segaud, M.), 1971; Raymond, H., *Habitat et Pratique de L'espace* (with Haumont, N.), 1974; Raymond, H., *The Great Panopticon of Space*, 1976; Raymond, H., *Urbanistique et Société Baroque* (with Huet, B.), 1978; Raymond, H., *Architecture: Les Aventures Spatiales de la Raison*, 1984; Raymond, H., *L'Urbanistique en Sicile au 17ème et 18ème Siècles*, 1985; Raymond, H., *La Réconstruction Baroque de Avola, Noto et Lentini*, 1986.

Richard Rogers

It appears I can kiss goodbye to a knighthood

Richard Rogers, born in 1933 in Florence, Italy, went to the Architectural Association, London (1953-1959) and the School of Architecture, Yale University (1961-1962). Here he met Norman Foster and together they worked on various projects. Soon afterwards they formed *Team 4* with Sue Rogers and Wendy Foster (1963-1971). After this partnership ended Rogers worked with Renzo Piano (1971-1977). Between 1977 and 1984 he was in partnership with J. Young, M. Goldschmied and M. Davies. Since 1984 the practice has been carried out by a limited company which today trades under the name of the **Richard Rogers Partnership.** Research is taken very seriously by the office: the study of user needs and use patterns coupled with technology in building to achieve optimum social, technical and economic benefits is an important focus. In 1991 Rogers received a knighthood for his services to architecture.
Projects Centre Culturel d'Art Georges Pompidou, Paris, (F) 1971-1976; Lloyd's of London redevelopment, City of London, (GB) 1978-1986; Inmos Factory, Newport, (GB) 1982; Tokyo International Forum, Tokyo, (J) 1989; Human Rights Building, Strasbourg, (F) 1990; Zoofenster; Brau und Brunnen Building, Berlin, (D) 1991; Shanghai Lu Jia Zui, Masterplan for a new commerial centre, (PRC) 1992; Airport terminal, Marseille, (F) 1992.
Publications *Richard Rogers + Architects*, Architectural Monographs, Academy Editions, New York 1985; Appleyard, B., *Richard Rogers, a Biography*, London, 1986; Rogers, R., 'Belief in the Future is Rooted in the Memory of the Past', *R.S.A. Journal*, November 1988, pp. 873-884; Rogers, R., *A Modern View*, London 1991.

Martha Rosler

Are you upset about this?

Martha Rosler is an artist working primarily with photography and text, video and installation. She also writes about art and culture and teaches media and critical studies at Rutgers University, where she is director of graduate studies in art. Much of her work concerns information and power; a recurrent focus is the built environment and the organisation of space. Her project on homelessness and housing, including exhibitions and public forums held in New York in 1989, is documented in: Wallis, Brian (ed.), *If you lived here: The city in Art, Theory, and Social Activism,* Seattle 1991; A previous book, *Martha Rosler, Three Works*, includes the photo-text work 'The Bowery in two inadequate descriptive systems' and an essay on documentary. While organising an exhibition on homelessness in St. Louis (1992), she video-interviewed a man who grew up in the Pruitt-Igoe housing project and who watched its demolition – called the moment of birth of Post-Modernism in architecture – from his schoolhouse window.

Denise Scott Brown & Robert Venturi

Enrich life; not clarify it, because we live amidst confusion

Denise Scott Brown, born in 1931 in Nkana, Zambia, studied at the Architectural Association, London where she graduated in architecture and tropical architecture (1955). She also studied at the University of Pennsylvania, M.C.P. (1960) and the University of Pennsylvania, M. Arch. (1965). In 1967 the architectural office **Venturi, Rauch, Scott Brown** was established. Since 1992 it has been called **Venturi/Scott Brown and Associates (VSBA).** Scott Brown has the responsibility for the urban planning and urban design department of the office. She has taught and lectured at various universities in the USA: the University of Pennsylvania, School of Fine Arts (1960-1965), the University of California at Berkeley, the School of Environmental Design (1965-1968), Yale University, Department of Architecture (1967-1970) and since 1983 she has been a fellow of Princeton University, Butler College.
Besides their enormous building production, both Venturi and Scott Brown have theorised and written about what they think architecture should be. From

the seventies onwards they have proclaimed their architecture theory about the 'decorated shed'.

Publications Scott-Brown, D., *Learning from Las Vegas*, with R. Venturi and S. Izenour, Cambridge 1972; Scott-Brown, D., 'On Architectural Formalism & Social Concern', *Oppositions* 5, Summer 1976, pp. 99-112; 'Learning from Denise: The Role in Architecture of Denise Scott Brown', *Architectural Record*, July 1982, pp. 102-107; Scott-Brown, D., 'A Worm's-eye View of Recent Architectural History', *Architectural Record*, February 1984, pp. 69-81; Scott-Brown, D., *A View from The Campidoglio: Selected Essays, 1953-1984*, with R. Venturi, New York 1984; 'Urban Concepts. Denise Scott Brown', *Architectural Design* 60, Jan-February 1990.

Robert Venturi, born in 1925 in Philadelphia, USA, gained his Bachelor of Arts (1947) and Master of Fine Arts (1950) degrees at Princeton University. In the early fifties he spent two years in Italy at the American Academy in Rome (1954-1956) where he was impressed by Italian architecture, in particular by the Mannerist era. In his early building career he worked for Louis Kahn and E. Saarinen. Since 1980 he has been a faculty member at the University of Pennsylvania and assigned Ch. Shepard Davenport Professor of Architecture at Yale University (1979). In 1964 Venturi became a partner with Rauch and in the period 1967-1992 Venturi was associated with Rauch and Scott Brown. In the firm Venturi is responsible for architectural and urban design. From the beginning Venturi has expressed his architectural theories in publications. In 1966 he published *Complexity and Contradiction in Architecture*, New York (second ed. 1977), a decisively influential book on architecture throughout the world.

Projects Expo'82 building, Nashville, (USA) 1979; Molecular Biology Laboratory, Princeton University, (USA) 1985; Clinical Research Building, University of Pennsylvania, Philadelphia, (USA) 1990; MacDonald medical research laboratory, University of California, Los Angeles, (USA) 1991; The National Gallery, Sainsbury Wing, London, (GB) 1986-1991; Seattle Art Museum, Seattle, (USA) 1991; First prize competition entry for Stedelijk Museum extension, Amsterdam, (NL) 1992.

Publications 'Diversity, Relevance and Representation in Historicism, or Plus Ca Change', *Architectural Record*, June 1982, pp. 114-119; 'From Invention to Convention in Architecture', *Royal Society of Arts Journal* (Thomas Cubitt Lecture), London 1987; *On Houses and Housing*, VSBA, Academy Editions, London 1992.

Richard Sennett

May I say that the title you have chosen for my article – 'Some Remarks of a Sidewalk Superintendent' – does not mean in English what you think it means; it means an unemployed elderly person, rather than the English equivalent of a flaneur. I suggest you think further about this

Richard Sennett, born in 1943 in Chicago, USA, studied at the University of Chicago and at Harvard University. He is professor of sociology and of the humanities at New York University, USA. Sennett has published many works on urban history and social criticism.

Publications Sennett, R., *The Use of Disorder*, 1970; Sennett, R., *Families Against the City: Middle-class Homes of Industrial Chicago 1872-1890*, Cambridge, Mass. 1970; Sennett, R., *The Hidden Injuries of Class* (with J. Cobb), New York 1972; Sennett, R., *The Fall of Public Man*, New York 1977; Sennett, R., *Authority*, New York 1980; Sennett, R., *The Conscience of the Eye: The Design and Social Life of Cities*, New York 1990.

Alvaro Siza Vieira

At times I don't even know myself and that clearly creates problems

Alvaro Siza, born in 1933 in Matosinhos, Portugal, attended the School of Architecture, University of Porto (1949-1955) after having already begun a career as a painter and after having studied sculpture. His first built project was finished in 1954. From 1955-1958 he collaborated with F. Távora.
He has been visiting professor at the Ecole Polytechnique of Lausanne, the University of Pennsylvania, Los Andes University of Bogotá and the Graduate School of Design of Harvard University.

At the moment he teaches at the school of Architecture of Porto. The importance of his didactic work has led to the establishment of the Oporto School. He participated in SAAL in the seventies. SAAL (Servicio de Apoyo Ambulatorio Locale) was founded after the revolution of 24 April 1974. This organisation put up various programmes for social housing and gave less fortunate people a chance to participate during the thinking and realisation processes for their houses and surroundings. Many projects by Siza are social housing projects, later projects include public buildings. In 1992 he received the Pritzker Prize.

Projects Housing Bouça (SAAL), Porto, (P) 1973-1977; Housing São Victor (SAAL), Porto, (P) 1974-1977; Social Housing Schlesisches Tor, Berlin, (D) 1983; House A. Duarte, Ovar, (P) 1981-1984. Watertower, Aveiro, (P) 1989-1990; Oporto School of Architecture, Oporto, (P) 1993.

Publications 'A. Siza', *A + U*, December 1980; 'Architecture as Modification', *Casabella*, January, February 1984; 'Alvaro Siza, Poetic Profession', *Lotus Documents*, 1986; 'Alvaro Siza 1954-1988', *A & U*, June 1989.

Quinlan Terry

All I am trying to do is recreate a world that a lot of people think is dead. But I think it could come back

Quinlan Terry, born in 1937 in London, Great Britain, studied at the Architectural Association 1955-1960. After the AA he worked for one year in C. H. Elsom's office and then in the office of James Stirling and James Gowan. Between 1962 and 1973 he was partner with Raymond Erith and in those years they worked together developing the Classical tradition on a number of important buildings, including Kingswalden in Hertfordshire, the restoration of St. Mary's Church in Paddington Green and the design of a large temple in the Middle East. During this job he held a scholarship in Rome (1967-1968). After Erith's death in 1973, Terry continued to work in the Classical tradition. His projects include newstone and brick houses, commercial schemes, public buildings, garden and landscape architecture. He has also conducted many restorations and repairs, re-roofing,

alterations and refurbishment.

Projects extension Little Missenden Church, Buckinghamshire, (GB) 1977; Downing College, Cambridge, (GB) 1983; Hollands Farm, Great Oakley, Essex, (GB) 1983; Nos 5-8 Kent Terrace, Regents Park, London, (GB) 1984; Richmond Riverside, London, (GB) 1988; Brentwood Cathedral, Brentwood, GB, 1991.

Publications Terry, Q. 'A Question of Style', *A.D.* Vol. 49, no 3/4, 1979; Terry, Q., 'Seven Misunderstandings about Classical Architecture', Cat. *Quinlan Terry* (ed. Russell, F.), Academy Editions, 1981; 'Terry, Q., 'Postscript of Roman Sketch Book' 1968, in *In Opposition zur Moderne Aktuelle Positionen in der Architektur*, 1981; Aslet, C., *Quinlan Terry, the Revival of Architecture*, Harmondsworth 1986; *Quinlan Terry: Selected Works*, Academy Editions Monograph, London 1993

Bernard Tschumi

My pleasure has never surfaced in looking at buildings, at the 'great works' of the history or present of Architecture, but rather in dismantling them (to play with the words of Orson Welles: I don't like architecture, I like making architecture)

Bernard Tschumi, born in 1944 of French/Swiss parentage, studied at the Eidgenossische Technische Hochschule in Zürich where he got his degree in 1969. Tschumi has lectured at internationally known institutes, such as the Institute of Architecture and Urban Studies, New York (1976), the Architectural Association, London, (1970-1980), Princeton University (1980-1981), the Cooper Union (1980-1983). Since 1988 Tschumi has been Dean of Columbia University. After winning the international competition for the twenty-first century 'Parc La Villette'in Paris, he established **Bernard Tschumi Architects**, with offices in New York and Paris.
His projects can be divided into built and unbuilt projects.

Projects Joyce's Garden, London, (GB) 1977; New National Theatre (second prize), Tokyo, (J) 1986; New Country Hall, Strasbourg, (F) 1986; Joyce's Garden, La Villette, Paris, (F) 1983-1989; City Bridges, Lausanne, (CH) 1987-1988; Kansai International Airport, Osaka, (J) 1988; Library of France, Paris, (F) 1989;

Cultural Center, Fresnoy, (F) 1993.
Publications Tschumi, B., *Architectural Manifestoes*, London 1979; 'Bernard Tschumi Reviewed and Interviewed: Crime as Function', *Architectural Design* 2, 1979; 'Bernard Tschumi', *A + U*, June 1980; Tschumi, B., *The Manhattan Transcripts, Theoretical projects*, London 1981; 'Disjunctions', *Perspecta* 23, 1987 and *A + U*, September 1988; Tschumi, B., *Questions of Space, Lectures in Architecture*, B. Tschumi and Architectural Association, London, 1990.

Oswald Mathias Ungers

You know Seneca's saying: 'I don't need them all. I don't even need a hundred, and don't even need ten. One would be enough'

Oswald Mathias Ungers, born in 1926 in Kaisersesch/Eifel, Germany, studied at the Technical University of Karlsruhe (1947-1950). At the beginning of his career he did not build for years, being more fascinated by theories about architecture. In that time he lectured and wrote a lot. He lectured at the Technical University Berlin (1963-1968), Cornell University, Ithaca/New York (1969-1975), and in 1975 he became full professor of architecture at Cornell. Ungers also taught at Harvard University (1973-1978) and the University of California, Los Angeles (1974-1975). In the late seventies, Ungers established his own offices in Köln, Berlin, Frankfurt and Karlsruhe, Germany, and started working on the DAM, the Architectural Museum of Germany in Frankfurt am Main. In 1986 he was assigned professor at the Kunstakademie in Düsseldorf.
Projects Drawings for student housing, Enschede, (NL) 1963-1964; Project Embassy Deutschland, Rome, (I) 1964; Museum Berlin, Tiergarten, (D) 1965; Stadthäuser 'Steiner Haus', Marburg, (D) 1976; Messegebaüde, Frankfurt am Main, (D) 1980-1984; Deutsches Architektur Museum, Frankfurt am Main, (D) 1984; House of the architect himself, Köln 1957-1959 with library 1990.
Publications Ungers, O.M., *Sieben Variationen des Raumes über die Sieben Leuchter der Baukunst von John Ruskin*, Stuttgart 1985; Ullmann, G., 'Im Labyrinth des Quadrats', *Archithese* no 4, 1987; Neumeyer, F. (et al), *Oswald Mathias Ungers: Architektur 1951-1990*, Berlin 1991.

Gianni Vattimo

If, in this multicultural world, I set out my system of religious, aesthetic, political and ethnic values, I shall be acutely conscious of the historicity, contingency and finiteness of these systems, starting with my own

Gianni Vattimo, born in 1936 in Turin, Italy, studied philosophy and literature at the University of Turin (1954-1959) and received a research-scholarship of the Alexander von Humboldt Stiftung at the University of Heidelberg (1963-1964). At the university of his home city Vattimo has been professor in aesthetics, since 1964 and professor in theoretical philosophy, since 1982. He has been Dean at the Faculty of Literature and Philosophy at the University of Turin (1977-1980 & 1981-1984). Vattimo has been a visiting professor at the State University of New York, Albany (1972-1973), at Yale University (1981) and at New York University (1982).
Vattimo is known for his 'Weak thought' theory, and takes part in the international discussion on Post-Modernism.
He takes the philosophic Modern in the same way as Nietzsche, Heidegger, the Frankfurter Schule and the French Post-Modernists. His themes include the apology of Nihilism, the crisis of Humanism, the truth (and also the death) of Art, Nihilism and Post-Modernism, among others.
Publications by Vattimo, G., *Introduction à Heidegger*, Paris 1985; *Les Aventures de la Différence*, Paris 1985; *The End of Modernity: Nihilism and Hermeneutics in Post-Modern culture*, Cambridge 1988; *The Transparent Society*, Cambridge, 1992.

Francesco Venezia

I am not very interested in moral questions or irony in architecture. I am interested in the effort to benefit from everything that we have inherited from the past: techniques, precision, measurements, proportions, materials. This is the only thing I am interested in. A joke which has been built is no joke

Francesco Venezia, born in 1944 in Lauro (Campania), Italy, qualified from the Naples Architecture Faculty in 1970. He is professor of architectonical composition at the Genova Architectural Faculty, and works in Naples as a practising architect. He has participated in several exhibitions and international competitions, and his works, projects and articles have been published by many of the specialised magazines.
Projects Small open-air theatre, Salemi, Sicily, (I) 1980-1982; Public space, Salaparuta, Sicily, (I) 1986; Completion of a quarter, Monterusciello, Naples, (I) 1987; House at Palazzolo Acreide, Siracusa, (I) 1988-1989; Open-air theatre, Ruderi di Gibellina, (I) 1990; Gibellina Museum, (I) 1987; Monument for Tommaso Campanella, Gibellina, Trapani, (I) 1991.
Publications Venezia, F., *D'Ombre o l'architettura della apparenze reali; Salemi e il suo territorio; Scritti brevi*; 'Teatros y Antros' or 'Theatres and Grottos', *Quaderns* 175, October, November, December 1987, pp. 36-45; 'Architecture in Sicily of Francesco Venezia', *Casabella* 591, June 1992, pp. 58-63.

**Peter L. Wilson &
Julia B. Bolles-Wilson**

More than ever I believe that function follows form

Peter Wilson, born in 1950 in Melbourne, Australia, studied at the University of

Melbourne (1968-1970) and the Architectural Association, London (1972-1974). He lectured for ten years at the Architectural Association, London (1978-1988).
Julia Bolles was born in 1948 in Münster, Germany. She first studied at the University of Karlsruhe, Germany (1968-1976) and later she went to London to study at the Architectural Association (1978-1979). She taught at the Chelsea School of Art (1979-1985). After Wilson's lecture activities and Bolles' study at the AA had finished, they established their architectural office Wilson Partnership in London (1980-1988).
Since 1988 the practice has become the **Architekturbüro Bolles-Wilson and Partner**, London-Münster, to reflect current work in Germany. The office has three partners: Wilson, Bolles-Wilson and Kleffner. Eberhard Kleffner, born in 1947 in Ostbevern, Germany, went to the University of Karlsruhe (1968-1976).
Projects Opera, Tokyo, (J) 1985; Blackburn House (designed with Wright, C.), Hampstead, London, (GB) 1987; New city library, Münster, (D) 1987-1993; Centre for art and media technology (ZKM), Karlsruhe, (D) 1989; Kindergarten, Frankfurt, (D) 1988-1992; Sculpture hall, Documenta Kassel, (D) 1989; Berlin: Denkmal oder Denkmodell, (D) 1988; Waterfront Rotterdam, (NL) 1990- .
Publications 'Aedes. Western Objects-Eastern fields, Recent Projects by the Architektenbüro Bolles Wilson', *AA Files* 20, 1989; *Architekturbüro Bolles-Wilson, Münster City Library*, Münster 1990; 'Architekturbüro Bolles-Wilson', *El Croquis* 47, January 1991.

Index

506

508

510

Acknowledgements

Photo credits

Key: *t*=top, *c*=centre, *b*=bottom, *l*=left, *r*=right.
References are to the page numbers

Cover photomontage Jan van Toorn;
1 Ian Hamilton Finlay, Adorno's Hut, 1987, photo Antonio Reeve, courtesy Galerie Jule Kewenig, Frechen;
6-7 Joan Brossa, photo Gasull Fotografia;
13 17 20 photos Ole Bouman and Roemer van Toorn;
18 photo Teun Hocks, commission Prins Bernard Fonds, Amsterdam, courtesy Torch Gallery, Amsterdam 1990;
19 courtesy Regal Marketing Ltd.;
20 photo from Fernsehgalerie Gerry Schum, courtesy Jan Dibbets;
23 photo Bruchet (Transworld Features Holland bv, Paris Match);
28 29 30/photos Liesbeth Janson;
29*r***31***t-b* **35***t-b* **33** photos courtesy office Ando;
30*r* photo Tadao Ando;
31*c* photo Sir Norman Foster, courtesy office Foster;
32 courtesy Henny van der Steen Schakenraad;
34*t-b* photos M. Matsuoka, M., courtesy office Ando;
34-35*c* courtesy and photo Skeet McAuley;
36 39*c-b* **41 42***t-b* **43**/courtesy office Leon Krier;
38*t* photo Lex Verspeek (Hollandse Hoogte);
38*b* courtesy Royal Academy of Arts, London;
39*t* E. C. Venn, courtesy office Leon Krier;
40 photo Angela Pohl;
42/photo Ole Bouman and Roemer van Toorn collection Metropolitan New York City;
43*r* photo New York Times, January 22, 1989;
44 photos collection Architecture department Columbia University New York City;
45 47 photos Ole Bouman and Roemer van Toorn;
46*b* collection Gemäldegalerie im Kunsthistorischen Museum, Vienna;
46*t* **49/51** photos Grant Mudford (Esto);
49*r* photos office Gehry;
50 courtesy Barbara Kruger;
53*t* **57***c* **58***l-r* **64***t* **65***l-r* photos Dieter Leistner;
54 photo courtesy office Ungers;
56 photo Kai Falck, courtesy Wenzel – Hablik – Stiftung, Itzehoe;
59*c* **60 64***b* photos Ole Bouman and Roemer van Toorn;
66 70 71 photos Amos Rapoport;
67*r*, **68***r* photos Ole Bouman and Roemer van Toorn;
68/photo collection Architecture Department Columbia University New York City;
73 photo Errington (ABC Press Amsterdam);
74 78 79*t* **80 82***b* photos Ole Bouman and Roemer van Toorn;
75 Anglia TV, courtesy office Erith & Terry;
76 photos Nick Carter;
77 85 photos office Erith & Terry;
79*b* courtesy Artistic Treasures of Richmond, England;
82*t* collection National Gallery of Scotland, Edinburgh;

84 photo Charles Jencks;
87 photo Henri Cartier-Bresson (ABC Press Amsterdam, Magnum);
92 93 95 96*r-b* **97***bl-r* **99**/photos courtesy office Holl;
94/photo Paul Warhol, courtesy office Holl;
94*r* **96**/photos collection Architecture department Columbia University New York City;
97*b*/**98***r* **99**/full page-*r* photos Liesbeth Janson;
98/photo C. Accetta, courtesy Galleria Giorgio Persano, Torino;
98/full page photo Ole Bouman and Roemer van Toorn;
99*b* photo Steve Smith (ABC Press Amsterdam);
100 photos Ole Bouman and Roemer van Toorn;
102 103*t-b*/**105***c* photos courtesy office Venturi Scott Brown and Associates, Inc.;
103*br* courtesy Helander Gallery, Palm Beach, Florida;
104 105/*-r* **106**/**107***r* photos Matt Wargo courtesy office Venturi Scott Brown and Associates, Inc.;
106-107*c* courtesy Jeff Wall;
109*r* photo Ole Bouman and Roemer van Toorn;
109/**115** full page **113**/photos E. Hames Valentine;
110/**112***b* **113***c-r* photo office Coates & Branson;
110*r* photo Joe Nally (ABC Press Amsterdam);
111 pages from publication produced to accompany Ecstacity exhibition by Nigel Coates at the Architectural Association in London from 14 May to 26 June 1992;
112*t* photo Liesbeth Janson;
114 photo Henri Cartier-Bresson (ABC Press Amsterdam, Magnum);
115*cr* collection Stedelijk Museum Amsterdam;
117 120/photos courtesy office Venturi, Scott Brown and Associates, Inc.;
118 121*b* photos Tom Bernard, courtesy office Venturi, Scott Brown and Associates, Inc.;
120*c* ABC Press Amsterdam;
121*t* photo Craig Aurness (Transworld Features Holland bv);
121 124 125 photo Matt Wango, courtesy office Venturi, Scott Brown and Associates, Inc.) ;
127 photo and courtesy Vincent Mentzel;
128*t* photo Fridman;
128*c* **129 132**/**135***b* photos Ole Bouman and Roemer van Toorn;
134 photo René Burri (ABC Press Amsterdam);
135*c* Drawing worldmap by Michiel van Lith, Het Firmament Graphic Designers, Amsterdam;
137 full page Richard Einzig, courtesy office Rogers;
137*c* photo Seiji Okumiya, courtesy office Rogers;
138 139 140 141*t*/ **142 143***tl-tr* photos Eannon O'Mahony, courtesy office Rogers;
141*bl* courtesy office Rogers;
141*r* photo Ole Bouman and Roemer van

Toorn;
143*b* photo Geoff Beeckman, courtesy Art in Ruins;
144 courtesy Rob Scholte;
145*t* courtesy Charles Jencks;
145*bl* photo Liesbeth Janson;
145*br* photo Shigeo Ogawa;
146 photo Jason Winstanley;
147 148*b* **149***t* photos Dick Frank Studio, courtesy office Eisenman;
149*b* photo Roberto Gennari, courtesy office Eisenman;
151 photo and courtesy Chris de Jongh;
156 158/**160**/photos Ole Bouman and Roemer van Toorn;
157 159 160*r* **161 162-163** full page **162**/
163*t-b* photos courtesy office Galí;
162*t* photo Edo Kuiper, courtesy Michael Gibbs and Claudia Kölgen;
164 photo Ole Bouman and Roemer van Toorn;
165 photo Robert Mulder (Hollandse Hoogte);
169 photo courtesy office Moneo;
170*tl-tr* **171***bl-br* photos and courtesy Dida Biggi;
171*t* collection Georg Jizi Dokoupil, courtesy Rob Scholte;
172 photo Nancy Campbell courtesy Diller + Scofidio;
173 174*c* **176**/**177 175** photos courtesy Diller + Scofidio;
174*r* photo Ole Bouman and Roemer van Toorn;
174/photo Burt Glinn (ABC Press Amsterdam, Magnum;
176*r* **178***r* **179***b* photo Glenn Halvorson courtesy Diller + Scofidio;
179*t* courtesy Barbara Kruger;
181 182 183*c* **184 185***b* **186 188** photos Ole Bouman and Roemer van Toorn;
183/photos courtesy Bohigas, Martorell, Mackay;
185*t* photo José Azel (Transworld Features Holland bv);
190 191 194*t* photos Ole Bouman and Roemer van Toorn;
192*b* photo Digne Meller Marcovicz;
192-193*t* photo and courtesy Stuart Klipper;
196 photo Nasa;
198 199 200 201 202 203*c* photos office Hegger;
203*r* photo Ole Bouman and Roemer van Toorn;
204 208 209 212*tl-tr-bl-br* photos Ole Bouman and Roemer van Toorn;
205 full page photo E. Beaudouin;
205 212*c* sketch and photo courtesy office Siza;
208*b* photo Editorale Domus;
211 courtesy office O.M.A.;
215 photo Romano Cagnoni (ABC Press Amsterdam);
220*r* **224***r* photos Ole Bouman and Roemer van Toorn;
220/photo Robert Burley;
221 222 225*t*/**226***b* **227***r* photos Paolo Rosselli;
223*b* photo Burt Glinn (ABC Press Amsterdam, Magnum);
223*t* courtesy Olivia Parker;
224*b* photo Heinrich Helfenstein;
224/**225***bl-tr-br* photos courtesy office

Calatrava;
229 230 231/-*r* **232 233 234**; photos office Derossi;
231 full page menu 1993 courtesy Restaurant, Biffi Scala, Milan;
236 237 239 240 241*tr-br-bl* photos courtesy office Bolles & Wilson;
237 241*tl*/**242-243** full pages photos Samek Tomasz, courtesy office Bolles & Wilson);
238 photo Helene Binet and Shinkenchiku, courtesy office Bolles & Wilson;
242*t* photo ANP Amsterdam;
245/photo Kim Zwarts;
245*r* **246***r* **247**/**248**/**249**/**250 251**/**253**/ photos Ole Bouman and Roemer van Toorn;
255 photos Ole Bouman and Roemer van Toorn;
256 photo Jim Richardson;
258/photo Hans Werlemann, courtesy office O.M.A.;
258*r* photo Paul Warchol;
259*b* courtesy Toledo Museum of Art, Ohio;
261 photo Reimar Schefeld;
263 photo Roger Ressmeyer (ABC Press Amsterdam);
269 270 272 273/**275** full page photos Cary Markering, courtesy office Lafour & Wijk;
271 273*tr-br* **274** photos courtesy office Lafour & Wijk;
275*t* courtesy Gemeentemuseum Arnhem;
275*b* courtesy Hans van der Meer;
276 photo Liesbeth Janson;
277 278 photo Sina Baniahmad, courtesy Atelier Hollein;
279 photo Gerald Zugmann, courtesy Atelier Hollein;
280 281 283 full page photos courtesy Atelier Hollein;
282*t-c* **283***t-c-b* photos Ole Bouman and Roemer van Toorn;
282*b* photo Max Hetzler, Cologne;
284 285 286 288 291 289 photos courtesy office Tschumi;
287*c-b* photo Ole Bouman and Roemer van Toorn;
287*t* Arie Schippers (Hollandse Hoogte);
290 Newspaper comic from The Smithsonian Collection of Newspaper comics, Bill Blackbeard, Martin Williams, 1988 (Gasoline Alley, 1930, *The Chicago Tribune*);
294 photo Izak Salomons, courtesy office Hertzberger;
295/photo Aldo van Eyck;
296*t* photo Klaus Kinold, courtesy office Hertzberger;
296*b* **299 300***tl-b* **301 293** courtesy office Hertzberger;
299 302 photos Johan van der Keuken, courtesy office Hertzberger;
300*tr* photo Ole Bouman and Roemer van Toorn;
302-303 photo Klaas Koppe (Hollandse Hoogte);
305*b* photo Liesbeth Janson;
305*t* **306 308 308-309 309 310 311** photos Ole Bouman and Roemer van Toorn;
307 photo Leonard Freed (ABC Press Amsterdam, Magnum);
312 316*b* **313***t* photos Ole Bouman and Roemer van Toorn;
313*cr* photo Bob Krist (Transworld Features Holland bv);

316t illustration Antoine Buonomo and Georges Fessy, courtesy office Nouvel & Cattani;

317 320t 321t 324 photos Berget Gaston, courtesy Nouvel & Cattani ;

320b photo Oliver Boissière, courtesy office Nouvel & Cattani;

321b photo Nicolas Borel, courtesy office Nouvel & Cattani;

327 photo Lillian E. Svec;

332 334l-r 335t-b 336 337 339 photos courtesy office Alberts & Van Huut;

334c photo Lani Alberts, courtesy office Alberts & Van Huut;

334l illustration Ger Eikendal, courtesy office Alberts & Van Huut;

335c photo Ole Bouman and Roemer van Toorn;

340 photo Kenneth Jarecke (Transworld Features Holland bv);

341 342tl-tr 343 344 345 346cl-b-cr 347t-cl-b photos Tomio Ohashi, courtesy office Kurokawa,

342cr photo Thomas Höpker (ABC Press Amsterdam, Magnum);

346t Liesbeth Janson;

347cr courtesy collection Polanski, Paris;

348 courtesy Klee-Stiftung, Kunstmuseum, Bern;

350l photo Liesbeth Janson;

350r photo Ole Bouman and Roemer van Toorn;

351c-b-full page 352 353r 254c photos courtesy office Libeskind;

351t 353l photos Udo Hesse, courtesy office Libeskind;

254 photos Steven Gerrard, courtesy office Libeskind;

355r courtesy Hans Haacke;

357t 359 364tr 363 366 365tl photos Charles Jencks;

357c 362 courtesy Klaus Staeck;

360t photo Matt Wango, courtesy office Venturi, Scott Brown and Associates, Inc.;

360cr photo Louis Psi Hoyos, Courtesy New York magazine;

360bl photo Hugh Hales/Tooke;

361 photo Ian Lambot, courtesy office Foster;

364b courtesy Bernard Prinz;

364tl 365tr photos Ole Bouman and Roemer van Toorn;

365b photo Alan Wyllis, courtesy David Mach;

369 370 372b photos courtesy office Derossi;

372t photo Enzo Rizzi, courtesy office Derossi;

373 photo Gabriele Basilico, courtesy office Derossi;

374 377 378 photos Ole Bouman and Roemer van Toorn;

374-375b photo Liesbeth Janson;

377 courtesy Editions Chantal;

379 courtesy C. Hofman;

383t photo Photographic Department Faculty of Architecture TU-Delft;

383bl-br 385 387 386 photos office De Carlo;

384 389 photos Ole Bouman and Roemer van Toorn;

391 photo Antoinette Jongen (Transworld Features Holland bv, Black Star);

396 397 398 399tr-bl 403 400 401 403 photos courtesy office Kroll;

399tl photo Dieter Besch;

402 collection Mart Spruyt bv, Amsterdam, courtesy Jan van Toorn;

404 406 407 410-411 full page photos Ole Bouman and Roemer van Toorn;

405 407 409tr-br-bc photos courtesy office Bofill;

409l 410-411c 411cr photos Bartomeu Cruells, courtesy office Bofill;

412 photo Ole Bouman and Roemer van Toorn;

414c courtesy Diadalos;

415b photo Liesbeth Janson;

415cl photo Ben Johnson, courtesy office Foster;

415tr-br 417t-c-r 418 drawing photos courtesy Foster;

418cl photo Ries van Hulten, courtesy Dr. Ir. de Lange, TNO Delft;

418-419 full page 414 415t 416 417cl photos Richard Davies, courtesy office Foster;

419cr Advertisment Screen Machine, courtesy Fast Electronic GmbH, München;

421c photo Patrick Ward (ABC Press Amsterdam);

421l t courtesy Klaus Staeck;

422l courtesy Peter Dunn and Lorraine Leeson;

422r photo courtsy Olympia & York Canary Warf Limited;

424t poster Bladerunner The directors cut, Warner Bros;

424 426 427 photos Ole Bouman and Roemer van Toorn;

425 photo courtesy Turner-Krull Gallery, Los Angeles, California;

428 432 433 photos courtesy Jay Gorney Modern Art Gallery, New York City;

436 437 photos Ole Bouman and Roemer van Toorn;

438, 439 photos courtesy office Venezia;

442r courtesy Michel Boesveld;

444 photo Liesbeth Janson;

446l research by Drexel University (Joan M. Centrella) and University of Chicago (Adrian L. Melott);

446c 449 450t 451t photos Hans Werlemann, courtesy office O.M.A.;

447bl-br photo Stan Lee;

447tl-tr courtesy office O.M.A.;

450b 452 photos Ole Bouman and Roemer van Toorn;

451b photo courtesy Amsterdam waterfront corporation;

455 photo David James (ABC Press Amsterdam, Sygma);

460l photo Thomas Ruff, courtesy Stedelijk Museum Amsterdam;

460r 461 465 photos courtesy office Herzog & de Meuron;

462 463t photos Manuel Laguillo, courtesy office Herzog & de Meuron;

464 467tl-bc photos Margherita Krischanitz, courtesy office Herzog & de Meuron;

463bl-br photos Roemer van Toorn and Ole Bouman;

466 courtesy Dia Center for the Arts, New York City;

467cr photo and courtesy Thomas Ruff;

469 470c-r photos courtesy office Graves;

470l Herbert Moigdoll, courtesy office Graves;

471t-b photo Paschall/Taylor, courtesy office Graves;

471c photo Otto Baitz, courtesy office Graves;

472, photo courtesy Charles Jencks;

473 474 photo William Taylor, courtesy office Graves;

474, photo Steven Brooke, courtesy office Graves;

475, photo Hans Ulrich Reck, courtesy Kunstforum;

477 479 481t 483b photos courtesy office Hasegawa;

478 courtesy Wildenstein & Co., Inc., New York City;

480 482 484r photos Liesbeth Janson;

483t photo André Morin;

485 488 489 Ole Bouman and Roemer van Toorn;

491 advertisement in Dutch magazine HP/de tijd;

494 portrait Alberts and Van Huut, courtesy office Alberts & Van Huut;

494 portrait Ando, courtesy office Ando;

494 portrait Bofill, courtesy office Bofill;

494 portrait Calatrava, still from BBC television;

494 portrait De Carlo, photographic department, faculty of architecture, university of technology Delft;

495 portrait Coates, photo Cindy Palamo;

495 portrait Derossi, courtesy office Derossi;

495 portrait Diller and scofidio, courtesy Diller + Scofiodo;

495 portrait Eisenman, photomontage Dick Frank and Massimo Vignelli;

496 portrait Bohigas, photo Erica Lansner (Black Star, Transworld Features Holland bv);

496 portrait Galì, photo Erica Lansner (Black Star, Transworld Features Holland bv);

496 portrait Frampton, still from BBC television;

496 portrait Foster, photo Rudy Meisel, courtesy Foster;

496 portrait Gehry, photo Brian Yoo, courtesy office Gehry;

496 portrait Graves, photo William Taylor, courtesy office Graves;

497 portrait Harvey, courtesy David Harvey;

497 portrait Hasegawa, courtesy office Hasegawa;

497 portrait Hegger, courtesy office Hegger;

497 portrait Hertzberger, photo Giles Oliver, courtesy office Hertzberger;

497 portrait Herzog and Meuron, courtesy office Herzog & de Meuron;

497 portrait Holl, courtesy office Holl;

498 portrait Hollein, courtesy Atelier Hollein;

498 portrait Jencks, courtesy Jencks;

498 portrait Koolhaas, courtesy O.M.A.;

499 portrait Mandel, photographic department, faculty of architecture, university of technology Delft Delft;

499 portrait Krier, photo Celia Scott, courtesy office Krier;

499 sketch office members, courtesy office Kroll;

499 portrait Kurokawa, courtesy office Kurokawa;

499 portrait Lafour and Wijk, photo Rogier Fokke, courtesy office Lafour & Wijk;

499 portrait Libeskind, photo Idris Kolodziej, courtesy Libeskind;

499 portrait Moneo, photo Ole Bouman and Roemer van Toorn;

500 portrait Rogers, still from BBC television;

500 portrait Raymond, photographic department, faculty of architecture, university of technology Delft;

500 portrait Nouvel, photo Rita Scaglia, courtesy office Nouvel & Cattani;

500 portrait Rapoport, photo Bruce W. Buchanan, courtesy Amos Rapoport;

500 portrait Rosler, courtesy Jan van Eyck Academie Maastricht;

500 portrait Venturi and Scott Brown, photo J. T. Miller, courtesy Venturi Scott Brown and Associates Inc.;

501 portrait Sennett, courtesy Richard Sennett;

501 portrait Siza, courtesy office Siza;

501 portrait Terry, courtesy office Erith & Terry;

501 portrait Tschumi, courtesy office Tschumi;

502 portrait Ungers, photo Heinz-Günter Mebusch, courtesy office Ungers;

502 portrait Vattimo, courtesy Gianni Vattimo;

502 portrait Venezia, photo Enrico Pappalaro, courtesy office Venezia;

502 portrait Bolles and Wilson, courtesy office Bolles & Wilson.

Translation Acknowledgements

Interviews, article Venezia and Preface: Donald Gardner. Pictorial essays, introduction, introduction vectors and epilogue: Victor Joseph. Article Mandel and Raymond: Michael Gibbs.

Text Acknowledgements

Article Gianni Vattimo, pp 244-253
Another version of this text has been published as 'Myth Rediscovered', in Vattimo, Gianni, The Transparent Society, Cambridge, 1992, pp. 28-44.

Article Hal Foster, pp 554-261
Another version of this text has been published in K. Michael Hays and Carol Burns (ed.), Thinking the Present, Recent American Architecture, Princeton, 1990, pp. 110-122.

Article Richard Sennett, pp 304-311
An extended version of this text has been published as Sennett, Richard, The Conscience of the Eye, New York, 1990.

The Foundation has attempted to identify and credit individually each photographer and, wherever possible, contacted her or him for authorisation. If the Foundation has misattributed, the Foundation would be grateful to amend the acknowledgements in future editions.

Ole Bouman and Roemer van Toorn would like to thank for their collaboration

General editor, researcher and organiser
Dave Wendt

Design
Kees van Drongelen
Design assistants
Christine Baart, Harco van den Hurk *(practice)*

Final editors
Karst Bouman, Gerrie van Noord and
Erna Rijsdijk

Assistant editors
Machteld Bouman, Birgitte de Maar,
Ron Miltenburg, Ingrid Oosterheerd,
Ineke Schwartz, Arthur Wortmann and
Anouk de Wit

Assistants
Esther Agricola, Ché Anjie, Wilma Averesch,
Frank Bakker, Manon Beerman, Mirjam
Beerman, Titus Bouman, Arjen Hoogendoorn,
Anne Hoogewoning, Michel Korsse,
Liesbeth Leví, Suzanne Olde Monnikhof,
Pearl Perlmutter, Axel Roest, Hans Rijnja,
Petra Slegh and Yvonne Twisk

Production/publishing adviser
Johan Pijnappel

Translators
Donald Gardner, Michael Gibbs, Victor Joseph
and Stephan Piccolo

Advisory board
Tjeerd Dijkstra, Joop Doorman,
Kenneth Frampton, Marcel van Heck,
Guus Kemme, Frans Spruijt, Ed Taverne
and Jan van Toorn

**Members of the Board, Foundation The
Invisible in Architecture**
Hans Bos, Arnold van den Broek and
Hans van Dijk

**Assistants Series of Lectures *The Invisible in
Architecture* at the Faculty of Architecture
Delft University of Technology 1987-1988**
Herman Albers, Mirjam Beerman,
Rients Dijkstra, Oliver Draxler, Hans Ibelings,
Liesbeth Janson, Margot Knijn,
Arjen Knoester, Wilma Peterse, Angela Pohl,
Sjon van Rossem, Wienke Scheltens,
Joes Segal, Tessel van Toorn,
Frank van Unen, Steffen de Vries and
members of the board of the Stylos Student
Association

This book has been made possible with the financial aid of

- Ministry of Welfare, Health and Cultural Affairs, Rijswijk
- Ministry of Planning, Housing and Environment, Den Haag
- Prins Bernard Fonds, Amsterdam
- Faculty of Architecture, University of Technology, Delft
- Royal Institute of Dutch Architects, Amsterdam
- Rijnja Repro BV, Amsterdam
- Stylos Foundation, Delft
- Architectura & Natura International Booksellers, Amsterdam
- Architecten Werkgroep Th. J.A.M. van Esch en A.W.I. van der Hagen
- Architectenbureau Herlé, 's-Gravenhage
- Architectenbureau Jowa, Amsterdam
- Architectenbureau Nico H. Andriessen, B.V., Haarlem
- Architectenbureau Peter Schurink, Rotterdam
- Architectenbureau Pothoven, Amersfoort
- Architectenbureau Van den Broek en Bakema, Rotterdam
- Architectenbureau Vroom, Amsterdam
- Architectenburo ir. M. Schermelé, Rotterdam
- Architectengroep bv Ledderhof, Den Haag
- Architekten- en adviesburo Hamminga & Haverkort, Emmen
- Architekten- en ingenieursbureau Ir. J.W. Jansen, Baarn
- Architekten- en ingenieursbureau Mastenbroek BV
- Architektenbureau A.J. Kloosterman b.v., Harderwijk
- Architektenbureau Koldewijn - Drexhage, Rotterdam
- Architektenburo Eddie Verheugt, Bergen op Zoom
- Architektenburo Franse en van Hoof, Wassenaar
- Architektenburo Galis, Delft
- Architektenburo Hans Bik BV, Leiden
- Architektenburo Ir P.M.J. van Swieten, Leiden
- Architektenburo Ir. P.J. Trimp, 's-Hertogenbosch
- Architektenburo ir. Martin Wijnen, Amsterdam
- Architektenburo Irs. Vegter, Leeuwarden
- Architektenburo Visser en Beerman, Rotterdam
- Architektengroep Duintjer, Amsterdam
- Architektengroep Loerakker Rijnboutt Ruijssenaars Hendriks Mastenbroek Van Gameren bv, Amsterdam
- Atelier 06, Millingen aan de Rijn
- Atelier PRO, architecten bv, Den Haag
- B & D architekten, Leiden - Oosterbeek
- BEAR Architekten, Gouda
- Berent Stemerding, architekt, Amersfoort
- Bureau Van Droffelaar, Arnhem
- Buro Morsink, Oud Ootmarsum
- Buro Wiegerinck Architekten, Arnhem
- CH & Partners BNS BNT, stedebouw en landschap, Den Haag
- De Architekten Cie, Amsterdam
- Den Hartog Architecten, Doorn
- EGM architekten, Utrecht
- Heeling Krop Bekkering Stedebouwkundigen en Architekten, Groningen
- Henk Klunder Architekten, Rotterdam
- Henny Boesten architectenburo, Leidschendam
- Hoenders + partners architekten, Delft
- Homan,Osorio Lobato, Yanovshtchinsky Architectenmaatschap,'s Gravenhage
- Hpart Raadgevend Ingenieursburo ir R. Hajema en Partners, Assen
- Ir. L.W. Barneveld Architekt, Groningen
- J. L. C. Choisy, Presinge
- Jan Brouwer Associates, 's-Gravenhage
- Kleijer Architekten, Oosterbeek
- Kruisheer Elffers architecten/adviseurs, Rotterdam
- Kuiper Compagnons, bureau voor Ruimtelijke Ordening en Architektuur BV, Rotterdam
- Molenaar & van Winden, architecten, Delft
- OD 205 architektuur, stedebouw, onderzoek en landschap bv, Delft, Eindhoven
- Oostveen Architectuur, Breda
- OSTT architekten, Doetinchem
- Pamela van Duyvenboode, Wassenaar
- Peutz Architekten, Heerlen
- Rein van Wylick, Geldrop
- Roelf Steenhuis Architekten, Delft
- Schipper Verbeek Zijlstra Architekten, Zaandam
- Tauber Architecten, Alkmaar
- Team 4 - Nieuwland en Van der Vegte Architekten-adviseurs bv, Leeuwarden
- Team 4, architekten-adviseurs bv, Groningen
- Van den Heuvel de Wilde Architekten, Heerlen
- Van Hengstum interieurarchitekten, 's-Hertogenbosch
- Van Straalen Influence Communications, Gouda
- Vermeulen Windsant Architecten, Haarlem
- VHP/BDG Architekten/Stedebouwkundigen/Ingenieurs B.V., Rotterdam
- VVK Architectuur en StedebouwBV Amsterdam
- W.J. Neutelings, Architectuur BV, Rotterdam
- Wentink architekten, Baarn
- Werkplaats voor Architektuur, Utrecht
- Zwarts & Jansma Bureau voor Architektuur en Produktontwikkeling, Abcoude